Lonely planet

Cuba

Havana
p63

Varadero &
Matanzas
Province
p203

Villa Clara
Province
p259

Valle de Viñales
& Pinar del Río
Province
p177

Artemisa &
Mayabeque
Provinces
p149

Ciego de
Ávila
Province
p305

Cienfuegos
Province
p241

Trinidad &
Sancti Spíritus
Province
p279

Camagüey
Province
p323

Las
Tunas
Province
p343

Holguín
Province
p353

Isla de la Juventud &
Cayo Largo del Sur
p163

Granma
Province
p379

Santiago
de Cuba
Province
p399

Guantánamo
Province
p437

Brendan Sainsbury,
Wendy Yanagihara

Contents

PLAN YOUR TRIP

ON THE ROAD

VARADERO BEACH (P205)

FLAMINGO, CAYO COCO (P315)

PALACIO DE GOBIERNO (P244), CIENFUEGOS

Contents

COVID-19

We have re-checked every business in this book before publication to ensure that it is still open after the COVID-19 outbreak. However, the economic and social impacts of COVID-19 will continue to be felt long after the outbreak has been contained, and many businesses, services and events referenced in this guide may experience ongoing restrictions. Some businesses may be temporarily closed, have changed their opening hours and services, or require bookings; some unfortunately could have closed permanently. We suggest you check with venues before visiting for the latest information.

ON THE ROAD

CUEVA DE AMBROSIO
(P205), VARADERO

CENTRO HABANA (P83)

Contents

CURRENCY MATTERS

At the time of writing, money matters in Cuba are in a state of flux. The convertible (CUC$) was eliminated in January 2021 leaving Cuban pesos (CUP$) as the country's main currency. However, the US dollar also circulates in Cuba at a fixed rate of 1:24 against the peso (roughly the same as the erstwhile convertible). Early indications suggest that, moving forward, state-run enterprises will charge prices in Cuban pesos while private business people will prefer to be paid in US dollars. However, until the tourist industry fully reopens post-Covid, the details could be subject to change. We suggest that travelers arrive in Cuba with US dollars along with a non-US linked credit card and ATM card. Once in Cuba, US dollars can easily be changed for CUP$. ATMs also dispense CUP$.

Right: Gran
Teatro de la
Habana Alicia
Alonso (p85),
Havana

WELCOME TO

Cuba

Cuba and I go back a long way, from the economic chaos of the 1990s to the heady days of the Obama reopening. Yet no matter how many times I visit this plucky Caribbean nation with its bewildering bureaucracy and free-flowing music, I still return home with more questions than answers. One moment it's hot and frustrating, the next it's humbling and heart-warming. One day nothing adds up, the next day everything makes sense. From the cacophonous streets of Havana to the deserted beaches of the Isla de la Juventud, Cuba jolts you with its baffling uniqueness. Welcome to a country with no precedent.

By Brendan Sainsbury, Writer
🐦 @sainsburyb
For more about our writers, see p544

Cuba

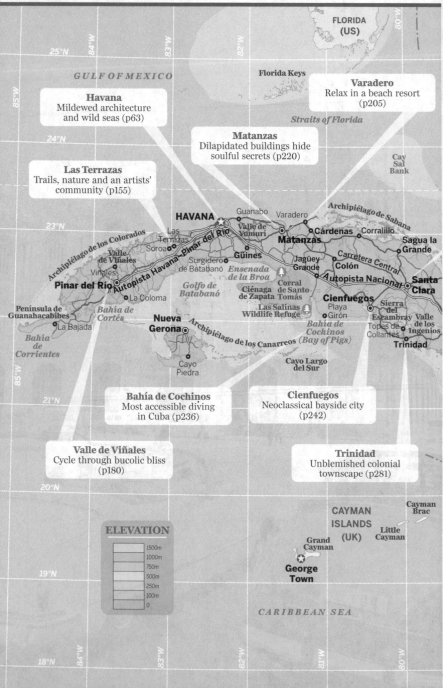

FLORIDA (US)

GULF OF MEXICO

Havana
Mildewed architecture and wild seas (p63)

Varadero
Relax in a beach resort (p205)

Florida Keys

Straits of Florida

Matanzas
Dilapidated buildings hide soulful secrets (p220)

Cay Sal Bank

Las Terrazas
Trails, nature and an artists' community (p155)

Archipiélago de Sabana

HAVANA
Guanabo   Varadero

Las Terrazas   Valle de Yumurí

Soroa   Pinar del Río   Cárdenas   Corralillo

Sagua la Grande

Archipiélago de los Colorados

Valle de Viñales

Viñales

Güines

Surgidero de Batabanó

Jagüey Grande

Colón

Carretera Central

Santa Clara

Pinar del Río   Autopista Havana-Pinar del Río

La Coloma

Ensenada de la Broa

Golfo de Batabanó

Corral de Santo Tomás

Autopista Nacional

Península de Guanahacabibes

La Bajada

Bahía de Cortés

Nueva Gerona

Ciénaga de Zapata

Cienfuegos

Sierra del Escambray

Valle de los Ingenios

Bahía de Corrientes

Archipiélago de los Canarreos

Las Salinas Wildlife Refuge

Playa Girón

Bahía de Cochinos (Bay of Pigs)

Topes de Collantes

Trinidad

Cayo Piedra

Cayo Largo del Sur

Bahía de Cochinos
Most accessible diving in Cuba (p236)

Cienfuegos
Neoclassical bayside city (p242)

Valle de Viñales
Cycle through bucolic bliss (p180)

Trinidad
Unblemished colonial townscape (p281)

CAYMAN ISLANDS (UK)

Cayman Brac

Little Cayman

ELEVATION

	1500m
	1000m
	750m
	500m
	250m
	100m
	0

Grand Cayman

George Town

CARIBBEAN SEA

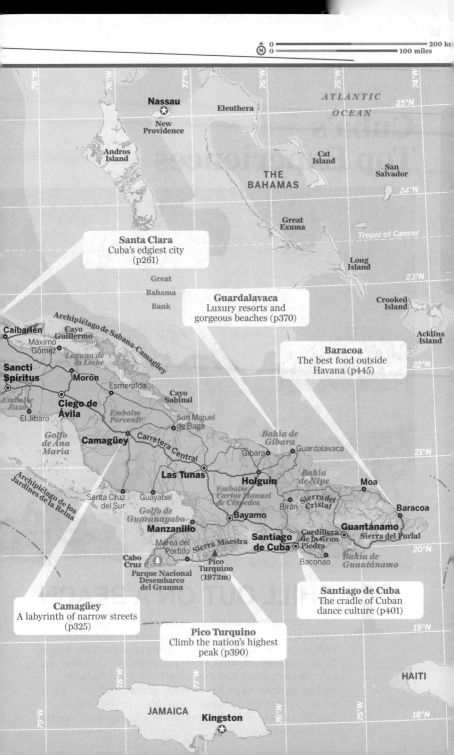

0 200 kr
0 100 miles

Nassau ✪
New
Providence

Eleuthera

Andros
Island

Cat
Island

San
Salvador

THE
BAHAMAS

24°N

25°N

ATLANTIC
OCEAN

Santa Clara
Cuba's edgiest city
(p261)

Great
Bahama
Bank

Great
Exuma

Tropic of Cancer

Long
Island

23°N

Guardalavaca
Luxury resorts and
gorgeous beaches (p370)

Crooked
Island

Acklins
Island

Baracoa
The best food outside
Havana (p445)

22°N

Caibarién

Cayo
Guillermo

Máximo
Gómez

Archipiélago de Sabana-Camagüey

Laguna de
la Leche

**Sancti
Spíritus**

Morón

Esmeralda

Cayo
Sabinal

Embalse
Zaza

**Ciego de
Ávila**

El Jíbaro

Embalse
Porvenir

San Miguel
de Bagá

Bahía de
Gibara

Guardalavaca

Golfo
de Ana
María

Camagüey

Carretera Central

Gibara

21°N

Las Tunas

Archipiélago de los
Jardines de la Reina

Santa Cruz
del Sur

Guayabal

Holguín

Embalse
Carlos Manuel
de Céspedes

Bahía
de Nipe

Moa

Golfo de
Guacanayabo

Bayamo

Birán

Sierra del
Cristal

Baracoa

Manzanillo

**Santiago
de Cuba**

Cordillera
de la Gran
Piedra

Guantánamo
Sierra del Purial

Marea del
Portillo

Sierra Maestra

Cabo
Cruz

Pico
Turquino
(1972m)

Baconao

Bahía de
Guantánamo

20°N

Parque Nacional
Desembarco
del Granma

Camagüey
A labyrinth of narrow streets
(p325)

Santiago de Cuba
The cradle of Cuban
dance culture (p401)

19°N

Pico Turquino
Climb the nation's highest
peak (p390)

HAITI

JAMAICA

Kingston ✪

18°N

Cuba's Top Experiences

 CHILL OUT ON A BEACH

Beaches are to Cuba what churches are to Italy and national parks are to Canada – well-loved, beautiful, and extremely varied. Picture long strips of white-sand backed by massive resorts that attract tourists by the planeload; wild, deserted eco beaches on off-shore cays where turtles lay their eggs; little-visited black-sand beaches where pirates once roamed; and unashamedly nudist beaches where bold foreign travelers lounge with mojitos.

Above: Varadero beach (p205)

Varadero

With 21km of unbroken white sand; a raft of sporty water activities including kitesurfing and sea kayaking, and a ton of hotels from modest two-stars to lavish all-inclusives, it's inconceivable that anyone could be disappointed with Varadero. One of the best beaches in the world. Period. p205

Right: Varadero watersports (p207)

Playa Pilar

Named for Hemingway's famous fishing boat, Pilar is straight out of the book of Caribbean tourist brochure clichés. Backed by the Caribbean's largest sand dunes and invaded by a couple of new hotels, it's caressed by waves so warm it's akin to sitting in a hot tub. p318

Above: Walkway, Playa Pilar

Cayo Largo del Sur

It seems almost unfair that some of Cuba's finest, widest and aptly named beaches (Playa Paraíso!) occupy a small southern cay reserved exclusively for tourists. Retire to the clapboard beach bar, order a piña colada and try not to feel guilty. p172

Above: Playa Paraíso (p173)

2 AMAZING ARCHITECTURE

Often spectacular yet rarely constant, Cuban architecture displays a definable 'Cuban-ness' that sets it apart from other genres. Drawing on a medley of influences, older colonial buildings retain strong hints of baroque, faint whiffs of mudéjar, echoes of gothic and large doses of neoclassicism. Moving into the 20th century, more recent architectural heirlooms have embraced lavish eclecticism, streamlined art deco and flamboyant art nouveau.

Habana Vieja

The detailed, meticulous, lovingly curated restoration of Havana's colonial core has created one of the historical wonders of the Americas, a kind of Hispanic 'Rome' where the past can be peeled off in layers. p67

Above: Catedral de la Habana (p67)

Trinidad

Soporific Trinidad went to sleep in 1850 and never really woke up. This strange twist of fate is good news for modern travelers, who can roam freely through the perfectly preserved mid-19th-century sugar town like voyeurs from another era. p281

Top: Trinidad houses

Camagüey

Always keen to be different, Camagüey was founded on a street grid that deviated from almost every other colonial city in Latin America. Here the lanes are labyrinthine, hiding Catholic churches, triangular plazas and a growing ensemble of boutique hotels encased in restored buildings. p325

Above: Calle Maceo (p336)

3 CREATIVE ART

Challenging accepted norms, creeping underneath censorship, and pushing the cultural zeitgeist; Cuban art can compete with the finest in the world. For proof, check out the modernist masterworks of Wifredo Lam, walk the paint-daubed streets of Havana, pop into private studios in Matanzas or listen to the creative chatter in a Camagüey coffee bar. It'll change your perspective of what this country is all about.

Museo Nacional de Bellas Artes

A dual-campus national art museum presenting a gorgeously curated history of Cuban art, from the derivative landscapes of the 19th century to the precocious brush strokes of the present day. World class! p85

Below left: Museo Nacional de Bellas Artes edifice

POSSOHH/SHUTTERSTOCK ©

Calle Narváez

Mantanzas is experiencing a nascent cultural reawakening, and its new waterside art street is lined with strange envelope-pushing sculptures, clay-splattered galleries, and junk-decorated cafes. p224

Top right: Matanzas (p220)

Fusterlandia

Nothing can prepare you for Fusterlandia, a small neighborhood on the periphery of Havana where street art has run amok. p94

Right: Taller-Estudio José Fuster (p94)

4 REVOLUTIONARY HISTORY

ITZAVU/SHUTTERSTOCK ©

S FORSTER/SHUTTERSTOCK ©

ARTIST: JOSE RODRIGUEZ FUSTER. IMAGE: JOCINEMATOGRAPHERY/ SHUTTERSTOCK ©

An improbable escape from a shipwrecked leisure yacht, handsome bearded guerrillas meting out Robin Hood–style justice and a classic David versus Goliath struggle between repressive colonizers and fiery rebels: Cuba's revolutionary escapades read like the pages of a barely believable movie script. Not surprisingly, reminders and monuments are everywhere, telling the story of a proud, spirited and independently minded people.

La Plata

Castro's bolt-hole in the Sierra Maestro went undiscovered for nearly two years in the 1950s. These days the former guerrilla HQ is firmly on the adventure tourist trail, although the modest war-camp has changed little since Fidel and Che used it. p388

Bayamo

The city that sparked the first cries of Cuban independence broadcasts a handful of sights honoring Carlos Manuel de Céspedes and his bid to kick out the Spanish. p381

Museo de la Revolución

Encased in a lavish palace, this encyclopedic museum tells the sometimes poetic, sometimes prosaic story of Cuba's revolutionary history with *mucho* propaganda. p83

Above: Tank, Museo de la Revolución

5 UNDERWATER ADVENTURES

There will be objections, of course, but let's say it anyway: Cuba is home to the best diving in the Caribbean. The reasons? Unrivaled water clarity, undisturbed reefs and sheltered Caribbean waters brimming with glowing fish. Accessibility for divers varies from the swim-out walls of the Bahía de Cochinos to the hard-to-reach subaquatic nirvana of the Jardines de la Reina archipelago.

INSPIRED BY MAPS/SHUTTERSTOCK ©

RICHARD SEMIK/SHUTTERSTOCK ©

Playa Girón

This could be the best diving and snorkeling in Cuba. Fabulous instructors, easy shore access, sheltered cenotes and interesting wrecks, all packaged in one of Cuba's friendliest towns. p235

Top: Cueva de los Peces (p236)

María la Gorda

The long journey to Cuba's western tip is worth it if you're heading for the 32 dive sites of María la Gorda, famous for their black coral. p200

Above: Snorkelling María la Gorda

Isla de la Juventud

Not many travelers make it to the undeveloped, hard-to-reach Isla, but 90% of those that do come for the exquisite diving. Pristine caves, passages and tunnels support dense coral and sponges. p165

Above: Isla coral reef (p170)

6 TROPICAL LANDSCAPES

YGON1970/SHUTTERSTOCK ©

ALBERTO CARRERA/SHUTTERSTOCK ©

TUPUNGATO/SHUTTERSTOCK ©

Zapata

A vast swamp full of crocodiles, mangroves, mosquitoes and abundant birdlife, Zapata is Cuba's largest remaining slice of wilderness. Access is by jeep, boat or on foot.
p230
Left: Zapata swampland

Parque Nacional Alejandro de Humboldt

One of the last remaining tracts of virgin jungle in the Caribbean, this mostly roadless park is home to immense rivers and the world's smallest frog.
p454
Left: Bridge on a park trail

Guanahacabibes

Shipwrecks, virgin beaches, petrified forests, and crabs crawling across the (only) roadway in their thousands, this long sliver of land that pokes like a spear toward Mexico is wild, unpopulated, and hard to pronounce. All the more reason to visit.
p199

Verdant, biodiverse and unsullied by strip malls and suburban sprawl, Cuba's surprisingly varied tropical landscapes are often overlooked in favor of the lucrative strips of sand that line the coast. But, speckled with swamps, jungle, mountains and limestone karst topography, the country's biospheres and national parks are equally rich in flavor. Flora and fauna abound and an increasing number of trails penetrate the easy-to-access hot spots.

7 SMALL TOWNS

Tourists cram the resorts, culture vultures head to the big cities, while Cuba's small towns are ideal places to slip under the radar and dip into the unofficial and uncensored aspects of Cuban life. Stay in a casa particular, sink into a rocking chair on a dimly-lit porch and discuss everything from cigar *vitolas* (sizes) to baseball statistics over a bottle of fiery local rum.

Viñales

Craggy *mogotes* (limestone monoliths), impossibly green tobacco fields, ambling oxen and spirit-lifting viewpoints at every turn, Viñales' slow rural vibe attracts a ton of tourists, but they can't detract from its underlying tranquility. p180

Below left: Viñales plantation

Gibara

A wonderfully authentic seafront town with an imperceptible air of mystery, Gibara has taken great strides in improving its demeanor after hard times and hurricanes. Home to a quirky film festival. p364

Top right: Gibara view

Remedios

Bastion of historic boutique hotels, colonial-era casas particulares and the loudest, craziest festival in Cuba, Remedios is a small town making a big city noise. p271

Right: Remedios street scene

8 MANY STYLES OF MUSIC

ROBERTO MACHADO NOA/LIGHTROCKET VIA GETTY IMAGES ©

ULRICH HEINSEN/SHUTTERSTOCK ©

TUPUNGATO/SHUTTERSTOCK ©

If you've been in Cuba for more than a day and still haven't heard any live music, you're clearly need to take out your ear plugs. Welcome to one of the most musically diverse countries on the planet, where street shoppers stroll to the beat of the bongos, guitars blast out of every other bar and singing is just another form of verbal communication. Wise up on salsa, son and reggaetón and get into the groove.

Fábrica de Arte Cubano

Art emporium extraordinaire, cutting-edge music venue, gathering spot for the most innovative people in Cuba, come to Havana's art 'factory' and be blinded by the capital's leading cultural lights. p132

Casa de la Trova, Santiago de Cuba

Legendary cultural venue in the birthplace of many of Cuba's traditional musical genres, this wonderful New Orleans style building pulsates with rhythms, energy and history. p420

Above: Performance at la Casa

Jazz Club la Zorra y El Cuervo

Hot dark basement jazz club in Havana that sees Cuban improvisors let loose with freestyle Latin riffs. p133

Need to Know

For more information, see Survival Guide (p505)

Currency
Cuban peso (CUP$; also called *moneda nacional*, MN$)

Language
Spanish

Visas
Regular tourists who plan to spend up to two months in Cuba do not need visas. Instead, you get a *tarjeta de turista* (tourist card).

Money
Private businesses prefer cash. State-run resorts and hotels favor (non-US) credit cards. There are a growing number of ATMs.

Cell Phones
Check with your service provider to see if your phone will work (GSM or TDMA networks only). International calls are expensive. You can pre-buy services from the state-run phone company, Cubacel.

Time
Eastern Standard Time GMT/UTC minus five hours

When to Go

Havana
GO Nov–Mar

Camagüey
GO Nov–Mar

Guardalavaca
GO Nov–Mar

Baracoa
GO Nov–Mar

Santiago de Cuba
GO Nov–Mar

Dry climate
Tropical climate, wet & dry seasons

High Season
(Nov–Mar, Jul & Aug)

➡ Prices are 30% higher and hotels may require advance bookings.

➡ Prices are at their highest around Christmas and New Year.

➡ Weather is cooler and drier November to March.

Shoulder
(Apr & Oct)

➡ Look out for special deals outside of peak season.

➡ Prices and crowds increase over Easter.

➡ October can be wet and stormy.

Low Season
(May, Jun & Sep)

➡ Some resort hotels offer fewer facilities or shut altogether.

➡ There's a hurricane risk between June and November and a higher chance of rain.

Useful Websites

BBC (www.bbc.co.uk) Interesting correspondent reports on Cuba.

Cubacasas.net (www.cubacasas.net) Information, photos and contact details for casas particulares (rooms in private homes).

Info Cuba (www.cubainfos.net) Excellent collection of web pages focusing mainly on Cuba's resort areas. In French and English.

Havana Times (www.havanatimes.org) A regularly updated and relatively objective site dedicated exclusively to Cuban news.

Lonely Planet (www.lonelyplanet.com/cuba) Destination information, articles, hotel reviews, traveler forum and more.

Important Numbers

To call Cuba from abroad, dial your international access code, Cuba's country code (🕾53), the city or area code, and the local number.

Emergency	🕾106
Directory assistance	🕾113
Police	🕾106
Fire	🕾105

Exchange Rates

Argentina	ARS$1	CUP$0.25
Australia	A$1	CUP$18.64
Canada	C$1	CUP$20.00
Europe	€1	CUP$29.40
Japan	¥100	CUP$0.22
Mexico	MXN$1	CUP$1.21
New Zealand	NZ$1	CUP$17.36
UK	£1	CUP$34.27
US	US$1	CUP$24.24

For current exchange rates, see www.xe.com.

Daily Costs

At the time of writing, money matters in Cuba are in a state of flux. See the box on p5 for more information.

At the time of research the CUC$ was still in use, and so many of the prices in this book are given as the US$ equivalent. Please check the conversions to CUP$ before traveling.

Budget:
Less than USD$80

➡ Casa particular (room in a private home): USD$25–45

➡ Meal in government-run restaurant: USD$10–15

➡ Museum entry: USD$1–5

Midrange:
USD$80–170

➡ Mid-range hotel: USD$50–120

➡ Meal in *paladar* (private restaurant): USD$15–25

➡ Bus travel: Havana–Trinidad USD$25

Top end:
More than USD$170

➡ Resort or historic hotel: USD$200–300

➡ Car hire or taxi: USD$70–80

➡ Evening cabaret: USD$35–60

Opening Hours

Banks 9am to 3pm Monday to Friday

Cadeca money exchanges 9am to 7pm Monday to Saturday, 9am to noon Sunday. Many top-end city hotels offer money exchange late into the evening.

Pharmacies 8am to 8pm

Post offices 8am to 5pm Monday to Saturday

Restaurants 10:30am to 11pm

Shops 9am to 5pm Monday to Saturday, 9am to noon Sunday

Arriving in Cuba

Aeropuerto Internacional José Martí (Havana) There are no regular buses or trains running direct from the airport into the city center. Taxis cost USD$25 to USD$30 and take 30 to 40 minutes to reach most of the city-center hotels. You can change money at the bank in the arrivals hall.

Other international airports Cuba has nine other international airports, but none of them has reliable public transport links; your best bet is always a taxi. Agree fares beforehand.

Getting Around

Bus The most efficient and practical option. State-run Víazul links most places of interest to tourists on a regular daily schedule. Cubanacán runs a less comprehensive service. Local buses are crowded and have no printed schedules.

Car Rentals are quite expensive and driving can be a challenge due to the lack of signposts and ambiguous road rules. Cars are often in short supply.

Taxi *Colectivos* (shared taxis) are a good option over longer distances if you are traveling in a small group. Fares can be split four ways, meaning *colectivos* are almost as cheap as buses.

Train Cuba's extensive rail network was recently upgraded with new carriages from China. Trains are still slow, but at least they're now more comfortable.

For much more on **getting around**, see p518.

First Time Cuba

For more information, see Survival Guide (p505)

Checklist

➡ Procure plenty of cash (preferably US dollars including small denominations for tips) and check the status of your credit/debit cards in Cuba with your home bank.

➡ Print out a copy of your medical insurance to show at the airport.

➡ Check when booking your flight that your tourist card is included in your package.

➡ Book ahead for accommodations and bus tickets.

What to Pack

➡ Latin American Spanish dictionary/phrasebook

➡ Plug adapters for European *and* US sockets

➡ Good money belt that fits snugly around your waist

➡ Basic first aid and required medications

➡ Insect repellent, sunscreen and sunglasses

➡ Stash of cash in US dollars, euros, Canadian dollars or pound sterling

➡ Antiseptic handwash and/ or wipes

Top Tips for Your Trip

➡ For a glimpse of the real Cuba and a chance to put your money directly into the pockets of individual Cubans, stay in a casa particular (private homestay).

➡ Carry toilet paper and antiseptic handwash, and drink bottled water.

➡ Avoid driving in Havana. The city has various public transportation options and reasonably priced taxis. Most neighborhoods are walkable.

➡ Thanks to heavy bureaucracy, answers to simple requests aren't always straightforward. Probe politely and ask at least five different people before you make important decisions.

➡ Bring a sweater/jacket for buses – the air-conditioning is often freezing.

➡ US travelers shouldn't rely on credit/debit cards – despite diplomatic talk, their use in Cuba still hasn't been activated.

➡ Book ahead for accommodations and transport, especially in peak season.

What to Wear

Cuba is a hot, humid country that, thankfully, has a casual approach to clothing. Locals generally opt for shorts, sandals and T-shirts; women favor tight-fitting Lycra, men looser *guayabera* shirts (invented in Cuba). There are only two nude beaches in Cuba, frequented almost exclusively by foreigners. Cinemas and theaters usually have a 'no shorts' rule for men.

What to Buy

Cuba is not a great shopping destination per se. However, if you're in the market for rum, cigars, coffee, unique local art, handmade crafts, or Cuba-themed souvenirs, you're in luck. Havana has the best array of shops. The resort areas are also well endowed with well-stocked souvenir outlets. For more interesting paraphernalia, gravitate to one of the private vendor markets located in most provincial cities.

Money

The Cuban peso (CUP$) is pegged at 24:1 to the US dollar. Both currencies are used in Cuba. Private businesses prefer dollars.

Bargaining

Cuba's socialist economy doesn't have a history of bargaining, though there may be some room for maneuver on prices at private enterprise markets.

Tipping

Tipping in Cuba is important. It is always preferable to tip in US dollars. Even a US$1 tip (worth CUP$24) can go a long way.

Resorts/hotels Tip for good service with bellboys, room maids.

Musicians Carry small notes to tip musicians in bars/restaurants.

Restaurants Standard 10%, or up to 15% if service is excellent.

Taxis Tip 10% if you are on the meter, otherwise agree full fare beforehand.

Language

Cubans working in the tourist industry are usually proficient in English as well as other European languages. Elsewhere, Spanish predominates. Many casa particular (private homestay) owners speak limited or no English, and most museums print explanations in Spanish. Bring a phrasebook or install a language app on your phone before travel.

Salsa dancing, Havana (p63)

Etiquette

Cuba is an informal country with few rules of etiquette.

Greetings Shake hands with strangers; a kiss or double-cheek kiss is appropriate between people (men–women and women–women) who have already met.

Conversation Although they can be surprisingly candid, Cubans aren't keen to discuss politics, especially with strangers and if it involves being openly critical of the government.

Dancing Cubans don't harbor any self-consciousness about dancing. Throw your reservations out of the window and let loose.

Eating

Private restaurants Although slightly pricier than their state-run equivalents, private restaurants nearly always offer the best, freshest food and the highest quality service.

Casas particulares Cuban homestays invariably serve a massive breakfast for around USD$5; some also offer an equally large and tasty dinner made from the freshest ingredients.

Hotels & resorts The all-inclusives offer buffet food of an international standard but after a week it can get a bit bland.

State-run restaurants Varying food and service from top-notch places in Havana to unimaginative rations in the provinces. Prices are often lower than private places.

What's New

Crippled by the coronavirus pandemic, deteriorating relations with the US, and deep economic problems including food shortages and sweeping price rises, 2020–21 was a bad year in a country wearily accustomed to bad years. Faced with tightened travel restrictions, fewer tourists and the dramatic collapse of an important economic ally (Venezuela), Cuba's future remains shaky and uncertain.

Currency Reform

In January 2021 Cuban convertibles (CUC$) were taken out of circulation for good. Prices in state-run businesses are now charged in Cuban pesos (CUP$) pegged at 24:1 to the US dollar. The 10% commission formerly levied on US dollars was abolished in July 2020 and American money has effectively replaced convertibles as Cuba's second currency.

New Trains

Cuba's undistinguished railway network appeared to turn a corner in July 2019 when, for the first time in nearly 20 years, the system received new rolling stock in the form of modern train carriages from China, along with a revamped timetable.

Reopened Capitolio

After six years of renovations, Havana's emblematic Capitolio Nacional (p85) reopened in time for the city's 500th anniversary celebrations in 2019. Guided tours unlock the wonders of its grandiose interior.

Sagua La Grande

This erstwhile sugar-producing town in Villa Clara Province has put itself back on the independent tourist map with a palatial new hotel and a restored town center.

First Specific LGBTIQ+ Hotel

One of three new Muthu hotels on Cayo Guillermo, the Gran Muthu Rainbow opened in December 2019 just before it

---

LOCAL KNOWLEDGE

WHAT'S HAPPENING IN CUBA

Two steps forward, one step back. It's a familiar mantra in Cuba's recent history and, as the 2010s turned into the 2020s, it was Groundhog Day again. Between 2017 and 2020, three separate rulings by the Trump administration decapitated the post-Obama boom in American tourism and shifted US–Cuban relations back to the days of schoolyard squabbling and petty insults lobbed across the Straits of Florida. And then came the coronavirus pandemic.

In March 2020, when Cuba closed its doors to the outside world, tourism figures – which had already been faltering – fell off a cliff. Although the country attempted a tentative reopening of targeted resort areas in July 2020, a Covid-paranoid world wasn't buying.

The fallout from the pandemic, coupled with food shortages, loss of remittances from abroad and a complicated restructuring of the national currency continues to sow uncertainty in Cuba and create a source of existential worry, especially among private business people.

was forced to close again due to the pandemic. It is Cuba's first specific state-run LGBTIQ+ hotel.

Villa Clara Resorts

Cayo las Brujas (Witch's Key) has become slightly less bewitching with the construction of four new hotels in less than two years on the 7 sq km island in Villa Clara Province.

Trinidad Train

The Valle de los Ingenios train (p293) is running out of Trinidad again after a long hiatus. The steam-powered loco puffs sedately through the Unesco-rated scenery of this once profitable sugar-growing valley, stopping at Manaca Iznaga.

Cayo Guillermo Luxury Hotel

The Swiss-based Kempinski hotel group opened up their second Cuban hotel – a luxury five-star resort on Cayo Guillermo – in December 2019. The resort's attractive over-the-water villas lend it a classy desert island feel.

Tapas Revolution

Over 100 years after cutting colonial ties, the Cubans have finally embraced Spain's finest food creation – tapas. Bars and restaurants offering small bites (some with Cuban twists) are proliferating everywhere from Havana to Holguín.

Cayo Cruz

Cayo Cruz is a previously undeveloped key off the northern coast of Cuba that has recently opened two new hotels with a third on the way. in 2021. The island is 25km-long and lined with beaches. It's attached to Cayo Coco by a new road and causeway.

Bike-Sharing

In November 2018 Havana inaugurated Cuba's first bike-sharing scheme called Ha'Bici (p142). Centered on Habana Vieja, it comprises a modest collection of 60 bikes and seven service stations.

LISTEN, WATCH & FOLLOW

For inspiration, visit www.lonelyplanet.com/cuba/articles.

Cubacasas.net Comprehensive and well-researched website dedicated primarily to promoting casas particulares (private homestays) but also providing a wealth of information about all aspects of independent travel in Cuba.

On Cuba Travel (www.oncubatravel.com/) Offers a downloadable pdf magazine and a regularly updated free blog about all things Cuban.

Granma (http://en.granma.cu) Cuba's main national newspaper published online in Spanish, English, French, German, Italian and Portuguese.

Yoani Sánchez (https://generacionyen.wordpress.com/) Widely read Cuban blogger who has garnered multiple international media awards.

FAST FACTS

Food trend Tapas bars

Doctor to patient ratio 1:149

Car ownership per 1000 people 38

Population 11.3 million

POPULATION PER SQ KM

CUBA   USA   UK

† ≈ 4 people per sq km

Accommodations

Find more accommodation reviews throughout the On the Road chapters (from p61)

Accommodations Types

Casas particulares Cuban homes that rent rooms to foreigners; an authentic and economic form of cultural immersion. There are thousands of casas across the country and most offer good value along with comfortable (if not luxurious) facilities.

Campismos Cheap, rustic accommodations in rural areas, usually in bungalows or cabins. There are over 80 in Cuba but only around a dozen rent to non-Cubans.

Boutique hotels The government-run company Cubanacán offers a range of 'boutique hotels' encased in refurbished historic buildings in Cuba's provincial towns. They are branded as 'E-hotels' after the Encanto brand.

State-run hotels Most Cuban hotels are government-owned. Prices and quality range from cheap Soviet-era digs to high-flying colonial chic. By far the biggest company is Gaviota, which runs mostly large resorts. Gran Caribe operates upmarket hotels spearheaded by Havana's emblematic Hotel Nacional. Cubanacán specializes in boutique hotels while Islazul offers cheap (sometimes dogeared) hotels favored by Cuban guests.

Resorts Large international-standard hotels in resort areas that sell all-inclusive packages. Well-represented international chains include Meliá, Blau, Memories and Iberostar.

Price Ranges

The following price ranges refer to a double room with bathroom in high season.

Havana / Rest of Cuba

$ less than US$70 / less than US$50

$$ US$70–$150 / US$50–$120

$$$ more than US$150 / more than US$120

Best Places to Stay

Best on a Budget

In this price range, accommodations consist almost entirely of casas particulares (rooms in a private homes) and campismos (rural cabins).

Although casa prices have crept up a little in the last few years, most still cost between US$25 and US$35. For this you can usually expect hot water, air-conditioning and a private bathroom. Breakfast is normally US$5 extra.

➡ Roy's Terrace Inn (p413), Santiago de Cuba

➡ Alojamiento Maité (p311), Morón

➡ Hostal Peregrino Consulado (p108), Havana

➡ Hostal Luis (p237), Playa Girón

➡ Casa Yamicel (p448), Baracoa

Best for Families

Since casas particulares are nearly always located in family homes, they are particularly well suited for catering to families traveling with kids. A large number of rooms have extra beds or can procure one quickly.

Many of Cuba's all-inclusive resorts are family-friendly and offer specific kids' activities as well as entertainment programs.

➡ Blau Varadero (p211), Varadero

➡ Hotel Playa Pesquero (p369), Playa Pesquero

➡ Pullman Cayo Coco (p315), Cayo Coco

➡ Casa Colonial Ykira (p448), Baracoa

➡ Casa Daniela (p183), Viñales

Best for Solo Travelers

Single hotel rooms can be pricey in Cuba, with travelers often having to cough up around 70% of the price of a double. Solo travelers can save money by staying in a casa particular. Prices here are nearly always 'per room' as opposed to 'per person,' but they rarely exceed US$35 per night outside of Havana. Casas also put you into contact with local people, meaning it's easier to make friends.

➡ Hostal El Encinar (p106), Havana

➡ 'Villa Colonial' – Frank & Arelys (p271), Remedios

➡ Casa Terraza Pavo Real (p414), Santiago de Cuba

➡ Villa Bely (p373), Guardalavaca

➡ Beny's House (p208), Varadero

Best for History

With four cities listed as Unesco World Heritage sites and several more deserving of the label, Cuba has plenty of attractive historic buildings reborn as hotels and private homestays. Factor in wonderful architecture and a tangible history-evoking atmosphere, and you can overlook the sometimes lackluster service.

➡ Hotel Ordoño (p367), Gibara

➡ Hostal Conde de Villanueva (p107), Havana

➡ Hotel Sagua (p274), Sagua La Grande

➡ Hotel Nacional (p112), Havana

➡ Hotel La Unión (p248), Cienfuegos

➡ Hotel Imperial (p416), Santiago de Cuba

Booking

It is always cheaper to book big hotels and resorts in advance. Most Cuban resorts are all-inclusive and sell packages (flights included) through agencies abroad.

Despite the abundance of casas particulares in Cuba, it is still advisable to book ahead in peak season (November to April).

Santiago de Cuba (p401)

Prices don't vary much. In recent years it has become possible to prebook a wide selection of casas with a credit card using popular accommodation portals such as Airbnb and Booking.com.

Lonely Planet (lonelyplanet.com/cuba) Find more independent reviews, as well as recommendations on the best places to stay.

Gaviota (www.gaviotahotels.com) Government-owned company that runs nearly 50 Cuban hotels.

Cubacasas (www.cubacasas.net) Lists and reviews hundreds of casas particulares across Cuba with contact details and photos.

Cuba Junky (www.cuba-junky.com) Has a directory of casas particulares available as an iPhone/android app.

Month by Month

TOP EVENTS

Carnaval de Santiago de Cuba, July

Festival Internacional de Ballet de la Habana, October

Las Parrandas, December

Festival Internacional de Jazz, January

Ciudad Metal November

January

The tourist season hits full swing, and the whole country has added buoyancy. Cold fronts bring occasionally chilly evenings.

✵ Día de la Liberación

As well as seeing in the New Year with roast pork and a bottle of rum, Cubans celebrate January 1 as the triumph of the revolution, the anniversary of Fidel Castro's 1959 victory.

✵ Incendio de Bayamo

Bayamo residents remember the 1869 burning of their city with music and theatrical performances in an *espectáculo* (show) culminating in particularly explosive fireworks.

✵ Festival Internacional de Jazz

The cream of Cuban music festivals arrives every January like a late Christmas present. In the past it has attracted the greats, Dizzy Gillespie and Max Roach among them, along with a perfect storm of Cuban talent.

February

Peak tourist season continues and high demand can lead to overbooking, particularly in the rental-car market. Calm seas and less fickle weather promote better water clarity, making this an ideal time to enjoy diving and snorkeling.

✵ Feria Internacional del Libro

First held in 1930, the International Book Fair is headquartered at Havana's Fortaleza de San Carlos de la Cabaña, but it later goes on the road to other cities.

Highlights include book presentations, special readings and the prestigious Casa de las Américas prize. (p105)

🏃 Diving with Clarity

Calm conditions promote clear water for diving, particularly on Cuba's south coast. The country's prime diving nexuses, La Isla de la Juventud and Playa Girón, have ideal conditions for underwater photography.

✵ Habanos Festival

Trade fairs, seminars, tastings and visits to tobacco plantations draw cigar aficionados to Havana for this annual cigar festival (www.habanos.com) with prizes, rolling competitions and a gala dinner.

March

Spring offers Cuba's best wildlife-watching opportunities, particularly of migrant birds. With dryer conditions, it is also an ideal time to indulge in hiking, cycling or numerous other outdoor activities.

✨ Festival de la Trova 'Pepe Sánchez'

Held since 1962 in honor of *trova* (international poetic singing) pioneer Pepe Sánchez, this festival invades the parks, streets and music houses of Santiago de Cuba in a showcase of the popular verse/song genre.

✨ Carnaval – Isla de la Juventud

This is the big annual party on the otherwise soporific Isla de la Juventud, a knees-up involving parades characterized by giant puppet-like heads, a rodeo, sports competitions and perhaps just a little drinking. (p167)

🏃 Birdwatching

March is a crossover period when migrant birds from both North and South America join Cuba's resident endemics en route for warmer or colder climes. There's no better time to polish off your binoculars.

✨ Semana de la Cultura Baracoesa

Beginning in late March, and culminating on April 1, Baracoa commemorates the landing of Antonio Maceo at Duaba in 1895, with a raucous carnival along the Malecón, expos of its indigenous music *nengón* and *kiribá,* and various culinary offerings. (p448)

Top: Street performers, Carnaval de la Habana (p32), Havana

Bottom: Cuban emerald hummingbirds can be seen in the Gran Parque Natural Montemar (p233)

DENNIS KARTENKAEMPER/SHUTTERSTOCK ©

April

Economy-seeking visitors should avoid the Easter period, which sees another spike in tourist numbers and prices. Otherwise April is a pleasant month with good fly-fishing potential off the south coast.

✩✩ Bienal Internacional del Humor

Cuba's unique humor festival takes place in odd-numbered years in San Antonio de los Baños in out-of-the-way Artemisa Province. Headquartered at the celebrated Museo del Humor, talented scribblers try to outdo each other by drawing ridiculous caricatures. (p151)

May

May marks the lull between the foreign crowds of winter and the domestic barrage of summer. Look out for special deals offered by resort hotels and significantly cheaper prices all round.

✩✩ Romerías de Mayo

This religious festival takes place in the city of Holguín during the first week of May and culminates with a procession to the top of the city's emblematic Loma de la Cruz, a small shrine atop a 275m hill. (p357)

Top: Music can often be heard on the streets of Havana (p63)

Bottom: Loma de la Cruz (p356), Holguín

Dia Internacional Contra Homophobia, Transfobia y Bifobia

Cuba's biggest pride parade has been held on May 17 since 2008. *Congas* (musical groups) wielding drums, trumpets and rainbow flags fan out along Havana's Calle 23, the climax of a three-week LGBTIQ+ campaign that includes workshops, discussion groups and art expos.

Cubadisco

An annual get-together of foreign and Cuban record producers and companies in Havana, Cubadisco hosts music concerts, a trade fair and a Grammy-style awards ceremony that encompasses every musical genre from chamber music to pop.

June

The Caribbean hurricane season begins inauspiciously. A smattering of esoteric provincial festivals keeps June interesting. Prices are still low and, with the heat and humidity rising, travelers from Europe and Canada tend to stay away.

Jornada Cucalambeana

Cuba's celebration of country music, and the witty 10-line *décimas* (stanzas) that go with it, takes place about 3km outside unassuming Las Tunas at Motel el Cornito, the former home of erstwhile country-music king, Juan Fajardo 'El Cucalambé.' (p345)

Fiestas Sanjuaneras

This feisty carnival in Trinidad on the last weekend in June is a showcase for the local *vaqueros* (cowboys), who gallop their horses through the narrow cobbled streets.

July

High summer is when Cubans vacation; expect the beaches and cheaper accommodations to be mobbed. The July heat also inspires two of the nation's hottest events: Santiago's Carnaval and the annual polemics of July 26.

Festival del Caribe, Fiesta del Fuego

The Festival del Fuego in early July kicks off an action-packed month for Santiago with exhibitions, song, dance, poetry and religious-tinged rituals from all around the Caribbean. (p411)

Festival Internacional 'Boleros de Oro'

Organized by Uneac, Cuba's artists and writers union, the Boleros de Oro was created by Cuban composer and musicologist José Loyola Fernández in 1986 as a global celebration of this distinctive Cuban musical genre. Most events take place in Havana's Teatro Mella. (p136)

Festival Internacional de Cine de Gibara

Gibara's celebration of indie cinema has been an annual event since 2003, when it was inaugurated by late Cuban film director Humberto Sales. Formerly a competition for budget movies, it has recently widened its reach to anything independent or avant-garde. (p368)

Carnaval de Santiago de Cuba

Arguably the biggest and most colorful carnival in the Caribbean, the famous Santiago shindig at the end of July is a riot of floats, dancers, rum, rumba and more. Come and join in the very *caliente* (hot) action. (p411)

Día de la Rebeldía Nacional

On July 26 Cubans 'celebrate' Fidel Castro's failed 1953 attack on Santiago's Moncada Barracks. The event is a national holiday and a chance for party leaders to deliver bombastic speeches. Expect *un poco* politics and *mucho* eating, drinking and being merry.

August

While Santiago retires to sleep off its hangover, Havana gears up for its own annual celebration. Beaches still heave with holidaying Cubans while tourist hotels creak under a fresh influx of visitors from Mediterranean Europe.

⭐ Carnaval de la Habana

Parades, dancing, music, colorful costumes and striking effigies – Havana's annual summer shindig might not be as famous as its more rootsy Santiago de Cuba counterpart, but the celebrations and processions along the Malecón leave plenty of other city carnivals in the shade.

⭐ Festival Internacional 'Habana Hip-Hop'

Organized by the Asociación Hermanos Saíz – a youth arm of Uneac – the annual Havana Hip-Hop Festival is a chance for the island's young musical creators to improvise and swap ideas.

September

Peak hurricane season. Tourist numbers hit a second trough. The storm-resistant take advantage of cheaper prices and near-empty beaches. But beware – some facilities close down completely.

⭐ Fiesta de Nuestra Señora de la Caridad

Every September 8, religious devotees from around Cuba partake in a pilgrimage to the Basílica de Nuestra Señora del Cobre, near Santiago, to honor Cuba's venerated patron saint (and her alter ego, the Santería *orisha*, Ochún). (p429)

October

Continuing storm threats and persistent rain keep most travelers away. While the solitude can be refreshing in Havana, life in the peripheral resorts can be deathly quiet and lacking in atmosphere.

⭐ Festival del Bailador Rumbero

During the 10 days following October 10, Matanzas rediscovers its rumba roots in this festival with talented local musicians performing in various city venues. (p222)

⭐ Festival Internacional de Ballet de la Habana

Hosted by the Cuban National Ballet, this annual festival brings together dance companies, ballerinas and a mixed audience of foreigners and Cubans for a week of expositions, galas, and classical and contemporary ballet. It has been held in even-numbered years since its inception in 1960. (p105)

November

Get ready for the big invasion from the north – and a hike in hotel rates. Over a quarter of Cuba's tourists come from Canada; they start arriving as soon as the Canadian weather turns frigid.

⭐ Fiesta de los Bandas Rojo y Azul

Considered one of the most important manifestations of Cuban campesino (farmer) culture, this esoteric fiesta in the settlement of Majagua, in Ciego de Ávila Province, splits the town into two teams (red and blue) that compete against each other in boisterous dancing and music contests.

🏃 Marabana

The popular Havana marathon draws between 2000 and 3000 competitors from around the globe. It's a two-lap course – though there is also a half-marathon, and 5km and 10km races. (p105)

⭐ Ciudad Metal

Decidedly edgy when it was first established in Santa Clara in 1990, this celebration of hardcore punk and metal sees Cuban bands setting up in the local baseball stadium and quite literally rocking the rafters. (p265)

December

Christmas and the New Year see Cuba's busiest and most expensive tourist spike. Resorts nearly double their prices and rooms sell out fast. The nation goes firework-crazy in a handful of riotous festivals. Book ahead!

✯✯✯ Benny Moré International Music Festival

The Barbarian of Rhythm is remembered in this annual celebration of his suave music, headquartered in the singer's small birth town of Santa Isabel de las Lajas in Cienfuegos Province. (p247)

✯✯✯ Festival Internacional del Nuevo Cine Latinoamericano

Widely lauded celebration of Cuba's massive film culture with plenty of nods to other Latin American countries. Held at various cinemas and theaters across Havana. (p106)

✯✯✯ Festival Nacional de Changüí

Since 2003, the city of Guantánamo has celebrated its indigenous music in this rootsy music festival. Look out for Elito Revé (son of Elio) and his orchestra. (p440)

✯✯✯ Procesión de San Lázaro

Every year on December 17, Cubans descend en masse on the venerated Santuario de San Lázaro in Santiago de las Vegas, on the outskirts of Havana. Some come on bloodied knees, others walk barefoot for kilometers to exorcize evil spirits and pay off debts for miracles granted. (p103)

✯✯✯ Las Parrandas de Remedios

A firework frenzy that takes place every Christmas Eve in Remedios in Villa Clara Province, Las Parrandas sees the town divide into two teams that compete against each other to see who can come up with the most colorful floats and the loudest bangs! (p271)

✯✯✯ Las Charangas de Bejucal

Didn't like Las Parrandas? Then try Bejucal's Las Charangas, Mayabeque Province's cacophonous alternative to the firework fever further east. The town splits into the exotically named *Espino de Oro* (Golden Thorn) and *Ceiba de Plata* (Silver Silk-Cotton Tree).

PARRANDAS FESTIVALS

Peculiar to the former Las Villas region of Cuba, Las Parrandas take place only in towns in Villa Clara, Ciego de Ávila and Sancti Spíritus provinces. Though each festival is different, there are some generic party tricks, such as fireworks, decorative floats and opposing neighborhoods competing for the loudest, brightest and wildest stunts. Camajuani, Caibarién, Mayajigua and Chambas all have raucous celebrations, but the biggest party of all erupts annually in Remedios on December 24.

Plan Your Trip
Itineraries

STRAITS OF FLORIDA

HAVANA

Viñales

Santa Clara

Cienfuegos

Trinidad

Camagüey

Baracoa

Bayamo

Santiago de Cuba

CARIBBEAN SEA

18 DAYS ## The Classic Itinerary

It's your first time in Cuba and you want to see as many eye-opening sights as possible countrywide. Even better, you don't mind a bit of road travel. This itinerary ferries you between the rival cities of Havana and Santiago, bagging most of the nation's historical highlights on the way. Víazul buses link all of the following destinations.

Fall in love with classic Cuba in **Havana**, with its museums, forts, theaters and rum. Three days is the bare minimum here to get

to grips with the main neighborhoods of Habana Vieja, Centro Habana and Vedado.

Head west next to the bucolic bliss of **Viñales** for a couple of days of hiking, caving and relaxing on a rocking chair on a sun-kissed colonial porch. Daily buses connect Viñales with French-flavored **Cienfuegos**, an architectural monument to 19th-century neoclassicism. After a night of Gallic style and Cuban music, travel a couple of hours down the road to colonial **Trinidad**, with more museums per head than anywhere else in Cuba. The casas particulares (rooms in private homes) resemble historical monuments

Habana Vieja (p67), Havana

here, so stay three nights. On the second day you can break from the history and choose between the beach (Playa Ancón) or the natural world (Topes de Collantes).

Santa Clara is a rite of passage for Che Guevara pilgrims visiting his mausoleum but also a great place for luxurious private rooms and an upbeat nightlife. Check out Club Mejunje and have a drink in dive bar La Marquesina. Further east, **Camagüey** invites further investigation with its maze of Catholic churches and giant *tinajones* (clay pots).

Laid-back **Bayamo** is where the revolution was ignited, and it has an equally sparky street festival should you be lucky enough to be there on a Saturday. Allow plenty of time for the cultural nexus of **Santiago de Cuba**, where seditious plans for rebellion have been routinely hatched. The Cuartel Moncada, Cementerio Santa Ifigenia and Morro Castle will fill a busy two days. Save the best till last with a long, but by no means arduous, journey over the hills and far away to **Baracoa** for two days' relaxing with the coconuts, chocolate and other tropical treats.

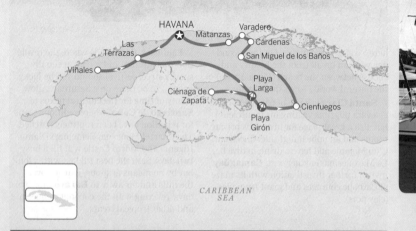

GULF OF
MEXICO

HAVANA
Matanzas
Varadero
Cárdenas
Las
Terrazas
San Miguel de los Baños
Viñales
Playa
Larga
Ciénaga de
Zapata
Cienfuegos
Playa
Girón

CARIBBEAN
SEA

1 WEEK Escape from Varadero

Varadero has some cheap packages and is a popular gateway into Cuba, but once you've pacified your partner/kids and had your fill of the beach, what else is there for a curious Cuban adventurer to do? Plenty. Víazul or Conectando buses link the following places.

Take a bus west, stopping off for lunch in **Matanzas**, where Cuban reality will hit you like a sharp slap to the face. Investigate the Museo Farmacéutico, take a peep inside the Teatro Sauto and stroll Calle Narváez, the city's fabulous art street. For a slow approach to Havana, divert through the Escaleras de Jaruco for spectacular coastal views of Mayabeque Province. Book a night in a fine colonial hotel in **Havana** and spend the next day admiring the copious sights of the old quarter, Habana Vieja. Essential stops include the cathedral, the Museo de la Revolución and a stroll along the Malecón.

The next day, head west to **Las Terrazas**, an eco-resort that seems a million miles from the clamorous capital (it's actually only 55km). You can bathe and birdwatch at the same time in the Baños del San Juan and recuperate with a night in the Hotel Moka. An optional two-day extension of this itinerary lies further west in **Viñales**, a resplendent yet bucolic Unesco World Heritage site where you can decamp to a casa particular (homestay), eat some of the best roast pork in Cuba (the world?), go for a hike and then slump into a rocking chair on a rustic colonial porch.

Going back east, skip the touristy Boca de Guamá and stop instead at **Playa Larga** for an afternoon of beach sloth. Procure a night or two of accommodations at a homestay in **Playa Girón**, where you can either dive or plan wildlife forays into the **Ciénaga de Zapata**. A couple of hours east lies the city of **Cienfuegos**, an elegant last stopover with fine boutique hotels and sunset cruises on the bay.

On the leg back to Varadero you can uncover a dustier, time-warped Cuba in half-ruined **San Miguel de los Baños** back in Matanzas Province, an erstwhile spa that harbors a grand abandoned hotel. Last stop before returning to your Varadero sunbed is **Cárdenas**, home to three superb museums.

Top: Matanzas (p220)
Bottom: Harbor, Cienfuegos (p242)

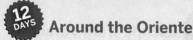

12 DAYS
Around the Oriente

The Oriente is like another country; they do things differently here, or so they'll tell you in Havana. This circuit allows you to bypass the Cuban capital and focus exclusively on the culturally rich, fiercely independent eastern region. With poor transport links, a rental car is useful here.

Make your base in **Santiago de Cuba**, city of revolutionaries, culture and *folklórico* dance troupes. There's tons to do here pertaining to history (Morro Castle), music (Cuba's original Casa de la Trova) and religion (Basílica de Nuestra Señora del Cobre). On the second day, reserve time to explore east into the Parque Baconao and the ruined coffee farms around **La Gran Piedra**.

Regular buses travel east into the mountains of Guantánamo Province. Pass a night in **Guantánamo** to suss out the *changüí* music (local fusion of African and Spanish sounds) before climbing the spectacular road La Farola into **Baracoa**, where three days will bag you the highlights – beach time at Playa Maguana, a sortie into the Parque Nacional Alejandro de Humboldt and a day absorbing the psychedelic rhythms of the town itself.

Heading north via Moa is a tough jaunt, with taxis or rental cars required to get you to **Cayo Saetía**, an isolated key with an on-site hotel where lonesome beaches embellish a former hunting reserve.

Pinares del Mayarí ecological area sits within the pine-clad mountains of the Sierra Crystal amid huge waterfalls and rare flora. Hiking married with some rural relaxation make excellent bedfellows at the region's eponymous hotel. If you have half a day to spare, consider a side trip to **Museo Conjunto Histórico de Birán** to see the surprisingly affluent farming community that spawned Fidel Castro.

Take a day off in hassle-free **Bayamo** with its smattering of small-town museums before tackling **Manzanillo**, where Saturday night in the main square can get feisty. More-adventurous transport options will lead you down to Niquero and within striking distance of the largely deserted **Parque Nacional Desembarco del Granma**, famous for uplifted marine terraces and aboriginal remains. Linger in one of **Marea del Portillo's** low-key resorts before attempting the spectacular but potholed coast road back to Santiago.

Top: Santiago de Cuba (p401)
Bottom: La Farola (p444)

Cuba: Off the Beaten Track

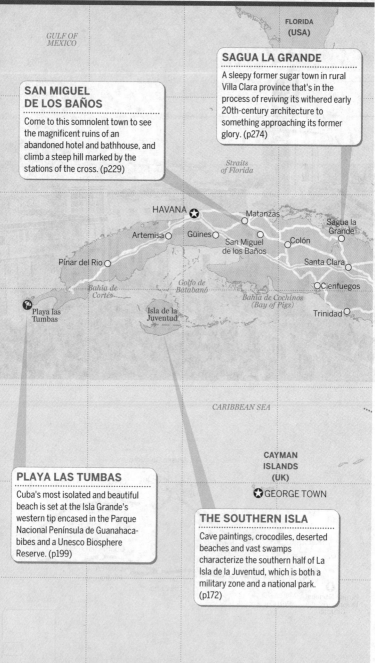

GULF OF
MEXICO

FLORIDA
(USA)

SAGUA LA GRANDE

A sleepy former sugar town in rural
Villa Clara province that's in the
process of reviving its withered early
20th-century architecture to
something approaching its former
glory. (p274)

SAN MIGUEL
DE LOS BAÑOS

Come to this somnolent town to see
the magnificent ruins of an
abandoned hotel and bathhouse, and
climb a steep hill marked by the
stations of the cross. (p229)

Straits
of Florida

HAVANA

Matanzas

Sagua la
Grande

Artemisa   Güines   Colón

San Miguel
de los Baños

Pínar del Rio

Santa Clara

Bahía de
Cortés

Golfo de
Batabanó

Cienfuegos

Bahía de Cochinos
(Bay of Pigs)

Playa las
Tumbas

Isla de la
Juventud

Trinidad

CARIBBEAN SEA

CAYMAN
ISLANDS
(UK)

GEORGE TOWN

PLAYA LAS TUMBAS

Cuba's most isolated and beautiful
beach is set at the Isla Grande's
western tip encased in the Parque
Nacional Península de Guanahacabibes and a Unesco Biosphere
Reserve. (p199)

THE SOUTHERN ISLA

Cave paintings, crocodiles, deserted
beaches and vast swamps
characterize the southern half of La
Isla de la Juventud, which is both a
military zone and a national park.
(p172)

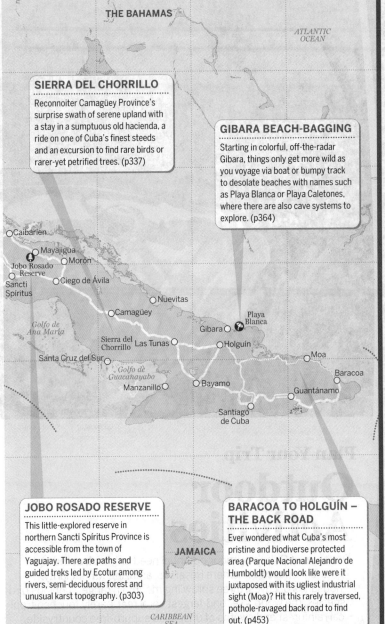

SIERRA DEL CHORRILLO

Reconnoiter Camagüey Province's surprise swath of serene upland with a stay in a sumptuous old hacienda, a ride on one of Cuba's finest steeds and an excursion to find rare birds or rarer-yet petrified trees. (p337)

GIBARA BEACH-BAGGING

Starting in colorful, off-the-radar Gibara, things only get more wild as you voyage via boat or bumpy track to desolate beaches with names such as Playa Blanca or Playa Caletones, where there are also cave systems to explore. (p364)

JOBO ROSADO RESERVE

This little-explored reserve in northern Sancti Spíritus Province is accessible from the town of Yaguajay. There are paths and guided treks led by Ecotur among rivers, semi-deciduous forest and unusual karst topography. (p303)

BARACOA TO HOLGUÍN – THE BACK ROAD

Ever wondered what Cuba's most pristine and biodiverse protected area (Parque Nacional Alejandro de Humboldt) would look like were it juxtaposed with its ugliest industrial sight (Moa)? Hit this rarely traversed, pothole-ravaged back road to find out. (p453)

0 — 200 km
0 — 100 miles

THE BAHAMAS

ATLANTIC OCEAN

Caibarién
Mayajigua
Jobo Rosado Reserve
Morón
Sancti Spíritus
Ciego de Ávila
Golfo de Ana María
Nuevitas
Camagüey
Sierra del Chorrillo
Las Tunas
Santa Cruz del Sur
Golfo de Guacanayabo
Manzanillo
Bayamo
Santiago de Cuba
Gibara
Playa Blanca
Holguín
Moa
Baracoa
Guantánamo

JAMAICA

CARIBBEAN SEA

Scuba diving, Jardines de la Reina (p314)

Outdoor Activities

Doubters of Cuba's outdoor potential need only look at the highlights: six Unesco Biosphere Reserves, amazing water clarity, thousands of caves, three sprawling mountain ranges, copious bird species, the world's second-largest coral reef, barely touched tropical rainforest and swaths of unspoiled suburb-free countryside.

Helpful Tips

Accessibility

Access to many parks and protected areas in Cuba is limited and can only be negotiated with a prearranged guide or on an organized excursion. If in doubt, consult Ecotur (p142) travel agency.

Private Guides

Since the loosening of economic restrictions in 2011, it has become legal for private individuals to set up as outdoor guides in Cuba, though, as yet, there are few full-blown non-government travel agencies. Most private guides operate out of casas particulares (rooms in private homes) or hotels and many are very good. If you are unsure whether your guide is official, ask to see their government-issued license first.

Prebooking Tours

The following agencies organize outdoor tours from outside Cuba:

Scuba en Cuba (www.scuba-en-cuba.com) Diving trips.

Explore (www.explore.co.uk) Offers an eight-day walking trip.

WowCuba (www.wowcuba.com) Specializes in cycling trips.

Need to Know

Travelers in search of adventure who've already warmed up on rum, cigars and all-night salsa dancing won't get bored in Cuba. Hit the highway on a bike, fish (as well as drink) like Hemingway, hike on guerrilla trails, fly over an ecovillage on a zip line, or rediscover a sunken Spanish shipwreck off the shimmering south coast.

Thanks to the dearth of modern development, Cuba's outdoors is refreshingly green and free of the smog-filled highways and ugly suburban sprawl that infect many other countries.

While not on a par with North America or Europe in terms of leisure options, Cuba's facilities are well established and improving. Services and infrastructure vary depending on what activity you are looking for. The country's diving centers are generally excellent and instructors are of an international caliber. Naturalists and ornithologists in the various national parks and flora and fauna reserves are similarly conscientious and well qualified. Hiking has traditionally been limited and frustratingly rule-ridden, but opportunities have expanded in recent years, with companies such as Ecotur offering a wider variety of hikes in previously untrodden areas and even some multiday trekking. Cycling is refreshingly DIY, and all the better for it. Canyoning and climbing are newer sports in Cuba that have a lot of local support but limited official backing – as yet.

It's possible to hire reasonable outdoor gear in Cuba for most of the activities you will do, although it may not always be top quality. If you do bring your own supplies, any gear donated at the end of your trip to individuals you meet along the way (headlamps, snorkel masks, fins etc) will be greatly appreciated.

Diving

If Cuba has a stand-out activity, it is scuba diving. Even Fidel Castro in his younger days liked to don a wetsuit and escape beneath the iridescent waters of the Atlantic or Caribbean (his favorite dive site was – apparently – the rarely visited Jardines de la Reina archipelago). Indeed, so famous was the Cuban leader's diving addiction that the CIA allegedly once considered an assassination plot that involved inserting an explosive device inside a conch and placing it on the seabed.

Excellent dive sites are numerous in Cuba. Focus on the area or areas where you want to dive rather than trying to cover multiple sites. The best areas – the Jardines de la Reina, María la Gorda and the Isla de la Juventud – are all fairly isolated, requiring travel time (and pre-planning). The more sheltered south coast, in particular Playa Girón, has the edge in terms of water clarity and dependable weather, though the north coast, offering easy access to one of the world's largest reefs, is no slouch.

What makes diving in Cuba so special is its unpolluted ocean, clear water conditions (average underwater visibility is 30m to 40m), warm seas (mean temperature is 24°C), abundant coral and fish, simple access (including a couple of excellent swim-out reefs) and fascinating shipwrecks. Cuba was a nexus for weighty galleons in the 17th and 18th centuries, and rough seas and skirmishes with pirates sunk many of them.

Diving Centers

In all, Cuba has 25 recognized diving centers spread over 17 different areas. The majority of the centers are managed by Marlin Náutica y Marinas (www. nauticamarlin.com), though you'll also find representation from Gaviota (p142). Though equipment can sometimes be a little worn, you can generally expect safe, professional service with back-up medical support. Environmentally sensitive diving is where things can get wobbly, and individuals should educate themselves about responsible diving. As well as being Scuba Schools International (SSI), American Canadian Underwater Certification (ACUC) and Confédération Mondiale de Activités Subaquatiques (CMAS) certified, most dive instructors are multilingual, speaking a variety of Spanish, English, French, German and Italian. Because of US embargo laws, Professional Association of Diving Instructors (PADI) certification is generally not offered in Cuba.

Dives and courses are comparably priced island-wide, from US$25 to US$50 per dive, with a discount after four or five dives. Full certification courses are US$310 to US$365, and 'resort' or introductory dives cost US$50 to US$60.

La Boca, Playa Ancón (p291)

especially, but also in Varadero and in the Cienfuegos and Guajimico areas. If you intend to do a lot of snorkeling, bring your own gear, as the rental stuff can be tattered and buying it in Cuba will mean you'll sacrifice both price and quality.

Snorkeling

You don't have to go deep to enjoy Cuba's tropical aquarium. Snorkelers can glide out from the shore at Playa Girón in the Bay of Pigs, or Playa Coral and Playa Jibacoa on the north coast east of Havana. Otherwise, most dive operators can also organize snorkeling for cheaper rates.

Good boat dives for snorkeling happen around Isla de la Juventud and Cayo Largo

Boating & Kayaking

Boat rental is available on many of the island's lakes. Good options include the Laguna de la Leche, Laguna la Redonda and the Liberación de Florencia, in Ciego de Ávila Province, and Embalse Zaza in Sancti Spíritus Province. You can also rent rowboats and head up the Río Canímar near Matanzas, oaring between the jungle-covered banks of this mini-Amazon.

Kayaking as a sport is pretty low-key in Cuba, treated more as a beach activity in the plusher resorts. Most of the tourist beaches will have Náutica points that rent out simple kayaks, good for splashing around in but not a lot else.

Varadero (p205)

Fishing

Deep-Sea Fishing

Hemingway wasn't wrong. Cuba's fast-moving Gulf Stream along the north coast supports prime game fishing for sailfish, tuna, mackerel, swordfish, barracuda, marlin and shark pretty much year-round. Deep-sea fishing is a rite of passage for many and a great way to wind down, make friends, drink beer, watch sunsets and generally leave the troubles of the world behind. Not surprisingly, the country has great facilities for sport anglers, and every Cuban boat captain seems to look and talk as if he's walked straight from the pages of a Hemingway classic.

Cuba's best deep-sea fishing center is Cayo Guillermo, the small island (then uninhabited) that featured in Hemingway's *Islands in the Stream*. Papa may no longer be in residence, but there's still an abundance of fish. Another good bet is Havana, which has two marinas, one at Tarará and the other – better one – at Marina Hemingway to the west.

Elsewhere, all of Cuba's main resort areas offer excursions for deep-sea fishing at similar rates. Count on paying approximately US$310 per half-day for four people, including crew and open bar.

Fly-Fishing

Fly-fishing is undertaken mainly on shallow sand flats easily reached from the shoreline. Classic areas to throw a line are Las Salinas in the Ciénaga de Zapata, the protected waters surrounding Cayo Largo del Sur, parts of the Isla de la Juventud and – most notably – the uninhabited nirvana of the Jardines de la Reina archipelago. The archipelago is a national park and heavily protected. It is not unheard of to catch 25 different species of fish in the same day here.

A 'grand slam' for fly-fishers in Cuba is to bag tarpon, bonefish and permit in the same day; bag a snook as well and they call it a 'superslam.' The best fishing season in this part of Cuba is February to June. The remoteness of the many islands, reefs and sand flats means fishing trips are usually organized on boats that offer on-board accommodations. They are coordinated

Kiteboarding, Cayo Guillermo (p318)

Kiteboarding

With stiff east-northeast winds fanning its jagged northern coastline, it was only a matter of time before the country's excellent kiteboarding potential was discovered by Cubans (and visiting tourists). The sport is still relatively new in Cuba, although several good operators have now established themselves at various points along the north coast, offering equipment rental and courses. The main kitesurfing hubs are Havana (more specifically Tarará), Varadero and, best of all, Cayo Guillermo. There are also small scenes at Playa Santa Lucía and Guardalavaca. Havana Kiteboarding Club (p318) maintains an operation in Cayo Guillermo. Barracuda Scuba Diving Center (p207) is among several operators in Varadero.

Prices vary considerably, but two-hour basic courses cost from around US$80, and equipment rental starts at US$35 per day. Kite operators can also help arrange accommodations packages at various beachside hotels. Check the websites.

Hiking & Trekking

European hikers and North American wilderness fiends take note: while Cuba's trekking potential is enormous, the traveler's right to roam is restricted by badly maintained trails, poor signage, a lack of maps and rather draconian restrictions about where you can and cannot go without a guide. Hiking for recreation isn't as ingrained in the culture here as it is in, say, Canada or Germany. Instead, many park authorities tend to assume that all hikers want to be led by hand along short, relatively tame trails that are rarely more than 5km or 6km in length. You'll frequently be told that hiking alone is a reckless and dangerous activity, despite the fact that Cuba harbors no big fauna and no poisonous snakes. The best time of year for hiking is outside the rainy season and before it gets too hot (December to April).

The dearth of available hikes isn't always the result of nitpicking restrictions. Much of Cuba's trekkable terrain is in ecologically sensitive areas, meaning access is carefully managed and controlled.

through a company called Avalon (www. cubandivingcenters.com).

The north coast hides a couple of good fly-fishing havens. Most noted are the still-uninhabited keys of Cayo Romano and Cayo Cruz in the north of Camagüey Province. Trips are coordinated by Avalon and based at a hotel on Cayo Cruz.

Freshwater Fishing

Freshwater fishing in Cuba is lesser known than fly-fishing but equally rewarding, and many Americans and Canadians home in on the island's numerous lakes. Freshwater fly-fishing is superb in the vast Ciénaga de Zapata in Matanzas, where enthusiasts can arrange multiday catch-and-release trips. *Trucha* (largemouth bass) was first introduced into Cuba in the early 20th century by Americans at King's Ranch and the United Fruit Company. Due to favorable environmental protection, the fish are now abundant in many Cuban lakes. Good places to cast a line are the Laguna del Tesoro in Matanzas, the Laguna de la Leche and Laguna la Redonda in Ciego de Ávila Province, Embalse Zaza in Sancti Spíritus and Embalse Hanabanilla in Villa Clara – 7.6kg specimens have been caught here!

Top: Salto del Caburni (p294), Topes de Collantes

Bottom: Hiking El Yunque (p453), near Baracoa

Multiday hiking in Cuba has improved in the last couple of years and, though information is still hard to get, you can piece together workable options in the Sierra Maestra and the Sierra del Escambray. The most popular by far is the three-day trek to the summit of Pico Turquino. There are also long day hikes available in the forests around Soroa in Artemisa Province.

More challenging day hikes include El Yunque, a mountain near Baracoa; the Balcón de Iberia circuit in Parque Nacional Alejandro de Humboldt; and some of the hikes around Las Terrazas and Viñales.

Topes de Collantes probably has the largest concentration of hiking trails in its protected zone (a natural park). Indeed, some overseas groups organize four- to five-day treks here, starting near Lago Hanabanilla and finishing in Parque El Cubano. Inquire in advance at the Carpeta Central information office in Topes de Collantes if you are keen to organize something on behalf of a group.

Other, tamer hikes include Cueva las Perlas and Del Bosque al Mar in the Península de Guanahacabibes, the El Guafe trail in Parque Nacional Desembarco del Granma and the short circuit in Reserva Ecológica Varahicacos in Varadero. Some of these hikes are guided and all require the payment of an entry fee.

If you want to hike independently, you'll need patience, resolve and an excellent sense of direction. Try experimenting first with Salto del Caburní or Sendero La Batata in Topes de Collantes or the various hikes around Viñales. There's a beautiful, little-used DIY hike on a good trail near Marea del Portillo and some gorgeous options around Baracoa – ask the locals!

Cycling

Riding a bike in Cuba is *the* best way to discover the island in close-up. Decent, quiet roads, wonderful scenery and the opportunity to get off the beaten track and meet Cubans in rural areas make cycling here a pleasure, whichever route you take. For casual pedalers, daily bike rental is sometimes available and has become more widespread in recent years. Some hotels lend or rent bikes for about US$3 to US$7 per day. The bigger all-inclusive resorts in Varadero and Guardalavaca are the best bet as they sometimes include bike use as part of the package, although it's unlikely the bikes will have gears. If you're staying in a casa particular (room in a private home), your host will generally be able to rustle up something roadworthy. Some casa owners have even started renting out foreign-made bikes good enough for tack-

BEST HIKES

HIKE	SOLO OR GUIDED	START/FINISH	DISTANCE	GRADE	FEATURES
Pico Turquino	guided	Alto del Naranjo/ Las Cuevas	17km	hard	mountain, birdwatching
Salto del Caburní	solo	Topes de Collantes	6km	medium	waterfall, natural swimming pool
El Guafe	solo	Parque Nacional Desembarco del Granma	3km	easy	flora, archaeological sites
Balcón de Iberia	guided	Parque Nacional Alejandro de Humboldt	6km	easy	flora, fauna, natural swimming pool
El Brujito	guided	Soroa	15km	medium	ecoforest, birdwatching, coffee plantations
El Yunque	guided	Campismo El Yunque	8km	medium-hard	mountain, flora

Horseback riding, Viñales (p180)

ling rural day trips (bank on paying US$10 to US$15 a day).

Serious cyclists contemplating a multi-day Cuban cycling tour should bring their own bikes from home, along with plenty of spare parts. Since organized bike trips have long been common in Cuba, customs officials, taxi drivers and hotel staff are used to dealing with boxed bikes.

Cycling highlights include the Valle de Viñales; the countryside around Trinidad, including the flat spin down to Playa Ancón; the quiet lanes that zigzag through Guardalavaca; and the roads out of Baracoa to Playa Maguana (northwest) and Boca de Yumurí (southeast). For a bigger challenge try La Farola between Cajobabo and Baracoa (21km of ascent), the bumpy but spectacular coast road between Santiago and Marea del Portillo – best spread over three days with overnights in Brisas Sierra Mar los Galeones and Campismo la Mula – or, for real wheel warriors, the insanely steep mountain road from Bartolomé Masó to Santo Domingo in Granma Province. Havana has recently sprouted a bike-sharing scheme and a couple of private operators offering bike tours.

With a profusion of casas particulares offering cheap, readily available accommodations, cycle touring is a joy here as long as you keep off the Autopista and steer clear of Havana.

Off-road biking has not yet taken off in Cuba and is generally not permitted.

Horseback Riding

Cuba has a long-standing cowboy culture, and horseback riding is available countrywide in both official and unofficial capacities. If you arrange it privately, make sure you check the state of the horses and equipment first. Riding poorly kept horses is both cruel and potentially dangerous.

The state-owned catering company Palmares owns numerous rustic ranches across Cuba that are supposed to give tourists a feel for traditional country life. All of these places offer guided horseback riding, usually for around US$6 to US$8 per hour. You'll find good ranchos in Florencia in Ciego de Ávila Province and Finca La Belén (p338) in Camagüey Province.

USEFUL AGENCIES

Ecotur Runs organized hiking, trekking, fishing and birdwatching trips to some of the country's otherwise inaccessible corners. It has offices in every province and a main HQ (p142) in Havana.

Campismo Popular (www.campismopopular.cu) Runs Cuba's 80-plus campismos (cheap rustic accommodations). It has Reservaciones de Campismo offices in every provincial capital.

Marlin Náutica y Marinas (www.nauticamarlin.com) State-run company that oversees many of Cuba's marinas. It also offers fishing, diving, boating and other water-based excursions.

La Guabina (p199) is a horse-breeding center near the city of Pinar del Río that offers both horse shows and horseback-riding adventures.

Trinidad and Viñales are two of the best and most popular places in Cuba for horse riding.

Rock Climbing

The Valle de Viñales has been described as having some of the best rock climbing in the western hemisphere. There are more than 150 routes now open (at all levels of difficulty, with several rated as YDS Class 5.14) and the word is out among the international climbing crowd, who are creating their own scene in one of Cuba's prettiest settings. Independent travelers will appreciate the free rein that climbers enjoy here.

Though you can climb year-round, the heat can be oppressive, and locals stick to an October to April season, with December to January being the optimum months. For more information, visit Cuba Climbing (www.cubaclimbing.com) or head straight to Viñales.

It is important to note that, though widely practiced and normally without consequence, the legality of climbing in Cuba inhabits one of the country's many gray areas. It was technically banned in 2012, but still widely practiced by locals and visitors. By 2019 it was even quietly being promoted, with climbing areas marked on local maps at Viñales' tourist office. The government has always come down harder on Cubans than tourists; as a foreigner, you're unlikely to get arrested or even warned for climbing, but you will be undertaking the activity at your own risk (don't expect any helicopter rescues). Take extreme care and do not, under any circumstances, do anything that damages the delicate ecosystem. Most of Viñales' private climbing guides are highly experienced.

Caving

The karst landscapes of Cuba are riddled with caves – more than 20,000 and counting – and cave exploration is available to both casual tourists and professional speleologists. The Gran Caverna de Santo Tomás (p188), near Viñales, is Cuba's largest cavern, with over 46km of galleries, and offers guided tours. The Cueva de los Peces (p236), near Playa Girón, is a flooded *cenote* (sinkhole) with colorful snorkeling. The Cuevas de Bellamar (p219) near Matanzas also has daily tours, while the bat-filled Cueva de Ambrosio (p205) in Varadero can be explored independently.

Caving specialists have virtually unlimited caves from which to choose. With advance arrangements, you can explore deep into the Gran Caverna de Santo Tomás or visit the Cueva Martín Infierno in Cienfuegos Province, which has the world's largest stalagmite. The Cueva San Catalina, near Varadero, is famous for its unique mushroom formations. Speleo-diving is also possible, but only for those already highly trained.

Plan Your Trip
Family Travel

Just as Cuba is stuck in time for adults, it's also unashamedly retro for children. There's something wonderfully old-fashioned about kids' entertainment here, which is less about sophisticated computer games and more about messing around in the plaza with an improvised baseball bat and a rolled-up ball of plastic.

Cuba for Kids

There are certain dichotomies regarding child facilities in Cuba. On the one hand, Cuban society is innately family-friendly, child-loving and tactile; on the other, economic challenges have meant that common 'Western' provisions such as pushchair ramps, changing tables and basic safety measures are often thin on the ground. If you're traveling with teenagers, note that Cuba's intermittent internet service could throw your phone-addicted offspring into a temporary strop.

The one place where you'll find generic international standards of service is in the modern resorts, most of which have dedicated and professionally run 'kids' clubs.'

Children's Highlights

Forts & Castles

Fortaleza de San Carlos de la Cabaña, Havana (p99) This huge fort has museums, battlements and a nightly cannon ceremony with soldiers in period costume.

Castillo de San Pedro de la Roca del Morro, Santiago (p410) This Unesco-listed fort is best known for its exciting pirate museum.

Castillo de la Real Fuerza, Havana (p71) This centrally located fort has a moat, lookouts and scale models of Spanish galleons.

Best Regions for Kids

Havana

The streets of Habana Vieja can't have changed much since the days of the *Pirates of the Caribbean,* so your kids' imaginations will be allowed to run wild in forts, squares, museums and narrow streets. Havana also has an aquarium (Acuario Nacional) and several beaches a short hop away.

Varadero

Cuba's biggest resort has the largest – if most predictable – stash of specifically tailored kids' activities, including nighttime shows, organized sports, beach games and boat trips.

Trinidad

The south coast's southern gem is awash with economic casas particulares (private homestays), an ideal opportunity for your kids to mix and mingle with Cuban families. Throw in an excellent beach (Playa Ancón), easily accessible snorkeling waters and a profusion of pleasant pastoral activities (horseback riding is popular), and you've got the perfect nonresort family option.

Playgrounds

Parque Maestranza, Havana (p69) Bouncy castles, fairground rides and sweet snacks overlooking Havana harbor.

Barbeparque, Havana (p82) Barber-themed kids' park that forms part of a Habana Vieja community project.

Parque Lenin, Havana (p101) More 'rustic' playground rides, boats, a train, and horses for rent.

Animal Encounters

Acuario Nacional, Havana (p97) Various reproductions of Cuba's coastal ecosystems including a marine cave and a mangrove forest at the nation's main aquarium in the Miramar district.

Criadero de Cocodrilos (p232) Of the half-dozen croc farms spread across the country, the best is in Guamá, Matanzas Province.

Horseback riding Possible all over Cuba and usually run out of rustic *fincas* (farms) in rural areas such as Pinar del Río and Trinidad.

Festivals

Las Parrandas, Remedios (p271) Fireworks, smoke and huge animated floats: Remedios' Christmas Eve party is a blast for kids *and* adults.

Carnaval de Santiago de Cuba (p411) A colorful celebration of Caribbean culture with floats and dancing that takes place every July.

Carnaval de la Habana (p32) More music, dancing and effigies, this time along Havana's Malecón in August.

Planning

Travelers with kids are not unusual in Cuba and the trend has proliferated in recent years with more Cuban-Americans visiting their families with offspring in tow; these will be your best sources for on-the-ground information. Be forewarned that physical contact and human warmth are typically Cuban: strangers will effusively welcome your kids, give them kisses or take their hands with regularity. Chill, it's all part of the Cuban way.

Local children run around freely in Cuba and, with strong local community organizations, the safety of your child shouldn't be a problem as long as you take normal precautions. Be careful with the unforgiving

motorized traffic, watch for unprotected roadworks and be aware of the general lack of modern safety equipment.

Your kids shouldn't need any specific pre-trip inoculations for Cuba, though you should check with your doctor about individual requirements before departing. Medicines are in short supply in Cuba, so take all you think you might need. Useful supplies include acetaminophen, ibuprofen, anti-nausea medicines and cough drops. Insect repellent is also helpful in lowland areas. Diapers and baby formula can be hard to find; bring your own. A copy of your child's birth certificate containing the names of both parents could also prove useful, especially if you have different surnames.

Car seats are not mandatory in Cuba, and taxi and rental-car firms don't carry them. Bring your own if you're planning on renting a car. High chairs in restaurants are also almost nonexistent, though wait staff will try to improvise. The same goes for travel cribs. Cuba's pavements weren't designed with strollers in mind. If your child is small enough, carry him/her in a body harness.

Casas particulares (rooms in private homes) are nearly always happy to accommodate families and are exceptionally child-friendly. Resort hotels are family-friendly too.

For all-round information and advice, check out Lonely Planet's *Travel with Children*.

Dining

With a dearth of exotic spices and an emphasis on good, plain food, kids in Cuba are often surprisingly well accommodated. The family-oriented nature of life on the island certainly helps. Few eating establishments turn away children, and wait staff in most cafes and restaurants will, more often than not, dote on your boisterous young offspring and go out of their way to try to accommodate tastes. Rice and beans are good staples, and chicken and fish are relatively reliable sources of protein. The main absent food group – though your kid probably won't think so – is a regular supply of fresh vegetables.

Plan Your Trip

US Travelers to Cuba

In the space of four years, US–Cuban relations went from cagey cooperation to the prickly squabbling of yore. The Trump administration introduced three new sets of restrictions for US travelers between 2017 and 2020, wiping out the historic reopening instituted by Obama several years before. Many Cubans are hoping that the new Biden administration will turn the clock back. But with the pandemic still affecting many policy decisions, they may be in for a long wait.

Current Restrictions

During four tumultuous years, the Trump administration placed three sets of restrictions on travel to Cuba for Americans. The first, announced in June 2017, prohibited US citizens from partaking in individual 'people-to-people' trips to Cuba and also banned any financial dealings with the Cuban military body, GAESA. This effectively stopped Americans from staying in Cuba's state-run hotels managed by the Gaviota brand and prevented them from using many of the country's car-rental agencies, state-run restaurants, marinas and tours.

In June 2019, a second set of regulations prohibited US cruise ships from calling at Cuban ports, reversing a historic opening initiated by Obama in 2016. The ruling also forbade organized groups from visiting Cuba through authorized US travel providers – the so-called people-to-people trips.

A third set of restrictions passed just before the presidential elections in 2020, banned American travelers from staying in all state-run hotels and ended the legal importation of Cuban alcohol and tobacco into the US. At the time of research, President Joe Biden's administration had yet to announce any major reforms.

What's Allowed

As of 2021, a handful of reforms from the Obama-era 'opening' remain in place.

Cuba–US travel rules change regularly. For more information and updates, check the US Department of the Treasury's webpage: https://www.treasury.gov/resource-center/sanctions/programs/pages/cuba.aspx.

Flights

US airlines continue to offer scheduled flights to Cuba (Havana only) from half a dozen US airports.

Organized Tours

Several US companies have re-registered under a different license category and continue to run tours.

Accommodations

Qualifying American travelers can book private homestays through Airbnb.

Diplomatic Relations

The US and Cuba maintain diplomatic relations and the US has an embassy in Havana.

MONEY

Despite optimistic political rhetoric, US credit cards still don't work in Cuba. It is thus necessary to come armed with plenty of cash. Since 2020, US dollars have been legal to use in Cuba. Cuban pesos (CUP$) are pegged 24:1 with the US dollar.

Travel to Cuba

Despite recent bans on cruise ships and 'people-to-people' trips, US citizens can still apply for a 'general license' to travel to Cuba under 11 different categories listed by the US Department of the Treasury. These range from the specific (public performances or athletic competitions) to the vague ('support for the Cuban people'). Independent travelers with no specific affiliations are best off qualifying under the 'support for the Cuban people' category, a relatively open classification.

General licenses are self-qualifying and require no long-winded paperwork. To avoid any legal ramifications when returning to the US, you are advised to draw up a detailed trip itinerary before you go and to keep all receipts and addresses of places where you stayed and visited for five years after your return.

Essential bedtime reading for all US citizens wishing to undertake travel to Cuba is the regularly updated fact sheet on the Department of the Treasury website: www.treasury.gov/resource-center/sanctions/Programs/pages/cuba.aspx

Getting There

With cruise ships no longer calling at Cuban ports, flights are the only option for Cuba-bound travelers. Scheduled services from the US, reintroduced by the Obama administration in 2016, continue to run from half a dozen US airports, with Miami being the main gateway. Cooperating airlines include JetBlue, American, Delta, Southwest and United.

Airlines should provide you with the necessary Cuban tourist card before you embark (double-check when booking). Prices range from US$50 to US$85 depending on which airline you fly with.

Non-Americans traveling to Cuba from the US face the same restrictions as US travelers. To avoid complications, it is thus far easier for non-Americans to fly direct from their home country, changing, if necessary, in Canada or Mexico.

Where to Stay

The Trump restrictions prohibit Americans from staying at any hotel run by the Cuban government. Thankfully, this is a blessing in disguise. Cuba's state-run hotels aren't its best accommodations. You're far better off staying in one of the country's thousands of safe, homely casas particulares (rooms in private homes). Here, you'll not only get better food and service, you'll also receive a candid and uncensored view of Cuban life.

You can book private accommodations in Cuba in advance with a credit card through Airbnb. Most casas particulares cost between US$25 to US$45 per night.

Tours from the US

Although the Trump administration ended group people-to-people trips in 2019, several US companies have continued to offer licensed Cuba tours by re-registering under the US Department of the Treasury's 'support for the Cuban people' category.

Cuba Travel Services (www.cubatravelservices.com) Great source of general travel information for US travelers. The company also arranges flights, accommodations, car rental and travel packages.

Cuban Adventures (www.cubagrouptour.com) Australian-based company specializing in Cuba travel that also runs licensed trips for US travelers.

GeoEx (www.geoex.com) Runs luxury people-to-people trips of six to eight days' duration from the US, plus opportunities to build your own custom trip. Tours can include everything from meeting diplomats to delving into Cuba's complex religious rites.

Insight Cuba (www.insightcuba.com) A well-established registered Cuba operator serving American travelers. Insight's trips include a one-week jazz-themed excursion and a trip to run the Havana marathon in November.

Road Scholar (www.roadscholar.org) The largest non-profit provider of learning adventures in Cuba, with six trips including birdwatching, community art projects and organic farm visits.

Regions at a Glance

Cuba's provinces are splayed end to end across the main island, with the oft-forgotten comma of Isla de la Juventud hanging off the bottom. All of them have coast access and are embellished with beautiful beaches, the best hugging the north coast. Equally stimulating are the vivid snippets of history, impressive colonial architecture and potent reminders of the 1959 revolution. The country's highest mountain range, the Sierra Maestra, rises in the east with another significant range, the Sierra del Escambray, positioned south-central. Cuba's main wilderness areas are the Zapata swamps, the marine terraces of Granma, the tropical forests of Guantánamo and the uninhabited (for now) northern keys. Urban highlights include Havana, Santiago de Cuba, Camagüey and colonial Trinidad.

Havana

Museums
Architecture
Nightlife

Museos Históricos

The capital's 4-sq-km historic center has history wherever you look and museums dedicated to everything from chocolate to playing cards. Kick off with the Museo de la Revolución, garner more cultural immersion in the Museo de la Ciudad and schedule at least half a day for the fine Museo Nacional de Bellas Artes.

Eclectic Architecture

Havana's architecture is not unlike Cuba's diverse natural environment: hard to categorize and sometimes a little – well – weird. Stroll the streets of Habana Vieja and Centro Havana and choose your own highlights.

Life is a Cabaret

Every Cuban music style is represented in Havana, from street rumba to glitzy cabaret, making it the best place in the country for live concerts, spontaneous busking and racy nightlife.

p63

Artemisa & Mayabeque Provinces

Beaches
Eco-tourism
Coffee Ruins

Secret Beaches

Playing second fiddle to Varadero on the main highway between Havana and Matanzas, Mayabeque Province has its own unheralded and rather delightful beaches, spearheaded by Playa Jibacoa, which has just two resorts compared to Varadero's 60.

Small Footprints

The small white eco-village of Las Terrazas was practicing environmentally friendly living long before the urgency of the Special Period or the adoption of eco-practices worldwide. Today it carries on much as it has always done: quietly, confidently and – above all – sustainably.

Plantation Past

Las Terrazas has dozens of abandoned coffee farms, half-covered by encroaching jungle, while Artemisa has its own Antiguo Cafetal Angerona, a larger, more refined, but no-less-weathered ruin that once functioned as a coffee plantation employing 450 enslaved people.

p149

Isla de la Juventud & Cayo Largo del Sur

Diving
Wildlife
History

Into the Blue

Outside the hard-to-access Jardines de la Reina archipelago, La Isla offers the best diving in Cuba and is the main reason many people come here. Ultraclear water, abundant sea life and a protected marine park at Punta Francés are the high points.

Rejuvenated Fauna

If you missed it in the Ciénaga de Zapata, La Isla is the only other place in the world where you can view the Cuban crocodile in its natural state. It has been successfully reintroduced into the Lanier Swamp.

Cuba's Alcatraz

Not one but two of Cuba's verbose spokesmen were once imprisoned on the archipelago's largest outlying island that also doubled as a big jail: José Martí and Fidel Castro. Their erstwhile incarceration sites are riddled with historical significance.

p163

Valle de Viñales & Pinar del Río Province

Diving
Food
Flora & Fauna

Divers' Dream

Isolated at the westernmost tip of the main island, María la Gorda has long lured travelers for its spectacular diving, enhanced by electrically colored coral, huge sponges and gorgonians, and a knowledgeable but laid-back dive community.

Roast Pork

There's nothing like a true Cuban pork roast and there's no place better to try it than among the *guajiros* (country folk) of Viñales who offer up humongous portions of the national dish with trimmings of rice, beans and root vegetables.

Parks of Pinar

With more protected land than any other province, Pinar is a green paradise. Go hiking in Parque Nacional Viñales, spot a sea turtle in Parque Nacional Península de Guanahacabibes or train your binoculars on the feathered action around Cueva de los Portales.

p177

Varadero & Matanzas Province

Diving
Flora & Fauna
Beaches

Accessible Aquatics

Bahía de Cochinos (Bay of Pigs) might not have Cuba's most spectacular diving, but it certainly has its most accessible. You can glide off from the shore here and be gawping at coral-encrusted drop-off walls within a few strokes.

Swamp Life

In contrast to the resort frenzy on the north coast, Matanzas' southern underbelly is one of Cuba's last true wildernesses and an important refuge for wildlife, including Cuban crocodiles, manatees, bee hummingbirds and tree rats.

Sands of Varadero

Even if you hate resorts, there's still one reason to go to Varadero – an unbroken 21km ribbon of golden sand that stretches the whole length of the Península de Hicacos. It's one of the longest and finest beaches in the world.

p203

Cienfuegos Province

Architecture
Music
Diving

French Classicism

Despite its position as one of Cuba's newer cities, founded in 1819, Cienfuegos retains a remarkably homogeneous urban core full of classical facades and slender columns heavy with the essence of 19th-century France, from where it drew its inspiration.

Benny Moré Trail

Benny Moré, Cuba's most legendary musician, who ruled the clubs and dance halls in the 1940s and '50s, once called Cienfuegos the city he liked best. Come see if you agree and, on the way, visit the village where he was born.

Secrets of Guajimico

Welcome to one of Cuba's least-discovered diving spots, run out of a comfortable campismo (cheap, rustic accommodations) on the warm, calm south coast and renowned for its coral gardens, sponges and scattered wrecks.

p241

Villa Clara Province

Beaches
History
Nightlife

Spectacular Keys

Cuba's newest resorts on the keys off the coast of Villa Clara hide some stunning and still relatively uncrowded beaches, including the publicly accessible Las Gaviotas on Cayo Santa María and the more-refined Playa el Mégano and Playa Ensenachos on Cayo Ensenachos.

Che Guevara

Love him or hate him, his legacy won't go away, so you might as well visit Santa Clara to at least try to understand what made the great *guerrillero* (warrior) tick. The city hosts Che's mausoleum, a museum cataloguing his life and the historic site where he ambushed an armored train in 1958.

Student Scene

The city of Santa Clara has the edgiest and most contemporary nightlife scene in Cuba, where local innovators are constantly probing for the next big thing.

p259

Trinidad & Sancti Spíritus Province

Museums
Hiking
Music

Revolution to Romance

Trinidad has more museums per square meter than anywhere outside Havana, and they're not token gestures either. Themes include history, furniture, counterrevolutionary wars, ceramics, contemporary art and romance.

Trails & Topography

Topes de Collantes has the most comprehensive trail system in Cuba and showcases some of the best scenery in the archipelago, with waterfalls, natural swimming pools, precious wildlife and working coffee plantations. Further trails can be found in the less-heralded Alturas de Banao and Jobo Rosado Reserves.

Spontaneous Sounds

In Trinidad – and to a lesser extent Sancti Spíritus – music seems to emanate out of every nook and cranny, much of it spontaneous and unrehearsed. Trinidad, in particular, has the most varied and condensed music scene outside Havana.

p279

Ciego de Ávila Province

Fishing
Beaches
Festivals

Hemingway's Haunts

Cayo Guillermo has all the makings of a fishing trip extraordinaire: a warm tropical setting; large, abundant fish; and the ghost of Ernest Hemingway to follow you from port to rippling sea and back. Pack a box of beer and follow the Gulf Stream.

Cayo Coasts

Coloradas, Prohibida, Flamingo and Pilar – the beaches of the northern cayos lure you with their names as much as their reputations and, when you get there, there's plenty of room for everyone.

Fiestas & Fireworks

No other province has such a varied and – frankly – weird stash of festivals. Ciego is home to an annual cricket tournament, rustic country dancing, voodoo rites and explosive fireworks.

p305

Camagüey Province

Diving
Architecture
Beaches

Feeding Sharks

OK, the resorts aren't exactly refined luxury, but who cares when the diving's this good? Playa Santa Lucía sits astride one of the largest coral reefs in the world and is famous for its shark-feeding show.

Urban Maze

Camagüey doesn't conform to the normal Spanish colonial building manual when it comes to urban layout, but that's part of the attraction. Lose yourself in Cuba's third-largest city that has been a Unesco World Heritage site since 2008.

Limitless Sand

The beaches on the province's north coast are phenomenal. There's 20km-long Playa Santa Lucía, the Robinson Crusoe–like Playa Los Pinos on Cayo Sabinel, and the shapely curve of Playa Los Cocos at the mouth of the Bahía de Nuevitas.

p323

Las Tunas Province

Beaches
Art
Festivals

Eco-Beaches

Hardly anyone knows about them, but they're still there. Las Tunas' northern eco-beaches are currently the preserve of local Cubans, seabirds and the odd in-the-know outsider. Come and enjoy them before the resort-building bulldozers wreck the tranquility.

City of Sculptures

Scout around the congenial streets of the provincial capital Las Tunas and you'll uncover an esoteric collection of revolutionary leaders, two-headed Taíno chiefs and oversize pencils crafted in stone.

Country Music

The bastion of country music in Cuba, Las Tunas hosts the annual Cucalambeana festival, where songwriters from across the country come to recite their quick-witted satirical *décimas* (verses).

p343

Holguín Province

Beaches
Ecotourism
Archaeology

Little-Known Beaches

Most tourists gravitate to the well-known beaches of Playa Pesquero and Guardalavaca that are backed by big resorts. Less touted, but equally *linda* (pretty), are Playa Caleta near Gibara and Las Morales near Banes.

Mountains & Keys

Strangely, for a province that hosts Cuba's largest and dirtiest industry (the Moa nickel mines), Holguín has a profusion of green escapes tucked away in pine-clad mountain retreats or hidden on exotic keys. Discover Cayo Saetía and Pinares de Mayarí.

Pre-Columbian Culture

Holguín preserves Cuba's best stash of archaeological finds. The region's long-lost pre-Columbian culture is showcased at the Museo Chorro de Maita and its adjacent reconstructed Taíno village. There are more artifacts on display at the Museo Indocubano Bani in nearby Banes.

p353

Granma Province

History
Hiking
Festivals

Revolutionary Sites

History is never as real as it is in Cuba's most revolutionary province. Here you can hike up to Castro's 1950s mountaintop HQ, visit the sugar mill where Céspedes first freed his enslaved people or ponder the poignant spot where José Martí fell in battle.

Bagging a Peak

With the Sierra Maestra overlaying two national parks, Granma has tremendous hiking potential, including the trek up to the top of the nation's highest peak, Pico Turquino.

Street Parties

Granma is famous for its street parties. Towns such as Bayamo and Manzanillo have long celebrated weekly alfresco shindigs with whole roast pork, chess tournaments and music provided by old-fashioned street organs.

p379

Santiago de Cuba Province

Dance
History
Festivals

Folklórico Groups

As magical as they are mysterious, Santiago's *folklórico* (traditional Latin American dance) troupes are a throwback to another era when enslaved people hid their traditions behind a complex veneer of singing, dancing and syncretized religion.

Revolutionary Legacy

Cuba's hotbed of sedition has inspired multiple rebellions and many key sites can still be visited. Start at Moncada Barracks and head south through the birth houses of local heroes Frank País and Antonio Maceo, to the eerily named Museo de la Lucha Clandestina (Clandestine War Museum).

Caribbean Culture

Santiago has a wider variety of annual festivals than any other Cuban city. July is the top month, with the annual Carnaval preceded by the Festival del Caribe, celebrating the city's rich Caribbean culture.

p399

Guantánamo Province

Flora & Fauna
Hiking
Food

Endemic Eden

Guantánamo's historical isolation and complex soil structure have led to high levels of endemism, meaning you're likely to see plant and animal species here that you'll see nowhere else in the archipelago. Aspiring botanists should gravitate toward Parque Nacional Alejandro de Humboldt.

Unsung Trails

As Baracoa grows as an ecological center, hiking possibilities are opening up. Try the long-standing treks up El Yunque or into Parque Nacional Alejandro de Humboldt, or tackle newer trails around the Río Duaba or to the beaches near Boca de Yumurí.

Coconut & Cocoa

What do you mean you didn't come to Cuba for the food? Baracoa is waiting to blow away your culinary preconceptions with a sweet-and-spicy mélange of dishes concocted from the ubiquitous cocoa, coffee, coconuts and bananas.

p437

On the Road

AT A GLANCE

POPULATION
2.1 million

TALLEST BUILDING
Torre López-Callejas:
154m

BEST TAPAS
Lamparilla 361 Tapas
& Cervezas (p117)

BEST COCKTAILS
El del Frente (p117)

**BEST BOUTIQUE
HOTEL**
Malecón 663 (p109)

WHEN TO GO

Nov–Apr
Peak season lends
extra life to the
city and welcomes
plenty of festivals.
Cold fronts bring
fresher weather.

May–Aug
Hot, but fun,
especially if you time
your visit to coincide
with Havana's
ostentatious
Carnaval.

Sep–Oct
Avoid crowds and
heat in these quieter
but wetter months.

Malecón (p83)
KAMIRA/SHUTTERSTOCK ©

Havana

O n first impressions, Havana can seem like a confusing jigsaw puzzle, but work out how to put the pieces together and a beautiful picture emerges.

No one could have invented this hot, sultry, eternally stoic city. It's too audacious, too contradictory and – despite 60 years of withering neglect – too damned beautiful. How it does it is anyone's guess. Maybe it's the long history of piracy, colonialism and mobster rule. Perhaps it's the survivalist spirit of a populace scarred by two independence wars, a revolution and a US trade embargo. Or possibly it's something to do with the indefatigable salsa energy that ricochets off walls and emanates most emphatically from the people. Don't come here with a list of questions; just bring an open mind and prepare for a long, slow seduction.

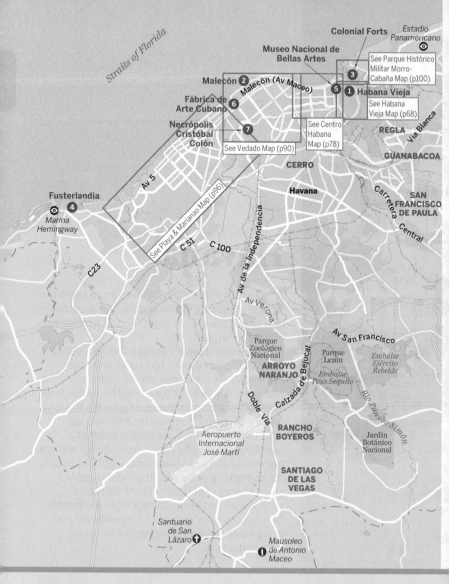

Havana Highlights

1 **Habana Vieja** (p67)
Letting your imagination spill over on the evocative cobbled streets of 'Old Havana.'

2 **Malecón** (p83) Hanging out with the *habaneros* amid crashing waves and wandering troubadours.

3 **Colonial Forts** (p99)
Seeing the sturdy bastions

that once protected Havana from its cutthroat enemies.

4 **Fusterlandia** (p94)
Getting an insight into the amazing experimental street art of José Fuster.

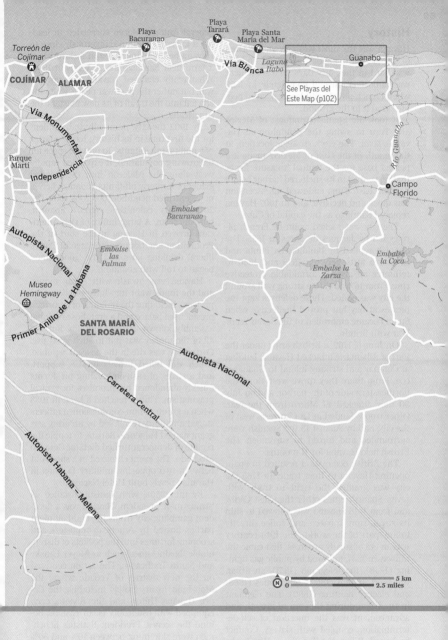

History

Havana was the most westerly and isolated of Diego Velázquez' original villas, and life was hard in the early days. The settlement was almost eradicated completely in 1538 when French pirates and local enslaved people razed it to the ground.

It took the Spanish conquest of Mexico and Peru to swing the pendulum in Havana's favor. The city's strategic location, at the mouth of the Gulf of Mexico, made it a perfect base for the annual 'treasure fleets' that regrouped in its sheltered harbor before heading east. Thus endowed, its ascension was quick and decisive, and in 1607 Havana replaced Santiago as the capital of Cuba.

The city was sacked again by French pirates led by Jacques de Sores in 1555. The Spanish replied by building La Punta and El Morro forts between 1558 and 1630 to reinforce an already formidable protective ring. From 1674 to 1740 a strong wall around the city was added. These defenses kept the pirates at bay but proved ineffective when Spain became embroiled in the Seven Years' War with Britain.

On June 6, 1762, a British army under the Earl of Albemarle attacked Havana, landing at Cojímar and striking inland to Guanabacoa. From there they drove west along the northeastern side of the harbor, and on July 30 they attacked El Morro from the rear. Other troops landed at La Chorrera, west of the city, and by August 13 the Spanish were surrounded and forced to surrender. The British held Havana for 11 months.

The British occupation resulted in Spain opening Havana to freer trade. In 1765 the city was granted the right to trade with seven Spanish cities other than just Cádiz, and from 1818 Havana was allowed to ship its sugar, rum, tobacco and coffee directly to any part of the world. The 19th century was an era of steady progress: first came the railway in 1837, followed by public gas lighting (1848), the telegraph (1851), an urban transport system (1862), telephones (1888) and electric lighting (1890). The elephant in the room during this era of growth and advancement was the question of self-determination, coupled with slavery. Conflict beckoned. When the Ten Years' War broke out in 1868, the violence never reached Havana, where rich pro-colonial landholders maintained their power base. Similarly, the Independence War (1895–98) was also confined largely to the east, although this time general Antonio Maceo succeeded in leading a guerrilla column dangerously close to Havana before being killed in a skirmish at a farm near Santiago de las Vegas in 1896. What really changed Havana was not the war, but rather the post-war peace, when the city fell into the thrall of its new masters, the Americans.

By 1902 the city, nominally independent for the first time in its history, had a quarter of a million inhabitants. To provide space for its growing population, it expanded rapidly west along the Malecón into the wooded glades of formerly off-limits Vedado where a new gentrified neighborhood took root. The 20th-century colonizers weren't Spanish, but American. A large influx of rich Americans arrived in Havana at the start of the Prohibition era, taking advantage of Cuba's liberal drinking laws and the 'good times' began to roll with abandon.

Havana was awash with sugar money and the funds went into huge public works projects, including the building of an ornate presidential palace and a grandiose national assembly known as the Capitolio. But not all of the money was put to such good use. Corruption was rife in the nascent republic, which still relied heavily on US support, and a string of cash-embezzling presidents quickly abandoned big promises for cynical pragmatism. Things reached a head in 1933 when a group of non-commissioned officers staged a military revolt, led by an army sergeant named Fulgencio Batista, to topple the regime of democrat turned dictator Gerardo Machado. The event climaxed in a shoot-out between two opposing military factions in Havana's newly built Hotel Nacional.

By the 1950s, with Batista installed as 'strong man' president, Havana was a decadent gambling city frolicking amid all-night parties hosted by American mobsters and scooping fortunes into the pockets of disreputable 'businessmen' such as Meyer Lansky and Santo Trafficante. The action centered on the new district of Vedado where the Mob built luxury hotels including the Capri, Habana Hilton and the Riviera, each equipped with ostensibly 'clean' casinos. Behind the scenes, President Batista's henchmen were skimming between 10% and 30% of the profits. Meanwhile, Havana continued to expand outwards, most notably along the coast west of the Río Almendares into the Beverly Hills–like neighborhood known as Miramar.

LOCAL KNOWLEDGE

HAVANA VIEJA - A PLAN OF ATTACK

Awash with museums, galleries, historic hotels and colonial plazas, Habana Vieja can be a bit overwhelming for first-time visitors. To tackle it properly, grab a cup of coffee (Plaza Vieja has some good spots), sit down with a map, and draw up a strategic plan of attack. The motto: you won't have time to see everything.

Habana Vieja's essential business revolves around its four main squares, all clustered in close proximity to each other on the eastern side of the neighborhood. Intimate Plaza de la Catedral (see below) faces the not-to-be-missed cathedral and has some fine restaurants squeezed into a nearby alley. Shady Plaza de Armas (p74) is overlooked by the emblematic Museo de la Ciudad and Havana's oldest fort. Breezy Plaza de San Francisco de Asís (p74) has some thought-provoking public sculpture, while Plaza Vieja (p75) sports the most varied body of architecture and the best array of after-dark bars and lounges.

Interesting connecting streets include Calle Oficos, Calle Obispo (with a beautiful din of competing live music after 6pm) and Calle Mercaderes, with its historic ensemble of shops. The rest of the quarter's dense grid is yours for the taking, a potluck of rusting 'yank tanks,' hole-in-the-wall restaurants and socialism on a shoestring. Anyone vaguely hip should gravitate toward Plaza del Cristo (p81), a dandy collection of spirited bars.

Of more recent interest to travelers is the emerging San Isidro quarter of Habana Vieja, embedded in the grid of streets south of Calle Acosta. Now an official art district supported by the Office of the City Historian, it's worth a wander for its galleries and murals.

◉ Sights

◉ Habana Vieja

Havana's Old Town – the site where the city first took root in 1519 – is one of the historical highlights of Latin America, an architectural masterpiece where fastidiously preserved squares and grandiose palaces sit alongside a living, breathing urban community still emerging from decades of economic austerity. The result is by turns grand and gritty, inspiring and frustrating, commendable if a little rough around the edges. No one should leave Cuba without seeing it.

◉ Plaza de la Catedral & Around

★ **Plaza de la Catedral**   SQUARE
(Map p68) Habana Vieja's most uniform square is a museum to Cuban baroque, with all the surrounding buildings, including the city's beguiling asymmetrical cathedral, dating from the 1700s. Despite this homogeneity, it is actually the newest of the four squares in the Old Town, with its present layout dating from the 18th century.

On the square's eastern side, the **Casa del Lombillo** was built in 1741 and once served as a post office (a stone-mask ornamental mailbox built into the wall is still in use). Since 2000 it has functioned as an office

for the City Historian. On the western side is the majestic **Palacio de los Marqueses de Aguas Claras**, completed in 1760 and widely lauded for the beauty of its shady Andalusian patio. Today it houses the **Restaurante Paris** (Map p68; San Ignacio No 54; meals USD$15-20; ⊙noon-midnight). The south side is taken up by the resplendent **Palacio de los Condes de Casa Bayona**, built in 1720, which today hosts the **Museo de Arte Colonial** (Map p68; San Ignacio No 61; USD$2; ⊙9:30am-4:45pm).

★ **Catedral de la Habana**   CATHEDRAL
(Map p68; cnr San Ignacio & Empedrado; ⊙9am-4:30pm Mon-Fri, to noon Sat & Sun) FREE Described by novelist Alejo Carpentier as 'music set in stone,' Havana's incredible cathedral, dominated by two unequal towers and framed by a theatrical baroque facade, was designed by Italian architect Francesco Borromini. Construction of the church was begun by Jesuits in 1748 and work continued despite their expulsion in 1767. When the building was finished in 1787, the diocese of Havana was created and the church became a cathedral – it's one of the oldest in the Americas.

The remains of Christopher Columbus were brought here from Santo Domingo in 1795 and interred until 1898, when they were moved to Seville Cathedral in Spain.

Habana Vieja

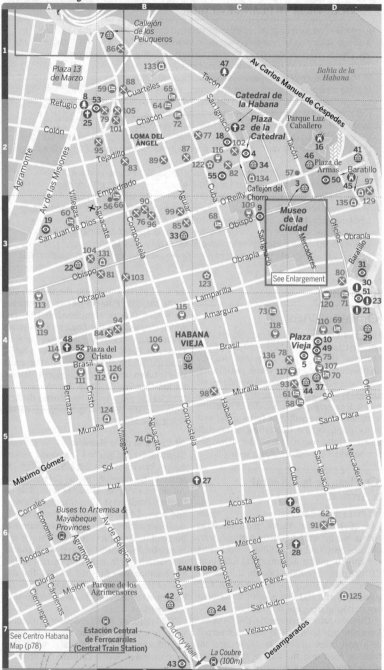

A curiosity of the cathedral is its interior, which is neoclassical rather than baroque and relatively austere. Frescoes above the altar date from the late 1700s, but the paintings that adorn the side walls are copies of originals by Bartolomé Esteban Murillo and Peter Paul Rubens. You can climb the smaller of the towers for USD$1.

Taller Experimental de Gráfica   ARTS CENTER
(Map p68; ☎ 7-801-3179; tgrafica@cubarte.cult. cu; Callejón del Chorro No 6; ⊙ 10am-4pm Mon-Fri) `FREE` Easy to miss at the end of a short cul-de-sac, this is one of Havana's most cutting-edge art workshops, which also offers the possibility of engraving classes. Group classes (up to 12 pupils) for one/two/three weeks cost USD$200/280/400. Make arrangements at least a few days in advance in person or by email. No classes in August.

**Centro de Arte
Contemporáneo
Wifredo Lam**   CULTURAL CENTER
(Map p68; cnr San Ignacio & Empedrado; USD$3; ⊙10am-5pm Mon-Sat) At the corner of Plaza de la Catedral, this cultural center named after the island's most celebrated painter is hit or miss depending on what is or isn't showing. Rather than displaying Lam's paintings, it hosts temporary exhibitions of contemporary art and reaches its apex during the sporadic Biennial (usually held every three years in April).

Parque Maestranza   PARK
(Map p68; Av Carlos Manuel de Céspedes; USD$3; ⊙10am-5pm Wed-Sun) Overlooking the harbor is this small-scale Cuban-style playground (for children aged four to 12), with inflatable castles and other games.

◉ Plaza de Armas & Around

★**Museo de la Ciudad**   MUSEUM
(Map p68; Tacón No 1; USD$3; ⊙9:30am-6pm) Even with no artifacts, Havana's city museum would be a tour de force, courtesy of the opulent palace in which it resides. Filling the whole western side of Plaza de Armas, the **Palacio de los Capitanes Generales** dates from the 1770s and is a textbook example of Cuban baroque architecture, hewn out of rock from the nearby San Lázaro quarries. A museum has been here since 1968.

From 1791 until 1898 the palace was the residence of the Spanish captains general. From 1899 until 1902 the US military governors were based here, and during the first

Habana Vieja

two decades of the 20th century the building briefly became the presidential palace. These days the museum is wrapped regally around a splendid central courtyard adorned with a white-marble statue of Christopher Columbus (1862). Artifacts (some of them a tad dusty) include period furniture, military uniforms and antique horse carriages, but the real history-defining highlights are the boat used by Antonio Maceo to cross the Trocha de Mariel in 1896, a cannon captured by the Mambís (Cuban Independence War soldiers) from the Spanish in 1897, and Cuba's first flag, raised by Narciso López in Cárdenas in 1850. Audio guides (USD$5) are available in Spanish and English.

Palacio del Segundo Cabo MUSEUM
(Map p68; ☏ 7-801-7176; http://segundocabo.ohc.cu; O'Reilly No 4; USD$10; ◷ 9:30am-5pm Tue-Sat, to 1pm Sun; ⊛) **FREE** Wedged into Plaza de Armas' northwestern corner, this beautiful baroque building was constructed in 1772 as the headquarters of the Spanish vice-governor. After several reincarnations as a post office, the palace of the Senate, the Supreme Court, and the National Academy of Arts and Letters, the building reopened in 2016 as a multifarious museum dedicated to Cuban-European cultural relations. It's masterfully done, using modern media devices to highlight various facets of Cuba and Europe's interwoven history.

Spread over two floors, the interconnecting rooms include a timeline 'tunnel,' a couple of cube-activated screens broadcasting different elements of Cuba's history, an interactive trajectory of Cuban-European musical forms, and a comparative study of the architectural development of Havana and Barcelona. Aided by EU funding, it's the best new museum in Havana for a long time.

Castillo de la Real Fuerza   FORT
(Map p68; Plaza de Armas; USD$3; ☺9:30am-5pm Tue-Sun) On the seaward side of Plaza de Armas is one of the oldest existing forts in the Americas, built between 1558 and 1577 on the site of an earlier fort destroyed by French privateers in 1555. The imposing castle is ringed by an impressive moat and shelters the Museo de Navegación, which covers the history of the fort and Old Town, and its connections with the Spanish empire. Look out for the huge scale model of the Santísima Trinidad galleon.

The west tower is crowned by a copy of a famous bronze weather vane called La Giraldilla. The original was cast in Havana in 1632 by Jerónimo Martínez Pinzón and is popularly believed to be of Doña Inés de Bobadilla, the wife of gold explorer Hernando de Soto. The original is now kept in the Museo de la Ciudad (p69), and the figure also appears on the Havana Club rum label.

Habana Vieja

WALKING TOUR OF OLD HAVANA

This easy 'four plaza' walking tour, though less than 2km in length, could fill a day with its museums, shops, bars and street theater. It highlights Havana's unique historical district, built up around four main squares.

Start at ❶ **Catedral de la Habana**, which anchors the Plaza de la Catedral. This compact square has bags of atmosphere and is always awash with interesting characters.

Then take Calle Empedrado followed by Calle Mercaderes to Plaza de Armas, once used for military exercises and still guarded by the ❷ **Castillo de la Real Fuerza**. The fort's museum is worth a quick look. Worth more time is the Museo de la Ciudad in the ❸ **Palacio de los Capitanes Generales**; eschew the on-site guides and wander alone.

Walk up ❹ **Calle Obispo** next, Havana's busy main drag, before turning left into ❺ **Calle Mercaderes**, where old shops and several museums make ambling a pleasure.

Turn left on Calle Amargura and dive into Plaza de San Francisco de Asís, dominated by ❻ **Iglesia y Monasterio de San Francisco de Asís**. Make a note of upcoming classical concerts (great acoustics) and try to take in the church's impressive religious-art museum. Turn right on Calle Brasil and you'll enter ❼ **Plaza Vieja**, home to a planetarium and several museum-galleries. And when you're museumed out, crash at Factoria Plaza Vieja for a smooth microbrewed beer.

RICHARD CAVALLERI/SHUTTERSTOCK ©

Catedral de la Habana

The cathedral's interior was originally baroque, like its main facade. However, in the early 19th century, a renovation project redecorated the church's inner sanctum in a more sober classical tone.

Plaza de la Catedral

Palacio de los Capitanes Generales

An interesting feature of this sturdy building is the marine fossils embedded in its limestone walls. The street outside is lined with wooden bricks designed to deaden the sound of horses' hooves.

Calle Obispo

The lower section of Obispo is an architectural crossroads. The row of buildings on the south are the oldest town houses in Havana, dating from the 1570s. Opposite is the Hotel Ambos Mundos, Hemingway's 1930s hangout.

HALFSHADOW/GETTY IMAGES ©

MUSEUMS

Dip into some of the museums you will pass on the way (in order):

Museo de Arte Colonial Colonial furniture

Museo de Navegación Maritime history

Museo de la Ciudad City history

Museo de Pintura Mural Frescoes

Maqueta de La Habana Vieja Scale model of Havana

Museo de Naipes Playing cards

Castillo de la Real Fuerza

The highlight of this fort's on-site maritime museum is a 4m-long model of the *Santíssima Trinidad*, a ship built in Havana in the 1760s that fought at the Battle of Trafalgar in 1805.

Calle Mercaderes

Pedestrian-friendly 'Market St' is notable for its esoteric shops. On the corner of Calle Obrapía sits the Casa de la Obra Pía, one of the first renovation projects of city historian Eusebio Leal Spengler in 1968.

Iglesia y Monasterio de San Francisco de Asís

Once Havana's tallest building, the bell tower of this former church-monastery was originally topped by a statue of St Francis of Assisi; the figure fell off during an 1846 hurricane.

Barillo

Cuba tacón

② ③

Plaza de Armas

④

Oficios

⑤

Mercaderes

Baratillo

Plaza de San Francisco de Asís ⑥

Obispo

Obrapía

San Ignacio

Lamparilla

Amargura

Cuba

Brasil

⑦

Muralla

Sol

Plaza Vieja

Plaza Vieja's buildings were constructed as private residences rather than municipal buildings. They housed some of Havana's richest families, who would gather to watch the plaza's gory public spectacles, including executions.

Plaza de Armas SQUARE

(Map p68) Havana's oldest square was laid out in the early 1520s, soon after the city's foundation, and was originally known as Plaza de Iglesia after a church – the Parroquial Mayor – that once stood on the site of the present-day Palacio de los Capitanes Generales. The name Plaza de Armas (Square of Arms) wasn't adopted until the late 16th century, when the colonial governor, then housed in the Castillo de la Real Fuerza, used the site to conduct military exercises.

Today's plaza, along with most of the buildings around it, dates from the late 1700s.

In the center of the square, which is lined with royal palms, is a marble **statue of Carlos Manuel de Céspedes** (Map p68; Plaza de Armas), the man who set Cuba on the road to independence in 1868. The statue replaced one of unpopular Spanish king Ferdinand VII in 1955.

Palacio de Los Condes de Santovenia PALACE

(Map p68; Calle Baratillo No 9) Lining Plaza de Armas, Los Condes de Santovenia is the former stately palace of the counts of Santovenia and today houses the five-star Hotel Santa Isabel (p108). It dates from the 1780s and was converted into the luxurious accommodations in 1867, making it one of Habana's oldest hotels. Habaguanex (the City Historian's renovation arm) gave the place a much-needed makeover in the 1990s, which was good enough for former US president Jimmy Carter, who stayed here during his groundbreaking 2002 visit.

Museo El Templete MUSEUM

(Map p68; Plaza de Armas; USD$2; ⊙8:30am-6pm) This museum is housed in the tiny neoclassical Doric chapel on the eastern side of Plaza de Armas, and was erected in 1828 at the point where Havana's first Mass was held beneath a ceiba tree in November 1519. A similar ceiba tree has now replaced the original. Inside the chapel are three large paintings of the event by French painter Jean-Baptiste Vermay (1786–1833).

⊙ **Plaza de San Francisco de Asís & Around**

Plaza de San Francisco de Asís SQUARE

(Map p68) Facing Havana harbor, the breezy Plaza de San Francisco de Asís first grew up in the 16th century when Spanish galleons stopped quayside on their passage from the Caribbean to Spain. A market took root in the 1500s, followed by a church in 1608, though when the monks complained of too much noise, the market was moved a few blocks south to Plaza Vieja.

The plaza underwent a full restoration in the late 1990s and is most notable for its uneven cobblestones and the white-marble **Fuente de los Leones** (Fountain of Lions; Map p68; Plaza de San Francisco de Asís), a fountain carved by Italian sculptor Giuseppe Gaggini in 1836. A more modern statue outside the square's famous church depicts **El Caballero de París** (Map p68), a well-known street person who roamed Havana during the 1950s, engaging passersby with his philosophies on life, religion, politics and current events. The square's newest sculpture (added in 2012) is **La Conversación** (Map p68; Plaza San Francisco de Asís) by French artist Etienne, a modernist bronze rendition of two seated people talking.

The cruise terminal is directly opposite the square.

Iglesia y Monasterio de San Francisco de Asís MUSEUM

(Map p68; Oficios, btwn Amargura & Brasil; museum USD$2; ⊙9:30am-4:30pm) Originally constructed in 1608 and rebuilt in baroque style from 1719 to 1738, this church-convent ceased to have a religious function in the 1840s after being 'desecrated' by the Protestant British during the Seven Years' War. In the late 1980s crypts and religious objects were excavated; these were later incorporated into the **Museo de Arte Religioso**, which displays religious paintings, silverware, woodcarvings and ceramics. Visitors can examine the convent's old cloisters and climb the rickety tower for an extra USD$1.

The former church is more famous today as Havana's premier classical-music venue. Weekly concerts (6pm Saturday) are held in the nave, which benefits from excellent acoustics.

Museo del Ron MUSEUM

(Map p68; ☎7-862-3832, 7-862-4108; www.havanaclubmuseum.com; San Pedro No 262, cnr Sol; incl guide USD$7; ⊙9am-5pm Mon-Thu, to 4pm Fri-Sun) You don't have to be an Añejo Reserva quaffer to enjoy the Museo del Ron in the Fundación Havana Club, but it probably helps. The museum, with its quintilingual guided tour, shows rum-making antiquities and the complex distilling process in a scale model. A tasting of a seven-year-old *añejo*

SAN ISIDRO – A 21ST CENTURY ART DISTRICT

Bereft of the historical monuments common in other parts of Habana Vieja, the populous San Isidro quarter has been largely ignored by outsiders – until recently. Before the revolution it was a well-known den of iniquity harboring gamblers, pimps and contraband goods; then, from the 1960s onward, it became a tightly packed grid of decaying social housing. The turnaround came in 2016, when the founding of a community art project in collaboration with the Office of the City Historian set the formerly drab streets alight with vivid murals and art galleries.

One of the main players in the neighborhood's revival is Adán Perugorría, keyboardist in rock-funk band Nube Roja and manager of art space Galería-Taller Gorría (p76), which was founded by his famous father, Jorge (who starred in the film *Fresa y chocolate* and the TV miniseries *Cuatro estaciones en La Habana*), on the site of a former bakery.

With the help of several US-based artists, including Cuban-American Abstrk and New Yorker Stephen Palladino, the Gorría gallery has overseen the development of San Isidro's cultural traditions into evocative murals depicting everything from masked faces to abstract animals and birds.

Perugorría and his crew also organize a multicultural one-day festival every other month with new murals, music concerts, body painting and theater performances in the quarter's streets and small parks.

The San Isidro district is roughly demarcated by the grid of streets south of Calle Acosta, including Merced, San Isidro and Picota.

(aged rum) is included at the end of the tour. Reservations can be made online.

There's a bar and shop on-site, but the savvy reconvene at Bar Dos Hermanos (p130) next door. The museum also offers rum-tasting (USD$12) and cocktail-making (USD$15) workshops.

Catedral Ortodoxa
Nuestra Señora de Kazán   CHURCH
(Map p68; Av Carlos Manuel de Céspedes, btwn Sol & Santa Clara) One of Havana's newer buildings, this beautiful gold-domed Russian Orthodox church was built in the early 2000s and consecrated at a ceremony attended by Raúl Castro in October 2008. The church was part of an attempt to re-ignite Russian–Cuban relations after they went sour in 1991. The interior glows with gold leaf.

Lonja del Comercio   ARCHITECTURE
(Map p68; Plaza de San Francisco de Asís) This large, box-shaped building on Plaza de San Francisco de Asís is a former commodities market erected in 1909. The building was completely renovated in 1996 by the City Historian and today provides office space for foreign companies with joint ventures in Cuba. You can enter the Lonja to admire its central atrium and futuristic interior. It also houses a cafe-restaurant, El Mercurio (Map p68; Plaza de San Francisco de Asís; mains USD$6-12; ⊙7am-11pm), named after the

bronze figure of the god Mercury that sits atop a dome on the roof.

⊙ Plaza Vieja & Around

★Plaza Vieja   SQUARE
(Old Square; Map p68) Laid out in 1559, Plaza Vieja is Havana's most architecturally eclectic square, where Cuban baroque nestles seamlessly next to Gaudí-inspired art nouveau. Originally called Plaza Nueva (New Square), it was initially used for military exercises and later served as an open-air marketplace.

During the regime of Fulgencio Batista an ugly underground parking lot was constructed here, but this monstrosity was demolished in 1996 to make way for a massive renovation project. Sprinkled liberally with bars, restaurants and cafes, Plaza Vieja today has its own microbrewery, the Angela Landa primary school, a beautiful fenced fountain and, on its western side, some of Havana's finest *vitrales* (stained-glass windows). A number of cool bars and cafes give it a sociable buzz in the evenings.

Planetario   PLANETARIUM
(Map p68; ☑7-864-9544; Mercaderes No 311; USD$10; ⊙10am-3pm Wed-Sun) Aimed more at Cubans than tourists who may be used to more technical wizardry, Havana's planetarium includes a scale reproduction of the solar system inside a giant orb, a simulation

of the Big Bang, and a theater that allows viewing of more than 6000 stars. It's only accessible by guided tour booked in advance. Tours take place Wednesday to Sunday and can be booked (in person) on Monday and Tuesday. There are four tours daily and two on Sunday.

Palacio de los Condes de Jaruco   GALLERY
(Map p68; Muralla No 107) FREE This muscular mansion on Plaza Vieja's southwestern corner is one of the square's oldest, constructed in 1738 from local limestone in a transitional *mudéjar*-baroque style. Rich in period detail, it is typical of merchant houses of the era. For many years it was the residence of the exalted counts of Jaruco. Today it's the HQ of Cuba's main cultural foundation.

Cámara Oscura   LANDMARK
(Map p68; Plaza Vieja; USD$2; ⊙9:30am-4:45pm Tue-Sun) At the northeastern corner of Plaza Vieja in a tall, narrow edifice is this clever optical device providing live, 360-degree views of the city from atop a 35m-tall tower. Explanations are in Spanish and English.

Museo de Naipes   MUSEUM
(Map p68; Muralla No 101; ⊙9:30am-5pm Tue-Sun) FREE Encased in Plaza Vieja's oldest building is this quirky playing-card museum, with a 2000-strong collection that includes rock stars, rum drinks and round cards.

◉ San Isidro & Around

Iglesia y Convento de Nuestra Señora de la Merced   CHURCH
(Map p68; Cuba No 806; ⊙8am-noon & 3-5:30pm) Bizarrely overlooked by the tourist hordes, this baroque church in its own small square has Havana's most sumptuous ecclesiastical interior, as yet only partially restored. Beautiful gilded altars, frescoed vaults and a number of valuable old paintings create a sacrosanct mood. There's a quiet cloister adjacent.

Galería-Taller Gorría   GALLERY
(Map p68; ☑7-864 6713; www.galeriatallergorria.com; San Isidro 214, btwn Compostela & Picota; ⊙10am-6pm Tue-Sat) FREE Anchoring an art project in the San Isidro quarter of Habana Vieja, this bold contemporary gallery

---

HISTORICAL JIGSAW

Never in the field of architectural preservation has so much been achieved by so many with so few resources. You hear plenty in the international press about the sterling performance of the Cuban education and health-care systems but relatively little about the remarkable work that has gone into preserving the country's valuable but seriously endangered historical legacy, most notably in Habana Vieja.

A work in progress since the late 1970s, the piecing back together of Havana's Old Town after decades of neglect has been a foresighted and miraculous process, considering the economic odds stacked against it. The genius behind the project is Eusebio Leal Spengler, Havana's celebrated City Historian, who, unperturbed by the tightening of the financial screws during Cuba's Special Period, in 1994 set up Habaguanex, a holding company that earns hard currency through tourism. The money Habaguanex grosses is reinvested in the city, shared between historical preservation (to attract more tourists) and citywide urban regeneration (to benefit ordinary *habaneros*).

Eschewing the temptation to turn Havana's old quarter into a historical theme park, Leal has sought to rebuild the city's urban jigsaw as an authentic 'living' center that provides tangible benefits for the neighborhood's 82,000-plus inhabitants. As a result, schools, neighborhood committees, care homes for seniors and centers for children with disabilities sit seamlessly alongside cleaned-up colonial edifices. Every time you put your money into a Habana Vieja hotel, museum or restaurant, you are contributing not just to the quarter's continued restoration but to a raft of projects that directly benefit the local population.

Today, the Office of the City Historian splits its annual tourist income (reported to be in excess of US$160 million) between further restoration (45%) and social projects in the city (55%), of which there are now more than 400. So far, one quarter of Habana Vieja has been returned to the height of its colonial-era splendor, with ample tourist attractions including 20 Habaguanex-run hotels, four classic forts and over 30 museums.

is the brainchild of Cuban actor and artist Jorge Perugorría (who starred in the Oscar-nominated *Fresa y chocolate*) but is overseen by his son Adán, a classical pianist and keyboard player in Cuban rock-funk band Nube Roja. The gallery cooperates with the Office of the City Historian to organize cultural events and plan artistic murals in the surrounding streets.

Despite being little trodden by tourists, San Isidro is sprouting some of the city's most thought-provoking street art. Walk along Calles Merced, San Isidro, Acosta and Picota to see what's new.

Museo-Casa Natal de José Martí MUSEUM
(Map p68; Leonor Pérez No 314; USD$2; ⊙ 9:30am-5pm Tue-Sat, to 1pm Sun) Opened in 1925, this tiny museum, set in the house where the apostle of Cuban independence was born on January 28, 1853, is considered to be the oldest in Havana. The Office of the City Historian took the house over in 1994, and its succinct stash of exhibits devoted to Cuba's national hero continues to impress.

**Iglesia y Convento de
Nuestra Señora de Belén** CONVENT
(Map p68; Compostela, btwn Luz & Acosta; ⊙9:30am-4:30pm Mon-Fri, to noon Sat) FREE
This huge building dating from the early 18th century first functioned as a free school and convalescent home run by the Belemitas order. It was taken over by the Jesuits after they returned to Cuba in the 1850s and they ran it for 75 years as a college with an attached meteorological station that studied climate science. In 2019 a museum dedicated to meteorology and climatology was opened to honor the convent's erstwhile role. It's spread over five floors in the main tower.

The Belén was abandoned in 1925 when the Jesuits moved their college to Marianao. It subsequently fell into disrepair, exacerbated in 1991 by a damaging fire. The City Historian reversed the decline in the late 1990s, using tourist coffers to transform it into an active community center for those with physical and mental disabilities, and the elderly (there are 18 apartments for senior citizens). The convent's former church is currently being refurbished.

**Iglesia Parroquial
del Espíritu Santo** CHURCH
(Map p68; Acosta 161; ⊙8am-noon & 3-6pm) Havana's oldest surviving church has been heavily remodeled since its founding as a

hermitage, built by freed formerly enslaved black people in 1638. Most of the current edifice dates from the mid-19th century and exhibits Moorish, Gothic, neoclassical and Andaluz styles.

⊙ Calle Obispo & Around

Calle Obispo STREET
(Map p68) Narrow, chockablock Calle Obispo (Bishop's Street), Habana Vieja's main interconnecting artery, is packed with art galleries, shops, music venues and people. Four- and five-story buildings block out most of the sunlight, and the swaying throng seems to move in time to the beautiful din of competing live music that wafts out of every bar.

★Calle Mercaderes AREA
(Map p68) Cobbled, car-free Calle Mercaderes (Merchant's Street) has been extensively restored by the Office of the City Historian and is an almost complete replica of itself at its splendid 18th-century high-water mark. Interspersed with the museums, shops and restaurants are some working social projects, such as a maternity home and a papermaking cooperative.

Most of the myriad museums are free, including the Casa de Asia (Map p68; Calle Mercaderes No 111; ⊙10am-6pm Tue-Sat, 9am-1pm Sun) FREE, with paintings and sculpture from China and Japan; the Armería 9 de Abril (Map p68; Calle Mercaderes No 157; ⊙9am-5pm Tue-Sat, 1-5pm Mon) FREE, an old gun shop (now museum) stormed by revolutionaries on the said date in 1958; and the Museo de Bomberos (Map p68; cnr Mercaderes & Lamparilla; ⊙10am-6pm Mon-Sat) FREE, which has antediluvian fire equipment dedicated to 19 Havana firefighters who lost their lives in an 1890 railway blaze.

Just off Mercaderes down Obrapía, it's worth slinking into the gratis Casa de África (Map p68; Obrapía No 157; ⊙9:30am-5pm Tue-Sat, to 1pm Sun) FREE, which houses sacred objects relating to Santería and the secret Abakuá fraternity collected by ethnographer Fernando Ortíz.

The corner of Mercaderes and Obrapía has an international flavor, with a bronze statue of Latin America liberator Simón Bolívar (Map p68; cnr Mercaderes & Obrapía); across the street you'll find the Museo de Simón Bolívar (Map p68; Calle Mercaderes No 160; ⊙9am-5pm Tue-Sat, to 1pm Sun) FREE, dedicated to Bolívar's life. The Casa de México Benito Juárez (Map p68; Obrapía No

Centro Habana

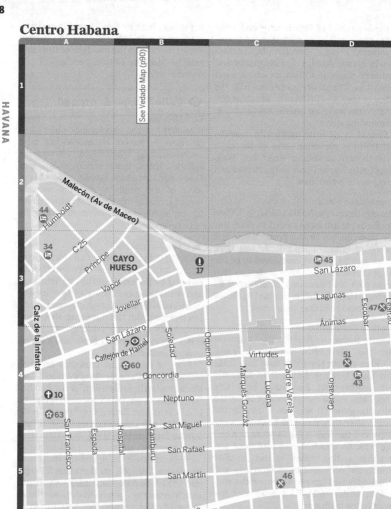

See Vedado Map (0g0)

Malecón (Av de Maceo)

CAYO HUESO

Calz de la Infanta

Humboldt

C 25

Príncipe

Vapor

Jovellar

San Lázaro

Callejón de Hamel

Concordia

Neptuno

San Miguel

San Rafael

San Martín

Zanja

Salud

Pocito

San Francisco

Espada

Hospital

Aramburu

Soledad

Oquendo

Marqués Gonzáz

Lucena

Padre Varela

Santiago

Virtudes

Gervasio

Escobar

Lealtad

San Lázaro

Lagunas

Ánimas

44

34

7

60

10

63

17

45

47

51

43

46

50

Av Salvador Allende

Calz de Ayestarán

Retiro

Árbol Seco

Maloja

Sitio

Oquendo

Marqués Gonzáz

San Carlos

Padre Varela

Escobar

Lealtad

Enrique Barnet

Peñalver

69

15

25

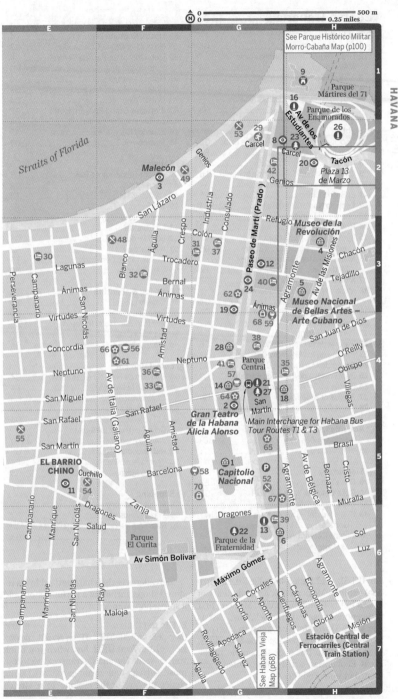

Centro Habana

116; USD$1; ⊗10:15am-5:45pm Tue-Sat, 9am-1pm Sun) exhibits Mexican folk art and plenty of books but not a lot on Juárez (Mexico's first indigenous president) himself. Just east is the **Casa Oswaldo Guayasamín** (Map p68; Obrapía No 111; ⊗9am-4:30pm Tue-Sun) **FREE**, now a museum but once the studio of the great Ecuadorian artist who painted Fidel Castro in numerous poses.

Mercaderes is also characterized by its restored shops, including a perfume store and a spice shop. Wander at will.

El Ojo del Ciclón   GALLERY
(Map p68; ☑7-861-5359; O'Reilly No 501, cnr Villegas; ⊗10am-7pm) **FREE** Just when you think you've seen Havana's strangest, weirdest, most surreal and avant-garde art, along comes the 'eye of the cyclone' to re-stretch

your imagination. The abstract gallery displays the work of Cuban visual artist Leo D'Lázaro and it's pretty mind-bending stuff – giant eyes, crashed cars, painted suitcases and junk reborn as art. Imagine Jackson Pollock sitting down for tea with JRR Tolkien and John Lennon.

Some of the art is semi-interactive: you can hit a punching bag, play a bizarre game of table football or hang your bag on a masked metal scarecrow. If that's not outlandish enough, come back for the tango classes on Friday and Sunday at 8pm.

Plaza del Cristo   SQUARE
(Map p68) A little apart from the historical core, Plaza del Cristo hasn't benefited from a full restoration yet and this adds subtly to its charm. Here you can sidestep boisterous games of football, listen to the musical outpourings of several cool bars or sit down with half the neighborhood and hook up to the local wi-fi hot spot (in Cuba even the internet is a socially interactive experience!).

The square's chunkiest edifice is the **Parroquial del Santo Cristo del Buen Viaje** (Map p68; Plaza del Cristo; ⊘9am-noon), a recently renovated 18th-century church where sailors once came to pray before embarking on long voyages.

Edificio Bacardí   LANDMARK
(Bacardí Bldg; Map p68; Av de las Misiones, btwn Empedrado & San Juan de Dios; ⊘hours vary) Finished in 1930, the magnificent Edificio Bacardí, once the HQ of Cuba's erstwhile rum dynasty, is a triumph of art deco architecture, with a host of lavish finishes utilizing red granite, green marble, terra-cotta reliefs and glazed tiles. Though 12 stories high, it's hemmed in by other buildings these days, so it's hard to get a panoramic view of the structure from street level. Notwithstanding, the opulent bell tower can be glimpsed from all over Havana.

Art deco aficionados can scout around the lobby, where a mediocre bar welcomes you. Note that trips up to the tower for eagle's-eye views of the city were suspended at research time.

Edificio Santo Domingo   MUSEUM
(Map p68; Mercaderes, btwn Obispo & O'Reilly; ⊘9:30am-5pm Tue-Sat, to 1pm Sun) **FREE** The block behind Plaza de Armas was the original home of Havana's university, from 1728 to 1902. The university was once part of a convent. The office block you see today was built by the Office of the City Historian in

2006 over the skeleton of an uglier 1950s office, the roof of which was used as a helicopter landing pad. It's been ingeniously refitted using the convent's bell tower and baroque doorway – an interesting juxtaposition of old and new.

Many of the university's arts faculties have reinhabited the space, while a small 1st-floor art gallery displays some priceless paintings by Cuban old masters such as José Nicolás de la Escalera, plus a couple of more modern works by Victor Manuel Valdés.

Casa de la Obra Pía   HISTORIC BUILDING
(Map p68; Obrapía No 158; ⊘10:30am-5:30pm Tue-Sat, 9:30am-2:30pm Sun) **FREE** One of the more muscular sights around Calle Mercaderes is this typical Havana aristocratic residence, constructed around 1648 and rebuilt in 1780. Baroque decoration, including an intricate portico made in Cádiz, Spain, covers the facade. The house today functions as a decorative-arts museum, containing a potpourri of period furniture from Chinese to French. It was one of the first structures to be rehabilitated by the City Historian in the early 1980s.

A local embroidery cooperative maintains an HQ here, and you'll spy some old Singer sewing machines not yet requisitioned by Havana's hipsters. Beware: opening hours can be temperamental.

Maqueta de La Habana Vieja   MUSEUM
(Map p68; Mercaderes No 114; USD$2; ⊘9:30am-5pm Tue-Sat, to 1pm Sun; ⊕) Herein lies a 1:500 scale model of Habana Vieja, complete with an authentic soundtrack meant to replicate a day in the life of the city. It's incredibly detailed and provides an excellent way of geographically acquainting yourself with the city's historical core.

Also here is a small cinema, the **Cinematógrafo Lumière** (tickets USD$2), that shows nostalgia movies for senior citizens, and a 25-minute documentary about Habana Vieja's restoration for visitors at 2pm.

Museo de la
Farmacia Habanera   MUSEUM
(Map p68; cnr Brasil & Compostela; ⊘9am-5pm) **FREE** A few blocks east of Plaza del Cristo, this grand wood-paneled store founded in 1886 by Catalan José Sarrá has been restored as both a museum and a working pharmacy for the local population. The small museum section displays an elegant mock-up of an old drugstore with some interesting historical explanations.

Museo 28 Septiembre de los CDR   MUSEUM
(Map p68; Obispo, btwn Aguiar & Habana; USD$2; ⊙9am-5pm) A pale-pink building on Obispo dedicates two floors to a rather one-sided dissection of the nationwide Comites de la Defensa de la Revolución (CDR; Committees for the Defense of the Revolution). Commendable neighborhood-watch schemes or grassroots spying agencies? Sift through the propaganda and decide.

Museo de Pintura Mural   MUSEUM
(Map p68; Obispo, btwn Mercaderes & Oficios; ⊙10am-6pm) FREE A simple museum that exhibits some beautifully restored original frescoes in the Casa del Mayorazgo de Recio, popularly considered to be Havana's oldest surviving house. It has been renovated and, at the time of research, only the ground floor was open.

◉ La Loma de Ángel & Around

Plazuela de Santo Ángel   PLAZA
(Map p68) This lovely, intimate plaza behind the Iglesia del Santo Ángel Custodio has benefited from a recent beautification project that has installed several private restaurants, along with a statue of the fictional heroine Cecilia Valdés, who is watched over by a bust of the author who created her, Cirilo Villaverde.

Iglesia del Santo Ángel Custodio   CHURCH
(Map p68; Compostela No 2; ⊙during Mass 7:15am Tue, Wed & Fri, 6pm Thu, Sat & Sun) Originally constructed in 1695, this church was pounded by a ferocious hurricane in 1846, after which it was entirely rebuilt in neo-Gothic style. Among the notable historical and literary figures to have passed through its handsome doors are 19th-century Cuban novelist Cirilo Villaverde, who set the main scene of his novel *Cecilia Valdés o la loma del ángel* here. Other notables include Félix Varela and José Martí, who were baptized in the church in 1788 and 1853, respectively.

Arte Corte   MUSEUM
(Map p68; ☑7-861-0202; www.artecorte.org; Aguiar No 10, btwn Peña Pobre & Av de las Misiones; ⊙10am-6pm Tue-Sat) FREE The brainchild of Gilberto Valladares, aka 'Papito,' this novel hairdressing salon is also a school and a small museum to the barber's art. Even better, with a little help from his friends (including the City Historian), Papito's barber theme has taken over the whole street, unofficially rechristened Callejón de los Peluqueros (Hairdresser's Alley) and now supported by more than 20 independent businesses.

Nearby there's a children's park with barber-themed apparatus, and down the street is Figaro's restaurant, named after the main character in *The Barber of Seville*.

Barbeparque   PARK
(Map p68; Av de las Misiones, btwn Peñapobre & Cuarteles; ⊙10am-7pm Tue-Sun) FREE A project of Arte Corte inaugurated in December 2013 in collaboration with the Office of the City Historian, Barbeparque is a whimsical space that invites kids to think about the haircuts they see and wear. The small park includes a cafeteria and, yes, a barber shop!

Statue of General Máximo Gómez   MONUMENT
(Map p78; cnr Malecón & Paseo de Martí) On a large traffic island overlooking the mouth of the harbor is a rather grand depiction of Máximo Gómez, a war hero from the Dominican Republic who fought tirelessly for Cuban independence in both the 1868 and 1895 conflicts with the Spanish. The impressive statue of him sitting atop a horse was created by Italian artist Aldo Gamba in 1935 and faces heroically out to sea.

Parque de los Enamorados   PARK
(Map p78) In Parque de los Enamorados (Lovers' Park), surrounded by speeding traffic, lies a section of the colonial Cárcel (Map p78; aka Tacón Prison), built in 1838. Many Cuban patriots, including José Martí, were imprisoned in this brutal place, which sent inmates to perform hard labor in the nearby San Lázaro quarry. The prison was demolished in 1939, and this park is dedicated to the memory of those who suffered so terribly within its walls. Two tiny cells and a chapel are all that remain.

Behind the park, the beautiful wedding-cake-like building (art nouveau with a dash of eclecticism) flying the Spanish flag is the old Palacio Velasco (Map p78; Cárcel No 51), now the Spanish embassy.

Beyond that, on a traffic island, is the Memorial a los Estudiantes de Medicina (Map p78). A fragment of wall encased in marble, it marks the spot where eight Cuban medical students were shot by the Spanish in 1871 in reprisal for allegedly desecrating the tomb of a Spanish journalist.

Castillo de San Salvador de la Punta FORT
(Map p78; USD$2; ☺ museum 9:30am-5pm Tue-
Sat, to noon Sun) One in a quartet of forts
defending Havana harbor, La Punta was designed by Italian military engineer Bautista
Antonelli and built between 1589 and 1600.
It underwent comprehensive repairs after
the British shelled it during their successful
1762 Havana raid. During the colonial era a
chain was stretched 250m to the castle of El
Morro (p98) every night to close the harbor
mouth to shipping.

The castle's **museum** is really just a few
information boards chronicling its history
(in Spanish), but there are good views from
the battlements, where you can also admire
the huge Parrott cannons dating from the
mid-19th century.

◉ Centro Habana

Centro Habana's crowded residential grid
offers an uncensored look at Cuba without
the fancy wrapping paper. On its potholed
but perennially action-packed streets, elderly men engage in marathon games of dominoes, Afro-Cuban drums beat out addictive
rumba rhythms and sorrily down-at-heel
buildings give intriguing hints of their illustrious previous lives. Juxtaposed against
this ebullient but spectacularly dilapidated
quarter is the very different world of Parque
Central and El Prado, a busy, tourist-heavy
zone crammed with Havana's poshest hotels and some of its finest museums.

★ Malecón   WATERFRONT
(Map p78) The Malecón, Havana's evocative 7km-long sea drive, is one of the city's
most soulful and quintessentially Cuban
thoroughfares, and long a favored meeting
place for assorted lovers, philosophers, poets, traveling minstrels, fishers and wistful
Florida-gazers. The Malecón's atmosphere
is most potent at sunset, when the weak
yellow light from creamy Vedado filters like
a dim torch onto the buildings of Centro
Habana, lending their dilapidated facades a
distinctly romantic quality.

Laid out in the early 1900s as a salubrious oceanside boulevard for Havana's pleasure-seeking middle classes, the Malecón
expanded rapidly eastward in the century's
first decade, with a mishmash of architecture that mixed sturdy neoclassicism with
whimsical art nouveau. By the 1920s the
road had reached the outer limits of Vedado, and by the early 1950s it had metamor-
phosed into a busy six-lane highway that
carried streams of wave-dodging Buicks
and Chevrolets from the gray hulk of the
Castillo de San Salvador de la Punta to the
borders of Miramar. Today the Malecón
remains Havana's most authentic open-air
theater, sometimes dubbed 'the world's
longest sofa,' where the whole city comes to
meet, greet, date and debate.

Fighting an ongoing battle with the cor-
rosive effects of the ocean, many of the
thoroughfare's magnificent buildings now
face decrepitude, demolition or irrevocable
damage. To combat the problem, 14 blocks
of the Malecón have been given special status by the Office of the City Historian in an
attempt to stop the rot.

The Malecón is particularly evocative
when a cold front blows in and massive
waves crash over the sea wall. The road is
often closed to cars at these times, meaning
you can walk right down the middle of the
empty thoroughfare (and get very wet).

★ Museo de la Revolución   MUSEUM
(Map p78; Refugio No 1; USD$8, guided tours
USD$2; ☺ 9:30am-4pm) This emblematic
museum is set in the former **Presidential Palace**, constructed between 1913 and
1920 and used by a string of Cuban presidents, culminating in Fulgencio Batista.
The world-famous Tiffany's of New York
decorated the interior, and the shimmering
Salón de los Espejos (Hall of Mirrors) was
designed to resemble the eponymous room
at the Palace of Versailles.

The museum, designed primarily to
help Cubans understand their own history, descends chronologically from the top
floor, focusing on the events leading up to,
during and immediately after the Cuban
Revolution. It presents a sometimes scruffy
but always compelling story, told in English and Spanish, and tinted with *mucho*
propaganda.

The palace's sweeping central staircase,
guarded by a bust of José Martí, still retains
the bullet holes made during an unsuccessful attack in March 1957 by a revolutionary student group intent on assassinating
Batista.

The stairs take you up to the 2nd floor
and several important exhibit-free rooms,
including the **Salón Dorado** (decorated
in Louis XVI style and once used for ban-
quets), the **Despacho Presidencial** (President's Office, where Fidel Castro was sworn
in in 1959) and the **capilla** (chapel, with a
Tiffany chandelier).

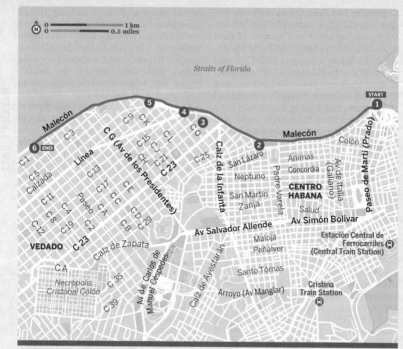

N
0   1 km
0   0.5 miles

Straits of Florida

START
1

Malecón

5

4

3

2

Malecón

Colón

C 9   CK

C 3

C G (Av de los Presidentes)

C-15   CJ   21

CH

CL

CO

C 23

C 25

Calz de la Infanta

San Lázaro

Animas

Concordia

Av de Italia (Galiano)

Paseo de Martí (Prado)

6 END

Línea

C 13

C-17

C E

CD

C 29

Neptuno

Padre Varela

CENTRO HABANA

C-1

C-5

Calzada

C-11

C-3

Paseo

CC

CA

CB

San Martín

Zanja

Salud

Av Simón Bolívar

C-7

C-9

C-4

C-19

C 2

Av Salvador Allende

VEDADO

C 23

Calz de Zapata

Maloja

Peñalver

Estación Central de Ferrocarriles
(Central Train Station)

C A

Necrópolis
Cristóbal Colón

C 35

Av de Carlos de Manuel Céspedes

Calz de Ayestarán

Santo Tómas

Arroyo (Av Manglar)

Cristina
Train Station

C 39

🏃 City Walk
The Malecón

START MALECÓN & PRADO
END MALECÓN & PASEO
LENGTH 5.5KM; TWO HOURS

Havana's 7km-long Malecón is one of the world's great promenades and the city's quintessential walk. Marking the beginning of the Malecón, the 16th-century **1 Castillo de San Salvador de la Punta** (p83) predates the sea drive by three centuries. It guards the entrance to Havana harbor and its walls face off against the larger Morro fort opposite.

The first break in the sea drive heading west is a small park with a dashing **2 statue of Antonio Maceo** (Map p78), the Cuban independence war hero, atop his horse. Behind the park rises the concrete mass of the Hospital Nacional Hermanos Ameijeiras. An underpass links the park to the walkway.

On a rocky knoll known as the Loma de Taganana, the **3 Hotel Nacional** (p89) dominates the Malecón at the intersection with Calle 23 (La Rampa). Far more than just a hotel, it's also a national monument, a top cabaret venue and an architectural marvel.

A rare monument honoring Americans in Cuba, the **4 Monumento a las Víctimas del Maine** (p93) commemorates the 266 US Marines killed when the US battleship *Maine* exploded in Havana harbor in 1898, an incident that helped spark the Spanish–American War. An eagle atop the monument was toppled in 1959 during a moment of high revolutionary fervor.

The former US Interests Section office was converted back into the **5 US Embassy** (p94) in 2015, and the Stars and Stripes flies here once again. The propaganda boards that used to dominate the environs have quietly disappeared, although the parade ground in front is still called the Tribuna Anti-Imperialista José Martí.

Still further west along the Malecón, end your walk at the striking modernist **6 Hotel Riviera** (p113). It opened in 1957 as a hotel-cabaret-casino, the property of US gangster Meyer Lansky. A year later the Cuban government appropriated the hotel as Lansky fled to the Bahamas. Today the building retains the over-the-top design of its brief 1950s heyday.

In front of the building is a fragment of the former city wall, as well as an SAU-100 tank used by Castro during the 1961 Bay of Pigs battle. In the space behind you'll find the Pavillón Granma, containing a replica of the 18m yacht that carried Castro and 81 other revolutionaries from Tuxpán, Mexico, to Cuba in December 1956. The boat is encased in glass and guarded 24/7, presumably to stop anyone from breaking in and sailing off to Florida in it. The pavilion is surrounded by other vehicles associated with the revolution, including planes, rockets and an old postal van that was used as a getaway car during the 1957 attack.

★ **Museo Nacional de Bellas Artes – Arte Cubano**   MUSEUM
(Map p78; www.bellasartes.co.cu; Trocadero, btwn Agramonte & Av de las Misiones; USD$5, under 14yr free; ⊙9am-5pm Tue-Sat, 10am-2pm Sun) The Bellas Artes' 'Colección de Arte Cubano' houses purely Cuban art. Works are displayed in chronological order, starting on the 3rd floor, and are surprisingly varied. Artists to look out for include Guillermo Collazo, considered to be the first truly great Cuban artist; Rafael Blanco, with his cartoon-like paintings and sketches; Raúl Martínez, a master of 1960s Cuban pop art; and the Picasso-like Wifredo Lam.

Museo Nacional de Bellas Artes – Arte Universal   MUSEUM
(Arte Universal; Map p78; www.bellasartes.co.cu; San Rafael, btwn Agramonte & Av de las Misiones; USD$5, under 14yr free; ⊙9am-5pm Tue-Sat, 10am-2pm Sun) Since 2001 Havana's international collection, displaying art from 500 BCE to the present day, has been exhibited on three floors of the Palacio de los Asturianos. Its undisputed highlight is its Spanish collection, with canvases by Francisco de Zurbarán, Bartolomé Esteban Murillo and Jusepe de Ribera, and a tiny work by Diego Velázquez. Also worth perusing are the 2000-year-old Roman mosaics, Greek pots from the 5th century BCE, and a suitably refined canvas by Thomas Gainsborough (in the British room).

★ **Capitolio Nacional**   HISTORIC BUILDING
(Map p78; cnr Dragones & Paseo de Martí; guided tour USD$10; ⊙10am-4pm Tue, Thu & Sun, to noon Wed & Sat) The incomparable Capitolio Nacional is Havana's most ambitious and grandiose building, constructed after the post-WWI boom ('Dance of the Millions') gifted the Cuban government a seemingly bottomless vault of sugar money. Similar to the Capitol in Washington, DC, but actually modeled on the Panthéon in Paris, the building was initiated by Cuba's US-backed dictator Gerardo Machado in 1926 and took 5000 workers three years, two months and 20 days to construct, at a cost of US$17 million.

Formerly the Capitolio was the seat of the Cuban Congress, then from 1959 to 2013 it housed the Cuban Academy of Sciences and the National Library of Science and Technology. The building underwent a massive refurbishment between 2013 and 2019, reopening in time for Havana's 500th anniversary. Guided tours leave on the hour and take in most of the main features, including the palatial hallways, the chamber of representatives and the more recently established **Tumba del Mambí Desconocido (Tomb of the Unknown Soldier)**.

Constructed with white Capellanía limestone and block granite, the building has an entrance guarded by six rounded Doric columns atop a staircase that leads up from Paseo de Martí (Prado). Looking out over the Havana skyline is a 62m stone cupola topped with a replica of 16th-century Florentine sculptor Giambologna's bronze statue of Mercury in the Palazzo del Bargello. Set in the floor directly below the dome is a copy of a 24-carat diamond. Highway distances between Havana and all sites in Cuba are calculated from this point.

The entryway is accessed by a sweeping 55-step staircase guarded by two giant statues carved by Italian sculptor Angelo Zanelli: *El Trabajo* and *La Virtud Tutelar*. The main doors open into the **Salón de los Pasos Perdidos** (Room of the Lost Steps, so named because of its unusual acoustics), at the center of which is a magnificent statue of *La República*, an enormous bronze woman standing 17.6m tall and symbolizing the mythic Guardian of Virtue and Work. The 30-tonne statue is covered in gold leaf and is the third-largest indoor statue in the world. It was carved by Zanelli in Rome and shipped to Cuba in three pieces.

★ **Gran Teatro de la Habana Alicia Alonso**   THEATER
(Map p78; ☑7-861-3077; Paseo de Martí No 458; guided tours USD$5; ⊙9:30am-4pm Mon-Sat, 9:15am-12:15pm Sun) The neobaroque Gran Teatro de la Habana Alicia Alonso, erected as a Galician social club between 1907 and 1914, features highly ornate and even exuberant architectural details. It's the official

stage for the Cuban National Ballet Company and the headquarters of the biennial International Ballet Festival (p105). Dance presentations, ranging from ballet to contemporary dance to Spanish-influenced choreography by companies from all over the country and abroad, are the highlights every weekend. There are daily guided tours.

Formerly known as Centro Gallego, the theater was built around the Teatro Tacón, attached to the social club since 1838. The Tacón opened with five masked Carnaval dances, which forms the basis for the claim that it's the oldest operating theater in the western hemisphere. Over its 180 years it has hosted international figures such as Enrico Caruso, Anna Pavlova, Maya Plisetskaya and Sarah Bernhardt, as well as remarkable companies such as the American Ballet Theatre, the Royal Ballet, Antonio Gades Ballet and the Ballet of Buenos Aires.

Still standing the test of time, the theater was renovated in 2015 and sparkles afresh from its perch in Parque Central. Its facilities include a 1500-seat main hall, a concert hall, conference rooms and an art gallery.

Paseo de Martí   HISTORIC SITE
(El Prado; Map p78) Construction of this stately European-style boulevard – the first street outside the old city walls – began in 1770, and work was completed in the mid-1830s during the term of Captain General Miguel Tacón (1834–38). The original idea was to create a boulevard as splendid as any found in Paris or Barcelona (El Prado bears more than a passing resemblance to Las Ramblas). The famous bronze lions that guard the central promenade at either end were added in 1928.

Notable Prado buildings include the neo-Renaissance Palacio de los Matrimonios (Map p78; Paseo de Martí No 302), the streamline-moderne Teatro Fausto and the neoclassical Escuela Nacional de Ballet (Map p78; cnr Paseo de Martí & Trocadero), Alicia Alonso's famous ballet school.

These days the Prado hosts a respected alfresco art market on weekends and countless impromptu soccer matches during the week.

Although officially known as Paseo de Martí, the street is almost universally referred to by its old name, Prado.

Taller Comunitario José Martí   GALLERY
(Map p78; Paseo de Martí, btwn Neptuno & Virtudes; ⊙10am-9pm) Workshop-gallery of an avant-garde artists' collective comprising around a dozen artists. Enter via the radiant mural in El Prado to admire and/or buy probing, cutting-edge creations and chat to their makers.

Hotel Inglaterra   HISTORIC BUILDING
(Map p78; Paseo de Martí No 416) Havana's oldest hotel opened its doors in 1856 on the site of a popular bar called El Louvre (the hotel's alfresco bar still bears that name). Facing leafy Parque Central, the building exhibits the neoclassical design features in vogue at the time, complemented by a lobby beautified with Moorish tiles. At a banquet here in 1879, José Martí made a speech advocating Cuban independence, and much later US journalists covering the Spanish–American War stayed at the hotel.

Parque Central   PARK
(Map p78) Diminutive Parque Central is a verdant haven from the belching buses and roaring taxis that ply the Paseo de Martí. Long a microcosm of daily Havana life, the park was expanded to its present size in the late 19th century after the city walls were knocked down. The 1905 marble statue of José Martí (Map p78) at its center was the first of thousands to be erected in Cuba. It's surrounded by 28 palm trees.

Hard to miss over to one side is the group of baseball fans who linger 24/7 at the famous Esquina Caliente (literally, 'hot corner'), discussing form, tactics and the Havana team's prospects in the playoffs.

Parque de la Fraternidad   PARK
(Map p78) Leafy Parque de la Fraternidad was established in 1892 to commemorate the fourth centenary of the Spanish landing in the Americas. A few decades later it was remodeled and renamed to mark the 1927 Pan-American Conference. The name is meant to signify American brotherhood, hence the many busts of Latin and North American leaders that embellish the green areas, including one of US president Abraham Lincoln.

Today the park is the terminus of numerous metro bus routes, and is sometimes referred to as 'Jurassic Park' because of the plethora of photogenic old American cars now used as *almendrones* (collective taxis) that congregate around here.

Old City Wall   HISTORIC SITE
(Map p68) In the 17th century, anxious to defend the city from attacks by pirates and overzealous foreign armies, Cuba's paranoid colonial authorities drew up plans for the construction of a 5km-long city wall.

Built between 1674 and 1740, the wall on completion was 1.5m thick and 10m high, running along a line now occupied by Av de las Misiones and Av de Bélgica.

Among the wall's myriad defenses were nine bastions and 180 big guns aimed toward the sea. The only way in and out of the city was through 11 heavily guarded gates that closed every night and opened every morning to the sound of a solitary gunshot. From 1863 the walls were demolished, but a few segments remain, the largest of which stands on Av de Bélgica close to the train station.

Callejón de Hamel   STREET
(Map p78; btwn Aramburu & Hospital) There are at least four reasons that you should incorporate this community-driven back alley into any serious Havana outing: 1) it's the unofficial HQ of Havana's Afro-Cuban community; 2) it's replete with inspired street art, much of it executed with recycled materials (this is where your old bathtub gets a new life); 3) it's an essential stop for anyone trying to understand Cuba's complex syncretic religions; and 4) the denizens put on hypnotic live rumba shows (p133) every Sunday.

Convento & Iglesia del Carmen   CHURCH
(Map p78; cnr Calzada de la Infanta & Neptuno; ⊙7:30am-noon & 3-7pm Tue-Sun) This little-visited church's bell tower dominates the Centro Habana skyline and is topped by a huge statue of Nuestra Señora del Carmen, but the real prizes are inside: rich Seville-style tiles, a gilded altarpiece, ornate woodcarving and swirling frescoes. Surprisingly, the church was only constructed in 1923, to house a Carmelite order. The building is considered 'eclectic.'

El Barrio Chino   AREA
(Map p78) One of the world's more surreal Chinatowns, Havana's Barrio Chino is notable for its lack of Chinese residents – most Chinese people left Havana as soon as a newly inaugurated Fidel Castro uttered the word *socialismo* in the early 1960s. Nevertheless, it's worth a wander for its novelty and its handful of decent restaurants.

The first Chinese arrived on the island as contract laborers in the late 1840s following the decline of the transatlantic slave trade. By the 1920s Havana's Chinatown had become the biggest Asian neighborhood in Latin America, a bustling hub of industry that spawned laundries, pharmacies,

theaters and grocery stores. The slide began in the early 1960s, when thousands of business-minded Chinese relocated to the US. Recognizing the tourist potential of the area in the 1990s, the Cuban government invested in rejuvenating the district's historical character with bilingual street signs, a large pagoda-shaped arch at the entrance to Calle Dragones, and incentives for local Chinese businesspeople to promote restaurants. Today most of the action centers on narrow Calle Cuchillo and its surrounding streets.

Iglesia del Sagrado Corazón de Jesús   CHURCH
(Map p78; Av Simón Bolívar, btwn Gervasio & Padre Varela; ⊙ hours vary) A little out of the way but well worth the walk is this inspiring marble creation with a distinctive white steeple – it's one of Cuba's few Gothic buildings. The church is rightly famous for its magnificent stained-glass windows, and the light that penetrates through the eaves first thing in the morning (when the church is deserted) gives the place an ethereal quality.

Fuente de la India   MONUMENT
(Map p78; Paseo de Martí) Spare a glance for this white Carrara-marble fountain, carved by Giuseppe Gaggini in 1837 for the Count of Villanueva and now situated on a traffic island in front of Hotel Saratoga. It portrays a regal indigenous woman adorned with a crown of eagle's feathers and seated on a throne surrounded by four gargoylesque dolphins.

In one hand the woman holds a horn-shaped basket filled with fruit, in the other a shield bearing the city's coat of arms – a golden key between two mountains, a sun above the sea, three stripes emblazoned on a white background, and a royal palm.

Real Fábrica de Tabacos Partagás   FACTORY
(Map p78; San Carlos No 816, btwn Peñalver & Sitio; tours USD$10; ⊙ tours every 15min 9am-2pm Mon-Fri) One of Havana's oldest and most famous cigar businesses, the Real Fábrica de Tabacos Partagás was founded in 1845 by Spaniard Jaime Partagás. In 2013 the factory moved from its original location behind the Capitolio (p85) to its current digs just off Calle Padre Varela in Centro Habana. It's the only cigar factory in Havana offering reliable tours. Tickets must be bought beforehand in the lobby of the Hotel Saratoga (p111).

**Asociación Cultural
Yoruba de Cuba** MUSEUM
(Map p78; Paseo de Martí No 615; USD$5; ⊙9am-
4:30pm Mon-Sat) To untangle the mysteries
of the Santería religion, its saints and their
powers, decamp to this museum–cultural
center. Aside from sculpted effigies of the
various *orishas* (deities), the association
hosts *tambores* (Santería drum ceremonies)
on Friday at 6pm (USD$5). Check the no-
ticeboard at the door for details. Note that
there's a church dress code for the *tambores*
(no shorts or tank tops).

◉ Vedado

Majestic, spread-out Vedado is Havana's
once-notorious Mafia-run district. During
Cuba's 50-year dalliance with the US, this
was the city's commercial hub and in many
ways it still is, although now the nightlife is
less tawdry, the casinos have become discos,
and the hotels are as much historical relics
as havens of luxury.

Aside from its small clutch of modernist *rascacielos* (skyscrapers), Vedado is a
largely leafy residential quarter bisected by
two wide Parisian-style boulevards and anchored by the bombastic Plaza de la Revolución and the eerily beautiful Necrópolis
Cristóbal Colón.

★**Necrópolis Cristóbal Colón** CEMETERY
(Map p90; USD$5; ⊙8am-6pm, last entry 5pm)
Havana's main cemetery (a national monument), one of the largest in the Americas,
is renowned for its striking religious ico-
nography and elaborate marble statues.
Far from being eerie, a walk through these
57 hallowed hectares can be an educational
and emotional stroll through the annals of
Cuban history. A map (USD$1) showing the
graves of assorted artists, sportspeople, politicians, writers, scientists and revolutionaries is for sale at the entrance.

Enter via the splendid Byzantine-
Romanesque gateway, the **Puerta de la
Paz**; the tomb of independence leader **General Máximo Gómez** (1905) is on the right
(look for the bronze face in a circular me-
dallion). Further along past the first circle,
and also on the right, are the **firefighters
monument** (1890) and the neo-Romanesque **Capilla Central** (1886), in the center
of the cemetery. Just northeast of the chapel
is the graveyard's most celebrated (and visited) tomb, that of Señora Amelia Goyri, better known as La Milagrosa (the Miraculous
One), who died while giving birth on May

3, 1901. The marble figure of a woman with
a large cross and a baby in her arms is easy
to find due to the many flowers piled on the
tomb and the local devotees in attendance.
For many years after her death her heartbro-
ken husband visited the grave several times
a day. He always knocked with one of four
iron rings on the burial vault and walked
away backwards so that he could see her for
as long as possible. When the bodies were
exhumed some years later, Amelia's body
was uncorrupted (a sign of sanctity in the
Catholic faith), and the baby, who had been
buried at its mother's feet, was allegedly
found in her arms. As a result, La Milagrosa
became the focus of a huge spiritual cult in
Cuba, and thousands of people come here
annually with gifts, in the hope of fulfilling
dreams or solving problems. In keeping with
tradition, pilgrims knock with the iron ring
on the vault and walk away backwards when
they leave.

As important as La Milagrosa among the
Santería community, the '**tomb of Hermano José**' marks the grave of a woman called
Leocadia Pérez Herrero, a black Havana
medium known for her great acts of charity among the poor in the early 20th century. Leocadia said that she consulted with
a Santería priest called Hermano José who
encouraged and guided her in her generous
acts. As a spiritual and superstitious person,
she always kept a painting of Hermano José's image in her house, and when she died
in 1962 the canvas was buried alongside her.
Today followers of Santería venerate Hermano José and regularly come to Leocadia's
grave to ask for charitable favors. In keeping with Santería tradition, they often leave
flowers, glasses of rum, half-smoked cigars
or sacrificed chickens on the grave.

Also worth looking out for are the graves
of novelist Alejo Carpentier (1904–80), sci-
entist Carlos Finlay (1833–1915), the Martyrs
of Granma and the Veterans of the Independence Wars.

★**Museo Napoleónico** MUSEUM
(Map p90; San Miguel No 1159; USD$3; ⊙9:30am-
5pm Tue-Sat, to 12:30pm Sun) Without a doubt
one of the best museums in Havana and
thus in Cuba, this magnificently laid-out collection of 7000 objects associated with the
life of Napoleon Bonaparte was amassed by
Cuban sugar baron Julio Lobo and politician
Orestes Ferrara.

Highlights include sketches of Voltaire,
paintings of the Battle of Waterloo, china,

furniture, an interesting recreation of Napoleon's study and bedroom, and one of several bronze Napoleonic death masks made two days after the emperor's death by his personal physician, Dr Francisco Antommarchi. It's set over four floors of a beautiful Vedado mansion next to the Universidad de la Habana and has stunning views from its 4th-floor terrace.

Hotel Nacional   HISTORIC BUILDING

(Map p90; cnr Calles O & 21; ☺ free tours 10am & 3pm Mon-Fri, 10am Sat) Far more than just a hotel, the Nacional, built in 1930 as a copy of the Breakers Hotel in Palm Beach, Florida, is a national monument and one of Havana's architectural emblems. Even if you're not staying here, reserve time to admire the Moorish lobby, stroll the breezy grounds and have a drink in the famous terrace bar overlooking the Malecón. Ask in the lobby about free tours.

The hotel's notoriety was cemented in October 1933 when, following a sergeants' coup by Fulgencio Batista that toppled the regime of Gerardo Machado, 300 aggrieved army officers took refuge in the building hoping to curry favor with resident US ambassador Sumner Welles, who was staying there. Much to the officers' chagrin, Welles promptly left, allowing Batista's troops to open fire on the hotel, killing 14 officers and injuring seven. More were executed later, after they had surrendered.

In December 1946 the hotel gained infamy of a different kind when US mobsters Meyer Lansky and Lucky Luciano used it to host the largest ever get-together of the North American Mafia, who gathered here under the guise of a Frank Sinatra concert.

These days the hotel maintains a more reputable face and the once famous casino is long gone, though the spectacular Parisian cabaret is still a popular draw.

Museo de Artes Decorativas   MUSEUM

(Map p90; Calle 17 No 502, btwn Calles D & E; USD$5; ☺ 9:30am-4pm Tue-Sat) One of Havana's best museums dazzles like a European stately home. It's replete with all manner of architectural features, including rococo furniture, Chinese screens and an art deco bathroom. Equally interesting is the building itself, which is of French design and was commissioned in 1924 by the wealthy Gómez family, who built the Manzana de Gómez shopping center in Centro Habana.

Walking around you'll encounter a weighty collection of porcelain, ceramics and glassware amassed by former lady of the house María Gómez Mena, who was known for throwing lavish parties before the 1959 revolution put an end to wanton extravagance. The garden is a more Italian affair, guarded by statues and busts denoting the four seasons.

Memorial a José Martí   MONUMENT

(Map p90; Plaza de la Revolución; USD$3; ☺ 9:30am-4pm Mon-Sat) Center stage in Plaza de la Revolución is this monument, which at 138.5m is Havana's tallest structure. Fronted by an impressive 17m marble statue of a seated Martí in a pensive *Thinker* pose, the memorial houses a museum (the definitive word on Martí in Cuba) and a 129m lookout (reached via a small USD$2 lift) with fantastic city views.

Parque Lennon   PARK

(Map p90; cnr Calles 17 & 6) If you prefer John Lennon to Vladimir Lenin (both 20th-century personalities have a park named after them in Havana), decamp to this small square of green in Vedado, where a hyper-realistic statue of the former Beatle – unveiled by Fidel Castro on the 20th anniversary of Lennon's death – takes center stage.

The Beatles, and Lennon in particular, are icons in Cuba, despite being banned by the government in the 1960s for their 'corrupting' influence. Castro ultimately saw the light, belatedly hailing the band as revolutionaries during the statue's unveiling in 2000. The bronze Lennon doesn't lack company and you'll likely have to wait in line to grab a photo.

Plaza de la Revolución   SQUARE

(Map p90) Conceived by French urbanist Jean-Claude Forestier in the 1920s, the gigantic Plaza de la Revolución (known as Plaza Cívica until 1959) was part of Havana's 'new city,' which grew up between 1920 and 1959. As the nexus of Forestier's ambitious plan, the square was built on a small hill (the Loma de los Catalanes) in the manner of Paris' Place de l'Étoile, with various avenues fanning out toward Río Almendares, Vedado and Parque de la Fraternidad in Centro Habana.

Surrounded by gray, utilitarian buildings constructed in the late 1950s, the square today is the base of the Cuban government and a place where large-scale political rallies are held. In January 1998 one million people (nearly one tenth of the Cuban population)

Vedado

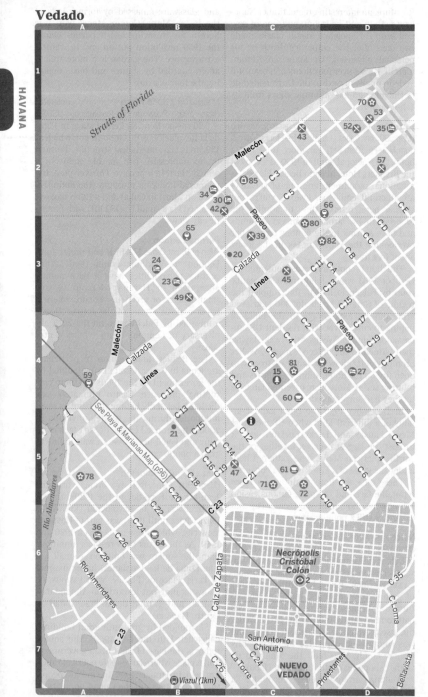

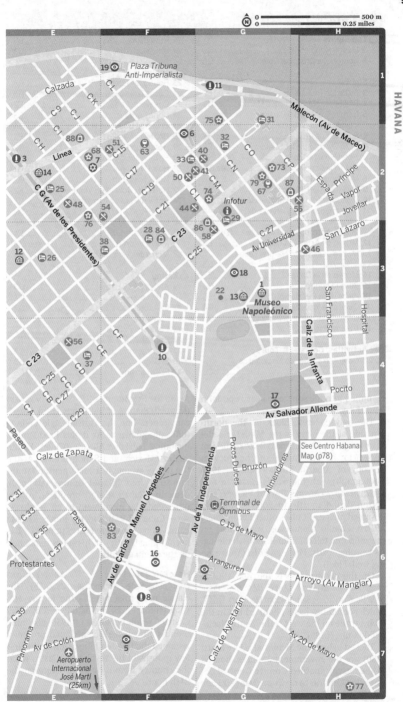

0 ___ 500 m
0 ___ 0.25 miles

Plaza Tribuna Anti-Imperialista

Calzada

C K

C J

C 9

C I

C H

Línea

C G (Av de los Presidentes)

Malecón (Av de Maceo)

Infotur

Museo Napoleónico

C O

C P

C N

C M

C L

Espada

Príncipe

Vapor

Jovellar

San Lázaro

Av Universidad

C 27

San Francisco

Hospital

Calz de la Infanta

See Centro Habana Map (p78)

Av Salvador Allende

C 23

C F

C E

C D

C C

C B

C 25

C 27

C A

C 29

Paseo

Calz de Zapata

C 31

C 33

C 35

C 37

Protestantes

C 39

Panorama

Av de Colón

Aeropuerto Internacional José Martí (25km)

Av de Carlos de Manuel Céspedes

Av de la Independencia

Pozos Dulces

Bruzón

Almendares

Terminal de Ómnibus

C 19 de Mayo

Aranguren

Arroyo (Av Manglar)

Calz de Ayestarán

Av 20 de Mayo

Vedado

crammed into the square to hear Pope John Paul II say Mass.

The ugly concrete block on the northern side of the plaza is the **Ministerio del Interior** (Map p90; Plaza de la Revolución), well known for its huge mural of Che Guevara (a copy of Alberto Korda's famous 1960 photograph) with the words *Hasta la victoria siempre* (Always Toward Victory) emblazoned underneath. In 2009 a similarly designed image of Cuba's other heroic *guerrillero,* Camilo Cienfuegos, was added on the adjacent telecommunications building. Its wording reads: *Vas bien Fidel* (You're going well, Fidel).

On the eastern side is the 1957 **Biblioteca Nacional José Martí** (Map p90; Plaza de la Revolución; ⊙8am-9:45pm Mon-Sat) FREE, which sometimes has a photo exhibit in the lobby, while on the west is the Teatro Nacional de Cuba (p135).

Tucked behind the Memorial a José Martí (p89) are the governmental offices, housed in the heavily guarded **Comité Central del Partido Comunista de Cuba** (Map p90; Plaza de la Revolución).

Av de los Presidentes   MONUMENT
(Map p90) Statues of illustrious Latin American leaders line the Parisian-style Calle G (officially known as Av de los Presidentes), including Salvador Allende (Chile), Benito Juárez (Mexico) and Simón Bolívar. At the top of the avenue is a huge marble **Monumento a José Miguel Gómez** (Map p90), depicting Cuba's second president. At the other end, the monument to his predecessor – Cuba's first president, Tomás Estrada Palma (long considered a US puppet) – has been toppled, with just his shoes remaining on the original plinth.

Hotel Habana Libre   NOTABLE BUILDING
(Map p90; Calle L, btwn Calles 23 & 25) This classic modernist hotel – the former Havana Hilton – was commandeered by Fidel Castro's revolutionaries in 1959 just nine months after it had opened, and promptly renamed the Habana Libre. During the first few months of the revolution, Castro ruled the country from a luxurious suite on the 24th floor.

A 670-sq-meter Venetian-tile mural by Amelia Peláez is splashed across the front of the building, while upstairs Alfredo Sosa Bravo's *Carro de la revolución* utilizes 525 ceramic pieces. There are some good shops, and an interesting photo gallery displaying snaps of the all-conquering *barbudos* (literally 'bearded ones') lolling around with their guns in the hotel's lobby in January 1959.

Monumento a las Víctimas del Maine
MONUMENT

(Map p90; Malecón) West beyond the Hotel Nacional (p89) is a monument (1926) to the 266 American marines who were killed when the battleship USS *Maine* blew up mysteriously in Havana harbor in 1898. The American eagle that once sat on top was decapitated soon after the 1959 revolution. Despite rumors to this effect, its replacement in the form of a dove sculpted by Pablo Picasso never materialized.

Quinta de los Molinos
GARDENS

(Map p90; cnr Av Salvador Allende & Luaces; tours USD$5; ⏰tours 10am Thu-Sun) The former stately residence of Independence War general Máximo Gómez, the Quinta sits in lush surroundings that have been managed as botanical gardens since 1839. While the former Gómez residence is closed, some of the grounds – with 160 tree species, 40 bird species and the tiny, colorful polymita snails that are endemic to Cuba – can be explored. There's also a butterfly enclosure, the first of its type in the country. Access is by guided visit only.

Museo de la Danza
MUSEUM

(Map p90; Línea No 365, cnr Av de los Presidentes; USD$2; ⏰10am-6pm Mon-Sat) Essentially a homage to Cuban ballet, this well-laid-out exhibition space in an eclectic Vedado mansion displays objects from Cuba's rich dance history. Most artifacts are drawn from the collection of former ballerina Alicia Alonso, who died in 2019.

Universidad de la Habana
UNIVERSITY

(Map p90; cnr Calles L & San Lázaro) Founded by Dominican monks in 1728 and secularized in 1842, Havana's university began life in Habana Vieja before moving to its present site in 1902. The existing neoclassical complex dates from the second quarter of the 20th century, and today some 30,000 students take courses here in social sciences, humanities, natural sciences, mathematics and economics.

Perched on a Vedado hill at the top of the famous *escalinata* (stairway), near the Alma Mater statue, the Plaza Ignacio Agramonte (the university's central quadrangle) displays a tank captured by Fidel Castro's rebels in 1958. Directly in front is the Librería Alma Mater (library) and, to the left, the Museo de Historia Natural Felipe Poey (Map p90; Universidad de la Habana; USD$1; ⊘ 9am-noon & 1-4pm Mon-Fri Sep-Jul), the oldest museum in Cuba, founded in 1842 by the Royal Academy of Medical, Physical and Natural Sciences. Many of its specimens of Cuban flora and fauna date from the 19th century. Upstairs in the faculty of biology is the Museo Antropológico Montané (Map p90; Universidad de la Habana; USD$1; ⊘ 9am-noon & 1-4pm Mon-Fri Sep-Jul), established in 1903, with a rich collection of pre-Columbian artifacts, including the 10th-century wooden Ídolo de Tabaco.

US Embassy   LANDMARK
(Map p90; https://cu.usembassy.gov; Calzada, btwn Calles L & M) Arguably the world's most famous US embassy, this modernist seven-story building on the Malecón with its high security fencing first opened in 1953, but it closed abruptly in 1961 when the US and Cuba cut diplomatic relations. It reopened as the US Interests Section, set up by the Carter administration in 1977, and in July 2015 it was rebranded an embassy thanks to the political thaw instigated by the Obama administration.

In 2018 most of the staff were withdrawn due to a mysterious wave of alleged 'sonic attacks.'

The embassy faces the Plaza Tribuna Anti-Imperialista (also known as Plaza de la Dignidad), once a site of major protests directed against the US. The mass of flagpoles was put up by the Cubans to block out an electronic message board mounted on the former Interests Section that flashed up messages, or propaganda, depending on which side of the fence you're on (!).

Edificio Focsa   LANDMARK
(Focsa Bldg; Map p90; cnr Calles 17 & M) Unmissable on the Havana skyline, the modernist Edificio Focsa was built between 1954 and 1956 in a record 28 months using pioneering computer technology. In 1999 it was

listed as one of the seven modern engineering wonders of Cuba. With 39 floors housing 373 apartments, on its completion it was the second-largest concrete structure of its type in the world, built entirely without the use of cranes.

When it fell on hard times in the early 1990s, the upper floors of the Focsa became nests for vultures, and in 2000 an elevator cable snapped, killing one person. Rejuvenated in the 2010s, this Havana giant nowadays contains residential apartments and a top-floor restaurant with spectacular views.

◉ Playa & Marianao

Playa, west of Vedado across the Río Almendares, is a large, complex municipality. For the sake of clarity, it can be split into several contrasting subneighborhoods. Gracious Miramar is a leafy diplomatic quarter of broad avenues, geriatric banyan trees and fine private restaurants; Cubanacán, further west, plays host to scientific fairs, business conventions, and biotechnological and pharmaceutical research institutes; Jaimanitas, hugging the shoreline, broadcasts the street-art extravaganza Fusterlandia; while Santa Fé is anchored by Marina Hemingway, Havana's premier, if slightly decrepit, boat marina. The separate municipality of Marianao is south of Playa.

★Fusterlandia   PUBLIC ART
(cnr Calle 226 & Av 3, Jaimanitas) FREE Where does art go after Antoni Gaudí? For a hint, head west from central Havana to the seemingly low-key district of Jaimanitas, where artist José Fuster has turned his home neighborhood into a masterpiece of intricate tile work and kaleidoscopic colors – a street-art wonderland that makes Barcelona's Park Güell look positively sedate. Imagine maximal-impact Gaudí relocated to a tropical setting.

The result is what is unofficially known as Fusterlandia, an ongoing project first hatched around 20 years ago that has covered several suburban blocks with whimsical but highly stylized public art. The centerpiece is Fuster's own house, Taller-Estudio José Fuster (⌨ 5-281-5421, studio 7-271-3028; cnr Calle 226 & Av 3, Jaimanitas; ⊘ 9:30am-5pm Mon-Fri, to 4pm Sat & Sun) FREE, a sizable residence decorated from roof to foundations with art, sculpture and – above all – mosaic tiles of every color and description. The overall impression defies written description (just *go!*): it's a fantastical mishmash of spiraling walkways, rippling

THE RISE OF THE GRAFITEROS

Art in Cuba has always been one of the most effective forms of social commentary. Subtly nuanced works by Cuban artists are often loaded with hidden messages or *dos sentidos* (double meaning) and can deliver a power political message. Yet, while heavy-handed censorship has been relaxed since the 1980s, artists must still be careful how they frame their ideas. Large, tourist-attracting street-art projects such as Fusterlandia are generally tolerated; direct attacks on the government are not.

Unauthorized graffiti is a relatively new phenomenon in Havana that would not have been possible 15 years ago. One of the city's most daring and visible *grafiteros* goes by the moniker 2+2=5. The name itself is subversive, a reference to the slogan in George Orwell's novel *Nineteen Eighty-Four* through which a one-party state legitimized its false dogma. Since 2016, 2+2=5 has used a recurring character, '*supermalo*,' a cartoonish minion masked by a balaclava, to make comments about contemporary culture. *Supermalo* features all over Havana in places such as the emerging San Isidro art district in Habana Vieja and ruined tenements on the Malecón. He is often joined by work from other *grafiteros*, such as Yulier P, known for his contorted human faces, and Cuban-American Abstrk, whose magnificent reclining woman decorates a small sports park opposite the Museo de la Revolución.

pools and sunburst fountains. The work mixes homages to Pablo Picasso and Gaudí with snippets of the style of Paul Gauguin and Wifredo Lam, magic realism, maritime motifs, aspects of Santería, the curvaceous lines of *modernisme*, and a large dose of Fuster's own Cubanness, which runs through almost everything. Look for the Cuban flags, a mural of the *Granma* yacht, and the words 'Viva Cuba' emblazoned across eight chimney pots.

Fusterlandia stretches way beyond Fuster's own residence. Over half the neighborhood has been given similar treatment, from street signs to bus stops to the local doctor's house. Wandering around its quiet streets is a surreal and psychedelic experience.

Jaimanitas is located just off Quinta Avenida (Av 5) in the far west of Playa, sandwiched between Club Havana and Marina Hemingway. A taxi from central Havana will cost USD$12 to USD$15.

Iglesia Jesús de Miramar　　　CHURCH
(Map p96; cnr Av 5 & Calle 82, Miramar; ☺9am-noon & 4-6pm) Despite its modernity, Playa cradles Cuba's second-largest church, an aesthetically pleasing neo-Romanesque structure topped by a giant dome. Built in 1948, it protects Cuba's largest pipe organ and – best of all – a set of truly amazing Stations of the Cross painted directly onto the walls by Spaniard Cesareo Hombrados Oñativia in the 1950s.

Memorial de la Denuncia　　　MUSEUM
(Map p96; ☎7-203-0120; cnr Av 5 & Calle 14, Miramar; USD$2; ☺9:30am-5pm Tue-Sat) The former Museum of the Ministry of the Interior

was remodeled in 2017 to form this far more interesting (if propaganda-ridden) look at US actions against Cuba in the last 60 years. The entrance stairway is covered with more than 3000 crosses, denoting people killed in skirmishes involving the US or other foreign powers since 1959, from the Bay of Pigs to the 1976 bomb aboard Cubana flight 455.

While you'll only get one side of the story here, the modern exhibits are well presented and the intriguing tales, from plots to kill Fidel Castro to the interminable ebbing and flowing of the embargo, are morbidly compelling.

Marina Hemingway　　　MARINA
(cnr Av 5 & Calle 248, Santa Fé) Havana's premier marina was constructed in 1953 in the small coastal community of Santa Fé. After the revolution it was nationalized and named after Fidel Castro's favorite *Yanqui*. The marina has four 800m-long channels, a dive center, a motley collection of shops and restaurants, and two hotels, and is only worth visiting if you're docking your boat or utilizing the water-sports facilities.

Like much of Cuba's infrastructure, the place retains a strangely abandoned air and is crying out for a renovation.

El Bosque de la Habana　　　PARK
(Map p96; Kohly) Running along the banks of the Río Almendares, below the bridge on Calle 23, is this welcome oasis of greenery and fresh air in the heart of the chaotic city. The 'Bosque' might not be the Bois de Boulogne (witness the stray dogs and unsightly litter),

Playa & Marianao

but it *is* a work in progress and far healthier than it was in the 1990s.

The lower park (closer to the bridge) is usually called **Parque Almendares** and is more developed, with a stash of so-so facilities, including an antiquated miniature golf course, the Anfiteatro Parque Almendares (a small outdoor performance space) and a kids' playground. South of the bridge, the so-called **Parque Metropolitano** is wilder and more bewitching, with giant trees shrouded by hanging curtains of vines. Several paths wind their way through the greenery between the road and the river, and Santería ceremonies are sometimes performed here. It's a beguiling spot, and potentially even more so if the city can sort out the litter problem.

Club Habana HISTORIC BUILDING
(☑ 7-204-5700; Av 5, btwn Calles 188 & 192, Náutico; day pass weekday/weekend USD$25/30; ☺ 9am-7pm) This fabulously eclectic 1928

mansion in Flores once housed the Havana Biltmore Yacht & Country Club. These days the establishment has swung full circle and it is again a popular hangout for diplomats and affluent visitors. The club has its own well-raked beach (technically the closest to central Havana), swimming pools (note plural), tennis courts, bar, restaurant and health club.

In the 1950s the place gained brief notoriety when it famously denied entry to Cuban president Fulgencio Batista on the grounds that he was black. Fidel Castro had better luck when he dropped by for dinner some 30 years later, and the club remains one of the few places where he dined in public.

Fundación Naturaleza y El Hombre MUSEUM
(Map p96; ☑ 7-209-2885; www.fanj.cult.cu; Av 5B No 6611, btwn Calles 66 & 70, Miramar; USD$2; ☺ 9am-3pm Mon-Fri) This tiny museum seems to confirm the adage 'small is beautiful.' It displays artifacts from a 17,422km canoe trip

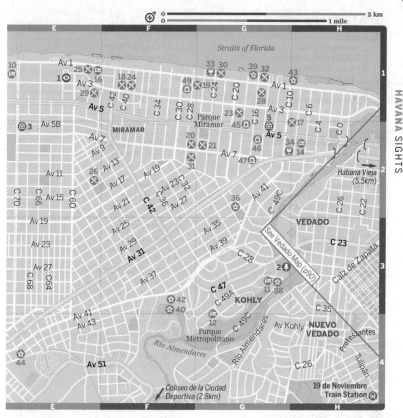

from the Amazon source to the sea that was led by Cuban intellectual and anthropologist António Núñez Jiménez in 1987. Exhibits in the astounding array of items include one of Cuba's largest photography collections, books written by the prolific Núñez Jiménez, his beloved canoe, and a famous portrait of Fidel Castro by Ecuadorian painter Oswaldo Guayasamín.

The museum is part of a nonprofit foundation and one of Havana's most rewarding small sights.

Museo de la Alfabetización   MUSEUM
(Map p96; cnr Av 29E & Calle 76, Marianao; ⊙8am-noon & 1-3pm Tue-Fri, 8am-noon Sat) **FREE** The former Cuartel Colombia military airfield at Marianao is now a school complex called Ciudad Libertad. Pass through the gate to visit this inspiring museum, which describes the 1961 literacy campaign during which 100,000 youths aged 12 to 18 spread out across Cuba to teach reading and writing to farmers, workers and seniors.

In the center of the traffic circle, opposite the entrance to the complex, is a tower in the form of a syringe. It commemorates Carlos Juan Finlay, who discovered the cause of yellow fever in 1881.

Acuario Nacional   AQUARIUM
(Map p96; ☑7-202-5872; cnr Av 3 & Calle 62, Miramar; adult/child USD$10/7; ⊙10am-6pm Tue-Sun; ⊕) Founded in 1960, the national aquarium is a Havana institution designed primarily for Cuban visitors, who arrive by the legion. Overseas visitors, be warned: the rather dilapidated facilities and limited selection of things to see are not on par with aquariums elsewhere.

Saltwater fish are the specialty, but there are also sea lions and dolphins, including hourly dolphin shows. Note that dolphin performances are widely criticized by animal-welfare groups, who say that captivity for such complex marine mammals is debilitating and stressful.

Playa & Marianao

◉ Regla, Guanabacoa & the Forts

Regla and Guanabacoa are two small towns on the eastern side of Havana harbor that got swallowed up during Havana's urban growth. Slow paced and little visited by tourists, the municipalities retain an independent-minded and culturally distinct spirit. There are other spirits here, too: Guanabacoa is sometimes called *el pueblo embrujado* ('the bewitched town') for its strong Santería traditions, while Regla – another Santería hotbed – was once known for its bolshie revolutionary politics.

Abutting the harbor further north are Havana's colossal military forts, testament to the 400-year Spanish reign.

★ **Parque Histórico Militar Morro-Cabaña**   FORT

(Map p100; per fort USD$6; ☺10am-10pm) This unmissable military park, included in the Habana Vieja Unesco World Heritage site, is arguably the most formidable defensive complex in Spain's erstwhile colonial empire. It's comprised of two strapping forts: El Morro, and La Cabaña, a sprawling minicity of a military bastion famed for its sunset-over-the-Malecón views and legendary *cañonazo* ceremony.

★ **Castillo de los Tres Santos Reyes Magnos del Morro**   FORT

(El Morro; Map p100; USD$6, lighthouse USD$2; ☺10am-6pm) This wave-lashed fort with its emblematic lighthouse was erected between 1589 and 1630 to protect the entrance to Havana harbor from pirates and foreign invaders (French corsair Jacques de Sores had sacked the city in 1555). Perched high on a rocky bluff above the Atlantic, the fort has an irregular polygonal shape, 3m-thick walls and a deep protective moat, and is a classic example of Renaissance military architecture.

For more than a century the fort withstood numerous attacks by French, Dutch and English privateers, but in 1762, after a 44-day siege, a 14,000-strong British force captured El Morro by attacking from the landward side. The Castillo's famous lighthouse was added in 1844.

Aside from fantastic views over the sea and the city, El Morro hosts several exhibits, including a riveting account of the fort's siege and eventual surrender to the British that uses words (in English and Spanish) and paintings.

★ **Fortaleza de San Carlos de la Cabaña**   FORT

(La Cabaña; Map p100; before/after 6pm USD$6/8; ⊙10am-10pm) This 18th-century colossus was built between 1763 and 1774 on a long, exposed ridge on the east side of Havana harbor to fill a weakness in the city's defenses. In 1762 the British had taken Havana by gaining control of this strategically important ridge, and it was from here that they shelled the city mercilessly into submission. In order to prevent a repeat performance, Spanish king Carlos III ordered the construction of a massive fort that would repel future invaders.

Measuring 700m from end to end and covering a whopping 10 hectares, it is the largest Spanish colonial fortress in the Americas. The impregnability of the fort meant that no invader ever stormed it, though during the 19th century Cuban patriots faced firing squads here. Dictators Gerardo Machado and Fulgencio Batista used the fortress as a military prison, and immediately after the revolution Che Guevara set up his headquarters inside the ramparts to preside over another catalog of grisly executions (this time of Batista's officers).

These days the fort has been restored for visitors, and you can spend at least half a day checking out its wealth of attractions.

As well as bars, restaurants, souvenir stalls and a cigar shop (containing the world's longest cigar), La Cabaña hosts the Museo de Fortificaciones y Armas (Map p100; with La Cabaña ticket free; ⊙10am-6pm) and the engrossing Museo de Comandancia del Che (Map p100; with La Cabaña ticket free; ⊙10am-10pm). The nightly 9pm cañonazo ceremony (p105) is a popular evening excursion in which actors dressed in full 18th-century military regalia reenact the firing of a cannon over the harbor. You can visit the ceremony independently or as part of an excursion.

Estatua de Cristo   MONUMENT

(Map p100; Casablanca) This impossible-to-miss statue on a rise on the harbor's eastern side was created by Jilma Madera in 1958. It was promised to President Batista by his wife after the US-backed leader survived an attempt on his life in the Presidential Palace in March 1957, and was (ironically) unveiled on Christmas Day 1958, one week before the dictator fled the country. As you disembark the Casablanca ferry, follow the road uphill for about 10 minutes until you reach the monument.

The views from up here are stupendous and it's a favorite nighttime hangout for the local youth.

★ **Iglesia de Nuestra Señora de Regla**   CHURCH

(Regla; ⊙7:30am-6pm) As important as it is diminutive, Iglesia de Nuestra Señora de Regla, which sits close to the dock in Regla, has a long and colorful history. Inside on the main altar you'll find La Santísima Virgen de Regla.

The Virgin, represented by a black Madonna, is venerated in the Catholic faith and associated in the Santería religion with Yemayá, the *orisha* of the ocean and the patron of sailors (and always represented in blue). Legend claims that this image was carved by St Augustine 'The African' in the 5th century, and that in 453 a disciple brought the statue to Spain to safeguard it from barbarians. The small vessel in which the image was traveling survived a storm in the Strait of Gibraltar, so the figure was recognized as the patron of sailors. In more recent times, rafters attempting to reach the US have evoked the protection of the Black Virgin.

To shelter a copy of the image, a hut was first built on this site in 1687 by a pilgrim named Manuel Antonio. This structure was destroyed in a 1692 hurricane. A few years later a Spaniard named Juan de Conyedo built a stronger chapel, and in 1714 Nuestra Señora de Regla was proclaimed patron of the Bahía de la Habana. In 1957 the image was crowned by the Cuban Cardinal in Havana cathedral. Every year on September 7 thousands of pilgrims descend on Regla to celebrate the saint's day, and the image is taken out for a procession (p105) through the streets.

The current church dates from the early 19th century and is always busy with devotees from both religions stooping in silent prayer before the images of the saints that fill the alcoves. In Havana there is probably no better (public) place to see the layering and transference between Catholic beliefs and African traditions.

Parque Histórico Militar Morro-Cabaña

Parque Histórico Militar Morro-Cabaña

Museo Municipal de Regla MUSEUM
(Martí No 158, Regla; USD$2; ⊙9am-5pm Mon-Sat, to noon Sun) If you've come to see Regla's church you should also check out this important museum. Don't be put off by its superficial dinginess – there are some valuable relics inside. Located a few blocks up the main street from the ferry, it records Regla's history and Afro-Cuban religions. Don't miss the Palo Monte *ngangas* (cauldrons) and the masked Abakuá dancing figurines.

There's also an interesting small exhibit on Remigio Herrero, first *babalawo* (priest) of Regla, and a bizarre statue of Napoleon with his nose missing.

Iglesia de Guanabacoa CHURCH
(cnr Pepe Antonio & Adolfo del Castillo Cadenas, Guanabacoa; ⊙parochial office 8-11am & 2-5pm Mon-Fri) This church, in Parque Martí in the center of Guanabacoa, is also known as the

Iglesia de Nuestra Señora de la Asunción. It was designed by Lorenzo Camacho and built between 1721 and 1748 with a Moorish-influenced wooden ceiling that's still beautifully intact.

The gilded main altar and nine lateral altars are worth a look, and there's a painting of the Assumption of the Virgin at the back. In typical Cuban fashion, the main doors are usually locked; knock at the parochial office out back if you're keen to see inside.

Museo Municipal de Guanabacoa MUSEUM
(Martí No 108, Guanabacoa; USD$2; ⊙9am-5:30pm Tue-Sat, to 1pm Sun) Guanabacoa's main museum, like Regla's, is an important shrine to Santería, though you'll need to see past the run-down facilities and impassive 'guides' to appreciate it. The collection is small but concise; rooms are dedicated to the various Santería deities, with a particular focus on

the *orisha* Elegguá. Equally fascinating are rare artifacts from the Palo Monte and Abakuá religions.

The museum also acts as a cultural center of sorts and puts on sporadic rumba and folkloric shows. Inquire within.

◉ Habana del Este

Habana del Este is home to Playas del Este, a multiflavored if slightly unkempt beach strip situated 18km east of Habana Vieja. While the beaches here are sublime, the accompanying resorts aren't exactly luxurious. Rather, Playas del Este has a timeworn and slightly abandoned air, and aspiring beach loungers might find the ugly Soviet-style hotel piles more than a little incongruous. But for those who dislike modern tourist development or are keen to see how Cubans get out and enjoy themselves, Playas del Este is a breath of fresh (sea) air.'

The beach strip proper begins at Tarará, home to eastern Havana's main marina and, more recently, *the* place to partake in kiteboarding, courtesy of its stiff winds.

Most foreign day-trippers who come to Playas del Este utilize the three beaches directly east of Tarará, namely El Mégano, Santa María del Mar (the busiest) and Boca Ciega (Havana's unofficial gay beach). This section of coast is backed by eastern Havana's three nothing-to-write-home-about all-inclusive accommodations, but it also has enough basic facilities to justify a comfortable day trip.

◉ Outer Havana

Spread out like a fan on three sides of downtown, Havana's little-visited suburban municipalities hide a handful of disparate sights that can make interesting half-day and day trips from the city center. Santiago de las Vegas and Santa María del Rosario are former rural settlements that have been incorporated into the larger metropolis without losing their soporific air; San Francisco de Paula trades off its association with famous former resident Ernest Hemingway; and Arroyo Naranjo encircles the city's largest green space, Parque Lenin, and hosts Havana's expansive botanical gardens.

◉ Arroyo Naranjo & Boyeros

Parque Lenin   PARK
(⊙ hours vary) **FREE** Parque Lenin, in Arroyo Naranjo municipality, 20km south of central

Havana, is the city's largest recreational area. Constructed between 1969 and 1972 on the orders of Celia Sánchez, a long-time associate of Fidel Castro's, it's one of the few developments in Havana from this era. The 670 hectares of parkland and beautiful old trees surround an artificial lake and provide a quintessential weekend escape for local families, who pile in with their picnics loaded up in old American cars.

Although the park itself is attractive enough, its mishmash of facilities has fallen on hard times since the 1990s. Taxi drivers complain it's *muy abandonado* and wax nostalgic about when 'Lenin' was an idyllic weekend getaway for scores of pleasure-seeking *habaneros*. These days, despite the weekend hordes, the park has a neglected and surreal air. Help has long been promised but tends to be sporadic and short-lived. An amusement park that reopened a decade ago with Chinese money is already showing signs of wear, and the park's emblematic steam train has no reliable schedule.

Most attractions are open 9am to 5pm Tuesday to Sunday, and admission to the park itself is free. Horseback riding is perennially popular, but try to hire a mount from the Centro Ecuestre (p104) rather than the army of hustlers who hang around outside the park entrance and who often ride maltreated horses. For the most fun, join the Cubans who congregate around the park's cheap *parrilladas* (barbecues), sharing bottles of rum and dancing away their cares to the strains of salsa and/or reggaeton.

The P-13 bus will get you close to the park, but to catch it you'll have to first get to Vibora. The best way to do this is to get on the P-9 bus at Calles 23 and L in Vedado.

Jardín Botánico Nacional   GARDENS
(Carretera del Rocio; USD$4; ⊙ 10am-5pm Wed-Sun) Havana's curiously under-visited 600-hectare botanical garden suffers from an out-of-town location and poor transport links (get a taxi). It opened in 1984 after 16 years of development and is hailed for its collection of 250 species of palm tree, ethno-botanical crop displays and tranquil **Japanese Garden** (1989). Multilingual guided tours are conducted on a mini-train (not as tacky as it sounds) or in your own vehicle, should you have one (the guide will come with you).

Between November and February the garden is an excellent spot for observing migratory birds. It is also known for its

Playas del Este

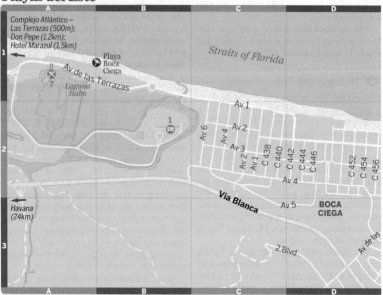

Playas del Este

😴 Sleeping
1 Bravo Club Hotel Arenal	B2
2 Gilberto & Blanca	F2
3 Hostal Las Terrazas de Teresa	F2
4 Villa Cloty	F2

🍴 Eating
5 Chicken Little	H2
6 Il Piccolo	H2
7 Mi Cayito	A1
8 Pan.com	F2
9 Restaurante 421	E3

vegetarian **Restaurante el Bambú** (Jardín Botánico Nacional; buffet USD$12; ⏰1-3pm; 🍴), which serves a meat-free buffet daily. There's a separate *ranchón* (rustic, open-sided restaurant) serving à la carte meat dishes for carnivores.

👁 San Francisco de Paula

★**Museo Hemingway**   MUSEUM
(📞7-692-0176; cnr Vigía & Singer; USD$5; ⏰10am-4:30pm Mon-Sat) In 1940 American novelist Ernest Hemingway bought the Finca la Vigía, a villa on a hill in San Francisco de Paula, 15km southeast of Havana, where he lived continuously for 20 years. When he departed, tired and depressed, for the US

in 1960 soon after the Castro revolution, he generously donated his house to the 'Cuban people.' It is now a museum and almost unchanged since the day he left.

To prevent the pilfering of objects, visitors are not allowed inside the house (La Casona), but there are enough open doors and windows to allow a proper glimpse of Papa's universe. Inside the house there are books everywhere (including beside the toilet), a large Victrola and record collection, and a disturbing array of trophy animal heads.

A three-story tower next to the main house contains a tiny typewriter, a telescope and a comfortable lounger, and offers suitably inspiring views north toward the distant city. In the heavily wooded grounds below you'll encounter the swimming pool where Ava Gardner once swam naked, a cockfighting ring and Hemingway's beloved fishing boat, *Pilar*, grounded on what was once his tennis court.

In 2019, in a rare show of Cuban-American cooperation, a restoration center was built on the site to preserve Hemingway's work.

To reach San Francisco de Paula, take metro bus P-7 (Alberro) from Parque de la Fraternidad in Centro Habana. Tell the driver you're going to the museum. You get off in San Miguel del Padrón; the house entrance

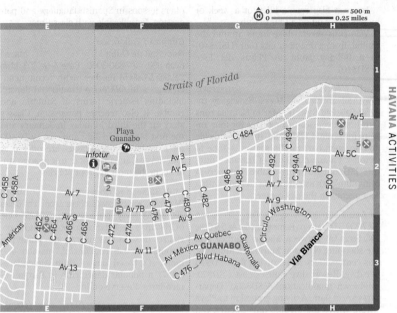

is on Calle Vigía, 200m east of the main road, Calzada de Guines.

◉ Santa María del Rosario

**Iglesia de Nuestra
Señora del Rosario**   CHURCH
(Calle 24, btwn 31 & 33, Santa María del Rosario; ⊘8am-6pm Tue-Sun) Havana is a city of many secrets, but few are as serendipitous as the church also known as the Catedral de los Campos de Cuba (cathedral of the Cuban countryside), a diminutive ecclesial beauty built in 1760 in classic baroque style on the Old Town square of Santa María del Rosario. The church is known for its gleaming gold interior, made up of a gilded mahogany altar and some equally sumptuous side altars fashioned in the churrigueresque style.

The paintings on the ceiling are by José Nicolás de la Escalera (1734–1804), an early Cuban-born artist. One is thought to contain the first known depiction of an enslaved black person in Cuban art.

◉ Rincón

Santuario de San Lázaro   CHURCH
(Carretera San Antonio de los Baños; ⊘7am-6pm) You can make your own journey to the site of Cuba's biggest annual pilgrimage, tucked away in the village-like Havana suburb of Rincón. The saint inside the church is San Lázaro (represented by the *orisha* Babalú Ayé in the Santería religion), the patron saint of healing and the sick. Hundreds come to light candles and lay flowers daily. Thousands come on December 17 to pray for respite from illness or to give thanks for cures.

There's a small museum displaying a raft of previous offerings to San Lázaro in a chapel next door.

🏃 Activities

Havana's two marinas, Marina Tarará (east) and Marina Hemingway (west), lie in its outer suburbs. Both offer numerous fishing, diving and boating opportunities.

With its spectacular Malecón sea drive, Havana possesses one of the world's most glorious municipal jogging routes. Several top-end hotels have gyms, and plenty more have pools.

Vélo Cuba   CYCLING
(Map p78; ☑7-836-8820; www.veloencuba.com; Paseo de Martí, cnr Carcel; ⊘9am-5:30pm) If you want more flexibility than the Ha'Bici (p142) bike-sharing scheme, you can rent two wheels from Vélo Cuba, which shares the same HQ as Ha'Bici. Bikes are slightly more expensive (USD$6 for two hours) but are proper hybrids, as opposed to city bikes, and capable of much longer journeys.

You can also rent a bike for a week or more and set off on a tour of Cuba.

Vélo runs several bike tours around the capital, from a one-hour city tour (USD$40) to a full-day jaunt to Playas del Este (USD$40).

Marlin Náutica WATER SPORTS
(www.nauticamarlin.com; Marina Hemingway, cnr Av 5 & Calle 248, Santa Fé) Marlin Náutica runs four-hour deep-sea-fishing trips for four anglers for around USD$330, including tackle and an open bar; marlin season is June to October. Catamaran tours of Havana's littoral (USD$65) are also available (four-person minimum). It's usually easier to book with a tour agency in the city center.

La Aguja Marlin Diving Center DIVING
(☑7-209-3377; Marina Hemingway, cnr Av 5 & Calle 248, Santa Fé) Between Marlin Náutica and the shopping center at Marina Hemingway, this center offers scuba diving for USD$40 per dive. Resort dive courses cost USD$70, full-blown qualifications USD$350. Departures are at 9am. A diving excursion to Playa Girón, where the diving's much better, can also be arranged.

Centro Ecuestre HORSE RIDING
(Parque Lenin; ⊙9am-5pm) The stables in the northwestern corner of Parque Lenin (p101) are run by environmental agency Flora y Fauna. Nominally, Centro Ecuestre offers riding for around USD$12 per hour, although, like most things in the park, the service isn't 100% reliable.

That said, if you'd like to ride in Parque Lenin it's better to go with these guys rather than the touts at the park entrance, who often ride maltreated horses.

Marlin Náutica Tarará WATER SPORTS
(☑7-796-0240; www.nauticamarlin.com; cnr Av 8 & Calle 17, Tarará) Yacht charters, deep-sea fishing and scuba diving are offered at Marina Tarará, 22km east of Havana. It's generally easier to organize activities at a hotel tour desk in Havana before heading out. Prices are similar to those at Marina Hemingway (eg USD$40 per dive).

⮞ Courses

★La Casa del Son DANCING
(Map p68; ☑7-861-6179; www.bailarencuba.com; Empedrado No 411, btwn Compostela & Aguacate; per hour from USD$10; ⊙9am-7pm Mon-Sat) A highly popular private dance school based in an attractive 18th-century house. It also

offers lessons in Spanish language and percussion. Very flexible with class times.

Conjunto Folklórico Nacional de Cuba DANCING
(Map p90; ☑7-830-3060; Calle 4 No 103, btwn Calzada & Calle 5) Teaches highly recommended classes in *folklórico* (traditional dance), including esoteric forms of Santería and rumba. It also teaches percussion. Classes start on the third Monday in January and the first Monday in July, and cost USD$500 for a 15-day course. Classes are offered at four levels; an admission test places students in the most appropriate class.

Club Salseando Chévere DANCING
(Map p96; www.salseandochevere.com; cnr Calles 49C & 28A, Kohly; per hour from USD$25) One of Havana's best dance schools, which specializes in salsa lessons, can also guide you through rumba, *chachachá*, mambo and more. It's based out of Club Almendares, (p137), a popular dance club in Parque Almendares. Reserve online.

Universidad de la Habana LANGUAGE
(Map p90; ☑7-831-3751, 7-832-4245; www.uh.cu; Edificio Varona, 2nd fl, Calle J No 556) The university's FLEX (School of Foreign Languages) faculty offers Spanish courses year-round, beginning on the first Monday of each month. Costs start at USD$200 for 40 hours (two weeks) and go up to a nine-month intensive course (USD$1798). You must sit a placement test to determine your level (graded one to five).

It's always best to make arrangements before you travel. For the FLEX page on the university website, choose 'Lenguas Extranjeras' under the 'Facultades' heading at the bottom of the home page.

Paradiso CULTURAL
(Map p96; ☑7-214-0701; Av 5 No 8202, btwn Calles 82 & 84, Miramar) A cultural agency that offers an astounding array of courses of between four and 12 weeks on everything from Afro-Cuban dance to ceramics.

⮞ Tours

State-run tourist agencies, such as Gaviota (p142), Cubanacán (p142) and Cubatur (p142) generally offer a similar array of tours. The most popular are city tours, Hemingway tours and tours for the *cañonazo* ceremony (the firing of the cannons at the Fortaleza de San Carlos de la Cabaña). You'll pay USD$15 to USD$20 per person.

San Cristóbal Agencia de Viajes (p142), the agency run by the City Historian, does a few more interesting specialist tours focusing on topics such as religion, art and architecture.

Several private tour operators have taken off in recent years, with quirky little excursions such as the Havana 'Mob tour' with Havana Super Tour. Guided bike tours are also available.

Infotur (p142) is Cuba's state-run information agency, with offices at the airport, Habana Vieja and elsewhere. It can furnish you with further details about these and other tours. Prices change regularly and often depend on group size.

★ **Free Walking Tour Havana**   WALKING
(Map p68; ☑5-818-6958; www.freewalkingtour havana.com) These wonderfully insightful tours kick off at the Plazuela de Santo Ángel (p82) at 9:30am and 4pm daily. Look for a guide with a white umbrella. There are two options: Habana Vieja (three hours) and Centro Habana (two hours); tours are offered in Spanish or English. Reserve online or phone ahead. A well-earned tip for your guide goes a long way.

★ **Havana Super Tour**   TOURS
(Map p78; ☑5-265-7101; www.campanario63.com; Campanario No 63, btwn San Lázaro & Lagunas; tours USD$60) One of Havana's first private tour companies, Super Tour runs all its trips in classic American cars. The two most popular are the art deco architectural tour and the 'Mob tour,' uncovering the city's pre-revolution Mafia haunts. If you're short on time, the full-blown Havana day tour (USD$150) will whip you around all of the city's key sights.

Also on offer is a day trip to Viñales (USD$250), including lunch, a cocktail, a guide and transport.

★ **Ruta Bikes**   CYCLING
(Map p90; ☑5-247-6633; www.rutabikes.com; Calle 16 No 152; city tour USD$30; 🚲) This was Havana's first decent bicycle-hire and -tour company when it started in 2013. Its cycling tours have proven to be consistently popular, particularly the three-hour classic city tour, which takes in the Bosque de la Habana, Plaza Vieja, Plaza de la Revolución and the Malecón. Book via phone or email at least a day ahead. Kids welcome.

It also rents sturdy, well-maintained bikes from USD$15 per day.

🎎 Festivals & Events

Cañonazo Ceremony   CULTURAL
(⊙9pm nightly) The *cañonazo* ceremony, held in La Cabaña fort (p99), is a theatrical show during which actors dressed in full 18th-century military regalia reenact the firing of a cannon over Havana harbor – a ritual that used to signify the closing of the city gates.

You can visit the ceremony independently or as part of an excursion. Arrive early, as it's popular.

Feria Internacional del Libro   LITERATURE
(⊙Feb) Headquartered in La Cabaña fort (p99), this book fair kicks off in Havana before going on tour around the country, ending in Santiago de Cuba. Attracting international publishing companies, book lovers and tourists alike, the fair includes book presentations and music concerts at night. It's dedicated to a different country and author each year.

Fiesta de Nuestra Señora de Regla   RELIGIOUS
September 7 is the feast day of the Virgin of Regla – Yemayá in the Santería religion – and a special day in Regla, wherein lies her sanctuary. The statue of the Virgin is taken from behind the altar in the Iglesia de Nuestra Señora de Regla (p99) and paraded around the district amid huge crowds. Devotees offer prayers while tossing flowers into the sea.

Festival Internacional de Ballet de la Habana   DANCE
(www.balletcuba.cult.cu; ⊙Oct & Nov) Cuba demonstrates its ballet prowess at this biennial festival, with energetic leaps and graceful pirouettes starting in late October in even-numbered years. International companies such as the American Ballet Theatre and Moscow's Bolshoi join the celebrations at Gran Teatro de La Habana Alicia Alonso (p85), Teatro Nacional (p135) and Teatro Mella (p136), among other venues.

Marabana   SPORTS
(www.maratondelahabana.com; ⊙Nov) As international participants continue to rise every year, Marabana is establishing itself as one of the most popular 10km/half-marathon/marathon courses on the Latin American circuit. At the crack of a 7am starting pistol, runners take in Havana's iconic Malecón just as the sun is rising.

Festival Internacional del Nuevo Cine Latinoamericano FILM
(www.habanafilmfestival.com; ☉ Dec) Widely lauded celebration of Cuba's massive film culture, with plenty of nods to other Latin American countries. Held at various cinemas and theaters across the city.

🛏 Sleeping

🛏 Habana Vieja

Habana Vieja specializes in meticulously restored historic hotels, ostensibly managed by the Office of the City Historian but owned by state-run agency Gaviota. Stay in a former palace, a revitalized mansion or an erstwhile convent. There's also a large and growing quota of casas particulares (private homestays), which offer good quality at an affordable price.

Greenhouse CASA PARTICULAR $
(Map p68; ☎ 7-862-9877; fabio.quintana@ infomed.sld.cu; San Ignacio No 656, btwn Merced & Jesús María; r USD$30-40; ✳) A fabulous Old Town casa run by Eugenio and Fabio, who have added superb design features to their huge colonial home. Check out the terrace fountain and the backlit model of Havana on the stairway. There are seven rooms in this virtual hotel, packed with precious period furnishings and gorgeous wooden beds; two rooms share a bathroom.

Hostal El Encinar CASA PARTICULAR $
(Map p68; ☎ 7-860-1257; www.hostalperegrino. com; Chacón No 60/Altos, btwn Cuba & Aguiar; s/d/tr incl breakfast USD$30/40/45; ✳) This outpost of Centro Habana's popular Hostal Peregrino (p108) is like a little hotel for independent travelers. Eight rooms, all with private bathroom, approach boutique standard, with classy tile work, hairdryers, TVs and minibars. There's a comfortable lounge area and a delightful roof terrace overlooking the bay and La Cabaña fort (p99).

Casa Villegas 66 CASA PARTICULAR $
(Map p68; ☎ 7-861-7321; Villegas No 66, btwn San Juan de Dios & Empredado; r from USD$60; ✳) These two rooms in a private 1st-floor apartment amid the action of Habana Vieja are set back far enough from the street to deaden the noise. The house has an art deco facade and a colonial-style interior. Two small but well-designed bedrooms have good beds and modern bathrooms.

Hostal Las Maletas CASA PARTICULAR $
(Map p68; ☎ 7-867-1623; www.hostallasmaletas. com; Empedrado No 409, btwn Aguacate & Compostela; r USD$45-55; ✳ 🛜) A good place to rest your *maletas* (suitcases) for a while, this private '*hostal*' has all the classic Habana Vieja calling cards: high ceilings, spiral staircases and creaky rocking chairs. It's pricier than smaller casas particulares but still a good deal cheaper than some of Havana's crappier state-run hotels – and it has much better service.

Casa Azul Havana CASA PARTICULAR $
(Map p68; ☎ 7-801-5304; Habana No 54, btwn Cuarteles & Peña Pobre; r USD$50; ✳) In the Loma del Ángel, Habana Vieja's emerging chic quarter, this white-and-blue house has an interesting mélange of rooms furnished with elegant side tables, ostentatious headboards and a bit of glitter. Bathrooms are huge, breakfasts are equally gigantic and – big bonus – there's a roof terrace to elevate you above Habana Vieja's urban sprawl.

Mind the spiral staircase on the way down – especially after several mojitos.

Ana y Surama CASA PARTICULAR $
(Map p68; ☎ 7-862-2717; San Ignacio No 454, btwn Sol & Muralla; r with/without bathroom USD$50/40; ✳) This lovely 2nd-floor casa steps from Plaza Vieja is dripping with Cuban character, from its antique chandeliers to its lurid curtains and bedspreads. Rooms are large (a couple have shared bathrooms), while the surfeit of baroque furniture might leave you thinking you've woken up in a tropical version of *Downton Abbey*.

Jesús & María CASA PARTICULAR $
(Map p68; ☎ 7-851-1378; jesusmaria2003@yahoo.com; Aguacate No 518, btwn Sol & Muralla; r USD$30-35; ✳) At this old-school casa you'll have to walk through the family sitting area, ducking deftly beneath the TV, in order to get to your room. Inside, the house morphs into something bigger, with an ample terrace (equipped with rockers) where you can enjoy an equally ample breakfast. The five spotless rooms come with safe boxes and comfortable beds.

Hostal La Maestranza HOTEL $$
(Map p68; ☎ 5-597-7099; Cuba No 82, btwn Cuarteles & Chacón; s/d/ste USD$100/125/150; 🅿 ✳) One of several emerging private hotels in Habana Vieja, the Maestranza enjoys an excellent location practically opposite the cathedral (p67). Five rooms and one suite share a narrow atrium and small bar where

an ample breakfast is laid on. While simple in design, the superclean rooms have high ceilings, original tiles and atmospheric backlighting behind the bedheads.

Penthouse Plaza Vieja CASA PARTICULAR $$

(Map p68; ☎7-801-2084; penthouseplazavieja@gmail.com; Mercaderes No 315-317, apt 16; r incl breakfast USD$90; ﹡) A private penthouse in a historic central square – this place would cost thousands anywhere else, but in Havana you can still bag it for as little as USD$60. Fidel and Bertha's two rooms high above Plaza Vieja share a leafy terrace guarded by a Santería shrine.

Conde de Ricla Hostal HOTEL $$

(Map p68; ☎5-291-6323; www.condedericlahostal.com; San Ignacio No 402, btwn Sol & Muralla; d/ste incl breakfast USD$100/150; ﹡@🛜) The Ricla (named for a Spanish count) is a seven-room family-run hotel with a to-die-for location at the corner of Plaza Vieja. Rooms are gleaming white, with original floor tiles, minibars, flat-screen TVs and plenty of space, and there's a spectacular roof terrace where breakfast is served.

Hostal Conde de Villanueva HOTEL $$$

(Map p68; ☎7-862-9293; www.gaviotahotels.com; Mercaderes No 202; s/d USD$235/305; ﹡@🛜) Restored under the watchful eye of the City Historian in the late 1990s, the former residence of the Count of Villanueva, a 19th-century railway-building magnate, has been converted from a grandiose city mansion into a nine-bedroom hotel with a tobacco-growing theme. Its centerpiece is a foliage-filled inner courtyard complete with resident peacock.

Upstairs suites contain stained-glass windows, chandeliers and arty sculptures; one suite has a whirlpool bathtub. On the mezzanine floor you'll also find one of Havana's best tobacco stores (p138), with an in-house roller.

Hotel Palacio Cueto HISTORIC HOTEL $$$

(Map p68; ☎7-823-4100; www.gaviotahotels.com; cnr Muralla & Mercaderes; s/d USD$209/324; ﹡@🛜) After interminable renovations, Havana's finest art nouveau building once again hosts a hotel. Before you even go inside you can award five stars for the Cueto's location, at the corner of Plaza Vieja, and its facade, a rippling collection of elegant pillars and curvaceous balconies.

The rooms are more minimalist than art nouveau, although there are subtle curves in the chairs, mirrors and bedheads. The roof terrace has a more flamboyant allure, with its tiled benches and wavy turrets recalling the *modernisme* of Gaudí's Barcelona. Services include spa, sundeck and swish lobby bar. Conceived in 1906, the building once housed a warehouse and a hat factory before it was rented by José Cueto in the 1920s as the Palacio Vienna hotel. The structure sat empty and unused from the early 1990s until its 2019 reopening.

Hotel Los Frailes HISTORIC HOTEL $$$

(Map p68; ☎7-862-9383; www.gaviotahotels.com; Brasil No 8, btwn Oficios & Mercaderes; d/ste USD$167/260; ﹡@🛜) There's nothing austere about Los Frailes (The Friars), despite the monastic theme (staff wear hooded robes), inspired by the nearby San Francisco de Asís convent (p74). Instead, this is the kind of hotel you'll look forward to coming back to after a long day, to recline in large, historical rooms in your monkish dressing gown, with candlelight flickering on the walls.

Hotel Palacio del Marqués de San Felipe y Santiago de Bejucal HOTEL $$$

(Map p68; ☎7-864-9191; www.gaviotahotels.com; cnr Oficios & Amargura; s/d USD$209/334; ﹡@🛜) Cuban baroque meets modern minimalism in this restored palace in the blustery Plaza de San Francisco de Asís, the erstwhile home of countless counts, dons and marquises. Thanks to its recent refurbishment, there's a classier and more contemporary feel to proceedings here, reflected in both decor and quality of service.

Expect cool 21st-century bathrooms, fluffy robes, deluxe bedcovers and a handsome little restaurant. The suites are enormous and come equipped with large, round whirlpool tubs.

Hotel Palacio O'Farrill HOTEL $$$

(Map p68; ☎7-860-5080; www.habaguanexhotels.com; Cuba No 102-108, btwn Chacón & Tejadillo; d/ste USD$167/260; ﹡@🛜) Not an Irish joke but one of Havana's more impressive period hotels, the Hotel Palacio O'Farrill is a staggeringly beautiful colonial palace that once belonged to Don Ricardo O'Farrill, a Cuban sugar entrepreneur who was descended from an Irish noble family. Compared to the lavish communal areas, the bedrooms are plainer and more modest.

Taking the Emerald Isle as its theme, the hotel has plenty of greenery in its plant-filled 18th-century courtyard. The 2nd floor, added in the 19th century, provides grandiose neoclassical touches, while the 20th-century top floor merges seamlessly with the magnificent architecture below.

Hotel Raquel
HOTEL $$$

(Map p68; ☏7-860-8280; www.gaviotahotels.com; cnr Amargura & San Ignacio; d/ste USD$209/324; ❄@🖭) A beauty of a building and one of the few genuine art nouveau structures in Havana, the Raquel induces historical hallucinations with its grandiose columns, sleek marble statues and intricate stained-glass ceiling. Behind its impressive lobby, the rooms are a little shabbier (some have no exterior windows), with maintenance issues not always ironed out as quickly as they should be.

As consolation, there's a small gym and sauna, an occasional band playing when you eat breakfast, and a great central location.

Hotel Ambos Mundos
HOTEL $$$

(Map p68; ☏7-860-9529; www.gaviotahotels.com; Obispo No 153; s/d USD$167/260; ❄@🖭) This pastel-pink Havana institution was Hemingway's hotel of choice before he bought a house in Havana in 1939 (he's said to have penned his seminal guerrilla classic *For Whom the Bell Tolls* in room 511). Small, sometimes windowless rooms suggest overpricing, but the lobby bar is classic enough (follow the romantic piano melody) and the creaky metal lift adds character.

It's an obligatory pit stop for anyone on a world tour of 'Hemingway once fell over in here' bars.

Hotel Santa Isabel
HOTEL $$$

(Map p68; ☏7-860-8201; www.gaviotahotels.com; Baratillo No 9; d/ste incl breakfast USD$209/324; ❄@🖭) Considered one of Havana's finest hotels as well as one of its oldest (operations began in 1867), the Santa Isabel is housed in the Palacio de Los Condes de Santovenia (p74), former crash pad of the esteemed counts of Santovenia. This three-story, multi-arched baroque beauty has large rooms full of historic charm and attractive Spanish-colonial furniture, although maintenance can be subpar.

🛏 Centro Habana

Centro Habana has the most economical stash of casas particulares in the city. More expensive hotels line Prado and Parque Central. There's a noticeable gap in the mid-range accommodation market.

★ Casa 1932
CASA PARTICULAR $

(Map p78; ☏5-264-3858, 7-863-6203; www.casahabana.net; Campanario 63, btwn San Lázaro & Lagunas; r USD$20-60; ❄🖭) Every piece of furniture has a story to tell at the carefully curated home of Luís Miguel, a cool connoisseur of art deco who offers his house as both boutique private homestay and museum to the 1930s, when his preferred architectural style was in vogue.

You can ask about the provenance of any number of assembled collectibles, including ornamental mirrors, French statuettes and pre-revolutionary casino chips as you enjoy the vintage atmosphere in one of three comfortable rooms and tuck into huge breakfasts (pancakes and peanut butter included!).

The biggest bonus, however, is Luís Miguel himself, a mine of local history and culture who runs his own tour company, Havana Super Tour (p105).

★ Hostal Peregrino Consulado
CASA PARTICULAR $

(Map p78; ☏7-861-8027; www.hostalperegrino.com; Consulado No 152, btwn Colón & Trocadero; s/d/tr/apt USD$30/40/45/50; ❄@) Pediatrician Julio Roque and his wife, Elsa, have expanded their formerly two-room casa particular into a web of accommodations. The HQ, Hostal Peregrino, offers five rooms and three attached apartments a block from Paseo de Martí and is one of the most professionally run private houses in Cuba.

Airport pickup, breakfast, laundry service and cocktail bar are available at extra cost, but Julio, Elsa and staff will provide you with a wealth of local information and tips free of charge. The family offers two other places to stay, one in Habana Vieja and the other in Calle Lealtad. They're all bookable through the same number.

Hostal Neptuno 1915
CASA PARTICULAR $

(Map p78; Amistad No 204, btwn Neptuno & San Miguel; r from USD$50; ❄🖭) Giving little away at street level, this private accommodations is an island of tranquility amid the Centro Habana maelstrom. Seven delightful rooms, adorned with original art, elegant furniture and deluxe modern bathrooms, surround a small 1st-floor patio and reception-lounge. Here you can recline in tasteful comfort as the rhythms of the gritty neighborhood pulsate around you.

La Casa de Concordia
CASA PARTICULAR $

(Map p78; ☏7-862-5330; Concordia No 421, btwn Escobar & Gervasio; r USD$50; ❄) A casa particular in one of Centro Habana's arterial streets, this place has grown to take on mini-hotel proportions. It now has 11 rooms, but you'll still feel as though you've joined an extended Cuban family when you stay here. Rooms marry solid 20th-century furniture with modern bathrooms and plant-filled communal areas.

The Concordia is right in the middle of Centro Habana's hectic but wonderfully theatrical 'hood and you'll really feel part of it all here.

Casa Colonial
Yadilis & Yoel
CASA PARTICULAR $

(Map p78; ☑7-863-0565; www.casacolonialyadilisyyoel.com; Industria No 120/Altos, btwn Trocadero & Colón; r USD$30-35; ✳🗺) Marrying sharp professionalism and excellent service without compromising the warmth and generosity that make Cuba so special, this venerable establishment is one of the best accommodations deals in the city. Recently expanded to include two additional buildings nearby, it offers smart, clean rooms right in the middle of the city's liveliest neighborhood.

Whether you're from Croatia or Camagüey, you'll immediately feel at home.

Casa de Lourdes
& José
CASA PARTICULAR $

(Map p78; ☑7-863-9879; Águila 168b, btwn Ánimas & Trocadero; r USD$25-30; ✳) Located in the midst of Centro, this place with wonderful hosts has three en suite rooms and set-you-up-for-the-day breakfasts. If you like good old-fashioned hospitality and the feeling that you're staying with a tight-knit Cuban family, look no further.

Lourdes Cervantes
CASA PARTICULAR $

(Map p78; ☑7-879-2243; lourdescepa@gmail.com; Calzada de la Infanta No 17, apt 10, btwn Calles 23 & Humboldt; r USD$35; ✳🗺) On the border of Vedado and Centro Habana, just a baseball-bat swing from the Hotel Nacional and Malecón, this 1st-floor apartment offers two large rooms with balconies. The bathroom is large but shared. Lourdes is a great hostess and fluent in English and French.

Dulce Hostal –
Dulce María González
CASA PARTICULAR $

(Map p78; ☑7-863-2506; Amistad No 220, btwn Neptuno & San Miguel; r USD$25; ✳) This house is all about the lovely hostess, Dulce, who has been renting out just one room in her neocolonial house for well over a decade. Nothing has changed (including the price)

– it's still as clean, friendly, welcoming and down-to-earth as it was on day one.

Duplex Cervantes
APARTMENT $$

(Map p78; ☑5-254-2232, 5-254-3629; duplexcervantes@gmail.com; Espada No 7, apts 308 & 312, btwn Calle 25 & Calzada de la Infanta; 2/3-bed apt USD$70/105; P✳) Two fully renovated, tastefully minimalist duplex apartments, one with two bedrooms, the other with three, are on offer here. Both apartments have separate bathroom, lounge-dining room, kitchen and balcony. They're three floors up, on the border of Centro Habana and Vedado. English, French and Italian are spoken by the friendly owners. Large breakfasts go for USD$5 extra.

The apartments can be rented on a single-room basis with shared bathroom (USD$35), subject to availability. Inquire when booking.

★Malecón 663
BOUTIQUE HOTEL $$$

(Map p78; ☑7-860-1459; www.malecon663.com; Malecón No 663, btwn Gervasio & Belascoaín; d USD$210-250, ste USD$290; ✳🗺) 🅿 A work of creative genius on the Malecón, this French-run hotel is a whimsical mélange of art, recycling, comfort and sophistication. The four rooms are individually themed (art deco, vintage, contemporary and eclectic), but all are doused with Cuban flavor, from AfroCuban religions to carnivals to cutting-edge street art.

The pièce de la résistance is the 3rd-floor suite with its curvaceous chairs, tiled bathtub, and private bar (now that's what you call room service!) with a terrace that overlooks the Malecón. Nonguests can enjoy a downstairs cafe crammed with artistic creations based on Cuba's recycling ethic, and a rooftop terrace that mixes fine mojitos after 6pm; the terrace also has a Jacuzzi (for guests only). A very cool concept store on the ground floor, close to the entrance, sells unique locally made fashion accessories.

★Hotel Iberostar
Parque Central
HOTEL $$$

(Map p78; ☑7-860-6627; www.iberostar.com; Neptuno, btwn Agramonte & Paseo de Martí; r incl breakfast USD$490-570; P✳@🗺🏊) For over two decades the Iberostar Parque Central has been Havana's most consistent international-standard hotel, despite newer competition, with service and business facilities on par with top-ranking five-star establishments elsewhere in the Caribbean. Although the chic lobby and classily furnished rooms

BACK IN THE USSR

American and Spanish culture is widely represented in Havana, but evidence of Cuba's 30-year *amistad* (friendship) with the Russians is less celebrated.

For an eerie feeling that you're back in the USSR, look closely at the traffic. Contrary to what glossy coffee-table books would have you believe, the most common car in Cuba isn't an Eisenhower-era Chevy or an antediluvian Oldsmobile but the slightly less sexy Russian Lada, closely followed by its oft-forgotten cousin, the ghastly Moskvitch. And there's more to these cars than meets the eye. Many of the antique American automobiles so beloved by tourists have been hybridized with Lada or Moskvitch engines due to the unavailability of spare parts in Cuba.

Soviet subtleties are also present in the city's architecture, especially in the utilitarian apartment blocks constructed in the 1970s and '80s by Cuba's *micro brigadas* (small armies of workers responsible for building much of the post-revolution housing). One building that particularly stands out (like a sore thumb) is the Russian embassy in Miramar, which looks like a giant concrete robot. Its unusual design has been described as everything from constructivist to thuggish. Equally monolithic is the Hospital Nacional Hermanos Ameijeiras on the Malecón, a building that wouldn't look out of place in Moscow.

While you won't find too many Cubans longing for a return to the era of collective farms and nuclear brinkmanship, there has been a small outbreak of Soviet nostalgia in Havana of late. A notable Soviet-phile is Nazdarovie, a private restaurant on the Malecón serving Russian food against a backdrop of Soviet propaganda posters from the 1970s. It has recently been joined by Tabarish in Habana Vieja, another exponent of goulash, chicken Kiev and Russian dolls lined up on the bar.

may lack the historical riches of Habana Vieja accommodations, the ambience is far from antiseptic.

Bonus facilities include a full-service business center, a rooftop swimming pool/fitness center/Jacuzzi, an elegant lobby bar, the celebrated El Paseo restaurant, and excellent international telephone and internet access. There's also an even swankier wing across Calle Virtudes, connected to the rest of the hotel by an underground tunnel. As well as state-of-the-art rooms, the wing includes its own luxurious restaurant, cafe and reception area.

⭐ **Iberostar**
Grand Packard Hotel   LUXURY HOTEL $$$
(Map p78; ☑7-823-2100; www.iberostar.com; Paseo de Martí, btwn Cárcel & Genios; d/ste $250/395; P❋@🛜🏊) An infinity pool overlooking the harbor is just one highlight of this 321-room hotel, centrally located at the entrance to the bay. Accommodation is elegant and modern, with minimalist decor, open spaces, and bright white rooms and suites. Spanish-influenced gastronomy meets Cuban flavors in the hotel's six restaurants and three bars, including a tapas bar and a cigar lounge.

In anticipation of the city's 500th anniversary in 2019, the hotel was built on the site of the former Biscuit Hotel, said to have hosted poet Pablo Neruda and actor Marlon Brando in the 1950s.

Gran Hotel
Manzana Kempinski   LUXURY HOTEL $$$
(Map p78; ☑7-869-9100; www.kempinski.com/en/havana/gran-hotel-kempinski-la-habana; San Rafael, btwn Av de las Misiones & Agramonte; d/ste USD$500/800; ❋🛜🏊) Swiss hotel chain Kempinski runs this self-proclaimed 5½-star hotel in the heart of Old Havana. Covering the entire block, the luxurious property features 246 large rooms and suites on five floors with views over the old city and Parque Central (p86). Facilities include a cigar lounge, a spa and fitness center, a rooftop swimming pool and a panoramic, guests-only bar-restaurant.

The original European-style building dates to 1894 and existed as a multifarious property, hosting offices and a shopping arcade until the 1980s. Today the entire ground floor is bedecked in retail colors, with names such as Mango, L'Occitane en Provence, Lacoste, Mont Blanc and other international brands that have few devotees in Cuba. The hotel decor is sophisticated and modern, with green, light blues and violets enlivening the predominant white and light grays.

Hotel Sevilla
HOTEL **$$$**

(Map p78; ☑ 7-860-8560; www.hotelsevilla-cuba. com; Trocadero No 55, btwn Paseo de Martí & Agramonte; s/d incl breakfast USD$200/308; P ✽ @ 🛜 ⛱) Al Capone once hired out the whole 6th floor, Graham Greene used room 501 as a setting for *Our Man in Havana*, and the Mafia requisitioned the place as operations center for its pre-revolutionary North American drug racket. Nowadays the Moorish Sevilla still packs a punch, with an ostentatious lobby that could have been ripped straight out of Granada's Alhambra.

Spacious rooms with Sevillian tiles on the headboards get periodic upgrades, and the 9th-floor restaurant where you're serenaded by violin over breakfast is an 'experience,' but you're paying more for history here than modern facilities or snappy service.

Hotel Saratoga
HOTEL **$$$**

(Map p78; ☑ 7-868-1000; www.saratogahotel-cuba.com; Paseo de Martí No 603; d/ste USD$506/605; P ✽ @ 🛜 ⛱) The mint-green Saratoga is an architectural work of art that stands imposingly at the intersection of Paseo de Martí and Dragones, with fantastic views toward the Capitolio (p85). Sharp, if officious, service is a feature here, as are extra-comfortable beds, power showers, a truly decadent rooftop swimming pool and an exquisite hotel bar.

Unsurprisingly, all this luxury comes at a price: the Saratoga is eye-wateringly expensive. Then again, it's perhaps the best hotel in Cuba.

Hotel Telégrafo
HOTEL **$$$**

(Map p78; ☑ 7-861-4741, 7-861-1010; www. gaviotahotels.com; Paseo de Martí No 408; d/ ste USD$167/260; ✽ @ 🛜) This bold royal-blue beauty at the northwestern corner of Parque Central (p86) juxtaposes old-style architectural features (the original building dates to 1888) with modern design flourishes, such as big, luxurious sofas, a huge, winding central staircase and an intricate mosaic on the wall of the downstairs bar. Rooms have bathtubs, cushioned bedheads and mirrored wardrobes.

Hotel Inglaterra
HOTEL **$$$**

(Map p78; ☑ 7-860-8595; www.hotelinglaterra-cuba.com; Paseo de Martí No 416; s/d USD$169/260; ✽ @ 🛜) There's no doubt that the Inglaterra is a Havana icon: it's the city's oldest hotel, where José Martí once stayed the night. But while the tiled Moorish lobby is still magnificent and the busy El Louvre bar out front a beehive of music and action, the Inglaterra remains a better place to hang out than to stay.

Rooms have been modernized relatively recently, with new beds and scarlet accents, but they're a variable bunch, and some at the back are dark and windowless.

🛏 Vedado

Vedado retains a cluster of mid-20th-century hotels built with Mafia money that exude the essence of the 1940s and '50s. Most notable is the Hotel Nacional (p112), now a national monument. The neighborhood also has a good selection of increasingly luxurious casas particulares, and more recently some private boutique hotels have sprung up.

Hostal Havaniko
CASA PARTICULAR **$**

(Map p90; ☑ 7-837-4850; hostalhavaniko@gmail. com; Calle I No 457, btwn Calles 21 & 23; r USD$40-50; ✽) This casa particular, currently into its third owners, has had numerous incarnations, all of them good. It's located in the middle of Vedado's nightlife zone and centered on a high-walled patio with plenty of greenery and a fountain. The seven rooms are hotel standard and accented with murals, tiles and terra-cotta bricks. It was completely renovated in 2019.

Bank on fridges, safe boxes, hairdryers and space to chill on the terrace. Breakfast is USD$5 extra, parking USD$2.

Marta Vitorte
CASA PARTICULAR **$**

(Map p90; ☑ 7-832-6475; www.casamarta inhavana.com; Calle G No 301, apt 14, btwn Calles 13 & 15; r USD$40-60; P ✽) Marta has lived in this apartment block on Av de los Presidentes since the 1960s. One look at the view and you'll see why: the glass-front wraparound terrace, taking in 270 degrees of Havana's pockmarked panorama, makes it seem as though you're standing atop the Martí monument (p89). Not surprisingly, the four rooms are deluxe, with lovely furnishings, minibars and safes.

Then there are the breakfasts, the laundry, the parking space, the elegant dining room... Marta also rents two self-contained luxury apartments nearby (USD$100 to USD$180).

Marques de Liz
CASA PARTICULAR **$**

(Map p90; ☑ 5-264-4756; Calle 25 No 715, btwn Calles D & E; r USD$45-60; ✽ 🛜) A handsome neoclassical house located in a quiet street, the 'Liz' has four rooms of varying configurations. All have kettles, microwaves and stocked fridges. Some have larger kitchenettes, and one has a sunny balcony overlooking Av 25. The bathrooms are large and luxuriously modern, and tempting bottles of wine and rum are left in your room (to purchase).

Doña Lourdes
CASA PARTICULAR $

(Map p90; ☑7-830-9509; Calle 17 No 459, btwn Calles E & F; r USD$30-35; ☀) Opposite the Museo de Artes Decorativas (p89), this unassuming 1st-floor casa is in a pleasant tucked-away nook. There's one rented room, located upstairs in a typically regal early-20th-century Vedado residence with a large communal balcony overlooking the street. Lovely hosts, too.

Mercedes González
CASA PARTICULAR $

(Map p90; ☑7-832-5846; www.mercybed breakfast.com; Calle 21 No 360, 2nd fl, btwn Calles G & H; r USD$35-45; ☀) Mercy's four rooms at this long-standing rental spread across two 2nd-floor apartments just off Av de los Presidentes have a passionate following. The hostess is lovely, and the rooms and common areas (with an extensive book collection) have a refined art deco feel. Mercy offers a good breakfast and can help with trip planning.

Casa Lizette
CASA PARTICULAR $

(Map p90; ☑7-830-1226; lizette2602@gmail.com; Calle 3 No 580, btwn Calles 8 & 10; r USD$40; ☀) A relatively modern self-contained house with private entry in western Vedado, a block from the Malecón and handily placed for nearby restaurants and the fabulous Fábrica de Arte Cubano (p132). Lizette's three rooms share a dining room and lounge, and there's access to a terrace with rocking chairs out back.

La Casa de Ana
CASA PARTICULAR $

(Map p90; ☑7-833-5128; www.anahavana.com; Calle 19 No 1422, btwn Calles 26 & 28; USD$35; ☀ @) Don't be put off by the out-of-the-way location (western Vedado): there's plenty going on in this neck of the woods, and the highly professional Casa de Ana will put you straight about everything from cheap transportation to where to find the best mojitos. Rooms are modern and clean, and service goes far beyond the call of duty. Book well ahead.

★ El Candil
Boutique Hotel
BOUTIQUE HOTEL $$

(Map p90; ☑7-833-1209; www.hotelcandil.com; Calle 2 No 457, btwn 19 & 21; r USD$150; ☀ ☎ ☀) Boutique hotels are a new thing in Cuba, and the five-room Candil is setting a high bar, occupying a distinguished early-20th-century villa decked out with the discreet elegance of the era but with some welcome modern additions. There's a curtain-draped front porch, a sun-splashed rooftop bar and plunge pool, plus wall-mounted flat-screen TVs and air-con units in all five rooms.

★ Casavana Cuba
CASA PARTICULAR $$

(Map p90; ☑5-804-9258; www.casavanacuba. com; Calle G No 301, 5th fl, btwn Calles 13 & 15; r/ ste from USD$130/170; ☀) What started as a casa particular has morphed into a de facto private hotel of four-star quality. Spread over three floors (4, 5 and 11) in a residential *rascacielo* (skyscraper), Casavana's huge rooms choose modern minimalism over antique clutter, but there are elegant touches and bright common areas with floors so polished you can virtually see your face in them.

Behold the carved wooden beds and then drink in the wondrous views from your personal balcony. It's a little pricier than your average casa but well worth it. Book online.

Boutique Hotel
5tay8 Vedado
BOUTIQUE HOTEL $$

(Map p90; ☑7-881-2671; www.boutiquehotel vedado.website; Av 5, cnr Calle 8; d from USD$115; P ☀) An exceptionally striking private hotel inhabiting a dignified villa, the 5 & 8 effortlessly mixes the modernity of Miami with the indefinable magic of Havana. The building itself is a beauty, with vines cascading down two stories from arched windows, plus a roof terrace (with illuminated bar) licked by gentle sea breezes.

Inside, you'll be greeted by elegant and spacious rooms equipped with top-of-the-range bathrooms and punctuated by cutting-edge design. One room has arty graffiti scrawled onto the walls of the toilet.

★ Hotel Nacional
HOTEL $$$

(Map p90; ☑7-836-3564; www.hotelnacionalde cuba.com; cnr Calles O & 21; s/d/tr USD$234/ 338/465; P ☀ @ ☎ ☀) The icing on the cake of Cuban hotels and a flagship of the government-run Gran Caribe chain, the neoclassical/neocolonial/art deco (call it eclectic) Hotel Nacional is as much a city monument as an international accommodation option.

113

HAVANA SLEEPING

Even if you don't stay here, find time to sip at least one minty mojito in the exquisite oceanside bar.

Steeped in history and furnished with rooms that have plaques advertising details of illustrious past occupants, the towering Havana landmark sports two swimming pools, a sweeping manicured lawn, a couple of lavish restaurants and its own top-class cabaret, the Parisién (p136). While the rooms might lack some of the gadgets of deluxe Varadero, the ostentatious communal areas and the ghosts of Winston Churchill, Frank Sinatra, Lucky Luciano and Errol Flynn that haunt the Moorish lobby make for a fascinating and unforgettable experience.

Hotel Meliá Cohiba   HOTEL $$$

(Map p90; ☑ 7-833-3636; www.meliacuba.com; Paseo, btwn Calles 1 & 3; s/d USD$527/570; P ✴ @ 🛜 ☒) Cuba's most businesslike city hotel is an oceanside concrete giant built in 1994 (it's the only building from this era on the Malecón) that will satisfy the highest of international expectations with its knowledgeable staff and modern, well-polished facilities. After a few weeks in the Cuban outback you'll feel as though you're on a different planet here.

For workaholics there are special 'business-traveler rooms,' and 59 units have Jacuzzis. On the lower levels gold-star facilities include a shopping arcade, one of Havana's plushest gyms, and premier nightlife option the Habana Café (p136). Book online for better rates.

Hotel NH Capri   HOTEL $$$

(Map p90; ☑ 7-839-7200; cnr Calles 21 & N; s/d USD$165/220; P ✴ @ 🛜 ☒) After spending over a decade as a rotting ruin, the Capri was reborn in 2014 as a quieter, less notorious version of its former self. Rather like *The Godfather: Part II* (in which it was fictionally depicted), the Capri II is just as good as the original, with a sharp minimalist lobby, a rooftop pool and slickly modern yet unostentatious rooms.

Built in modernist style with Mafia money in 1957, the 19-floor hotel in its (brief) heyday was owned by mobster Santo Trafficante, who used American actor George Raft as his debonair front man. When Fidel Castro's guerrillas came knocking in January 1959, Raft allegedly told them where to stick it and slammed the door in their faces.

The hotel has also featured in two movies: Carol Reed's *Our Man in Havana* and Mikhail Kalatozov's *Soy Cuba* (in an astounding 'tracking shot'). It was also the setting for Michael Corleone's meeting with Hyman Roth in *The Godfather: Part II*, though due to the embargo director Francis Ford Coppola shot the scenes in the Dominican Republic.

Hotel Habana Libre   HOTEL $$$

(Map p90; ☑ 7-834-6100; www.meliacuba.com; Calle L, btwn Calles 23 & 25; d/ste incl breakfast USD$464/495; P ✴ @ 🛜 ☒) This icon of the Havana skyline opened in March 1958 on the eve of President Batista's last waltz. Originally the Havana Hilton, it was commandeered by Fidel Castro's rebels in January 1959 and used as their temporary HQ. Now managed by Spain's Meliá chain, it's by turns spectacular (behold the views!) and sloppy (iffy plumbing, shaky elevators). Renovations are ongoing.

The hotel's communal areas with their retro '70s design features outshine the less illustrious rooms, although some of the upper-floor suites have been dragged into the 21st century. The 25th-floor El Turquin cabaret (p136) with its retractable roof is a city institution.

Hotel Riviera by Iberostar   HOTEL $$$

(Map p90; ☑ 7-836-4051; www.iberostar.com; cnr Paseo & Malecón; s/d USD$200/280; P ✴ @ ☒) Magnificently retro or dog-eared and dated – the hotel that mobster Meyer Lansky built in 1957 is a bit of both. The lobby, with its sharp modernist lines and Vegas-style ostentation, looks like a set from *The Godfather: Part II*, while the rooms are less striking.

Hotel ROC Presidente   HOTEL $$$

(Map p90; ☑ 7-838-1801; www.roc-hotels.com; cnr Calzada & Calle G; s/d USD$180/260; P ✴ @ 🛜 ☒) This art deco-influenced hotel on Av de los Presidentes wouldn't be out of place near Times Sq in New York. Built in 1928, the same year as the nearby **Hotel Victoria** (Map p90; ☑ 7-833-3510; www.nh-collection.com; Calle 19 No 101; s/d incl breakfast $165/220; ✴ @ 🛜 ☒), the Presidente is similar but larger, with more officious staff. Unless you're a walker or fancy getting some elbow exercise on Havana's crowded buses, the location can be awkward.

🛏 Playa & Marianao

Playa's hotels are the preserve of diplomats, the convention crowd and people whose flights have been bumped. There are some good ones among the dross, but the general location is detached from Havana's main sights and you'll need taxis or strong legs to get around.

Casa Guevara Alba   CASA PARTICULAR $

(Map p96; ☑ 7-202-6515; mt_alba@yahoo.es; Av 5F No 9611, btwn Calles 96 & 98, Náutico; r USD$40-60; P ❋) A welcoming homestay close to Playa's main hotel zone that outsmarts most of the hotels in terms of price, service and comfort. On offer are two apartments with bedrooms, sitting rooms, terraces, bathrooms and use of a kitchen. It's modern for Cuba but still has plenty of character.

Hotel Villa Eulalia   BOUTIQUE HOTEL $$

(Map p96; ☑ 7-203-5724; Av 5, cnr Calle 6, Miramar; s/d incl breakfast USD$87/136; ❋ 🛜) Guarding the entry to the diplomatic 'hood of Miramar, the Eulalia is a fairly new hotel set in an old mansion that was recently floated as one of Cubanacán's Encanto boutique brand. It's small (with seven rooms), discreet and self-contained, with bar-restaurant, breakfast room and salubrious garden.

Villa Teresa   CASA PARTICULAR $$

(Map p96; ☑ 7-202-2799; marlene7667@ yahoo.es; Av 1 No 4401, cnr Calle 44, Miramar; r incl breakfast USD$100; P ❋ 🛜) This private rental option opposite the Hotel Copacabana in a conspicuously modern lily-white house looks as though it's just been towed in from the Florida Keys. The four tastefully decorated rooms evoke the feel of a boutique hotel, with good art, large beds and fully stocked minibars. Breakfast is served in the open-plan dining area and lounge.

★ Hotel Meliá Habana   HOTEL $$$

(Map p96; ☑ 7-204-8500; www.meliacuba.com; Av 3, btwn Calles 76 & 80, Miramar; s/d USD$500; P ❋ @ 🛜 ⛱) A little brutal from the outside but beautiful within, Miramar's Hotel Meliá Habana is one of the city's best-run and best-equipped accommodations options. The 409 rooms (some wheelchair accessible) are positioned around a salubrious lobby with abundant hanging vines, marble statues and extravagant water features. Outside, Cuba's largest and most attractive swimming pool lies next to a desolate, rocky shore.

The polite service and excellent buffet restaurant round things off. Ignore the inflated rack rates and look online for better deals.

H10 Habana Panorama   HOTEL $$$

(Map p96; ☑ 7-204-0100; www.h10hotels.com; cnr Av 3 & Calle 70, Miramar; s/d/tr USD$146/192/269; P ❋ @ 🛜 ⛱) This flashy 'glass cathedral' on Playa's still-developing hotel strip is effectively a self-contained resort, which has its advantages when you're this far from the city center. Acres of blue-tinted glass and a vaguely aquamarine theme frame a monumental lobby, where space-age elevators whisk guests up to one of the 317 bright rooms that offer great views over Miramar and beyond.

Hotel el Bosque   HOTEL $$$

(Map p96; ☑ 7-204-9232; www.gaviotahotels. com; Calle 28A, btwn Calles 49A & 49C, Kohly; s/d USD$110/200; ❋ @ 🛜) El Bosque is part of the state-run Kohly-Bosque *complejo* (complex). Clean and friendly, it lies on the banks of the Río Almendares, surrounded by the Bosque de La Habana (p95) – the city's green lungs. The decor is a little behind the times, and like most Havana hotels it's overpriced for what you get, although the wooded grounds soften the blow a little.

Memories Miramar   HOTEL $$$

(Map p96; ☑ 7-204-3583/4; www.memories resorts.com; cnr Av 5 & Calle 74, Miramar; s/d USD$187/250; P ❋ @ 🛜 ⛱) This 427-room giant built in 2000 is one of Miramar's better hotels, roughly equivalent to a four-star place in Varadero. Rooms are large and comfortable, if not extravagant; breakfasts are plentiful; and there's a large, attractive pool area fringed by palm trees.

Additionally, there are plenty of sporty extras if the isolated location starts to grate, including tennis courts, said swimming pool, sauna, gym and games room.

🛏 Habana del Este

Most of eastern Havana's hotel accommodations center on Playas del Este, more specifically Playa Santa María del Mar, which sports three of only four all-inclusive options in the city of Havana. None of the hotels are a knockout, while some are downright ugly.

Further east, Guanabo has dozens of casas particulares but no decent hotels.

Villa Cloty   CASA PARTICULAR $

(Map p102; ☑ 7-786-2705; Av 5 No 4701, btwn Calles 470 & 472, Guanabo; r USD$35-45;

UNDERSTANDING JOSÉ MARTÍ

'Two fatherlands, have I; Cuba and the Night,' wrote poet, journalist, philosopher and all-round Renaissance man José Martí in 1882, perfectly summing up the dichotomies of late-19th-century Cuba, still as relevant today as they were 130 years ago.

Ironically, Martí – the brains behind Cuba's Second Independence War – remains the one figure who binds Cubans worldwide, a potent unifying force in a country fractiously divided by politics, economics and 145km of shark-infested ocean.

Born in Havana in 1853, Martí spent well over half his life outside the country he professed to love in sporadic exile, shunting between Spain, Guatemala, Venezuela and the US. But his absence hardly mattered. Martí's importance was in his words and ideas. An accomplished political commentator and a master of aphorisms, he was responsible in many ways for forming the modern Cuban identity and its dream of self-determination. It's difficult to meet a Cuban today who can't eloquently quote stanzas of his poetry. Similarly, there's barely a town or village across the country that doesn't have a statue or plaza named in his honor. The homage extends to the exile community in the US, where Cubans have named a radio station after him. Indeed, Martí is venerated across South and Central America, where he is often viewed as the ideological successor to Simón Bolívar.

A basic understanding of Martí and his far-reaching influence is crucial to understanding contemporary Cuba. Havana, the city of his birth, is dotted with poignant monuments, but there are important sites elsewhere. The following are the bare essentials:

Memorial a José Martí (p89) This giant tower (the tallest in Havana) has a massive statue of el Maestro at its foot and a comprehensive museum inside.

Museo-Casa Natal de José Martí (p77) Modest but lovingly curated birth house of Cuba's national hero.

Museo Finca el Abra (p167) Small, poignant house on the Isla de la Juventud where Martí was briefly imprisoned in 1870.

Cementerio Santa Ifigenia (p410) The apostle's beautiful mausoleum in Santiago de Cuba has a grand guard-changing ceremony every 30 minutes.

Dos Ríos Obelisk (Dos Ríos) Simple but appropriate monument marking where Martí died in battle in 1895 near Bayamo.

P ❄ ✖) Occupying a great spot on Guanabo's main drag, right by the beach, this place – rather unusually for a casa particular – benefits from its own pool, a kidney-shaped addition to the garden at the side. Bedrooms are well lit and clean (the one at the rear has sea views), and fruity breakfasts are served under a thatched roof in the lovely garden.

Gilberto & Blanca   CASA PARTICULAR $
(Map p102; ☑ 7-796-2171; gilberto@nauta.cu; Av 5 No 47012, btwn Calles 470 & 472, Guanabo; r USD$30-40; ❄) A friendly retired couple has this pleasant bungalow on Guanabo's main drag, a 100m dash from the beach, offering two rooms with private bathrooms. Ideal for families or groups of friends.

**Hostal Las Terrazas
de Teresa**   CASA PARTICULAR $
(Map p102; ☑ 7-796-6860; Calle 472 No 7b07, btwn Avs 7B & 9, Guanabo; apt USD$35; P ❄)

The three rooms here are realistically mini-apartments, with their own kitchens and eating areas. Teresa has put a lot of work into renovating her house and the gray-stone brickwork lends the spacious rooms a handsome glow. The terraces on different levels are great for relaxing with a drink.

Bravo Club Hotel Arenal   RESORT $$$
(Map p102; ☑ 7-797-1272; Laguna Boca Ciega; s/d/tr all-inclusive USD$150/250/320; P ❄ @ 🛜 ✖) The Arenal is undoubtedly Playas del Este's best hotel and the nearest decent all-inclusive resort to Havana. Situated by a small lagoon with boardwalk access to secluded Playa Boca Ciega, it lacks the panache of Cuba's northern cayos (keys), though its slightly dated architecture received a welcome spruce-up in 2016.

There's a free shuttle into Havana several days a week, and the Cuban beach town of Guanabo is accessible by horse and cart.

✕ Eating

✕ Habana Vieja

Habana Vieja's private restaurants are some of the city's most ambitious and are often housed in plush colonial digs. They've become more abundant and adventurous since the easing of economic restrictions in 2011.

The Old Town also has the most consistent stash of government-run restaurants in Cuba, many of them set up by the Office of the City Historian.

El Café   BREAKFAST $

(Map p68; 📞7-861-3817; www.facebook.com/
elcafehavana; Amargura 358, btwn Villegas & Aguacate; breakfast USD$3-7; 🕙9am-6pm; 🍽) There are many cafes in Havana these days, but only one El Café, a delicious mix of tight service, exceptional coffee and homemade sourdough sandwiches supplemented by all-day brunchy breakfasts. It's popular with indie travelers courtesy of its ample vegan and vegetarian options, including avocado and hummus varietals. Arrive early to get a seat.

Helad'oro   ICE CREAM $

(Map p68; 📞5-305-9131; Aguiar No 206, btwn Empedrado & Tejadillo; ice cream USD$1-4; 🕙11am-10pm) Back when Fidel Castro was 'king,' the government had a monopoly on many things. Controlled by the legendary Coppelia, ice cream rarely strayed beyond *fresa y chocolate* (strawberry and chocolate) flavors. Then along came the economic defrosting of the 2010s, ushering in Helad'oro, with its artisan ice cream dispensed in 30-plus flavors, including mamey and *desayuno tropical* (tropical breakfast). At USD$1 a scoop, it's Havana's cheapest indulgence.

Café Bohemia   TAPAS $

(Map p68; 📞7-836-6567; www.havanabohe
mia.com; San Ignacio No 364; tapas USD$6-10; 🕙10:30am-9:30pm; 🍽) Inhabiting a beautifully curated mansion on Plaza Vieja, Café Bohemia – named for a Cuban culture and arts magazine – manages to feel appropriately bohemian but also serves great cocktails, tapas and extremely addictive cakes.

The crispy baguettes are consistently good and the daily specials sometimes advertise vegan options. Seating spills into the busy beehive of the plaza, or you can stay more secluded in a colonial courtyard.

Café Suiza   CAFE $

(Map p68; 📞7-801-4023; Obispo No 453, btwn Aguacate & Villegas; mains USD$5-9; 🕙8:30am-10pm) Don't expect fondue and chocolates. This quick-fire cafe on Habana Vieja's main drag is named for one of the building's former owners rather than the Swiss-ness of its food. The deep, windowless interior is overlooked by a long bar that serves up burgers, salads and fruity smoothies.

Settle down for an elongated *pausa* – the live band in the evening will perform even if there are only two customers. No time to stop? A small booth out front overlooking Calle Obispo dispatches ice cream and irresistible tubs of *tres leches* cake.

Oasis Nelva   BREAKFAST $

(Map p68; 📞5-293-9758; Habana, cnr Muralla; crepes USD$4-8; 🕙8am-10pm; 🍽) Havana's experts on sweet and savory crepes have built a strong reputation on simple foundations. There's an eco-minded recycling aesthetic (jam jars for drinking glasses, old packing cases and tires for stools), along with cheap but generous cocktails, decent vegetarian options and a hearty USD$5 breakfast.

Jíbaro   CUBAN $

(Map p68; 📞5-346-8789; www.facebook.com/
therealjibaro; Merced 69, btwn Cuba & San Ignacio; mains USD$4-10; 🕙10am-midnight; 🍽) Located in a restored colonial mansion on the outskirts of Old Havana's oldest quarter, Jíbaro is a great option for authentic Cuban food and much-praised mocktails (unusual nonalcoholic cocktails). Local dishes take a modern twist without getting too chic. Stick to the basics and ask for stuffed *tostones* (fried plantain), *ropa vieja* (shredded beef) and black-bean cream.

A striking mural guards the doorway in Calle Merced.

Café del Ángel
Jacqueline Fumero   CAFE $

(Map p68; 📞7-862-6562; www.cafedelangeljf.
com; Compostela No 1, cnr Cuarteles; breakfasts USD$4-8; 🕙8am-11:30pm) Guarding the small, heavenly square behind the Iglesia del Santo Ángel Custodio (p82), minimalist Fumero (all white walls and clear plastic chairs) is run by a Cuban fashion designer. Its mega-popular outdoor tables are excellent perches for cocktails, egg-based breakfasts and intimate dissections of Havana street life. It also serves tapas-size food and iced coffee.

Sandwichería La Bien Paga
SANDWICHES $

(Map p68; Aguacate No 259; sandwiches USD$1-2.50; ⊙9am-6pm) If you're down to your last few Cuban convertibles, want something quick and simple, or fancy a proper Cuban sandwich without the Miami glitz, drop into this tiny snack shop that's barely big enough to swing a small kitten. A generous 'Cuban' (ham, cheese, pork and pickles) goes for a socialistic USD$2.

★Lamparilla 361 Tapas & Cervezas
TAPAS $$

(Map p68; ☑5-289-5324; Lamparilla No 361, btwn Aguacate & Villegas; tapas USD$5-12; ⊙noon-midnight) Havana's best tapas bar might also be its finest all-round eating establishment, with food, presentation and service down to a fine art. Inside the loungy, romantically lit restaurant there's plenty to look at as you enjoy ice-cold beer, fabulous cocktails, and creative but interestingly presented tapas (on plates, slates, pans and mini-shopping trolleys).

You'll need more than a postcard (or tweet) to list the standout food and drink items. Could they include the tapas-size lasagna, the meatballs served freshly made in the pan, the cornbread with sweet chicken, or the daiquiri that comes with a face iced onto it? It's all epic!

★Doña Eutimia
CUBAN $$

(Map p68; ☑7-861-1332; Callejón del Chorro 60c; mains USD$8-12; ⊙noon-10pm) The secret at Doña Eutimia is that there *is* no secret: just serve decent-size portions of the best Cuban food. Expect the likes of *ropa vieja* (shredded beef; there's also an interesting lamb version), epic *picadillo a la habanera* (spicy beef), glorious *lechón asado* (roast pork) and beautifully rustic roast chicken, all served with ample rice, beans and fried plantains.

This is trip-defining food of the highest order, and proof that Cuba's traditional cuisine, when prepared properly, can be pretty spectacular. The restaurant is located in a cul-de-sac near the cathedral. Reserve a day ahead.

★Lo de Monik
TAPAS $$

(Map p68; ☑7-864-4029; Compostela No 201, cnr Chacón; mains USD$10-15; ⊙8am-9:30pm) Eschewing colonial splendor for a French bistro feel, the Monk blends seamlessly into the increasingly chic Loma del Ángel quarter, with a bright-white interior and arguably the city's friendliest and chattiest staff.

Search the ever-changing blackboard menu for brunch or tapas ideas (fish tacos, well-stuffed Cuban baguettes, creamy cheesecake) and come back later for spectacular cocktails.

★El del Frente
INTERNATIONAL $$

(Map p68; ☑7-863-0206; O'Reilly No 303; mains USD$8-13; ⊙noon-midnight) When the owners of O'Reilly 304 (p118) wanted to expand their increasingly popular restaurant a few years back, they opened another one directly across the street and amusingly called it El del Frente ('The One in Front'). It's more of the same culinary genius, with a few bonuses – a roof terrace, retro 1950s design features and heady gin cocktails.

Partake in the lobster tacos, octopus salad or drinks from what are possibly Havana's best mixologists and enjoy it all under the stars. The entrance is through a modest door in Calle O'Reilly. Book ahead; it's insanely popular.

★El Rum Rum de la Habana
SEAFOOD $$

(Map p68; ☑7-861-0806; Empedrado No 256, btwn Cuba & Aguiar; mains USD$7-18; ⊙noon-midnight) Not every restaurant has a wine sommelier *and* a cigar sommelier, but this is Havana, and El Rum Rum (the name references both the drink and Cuban slang for 'gossip') can put you straight on every area of consumption. Everything is outstanding here, from the delicate seafood to the concert-worthy musical entertainment.

The menu's a feast of Cuban specialties full of subtle scents and sauces. There's *caldereta de mariscos* (a rich seafood stew), steak with three toppings, a paella worthy of Valencia, and about 10 ways of imbibing your mojito. Service, led by sommelier and owner Osiris Oramas, is exemplary, directing you toward the best rum and food flavors, and there are several spaces – including an air-conditioned VIP room – in which to eat.

Restaurante Antojos
INTERNATIONAL $$

(Map p68; ☑5-277-2577; www.restauranteantojos.com; Espada, btwn Cuarteles & Chacón; mains USD$7-12; ⊙11am-midnight) A place to satisfy your whims (*antojos*), particularly if you're feeling whimsical about daiquiris, generously stuffed pulled-pork baguettes or chunky *tostones* (fried plantain). Wander into the dessert realm (they serve 'em any time) and you'll be equally stirred, particularly if you choose a warm bowl of cinnamon-laced *arroz con leche* (rice pudding).

Occupying a handsome spot in cafe-lined Callejón de Espada, Antojos is relatively new to the game (it opened in February 2019) but already vying for promotion to Havana's gastronomic premier league.

5 Sentidos
INTERNATIONAL $$

(Map p68; ☑7-864 8699; www.paladar5sentidos. com; San Juan de Dios No 67, cnr Compostela; mains USD$10-18; ☺noon-4pm & 6:30-11pm) The romantically named five feelings (5 *sentidos*) ought to excite at least three of yours. The open kitchen allows for the free circulation of inviting aromas, the French-bistro decor (all painted wood and elegant chandeliers) is pleasing to the eye, and your taste buds won't leave unstimulated after you've savored the ceviche, octopus or melt-in-the-mouth lamb stew.

Cuba's reputation as a place to skip dessert comes a cropper here, too. The multi-textured 'chocolat' or the cream cheese coated in guava glaze could compete with anything in Michelin-starred, celebrity-chef-obsessed Europe or North America. The discreet but sharp service is similarly world class.

Il Rustico
ITALIAN $$

(Map p68; ☑5-539-4514; San Juan de Dios No 53, btwn Habana & Compostela; mains USD$5-10; ☺noon-10:30pm) With a Sicilian owner at the helm, furniture craftily made out of recycled wooden pallets, and a wood-fired pizza oven, Rustico can plausibly claim to serve Havana's best pizza.

The thin-crust pies – chewy, bubbled at the edges and not too busy on top – would make any Neapolitan proud. Sicilian staples such as *pasta alla norma* (with eggplant and tomatoes) make worthy menu-fellows.

Más Habana
INTERNATIONAL $$

(Map p68; ☑7-864-3227; www.facebook.com/ mashabanacuba; Habana No 308, btwn San Juan de Dios & O'Reilly; mains USD$8-16; ☺noon-midnight) There are multiple reasons you may request *más* (more) of Havana once you've visited this culinary institution. There's the effortlessly cool interior (*nuevo* industrial with artistic splashes), the happy-hour cocktails (daiquiris stand out), the modern renderings of classic Cuban food, and the thoroughly reasonable prices that draw both tourists and locals.

The small two-level interior has an attractive but refined ambience: it's Fábrica de Arte Cubano (p132) meets modern French bistro. It would be remiss not to mention the stuffed plantains, cinnamon-laced lamb and exceptionally tender octopus.

Trattoria 5esquinas
ITALIAN $$

(Map p68; ☑7-860-6295; Habana No 104, cnr Cuarteles; mains USD$5-11; ☺8am-11pm) Best Italian restaurant in Havana? There are a few contenders, but 5esquinas makes a strong claim. It has the full trattoria vibe, right down to the glow of the pizza oven and the aroma of roasted garlic. Visiting Italians won't be disappointed with the seafood pasta (generous on the lobster) or the crab-and-spinach cannelloni. Round off your meal with tiramisu.

Donde Lis
CUBAN $$

(Map p68; ☑7-860-0922; www.dondelis.com; Tejadillo No 163, btwn Habana & Compostela; mains USD$6-13; ☺noon-midnight) The Lis' interior is like a modern love letter to Havana: iconography from the Rat Pack era of the 1950s, reproduced 20th-century tropical art, and bright colors splashed onto old colonial walls. The menu is a carefully cultivated mélange of flavors, presenting Cuban staples with modern twists – octopus with guacamole, lobster enchilados – along with some Italian and Spanish cameos.

O'Reilly 304
INTERNATIONAL $$

(Map p68; ☑5-264-4725; O'Reilly No 304; meals USD$8-13; ☺noon-midnight) Fill a small bar-restaurant nightly with a buoyant crowd all happy to be enjoying potent cocktails, delectable food and Havana's tastiest plantain chips, and you've got a guaranteed recipe for success. As well as producing the best fruity alcoholic beverages in Havana, O'Reilly delivers its finest ceviche, tacos and fish, accompanied by a crispy mélange of vegetables.

The small interior is cleverly laid out to make the most of a mezzanine floor and the atmosphere is rarely anything less than electric. If it's busy, don't fret: turnover is high and tables can quickly vacate.

Buena Vista Curry Club
INDIAN $$

(Map p68; ☑7-862-7379; www.buenavistacurry club.com; Tejadillo No 24, cnr Cuba; mains USD$9-15; ☺12:30-11pm; ☑) Aiming to lure in spice-starved tourists (especially curry-loving Brits) and educate Cuban palates in the nuances of Indian food, the Buena Vista Curry Club is a brave venture in a country unaccustomed to fiery *phals* and spicy paneers.

If you came here purely out of curiosity, you'll be pleasantly surprised by the quality of the chicken tikka masala, blistered naan (yes, they have a tandoori oven) and aromatic basmati rice.

El Figaro
CUBAN **$$**
(Map p68; ☑ 7-861-0544; Aguiar No 18, btwn Peña Pobre & Av de las Misiones; mains USD$11-14; ⊙ 9am-midnight) This aptly named restaurant in Habana Vieja's 'barber's alley' is run by the grandson of the former chef to Meyer Lansky. He's revitalized the notorious mobster's favorite dish, lobster sautéed in coffee and cognac, and promises (with typical Cuban humor) to provide 'food without hairs in it.'

Old banknotes flutter like Tibetan prayer flags from the rafters inside the building, but for the best seats flop down at a table outside in traffic-free Calle Aguiar.

Tabarish
RUSSIAN **$$**
(Map p68; ☑ 7-801-4009; bar.tabarish@gmail.com; O'Reilly 465, cnr Villegas; mains USD$12-18; ⊙ 11am-midnight) Relocated from Miramar's residential area to bustling Calle O'Reilly, Tabarish is housed in a restored colonial building with high ceilings and wrought-iron columns. Dishes celebrate the friendly ties between Cuba and Russia; don't miss the *solyanka* (meat broth with salty vegetables) or the chicken Kiev. The open, well-lit seating areas get crowded on weekends. Cocktails are strong and well served.

La Vitrola
INTERNATIONAL **$$**
(Map p68; ☑ 5-285-7111; Muralla No 151, cnr San Ignacio; breakfast USD$5-8; ⊙ 8am-midnight) A retro '50s place on the corner of Plaza Vieja where the live band never seems to stop playing, La Vitrola is routinely swamped by tourists in the evening. It's far better, though, for its quieter alfresco breakfasts of fruit, coffee, toast and generous omelets, which come complete with a toothpick flag of your home country.

Nao Bar Paladar
SEAFOOD **$$**
(Map p68; ☑ 7-801-1263, 5-297-2804; Obispo No 1, btwn San Pedro & Baratillo; meals USD$7-18; ⊙ noon-midnight) Nao occupies a 200-year-old building near the docks and its decor plays on the seafaring theme. The small upstairs space is good for main courses (seafood dominates); the downstairs bar with outdoor seating excels in snacks.

Paladar Los Mercaderes
CUBAN, INTERNATIONAL **$$$**
(Map p68; ☑ 7-861-2437; Mercaderes No 207; meals USD$18-22; ⊙ 11am-11pm) This private restaurant in a historic building has to

be one of Cuba's most refined *paladares* (privately run restaurants) for ambience, service and food, both Cuban and international. Follow a marble staircase to a luxurious 1st-floor dining room where violinists play and the menu lists the provenance of the farm-to-table food: Cojímar sardines, Pinar del Río pork and Camagüeyan *ropa vieja* (shredded beef). While the ingredients are steadfastly local, the cooking techniques show international creativity, with such renderings as fish in Sri Lankan red-curry sauce and lobster in pineapple glaze.

Habana 61
CUBAN **$$$**
(Map p68; ☑ 7-801-6433; Calle Habana 61, btwn Cuarteles & Peña Pobre; mains USD$7-20; ⊙ noon-midnight) Habana 61's menu features Cuban classics with a fresh twist. The lobster is among its most popular dishes, but the traditional *ropa vieja* (shredded beef) is just as delicious. For a starter, don't miss the cold tomato soup with shrimp. Located in Old Havana's fast-developing Loma del Ángel quarter, this small restaurant is often full in high season. Book ahead.

La Imprenta
INTERNATIONAL **$$$**
(Map p68; Mercaderes No 208; meals USD$12-26; ⊙ noon-midnight) This attractive state-run restaurant has a resplendent interior filled with memorabilia from the building's previous incarnation as a printing works. The food also enjoys decorative presentation, especially if you go for a seafood skewer or a succulent lobster tail. Other draws include creative seafood medleys, chicken curry with pineapple, and a stash of decent wines.

Café del Oriente
FRENCH **$$$**
(Map p68; Oficios 112; meals USD$20-30; ⊙ noon-11pm) A posh, elegant side to Havana greets you as you walk through the door at this long-standing state-run establishment in Plaza de San Francisco de Asís. Options include smoked salmon, caviar (yes, caviar!), goose-liver pâté, lobster thermidor, steak *au poivre*, a cheese plate and a glass of port. Plus there's service by gents in tuxes.

✖ Centro Habana

In the past Centro Habana offered more limited fare than Habana Vieja and Vedado, though the culinary map is changing – some outstanding private restaurants now punctuate its dense grid. For something less ordinary, look out for Spanish clubs run by the Centro Asturianos and dip into the restaurant strip on Calle Cuchillo in the Barrio Chino (Chinatown).

Flor de Loto
CHINESE $

(Map p78; ☑ 7-863-5450; Salud No 303, btwn Gervasio & Escobar; mains USD$7-9; ☺ noon-midnight) Popularly considered to be Havana's best 'Chinese' restaurant, Flor de Loto has one major caveat: it isn't actually that Chinese at all. Sure, the rambling menu *does* list spring rolls, fried wontons and chop suey among its highlights, but the other 101 options are more closely aligned to the land of rice and beans.

The economical renditions of old-school Cuban classics, served in humongous portions, are what makes this place so good. Hence, you'll need several visits to appreciate the excellent breaded prawns, stewed rabbit, and chicken in pineapple sauce. The restaurant is camouflaged beneath Centro Habana's decaying facades and enjoys a dark, crowded and frigidly air-conditioned interior. A doorman works on crowd control. No bookings.

Nazdarovie
RUSSIAN $$

(Map p78; ☑ 7-860-2947; www.nazdarovie-havana. com; Malecón No 25, btwn Prado & Cárcel; mains USD$7-13; ☺ noon-midnight; ✱) Cuba's 31-year dalliance with bolshevism is relived in this popular restaurant in prime digs overlooking the Malecón. Upstairs, the decor is awash with old Soviet propaganda posters, brotherly photos of Fidel Castro and Nikita Khrushchev, and slightly less bombastic Russian dolls. The menu is in three languages (to get into the real spirit, try ordering in Russian).

Choices are simple but classic: beef stroganoff, chicken Kiev and borscht are all listed and they're all good. For a cocktail, try the James Bond option: a vodka martini (shaken, not stirred). From Russia with love.

Castas y Tal
CUBAN $$

(Map p78; ☑ 7-864-2177; Av de Italia No 51, cnr San Lázaro; mains USD$6-9; ☺ noon-midnight) Finding a balance by attracting Cubans (with economical prices and traditional recipes) and tourists (with creative 'fusion' touches), hip C&T is a bistro-style restaurant encased by the Centro Habana 'hood. High-quality, adventurous food, such as lamb with masala or chicken in orange sauce, is backed up with Cuban classics (lashings of rice and beans are served on the side).

Look out for the blackboard specials and admire the artistic presentation of your food when it arrives.

Barbra Restaurante Bar
INTERNATIONAL $$

(Map p78; ☑ 7-878-1699; Zanja, cnr Lucena; mains USD$8-15; ☺ 10am-11:45pm) Adding a Miami-esque flourish to the time-ravaged streets of Centro Habana, Barbra is a highly ambitious private restaurant that leaves a vivid impression with its polished glasses, formal service and decadent grand piano that anchors a large, glossy interior. The Cuban-Italian food matches the setting, especially if you opt for the peppery beef tenderloin or the extravagant ceviche.

Barbra's location on the cusp of the scruffy Barrio Chino (p87) adds to its diamond-in-the-rough demeanor.

Casa Miglis
SWEDISH $$

(Map p78; ☑ 7-864-1486; www.casamiglis.com; Lealtad No 120, btwn Ánimas & Lagunas; mains USD$6-12; ☺ noon-1am) There are many unusual juxtapositions at this Swedish-Cuban restaurant, hidden inside a battle-scarred tenement, where the cool Scandinavian-style interior is punctuated by the kind of avant-garde art that might have sprung from the mind of Ingmar Bergman. Then there's the food, a smorgasbord of international delights given extra zest by a couple of Swedish classics.

Tuck into toast *skagen* (prawns on toast), ceviche, Mexican chili and the crème de la crème: melt-in-your-mouth meatballs with mashed potato. The owner is a Swedish film director, hence the suspended chairs, empty picture frames, and zany little bar and performance space.

Los Nardos
SPANISH $$

(Map p78; ☑ 7-863-2985; Paseo de Martí No 563; mains USD$4-10; ☺ noon-midnight) Belonging to one of several Spanish aid societies in Havana (in this case the Asturianos), Nardos looks like another distressed Havana tenement from the outside but resembles a dark-wood, dark-lit gentlemen's club within. The Cuban-Spanish food is famously cheap and plentiful and served by speedy, waistcoated staff members. Paella, chicken and pork dishes don't break USD$5. Even the lobster's cheap!

This place was a godsend for Cubans during the Special Period, when private restaurants were practically nonexistent, and it has maintained its relevance, with a new generation of tourists now discovering it. There are actually three eating options in the building, all belonging to the Asturianos society; the folks at street level will point you in the right direction.

Castropol
SPANISH $$

(Map p78; ☑ 7-861-4864; Malecón 107, btwn Genios & Crespo; mains USD$11-14; ☺ noon-midnight) Spanish cultural societies have long had special legal status in Cuba, meaning that their restaurants (even in tougher times) have been able to offer decent food at good prices. Castropol, run by the Asturianos, was once one of the few quality eating joints in Havana and it continues to impress from its pretty perch on the Malecón.

The food, not surprisingly, displays Spanish influences. House paella and Galician octopus star but are backed up by Cuban-style lobster and chicken, both served with plenty of rice and beans. It's private-restaurant quality at state-restaurant prices – the perfect combo.

Restaurante Tien-Tan
CHINESE $$

(Map p78; ☑ 7-863-2081; Cuchillo No 17, btwn Rayo & San Nicolás; meals USD$7-12; ☺ 10:30am-11pm) One of the few authentic Chinese restaurants in Barrio Chino (p87), Tien-Tan (Temple of Heaven) is run by a Chinese-Cuban couple and serves an incredible 130 dishes. Try chop suey with vegetables or chicken with cashews and sit outside in action-packed Cuchillo, a narrow pedestrianized alley replete with cheap restaurants.

★La Guarida
INTERNATIONAL $$$

(Map p78; ☑ 7-866-9047; www.laguarida.com; Concordia No 418, btwn Gervasio & Escobar; mains USD$15-22; ☺ noon-4pm & 6pm-midnight) Only in Havana! The entrance to the city's most legendary private restaurant greets you like a scene out of a 1940s film noir. A decapitated statue lies at the bottom of a grand but dilapidated staircase that leads past lines of drying clothes to a wooden door, beyond which lie multiple culinary surprises.

La Guarida began to acquire its lofty reputation in the 1990s, when it was used as a location for the Oscar-nominated *Fresa y chocolate*. Regularly refined in the years since, the food is still up there with Havana's best, with the restaurant's pioneering brand of *nueva cocina cubana* driving both classic dishes (*ropa vieja*; shredded beef) and those that are unusual for Cuba (lamb tikka masala). Reservations recommended.

San Cristóbal
CUBAN $$$

(Map p78; ☑ 7-867-9109; San Rafael, btwn Campanario & Lealtad; meals USD$10-19; ☺ noon-midnight Mon-Sat) San Cristóbal was knocking out fine food long before the US president dropped by in March 2016, although the publicity attending Barack Obama's visit probably didn't hurt. Crammed into one of Centro Habana's grubbier streets, the restaurant has a museum-worthy interior crowded with old photos, animal hides, and a Santería altar flanked by images of Antonio Maceo and José Martí.

The menu is Cuban with a touch of Spain, and superbly prepared dishes are usually driven home with a complimentary glass of house rum. Obama had the *solomillo* (sirloin steak), while the First Lady had *tentación habanero* (fajitas with fried plantains). Since their visit, many other dignitaries have dined here.

✖ Vedado

Vedado's culinary scene is an evolving feast with more adventurous private restaurants opening all the time. It currently rivals Playa as Havana's (and Cuba's) top culinary district.

El Biky
CAFETERIA $

(Map p90; ☑ 7-870-6515; www.elbiky.com; cnr Calzada de la Infanta & San Lázaro; mains USD$4-11; ☺ 8am-midnight) Arriving like a breath of fresh air half a decade ago, Biky helped reinvent Havana's evolving brunch-lunch scene with its affordable quick-fire food, served in a modern cafe-restaurant hung with retro pre-revolution photos. It was so successful that it has since morphed into a 'gastronomic complex,' adding a cool bar and Havana's best bakery next door.

Cafetería Pilón
CAFE $

(Map p90; ☑ 5-323-2552; Calle 21, btwn Calles L & M; breakfast & snacks USD$3-6; ☺ 8am-10pm) Havana was once something of a desert for desserts – bad news for travelers who can't live without a 4pm appointment with a slice of chocolate cake. But help has arrived in the form of cafes such as Pilón, which are happy to fill those awkward dining gaps with brunches, all-day ice cream and the vitally important *merienda* (afternoon snack).

The waffles go down well at brunch, the ice cream melts nicely into a *sueño* (dream) milkshake, and the cakes (large, sweet and satisfying) pair perfectly with coffee.

Camino al Sol
VEGETARIAN $

(Map p90; Calle 3 No 363, btwn Paseo & Calle 2; mains USD$1-5; ☺10am-6pm Mon-Sat; 🖊) A decade ago Cuba and vegetarianism were about as compatible as Ronald Reagan and Leonid Brezhnev (ie: not very), but tastes have developed and the times they are a changin'. The completely meat-free Camino del Sol, while still a rarity in Havana, makes imaginative quiches, soups, pies and house-made pasta and displays them in a deli counter out front.

The pasta can be topped with several pesto-like sauces or taken home dry, or you can select something homemade from the deli and enjoy it in the bright, Ikea-style interior. Everything on the menu is under USD$5.

La Catedral
INTERNATIONAL $

(Map p90; 🖊7-830-0793; Calle 8 No 106, btwn Calzada & Calle 5; meals USD$4-6; ☺8am-11pm) It's not anywhere near the cathedral (p67), nor does it look particularly ecclesial – but no matter. The best thing about La Catedral is that, by offering very reasonable prices, it attracts a local Cuban clientele and not just visitors. The restaurant tackles a number of culinary genres, including pizza, burgers and a tremendous *tres leches* cake, and serves big portions.

If the size of the dishes defeats you, you can have them bagged up to go.

Topoly
IRANIAN $

(Map p90; 🖊7-832-3224; Calle 23 No 669, cnr Calle D; small plates USD$4-7; ☺10am-midnight) Cuba finds solidarity with Iran in Havana's first and still only Iranian restaurant, corralled in a lovely colonnaded mansion on arterial Calle 23. Sit on the wraparound porch beneath iconic prints of Gandhi, José Martí and Che Guevara, and enjoy pureed eggplant, lamb *brochetas* (shish kebabs), fantastic coffee, and tea in ornate silver pots.

Razones y Motivos
CUBAN $

(Map p90; 🖊7-832-8732; Calle F No 63, btwn Calles 3 & 5; mains USD$4-7; ☺noon-midnight) This two-piece restaurant has an open terrace upstairs (Motivos) with a barbecue and a no-frills international menu, and an air-conditioned space downstairs (Razones) plying slightly more upscale food, including steak. Neither is particularly fancy, and the reasonable prices attract a mainly Cuban clientele. The chefs do interesting things with lobster, flavoring it with pineapple sauce or coffee extract.

Woow Snack Bar
INTERNATIONAL $

(Map p90; Calle L No 414, cnr Calle 25; snacks USD$3-8; ☺11am-midnight) In a country where ordering food used to be a rather taxing experience, Woow makes it incredibly easy. It combines a handy location on Vedado's main crossroads, a bilingual menu, plenty of options for snacks (tacos) or bigger plates (a USD$20 fixed menu including one drink), excellent coffee and cake, ice-cold beer, and more than a passing nod to vegetarianism.

La Chuchería
AMERICAN $

(Map p90; Calle 1, btwn Calles C & D; snacks USD$2-7; ☺8:30am-midnight) Clinging to its perch close to the Malecón, this sleek sports bar looks as though it has floated across the straits from Florida like a returning exile. But what's run-of-the-mill in Miami is still vaguely exotic in Havana, as the tables of enthusiastic Cubans tucking into leafy salads, bumper sandwiches and stupendous ice cream and fruit milkshakes attest.

Better still, La Chuchería is cheap, quick and well air-conditioned. If you can handle the unimaginative reggaeton/Latin-pop videos played on repeat, pull up a plastic chair and observe how the line between *socialismo* and *capitalismo* is becoming ever more blurred.

Toke Infanta y 25
BURGERS $

(Map p90; 🖊7-836-3440; cnr Calzada de la Infanta & Calle 25; snacks USD$2-4; ☺7am-midnight) Buried amid the bruised edifices of Calzada de la Infanta on the border of Vedado and Centro Habana, Toke is a simple cafe serving economical *hamburguesas* (hamburgers), strong coffee and chocolate brownies any time of the day or night. It's become known as a gay-friendly spot due to its location next to a couple of nightclubs.

Coppelia
ICE CREAM $

(Map p90; cnr Calles 23 & L; ice cream from CUP$40; ☺10am-9:30pm Tue-Sat) Havana's celebrated ice-cream parlor, housed in a flying-saucer-like structure in a Vedado park, is as celebrated as much for its queues as for its ice cream. Insanely popular since it opened in 1966 (lasting through some very rough economic times), this state-run institution is about far more than mere ice cream.

Relationships have been forged here, fledgling novels drafted, birthday parties celebrated and Miami-bound escape plots hatched. The ultimate accolade came in 1993, when the Coppelia served as a location and major plot device in the Oscar-nominated

Cuban film *Fresa y chocolate* (the title alludes to two flavors of Coppelia ice cream: strawberry and chocolate).

Although there are better privately run ice-cream makers in Havana these days, the Coppelia remains part of city folklore, a place where you're guaranteed to meet Cubans at their leisure, either in the queue or at one of the compulsorily shared tables inside.

★ **Café Laurent** INTERNATIONAL **$$**
(Map p90; 7-832-6890; Calle M No 257, 5th fl, btwn Calles 19 & 21; mains USD$8-16; ⊙ noon-midnight) Talk about a hidden gem. The unsigned Café Laurent is a sophisticated fine-dining restaurant encased, incongruously, in a glaringly ugly 1950s apartment block next to the Focsa building (p94). Starched white tablecloths, polished glasses and lacy drapes furnish the bright modernist interior, while seafood risotto and artistically presented pork sautéed with dry fruit and red wine headline the Cuban-Spanish menu.

Take the creaky lift up five floors for a culinary surprise.

El Cimarrón CUBAN **$$**
(Map p90; www.elcimarron-cuba.com/paladar; Calle 14 No 1001, cnr Calle 19; mains USD$9-13; ⊙ 9am-midnight;) Family-run farm-to-table restaurant and social project that hosts evening *peñas* (music and dance performances), organizes cooking classes, and oversees an on-site casa particular. El Cimarrón (the name means 'runaway slave') wears many hats and succeeds on every level. There's a strong Afro-Cuban vibe in the art, bamboo furniture and percussive instruments, but the food's steadfastly *criolla*, with good vegetarian options.

Opera INTERNATIONAL **$$**
(Map p90; 7-831-2255; www.operahabana.com; Calle 5 No 204, btwn Calles E & F; mains USD$9-13; ⊙ noon-3pm & 7-10pm Wed-Mon;) Hitting the high notes of Cuban-Italian cuisine, Opera is housed in a colonnaded villa with a billiard table in the front room and the strains of *Carmen* or *Aida* fluttering over the sound system. The food is equally dramatic and embraces the Italian 'Slow Food' philosophy, encompassing homemade gnocchi stuffed with yucca and rabbit cooked in Bucanero beer.

Vegetarians are well catered for here. The eggplant-ratatouille appetizer provides a good overture and the fruit tartlet is a perfect coda. The wine list is extensive, but

sitting outside on a hot night it's hard to go past the sangria or a classic spritz.

Casa Mia Paladar CUBAN **$$**
(Map p90; 7-832-9735; Calle 1 No 103, btwn Calles C & D; mains USD$9-14; ⊙ 11:30am-11pm;) Rather than blinding you with fancy decor, clean-lined Casa Mia, abutting the Malecón, saves its surprises for the food, a simple menu that rests proudly on the classic foundations of Cuban cooking. The highlight in a medley of standouts is the *cerdo* cooked Pinar del Río style, which, as locals will tell you, is the melt-in-your-mouth pinnacle of Cuban pork. Back it up with sides of *moros y cristianos* (rice and beans) and fried plantains to enjoy the full fruits of the Cuban countryside in the heart of the city. The discreet but efficient table service is up there with the best in Havana.

La Cocina de Esteban INTERNATIONAL **$$**
(Map p90; 7-832-9649; www.lacocinade esteban.com; Calle L, cnr Calle 21; mains USD$9-15; ⊙ noon-midnight) A three-way explosion of Cuban, Italian and Spanish cuisine is guaranteed at this salubrious spot slap-bang in the middle of Vedado's hotel quarter. Bank on fine interpretations of risotto, pasta and grilled lobster. The venue is a regal mansion with inside and garden seating (and a fine rendition of Diego Velázquez' *Los borrachos* on the wall). Service is light on its feet, and lovely musical duos serenade diners in the evening.

Restaurante Habana Blues CUBAN **$$**
(Map p90; 7-835-6545; Calle H No 405, btwn Calles 17 & 19; mains USD$5-11; ⊙ noon-11:30pm) The dark, bluesy interior is backlit by a fabulous 3D mural of Havana's Morro castle (p98) and the waitstaff are all working actors from Cuban TV (check their caricature portraits in the entrance vestibule). First impressions set a high benchmark in this only-in-Havana restaurant that's popular with Cubans keen to enjoy economical plates of spicy prawns and caramelized ribs.

The restaurant is named for and pays homage to the 2005 movie *Habana Blues*, about two rock musicians struggling to make it during the Special Period, and much of the decor reflects the film. Reservations recommended.

El Idilio CUBAN **$$**
(Map p90; 7-830-7921; cnr Calles G & 15; meals USD$6-15; ⊙ noon-midnight) A bold, adventurous neighborhood joint with checked tablecloths, Idilio epitomizes the Cuban

culinary scene as it spreads its wings and flies. Anything goes here: pasta, ceviche and Cuban standards, or opt for the seafood medley, peeled off the barbecue before your very eyes.

Atelier
CUBAN $$$

(Map p90; ☑ 7-836-2025; Calle 5 No 511/Altos, btwn Paseo & Calle 2; meals USD$15-25; ⊗ noon-midnight) The first thing that hits you at Atelier is the stupendous wall art: huge, thought-provoking, religious-tinged paintings. Equally arresting is the antique wooden ceiling that might have been ripped from a *mudéjar* church, plus the terra-cotta roof terrace and old-school elegance. Eventually you'll get around to the food: Cuban with a French influence and scribbled onto an ever-changing menu.

Worth contemplating are the duck confit, rabbit, octopus salad or lobster tail (the specialty), all served on an interesting mélange of glass and china plates.

Decameron
INTERNATIONAL $$$

(Map p90; ☑ 7-832-2444; Línea No 753, btwn Paseo & Calle 2; mains USD$12-18; ⊗ noon-midnight; ☑) Nondescript from the outside, but far prettier within – thanks largely to its famous collection of antique clocks (don't be late, now!) – the Decameron is a stalwart *paladar* (privately owned restaurant) that was always good, still is good and probably always will be good. The food is Cuban with international inflections. People rave about the savory tuna tart, risotto and swordfish.

Le Chansonnier
FRENCH $$$

(Map p90; ☑ 7-832-1576; www.lechansonnier habana.com; Calle J No 257, btwn Calles 13 & 15; meals USD$12-20; ⊗ 12:30pm-12:30am) A great place to dine if you can find it (there's no sign), hidden in a faded mansion turned private restaurant with a revamped interior that is dramatically more avant-garde than the neoclassical facade. Food is served in various rooms inside. French wine and French flavors shine in house specialties such as rabbit with mustard, duck terrine and spare ribs.

Opening times can vary and it's often busy; phone ahead.

VIP Havana
MEDITERRANEAN $$$

(Map p90; ☑ 7-832-0178; Calle 9 No 454, btwn Calles E & F; mains USD$12-18; ⊗ noon-midnight) You don't have to be a very important person to eat at VIP Havana, but it probably helps. This is Havana posing as Miami, with a large central bar, drink shelves backlit with neon

striplights, and old black-and-white movies (including those of adopted hero Charlie Chaplin) running silently on a massive screen that takes up an entire wall.

VIP's atmosphere manages to be refined but not at all snobby, while the food dazzles with its Cuban lobster, Spanish-style tapas (including croquettes and Spanish omelet) and a lauded paella that comes in six varieties. It's recently added a garden space, the Rincón Criollo, with breezier pews.

✗ Playa & Marianao

Playa has been a bastion of some of Cuba's best private restaurants since the 1990s, and many of the stalwarts continue to impress despite an abundance of newer competition. There are also some surprisingly good state-run restaurants, many of them developed to satisfy the taste buds of diplomatic staff. It's worth the taxi fare of USD$10 to USD$15 from the city center to eat out here.

La Casa del Gelato
ICE CREAM $

(Map p96; ☑ 5-242-0870; cnr Av 1 & Calle 46, Miramar; ice cream USD$2-4; ⊗ 11am-11pm; ⊛) One of a small number of privately run ice-cream makers in Havana, this was one of the first in on the act and it's still one of the best. Unlike those closer to the city center, it has plenty of seating inside and out and, in addition to a rich array of flavors, sells cakes, sandwiches and Nespresso coffee.

La Carboncita
ITALIAN $

(Map p96; Av 3 No 3804, btwn Calles 38 & 40, Miramar; pasta & pizza USD$8-12; ⊗ noon-midnight) Small, discreet Miramar house turned Italian restaurant, with indoor and outdoor front-porch seating as well as a bar set up in what was formerly the garage. The pasta is homemade. Choose your varietal (ravioli, fettuccine) and then your sauce (there are more than 20 flavors, including vodka). The thin-crust pizzas are good and people speak glowingly of the 'flan' dessert.

El Palenque
INTERNATIONAL $

(Map p96; ☑ 7-208-8167; cnr Av 17A & Calle 190, Cubanacán; meals USD$3-10; ⊗ 10am-10pm) A huge place next to the **Pabexpo exhibition center** (Map p96; cnr Av 17 & Calle 180, Cubanacán) that sprawls beneath a series of open-sided thatched *bohíos* (traditional Cuban huts), Palenque offers an extensive menu at prices that attract Cubans and visitors alike. The cuisine is primarily Cuban, with locals and conference attendees tucking into roast pork, snapper or, for those with funds, lobster *mariposa* (USD$22).

Pan.com
FAST FOOD $

(Map p96; ☑ 7-204-4232; cnr Av 7 & Calle 26, Miramar; snacks USD$1-4; ☺ 10am-midnight) In Mc-Donald's-free Havana, Pan.com is about as fast as food gets. This small, state-run Cuban chain does hearty sandwiches (on proper Cuban bread!), cheap burgers and ice-cream milkshakes to die for. Join the diplomats under the breezy front canopy.

El Aljibe
CARIBBEAN $$

(Map p96; ☑ 7-204-1583/4; Av 7, btwn Calles 24 & 26, Miramar; mains USD$12-15; ☺ noon-midnight) Aljibe is a legend in Havana: a restaurant whose original incarnation predated the revolution and whose second coming in the 1990s revived its most renowned dish, the obligatory *pollo asado* (roast chicken in a bitter-orange sauce), served with as-much-as-you-can-eat helpings of white rice, black beans, fried plantain, French fries and salad for only USD$12.

Aljibe mark II has survived for 25 years. Even though it's run by the state, its consistent mix of quality food and zippy service is music to the ears of the diplomats bivouacked in the embassies nearby.

Paladar Vista Mar
SEAFOOD $$

(Map p96; ☑ 7-203-8328; www.restaurantevistamar.com; Av 1 No 2206, btwn Calles 22 & 24, Miramar; mains USD$10-18; ☺ noon-midnight Mon-Sat) The Vista Mar is one of half a dozen or so Havana *paladares* (private restaurants) that have been around since the 1990s, and it continues to excel despite competition. It inhabits a 1950s-era family home, facing the ocean and embellished by a beautiful infinity pool. The food is upmarket but classic, featuring ceviche, octopus and pork loin.

Amir Shisha
LEBANESE $$

(Map p96; ☑ 5-909-6313; Calle 40A, btwn Avs 1 & 3, Miramar; mains USD$8-12; ☺ noon-midnight) Lebanese food has recently gained traction in Havana, with several openings, including this restaurant in a tranquil glass-fronted house that evokes 1960s LA. Spinning the Middle Eastern magic are dishes such as *kafta* (oven-baked minced beef), *shish taouk* (marinated chicken kebab) and *shawarma* (shaved meat in pita bread), served against a backing track of Arabic-style music and dancing.

3 Chinitos
CAFETERIA $$

(Map p96; ☑ 7-202-4408; Calle 10, btwn Avs 3 & 5, Miramar; pizzas USD$6-15; ☺ 24hr; ☒) A popular place to eat well-loaded pizza, with cozy, old-fashioned touches such as vintage radios and old sewing machines that double as outdoor tables. One of the few places open 24/7 in the city, it's a go-to for families as well as night owls craving a late snack.

Siete Días
INTERNATIONAL $$

(Map p96; ☑ 7-209-6889; cnr Av 1 & Calle 14, Miramar; mains USD$8-14; ☺ noon-midnight) This seaside spot has a very decent menu, but it's really the ambience, location and view that make it so memorable. Housed in a beautiful mansion, the outdoor dining room–bar sits on Playa de 16, a lovely city beach known by anyone who grew up in Havana. It's a perfect place to watch the sunset with a drink in hand.

Casa Española
SPANISH $$

(Map p96; ☑ 7-206-9644; cnr Calle 26 & Av 7, Miramar; meals USD$8-16; ☺ noon-11pm) A medieval parody built in the Batista era by the silly-rich Gustavo Gutiérrez y Sánchez, this crenellated castle in Miramar has found new life as a Spanish-themed food complex cashing in on the Don Quixote legend. There are three options here: a restaurant, a cafe and a barbecue. The former is the most consciously Spanish, serving paella straight from the pan.

Papa's Complejo Turístico
CARIBBEAN $$

(cnr Av 5 & Calle 248, Santa Fé; meals USD$5-11; ☺ noon-3am) There's all sorts of stuff going on at this joint at Marina Hemingway, from beer-swilling boatmen to warbling *American Idol* wannabes hogging the karaoke machine. The eating options are equally varied, with a posh Chinese place (with dress code) and an outdoor *ranchón* (rustic, open-sided restaurant).

Dos Gardenias
CARIBBEAN $$

(Map p96; cnr Av 7 & Calle 28, Miramar; mains USD$7-10; ☺ noon-2am) Less a conventional eating space and more a tourist complex, Dos Gardenias sports two main restaurants (choose between a grill and a pasta place), a couple of shops and a music hot spot that's famous for its *boleros* (danceable Cuban ballads). The better singers start belting out their ballads soon after midnight, when punters waste no time migrating from the dinner tables to the dance floor.

THE RISE & FALL OF HAVANA'S MAFIA EMPIRE

There's a scene in Francis Ford Coppola's *The Godfather Part II* when mobster Hyman Roth, convening a meeting on the roof of a luxurious Havana hotel, is presented with a birthday cake decorated with a map of Cuba. In an act loaded with symbolism, Roth cuts into the cake with a knife and looks on calmly as his butlers serve it to his assembled Mafia guests.

While the film might be a thinly veiled work of fiction, the dramatic cake analogy is eerily accurate. Between 1952 and 1959 the Mafia, along with its opportunistic enabler Fulgencio Batista, divided up Cuba as if it were a large, creamy gâteau, turning Havana into a city of gambling and garishness, and inadvertently fueling the resentment that led to the rise of Fidel Castro.

Cuba's on-off marriage with the American Mafia first took root in the 1920s, when Prohibition in the US sent pleasure-seeking Americans flocking south to line up their rum cocktails in the bars of sensuous Havana. Al Capone was an early convert, financing an illegal molasses-supply racket for illicit Cuban rum factories. But the real deal – high-stakes gambling – didn't take off until after WWII.

Meyer Lansky and notorious Mafia don Charles 'Lucky' Luciano were the main second-phase instigators. In December 1946 the two mobsters coordinated the world's biggest ever Cosa Nostra get-together in Havana's Hotel Nacional under the cover of a Frank Sinatra concert. Hatching a plan to open the Cuban capital to narcotics, prostitution and large-scale gambling, the duo enlisted the clandestine support of ex-president Batista.

The plan reached fruition in March 1952 when a Batista coup toppled the government of Carlos Prío Socarrás and enacted laws that gave organized crime free rein in Cuba's corrupt capital. Over the next seven years Havana became a gambling and vice mecca to rival Las Vegas, a licentious vacation destination beloved by high-rolling tourists and the ever-grinning Batista (who personally bagged between 10% and 30% of all casino profits), but increasingly despised by anyone in Cuba who wasn't rich, American or part of the Mafia.

Grossly underestimating the popular force of Castro, the Mob was largely taken by surprise when the khaki-clad *barbudos* rolled into Havana in January 1959. Greeting them gruffly at the door of the Hotel Capri, famous Hollywood actor and Mafia stooge George Raft is said to have furiously slammed the door in their faces. The bravado wasn't to last. The Mafia might have been adept at dealing with random assassinations and extortion rackets, but a full-scale popular uprising was a different matter. With Che Guevara homing in on the city limits, Havana's residents took to the streets, focusing their ire on the casinos and clubs that had been fleecing them for so long. Hotels were ransacked, their slot machines and roulette wheels dragged outside to be trashed. One errant farmer even set his pigs loose inside the reception area of Meyer Lansky's million-dollar Hotel Riviera, where they unceremoniously crapped all over the furniture.

With the casinos in ruins and high-spending tourists flying back across the water to Florida, Lansky and his embezzling cronies packed their suitcases full of money, called their private planes and beat a hasty retreat to the US, tails between their legs. The era of loose morals and decadent gambling was over as quickly as it had begun.

★ **La Fontana** BARBECUE $$$
(Map p96; ☑ 7-202-8337; Av 3A No 305, Miramar; mains USD$13-28; ☉ noon-midnight) La Fontana, encased in a hard-to-find but beautiful house in Playa, is one of the best restaurants in Havana, a position it has enjoyed pretty much since its inception in 1995 (back in Cuba's culinary Stone Age). The secret: the restaurant has progressed with the times, adding space, dishes and multiple quirks such as fish ponds and live jazz.

These days there are several areas in which to drink and dine, each with a different ambience. The centerpiece is a brick-lined terrace and open grill, but there's also a trendy chill-out bar that mixes potent cocktails.

Fontana is famed for its barbecue or, more to the point, its full-on charcoal grill. Huge portions of meat and fish are served, so go easy on the starters, which include lobster ceviche, tuna tartare, and beef carpaccio with rocket.

La Corte del Príncipe ITALIAN $$$
(Map p96; ☑ 5-255-9091; cnr Av 9 & Calle 74, Miramar; mains USD$15-20; ☉ noon-3pm & 7pm-midnight Tue-Sun) An out-of-the-way location

has never seemed to hinder this restaurant, which has developed a loyal following over the years. The reason? It's probably the most authentic Italian joint in town, serving homemade pasta, eggplant parmigiana, epic prawns and focaccia (but not pizza). It even keeps Italian hours, closing briefly for an afternoon siesta.

La Cocina de Lilliam

FUSION $$$

(Map p96; 7-209-6514; www.lacocinadelilliam. com; Calle 48 No 1311, btwn Avs 13 & 15, Miramar; meals USD$15-30; noon-3pm & 7-11pm Tue-Sat) One of the oldest private restaurants in Havana (since 1994) and one that seems to have survived all the aches and pains of Cuba's economic roller coaster, entertaining illustrious guests along the way (Jimmy Carter came here in 2002).

The setting is a secluded villa and garden in residential Playa, and the food is a mélange of Cuban staples mixed with culinary rarities that range from salmon soufflé to stewed lamb. Though the private restaurant sector has exploded since 2011, Lilliam has maintained its prominence with classy service, creative food and a romantic setting amid trickling fountains and tropical ferns.

La Esperanza

INTERNATIONAL $$$

(Map p96; 7-202-4361; Calle 16 No 105, btwn Avs 1 & 3, Miramar; meals USD$8-17; 7-11pm Mon-Sat) La Esperanza recalls those old-school *paladar* (private restaurant) days when you felt you were dining in someone's home, and here you essentially are. The interior of this vine-covered house is a riot of quirky antiques, old portraits and refined 1940s furnishings, while the food includes such exquisite dishes as *pollo luna de miel* (chicken flambéed in rum) and lamb brochettes.

Doctor Café

CUBAN $$$

(Map p96; 7-203-4718; Calle 28, btwn Avs 1 & 3, Miramar; mains USD$12-20; noon-midnight) Ocean-flavored dishes such as ceviche, red snapper and grilled octopus are served in a fern-filled patio or a cooler indoor dining area; this doctor is obviously getting the treatment spot on. The food is from all over the globe, although the fish off the charcoal grill is the highlight. The menu is usually delivered verbally and changes daily.

El Tocororo

CARIBBEAN $$$

(Map p96; 7-202-4530; Calle 18 No 302, Miramar; meals USD$12-35; noon-11:45pm) Once considered one of Havana's finest government-run restaurants, along with El Aljibe (p125), El Tocororo has lost ground to private competition in recent years and is often criticized as overpriced. Nonetheless, the candlelit tables and grandiose interior make a visit worthwhile, while the menu, with such luxuries as lobster tail and pepper steak, still has the ability to surprise.

✖ Regla, Guanabacoa & the Forts

La Brisilla

CUBAN $$

(Cruz Verde, btwn Santa Ana & Segui, Guanabacoa; mains USD$6-11; noon-midnight) Unsignposted, hard to find and consequently almost 100% local, this is a rare private restaurant in Guanabacoa, where the food culture doesn't seem to have moved on much since the not-so-tasty '90s. You'll have to ask the way in Spanish, but the rabbit in red wine and the succulent lobster will please you as much as they'll surprise you.

Restaurante la Divina Pastora

INTERNATIONAL $$

(Map p100; Parque Histórico Militar Morro-Cabaña; mains USD$10-18; noon-11:30pm) Near Dársena de los Franceses and a battery of 18th-century cannons, this dramatically sited waterside restaurant lies in the shadow of La Cabaña fort (p99). Refurbished and reopened in late 2018, it's popular with tour groups and weddings. Fish is the specialty, but the food isn't anywhere near as spectacular as the sunset views.

Paladar Doña Carmela

CUBAN $$$

(Map p100; 7-867-7472; Calle B No 10; mains USD$16-35; noon-11pm) On the eastern side of the harbor in the small community near the forts, this private eating option gets filled up with tourists on their way to the nightly cañonazo ceremony (p105). The food is good but pricey, propped up by dishes such as octopus sautéed in garlic and whole roast pork cooked in a wood oven.

✖ Habana del Este

Pan.com

CAFE $

(Map p102; Av 5, btwn Calles 476 & 478, Guanabo; snacks USD$2-3; 8am-10pm) It's cheap, it's state run and it's pretty gritty inside, but this Cuban fast-food joint in Guanabo lures in locals with hot sandwiches on wonderful crusty Cuban bread that crumbles all over the table when you bite into it. Round off proceedings with a creamy USD$1 milkshake and you'll be more than ready for a hard day at the beach.

Mi Cayito
CUBAN $

(Map p102; ☑ 7-797-1339; Av de las Terrazas, Itabo; mains USD$5-12; ⊙ 10am-5pm) A small bar-restaurant reached via a raised boardwalk that overlooks Laguna Boca Itabo, a small lagoon abutting Playa Boca Ciega, Mi Cayito is a quiet spot surrounded by nature. It sells solid if unremarkable Cuban food.

You can rent kayaks or paddle boats at the dock from USD$1.50 per hour.

★ Ajiaco Café
CUBAN $$

(☑ 7-765-0514; cafeajiaco@gmail.com; Calle 92 No 267, btwn Avs 3E & 5, Cojímar; mains USD$4-12; ⊙ noon-midnight; ☑) 🍴 There are, arguably, two reasons to come to suburban Cojímar: 1) to pursue the ghost of Ernest Hemingway and 2) to visit this farm-to-table restaurant named for a quintessential Cuban stew that headlines a menu of Cuban classics, all executed with rustic creativity.

Here you can order fried chickpeas, pork ribs in a barbecue-and-honey sauce, or a unique shredded-beef and plantain pizza. Service in the open-sided country-style restaurant is exceptional, and the smooth coffee might just be the finest in Cuba.

Best of all, Ajiaco offers cooking classes (USD$50; 10am-1pm) that involve a visit to a nearby *finca* (farm) to choose ingredients, followed by time to prep, cook and eat your selected concoction back at the restaurant. Classes run daily if there are enough people.

Il Piccolo
ITALIAN $$

(Map p102; ☑ 7-796-4300; cnr Av 5 & Calle 502, Guanabo; pizzas USD$8-10; ⊙ noon-11pm) This Guanabo private restaurant has been around for eons and is an open secret among *habaneros*, some of whom consider its thin-crust wood-oven pizzas to be the best in Cuba. Out of the way and a little more expensive than Playas del Este's other numerous pizza joints, it's well worth the journey (take a horse and cart on Av 5).

Restaurante 421
INTERNATIONAL, CUBAN $$

(Map p102; ☑ 5-305-6900; Calle 462 No 911, btwn Avs 9 & 11, Guanabo; mains USD$5-12; ⊙ 9am-1am) Ask a local where to eat in Guanabo and they'll probably direct you up the gentle hill behind the main roundabout to this pleasant perch that has a surprisingly wide selection of Cuban favorites, mixed with international dishes such as paella, rabbit and the inevitable pizza. Sit on the breeze-lapped patio and enjoy the attentive service.

Chicken Little
INTERNATIONAL $$

(Map p102; ☑ 7-796-2351; Calle 504 No 5815, btwn Calles 5B & 5C, Guanabo; mains USD$6-9; ⊙ noon-11pm) Forgive the kitschy name – Chicken Little could yet make it big. Defying Guanabo's ramshackle image, this deluxe restaurant has polite waitstaff with welcome cocktails who'll talk you through a menu of pesto chicken, chicken in orange and honey, and at least a dozen more varieties.

Don Pepe
SEAFOOD $$

(Av de las Terrazas, Playas del Este; mains USD$5-18; ⊙ 10am-11pm) When the Guanabo pizza gets too much, head to this thatched-roof, beach-style restaurant about 50m from the sands of Playa Santa María. It specializes in seafood.

La Terraza de Cojímar
SEAFOOD $$

(☑ 7-766-5151; Calle 152 No 161, Cojímar; meals USD$7-15; ⊙ noon-11pm) Another shrine to the ghost of Hemingway, La Terraza specializes in seafood and does a roaring trade with the hordes of Papa fans who are bused in daily. The food is surprisingly mediocre, although the terrace dining room overlooking the bay is pleasant. More atmospheric is the old bar out front, where mojito prices haven't yet reached El Floridita levels.

🍴 Outer Havana

Casa 1740
CUBAN $

(María Capote, Parque Lenin; mains CUP$50-70; ⊙ 10am-5pm Wed-Sun) One of the quieter eating options in Parque Lenin (p101) is set in a small house south of the lake and is air-conditioned to replicate a chilly day in Canada. Food is straight up *comida criolla* (traditional Cuban). You can't go wrong with the *ropa vieja* (shredded beef) at CUP$50 (USD$2).

Las Ruinas
CARIBBEAN $$

(Cortina de la Presa, Parque Lenin; mains USD$6-10; ⊙ 11am-midnight Tue-Sun) One of Havana's more unusual restaurants, Las Ruinas sits atop the mossy stone ruins of a sugar mill, with classical statues, elegant staircases and a spectacular stained-glass screen by Cuban artist René Portocarrero adding dramatically to the visuals. Like most things in Parque Lenin (p101), it's beloved by Cuban families, who cherish the low prices, traditional food and *Alice in Wonderland* decor.

The restaurant was refurbished in 2017 and is arguably the most interesting feature to grace the park.

☕ Drinking & Nightlife

Havana's cafe scene is going through an interesting stage. Bland international franchises have yet to gain a foothold, but, with more freedom to engage in private business, local entrepreneurs are directing their creativity into a growing number of bohemian bars and cafes.

☕ Habana Vieja

★ **El Dandy** CAFE
(Map p68; ☑7-867-6463; www.bareldandy.com; cnr Brasil & Villegas; ⊙8am-1am) More stylish man-about-town than vain popinjay, El Dandy is an unpretentious cafe by day and a cool cocktail bar by night. A casual greeter shakes your hand at the door, efficient waitstaff take your order at the bar, and trendier-than-you customers pose like peacocks around the marble tables.

★ **Azúcar Lounge** LOUNGE
(Map p68; ☑7-860-6563; Mercaderes No 315; ⊙11am-midnight) From a 2nd-floor balcony, high above the architectural beauty contest that is Plaza Vieja, there's no better place in Cuba to savor a piña colada than Azúcar. With its lounge-y seating, trance-y music and Ikea-meets-avant-garde decor, this is an unashamedly trendy place to hang out, but it never feels exclusive. Tourists, premillennials and self-confessed squares will all feel welcome.

★ **El Chanchullero** BAR
(Map p68; www.el-chanchullero.com; Brasil, btwn Bernaza & Christo; ⊙1pm-midnight) *'Aquí jamás estuvo Hemingway'* (Hemingway was never here) reads the sign outside Chanchullero, with more than a hint of irony. It's a key point. Since the American author never frequented this roguish joint in Plaza del Cristo, the price of cocktails has remained refreshingly low (USD$2.50), meaning you can get as smashed as he once did.

El Chanchullero started as a small bar half a decade ago and, fueled by a recent expansion, it remains popular. Join the line outside. It's well worth the wait.

La Taberna del Son BAR
(Map p68; Brasil 104, btwn Cuba & San Ignacio; ⊙noon-midnight) A hurricane of Cuban energy, this tiny dive just off Plaza Vieja gives at least half of its space over to the nightly band, most of whom are older than the Rolling Stones – and just as energetic. The

crowd is half Cuban, half tourist, but all are armed with a desire to sink *muchos* mojitos. Dancing quickly becomes inevitable.

El Patchanka BAR
(Map p68; ☑7-860-4161; Bernaza No 162; ⊙1pm-1am) Live bands rock the rafters, locals knock back powerful USD$3 mojitos, and earnest travelers banter about Che Guevara's contribution to modern poster art in this gritty dive bar in Plaza del Cristo that looks comfortably lived in. Cultural interaction is the key here. By keeping prices low (lobster for USD$9), Patchanka attracts everyone.

The walls are decorated with graffiti from around the world, along with a cartoonish pirate ship sporting the name 'Patchanka' – the Spanish term for fusion-rock.

Art Pub BAR
(Map p68; ☑7-861-5014; Brasil No 306, btwn Aguacate & Compostela; ⊙noon-11pm) Worth incorporating into a neighborhood bar crawl, even if the 'pub' moniker is a bit misleading (the only beer it has is bottled Heineken). The eclectic interior is a potpourri of Cuban flags, retro Havana photos and random British motifs (football scarves, dartboards). The rum cocktails are potent enough, though, and, like all bona fide pubs it serves good food.

Espacios Old Fashioned BAR
(Map p68; ☑7-861-3895; Amargura No 258, btwn Habana & Compostela; ⊙noon-midnight) An offshoot of the hip Miramar bar (p132), Espacios inhabits a smaller abode in Habana Vieja but, like its bigger sibling, adorns its walls with eye-widening avant-garde art. You can eat here, but it's best as a place to sink a glass or cup of something containing caffeine, alcohol or perhaps just juice while checking out the art – and artists.

La Bodeguita del Medio BAR
(Map p68; Empedrado No 207; ⊙11am-midnight) Made famous thanks to the rum-swilling exploits of Ernest Hemingway (who by association instantly sends prices soaring), this is Havana's most celebrated bar. A visit has become de rigueur for tourists who haven't yet cottoned on to the fact that the mojitos are better and (far) cheaper elsewhere.

Patrons have included Salvador Allende, Fidel Castro, Nicolás Guillén, Harry Belafonte and Nat King Cole, all of whom have left their autographs on La Bodeguita's wall – along with thousands of others (save for the big names, the walls are repainted every few months). These days the clientele is less luminous, with package tourists from Varadero outnumbering bohemians.

El Floridita
BAR

(Map p68; Obispo No 557; ⊘11am-midnight) El Floridita was a favorite of expat Americans long before Hemingway dropped by in the 1930s, hence the name (which means 'Little Florida'). Bartender Constante Ribalaigua invented the daiquiri here soon after WWI, but it was Hemingway who popularized it and ultimately the bar christened a drink in his honor: the Papa Hemingway Special (a grapefruit-flavored daiquiri).

Hemingway's record – legend has it – was 13 doubles in one sitting. Any attempt to equal it at current prices (USD$6 for a shot) will cost you a small fortune – and a huge hangover. Inside there's a statue of the sage, usually commandeered by bevies of daiquiri-sinking tourists taking selfies.

Museo del Chocolate
CAFE

(Map p68; cnr Amargura & Mercaderes; ⊘9am-9pm) Chocolate addicts, beware: this state-run museum-cafe in Habana Vieja's heart is a lethal dose of chocolate, truffles and yet more chocolate (all made on the premises). Situated – with no irony intended – on Calle Amargura (literally, Bitterness St), it's more a cafe than a museum, with a cluster of marble tables set amid chocolate paraphernalia.

Not surprisingly, everything on the menu contains one all-pervading ingredient: have it hot, cold, white, dark, rich or smooth – the stuff is divine, whichever way you choose.

La Factoria Plaza Vieja
BAR

(Map p68; cnr San Ignacio & Muralla; ⊘11am-midnight) Havana's original microbrewery occupies a boisterous corner of Plaza Vieja and sells smooth, cold, homemade beer at sturdy wooden benches set up outside on the cobbles or in a bright, noisy beer hall. Gather a group together and you'll get one of three beer varieties (light, amber or dark) in a tall plastic tube with a tap at the bottom.

Café Taberna
BAR

(Map p68; cnr Brasil & Mercaderes; ⊘noon-midnight) Founded in 1772 and glowing after a 21st-century makeover, this drinking and eating establishment is a favorite of cruisers and tour groups, who prop up the long, long bar and sink a few cocktails before dinner. The music, which gets swinging around 8pm, doffs its cap more often than not to one-time resident mambo king Benny Moré. Skip the food.

Bar Dos Hermanos
BAR

(Map p68; San Pedro No 304; ⊘24hr) This once-seedy, now polished bar by the docks broadcasts a list of former rum-slugging patrons on a plaque by the door: Federico García Lorca, Marlon Brando, Errol Flynn and Ernest Hemingway (of course) among them. With its long wooden bar furnished with enough Havana Club rum bottles to inebriate an army of Hemingways, it still spins a little magic.

Café París
BAR

(Map p68; Obispo No 202; ⊘24hr) Rough-hewn Habana Vieja dive bar, with outdoor seating, a gregarious, tourist-heavy atmosphere and a constant diet of live music. On good nights (which is *most* nights), the rum flows and spontaneous dancing erupts.

Monserrate Bar
BAR

(Map p68; Obrapía No 410; ⊘noon-midnight) A couple of doors down from the famous Hemingway drinking haunt of El Floridita, Monserrate is a Hemingway-free zone, meaning the daiquiris are half the price.

Centro Habana

★ Café Arcángel
CAFE

(Map p78; ☑5-268-5451; www.cafearcangel.com; Concordia No 57; ⊘8:15am-6pm Mon-Sat, to 1pm Sun) Excellent coffee, fine croissants, suave non-reggaeton music and Charlie Chaplin movies playing on a loop in a scarred Centro Habana apartment – what more could you want?

Rooftop Bar, Hotel Inglaterra
BAR

(Map p78; Paseo de Martí No 416, btwn San Rafael & Neptuno; ⊘7pm-late) The rooms may have lost their luster, but the Inglaterra's open-air roof terrace remains one of the best free-entry bars in Havana for live music and evening libations. Turn up to watch the sunset and stick around as the resident band sends its syncopated rhythms floating over Parque Central (p86) with the baroque Gran Teatro theater (p85) sitting pretty in the background.

Siá Kará Café
BAR

(Map p78; ☑7-867-4084; www.facebook.com/siakaracafecuba; Barcelona, cnr Industria No 502; ⊘noon-2am) In Starbucks-free Havana, every cafe is individual and Siá Kará exhibits its character with graffiti-covered tables, an old tie collection and a parody of the *Mona Lisa* flipping the bird. Although ostensibly a bar-cafe, it serves everything from Varadero lobster to crusty chicken sandwiches. The cushioned benches under the stairs are the perfect place to crack open a thick novel.

Cafe El Louvre
CAFE

(Map p78; Paseo de Martí No 416, btwn San Rafael & Neptuno; ☉10am-midnight; 🛜) The animated sidewalk cafe at the Hotel Inglaterra (p111) is an open terrace bar where mojitos and Cuba libres are served well before noon. It's the perfect place to watch Havana's vibrant Parque Central (p86) to the soundtrack of the live bands that play here daily. Cocktails cost USD$4 to USD$7. In April 1879 El Louvre was where the young José Martí gave a fiery speech that jump-started the pro-independence movement.

Sloppy Joe's
BAR

(Map p78; 📞7-866-7157; cnr Agramonte & Ánimas; cocktails USD$4-8; ☉noon-1am Sun-Thu, to 3am Fri & Sat) Opened by young Spanish immigrant José García (aka 'Joe') in 1919, this bar earned its name for its dodgy sanitation and soggy *ropa vieja* (shredded-beef) sandwich. Legendary among expats before the revolution, it closed in the '60s after a fire but was reincarnated in 2013 behind the same noble neoclassical facade. And it's still serving decent cocktails and soggy sandwiches.

Granted, it's touristy these days, but the interior is true to its predecessor, as old black-and-white photos (most of which feature Frank Sinatra with a glass in his hand) testify.

🍸 Vedado

⭐Belview ArtCafé
CAFE

(Map p90; 📞7-832-5429; www.facebook.com/ belviewartcafe; Calle 6 No 412, cnr Calle 19; ☉9am-6pm Tue-Sun) Behold the backlit photo art, the sofa shoehorned into the trunk of an American car, and the globes doubling as lampshades. The Belview, bivouacked in a handsome Vedado mansion, is an explosion of thought-provoking art. Once you've worked out that you can order drinks as well as admire the graphics, you can place your order for coffee, cake, cocktails or tapas.

⭐Café Mamainé
BAR

(Map p90; 📞7-832-8328; Calle L No 206, btwn Calles 15 & 17; ☉8am-midnight Mon-Thu, to 3am Fri-Sun) 🖋 Art and coffee go together like Fidel and Che in this wonderfully reimagined mansion with an interior that features

revolving local art. Seating is arranged over a wooden mezzanine or shady side patio, the coffee is pleasantly strong, and the clientele is a mix of young students and people who look as though they've just performed at the Fábrica de Arte Cubano (p132).

Café Madrigal
BAR

(Map p90; Calle 17 No 302, btwn Calles 2 & 4; ☉6pm-2am Tue-Sun) Vedado flirts with bohemia in this dimly lit gay-friendly bar that might have materialized from Paris' Latin Quarter in the days of James Joyce and Ernest Hemingway. Order a *tapita* (small tapa) and a cocktail, and retire to the atmospheric art nouveau terrace, where the buzz of nighttime conversation competes with the racket of vintage American cars rattling past below.

La Esencia
BAR

(Map p90; 📞7-836-3031; www.facebook.com/ laesenciacuba; Calle B No 153, btwn Calzada & Línea; ☉6pm-3am Sat-Thu, from 5pm Fri) Housed in an 1880s mansion, La Esencia is among Havana's trendiest bars due to its ambience, retro-style decoration and consistent cocktails. It also operates as a full restaurant, but the tapas and pizzas are the best bet to accompany your next round of drinks. Friday's happy hour (5pm to 8pm) is popular among young students and professionals.

The music selection combines throwback and current video clips, Cuban all-time hits and international singles. At research time it hosted an LGBT night on Monday and karaoke on Wednesday.

Juguera de 6
JUICE BAR

(Map p90; Calle 6, btwn Calles 1 & 3; ☉9am-7pm Mon-Sat, to 1pm Sun) Tucked behind a residential building in sight of the Hotel Meliá Cohiba (p113), this small walk-up bar offers an astounding 97 fresh juice combinations using the best tropical-fruit flavors (including papaya, mango and pineapple) and sometimes vegetables, too. You can stand around with the locals and detox from last night's deep-fried pork for only CUP$6 a glass.

Bar-Restaurante 1830
CLUB

(Map p90; cnr Malecón & Calle 20; ☉noon-1:45am) If you want to salsa dance, this is *the* place to go: after the Sunday-night show literally everyone takes to the floor. It's at the far-western end of the Malecón with a water-facing terrace. Skip the food.

Cuba Libro
CAFE

(Map p90; ☑7-830-5205; www.cubalibrohavana.com; cnr Calles 24 & 19; ☺10am-7pm Mon-Sat; 🖭) ✎ Cafe, English-language bookshop, socially responsible community resource, and a great place for Cubans and non-Cubans to interact: Cuba Libro plays many roles. Hidden in a tranquil part of residential Vedado, it's an ideal spot to find out more about Havana below the radar. Grab a coffee, sink into a hammock in the garden and join the discussion.

Café Fresa y Chocolate
CAFE

(Map p90; Calle 23, btwn Calles 10 & 12; ☺9am-11pm) No ice cream here, just movie memorabilia. This is the HQ of the Cuban Film Institute and a nexus for coffee-quaffing students and art-house movie addicts. It's not fancy, but on the right night (Friday and Saturday) you can debate the merits of Pedro Almodóvar over Martin Scorsese on the pleasant patio before heading next door for a film preview.

Piano Bar Delirio Habanero
CLUB

(Map p90; ☑7-878-4275; cnr Paseo & Calle 39; cover USD$5-10; ☺from 6pm Tue-Sun) This sometimes suave, sometimes frenetic lounge upstairs at Teatro Nacional de Cuba (p135) hosts everything from young rap artists to smooth, improvised jazz. The sharp red-accented bar and performance space abut a wall of glass overlooking Plaza de la Revolución – it's impressive at night with the Martí memorial (p89) and the handsome Che Guevara mural alluringly backlit.

Café Cantante Mi Habana
CLUB

(Map p90; ☑7-879-0710; cnr Paseo & Calle 39; cover USD$10; ☺8pm-3am) Below the Teatro Nacional de Cuba (p135) (side entrance), this hip disco offers live salsa music and dancing as well as bar snacks and food. It has earned a reputation as being *the* place to go to meet cool, trendy Cubans in a laid-back *jinetero* (tout-free) environment. On Saturday it hosts a gay party with drag show called Divino.

No shorts, T-shirts or hats may be worn, and no under-18s are allowed.

Cabaret Las Vegas
CLUB

(Map p90; Calzada de la Infanta No 104, btwn Calles 25 & 27; entry USD$5; ☺10pm-4am) The Vegas was once a rough and slightly seedy local music dive, but these days it's better known for its late-night drag shows and is one of Havana's most reliable gay clubs.

🍺 Playa & Marianao

★ Café Fortuna Joe
BAR

(Map p96; ☑5-413-3706; cnr Calle 24 & Av 1, Miramar; ☺9am-midnight) There are a lot of seriously weird (in a good way) places to drink coffee in Havana, but Café Fortuna Joe stands alone, mainly because of its original seating. Forget the mismatched chairs so beloved by hipsters elsewhere; Fortuna's places to park yourself include a horse carriage, an old car, a bed and a cushioned toilet – no kidding. There's another, smaller Café Fortuna nearby, at Av 3 and Calle 28.

Espacios
COCKTAIL BAR

(Map p96; ☑7-202-2921; Calle 10 No 513, btwn Avs 5 & 7, Miramar; ☺noon-3am) This fabulously chilled tapas bar occupying an unsignposted villa in the diplomatic quarter is where hip *habaneros* come to consume cocktails and art. Inside, the place has the atmosphere of an informal house party, with fashionable factions of Havana's brainy and beautiful gathering in different rooms or holding court in the patio and garden.

There's food available, including wood-fired pizzas, but really Espacios is more about youthful energy, late-night libations and striking avant-garde art.

☆ Entertainment

Although it may have lost its pre-revolutionary reputation as a casino quarter, Vedado is still *the* place for nightlife in Havana. A wealth of high-quality cabaret, jazz, classical music, dance and cinema is on offer. Entertainment in Habana Vieja is emerging from a Rip Van Winkle–like slumber and becoming increasingly hip. Centro's nightlife is edgier and more local.

Live Music
★ Fábrica de Arte Cubano
LIVE PERFORMANCE

(Map p90; ☑7-838-2260; www.fac.cu; cnr Calle 26 & 11; USD$2; ☺8pm-2am Thu-Sun; 🎨) If only every city had a cultural venue as wide-ranging, inclusive and downright revolutionary as Havana's unique art factory. The brainchild of Cuban fusion musician X-Alfonso in 2014, this gallery/live-music venue/inspirational meeting place for anyone who can afford the USD$2 entry fee is where electrifying 'happenings' take place in a cavernous, Bauhaus-like interior.

Forget surly bouncers and elitist VIP passes. The Fábrica is a wonderfully cool

LOCAL KNOWLEDGE

GAY HAVANA

Havana's gay life ebbs and flows, though in recent years the city has become noticeably more open and tolerant. Legally, lesbians enjoy the same rights as gay men, though there is a less evident lesbian scene.

The focus of gay life is on the border of Centro Habana and Vedado in the 'triangle' that stretches between Calzada de la Infanta, Calle L and Calle 23 (La Rampa). Nightlife centers on gay-friendly venues such as the Pico Blanco club (Map p90; Calle O, btwn Calles 23 & 25; cover USD$5-10; ☺ from 9pm) in Hotel St John's and Cabaret Las Vegas (p132), both known for their drag shows. Sandwiched between the two is a pleasant little cafe called Toke Infanta y 25 (p122). Also worth a trip is the Café Cantante Mi Habana (p132) in Cuba's National Theater, which has a gay party on Saturday night. Gay film nights are held at the Instituto Cubano del Arte e Industria Cinematográficos headquarters (p140) in Vedado. Havana's gay beach is Playa Boca Ciega in Habana del Este.

Since 2008 Havana has openly celebrated gay pride with a big parade on May 17.

yet unpretentious place where you're encouraged to meet the performers as well as applaud them. Repertoires are as flexible as they are creative. Expect everything from classical cellists to Cuban rappers to arty T-shirt designers selling their latest creations.

For the best experience, arrive at the Fábrica early (it opens promptly at 8pm) to explore the revolving art exhibits, food outlets and music stages before the crowd arrives. There are numerous bars and performance spaces. Food and drink concessions don't accept cash; instead, you must run up a bill on a stamp card and pay (in cash) when you leave.

Various performances take place throughout the evening, usually starting around 9pm – follow the sounds. Free dance lessons are sometimes offered, and artists, designers and musicians mingle with the crowd. It's more than exciting.

The Fábrica is closed for the entire months of May, September and January. It is well worth planning your trip around these times – it's that good!

★ **Callejón de Hamel**
Live Rumba LIVE MUSIC
(Map p78; ☺ from noon Sun) Aside from its funky murals and psychedelic art shops, the main reason to come to this alleyway, Havana's high temple of Afro-Cuban culture, is the frenetic rumba music that kicks off every Sunday around noon.

For aficionados, this is about as raw and hypnotic as it gets, with interlocking drum patterns and lengthy rhythmic chants powerful enough to summon the spirit of the orishas (Santería deities).

Due to a liberal sprinkling of tourists these days, some argue that the callejón (back alley) has lost much of its charm. Don't believe them. This place still rocks – and rumbas!

Jazz Club la Zorra y El Cuervo LIVE MUSIC
(Map p90; ☑ 7-833-2402; cnr Calles 23 & O; USD$5-10; ☺ from 10pm) One in a duo of long-standing and highly lauded jazz clubs, the Vixen and the Crow opens its doors nightly at 10pm to long lines of committed music fiends. Enter through a red British phone box and descend into a diminutive and dark basement. The scene is more hot and clamorous than the Jazz Café and leans toward freestyle jazz.

Café Teatro Bertolt Brecht LIVE MUSIC
(Map p90; ☑ 7-832-9359; cnr Calles 13 & I; tickets USD$3) What pass for hipsters in Havana tend to congregate at this live-music venue known locally as No Se lo Digas a Nadie (Don't Tell Anyone) for the weekly concerts headlined by legendary music collective Interactivo (Wednesday around midnight). If you're curious about Cuban culture – and its future – roll up for an evening here. Be prepared to queue.

Jazz Café LIVE MUSIC
(Map p90; ☑ 7-838-3302; Galerías de Paseo, top fl, cnr Calle 1 & Paseo; cover after 8pm USD$10; ☺ noon-2am) This upscale joint, improbably located in a shopping mall (p140) overlooking the Malecón, is a kind of jazz supper club, with dinner tables and a decent menu. At night the club swings into action with live jazz, timba and, occasionally, straight-up salsa. It's definitely the suavest of Havana's jazz venues.

Basílica Menor de
San Francisco de Asís   CLASSICAL MUSIC

(Map p68; Plaza de San Francisco de Asís; tickets USD$5; ⊙from 6pm Sat) Plaza de San Francisco de Asís' glorious church, which dates from 1738, has been reincarnated as a 21st-century museum and concert hall. The old nave hosts choral and chamber music at least once a week (check the schedule at the door) and the acoustics are famously good. It's best to bag your ticket at least a day ahead.

Oratorio de San Felipe Neri   LIVE MUSIC

(Map p68; cnr Aguiar & Obrapía; USD$2; ⊙performances 7pm) The Neri has had many incarnations since its founding in 1693: first as a church under various religious orders (Oratorianas, Capuchinos, Carmelitas), then as a bank, and since 2004 as one of Havana's top venues for classical music (mainly choral).

Centro Andaluz   LIVE PERFORMANCE

(Map p78; ☑7-863-6745; Paseo de Martí No 104) Cubans have adopted and adapted many foreign music and dance forms, including flamenco. You can see Havana's best troupes here on Monday, Friday and Saturday at lunchtime and in the evening. The recently refurbished center is the former HQ of Havana's Andalusian social club, one of several prominent Spanish aid societies in the city.

El Tablao Centro Cultural Artex   LIVE MUSIC

(Map p78; Paseo de Martí No 458; cover USD$5; ⊙from 10pm) Bang in the city center, cleverly hidden in a basement beneath the Gran Teatro (p85), this dark club is perennially popular, particularly with mature locals, for its nightly shows that range from flamenco and *trova* (traditional poetic singing) to jazz and gay nights. The entrance is in Calle San Rafael.

El Guajirito   LIVE MUSIC

(Map p68; ☑7-863-3009; Agramonte No 660, btwn Gloria & Apodaca; show USD$30, incl dinner USD$50; ⊙9:30pm) Some label it a tourist trap, but this restaurant–entertainment space bivouacked upstairs in a deceptively dilapidated Havana tenement plays some of the most professional Buena Vista Social Club music you'll ever hear. Indeed, this is a Buena Vista Social Club of sorts.

True, there are plenty of tour-bus escapees crowding out the tables, and yes the food's a little anemic, but the musicianship of the horn-blasting, drum-thumping, lung-stretching band, most of whom are of pensionable age, ought to have the likes of

Compay Segundo smiling down from the great gig in the sky.

Casa de la Música   LIVE MUSIC

(Map p78; Av de Italia, btwn Concordia & Neptuno; USD$5-25; ⊙5pm-3am) One of two such establishments in the city, this legendary place is where Cubans and tourists who don't want to be treated like tourists go for full-on *caliente* (hot) music and dancing. All the big names play here, from Bamboleo to Los Van Van – and you'll pay peanuts to see them. Partly closed for renovations at research time; check ahead.

Submarino Amarillo   LIVE MUSIC

(Map p90; cnr Calles 17 & 6; USD$2-5; ⊙9pm-2am Mon, 2-7:30pm & 9pm-2am Tue-Sat, 2-10pm Sun) You can't escape the Beatles in Cuba; their iconic status is epitomized in clubs such as this one abutting Parque Lennon, where every tabletop is decorated with a different Beatles album cover. The Yellow Sub hosts all types of live music as long as it's in 4/4 time and answers to the name of 'rock.'

El Gato Tuerto   LIVE MUSIC

(Map p90; Calle O No 14, btwn Calles 17 & 19; drink minimum USD$5; ⊙noon-6am) Once the headquarters of Havana's alternative artistic and sexual scene, the 'one-eyed cat' is now a nexus for middle-aged lovers of traditional Cuban *boleros* (rhythmic ballads) and *filin* music (jazz crooning). Riotously popular with both tourists and locals, the venue is hidden just off the Malecón in a quirky two-story house with turtles swimming in a front pool.

The upper floor is taken up by a restaurant, while down below late-night revelers raise the roof in a chic nightclub.

Casa de las Américas   LIVE PERFORMANCE

(Map p90; ☑7-838-2706; www.casa.co.cu; cnr Calles 3 & G) Set up in 1959 by revolutionary Haydée Santamaría, a survivor of the attack on the Moncada Barracks, this powerhouse of Cuban and Latin American culture offers conferences, exhibitions, a gallery, a bookstore, concerts and an atmosphere of erudite intellectualism. Its literary award is one of the Spanish-speaking world's most prestigious. See the website for upcoming events.

El Hurón Azul   LIVE MUSIC

(Map p90; ☑7-832-4551; www.uneac.org.cu; cnr Calles 17 & H; ⊙hours vary) If you want to rub shoulders with socialist celebrities, hang out here at the Union of Cuban Writers and Artists (Uneac) social club, replete with priceless snippets of Cuba's under-the-radar cultural life. Most performances take place in the garden. Wednesday is Afro-Cuban rumba, Saturday is authentic *boleros* (ballads), and alternate Thursdays there's jazz and *trova*. You'll never pay more than USD$5.

Café Miramar
LIVE MUSIC

(Map p96; Av 5 No 9401, cnr Calle 94, Miramar; cover USD$2; ⊗Fri-Sun) A suitably refined little club for a suitably refined part of Playa, this venue encased in the Cine Teatro Miramar and affiliated with government agency AR-Tex is dedicated mainly to live jazz, although other elements (such as funk) are sometimes thrown into the mix. Things usually get jamming at 9pm-ish and there's cheap food.

Salón Rosado Benny Moré
LIVE MUSIC

(El Tropical; Map p96; ⏹7-206-1281; cnr Av 41 & Calle 46, Kohly; ⊗9pm-2am Thu-Sat, 5-10pm Sun) If you're looking for something inherently Cuban, tag along with the local *habaneros* for some very *caliente* action at this outdoor venue known colloquially as La Tropical. The long-standing club hosts live music and has changed its spots over the years – these days it's less Benny Moré and more Pupy y Los que Son Son, with occasional reggaeton thrown in.

Dancing is de rigueur, unless you can escape to one of the balconies for a drink. Entry prices and show nights vary – check the local grapevine first.

Casa de la Música
LIVE MUSIC

(Map p96; ⏹7-202-6147; Calle 20 No 3308, cnr Av 35, Miramar; matinee/night USD$10/15; ⊗5-9pm & 11pm-3am) Launched with a concert by renowned jazz pianist Chucho Valdés in 1994, this Miramar favorite is run by national Cuban recording company EGREM, and the programs are generally a lot more authentic than the cabaret entertainment you'll see at the hotels.

Platinum players such as NG La Banda, Los Van Van and Adalberto Álvarez y su Son play here regularly; you'll rarely pay more than USD$20 for entry. It has a more relaxed atmosphere than its Centro Habana namesake.

Teatro Karl Marx
LIVE MUSIC

(Map p96; ⏹7-209-1991; cnr Av 1 & Calle 10, Miramar) Size-wise the Karl Marx puts other Havana theaters in the shade, with a seating capacity of 5500 in a single auditorium. The very biggest events happen here, such as the closing galas for the jazz and film festivals,

and rare concerts by *trovadores* such as Silvio Rodríguez.

Don Cangrejo
LIVE MUSIC

(Map p96; Av 1 No 1606, btwn Calles 16 & 18, Miramar; cover USD$5; ⊗11pm-3am) The daytime restaurant of the Cuban fisheries becomes party central particularly on Friday night, with alfresco live music (often by big-name acts) and an atmosphere akin to that of an undergraduate freshers' ball. It's crowded and there are queues.

La Cecilia
LIVE MUSIC

(Map p96; ⏹7-204-1562; Av 5 No 11010, btwn Calles 110 & 112, Náutico; ⊗noon-midnight) This walled outdoor garden complex serves traditional Cuban food and keeps tour groups hydrated with mojitos, but it's best known for its big-band salsa music, which blasts out on weekend nights beneath the ferns and canopies.

Theater

⭐Gran Teatro de la Habana Alicia Alonso
THEATER

(Map p78; ⏹7-861-3077; cnr Paseo de Martí & San Rafael; tickets USD$30; ⊗box office 9am-6pm Mon-Sat, to 3pm Sun) Havana's fabulously renovated 'great' theater is open again and offering up the best in Cuban dance and music. Its specialty is ballet (it's the headquarters of the Cuban National Ballet), but it also stages musicals, plays and opera. Check the noticeboard for upcoming events.

Teatro Nacional de Cuba
THEATER

(Map p90; ⏹7-879-6011; cnr Paseo & Calle 39; per person USD$10; ⊗box office 10am-5pm & before performances) One of the twin pillars of Havana's cultural life, the Teatro Nacional de Cuba on Plaza de la Revolución is the modern rival to the Gran Teatro (p85) in Centro Habana. Built in the 1950s as part of Jean-Claude Forestier's grand city expansion, the complex hosts landmark concerts, foreign theater troupes and La Colmenita children's company.

The main hall, Sala Avellaneda, stages big events such as musical concerts and Shakespeare plays, while the smaller Sala Covarrubias along the back puts on a more daring program (the seating capacity of the two halls combined is 3300). The 9th floor is a rehearsal and performance space where the newest, most experimental stuff happens. The ticket office is at the far end of a separate single-story building beside the main theater.

Teatro Mella   THEATER
(Map p90; ☑ 7-833-8696; Línea No 657, btwn Calles A & B) Occupying the site of the old Rodi Cinema on Línea, Teatro Mella offers one of Havana's most comprehensive programs, including an international ballet festival, comedy shows, theater, dance and intermittent performances from the famous Conjunto Folklórico Nacional. American rock band Blondie played here in 2019.

The adjacent **Jardines del Mella** is a good place to chill with a drink before or after a performance.

Sala Teatro Hubert de Blanck   THEATER
(Map p90; ☑ 7-830-1011; Calzada No 657, btwn Calles A & B) This theater is named for the founder of Havana's first conservatory of music (1885). The Teatro Estudio based here is Cuba's leading theater company. You can usually see plays in Spanish on Saturday at 8:30pm and on Sunday at 7pm. Tickets are sold just before the performance.

Teatro Martí   THEATER
(Map p78; ☑ 7-866-7152; teatromarti@patrimo nio.ohc.cu; Dragones, btwn Agramonte & Paseo de Martí; adult USD$20) Known also as the 'theater of a hundred doors' (in reference to the French windows adorning its exterior), this neoclassical gem is a masterpiece of restoration. After 40 years in dereliction, it reopened in 2014 with decent air-conditioning and audio equipment, an orchestra pit, intricate wood- and ironwork, as well as an adjacent cafeteria and well-kept surrounding gardens.

Teatro América   THEATER
(Map p78; Av de Italia No 253, btwn Concordia & Neptuno) Housed in a classic art deco *rascacielo* (skyscraper), the América seems to have changed little since its theatrical heyday in the 1930s and '40s. It hosts variety, comedy, dance, jazz and salsa; shows are normally held on Saturday at 8:30pm and on Sunday at 5pm.

Cabaret

⭐ **Cabaret Parisién**   CABARET
(Map p90; ☑ 7-836-3564; Hotel Nacional, cnr Calles 21 & O; entry USD$35; ☺9pm) One rung down from Marianao's world-famous Tropicana, but cheaper and closer to the city center, the nightly Cabaret Parisién in the Hotel Nacional (p89) is well worth a look, especially if you're staying in or around Vedado. It's the usual mix of frills, feathers and seminaked women (and men), but the choreography is first class and the costumes wonderfully flamboyant.

Doors open at 9pm. There's a warm-up band and one cocktail is included.

Tropicana Nightclub   CABARET
(Map p96; ☑ 7-267-1871; Calle 72 No 4504, Marianao; tickets from USD$75; ☺from 10pm) An institution since its 1939 opening, the world-famous Tropicana was among the few bastions of Havana's Las Vegas–style nightlife to survive the revolution. Immortalized in Graham Greene's 1958 *Our Man in Havana,* the open-air cabaret show here has changed little since its 1950s heyday, with scantily clad *señoritas* descending from palm trees to dance Latin salsa amid bright lights. It's easily Havana's most popular cabaret and de rigueur on the bus-tour circuit, none of which takes away from the magnificence of the spectacle.

Habana Café   CABARET
(Map p90; Paseo, btwn Calles 1 & 3; USD$20; ☺from 9pm) A hip and trendy nightclub–cabaret show at the Hotel Meliá Cohiba (p113), laid out in 1950s American style but with live salsa music. After 1am the tables are cleared and the place rocks to 'international music' until the cock crows. Excellent value.

It's best to book ahead at the desk in the hotel lobby.

El Turquino   LIVE MUSIC
(Map p90; Hotel Habana Libre, Calle L, btwn Calles 23 & 25; USD$10; ☺from 10:30pm) On the 25th floor of the Hotel Habana Libre (p92), this well-known club puts on mediocre cabaret shows followed by much better live bands and dancing. The pièce de résistance is the retractable roof, which slides back when everyone hits the dance floor around midnight.

Dance

Centro Cultural El Gran Palenque   DANCE
(Map p90; Calle 4 No 103, btwn Calzada & Calle 5; USD$5; ☺3-6pm Sat) Founded in 1962, the high-energy Conjunto Folklórico Nacional de Cuba specializes in Afro-Cuban dancing (all of the drummers are Santería priests). See them perform here, and dance along during the regular Sábado de la Rumba – three full hours of mesmerizing drumming and dancing. This group also performs at Teatro Mella and internationally.

A major festival called FolkCuba unfolds here biannually, during the second half of January and the first half of July.

Club Almendares
DANCE
(Map p96; ☑7-204 4990; cnr Calles 49C & 28A, Kohly; USD$6; ⏰7pm-midnight) Go into the woods in El Bosque de la Habana (p95) for the weekly Fiesta del Casino, a popular open-air disco where a mix of Cubans and non-Cubans come to dance salsa. The event starts with a communal salsa lesson from Club Salseando Chévere (p104).

Cinema

Cine Yara
CINEMA
(Map p90; cnr Calles 23 & L) The first date (and first kiss) of many an enamored *cubano* has taken place at this classic modernist cinema on Vedado's main crossroads. It's also a major venue in the December film festival (p106).

Cine Charles Chaplin
CINEMA
(Map p90; ☑7-831-1101; Av 23, btwn Calles 10 & 12) One of Cuba's largest and best-equipped cinemas, the Chaplin shows nightly films of all types and sometimes runs a special season on one director. The lobby is a veritable museum of Cuban film posters and is worth a look at any time of day.

Cine 23 & 12
CINEMA
(Map p90; ☑7-833-6906; Calle 23, btwn Calles 12 & 14) One of a clutch of well-maintained cinemas on Vedado's movie strip, this is one of the HQs of Havana's film festival (p106). Since 2014 the 23 & 12 has hosted Havana's *cinemateca*, showing old classics and art-house movies.

Cine Infanta
CINEMA
(Map p78; Calzada de la Infanta No 357) A multiplex cinema that's plush by Cuban standards, Infanta is an important venue during December's international film festival (p106).

Cine la Rampa
CINEMA
(Map p90; Calle 23 No 111) Ken Loach movies, French classics, Cuban film festivals – catch them all at this Vedado staple, which houses the Cuban film archive.

Cultural

Centro Cultural Enguayabera
ARTS CENTER
(Calle 162, btwn Avs 7A & 7B, Alamar; ⏰11am-6:30pm Tue-Sun) In an old shirt factory abandoned in the 1990s, when it became a rubbish dump and public urinal, this state-sponsored community arts project was inspired by the Fábrica de Arte Cubano (p132)

SPECTATOR SPORTS

As economic standards nosedived in the early 1990s, the nation's sporting prowess moved in the other direction, peaking at the 1992 Barcelona Olympics, when Cuba (the world's 106th-largest nation) came fifth in the medal tally with 14 gold. Cubans continue to excel in baseball, boxing, volleyball and high jump (Javier Sotomayor has held the world record since 1993). Soccer is a growing sport, attracting an ever-expanding fan base, particularly since the 2014 FIFA World Cup. Havana's main stadiums are located in the peripheral municipalities of Playa, Cerro and Habana del Este. Going to a game is an experience. No bookings are required; just turn up, pay the nominal ticket price and find a (hard) seat.

Estadio Latinoamericano (Map p90; Zequiera No 312, Cerro; tickets USD$2) The largest stadium in the country holds 55,000 people and was built before the revolution in 1946. It's the home of Havana's Los Industriales baseball team. Entry to games costs small change. The season is from late October to April, with playoffs running until May.

Estadio Pedro Marrero (Map p96; cnr Av 41 & Calle 46, Kohly) This slightly down-at-heel Playa stadium holds 28,000 spectators and is home to FC Ciudad de La Habana, the city's main soccer team, which has won the Campeonato Nacional de Fútbol six times.

Estadio Panamericano The shabby Estadio Panamericano was built for the 1991 Pan American Games. It was fitted with a new athletics track in 2008 but still looks neglected and unloved. It's used mainly for athletics and soccer.

Coliseo de la Ciudad Deportiva (cnr Av de la Independencia & Vía Blanca, Cerro) This multiuse 15,000-capacity indoor sports arena opened in 1958. It's the headquarters of the national men's volleyball team, and in 2016 the surrounding grounds hosted the Rolling Stones' first Cuban rock concert.

in Vedado. Numerous funky venues are bivouacked under its cultural umbrella, including three small cinemas, a literary cafe, a theater and a crafts outlet.

The place is a shot in the arm for oft-forgotten Alamar, the ugly collection of '70s apartment blocks that gave birth to Cuban hip-hop and can now concentrate on fostering plenty more urban creativity. The center offers free entry and a wi-fi zone.

Circo Trompoloco CIRCUS
(Map p96; www.circonacionaldecuba.cu; cnr Av 5 & Calle 112, Náutico; USD$5-10; ⊙7pm Fri, 4pm & 7pm Sat & Sun; 🚼) Havana's permanent 'Big Top,' with a weekend matinee featuring strongmen, contortionists and acrobats.

Fundación Alejo Carpentier ARTS CENTER
(Map p68; ☑7-861-3667; www.fundacioncar pentier.cult.cu; Empedrado No 215; ⊙8am-4pm Mon-Fri) Check for cultural events at this baroque former palace of the Condesa de la Reunión (from the 1820s), where Carpentier set his famous novel *El Siglo de las luces*. It's near the Plaza de la Catedral.

Sport

Kid Chocolate SPECTATOR SPORT
(Map p78; Paseo de Martí) A boxing club directly opposite the Capitolio (p85) that usually hosts matches on Friday at 7pm. There have long been rumors of a refurb, but for the time being it remains scruffily atmospheric.

Rodeo Nacional RODEO
(☑7-643-8089; Parque Lenin; ⊙4pm Sun) In an arena in Parque Lenin, Rodeo Nacional, the biggest rodeo in Cuba, is held on Sunday (but not *every* Sunday, so check in advance). Rodeos in Cuba attract few tourists but are classic Cuban affairs and a great insight into rural culture. The big 'un, held here every March, is the Boyeros Cattlemen's International Fair.

🔒 Shopping

Sixty years of *socialismo* haven't done much for Havana's shopping scene. That said, there are some decent outlets for travelers and tourists, particularly for those seeking the Cuban shopping triumvirate of rum, cigars and coffee. Art is another worthwhile field: Havana's scene is cutting edge and ever changing, and browsers will find many galleries in which to while away many hours.

🔒 Habana Vieja

★**Clandestina** CLOTHING
(Map p68; ☑5-381-4802; www.clandestina.co; Villegas No 403, btwn Brasil & Muralla; ⊙10am-8pm Mon-Sat, to 5pm Sun) Cuba's first indie design store when it opened in 2015, Clandestina makes its own T-shirts, bags and accessories out of any old junk it can find, 99% of it Cuban. It's the most progressive and coolest thing around town right now, but it's also eco-conscious and deft at working in a tough economic climate.

★**Centro Cultural Antiguos Almacenes de Deposito San José** ARTS & CRAFTS
(Map p68; cnr Desamparados & San Isidro; ⊙10am-6pm Mon-Sat) Havana's multifarious handicraft market sits under the cover of an old shipping warehouse in Desamparados. Check your socialist ideals at the door: herein lies a hive of free enterprise and (unusually for Cuba) haggling. Possible souvenirs include paintings, *guayaberas* (men's shirts), woodwork, leather items, jewelry and numerous apparitions of the highly marketable El Che. It's as popular with Cubans as it is with tourists.

Piscolabis Bazar & Café HOMEWARES
(Map p68; www.piscolabishabana.com; San Ignacio 75, btwn Callejón del Chorro & O'Reilly; ⊙9:30am-7:30pm Mon-Sun) Perfectly located just steps from Havana's 18th-century cathedral (p67), this small but eclectic shop is run by a group of Cuban artists of various disciplines and features a wide range of decorative and functional items for the home, as well as jewelry and some clothing. The designers make modern creations from iconic objects of Cuba's past.

Librería Venecia BOOKS
(Map p68; Obispo No 502; ⊙10am-10pm) Wonderful little private bookshop in Calle Obispo selling yellowed secondhand tomes, esoteric film posters and other random print work that you won't find anywhere else in Havana.

Casa del Habano – Hostal Conde de Villanueva CIGARS
(Map p68; Mercaderes No 202; ⊙10am-6pm) One of Havana's best cigar shops, with its own roller, smoking room and expert sales staff. It's on the mezzanine floor inside the hotel (p107).

Casa Obbatalá
ARTS & CRAFTS

(Map p68; Muralla 456, btwn Villegas & Cristo; ⊙9am-5pm) This specialist religious shop in Habana Vieja sells all manner of Santería offerings and cult objects, almost exclusively to religious-minded locals. The assorted costumes, dresses and dolls come in a maelstrom of colors for the different *orishas* – yellow for Oshún, purple for Babalú Ayé, red for Changó and white for Obbatalá.

La Marca
BODY ART

(Map p68; ☎7-801-2026; www.lamarcabodyart.com; Obrapía 108c, btwn Oficios & Mercaderes; ⊙11am-7pm Mon-Sat) Should you want a more permanent memento of your time in Cuba, try La Marca, the first licensed tattoo shop on the island. The parlor is run by a group of young Cuban artists who maintain an international level of cleanliness and hygiene, and they sometimes host exhibitions by some of Cuba's leading artists.

La Casa del Café
COFFEE

(Map p68; cnr Baratillo & Obispo; ⊙9am-5pm) For a range of coffee and a decent taster cup, pop into La Casa del Café, just off Plaza de Armas.

Secondhand Book Market
BOOKS

(Map p68; cnr Baratillo & Jústiz; ⊙9am-7pm) Relocated from Plaza de Armas, much to the chagrin of many vendors, Havana's famous secondhand-book market now convenes in the open-air ruins of the former Casa de Jústiz y Santa Ana. It's the same mix of bibliophile stallholders selling well-thumbed copies of works by Fidel Castro, Che Guevara and Ernest Hemingway. There's no market on important holidays or if it rains.

Fundación Havana Club Shop
ALCOHOL

(Map p68; San Pedro No 262; ⊙9am-6pm) Havana Club rum, right from the source.

Palacio de la Artesanía
GIFTS & SOUVENIRS

(Map p68; Cuba No 64; ⊙9am-7pm) If only all shopping malls could be this attractive! Encased in an 18th-century colonial palace and gathered around a shaded central patio, this place offers one-stop shopping for souvenirs, cigars, crafts, musical instruments, CDs, clothing and jewelry at fixed prices. Join the gaggle of cruise-ship escapees and fill your bag.

Habana 1791
PERFUME

(Map p68; Mercaderes No 156, btwn Obrapía & Lamparilla; ⊙9:30am-6pm) A restored colonial-era shop on historic Calle Mercaderes that sells perfume made from tropical flowers, Habana 1791 retains the air of a working museum. Floral fragrances are mixed by hand – you can see the petals drying in a laboratory out back. Worth a sniff.

Taller de Serigrafía René Portocarrero
ART

(Map p68; ☎7-862-3276; Cuba No 513, btwn Brasil & Muralla; ⊙9am-4pm Mon-Fri) Paintings and prints by young Cuban artists are exhibited and sold here, with prices ranging from USD$30 to USD$150. You can also see the artists at work. Inquire about courses.

Museo del Tabaco
CIGARS

(Map p68; Mercaderes No 120; ⊙10am-5pm Mon-Sat) At Museo del Tabaco you can see various indigenous pipes and idols and buy some splendid smokes.

🏠 Centro Habana

★Memorias Librería
BOOKS

(Map p78; ☎7-862-3153; Ánimas No 57, btwn Paseo de Martí & Agramonte; ⊙9am-5pm) A shop full of beautiful artifacts, the Memorias Librería opened in 2014 as Havana's first genuine antique bookstore. Delve into its gathered piles and you'll find wonderful rare collectibles, including old coins, postcards, posters, magazines and art deco signs from the 1930s. Priceless!

Real Fábrica de Tabacos Partagás Store
CIGARS

(Map p78; Industria No 520, btwn Barcelona & Dragones; ⊙9am-6pm) Confusingly, the cigar shop affiliated with Havana's main cigar factory (p87) is still housed in the factory's old location behind the Capitolio (p85). Naturally, it sells some of Havana's best smokes, including the deep, earthy Partagás brand.

Plaza Carlos III
SHOPPING CENTER

(Map p78; Av Salvador Allende, btwn Arbol Seco & Retiro; ⊙10am-6pm Mon-Sat) After Plaza América in Varadero, this is probably Cuba's flashiest shopping mall – and there's barely a tourist in sight. The place has taken a step up in recent years: formerly empty shelves are now at least half full of consumer goods. For something with a unique Cuban touch, pop into **Baracoa**, a chocolate shop.

Vedado

ROX 950
JEWELRY

(Map p90; ✆7-832-9978; www.rox950.net; Línea No 256, btwn Calles I & J; ⊙8am-8pm Mon-Fri) ROX 950 is the creation of self-taught silversmith Rosana Vargas. She opened her first shop at this Vedado mansion in 2012, and today her work can be found in hotel shops and at international fairs. Her style is minimalist, with pure soft lines and geometric shapes, using silver, semiprecious stones...even corks! Ask for a quick tour of the workshop.

Vargas has sewn the seeds of silversmithing among youngsters of her community, hosting a yearly workshop called *En busca del sol* (In Search of the Sun).

Bazar Estaciones
GIFTS & SOUVENIRS

(Map p90; ✆7-832-9965; Calle 23 No 10, btwn Calles J & I; ⊙10am-9pm) This lovingly curated private shop sells some interesting and unique souvenirs (not the standard government-branded stuff). It's on the upper floor of a Vedado mansion right on the main drag.

Instituto Cubano del Arte e Industria Cinematográficos
GIFTS & SOUVENIRS

(Map p90; Calle 23, btwn Calles 10 & 12; ⊙10am-5pm) The best place in Havana for rare Cuban movie posters and DVDs. The small shop is inside the ICAIC (Cuban Film Institute) building and accessed through the Café Fresa y Chocolate (p132).

Galería de Arte Latinoamericano
ART

(Map p90; cnr Calles 3 & G; ⊙10am-4pm Mon-Fri) Situated in the Casa de las Américas (p134) and featuring art from all over Latin America.

Librería Centenario del Apóstol
BOOKS

(Map p90; Calle 25 No 164; ⊙10am-5pm Mon-Sat, 9am-1pm Sun) Great assortment of used books with a José Martí bias in downtown Vedado.

Andare – Bazar de Arte
GIFTS & SOUVENIRS

(Map p90; cnr Calles 23 & L; ⊙10am-6pm Mon-Fri, to 2pm Sat) A selection of old movie posters, antique postcards, T-shirts and, of course, all the greatest Cuban films on videotape are sold at this state-run shop next to the Cine Yara (p137).

Galerías de Paseo
SHOPPING CENTER

(Map p90; cnr Calle 1 & Paseo; ⊙9am-8pm) Across the street from the Hotel Meliá Cohiba (p113), this dated-looking relic from the 1980s with its tinted glass and curvaceous windows is considered upscale for Havana. It sells well-made clothes and other consumer items to tourists and affluent Cubans, and also hosts a small supermarket and the peerless Jazz Café (p133).

La Habana Sí
GIFTS & SOUVENIRS

(Map p90; cnr Calles 23 & L; ⊙10am-10pm Mon-Sat, to 7pm Sun) This government-run ARTex shop opposite the Hotel Habana Libre (p92) has a good selection of CDs, cassettes, books, crafts and postcards.

Playa & Marianao

★La Casa del Habano Quinta
CIGARS

(Map p96; ✆7-214-4737; cnr Av 5 & Calle 16, Miramar; ⊙10am-6pm Mon-Sat, to 1pm Sun) Arguably Havana's top cigar store – and there are many contenders. The primary reasons: it's well stocked, with well-informed staff, a comfy smoking lounge and a decent on-site restaurant. It also enjoys the on-off presence of many of Cuba's top cigar aficionados.

Alma Shop
ARTS & CRAFTS

(Map p96; ✆5-264-0660; www.almacubashop.com; Calle 18 No 314, btwn Avs 3 & 5, Miramar; ⊙10am-6pm Mon-Sat) Whether you're searching for jewelry, embroidered cushions or a vintage cigar humidor, this privately run shop is a great place to pick up a high-quality gift or souvenir. The owners have traveled across Cuba to carefully select pieces made by local artisans; each item is unique and handmade using natural or recycled materials.

Salomé Casa de Modas
CLOTHING

(Map p96; ✆7-203-5070; salomemodas@hotmail.com; Calle 28 No 118, btwn Avs 1 & 3, Miramar; ⊙10am-6pm Mon-Sat) Every single piece at this private boutique reflects authentic Cuban style. It specializes in all things linen – dresses, blouses, trousers and *guayaberas* (traditional men's Cuban shirts). Salomé's pieces are elegant but unpretentious, featuring pastel colors, pleats and embroidery.

All pieces are handmade by a team of tailors and an 82-year-old embroiderer who is said to have made clothes for revolutionary Celia Sánchez, Fidel Castro's secretary.

La Maison
CLOTHING

(Map p96; Calle 16 No 701, Miramar; ⊙9am-5pm) The Cuban fashion fascination is in high gear at this small boutique complex hidden in a Miramar villa. It has a limited selection of designer clothing, shoes, handbags, jewelry and cosmetics but is best known for its fashion shows (Thursday to Sunday) that take place around a leaf-infested swimming pool.

Miramar Trade Center   SHOPPING CENTER
(Map p96; Av 3, btwn Calles 76 & 80, Miramar; ⏰hours vary) Cuba's largest and most modern shopping and business center houses myriad stores, airline offices and embassies. Look out for the offbeat art installations, including a herd of elephants prancing through.

ⓘ Information

SAFE TRAVEL

Havana is not a dangerous city, especially when compared to other metropolitan areas in North and South America. There's almost no gun crime, violent robbery, organized gang culture, teenage delinquency, drugs or dangerous no-go zones. Stiff prison sentences for crimes such as assault have acted as a major deterrent for would-be criminals and kept organized crime at bay. Things to be aware of as a traveler:

➡ Petty theft and pickpocketing

➡ Short-changing in bars and restaurants

➡ Street hustlers selling cigars

➡ For women, sexist banter and unwanted attention from men

INTERNET ACCESS

Cuba's internet service provider is national phone company Etecsa. Etecsa runs various *telepuntos* (internet cafe–call centers) in Havana; the main ones are in **Centro Habana** (www.etecsa.cu; Águila No 565, cnr Dragones; ⏰8:30am-7pm) and **Habana Vieja** (Habana No 406, cnr Obispo; ⏰8:30am-7pm). Buy a one-hour user card (USD$1) with a scratch-off user code and *contraseña* (password), and either help yourself to a free computer or use it on your own device in one of the city's 100-plus wi-fi hot spots. Most Havana hotels that are rated three stars and up also have wi-fi. You don't generally have to be a guest to use it.

Popular **wi-fi hot spots** in Havana:

➡ La Rampa (Calle 23 between Calle L and Malecón) in Vedado

➡ Plaza del Cristo in Habana Vieja

➡ Outside the Hotel Deauville on the Malecón in Centro Habana

➡ Miramar Trade Center in Playa

MONEY

There are banks and ATMs in the Miramar Trade Center. The quickest and most hassle-free places to exchange money are in Cadecas. There are dozens of them across Havana and they usually have much longer opening hours and quicker service than banks.

Banco de Crédito y Comercio Vedado (✆7-833-7344; Calle 23, btwn Calles N & O; ⏰9am-3pm Mon-Fri), **Ciudad Panoramico** (Paseo Panamericano, Villa Panamericano; ⏰8:30am-3pm Mon-Fri, to 11am Sat). Expect lines.

Banco Financiero Internacional Habana Vieja (✆7-860-9369; cnr Oficios & Brasil; ⏰8:30am-3pm Mon-Fri)

Banco Metropolitano Centro Habana (Av de Italia No 452, cnr San Martín; ⏰8:30am-7:30pm Mon-Sat), **Vedado** (✆7-832-2006; cnr Calles 23 & J; ⏰8:30am-7:30pm Mon-Sat), **Vedado** (cnr Línea & Calle M; ⏰8:30am-3:30pm Mon-Fri), **Vedado** (Línea, btwn Paseo & Calle A; ⏰8:30am-3:30pm Mon-Fri), **Habana Vieja** (cnr Cuba & O'Reilly; ⏰9am-3pm Mon-Fri), **Miramar** (cnr Calle 42 & Av 31, Miramar; ⏰9am-3pm Mon-Fri), **Playa** (cnr Av 5 & Calle 84, Miramar; ⏰9am-3pm Mon-Fri)

Banco Popular de Ahorro Guanabo (Av 5 No 47810, btwn Calles 478 & 480, Guanabo; ⏰9am-3pm Mon-Fri)

Cadeca Centro Habana (Neptuno, btwn Industria & Consulado; ⏰8:30am-4pm Mon-Sat, to 11:30am Sun), **Habana Vieja** (cnr Oficios & Lamparilla; ⏰8:30am-8pm Mon-Sat, 9am-6pm Sun), **Habana Vieja** (Obispo No 257, btwn Cuba & Aguiar; ⏰8am-midnight), **Vedado** (cnr Calles 23 & J; ⏰8:30am-4pm Mon-Fri, to 11:30am Sat), **Vedado** (Hotel Meliá Cohiba, Paseo, btwn Calles 1 & 3; ⏰8am-11pm), **Vedado** (Mercado Agropecuario, cnr Calles 19 & A; ⏰8:30am-4pm Tue-Sat, to 11:30am Sun), **Miramar** (✆7-204-9327; Av 5A, btwn Calles 40 & 42, Miramar; ⏰8:30am-4pm Mon-Sat, to 11:30am Sun), **Playa** (✆7-207-9085; cnr Av 3 & Calle 70, Miramar; ⏰8am-8pm), **Guanabo** (Av 5 No 47612, btwn Calles 476 & 478, Guanabo; ⏰8:30am-4pm Mon-Sat, to 11:30am Sun)

ⓘ WHERE THE STREETS HAVE TWO NAMES

One of the most confusing aspects of Havana's geography is its street names. Almost every *calle*, *avenida* or *calzada* bears two denominations: a pre-1959 name and a newer alternative. Following the Cuban Revolution, the government elected to give practically every street in Cuba a new name, but, in a silent act of rebellion, the locals largely refused to adopt them. Today the old names endure and are nearly always used in colloquial speech (in many cases, the locals don't even know the new names). Meanwhile, the new names appear on street signs and officially printed maps. Confused? Welcome to Cuba!

LOCAL KNOWLEDGE

HAVANA'S BIKE SHARING SCHEME

Cycling in Havana is a tough sell. For Cubans the activity evokes memories of the austere Special Period. Notwithstanding, faced with a slow but noticeable rise in motor traffic over the last decade, the Office of the City Historian, in tandem with private company Vélo Cuba (p103), inaugurated **Ha'Bici** (Paseo de Martí, cnr Carcel; 1/2/4hr USD\$2/3/7; ⊙9am-5:30pm) in November 2018. For the time being, this bike-sharing scheme is focused on Habana Vieja.

Bikes can be hired and dropped off at seven service stations around the Old Town, including Ha'Bici HQ on Paseo de Martí (Prado). To help cyclists negotiate cars, pedestrians and other unique Havana obstacles (fruit carts, stray dogs, acrobats on stilts!), three streets – Luz, Compostela and Empredado – have been designated special cycling thoroughfares. Both Cubans and non-Cubans are welcome to use the program. Bikes have six gears and come with helmets and a lock. Bring your passport.

TOURIST INFORMATION

Infotur offices in Havana:

Airport (☑ 7-642-6101; Terminal 3, Aeropuerto Internacional José Martí; ⊙24hr)

Guanabo (Map p102; Av 5, btwn Calles 468 & 470, Guanabo; ⊙8:15am-4:15pm)

Habana del Este (Edificio los Corales, Av de las Terrazas, btwn Calles 10 & 11, Playas del Este; ⊙8:15am-4:15pm)

Vedado (Map p90; Calle L, btwn Calles 23 & 25; ⊙9:30am-noon & 12:30-5pm)

Habana Vieja (☑7-866-4153; Obispo No 524 btwn Bernaza & Villegas; ⊙9:30am-5:30pm)

Playa (Map p96; cnr Av 5 & Calle 112, Náutico; ⊙8:30am-noon & 12:30-5pm Mon-Sat)

TRAVEL AGENCIES

Cubanacán (☑7-537-4090; www.cubanacan. cu) In all Cubanacán hotels.

Cubatur (☑7-833-3569; cnr Calles 23 & L; ⊙8am-8pm) Also in most of the main hotels.

Ecotur (☑7-273-1542; www.ecoturcuba.tur. cu; Calle 13 No 18005, btwn Av 5 & Calle 182, Flores; ⊙9am-5pm Mon-Fri) Naturalistic excursions, mostly outside Havana.

Gaviota (☑7-867-1194; www.gaviotahotels. com; ⊙9am-5pm) In all Gaviota hotels.

San Cristóbal Agencia de Viajes (Map p68; ☑7-869-7490; www.viajessancristobal.cu; O'Reilly No 102, cnr Tacón; tours per person from USD\$20; ⊙8:30am-5:30pm Mon-Fri, to 12:30pm Sat) Office of the City Historian tours.

ⓘ Getting There & Away

AIR

Aeropuerto Internacional José Martí (www. havana-airport.org; Av Rancho Boyeros, Rancho Boyeros) is at Rancho Boyeros, 25km southwest of Havana via Av de la Independencia. There are five terminals. Terminal 1, on the southeastern side of the runway, handles only domestic flights. Terminal 2 is 3km away via Av de la Independencia and receives flights and charters from the US. All other international flights use Terminal 3, a well-ordered, modern facility at Wajay, 2.5km west of Terminal 2. Charter flights, mainly to Cuban destinations, use the Caribbean Terminal (also known as Terminal 5) at the northwestern end of the runway, 2.5km west of Terminal 3. Terminal 4 handles freight. Check carefully which terminal you'll be using.

Aerogaviota (☑7-203-0668; www. aerogaviota.com) is a Cuban airline run by the government tourist agency that handles mainly domestic flights to places such as Holguín and Cayo Coco.

Most airlines, including national carrier **Cubana de Aviación** (☑7-649-0410; www.cubana.cu; Airline Bldg, Calle 23 No 64, Vedado, Havana; ⊙8:30am-4pm Mon-Fri, to noon Sat), have offices in the **Airline Building** (Calle 23 No 64) in Havana's Vedado district.

BOAT

There are currently no international ferries calling at Havana.

Buses connecting with the hydrofoil service to the Isla de la Juventud leave from the **Terminal de Ómnibus** (Map p90; ☑7-878-1841; www.viazul. com; cnr Av de la Independencia & Calle 19 de Mayo), near Plaza de la Revolución, but they're often late. It's advisable to reserve and buy your bus-boat combo ticket at least a day ahead. Tickets are available at the **Naviera Cubana Caribeña (NCC) Kiosk** (☑7-878-1841; ⊙7am-noon), and cost USD\$50 for the boat and CUP\$5 for the bus. Bring your passport.

BUS

Víazul (www.viazul.com) covers most destinations of interest to travelers, in safe, air-conditioned coaches. Most buses are direct, except those to Guantánamo, Baracoa, Remedios and Cayo Santa María. Buses get busy, particularly in peak season (November through March), so it's wise to book up to a week ahead. You can also book online. Full schedules are available on the website. Some casa particular owners may offer help with prearranging bus tickets.

You board all Víazul buses at the Terminal de Ómnibus, just north of the Plaza de la Revolución. This is where you'll also have to come to buy tickets. Taxis charge around USD$5 for the ride from central Havana, or it's walkable if you have a light pack.

A newer alternative to the increasingly crowded Víazul buses is Conectando, run by Cubanacán, which offers six itineraries linking Havana with Viñales, Trinidad, Varadero and Santiago de Cuba. The smaller buses, which run daily, pick up from various hotels and charge similar prices to Víazul's. Tickets can be reserved via Infotur or any Cubanacán hotel rep.

Buses (Map p68) to points in Artemisa and Mayabeque provinces leave from Apodaca No 53, off Agramonte, near the main train station. They go to Güines, Jaruco, Madruga, Nueva Paz, San José, San Nicolás and Santa Cruz del Norte, but expect large crowds, and come early to get a peso ticket.

VÍAZUL DEPARTURES FROM HAVANA

Check the most up-to-date departure times at www.viazul.com.

Destination	Cost (USD$)	Duration (hr)	Frequency (daily)
Bayamo	44	13	3
Camagüey	33	9	5
Ciego de Ávila	27	7	4
Cienfuegos	20	4½	2
Holguín	44	12	3
Las Tunas	39	11½	5
Matanzas	7	2	4
Pinar del Río	11	3	3
Sancti Spíritus	23	5¾	3
Santa Clara	18	3¾	5
Santiago de Cuba	51	15	3
Trinidad	25	5-6	2
Varadero	10	3	4
Viñales	12	4	3

CAR & MOTORCYCLE

There are car-rental offices in most Havana hotels rated three stars and up. However, a recent spike in tourist numbers has meant that vehicles are often in short supply. Book ahead on www.transturcarrental.com.

Rental prices for an average-size vehicle are around USD$70 to USD$80 per day.

Traffic in Havana isn't as light as it used to be. However, once you get outside the city, the traffic quickly thins out. Beware: signposting can be poor in Cuba, especially in the suburbs of Havana. Get a good map.

TAXI

Full buses are the norm in Cuba these days as they become more utilized by Cubans and Cuban-Americans, as well as tourists. To counter the shortfall, many travelers are turning to *colectivos* (shared taxis). Taxis charge approximately USD$0.50 to USD$0.60 per kilometer. This translates to around USD$90 to Varadero, USD$90 to Viñales, USD$150 to Santa Clara, USD$120 to Cienfuegos and USD$160 to Trinidad. A *colectivo* can take up to four people, meaning you can share the cost. *Colectivos* can usually be organized through your casa particular, at an Infotur office or by negotiating at a standard pickup point. It's also usually pretty easy to arrange a *colectivo* at the main bus terminal.

TRAIN

Trains to most parts of Cuba depart from **La Coubre station** (Túnel de la Habana); the **Estación Central de Ferrocarriles** (Central Train Station; ☑ 7-862-1920, 7-861-8540; cnr Av de Bélgica & Arsenal) was being refurbished at the time of research. La Coubre is on the southwestern side of Habana Vieja; from the main station, head down Av de Bélgica toward the harbor and turn right. The ticket office is located 100m down the road on the right-hand side. If it's closed, try the Lista de Espera office adjacent, which sells tickets for trains leaving immediately. Kids under 12 travel half-price.

Cuba's railway system got a much-needed upgrade in 2019 and now utilizes modern carriages imported from China with air-con and refreshment facilities. Four scheduled trains depart from Havana several times a day. There are two classes and a limited number of seats for foreigners in each carriage. Reservations are accepted up to 30 days ahead.

Tren 1 Runs every other day between Havana and Santiago de Cuba (USD$70, 15 hours).

Tren 3 Runs every third day to Guantánamo (USD$75, 17 hours).

Tren 5 Runs every third day to Holguín (USD$60, 14 hours).

Tren 7 Runs every third day to Bayamo (USD$60, 15 hours) and Manzanillo (USD$65, 17¼ hours).

All trains call in at roughly a dozen stations en route, including Matanzas (USD$10, two hours), Santa Clara (USD$25, five hours), Ciego de Ávila (USD$35, 7½ hours), Camagüey (USD$45, 9½ hours) and Las Tunas (USD$55, 11½ hours). First-class tickets cost approximately USD$20 to USD$25 more.

There are also lines heading east to Morón and Cienfuegos, and west to Pinar del Río, but none of these routes were posting reliable timetables at the time of writing. Check at the

PUBLIC TRANSPORT OVERVIEW

Like many things in Cuba, Havana's transport system is a baffling one-off that even the locals sometimes struggle to understand. If you've got the energy, the best way to get around town is on foot, but for a full dose of Cuban immersion, test the waters with one or more of the following transport options.

Guaguas City buses that run along set routes. Most of the lines have a P prefix. *Guaguas* (pronounced wah-wahs) are hot, crowded and used mainly by locals. Fares are a standard USD$0.40.

Almendrones Primarily used by locals, *almendrones* (sometimes called *máquinas*) are shared taxis that run along fixed routes in Havana. They're usually wheezing old American cars that can squeeze in up to six passengers. They'll stop anywhere en route to pick up/drop off, if they have space. Passengers use a series of hand signals to indicate to drivers where they want to go. Fares are between CUP$10 and CUP$20, which translates to around USD$0.20.

Colectivos Communal taxis – usually station wagons (estate cars) – that run between major Cuban towns and carry up to four people. *Colectivos* are a good alternative to the often overcrowded Víazul buses. They can usually be booked through Infotur offices or at casas particulares. Alternatively, they sometimes hang around outside bus stations.

Coco taxis Small, three-wheeled taxis shaped like coconuts and painted yellow. Originally designed for the tourist market in the 1990s, Coco taxis have since been derided for their poor safety and price gouging.

Lada taxis Private taxis that are prohibited from waiting at standard taxi ranks and roam the streets in search of fares. They're generally cheaper than Cubataxi, but they're less luxurious (seat belts and air-con are practically nonexistent) and you'll have to hail one streetside. Agree fares before you get in.

Cubataxi Modern yellow taxis with air-con and meters usually leased from the state by private drivers. They pick up outside hotels and at taxi ranks, and cost more than Lada taxis.

Vintage cars Well-maintained vintage American cars (often convertibles) lovingly restored and used for city 'tours.' They generally cluster in and around Parque Central and charge around USD$40 per hour. The guiding qualities of your driver can vary. Hugely popular with tourists.

Bici-taxis Three-wheeled bicycle rickshaws that ply short inner-city routes, primarily in Habana Vieja. They should charge between USD$1 and USD$2 per ride. Agree on rates before you get in.

Havana Bus Tour Popular hop-on, hop-off double-decker that runs on three routes in Havana. All-day tickets cost USD$5 to USD$10.

---

station beforehand and bear in mind that, when running, these trains are slow, uncomfortable and unreliable.

🛈 Getting Around

TO/FROM THE AIRPORT

Public transportation from the airport into central Havana is practically nonexistent.

A standard taxi will cost you approximately CUC$25 (30 to 40 minutes).

True adventurers with light luggage and a tight budget can chance their arm on the P-12 metro bus from the Capitolio or the P-15 from the Hospital Nacional Hermanos Ameijeiras on the Malecón, both of which go to Santiago de las Vegas, stopping close to the airport (about 1.5km

away) on Av Rancho Boyeros. This is a lot easier for departing travelers, who will have better knowledge of local geography.

BOAT

Passenger ferries shuttle across the harbor to Regla and Casablanca, leaving every 15 or 20 minutes from the terminal **Emboque de Luz** (Map p68), at the corner of San Pedro and Santa Clara on the southeastern side of Habana Vieja. The fare is a flat 10 centavos, but foreigners are often charged USD$1. There's a quick bag search before you get on.

Cruise ships dock at the **Terminal Sierra Maestra – Cruise Terminal** (Map p68), adjacent to Plaza de San Francisco de Asís on the cusp of Habana Vieja.

BUS

The handy hop-on, hop-off **Habana Bus Tour** (Map p78) runs on two main routes: T1 and T3. The main stop is in Parque Central opposite the Hotel Inglaterra. This is the pickup point for bus T1, which runs from Habana Vieja via Centro Habana, the Malecón, Calle 23 and Plaza de la Revolución to La Cecilia at the western end of Playa; and bus T3, which runs from Centro Habana to Playas del Este (via Parque Histórico Militar Morro-Cabaña).

Bus T1 is an open-top double-decker. Bus T3 is an enclosed single-decker. All-day tickets for T1/T3 are USD\$10/5. Services run from 9am to 6pm, and routes and times are clearly marked on all bus stops. Beware: these bus routes and times have been known to change. Check the latest route maps at the bus stop in Parque Central.

Bus T2 is a shuttle that runs from La Cecilia to Marina Hemingway four times a day. It costs USD\$1 one way.

Havana's **metro bus service** calls on a relatively modern fleet of Chinese-made 'bendy' buses and is far less dilapidated than it used to be. These buses run regularly along 17 routes, connecting most parts of the city with the suburbs. Fares are 40 centavos (five centavos if you're using convertibles), which you deposit into a small slot in front of the driver when you enter. Cuban buses are crowded and little used by tourists. Guard your valuables closely.

All bus routes have the prefix P before their number:

P-1 La Rosita–Playa (via Virgen del Camino, Vedado, Línea, Av 3)

P-2 Alberro–Línea y G (via Vibora and Ciudad Deportiva)

P-3 Alamar–Túnel de Línea (via Virgen del Camino and Vibora)

P-4 San Agustín–Terminal de Trenes (via Playa, Calle 23, La Rampa)

P-5 San Agustín–Terminal de Trenes (via Lisa, Av 31, Línea, Av de Puerto)

P-6 Reparto Eléctrico–La Rampa (via Vibora)

P-7 Alberro–Capitolio (via Virgen del Camino)

P-8 Reparto Eléctrico–Villa Panamericano (via Vibora, Capitolio and harbor tunnel)

P-9 Vibora–Hospital Militar (via Cuatro Caminos, La Rampa, Calle 23, Av 41)

P-10 Vibora–Playa (via Altahabana and Calle 100)

P-11 Alamar–Vedado (via harbor tunnel)

P-12 Santiago de las Vegas–Capitolio (via Av Boyeros)

P-13 Santiago de las Vegas–Vibora (via Calabazar)

P-14 San Agustín–Capitolio (via Lisa and Av 51)

P-15 Alamar/Guanabacoa–Capitolio (via Av Boyeros and Calle G)

P-16 Santiago de las Vegas–Vedado (via Calle 100 and Lisa)

PC Hospital Naval–Playa (via Parque Lenin)

Infotur offices publish a free map of Havana metro bus routes called *Por La Habana en P*.

CAR & MOTORCYCLE

There are lots of car-rental offices in Havana but a big shortage of rentable cars. You are thus advised to make reservations from your home country at least one month in advance. There are three main state-run agencies: Cubacar, Via and Rex. All have offices at Aeropuerto Internacional José Martí's Terminal 3. Otherwise, there's a car-rental desk in any three-star (or higher) hotel. Prices vary depending on make of car, rental period and season. The cheapest you'll get is around USD\$60 per day. An average medium-size rental costs closer to USD\$80 per day.

Cubacar has desks at most of the big hotels, including Meliá Cohiba, Meliá Habana, Iberostar Parque Central, Habana Libre and Sevilla.

Rex Rent a Car (☎ 7-836-7788; www.rex.cu; cnr Línea & Malecón; ☺ 9am-5pm) rents fancy cars for extortionate prices.

Cupet-Cimex gas stations are in Vedado at Calles L and 17; Malecón and Calle 15; Malecón and Paseo near the Riviera and Meliá Cohiba hotels; and on Av de la Independencia (northbound lane) south of Plaza de la Revolución. All are open 24 hours a day.

1. Callejón de los Peluqueros 2. Callejón de Hamel 3. Callejón del Chorro 4. Callejón Espada

ALVARFUENTE/SHUTTERSTOCK ©

The Back Alleys of Havana

Havana has become known for its *callejones* (back alleys) in recent years, many of them organized around privately run community projects inspired by art, food and even hairdressing. Here is a leading quartet:

Callejón del Chorro

Habana Vieja's culinary alley was once a forgotten cul-de-sac that contained little more than a graphic artist's co-op. Today it is a beehive of mega popular private restaurants packed with alfresco seating and guarded by a gauntlet of over-keen waiters. Notwithstanding, the Chorro, just off Plaza de la Catedral, contains some of Havana's best restaurants, including Doña Eutimia (p117).

Callejón de Hamel

Havana's most famous back alley (p87) is located in a small subneighborhood of Centro Habana called Cayo Hueso and is dedicated to street art, live music, Afro-Cuban folklore and Santería.

Callejón Espada

Named after a reformist 19th-century Havana bishop, Espada cuts diagonally across the Habana Vieja grid in the genteel Loma del Ángel neighborhood. Reclaimed as a community project a few years ago, its repaved sidewalks are often filled with locals playing dominoes, or tourists sipping mojitos outside the bars and restaurants of Five Corners (Cinco Esquinas), where Espada merges with Calles Cuarteles and Habana.

Callejón de los Peluqueros

The short 100m stretch of Calle Aguiar on the north side of Habana Vieja has been transformed into a hairdressing-themed art project by a local barber named Gilberto Valladares, aka 'Papito,' in tandem with the Office of the City Historian. Anchored by Papito's own salon, which doubles as a museum called Arte Corte (p82), the street is augmented by an art studio, a clothing boutique, several restaurants and a kids' playground.

AT A GLANCE

POPULATION
934,000

**OLDEST COFFEE
PLANTATION RUINS**
Cafetal Buenavista
(p156): founded 1801

BEST COFFEE
Patio de María (p158)

BEST RESORT
Memories Jibacoa
Beach (p160)

BEST HIKE
Sendero La Serafina
(p156)

WHEN TO GO

May–Nov
The wettest and
warmest months.

Dec–Apr
Best for the beaches
at Playa Jibacoa,
although you'll
encounter higher
prices and more
tourists. Big parties
include Bejucal's
Las Charangas
in December the
International
Humor Festival in
San Antonio de los
Baños in April.

Soroa (p154), Artemisa Province
POOPEE/SHUTTERSTOCK ©

Artemisa & Mayabeque Provinces

Leap-frogged by almost all international visitors, Cuba's two smallest provinces, created by dividing Havana Province in 2010, are the preserve of more everyday concerns – like growing half of the crops that feed the nation, for example. But in among the patchwork of citrus and pineapple fields lies a smattering of small towns that will satisfy travelers always keen to peer around the next corner.

The only advertised tourist destination is Las Terrazas, Cuba's most successful ecoproject and an increasingly important nexus for trekking and birdwatching. East of Havana, Jibacoa's beaches are the domain of a trickle of Varadero-avoiding tourists who guard their secret tightly. Wander elsewhere and you'll be in mainly Cuban company (or none at all) contemplating sugar-plantation ruins, humorous one-of-a-kind museums and improbably riotous festivals. For a kaleidoscope of the whole region, take the ridiculously slow Hershey train through the nation's proverbial backyard and admire the view.

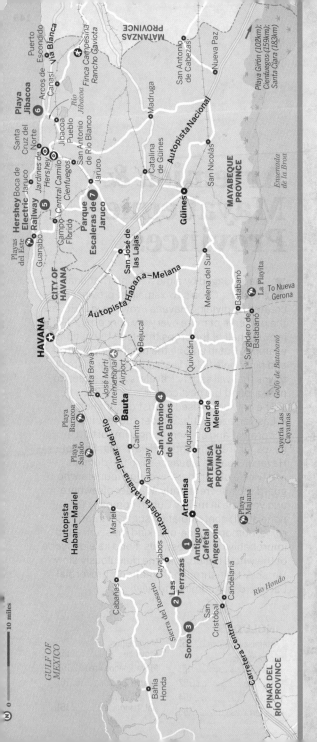

Artemisa & Mayabeque Provinces Highlights

1 **Antiguo Cafetal Angerona** (p152) Roaming the abandoned ruins of a once-mighty coffee plantation.

2 **Las Terrazas** (p155) Going green at Cuba's primary ecovillage, where the slopes have been replanted with trees, flowers, painters and poets.

3 **Soroa** (p154) Hiking in the so-called rainbow of Cuba amid giant ferns and diminutive orchids.

4 **Museo del Humor** (p151) Seeing the funny side of San Antonio de los Baños.

5 **Hershey Electric Railway** (p160) Escaping the tourist trails on the temperamental electric railway of an erstwhile chocolate czar.

6 **Playa Jibacoa** (p159) Bagging a beach retreat where you can snorkel direct from the shore.

7 **Parque Escaleras de Jaruco** (p161) Feasting with a view and weekending Havana folk amid the heights of Mayabeque.

History

Havana was founded on the site of modern-day Surgidero de Batabanó in 1515 but rapidly relocated; the region's role in shaping Cuba was to make it an almost exclusively agricultural one, with coffee and sugar the key crops. Western Artemisa was the center of the country's short-lived coffee boom from 1820 until 1840, when sugar took over as the main industry. Large numbers of enslaved people were recruited to work on the plantations during the second half of the 19th century, when Cuba became the center of the Caribbean slave trade; as such, the area became a focus for the events leading up to the abolition of slavery in the 1880s.

The success of the sugar industry swept over into the 20th century: sweets mogul Milton S Hershey turned to Mayabeque as a dependable source for providing sugar for his milk chocolate in 1914. This lucrative industry would later suffer under Fidel Castro, once the Americans and then the Russians ceased to buy Cuba's sugar at over-the-odds prices. The region was hard-hit economically, and this deprivation was perhaps best epitomized by the 1980 Mariel Boatlift, when a port on the coast west of Havana became the stage for a Castro-sanctioned (and Jimmy Carter–endorsed) mass exodus of Cubans to Florida.

A major step against the area's downturn was taken in 1968. Neglected land in western Artemisa Province, around the very coffee plantations that had once sustained it, was reforested and transformed into a pioneering ecovillage – now one of the region's economic mainstays propped up by tourism.

ARTEMISA PROVINCE

In many ways a giant vegetable patch for Havana, Artemisa Province's fertile delights include the ecovillage of Las Terrazas and the outdoor action on offer among the densely forested slopes of the Sierra del Rosario mountain range. Then there are myriad mystery-clad coffee-plantation ruins and the ever-inventive town of San Antonio de los Baños, which has spawned an internationally renowned film school as well as some of Cuba's top artists. On the north coast, good beaches and great back roads entice the adventurous.

San Antonio de los Baños

POP 32,500

Full of surprises, artsy San Antonio de los Baños, 35km southwest of central Havana, is Cuba on the flip side, a hard-working municipal town where the local college churns out wannabe cinematographers and the museums are more about laughs than crafts.

Founded in 1986 with the help of Nobel Prize–winning Colombian novelist Gabriel García Márquez, San Antonio's Escuela Internacional de Cine y TV invites film students from around the world to partake in its excellent on-site facilities, including an Olympic-sized swimming pool for practicing underwater shooting techniques. Meanwhile, in the center of town, an unusual humor museum makes a ha-ha-happy break from the usual stuffed-animal/revolutionary-artifact double act.

San Antonio is also the birthplace of music giant Silvio Rodríguez, born here in 1946. Rodríguez went on to write the musical soundtrack to the Cuban Revolution almost single-handed. His best-known songs include 'Ojalá,' 'La Maza' and 'El Necio.'

◉ Sights & Activities

Boat trips on the Río Ariguanabo take off from a boat dock at the Hotel Las Yagrumas. A motor boat will take you on an 8km spin for USD$3, while rowing boats go for USD$1 an hour.

Iglesia de San Antonio
de los Baños   CHURCH
(cnr Calles 66 & 41) This impressive early-19th-century church has twin towers and porthole windows, and is the largest, grandest religious building in Artemisa and Mayabeque.

Museo del Humor   MUSEUM
(cnr Calle 60 & Av 45; USD$2; ◷10am-6pm Tue-Sat, 9am-1pm Sun) Unique in Cuba is this fun selection of cartoons, caricatures and other entertaining ephemera. Among the drawings exhibited in a neoclassical colonial house are saucy cartoons, satirical scribblings and the first known Cuban caricature, dating from 1848. Visit in April of odd-numbered years for extra laughs at the Biennial of Graphic Humor (entries remain on display for several weeks during this period).

The museum houses the work of Cuba's foremost caricaturist, Carlos Julio Villar

Alemán, a member of Uneac (Unión de Escritores y Artistas de Cuba) and one-time judge at the festival. A few times monthly, music and ballet are also staged here.

Galería Provincial Eduardo Abela GALLERY
(Calle 58 No 3708, cnr Calle 37; ⊙noon-8pm, from 8am Sat, 8am-noon Sun) FREE This bold and groundbreaking art gallery is anything but provincial. The first room focuses on painting while others showcase poignant black-and-white photography. The gallery is named after city son Eduardo Abela, a Cuban artist and satirist most famous for creating *El Bobo* (The Fool), a cartoon character who poked fun at the Gerardo Machado dictatorship of the 1920s and '30s.

🛏 Sleeping

Hotel Las Yagrumas HOTEL **$$**
(☑47-38-44-60; Calle 40 y Final Autopista; s/d from USD$30/40; [P][❄][≋]) A hotel of untapped potential, Las Yagrumas, 3km north of San Antonio de los Baños, overlooks the picturesque but polluted Río Ariguanabo. Its 120 rooms with balconies and terraces (some river facing) are popular with peso-paying Cubans as opposed to foreign tourists, but many fixtures are falling apart. Sports facilities are better; there's table tennis and a gigantic pool (nonguests pay CUC$6).

🍴 Eating & Drinking

San Antonio's main shopping strip is Av 41, and there are numerous places to snack on peso treats along this street. Full-blown restaurants are thinner on the ground. If in doubt, head to Don Oliva.

Don Oliva CUBAN **$**
(☑47-38-23-70; Calle 62 No 3512, btwn Calles 33 & 35; mains USD$3-6; ⊙noon-11pm Wed-Sun) Some of the cheapest lobster in Cuba is served on Don Oliva's secluded covered patio – barely 35km from the costly cuisine of Havana – and it's not bad either. Not surprisingly this is a refreshingly untouristed private restaurant with prices displayed in *moneda nacional* (Cuban pesos). Opt for the seafood.

Taberna del Tío Cabrera CLUB
(Calle 56 No 3910, btwn Calles 39 & 41; ⊙2-5pm, to 1am Sat & Sun) An attractive garden club that puts on occasional comedy shows organized in conjunction with the Museo del Humor (p151). The clientele is a mix of townies, folk from surrounding villages and film-school students.

❶ Getting There & Away

Hard to get to without a car, San Antonio is supposedly connected to Havana's Estación 19 de Noviembre (USD$1.50, one hour, four trains a day), but information is scant and services are unreliable. A taxi should cost USD$35 one way from central Havana (45 minutes).

Artemisa

POP 48,000

Capital of the province it may be, but Artemisa isn't, by any stretch of the imagination, a tourist mecca. This farming town's days of affluence and appeal lie firmly embedded in the past. Having once attracted notables such as Ernest Hemingway and the Cuban poet Nicolás Guillén, and having grown wealthy on the back of 19th-century sugar and coffee booms, Artemisa's importance declined when the bottom fell out of the sugar and coffee industries. It's known today as the Villa Roja (Red Town) for the famous fertility of its soil, which still yields a rich annual harvest of tobacco, bananas and sugarcane.

Artemisa has scant accommodations for tourists – Soroa is the nearest good option. As if in compensation, it has one of provincial Cuba's nicest *bulevares* (pedestrianized shopping streets) and its most romantic and accessible coffee-farm ruins.

◉ Sights

Artemisa contains two national monuments, along with a restored section of the La Trocha Mariel-Majana, a defensive wall erected by the Spanish during the Wars of Independence.

★**Antiguo Cafetal Angerona** HISTORIC SITE
(⊙dawn-dusk) FREE The Antiguo Cafetal Angerona, 5km west of Artemisa on the road to the Autopista Habana–Pinar del Río (A4), was one of Cuba's earliest *cafetales* (coffee farms). Erected between 1813 and 1820 by Cornelio Sauchay, it once employed 450 enslaved people tending 750,000 coffee plants. Behind the ruined mansion lie the slave barracks, an old watchtower from which the slaves were monitored, and multiple storage cellars. Receiving few visitors, it's a great place to take creative photos as you quietly contemplate Cuba's past.

The atmospheric gray walls and arches surrounded by sugarcane and gnarly trees have the feel of a latter-day Roman ruin.

TRAINSPOTTING

The provincial town of Bejucal in Mayabeque Province is a workaday sort of place, with one notable exception: its foundational role in Cuba's fascinating rail history.

Bejucal was the destination of Cuba's first pioneering train, which chugged into action in November 1837, long before any other country in Latin America had a rail network and – ironically – 11 years before its colonial overlord, Spain, acquired one. The inaugural line ran for 27.5km, connecting Havana with Bejucal. This success was followed up by an 80km line from Camagüey to the port of Nuevitas on Cuba's north coast and by 1848 tramways were crisscrossing the streets of Havana, before any European city outside of Paris.

Until the beginning of the 20th century, 80% of Cuban railways were associated with the sugar industry. It wasn't until 1902 that the west–east passenger network was joined for the first time by US-Canadian railway magnate William Van Horne (builder of the first Canadian transcontinental railway), creating a line that stretched 1100km from Guane in Pinar del Río Province to Guantánamo in the east.

After the revolution and the US trade embargo that ensued, Cuba's once ground-breaking rail network struggled to find fuel and rolling stock. By the 2010s it had tragically became a national joke.

Artemisa and Mayabeque Provinces remain good turf for spotting old locomotives, including the temperamental electric Hershey train. Bejucal's station – the nation's first – is a gaily painted affair, although the railway museum here no longer operates. Of Cuba's other rail museums, the Museo del Ferrocarril in Havana was closed until further notice at the time of research, but there's the Museo de Agroindustria Azucarero Marcelo Salado (p274) near Caibarién in Villa Clara Province.

A couple of daily trains still pass through Bejucal from Havana's Estación Central meaning you can still run (read: chug) along that inaugural rail route.

Look for the stone-pillared gateway and sign on the right after you leave Artemisa.

The estate is mentioned in novels by Cirilo Villaverde and Alejo Carpentier, and James A Michener devotes several pages to it in *Six Days in Havana*.

Mausoleo a los Mártires
de Artemisa   MAUSOLEUM
(☑ 47-36-32-76; Av 28 de Enero; ⊙9am-5pm Tue-Sun) FREE Revolution buffs may want to doff a cap to the Mausoleo a los Mártires de Artemisa. Of the 119 revolutionaries who accompanied Fidel Castro in the 1953 assault on the Moncada Barracks, 28 were from the Artemisa region, including current Cuban vice-president Ramiro Valdés. Fourteen of the men buried below the cube-shaped bronze mausoleum died in the assault or were killed soon after by Batista's troops. A small subterranean museum contains combatants' photos and personal effects.

✖ Eating & Drinking

Los Nardis   CUBAN $
(cnr Calles 49 & 42; mains USD$3-6; ⊙noon-midnight Tue-Sun) Unsignposted, thus hard-to-find, private restaurant a block from the main drag (Av 28 de Enero) that serves unadorned Cuban dishes featuring *mucho* rice and beans.

Miguel's   CUBAN $
(Calle 45 No 4811, btwn Calle 48 & Calle 50; mains USD$2-4; ⊙10am-11pm) Cute *paladar* (privately-owned restaurant) serving unusual (for Artemisa) dishes including crab, tamales and *bistec uruguayo* (Uruguayan steak). Favored by locals.

Cafe Cubita   CAFE
(Búlevar, btwn Maceo & General Gómez; ⊙10am-10pm, to midnight Fri & Sat) This is one of the best outlets of Cuba's reinvigorated coffee chain, with comfortable seating, a comprehensive coffee menu and table service. Bonus: it does cheap (USD$1 to USD$2) toasted sandwiches on fresh Cuban bread. Practically everyone opts for the *café helado* (coffee ice-cream milk shake).

❶ Getting There & Away

Despite its proximity to Havana, travel to and from Artemisa can be problematic. Car or taxi is the easiest way in.

The bus station is on the Carretera Central in the center of Artemisa, but is served by local buses only (there are no written timetables).

Artemisa train station (Av Héroes del Moncada) is four blocks east of the bus station. There are supposed to be two trains a day from Havana (USD$2.20, two hours) at noon and midnight, but don't bank on it.

Soroa

POP 7200

Known appropriately as the 'rainbow of Cuba,' Soroa, a gorgeous natural area and tiny settlement 85km southwest of Havana, is the closest mountain resort to the capital. Located 8km north of Candelaria in the Sierra del Rosario, the easternmost and highest section of the Cordillera de Guaniguanico, the region's heavy rainfall (more than 1300mm annually) promotes the growth of tall trees and orchids. The area gets its name from Jean-Pierre Soroa, a Frenchman who owned a 19th-century coffee plantation in these hills. One of his descendants, Ignacio Soroa, created the park as a personal retreat in the 1920s, and only since the revolution has this luxuriant region been developed for tourism.

While it shares the same abundant flora as Las Terrazas, Soroa is generally quieter and receives fewer tourists. It's a great area to explore by bike.

Sights

Finca Excelencia   FARM

(☑5-306-4315; Carretera Soroa Km 11; USD$5; ☉dawn-dusk) Fitting right into the ecological rainbow of Soroa is this private farm where you can relax, learn about medicinal plants and even partake in a day of voluntary work (and learning). Stroll through the diligently tilled sloping grounds and feast your eyes upon 140 varieties of fruit (blended into juices and smoothies) and over 300 types of orchids. Higher up sit two *miradores* that teeter over tremendous views doused with a hundred different shades of green.

Orquideario Soroa   GARDENS

(Carretera Soroa Km 9; USD$3; ☉8:30am-4:30pm) Tumbling down a landscaped hillside garden next door to Hotel & Villas Soroa is this labor of love built in the late 1940s by Spanish lawyer Tomás Felipe Camacho, in memory of his wife and daughter. Camacho traveled round the world to amass his collection of 700 orchid species (the largest in Cuba), including many endemic plants. Though he died in the 1960s, the Orquideario, connected to the University of Pinar del Río, lives on with guided tours in Spanish or English.

Salto del Arco Iris   WATERFALL

(Carretera Soroa Km 8; USD$3; ☉9am-6pm) The vegetation-rich 'rainbow falls' is a 22m-high cascade on the Arroyo Manantiales. The entrance to the park encompassing it is to the right just before the Hotel & Villas Soroa. A path corkscrews to two viewpoints above and below the falls, which are at their most impressive in the May-to-October rainy season and at other times a trickle. You can swim here. There's also a roughshod snack bar.

Activities

Most of Soroa's activities can be arranged at the Hotel & Villas Soroa, including horseback riding and hikes. Alternatively, ask at your casa particular (private homestay). Other trails lead to a rock formation known as Labyrinth de la Sierra Derrumbada and an idyllic bathing pool, the Poza del Amor (Pond of Love). The hotel is also the main information point for the area.

⭐ Mirador Loma El Mogote   HIKING

(Carretera Soroa Km 8) Starting at the Baños Romanos (Carretera Soroa Km 8; per hour USD$5), take the signposted well-trodden path 2km uphill to the *mirador*, a rocky crag with an incredible sweeping panorama of all Soroa and the coastal flats beyond. A stone staircase provides access to the steep summit where hungry turkey vultures circle below.

El Brujito   HIKING

(per person USD$15) This hike goes to the tiny isolated village of El Brujito, still inhabited by the descendants of enslaved people who once worked on a former French-run coffee plantation. The village is pretty much self-sufficient and sports a school with just four pupils, all in different grades. This hike is around 15km and you'll need about seven hours to complete it with a guide.

Ruinas de los Cafetales Franceses   HIKING

(per person USD$12) The ruins of several French coffee farms – La Independencia, La Esperanza and La Merced – can be seen during this four-hour hike that pitches northeast from the Villa Soroa.

La Rosita   HIKING

(per person USD$12) For some great birdwatching, head out on one of the more adventurous trails in Soroa, to the former ecovillage of La Rosita (itself sadly destroyed by a hurricane), perched in the hills beyond the Hotel & Villas Soroa. Nevertheless, this is one of the rare opportunities to experience rural life as Cubans do – without the 'acting up' to tourists. Around 8km.

🛏 Sleeping

Nearly every house along the road from Candelaria to Soroa rents rooms, plus there are two hotels. Soroa makes an excellent alternative base for visiting Las Terrazas and, in its own way, is equally beautiful.

Maité Delgado   CASA PARTICULAR **$**
(☑5-227-0069; yeisondelg@nauta.cu; Carretera Soroa Km 7; r USD$25-30; [P]❋) A bright family home a 15-minute walk from most of the Soroa sights, Maité's is a slice of rustic heaven with rocking chairs on the porch, a verdant garden and five funky rooms decked out in various themes and styles (choose *yours*). Comfort in *el campo*.

Don Agapito   CASA PARTICULAR **$**
(☑5-812-1791; donagapitosoroa@nauta.cu; Carretera Soroa Km 8; r USD$20-25; [P]❋) Two well-lit, super-clean rooms and some professional touches, including several personalized maps of the province and the local walking trails, make a stopover at this private homestay right next to the Orquideario a real pleasure. The food is equally marvelous.

Casa Las Piedras   CASA PARTICULAR **$**
(☑5-336-4997; casalaspiedrassoroa@gmail.com; Carretera a Soroa Km 3.5; r USD$25; [P]❋) 🖋
Private homestay, ecofarm and diminutive restaurant, Las Piedras perfectly captures the spirit of Soroa. There are four bright independent rooms surrounded by lush greenery and your breakfast fruit is plucked fresh from the trees out back. The downside? You're a good 6km from Soroa's main sights so your own wheels will come in handy.

Hotel & Villas Soroa   RESORT **$$**
(☑48-52-35-34; Carretera Soroa Km 9; s/d/tr incl breakfast USD$49/78/105; [P]❋🛜🏊) You can't knock the setting of this place, nestled in a narrow valley amid stately trees and verdant hills, though you might wonder about the juxtaposition of these scattered block-like cabins against such a breathtaking natural backdrop. Isolated and tranquil, there are 80 renovation-craving rooms in a spacious complex just shouting-distance from the forest.

Castillo de las Nubes   BOUTIQUE HOTEL **$$$**
(Castle of the Clouds; ☑48-52-35-34; s/d/ste USD$150/175/250; [P]❋🛜🏊) A romantic faux-European castle with a circular tower on a hilltop 1.5km up a rough road beyond the Orquideario Soroa, the Castillo de las Nubes was built by wealthy farmer Antonio Arturo Bustamante in 1940, but was quickly abandoned after the revolution. In 2016 it reopened as a six-room boutique hotel with a bar-restaurant, small pool and expansive Soroa views in every direction.

🍴 Eating

All the accommodations in Soroa provide meals, with the casas particulares (private homestays) offering the best food. Good job, too, as there aren't many stand-alone restaurants.

Restaurante el Salto   CUBAN **$**
(Carretera Soroa Km 8; mains USD$5-12; ⊙9am-7pm; [P]) This simple place at the start of the path to the waterfall is one of the few independent eating options outside Soroa's hotels and casas particulares (private homestays). It serves basic Cuban food – high on bulk, if low on taste.

❶ Getting There & Away

The Havana–Viñales **Víazul** (www.viazul.com) bus stops in Las Terrazas, but not Soroa; you can cover the last 16km in a taxi for USD$15 (15 minutes). If staying at a casa particular (room in a private home), ask about lifts. Transfer buses (not to be depended upon) sometimes pass through Soroa between Viñales and Havana. Inquire at Hotel & Villas Soroa, or at Infotur in Viñales (p187) or Havana (p142).

The only other access to Soroa and the surrounding area is with your own wheels: car, bicycle or moped. The **Servi-Cupet gas station** is on the Autopista at the turnoff to Candelaria, 8km below Soroa.

Las Terrazas

POP 1200

The pioneering ecovillage of Las Terrazas dates back to a reforestation project in 1968. Today it's a Unesco Biosphere Reserve, a burgeoning activity center and the site of the earliest coffee plantations in Cuba. Not surprisingly, it attracts day-trippers from Havana by the busload.

Over-nighters can stay in the community's sole hotel, the mold-breaking Hotel Moka, a midrange ecoresort built between 1992 and 1994 by workers drawn from Las Terrazas to attract foreign tourists. Close by, in the picturesque whitewashed village that overlooks a small lake, there's a vibrant art community with open studios, woodwork and pottery workshops. But the region's biggest attraction is its verdant natural surroundings, which are ideal for hiking, relaxing and birdwatching.

◉ Sights

Cafetal Buenavista HISTORIC SITE

FREE The most moving ruins in Las Terrazas are about 1.5km up the hill from the **Puerta las Delicias** eastern gate, and accessible by road. Cafetal Buenavista is Cuba's oldest (now partially restored) coffee plantation, built in 1801 by French refugees from Haiti. Ruins of the quarters of some of the 126 enslaved people held by the French-Cuban owners here can be seen alongside the driers.

The attic of the master's house (now a restaurant) was used to store the beans until they could be carried down to the port of Mariel by mule. There are decent views from here, best appreciated on the Sendero las Delicias hike which incorporates the *cafetal*.

Casa-Museo Polo Montañez MUSEUM

(◉9am-5pm Mon-Fri) **FREE** The former lakeside house of local musician Polo Montañez, regarded as one of Cuba's finest-ever folk singers, is now a small museum containing various gold records and assorted memorabilia. It's right in Las Terrazas village, overlooking the lake. Polo's most famous songs include 'Guajiro Natural' and 'Un Montón de Estrellas;' they captured the heart of the nation between 2000 and 2002 with simple lyrics about love and nature. His stardom was short-lived, however: he died in a car accident near Las Terrazas in 2002.

San Pedro & Santa Catalina HISTORIC SITE

FREE These ruins of a 19th-century coffee estate are down a branch road at La Cañada del Infierno (Trail to Hell), midway between the Hotel Moka access road and the Soroa side entrance gate. A kilometer off the main road, just before the ruins of the San Pedro coffee estate, a bar overlooks a popular swimming spot. After this it's another kilometer to Santa Catalina. A trail (p154) leads on from here to Soroa.

Hacienda Unión HISTORIC SITE

FREE About 3.5km west of the Hotel Moka access road, the Hacienda Unión is a partially reconstructed coffee-estate ruin that features a country-style restaurant, a small flower garden known as the Jardín Unión and horseback riding (USD$8 per hour).

La Plaza PLAZA

(◉9am-5pm) In the middle of Las Terrazas village at the top of a large knoll, this mini-mall encompasses a cinema, a cafe, a library and a small ecomuseum that gives an overview of the community's short history.

All are generally open throughout the day, or can become so if you ask at the Oficinas del Complejo (p158).

Galería de Lester Campa GALLERY

(◉hours vary) **FREE** Several well-known Cuban artists are based at Las Terrazas, including Lester Campa, whose work has been exhibited internationally. Pop into his lakeside studio-gallery, on the right-hand side a few houses after Casa-Museo Polo Montañez.

🏃 Activities & Tours

The Sierra del Rosario has some of the best hikes in Cuba. They're all guided, so you can't officially do any of them on your own (nonexistent signposting deters all but the hardiest from trying). On the upside, most of the area's guides are highly knowledgeable, which means you'll emerge from the experience both fitter and wiser. There were five different hikes available at last visit, each costing USD$22 per person. Book at the Oficinas del Complejo (p158) or Hotel Moka.

★ Sendero la Serafina HIKING

(per person USD$22) The easy 6.4km La Serafina loop starts and finishes near the Oficinas del Complejo (p158). It's a well-known paradise for birdwatchers (there are more than 70 species on show). Halfway through the walk you will pass the ruins of the Cafetal Santa Serafina, one of the first coffee farms in the Caribbean. Reserve three hours for this guided excursion.

El Contento HIKING

(per person USD$22) This 9km ramble takes you through the reserve's foothills between the Campismo el Taburete (rustic accommodations for Cubans only) and the Baños del San Juan, taking in two coffee-estate ruins: San Ildefonso and El Contento. You'll have to hike 5km along a quiet road to get back to the start or arrange a taxi (around USD$3).

El Taburete HIKING

(per person USD$22) This 6km hike follows a direct route over the 452m Loma el Taburete, where a poignant monument is dedicated to the 38 Cuban guerrillas who trained in these hills for Che Guevara's ill-fated Bolivian adventure. It's a 5km walk along a quiet road (or USD$3 taxi ride) to and from the start of the hike.

Sendero las Delicias HIKING

(per person USD$22) This 3km route runs from near the Oficinas del Complejo (p158) to the

Cafetal Buenavista, incorporating some fantastic views and plenty of birdwatching opportunities. Book and pay at the Oficinas del Complejo or Hotel Moka .

Baños del San Juan SWIMMING
(incl lunch USD$15; ⊘9am-6pm) It's hard to envisage more idyllic natural swimming pools than those situated 3km to the south of Hotel Moka down an undulating paved road. These *baños* (baths) are surrounded by terraced rocks, where the clean, bracing waters cascade into a series of pools.

Riverside, there are a handful of open-air eating places, along with changing rooms, showers and overnight **cabins** (☑48-57-86-00; cabin s/d USD$15/25), though the spot still manages to retain a sense of rustic isolation.

Canopy Tour ADVENTURE
(per person USD$17) Cuba's original canopy tour and still its best has six zip lines that catapult you over Las Terrazas village and the Lago del San Juan like a turkey vulture in flight. The total 'flying' distance is 1600m. Professional instructors maintain high safety standards. To book the zip lining, get in touch with the Oficinas del Complejo (p158).

🛏 Sleeping

The ecofriendly Hotel Moka is Las Terrazas' emblematic hotel. From here, you can also book five rustic cabins 3km away in Río San Juan (single/double USD$15/25) or arrange tent camping (USD$12). There are also three villas (single/double USD$102/140) available for rent in the village.

There are a couple of casas particulares (rooms in private homes) on the eastern approach road to Las Terrazas, a kilometer or so outside the entrance to the reserve.

Hospedaje Villa Duque CASA PARTICULAR $
(☑5-322-1431; Carretera a Cayajabos Km 2, Finca San Andrés; r incl breakfast USD$25-30; P※) Ecotourism doesn't have to come at a cost. This farmhouse 2km before the eastern entrance of Las Terrazas has two spick-and-span rooms, a fridge full of beer, a wraparound balcony and farm breakfasts for USD$5 extra.

Hotel Moka RESORT $$
(☑48-57-86-00; www.lasterrazas.cu; s/d/tr USD$88/136/187; P※🛜🛝) 🍴 Cuba's self-proclaimed ecohotel might not qualify for the four stars it advertises, but who's arguing? With its trickling fountains, blooming flower garden and resident tree growing through the lobby, Moka certainly aims to integrate with its verdant surroundings. The 26 bright, spacious rooms have fridges, satellite TV and bathtubs with stupendous views (there are blinds for the shy).

Equipped with a bar, restaurant, shop, pool and tennis court, the hotel also acts as an information portal for the reserve and can organize everything from hiking to zip lining.

BIRTH OF AN ECO-PROJECT

Back in 1968, when the nascent environmental movement was a prickly protest group led by hippies with names like 'Swampy,' the forward-thinking Cubans – concerned about the ecological cost of island-wide deforestation – came up with an idea.

The plan involved taking a 50-sq-km tract of degraded western mountains land that had once supported a network of French coffee farms and reforesting it on terraced, erosion-resistant slopes. In 1971, with the first phase of the plan completed, the workers were tasked to create a reservoir, and on its shores construct a small settlement of white houses to provide much-needed housing for the area's disparate inhabitants.

The result was Las Terrazas, Cuba's first ecovillage, a thriving community of 1200 inhabitants whose self-supporting, sustainable settlement today includes a hotel, myriad artisan shops and a vegetarian restaurant that utilizes small-scale organic farming techniques. The project was so successful that, in 1985, the land around Las Terrazas was incorporated into Cuba's first Unesco Biosphere Reserve, the Sierra del Rosario.

In 1994, as the tourist industry was expanded to counteract the economic effects of the Special Period, Las Terrazas opened Hotel Moka, an environmentally congruous hotel designed by minister of tourism and green architect Osmani Cienfuegos, brother of the late revolutionary hero, Camilo.

Now established as Cuba's most authentic ecoresort, Las Terrazas operates on principles that include energy efficiency, sustainable agriculture, environmental education and a sense of harmony between buildings and landscape. Far from being degraded, the hills around Las Terrazas these days attract the country's most diverse and abundant birdlife.

HAVANA CLUB'S HUB

Some 30km west of the province-spanning Bacunayagua Bridge, Santa Cruz del Norte is a quiet town that's home to a famous rum factory: the Ronera Santa Cruz, producer of Havana Club rum. It's one of the biggest plants of its kind in Cuba.

Havana Club, founded in 1878 by the Arechabala family of Cárdenas, produced one of Cuba's finest rums (rivaling Bacardí) with much success in a huge factory in their hometown, until the revolution when the business was nationalized. The Arechabalas fled to the US where they gave up rum production and let the trademark lapse. In 1976 it was snapped up by the Cuban government and, the following year, they opened up a new distillery at Santa Cruz del Norte with the capacity to produce 30 million liters of rum annually. Although not sold in the US, the rum has since become an international hit and a defining symbol of Cuba, despite competing with a rival 'Havana Club' produced by Bacardí in Puerto Rico.

In 2007 the government opened a second Havana Club factory in San José de las Lajas, also in Mayabeque Province.

✗ Eating & Drinking

Las Terrazas has a scattered collection of country-style restaurants, open to the elements and purveying simple *comida criolla* (Creole food). In the village itself there are some more sophisticated offerings, including a bona fide vegetarian restaurant – a rarity in Cuba.

Fonda de Mercedes　　　　CUBAN $
(mains USD$6-8; ⏰9am-6pm) 🍴 On a terrace beside her home in an apartment block beneath Hotel Moka, Mercedes has been serving up vegetable soup and hearty home-cooked meat and fish dishes for years.

Casa del Campesino　　　CARIBBEAN $
(mains USD$5-8; ⏰9am-6pm; P) Of the *ranchónes* dotted around, this one adjacent to the Hacienda Unión, about 3.5km west of the Hotel Moka access road, is a visitor favorite. The only proviso: you'd better like rice and beans.

El Romero　　　　　　VEGETARIAN $
(📞48-57-85-55; Las Terrazas; mains USD$3-10; ⏰noon-9pm; 🍴) 🍴 One of Cuba's few full-blown ecorestaurants, El Romero specializes in vegetarian fare, uses solar energy, home-grown organic vegetables and herbs, and keeps its own bees. With over a decade of experience, it's become a deft hand at fabricating *cremas* (soups), pies, wild rice, tempuras and crepes in a country not overly schooled in meat-free diets.

Casa de Botes　　　　　SEAFOOD $$
(mains USD$5-9; ⏰9am-10pm) The community's fish specialist is suspended on stilts above Lago del San Juan – where you can first work up an appetite on a kayak.

Patio de María　　　　　　CAFE
(⏰9am-10pm) 🍴 Patio de María is a small, brightly painted coffee bar that dispatches one of the best brews in Cuba. The secret comes in the expert confection and the fact that Las Terrazas touts a coffee culture that goes back 220 years.

ℹ Information

Las Terrazas is 20km northeast of Hotel & Villas Soroa (p155) and 13km west of the Havana–Pinar del Río Autopista at Cayajabos. There are toll gates at both entrances to the Biosphere Reserve (per person USD$4). The eastern toll gate, Puerta las Delicias (p156), is a good source of information on the park, while the best place to get information and arrange excursions is at the **Oficinas del Complejo** (📞48-57-85-55, 4857-8700; ⏰8am-5pm), or at Hotel Moka (p157), perched behind trees above the village. Both places act as nexus points for the reserve.

For more information see: www.lasterrazas.cu

ℹ Getting There & Away

Two Víazul (www.viazul.com) buses a day currently stop next door to the Oficinas del Complejo; one bound for Pinar del Río and Viñales (USD$8, 2¼ hours), the other heading to Havana (USD$6, 1½ hours). Occasional transfer buses, which run when they have enough passengers, pass through bound for Havana or Viñales. Inquire at Hotel Moka (p157) or contact the Viñales office of Infotur (p187).

ℹ Getting Around

Most excursions around Las Terrazas organize transport, otherwise you'll have to rely on hire car, taxi or your own two feet to get around.

There's an **Essto gas station** 1.5km west of the Hotel Moka (p157) access road. Self-drivers should fill up here before heading east to Havana or west to Pinar del Río.

MAYABEQUE PROVINCE

Tiny Mayabeque, now the country's smallest province, is a productive little place, cultivating citrus fruit, tobacco, grapes for wine and the sugarcane for Havana Club rum, the main distillery of which is in Santa Cruz del Norte. Tourists, predominantly Cubans, come here principally for the sandy coast in the northeast, drawn by the good-value resorts that back onto beautiful beaches for a fraction of the price of a Varadero vacation. Inland, amid the workaday agricultural atmosphere, lie some luxuriant landscapes accentuated by the jungle-like terraces of Jaruco.

Playa Jibacoa Area

Playa Jibacoa is the Varadero that never was, or the Varadero yet to come – depending on your hunch. For the time being it's a mainly Cuban getaway, with a coastal branch road from the main Vía Blanca highway winding by two small all-inclusive resorts, a hotel-standard campismo (cheap rustic accommodations) and several other shoreline sleeping options thrown in for good measure. Punctuated by a series of small but splendid beaches and blessed with good snorkeling accessible direct from the shore, Jibacoa is backed by a lofty limestone terrace overlooking the ocean. The terrace offers excellent views and some short DIY hikes.

The Vía Blanca, running between Havana and Matanzas, is the main transport artery in the area, although few buses make scheduled stops here, making Playa Jibacoa a more challenging pit stop than it should be. Just inland are picturesque farming communities and tiny time-warped hamlets linked by the Hershey Electric Railway.

◉ Sights & Activities

Puente de Bacunayagua   BRIDGE
Marking the border between Havana and Matanzas provinces, this is Cuba's longest (314m) and highest (103m) bridge. Begun in 1957 and finally opened by Fidel Castro in September 1959, it carries the busy Vía Blanca across a densely wooded canyon that separates the Valle de Yumurí from the sea. There's a snack bar and observation deck (8am to 10pm) on the Havana side of the bridge, where you can sink some drinks in front of one of Cuba's most awe-inspiring views.

You'll be looking out over hundreds of royal palm trees standing like ghostly sentries on the sheering valley slopes and, in the distance, dark, bulbous hills and splashes of blue ocean.

The snack bar and observation deck are a favorite stopping-off point for tour buses and taxis, and aside from hiring a car, these are your only means of visiting.

Central Camilo Cienfuegos   LANDMARK
Standing disused on a hilltop like a huge rusting iron skeleton, this former sugar mill, 5km south of Santa Cruz del Norte, was one of Cuba's largest and a testimony to the country's previous production clout. Opened in 1916, it once belonged to the Philadelphia-based Hershey Chocolate Company, which used the sugar to sweeten its world-famous chocolate. The Hershey Electric Railway (p160) used to transport produce and workers between Havana, Matanzas and the small town that grew up around the mill.

The mill was closed in July 2002; the train technically still runs (offering the best views of the rusting factory), but was *roto* (broken) at last visit.

Jardines de Hershey   GARDENS
Once lush – now largely overgrown – gardens formerly owned by the famous American chocolate tycoon Milton Hershey who ran the nearby sugar mill. There's an element of charming wildness in the winding paths, abundant green foliage and partially dammed river, although the thatched-roof restaurants and other facilities are a little run-down. The spot is mainly enjoyed by Cuban families who come to swim and relax.

From Playa Jibacoa, it's a pleasant 4km walk south of Santa Cruz del Norte.

Finca Campesina
Rancho Gaviota   OUTDOORS
(☏47-61-47-02; incl meal USD$8; ☺10am-5pm)
🏇 This activities center, 12km inland from Puerto Escondido via the pretty, palm-sprinkled Valle de Yumurí, is usually incorporated into 'jeep safaris' from Matanzas and Varadero. The hilltop ranch overlooks a reservoir and offers horseback riding, kayaking and cycling, plus a massive feast of local Cuban fare. Huts showcase various elements of Cuban agriculture, such as coffee and sugarcane – with tastings.

ARTEMISA & MAYABEQUE PROVINCES PLAYA JIBACOA AREA

THE HERSHEY TRAIN

'Cow on the line,' drawls the bored-looking ticket seller. 'Train shut for cleaning,' reads a scruffy hand-scrawled notice. To locals, the catalog of daily transport delays is tediously familiar. While the name of the antique Hershey Electric Railway might suggest a sweet treat to most visitors, in Cuba it signifies a more bitter mix of bumpy journeys, hard seats and interminable waits.

Built in 1921 by US chocolate 'czar' Milton S Hershey (1857–1945), the electric-powered railway line was originally designed to link the American mogul's humongous sugar mill in Mayabeque Province with stations in Matanzas and the capital. Running along a trailblazing rural route, it soon became a lifeline for isolated communities cut off from the provincial transport network.

In 1959 the Hershey factory was nationalized and renamed Central Camilo Cienfuegos (p159) after Cuba's celebrated rebel commander. But the train continued to operate, clinging unofficially to its chocolate-inspired nickname. In the true tradition of the post-revolutionary 'waste not, want not' economy, it also clung to the same tracks, locomotives, carriages, signals and stations.

While a long way from *Orient Express*–style luxury, an excursion on today's Hershey train is an intriguing journey back in time to the days when cars were for rich people and sugar was king. For outsiders, this is Cuba as the Cubans see it, a microcosm of rural life with all its daily frustrations, conversations, foibles and – occasionally – fun.

The train seemingly stops at every house, hut, horse stable and hillock between Havana and Matanzas (USD$2.80, four hours). Getting off is something of a toss-up, but be careful where you alight, as you could end up in the middle of nowhere. Suffice to say, most travelers stay on board for the whole journey, treating the ride as a travel adventure as opposed to a transport solution.

The Hershey train was *roto* (broken) at last visit with no information on how or when it might run again. Check for updates in Havana or Matanzas before making plans.

Self-drivers should take the inland road for 2km to Arcos de Canasí and turn left at the fork for another 10km to the signpost.

🛏 Sleeping

Campismo los Cocos　　　　CAMPISMO $
(☑ 47-29-52-31; www.campismopopular.cu; r from USD$19; 🅿 ❄ 🏊) The newest and nicest of Cubamar's 80 or more campismos (cheap, rustic accommodations), Los Cocos has facilities to match a midrange hotel and a beachside setting that emulates the big shots in Varadero. Ninety self-contained cabins are clustered around a pool set in the crook of the province's low, steplike cliffs.

Villa Tropico　　　　RESORT $$
(☑ 47-29-52-05; www.gran-caribe.com; Vía Blanca Km 60; s/d all-inclusive USD$48/70; 🅿 ❄ @ 🛜 🏊) This small, well-landscaped resort has great snorkeling and large spick-and-span rooms in cute concrete bungalows. Posh it isn't. Instead it's marketed as a three-star and is popular with repeat-visit package tourists from Canada.

★ **Memories Jibacoa Beach**　　RESORT $$$
(☑ 47-29-51-22; www.memoriesresorts.com; r all-inclusive from USD$175; 🅿 ❄ @ 🛜 🏊) Who knew? One of Cuba's best all-inclusive resorts isn't in Varadero (or any other resort strip for that matter), but in the more tranquil confines of Jibacoa. The secret? This 250-room resort doesn't try too hard. The trickling fountains, 24-hour pool and narrow but idyllic beach are elegantly unpretentious.

Then there's the joy of the surf and turf surroundings – snorkeling from the shore (with gear lent free to guests), an on-site dive center (immersions from USD$25), and trekking into the uplifted terraces just inland. Coming from Matanzas, the turnoff is 13km west of the Puente de Bacunayagua (p159).

❶ Getting There & Away

If it's working (services were mostly suspended when we last visited), it is possible to get to Playa Jibacoa on the Hershey Electric Railway from Casablanca train station in Havana to **Jibacoa Pueblo** (USD$1.65, 2½ hours). There's no bus to the beach from the station and traffic is sporadic, so bank on hiking the last 5km – a not unpleasant walk if you don't have too much gear.

Otherwise, you'll need your own wheels or a *colectivo* (shared taxi) from Havana.

Jaruco

POP 24,000

Jaruco, set back from the coast between Havana and Matanzas, is a good day trip for travelers with a car, moped or bike who want to give the beaches a body-swerve and instead sample quintessential rural Cuba.

Jaruco village is awash with pastel-hued houses bunched along gently pitching streets that wouldn't look amiss in the Peruvian Andes. The **Parque Escaleras de Jaruco**, 6km west, is even more precipitous. With its jungle-like vegetation, unexpected viewpoints and narrow winding road, the wild park is serenely spectacular.

Reached via hushed unmarked lanes, the protected area features forests, caves and strangely shaped limestone cliffs. Havana residents come here for bucolic weekend breaks Thursday through Sunday, the park's only official opening days, but with a minor road bisecting the park between Tapaste (off the Autopista Nacional) and Jaruco, you can slip in any time.

This forgotten oasis has outstanding *miradores* (viewpoints) over Mayabeque province. The highest and best is crowned by **El Árabe**, a bewitching if slightly bizarre restaurant built in the style of a mosque with a domed tower accessed by a spiral staircase and an interior decked out with rich Moorish lamps. The food could do with some work though.

❶ Getting There & Away

It's 32km to Jaruco from Guanabo in a southeasterly direction via Campo Florido, and you can make it a loop by returning through Santa Cruz del Norte, 18km northeast of Jaruco via Central Camilo Cienfuegos. A taxi from Havana costs USD$35 one-way (40 minutes).

It's possible to get to Jaruco on a branch line of the Hershey Electric Railway (if it's working),

a slow and ponderous journey. Take the train to Camilo Cienfuegos (USD$1.40, two hours) then change onto a train south to **Jaruco station** (USD$1, 30 minutes).

Surgidero de Batabanó

POP 22,500

Spanish colonizers founded the original settlement of Havana on the site of Surgidero de Batabanó on August 25, 1515, but quickly abandoned it in favor of the north coast. Looking around the decrepit town today, with its tumbledown clapboard houses and grubby beachless seafront, it's not difficult to see why. The only reason you're likely to end up in this fly-blown port is during the purgatorial bus-boat trip to the Isla de la Juventud. Should there be unforeseen delays, either staying within the port confines or cabbing it back to Havana are more attractive propositions than the town itself.

Fidel Castro and the other Moncada prisoners disembarked here on May 15, 1955, after Fulgencio Batista granted them amnesty. They made a quick getaway.

Los Dos Hermanos (Calle 68 No 521; mains USD$2-5; ⊙noon-10pm), the best answer to any ferry delay, is situated in a cute clapboard house that was once an elegant hotel. It serves straight-up Cuban nosh quickly and without unnecessary ceremony. Dig in; your next decent meal (if you're heading to La Isla) could be a long way away.

❶ Getting There & Away

The ferry from Surgidero de Batabanó to the Isla de la Juventud is supposed to leave daily at 12:30pm with an additional sailing at 5:30pm on Wednesday, Friday and Sunday (2½ hours). It is highly advisable to buy your bus-boat combo ticket (USD$50.20) in Havana (from the office at the main Astro bus station; p142) rather than turning up and doing it here. More often than not convertible tickets are sold out to bus passengers.

For self-drivers, there's a **Servi-Cupet gas station** (Calle 64 No 7110, btwn Avenidas 71 & 73) in Batabanó town. The next Servi-Cupet station east is in Güines.

Playa Sirena (p173), Cayo Largo del Sur
DBDO/SHUTTERSTOCK ©

Isla de la Juventud & Cayo Largo del Sur

H istoric refuge from the law for everyone from 16th-century pirates to 20th-century gangsters, La Isla is perhaps the quirkiest castaway destination you'll ever see. Dumped like a crumpled apostrophe 100km off mainland Cuba, this pine-tree-clad island is the Caribbean's sixth-largest. But the Cayman Islands this isn't. Other tourists? Uh-uh. And if you thought mainland Cuba's towns were time-warped, you haven't seen island capital Nueva Gerona, where the main street doubles as a baseball diamond, and the food 'scene' is stuck in the Special Period. If you make it here, you're in for a true adventure. Diving some of the Caribbean's most pristine reefs is the main lure – get used to being becalmed with the coral, the odd crocodile and a history that reads like an excerpt from *Treasure Island*.

Further east, Cayo Largo del Sur is La Isla's polar opposite, a manufactured tourist enclave renowned for its wide, white-sand beaches.

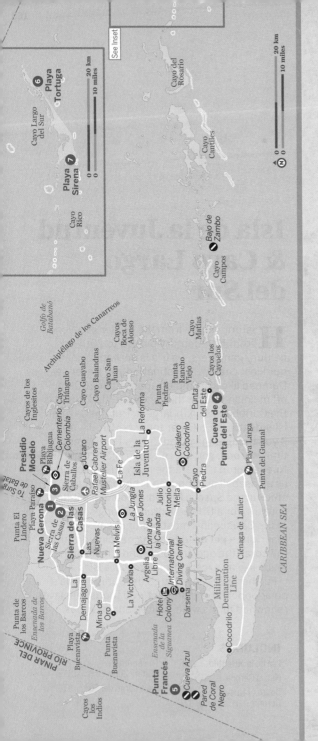

Isla de la Juventud & Cayo Largo del Sur Highlights

1 Nueva Gerona (p165)
Getting the lowdown on local life in the petite, sleepy island capital.

2 Sierra de las Casas (p167) Climbing the steep hills above Nueva Gerona to see the city (and island) splayed out below.

3 Presidio Modelo (p167) Exploring the ominous prison where Fidel Castro was once incarcerated.

4 Cueva de Punta del Este (p172) Seeing ancient cave paintings in the rarely visited militarized zone on the Isla de la Juventud.

5 Punta Francés (p171) Diving amid wrecks, walls, coral gardens and caves at arguably the best dive sites in Cuba.

6 Playa Tortuga (p173) Watching turtles nesting on the moonlit beaches of Cayo Largo del Sur.

7 Playa Sirena (p173) Trekking along the wide, white (sometimes nudist) beaches to Cayo Largo del Sur's finest stretch of sand.

History

La Isla's star-studded history starts with its first settlers, the Siboney, a pre-ceramic civilization who came to the island around 1000 BCE via the Lesser Antilles. They named their new homeland Siguanea and created a fascinating set of cave paintings, which still survive in Cueva de Punta del Este.

Columbus arrived in June 1494 and promptly renamed the island Juan el Evangelista, claiming it for the Spanish crown. But the Spanish did little to develop their new possession, which was knotted with mangroves and surrounded by shallow reefs.

Instead La Isla became a hideout for pirates, including Francis Drake and Henry Morgan. They called it Parrot Island, and their exploits are said to have inspired Robert Louis Stevenson's novel *Treasure Island*.

In December 1830 the Colonia Reina Amalia (now Nueva Gerona) was founded, and throughout the 19th century the island served as a place of imposed exile for independence advocates and rebels, including José Martí. Twentieth-century dictators Gerardo Machado and Fulgencio Batista followed this Spanish example by sending political prisoners – Fidel Castro included – to the island, which had by then been renamed a fourth time as Isla de Pinos (Isle of Pines).

As the infamous 1901 Platt amendment placed Isla de Pinos outside the boundaries of the 'mainland' part of the archipelago, some 300 US colonists also settled here, working the citrus plantations and building the efficient infrastructure that survives today (albeit a tad more dilapidated). By the 1950s La Isla had become a favored vacation spot for rich Americans, who flew in daily from Miami. Fidel Castro abruptly ended the decadent party in 1959.

In the 1960s and 1970s, thousands of young people from across the developing world volunteered to study here at specially built rural schools (most of which sit disused today). In 1978 their role in developing the island was officially recognized when the name was changed for the fifth time to Isla de la Juventud (Isle of Youth).

ISLA DE LA JUVENTUD

Large, very detached and set to a slow metronome, La Isla is both historically and culturally different from the rest of the Cuban archipelago. Mass sugar and tobacco production never existed here, and until the

Castro revolution the island yielded to a greater US influence – establishing eclectic expat communities that called on Cayman Island, American and Japanese ancestry.

Today the island, bereft of the foreign students that once populated its famous schools, is sleepy but extravagantly esoteric. Most Cubans have never visited its shores and foreigners sallying forth will need patience and perspective. The 'sights,' such as they are, include a sinister prison complex masquerading as a museum, a military zone you'll need a permit to enter and the nation's finest dive sites. The opportunities for getting (way) off the beaten track will appeal to escape artists, adventurers and committed contrarians.

Nueva Gerona

POP 46,000

Flanked by the Sierra de las Casas to the west and the Sierra de Caballos to the east, Nueva Gerona is a small, unhurried town that hugs the left bank of the Río las Casas, the island's only large river. Its museums and vivacious entertainment scene will detain, entertain and drain you for a day or two before you trundle out to explore the swashbuckling south, and it has virtually all of the island's somewhat scant services.

◉ Sights

◉ In Town

El Pinero MONUMENT
(Map p166; Calle 28) Two blocks east of Parque Guerrillero Heroico, you'll see a huge black-and-white ferry set up as a tatty memorial next to the river. This is El Pinero, the original boat used to transport passengers between La Isla and the main island. On May 15, 1955, Fidel and Raúl Castro, along with the other prisoners released from Moncada, returned to the main island on this vessel.

These days it's a meeting point for young reggaeton fanatics (read: very loud music) and the odd political rally.

Museo Municipal MUSEUM
(Map p166; Calle 30, btwn Calles 37 & 39; USD$1; ⊘9am-4:30pm Tue-Sun) In the former Casa de Gobierno (1853), the Museo Municipal houses a small historical collection that romps through the best of the island's past. It begins with a huge wall-mounted map of La Isla and continues through themed *salas*

Nueva Gerona

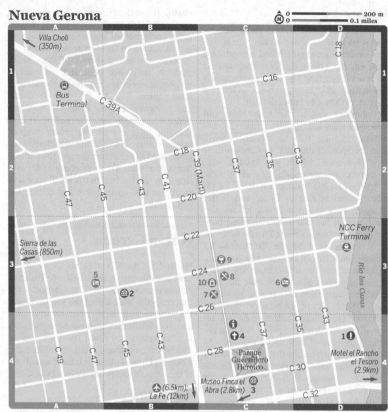

Nueva Gerona

(rooms) relating to indigenous peoples, pirates, US occupiers (most interestingly including gangster Charles 'Lucky' Luciano) and some local art.

Nuestra Señora de los Dolores   CHURCH
(Map p166; cnr Calles 28 & 39) On the northwest side of Parque Guerrillero Heroico, this dinky, Mexican colonial-style church was built in 1929, after the original was destroyed by a hurricane. In 1957 the parish priest, Guillermo Sardiñas, left Nueva Gerona to join Fidel Castro in the Sierra Maestra, the only Cuban priest to do so.

Museo Casa Natal Jesús Montané   MUSEUM
(Map p166; cnr Calles 24 & 45; ⊙9:30am-5pm Tue-Sat, 8:30am-noon Sun) **FREE** This museum documents the life of revolutionary Jesús Montané, who was born here, took part in the Moncada Barracks attack in 1953, fought alongside Fidel in the Sierra Maestra, and

served in the post-1959 government. It's a small but fascinating place and well worth 20 minutes of your time.

◎ Outside Town

★ Presidio Modelo   NOTABLE BUILDING

(guided visit USD$2; ◎ 8am-4pm Tue-Sat, to noon Sun) Welcome to the island's most impressive yet depressing sight. Located near Reparto Chacón, 5km east of Nueva Gerona, this striking prison was built between 1926 and 1931, during the repressive regime of Gerardo Machado. The four six-story and rather sinister-looking yellow circular blocks were modeled after those of a notorious penitentiary in Joliet, Illinois, and could hold 5000 prisoners at a time.

During WWII, assorted enemy nationals who happened to find themselves in Cuba (including 350 Japanese, 50 Germans and 25 Italians) were interned in the two rectangular blocks at the north end of the complex.

The Presidio's most famous inmates, however, were Fidel Castro and the other Moncada rebels, who were imprisoned here from October 1953 to May 1955. They were held separately from the other prisoners, in the hospital building at the complex's south end.

In 1967 the prison was closed and the section where Castro stayed was converted into a museum. There is one room dedicated to the history of the prison and several more focusing on the lives of the Moncada prisoners including Fidel (prisoner no. RN3859) who was briefly held in solitary confinement. Admission to the now skeletal circular blocks (the most moving part of the experience) is free.

Playa Bibijagua   BEACH

This unusual beach on the island's north coast, 4km to the east of Chacón, sports black sand rather than white, and pine trees rather than palms. Facilities begin and end with a peso restaurant, but there's plenty of low-key Cuban ambience. It's an easy bike ride from Nueva Gerona.

Playa Paraíso   BEACH

About 2km north of Chacón, Playa Paraíso is a dirty brown beach with good currents for water sports. The wharf was originally used to unload prisoners heading to the Presidio Modelo.

Cementerio Colombia   CEMETERY

The cemetery here contains the graves of Americans who lived and died on the island during the 1920s and 1930s. It's about 7km east of Nueva Gerona and 2km east of Presidio Modelo. Bus 38 passes by.

Presa El Abra   LAKE

(Carretera Siguanea; ◎ noon-5:30pm) Where have all the folk from Nueva Gerona gone? Gone to cool off in Presa El Abra, every one. On a scalding La Isla afternoon, you'd best join them. With verdant shores (perfect for picnics), this wide *presa* (reservoir) has a shaded outdoor restaurant (Carretera Siguanea Km 4; meals USD$1-4; ◎ noon-5:30pm; Ⓟ), plus various craft for aquatic shenanigans, including kayaks (USD$1.50 per hour) and aquatic bicycles (USD$3 per hour).

Museo Finca el Abra   MUSEUM

(Carretera Siguanea Km 2; USD$1; ◎ 9am-5pm Tue-Sat, to noon Sun) On October 17, 1870, the teenage José Martí spent nine weeks of exile at this farm-prison before his deportation to Spain. Legend has it that the revolutionary's mother forged the shackles he wore here into a ring, which Martí wore to his death. Set below the Sierra de las Casas, the old hacienda's surroundings are as much of an attraction as the museum. It's signed off the main road to Hotel Colony (a continuation of Calle 41), 3km southwest of Nueva Gerona.

The house is still occupied by descendants of Giuseppe Girondella, who hosted Martí here. A dirt road just before the museum leads north to the island's former marble quarry, clearly visible in the distance.

🏃 Activities

Sierra de las Casas   HIKING

Behold the view from the northernmost face of the craggy Sierra de las Casas! From the west end of Calle 22, a few hundred meters along a dirt track, a sinuous trail on the left heads toward the hills, at the foot of which is a deep cave and a local swimming hole. Beyond here a trail ascends steeply for around 1.5km to the mountaintop.

The view from the summit is amazing, taking in half the island, though the final stretch of the ascent is a bit closer to rock scrambling than hiking. For the sure-footed only.

🎉 Festivals & Events

Carnaval Pinero   CARNIVAL

(◎ Mar) A knees-up that includes parades with giant puppet-like heads, rodeo, sports competitions and perhaps just a little drinking. Held over three days in mid-March.

🛏 Sleeping

Casas particulares (private homestays) are your only town-center options and meals are provided; the owners will invariably meet arriving ferries. Nueva Gerona's two run-down state-operated hotels are south of town and are several years past their best-before date.

★ La Isla
CASA PARTICULAR $

(Map p166; ☑ 46-50-91-28; Calle 24, btwn Calles 45 & 47; r USD$15-20; ❄ 🛜 🐷) This fabulous place is worthy of any city on mainland Cuba. Run by a passionate *pinero* (person from the Isla) who knows and loves his island, it evokes La Isla's swashbuckling maritime history with wonderful murals, anchor motifs and six hotel-worthy rooms. Furthermore, it touts spacious terraces, a plunge pool and a brilliant 3rd-floor rooftop restaurant. Service is laid-back but impeccable.

Villa Gerona
CASA PARTICULAR $

(Map p166; ☑ 46-31-29-62; www.villagerona.com; Calle 35 No 2410, btwn Calles 24 & 26; r USD$20-25; ❄) A block from the ferry terminal, this place is handy if you've just staggered dull-eyed and disoriented off the boat (as Isla virgins are prone to do). With helpful owners, two well-scrubbed rooms and a large patio, it's a comfortable introduction to your island adventure.

Villa Choli
CASA PARTICULAR $

(☑ 46-32-31-47, 5-248-7916; Calle C No 4001a, btwn Calles 6 & 8; r USD$25; 🅿 ❄ @) Four serviceable rooms split between two floors with TV, internet access, secure parking space, plentiful food and – possibly the highlight – a great terrace with rockers and a hammock. A second terrace opens for alfresco grill-ups on occasion. There are bicycles for rent, and port pickup/tickets can be arranged. The convivial host Ramberto is an excellent cook.

Motel el Rancho el Tesoro
HOTEL $

(☑ 46-32-30-35; Autopista Nueva Gerona-La Fe Km 2; s/d USD$25/30; 🅿 ❄) Oh dear! This lackluster motel with a castellated frontage lies in a wooded area near the Río las Casas, 3km south of town. Inside, it's like a museum to kitsch with 34 sizable rooms propped up by a paltry state restaurant.

🍴 Eating

As far as food goes, La Isla is still living in the 1990s, bar a couple of welcome newer exceptions. After one night of fruitless searching,

most travelers sensibly elect to dine in their casa particular (private homestay). Sandwich and churros vendors set up on Martí (Calle 39) and peso ice-cream sellers appear spontaneously in the windows of various private houses.

★ El Galeon
CUBAN $

(Map p166; Calle 24, btwn Calles 45 & 47; mains USD$4-7; ⊙ 11:30am-10:45pm) A superb rooftop restaurant above the La Isla, El Galeon serves Havana-worthy Cuban classics off a smoking charcoal grill. Service is friendly and fast, the decor is nautical, traditional live music adds to the ambience, and mojitos cost just USD$1.50 – *and* they come round at least once with a top-up of rum!

You'll end the night surprised, satisfied and slightly sloshed.

Buena Vista 39
CUBAN $

(Map p166; ☑ 5-503-2666; www.buenavista39.com; Calle 39 No 2419, btwn Calles 24 & 26; mains USD$3-4; ⊙ 11am-11pm) Modest private restaurant up a staircase above Nueva Gerona's main drag (Calle 39) that serves the Cuban basics with a little more panache than the state-run places. Order the substantial dogfish and grab a seat on the first-floor terrace overlooking the street.

Restaurante Toti
CUBAN $

(Reparto Chacón; mains USD$2-5; ⊙ noon-midnight) Lobster fresh off the grill for USD$6 and a guitar duo serenading you as you dine? Sound too good to be true? It all happens at Toti, a deliciously modest private restaurant in the Chacón neighborhood up by the Presidio Modelo.

El Cochinito
CARIBBEAN $

(Map p166; cnr Calles 39 & 24; meals USD$1.50; ⊙ noon-10pm, closed Wed) The ominously named 'little pig' offers pork concoctions in a dark but disturbing interior decorated with pigs' heads (that look like they're squealing).

🍷 Drinking & Nightlife

Call it pent-up boredom, but Nueva Gerona likes a party. Venues on and around Calle 39 are pretty gritty. Others (eg El Pinero) are less 'venues' and more outdoor get-togethers.

El Pinero
CLUB

(Map p166; Calle 28, btwn Calle 33 & river; ⊙ from around 9pm) Extremely loud music and most of the town's teenagers and 20-somethings converge by the historic boat (p165) for alfresco dancing. Drink and snack stalls also set up shop. Fridays and Saturdays are liveliest.

La Rumba CLUB
(Map p166; Calle 24, btwn Calles 37 & 39; ⊘10pm-2am) Buy your drinks in the cage-like bar next door then head to the courtyard and hectic disco round the corner. This is hard dancing territory some nights, dead as a doorknob on others.

🛍 Shopping

Calle 39, also known as Calle Martí, is a pleasant pedestrian mall shaded by green-ery and decorated with sculptures by local artists. The shop displays aren't quite so handsome.

Suco Sucu GIFTS & SOUVENIRS
(Map p166; ☑46-32-10-07; Calle 39, btwn Calles 24 & 26; ⊘9am-5pm, to 1pm Sun) Nueva Gerona's (nay the Isla's) one-stop shop for souvenirs.

❶ Information

INTERNET ACCESS
Etecsa Telepunto (Calle 41 No 2802, btwn Calles 28 & 30; ⊘8:30am-7pm) Has internet terminals and sells cards for wi-fi (USD$1.50

---

❶ GETTING TO THE ISLA BY BOAT

Getting to La Isla by boat is an unnecessarily complicated and confusing affair. Few foreigners attempt it, while the trickle who do probably feel a bit like Columbus stumbling ashore when they arrive.

Bus-boat combo tickets are sold from the Naviera Cubana Caribeña (NCC) kiosk (p142) in Havana's main Terminal de Ómnibus (p142). There is one departure a day in either direction with a second (theoretically) on Wednesdays, Fridays and Sundays. The first departure requires a 7am check-in at Havana's Terminal de Ómnibus followed by a 90-minute bus ride to the seedy port of Surgidero de Batabanó. From here, the boat departs for Nueva Gerona at 12:30pm-ish (with strong emphasis on the 'ish'). It is wise to book tickets at least a day in advance. Beware, even the reservation process can take several hours. Tickets cost CUP$5 for the 90-minute bus journey and USD$50 for the 2½-hour ferry ride (NB that's two different currencies). The full journey time with *mucho* waiting takes around eight hours.

The second boat running on Wednesday, Fridays and Sunday leaves at 5:30pm, but check ahead as cancellations are not uncommon.

In the past, it was not possible to buy round-trip tickets, but thankfully this policy appears to have changed.

You'll need to get to the bus terminal at least two hours before departure to confirm your ticket. Be prepared for queues.

On arrival at the port in Surgidero de Batabanó, more lines usher you through airport-style security and into a waiting room for a likely period of one to two hours before the boat departs.

Do not show up independently in Batabanó with the intention of buying a ferry ticket direct from the dock. Although technically possible, a number of travelers have come unstuck here, being told that the tickets have been sold out through the NCC kiosk in Havana. Furthermore, bedding down overnight in Batabanó holds little appeal for travelers.

The return leg is equally problematic. If you haven't bought a return ticket, procure your passage from Nueva Gerona's NCC ferry terminal (Map p166; ☑46-32-44-15, 46-32-49-77; cnr Calles 31 & 24) soon after you arrive. The ferry leaves for Surgidero de Batabanó daily at 8am (USD$50), but you'll need to get there at least two hours beforehand to tackle the infamous queues. A second boat is supposed to leave at 1pm on Wednesdays, Fridays and Sundays (with a check-in time of 10:30am).

Before reserving tickets, ask if there are sufficient bus connections from Surgidero de Batabanó to Havana and, importantly, that you have a reservation.

Don't take anything as a given until you have booked your ticket. Isla boat crossings, rather like Cuban trains, tend to be late, break down or get canceled altogether. There are no printed schedules or reliable websites.

Traveling in either direction you'll need to show your passport. You'll also want to carry plenty of your own refreshments.

DREAM DIVING

Protected from sea currents off the Gulf of Mexico and blessed with remarkable coral and marine life, Isla de la Juventud offers some of the Caribbean's best diving: 56 buoyed and little-visited dive sites here will make you truly feel like a castaway. The dive sites are an underwater adventure park of everything from caves and passages to vertical walls and coral hillocks, while further east, in an area known as Bajo de Zambo, you can dive to the remains of some 70-odd shipwrecks.

The International Diving Center (see next page), run from Marina Siguanea just south of Hotel Colony on the island's west coast, is the center of diving operations. The establishment has a modern on-site recompression chamber along with the services of a dive doctor. It's from here that you can be transported out to the National Maritime Park at Punta Francés.

Boat transfers to Punta Francés take 90 minutes and deliver you to a gorgeous stretch of white-sand beach, from which most main dive sites are easily accessible. The cream of the crop is Cueva Azul (advanced), a trench of cerulean blue with a small *cueva* (cave) about 40m down, followed by Pared de Coral Negro (intermediate), a wall of black coral. You'll see lots of fish, including tarpon, barracuda, groupers, snooks and angelfish, along with sea turtles.

Diving costs start at USD$45 for one immersion with equipment. Inquire at Hotel Colony about diving and other nautical activities on offer first.

per hour). Pick up wi-fi in the main square or on Calle 39.

MEDICAL

Hospital General Héroes de Baire (☎ 46-32-30-12; Calle 39A) Has a recompression chamber.

Farmacia Principal McPal (cnr Calles 39 & 24; ☺ 24hr) Fairly basic but open-all-hours pharmacy.

MONEY

Banco Popular y Ahorro (cnr Calles 39 & 26; ☺ 8am-7pm Mon-Sat) Two ATMs.

TOURIST INFORMATION

Ecotur (Map p166; ☎ 46-32-71-01; reservas.ij@occ.ecotur.tur.cu; Calle 39, btwn Calles 26 & 28; ☺ 8am-4pm Mon-Fri) This ultra-helpful office organizes trips into the militarized zone (where the Cueva de Punta del Este cave paintings and Cocodrilo are located) and to Punta Francés and the Loma de la Cañada. Day passes to the Southern Military Zone are available here (USD$22 including an obligatory guide). It's best to book several days in advance.

ⓘ Getting There & Away

The most hassle-free and (often) cheapest way to get to La Isla is to fly. Unfortunately, most people have cottoned onto this, so flights are usually booked out weeks in advance.

Rafael Cabrera Mustelier Airport (code GER) is 5km southeast of Nueva Gerona.

Cubana Airlines (☎ 46-32-42-59; www.cubana.cu; Rafael Cabrera Mustelier Airport) flies here from Terminal 1 of Havana's Aeropuerto Inter-nacional José Martí (p516) at least twice daily from as little as USD$40 one way. There are no international flights.

There are no flights from Isla de la Juventud to Cayo Largo del Sur.

ⓘ Getting Around

BUS

Local buses are not especially reliable. Buses 431 and 436 to La Fe (26km) and 440 to Hotel Colony (45km) leave from the **terminal** (Map p166), a glorified bus stop, opposite the cemetery on Calle 39A, just northwest of the hospital.

CAR

Cubacar (☎ 46-32-44-32; cnr Calles 32 & 39; ☺ 7am-7pm) rents cars from USD$80 with insurance and mopeds for USD$25 a day. You'll need your own vehicle or a taxi to to enter the military zone (unless on an organized tour). Be warned: there aren't many cars available.

The **Oro Negro gas station** (cnr Calles 39 & 34) is in the center of town.

HORSE CARTS

Horse *coches* (carts) often park next to the Cubalse supermarket on **Calle 35**. You can easily rent one at USD$10 per day for excursions to the Presidio Modelo, Museo Finca el Abra, Playa Bibijagua and other nearby destinations. If you've got the time, you can be sure the driver will.

Many horses are overworked and in lamentable condition. It's best to give your business to healthy ones if there's an option, or take another mode of transport.

South of Nueva Gerona

The Isla's largely uninhabited interior is sprinkled with pine and palm trees and retains a strange, understated beauty. Now and then you'll encounter abandoned Soviet-era buildings, the international schools for which the island was once famous.

◉ Sights & Activities

Punta Francés   BEACH

This beach is the location of the National Maritime Park, accessible by a 90-minute boat ride from the marina just south of Hotel Colony. The white-sand beach is ground zero for divers who head for the reefs just offshore. However, it's also a fine place to lounge, swim, snorkel and enjoy a pristine paradise. Non-divers are welcome to use the boat. There's a small beach-shack restaurant.

Criadero Cocodrilo   CROCODILE FARM

(USD$5; ⊙ 7am-5pm) 🚣 This farm has played an important part in crocodile conservation in Cuba over the last few years and the results are interesting to see. Harboring more than 500 crocodiles of all shapes and sizes, the *criadero* (hatchery) acts as a breeding center, raising and then releasing groups of crocs back into the wild when they reach a length of about 1m.

To reach the farm, turn left 12km south of La Fe just past Julio Antonio Mella.

La Jungla de Jones   GARDENS

(USD$3; ⊙ dawn-dusk) Situated 6km west of La Fe, several kilometers off the main road (look for the sign), Jungla de Jones is a 'botanical garden' containing more than 80 tree varieties, established by two American botanists, Helen and Harris Jones, in 1902. These days it's poorly maintained and hopelessly overgrown, though the highlight, the aptly named Bamboo Cathedral, an enclosed space surrounded by huge clumps of craning bamboo, is still impressive. Paths wind through the hurricane-wracked grounds and past the ruins of the Jones' erstwhile residence.

Beyond the gate, you'll be met by a couple of local farmers, who'll offer to show you around.

International Diving Center   DIVING

(📞 46-39-82-82, ext 166) Run from Marina Siguanea 1km south of Hotel Colony, this is the Isla de la Juventud's center of dive operations. The dive boat leaves for Punta Francés at 9am (a 90-minute transfer), so arrive around 8am if you want to organize an excursion. Immersions cost USD$45.

Loma de la Cañada   HIKING

(guided hike USD$22) A steep 1.2km-long trail, named 'Hacia el Techo de la Isla' (toward the roof of the island) heads up this jungle-covered hill, which at 303m is the highest point on the Isla de la Juventud. You'll need to climb it with a guide from Ecotur in Nueva Gerona and you'll also need transport to get to the starting point near the pinprick settlement of Victoria.

Barely anyone does this walk, so it feels like virgin territory. It's possible to see half the island shimmering like the Garden of Eden from the summit. A friendly farmer who lives in a wooden abode at the trailhead will offer you guavas and fresh water on your return.

⌷ Sleeping

Hotel Colony   HOTEL $

(📞 46-39-81-81; r/bungalow from USD$32/40; 🅿 ❄ 🏊) Looking more like a hospital than a hotel from the outside, the Colony, 46km southwest of Nueva Gerona, originated in 1958 as part of the Hilton chain, but was confiscated by the revolutionary government. Today the complex has a mix of dull out-of-fashion rooms and large, bright newer bungalows. The clientele is split between in-the-know divers and Cubans belting out recorded music.

The water off the hotel's white-sand beach is shallow, with sea urchins littering the bottom. Take care if you decide to swim. A safer bet is the Colony's noisy pool. A long wharf stretches out hopefully into the Caribbean, though it's half-ruined these days. Snorkeling in the immediate vicinity of the hotel is mediocre, but the sunsets are to die for.

❶ Getting There & Away

Transport is tough on La Isla, and bus schedules make even the rest of Cuba seem efficient. Bus 440 travels several times daily to and from Hotel Colony from Nueva Gerona (departing from opposite the cemetery next to the hospital at 9:30am, 11am, 12:40pm and 2:30pm). Otherwise, your best bet to get to Hotel Colony is by taxi (approximately USD$35 from the airport), moped or rental car.

The Southern Military Zone

If the La Isla de la Juventud is Cuba's last frontier, the Southern Military Zone is a frontier on the frontier. Don't expect tanks and military bastions here. Instead what you'll find is deserted beaches, caves full of ancient pictographs, the Caribbean's tallest lighthouse and the Lanier Swamp, Cuba's second-largest wetland and home to a population of American crocodiles.

The southern Isla is also replete with other unusual wildlife. Look out for iguanas, deer, lizards and turtles.

◎ Sights

Cueva de Punta del Este   CAVE
(USD$5) The Cueva de Punta del Este, a national monument 59km southeast of Nueva Gerona, has been called the 'Sistine Chapel' of Caribbean indigenous art. Long before the Spanish conquest (experts estimate around AD 800), indigenous people painted some 235 pictographs on the walls and ceiling of several caves. The largest has 28 concentric circles of red and black, and the paintings have been interpreted as a solar calendar. Discovered in 1910, they're considered the most important of their kind in the Caribbean.

There's a small visitor center and meteorological station. The long, shadeless white beach nearby is another draw (for you and the mosquitoes – bring repellent).

Playa Larga   BEACH
Playa Larga is the star of La Isla's south-coast beaches, lying about 12km south of the village of Cayo Piedra. The long strip of white sand fronting a (usually) calm sea is clean, inviting and practically virgin. There are no facilities.

❶ Getting There & Away

The only way to enter this protected area is with a rental car or taxi. Cars can be rented at Cubacar (p170) in Nueva Gerona. Ecotur (p170) in Nueva Gerona can help with transport options.

Cocodrilo

A potholed road runs south from Cayo Piedra to the gorgeous white-sand beach of Playa Larga, then west 50km to the friendly village of Cocodrilo. Barely touched by tourism, and with a population of just 750, Cocodrilo was formerly known as Jacksonville, and was colonized in the 19th century by families from the Cayman Islands. You still occasionally meet people here who can converse in English. Through the lush vegetation beside the potholed road one catches glimpses of cattle, birds, lizards and beehives. The rocky coastline, sporadically gouged by small, white sandy beaches lapped by crystal-blue water, is magnificent.

❶ Getting There & Away

The only way to visit Cocodrilo is as part of a day trip organized through Ecotur in Nueva Gerona, for which you'll need either a rental car or a taxi.

CAYO LARGO DEL SUR

If you came to Cuba to witness colonial cities, exotic dancers, asthmatic Plymouths and peeling images of Che Guevara, then 38-sq-km Cayo Largo del Sur, 114km east of Isla de la Juventud, will hugely disappoint. If, instead, you booked tickets while dreaming of glittering white sandy expanses, coral reefs teeming with fish, out-of-the-catalog all-inclusive resorts and lots of fleshy Canadians and Italians wandering around naked, then this diminutive tropical paradise is the place for you.

---

❶ ENTERING THE SOUTHERN MILITARY ZONE

As the entire southern portion of La Isla beyond Cayo Piedra is a military zone, you must first procure a one-day pass and guide (USD$22) from Ecotur (p170) in Nueva Gerona. There are further fees for entry to the Cueva de Punta del Este, Playa Larga and Cocodrilo (USD$5 each). The obligatory guides speak Spanish, English, German, French and Italian (subject to availability). Hiring your own vehicle can be organized with Cubacar (p170) in Nueva Gerona (from USD$80 to USD$100). Traveling in the military zone is not possible without a guide or an official pass, so don't arrive at the Cayo Piedra checkpoint without either. As the whole excursion can wind up being rather expensive, it helps to split the transport costs with other travelers. For more up-to-date advice on the region, inquire at Ecotur in Nueva Gerona. Cuban nationals require 72 hours' notice to enter the military zone.

NATURISM ON CAYO LARGO DEL SUR

Naturism isn't part of the culture in Cuba, hence the only recognizable clothes-optional beaches are on the isolated holiday isle of Cayo Largo del Sur where, aside from a revolving army of flown-in hotel workers, no Cubans officially live.

Safe places to get naked on Cayo Largo include pockets of the main Lindarena beach in front of the tourist hotels as well as the east end of Playa Paraíso. More secluded is Playa Mal Tiempo on the headland between Playas Paraíso and Lindarena. Discretion is the key. None of the resorts on the island officially tolerate nudism within their grounds, and you'd be wise to cover up before visiting the beach bar. Nonetheless, naturism has a strong following among Playa Largo's tourists, many of whom are French-Canadian.

The only other bastion of public nudity in Cuba is similarly isolated Cayo Santa María (p274) in Villa Clara Province, where a small stretch of beach on the western edge of the island near the Hotel Meliá Buenavista is popular with naturists.

No permanent Cuban settlement has ever existed on the cayo. Instead, the island was developed in the early 1980s purely as a tourism enterprise. Cayo Largo del Sur is largely frequented by Italian tourists – several resorts here cater exclusively to them. The other all-inclusives are less picky. The heavenly beaches surpass most visitors' expectations of Caribbean paradise and are renowned for their size, emptiness and nesting turtles. Other natives include iguanas, flamingos and mosquitoes.

⊙ Sights

★ Playa Sirena   BEACH
Cayo Largo's (and, perhaps, Cuba's) finest beach is the broad westward-facing Playa Sirena, where 2km of powdery white sand is wide enough to accommodate several football pitches. Tourists on day trips from Havana and Varadero are often brought here. Thanks to calm seas, nautical activities (kayaks, catamarans) are available. Set back from the beach there's a restaurant (p175), along with showers and toilets. It is the only Cayo Largo beach with shade.

Just southeast is Playa Paraíso, a narrower and less shady but nonetheless wonderful strip of sand, serviced by a small bar.

Cayo Rico   ISLAND
A big day-trip destination, with boat excursions leaving from the hotels (for around USD$85 per person). Rico also has a simple beach restaurant that serves lunch (included). Cheaper excursions also leave from Marina Internacional Cayo Largo.

Playa Tortuga   BEACH
Beyond Playa los Cocos at the far end of the island is this beach, where sea turtles lay their eggs in the sand in the summer.

Centro de Rescate
de Tortugas Marinas   NATURE RESERVE
(USD$2; ⊙ 8am-noon & 1-4:30pm) A small, often-closed complex beyond the airstrip on the northwest end of the island in the settlement of Combinado. From May to September guides here can organize nighttime turtle-watching on the Cayo's beaches, one of only two places in Cuba where this is possible.

🏃 Activities

There are numerous activities available on the island, including snorkeling (from USD$25), windsurfing, sailing and tennis. Of note is the popular sunset catamaran cruise (USD$85) and a day trip to Havana by plane (USD$210). You can book any of these at the hotels.

Marina Internacional
Cayo Largo   DIVING, FISHING
(☑ 45-24-81-33) Just beyond the turtle farm in Combinado, this is the departure point for deep-sea fishing trips (USD$390 for four hours, minimum four people) and diving (USD$50 for one immersion including hotel transfer and equipment). Prices are more expensive here because you can't shop around. Transfers from the marina to Playa Sirena are free for island guests and depart during the morning.

Hiking & Cycling
The island's best hike is from Playa Sirena round to Sol Cayo Largo along the beach (7km) or vice versa. A broken path follows the dune ridge for much of the way if the tide is high. You can also procure a bicycle if you're staying in one of the resorts and head east beyond the Playa Blanca Beach Resort to some of the island's remoter beaches.

ISLA DE LA JUVENTUD & CAYO LARGO DEL SUR CAYO LARGO DEL SUR

Cayo Largo del Sur

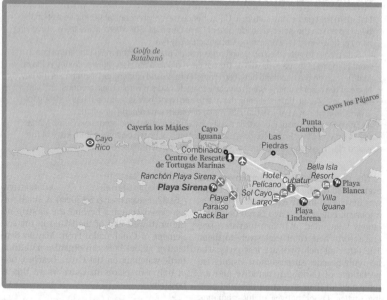

Golfo de
Batabanó

Cayos los Pájaros

Cayo
Rico

Cayería los Majáes
Cayo
Iguana

Punta
Gancho

Las
Piedras

Combinado
Centro de Rescate
de Tortugas Marinas

Bella Isla
Resort

Ranchón Playa Sirena
Playa Sirena

Hotel
Pelícano
Cubatur
Sol Cayo
Largo

Playa
Blanca

Playa
Paraíso
Snack Bar

Villa
Iguana

Playa
Lindarena

Sleeping

Cayo Largo del Sur's hotels face the 4km Playa Lindarena on the island's south side. Though largely shadeless, the beach is gorgeous and rarely crowded (although the sea can be choppy). Day-trippers can buy day passes to the Sol and Pelícano resorts starting from USD\$50 including lunch. Aside from the four large resorts, there are four small hotels reserved for Italian tourists.

Villa Marinera   RESORT \$\$
(☑ 45-24-80-80; www.grancaribehotels.com; Combinado; s/d all-inclusive USD\$80/120; P✳@🖧) The Marinera, a cohort of the Bella Isla Resort, is a little different from other Cayo Largo resorts. Rather than hugging the wide southern beach, it resides in the small administrative 'town' of Combinado. In this sense, it's ideal for people focused mainly on the water activities that leave from the adjacent marina.

★ **Sol Cayo Largo**   RESORT \$\$\$
(☑ 45-24-82-60; www.meliacuba.com; s/d all-inclusive from USD\$215/310; P✳@🖧) Under the tutelage of the Meliá chain, the four-star Sol Cayo Largo impresses with a Greek-temple-like lobby and trickling Italianate fountains. The beach out here is fantastic (and nudist) and the brightly painted (but

not luxurious) rooms all have terraces with sea views. To date, it's Cayo Largo's most exclusive resort and great if you want to escape the families and poolside bingo further east.

Villa Iguana   RESORT \$\$\$
(☑ 45-24-81-11; www.grancaribehotels.com; r all-inclusive from USD\$185; P✳@🖧) Salvaged from the wreckage of Hurricane Michelle in 2001, the Iguana is a small, modest place by modern Cuban all-inclusive standards. Its 196 rooms mix old refurbished units with wooden cabins linked by boardwalks. It styles itself as a 3½-star and is adults only.

Bella Isla Resort   RESORT \$\$\$
(☑ 45-24-80-80; www.grancaribehotels.com; s/d all-inclusive USD\$135/185; P✳@🖧) One of only two four-star hotels on Cayo Largo, this 306-room pile is set apart from the rest of the gang on an expansive stretch of Playa Blanca. Rather drab architecture is augmented by three different dining options and an array of sporting activities. It was extensively refurbished in 2018.

Hotel Pelícano   RESORT \$\$\$
(☑ 45-24-82-33; www.grancaribehotels.com; s/d all-inclusive USD\$235/335; ✳@🖧) This Spanish-style resort, flush on the beach 5km southeast of the airport, has 307 rooms in a series of three-story buildings and two-story

CARIBBEAN
SEA

duplex *cabañas* (cabins) built in 1993. This is the island's largest resort (by one room!) and it's most beloved by families (on an island not considered to be particularly family-friendly).

🍴 Eating & Drinking

Of the all-inclusives, the Sol Cayo Largo – allegedly – serves the best food.

For an away-day from the buffets, try the restaurant on Playa Sirena or one of a couple in the small administrative center of Combinado.

⭐**Ranchón Playa Sirena**   SEAFOOD $$$
(mains USD$11-20; ⊙9am-5pm) A rather fetching beach bar amid the Playa Sirena palm trees, with Latino Tom Cruises tossing around the cocktail glasses. Good food is also served here, and a buffet (USD$20) happens if enough tourists are around. It offers no-nonsense, salt-of-the-earth *comida criolla* (Creole food) including grilled *pargo* (red snapper) for USD$12 and lobster (USD$20).

Taberna el Pirata   CAFE, CLUB
(Combinado; ⊙8am-2am) Taberna el Pirata is primarily a haunt for boat hands, resort workers and the odd escaped tourist alongside Marina Internacional Cayo Largo. Icy beer, throat-burningly strong coffee, sandwiches and liquor in pleasant environs.

🛍 Shopping

Casa de Habano   CIGARS
(☎45-24-82-11; ⊙8am-8pm) Buy cigars at this shop in Combinado.

ℹ Information

SAFE TRAVEL

Due to dangerous currents, swimming is occasionally forbidden. This will be indicated by red flags on the beach. Mosquitoes can be a nuisance, too. Bring repellent.

MONEY

You can change money at the hotels. Combinado houses the island's main bank, **Bandec** (⊙8:30am-3pm Mon-Sat, 8am-noon Sun).

TOURIST INFORMATION

There's a **Cubatur** (☎45-24-82-58) in the Hotel Pelícano and further information offices in the Sol Cayo Largo and Playa Blanca resorts.

ℹ Getting There & Away

Vilo Acuña International Airport is a bright-enough place with a big snack bar and a souvenir stand. Several charter flights arrive directly from Canada and Italy weekly.

For pop-by visitors, daily flights from Havana to Cayo Largo del Sur with **Aerogaviota** (☎7-203-8686; Av 47 No 2814, btwn Calles 28 & 34, Kohly, Havana) or Cubana (p516) cost from USD$249 for a return trip. Included will be airport transfer at both ends and a boat trip from Cayo Largo's marina (but you don't have to go). The island makes a viable day trip from Havana, although you'll have to get up early for the airport transfer (all Cayo Largo flights depart between 7am and 8am from the drab airport at Playa Baracoa, a few miles west of Marina Hemingway). You can buy this trip at most Havana travel agencies and hotels, but they don't run every day. Book in advance.

ℹ Getting Around

Getting around diminutive Cayo Largo shouldn't present too many challenges.

A taxi or transfer bus can transport you the 5km from the airport to the hotel strip (included in your flight price).

There's a bus-boat transfer from the hotels to Playa Sirena two times a day (USD$5 round trip). Alternatively, you can charter a taxi for a similar price. Cars hang around outside the hotels.

The tiny settlement of Combinado is 1km north of the airport and 6km from the nearest resort.

The hotels have moped or ATV rental (USD$35 per day); Bella Isla Resort is best stocked because it's furthest from the 'action.'

Some of the hotels lend out bikes, which are flimsy but usually adequate for the short distances required.

Valle de Viñales (p180)
INSPIRED BY MAPS/SHUTTERSTOCK

Valle de Viñales & Pinar del Río Province

Tobacco is still king on Cuba's western fingertip, a rolling canvas of rust-red oxen-furrowed fields, tobacco-drying houses and sombrero-clad *guajiros* (country folk).

The crucible of this emerald land is the Valle de Viñales, a Unesco World Heritage site framed by a backdrop of distinctive *mogotes* (limestone monoliths) that beseech you to get hiking. Playing a tuneful second fiddle is the Península de Guanahacabibes, an uninhabited wilderness full of fertile ecosystems that abut a swath of 50-plus offshore dive sites.

People primarily come here to be close to nature, basing themselves in the serene hassle-free village of Viñales. From here, huge cave complexes call for torch-lit exploration, tobacco plantations lure recreational cigar smokers, beaches invite lazy contemplation and every horizon seems to be filled with a host of quintessential 'come to the Cuban countryside' images. So follow the fragrant aroma of tobacco and come here.

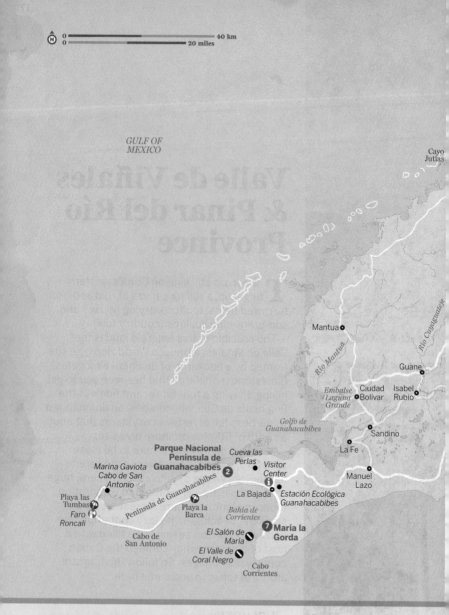

GULF OF
MEXICO

Cayo
Jutías

Mantua

Guane

Río Mantua

Río Cuyaguateje

Embalse
Laguna
Grande

Ciudad
Bolívar

Isabel
Rubio

Golfo de
Guanahacabibes

Sandino

La Fe

Parque Nacional
Península de
Guanahacabibes

Cueva las
Perlas

Visitor
Center

Manuel
Lazo

Marina Gaviota
Cabo de San
Antonio

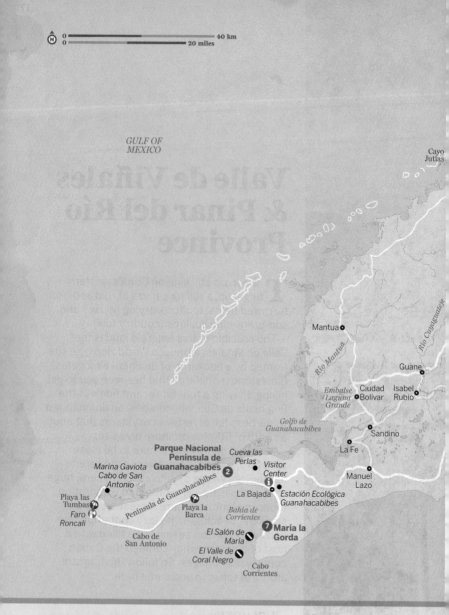2

Península de Guanahacabibes

La Bajada

Estación Ecológica
Guanahacabibes

Playa las
Tumbas

Faro
Roncali

Playa la
Barca

Bahía de
Corrientes

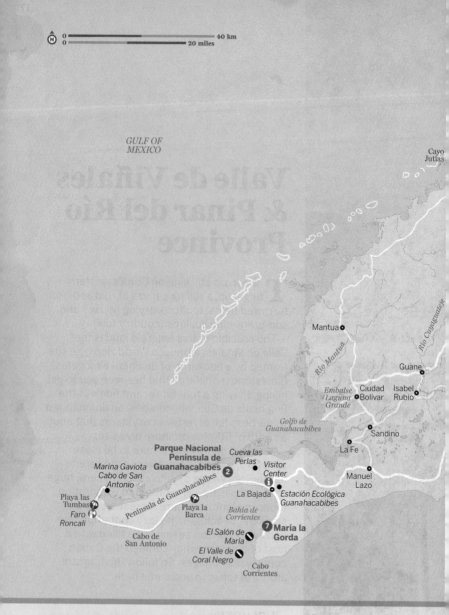7 María la
Gorda

Cabo de
San Antonio

El Salón de
María

El Valle de
Coral Negro

Cabo
Corrientes

0 ——— 40 km
0 ——— 20 miles

Pinar del Río Province Highlights

① **Parque Nacional Viñales**
(p188) Seeing, smelling and
tasting the agricultural beauty
of this wonderfully authentic
Unesco World Heritage site.

② **Parque Nacional
Península de
Guanahacabibes** (p199)
Going turtle-watching on
virgin beaches on the western
fingertip of the Cuban
mainland.

③ **Valle de Palmarito**
(p190) Riding a horse or hiking
into this pastoral valley in the
Parque Nacional Viñales.

④ **Gran Caverna de
Santo Tomás** (p188) Being
gobsmacked by the grottoes

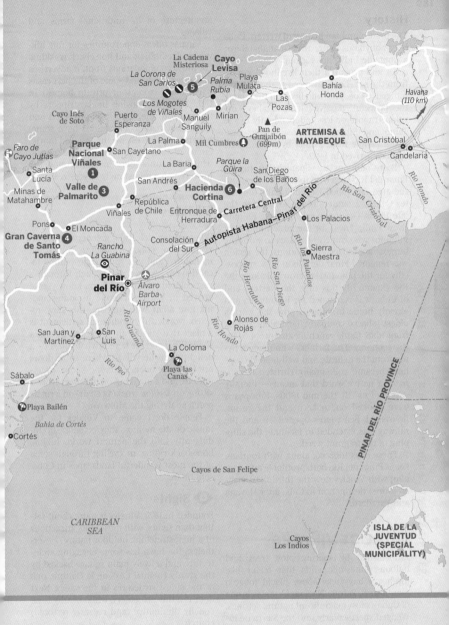

La Cadena Misteriosa
Cayo Levisa
La Corona de San Carlos
5
Palma Rubia
Playa Mulata
Bahía Honda
Havana (110 km)
Los Mogotes de Viñales
Manuel Sanguily
Mirian
Las Pozas
Cayo Inés de Soto
Puerto Esperanza
La Palma
Mil Cumbres
Pan de Guajaibón (699m)
ARTEMISA & MAYABEQUE
San Cristóbal
Faro de Cayo Jutías
Parque Nacional Viñales
1
San Cayetano
La Baria
Parque la Güira
San Diego de los Baños
Candelaria
Santa Lucía
San Andrés
Hacienda Cortina
6
Río San Cristóbal
Río Hondo
Minas de Matahambre
Valle de Palmarito
3
República de Chile
Entronque de Herradura
Viñales
Carretera Central
Los Palacios
Pons
El Moncada
Consolación del Sur
Autopista Habana–Pinar del Río
Río los Palacios
Sierra Maestra
Gran Caverna de Santo Tomás
4
Rancho La Guabina
Río Herradura
Río San Diego
Pinar del Río
Álvaro Barba Airport
Río Guamá
Río Hondo
Alonso de Rojás
San Juan y Martínez
San Luis
La Coloma
Río Feo
Playa las Canas
Sábalo
7 Playa Bailén
Bahía de Cortés
Cortés
Cayos de San Felipe
PINAR DEL RÍO PROVINCE
CARIBBEAN SEA
Cayos Los Indios
ISLA DE LA JUVENTUD (SPECIAL MUNICIPALITY)

of one of Latin America's largest subterranean cave systems.

5 **Cayo Levisa** (p192) Recharging your batteries on this dreamy key accessible only by boat.

6 **Hacienda Cortina** (p193) Walking around the recently restored, but still agreeably outlandish ruins of this huge rural estate.

7 **María la Gorda** (p200) Dipping down under the azure waters of one of Cuba's clearest and most colorful diving sites.

History

The pre-Columbian history of western Cuba is synonymous with the Guanahatabeys, a nomadic indigenous group who lived in caves and procured their livelihood largely from the sea. Less advanced than the other indigenous peoples who lived on the island, the peaceful, passive Guanahatabeys developed more or less independently of the Taíno and Siboney cultures further east. These people were extinct by the time the Spanish arrived in 1492.

Post-Columbus the Spanish left rugged Pinar del Río largely to its own devices, and the area developed lackadaisically only after Canary Islanders began arriving in the late 1500s. Originally called Nueva Filipina (New Philippines) for the large number of Filipinos who came to the area to work the burgeoning tobacco plantations, the region was renamed Pinar del Río in 1778, supposedly for the pine forests crowded along the Río Guamá. By this time the western end of Cuba was renowned for its tobacco and already home to what is now the world's oldest tobacco company, Tabacalera, dating from 1636. Cattle ranching also propped up the economy. The farmers who made a living from the delicate and well-tended crops here became colloquially christened *guajiros,* a native word that means – literally – 'one of us.' By the mid-1800s, Europeans were hooked on tobacco and the region flourished. Sea routes opened up and the railway was extended to facilitate the shipping of the fragrant weed.

These days tobacco, along with tourism, keeps Pinar del Río both profitable and popular, with Viñales now the third-most-visited tourist destination in Cuba after Havana and Varadero.

VALLE DE VIÑALES

Embellished by soaring pine trees and bulbous limestone cliffs that teeter like top-heavy haystacks above placid tobacco plantations, Parque Nacional Viñales is one of Cuba's most magnificent natural settings. Wedged spectacularly into the Sierra de los Órganos mountain range, this 11km-by-5km valley was recognized as a national monument in 1979, with Unesco World Heritage status following in 1999 for its dramatic steep-sided limestone outcrops (known as *mogotes*), coupled with the vernacular architecture of its traditional farms and villages.

Viñales offers opportunities for fine hiking, rock climbing and horseback trekking. On the accommodations front, it advertises first-class hotels and some of the best casas particulares (rooms in private homes) in Cuba. Despite drawing in day-trippers by the busload, the area's well-protected and spread-out natural attractions have somehow managed to escape the frenzied tourist circus of other less well-managed places, while the atmosphere in and around the town remains refreshingly hassle-free.

Viñales

POP 29,000

When Pinar del Río's greenery starts to erupt into craggy *mogotes* (limestone monoliths) and you spy a cigar-puffing local driving his oxen and plough through a rust-colored tobacco field, you know you've arrived in Viñales. Despite its long-standing love affair with tourism, this slow, relaxed, wonderfully traditional settlement is a place that steadfastly refuses to put on a show. What you see here is what you get – a delightful rustic village where front doors are left wide open, everyone knows everyone else and a night out on the tiles involves sitting on a *sillón* (rocking chair) on a rustic porch analyzing the Milky Way.

People don't come to Viñales for the music or the mojitos, they come to dip indulgently into the natural world, hiking, horseback riding, or cycling through some of the most wonderful landscapes in Cuba. Join them.

◉ Sights

Founded in 1875, Viñales is more about setting than sights, with most of its attractions of a lung-stretching outdoor nature. Nevertheless the town has some engaging architecture and a lively main square backed by the sturdy colonial Casa de la Cultura, one of the oldest structures in the valley. Next door is a tiny art gallery, while nearby is an equally diminutive (and recently restored) church.

Finca Agroecológica El Olivo   FARM
(☑ 48-69-66-54; www.olivovinalescuba.com; Carretera al Cementerio, Km 2; ⊙ 10am-noon)
✐ FREE Go directly to the source. Viñales' celebrated farm-to-table restaurant, Olivo

Valle de Viñales

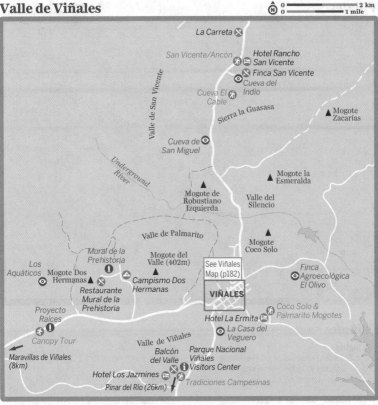

(p185), gets most of its ingredients from this farm in nearby Valle del Silencio. Run by the same family as the restaurant, the farm uses goats to make cheese, has a lake stocked with fresh fish (including tilapia), and copious fields and gardens swaying with well-nurtured crops. You're welcome to turn up for tours.

El Jardín Botanico de las Hermanas Caridad y
Carmen Miranda   GARDENS
(Salvador Cisneros; by donation; ☺8am-5pm) Just opposite the Servi-Cupet gas station as Cisneros swings north out of town, you'll spot an outlandish, vine-choked gate beckoning you in. This is the entrance to a sprawling garden, work on which began in 1918. Cascades of orchids bloom alongside plastic doll heads, thickets of orange lilies grow in soft groves and turkeys run amok. Knock on the door of the Little Red Riding Hood cottage and a guide will emerge to show you around.

Museo Municipal   MUSEUM
(Salvador Cisneros No 115; USD$1; ☺8am-5pm, to 4pm Sun) Positioned halfway down Cisneros, Viñales' pine-lined main street, the Museo Municipal occupies the former home of independence heroine Adela Azcuy (1861–1914) and tracks the local history. Five different guided hikes leave from here twice daily; check times at the museum a day prior to visiting.

La Casa del Veguero   FARM
(Carretera a Pinar del Río Km 24; ☺10am-5pm) To learn about the local tobacco-growing process, stop by this tobacco plantation just outside Viñales on the road south to Pinar del Río and see a fully functional *secadero* (drying house) in which tobacco leaves are cured from February to May. The staff give brief explanations, and you can buy loose cigars (the unbranded variety most Cubans smoke) here at discount prices. There's a restaurant too.

Viñales

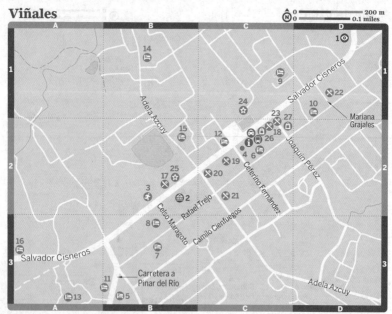

Viñales

◎ Sights

✪ Activities, Courses & Tours

⌂ Sleeping

◎ Eating

✪ Entertainment

◎ Shopping

🏃 Activities & Tours

While most activities in Viñales are located outside town, there's a handful – including some climbing routes – within easy walking distance. Even if you're staying in a private homestay, it's worth strolling the 2km uphill to the lovely Hotel La Ermita (p184) where you can **swim** (USD$8, including bar cover) in the gorgeous pool or book a

massage (USD$20 to USD$35). Hotel Los Jazmines (p184) has an equally amazing pool (USD$8, including bar cover), though the ubiquitous tour buses can sometimes kill the tranquility.

Bike Rental Point   CYCLING
(Salvador Cisneros No 140; bike hire per hour/day USD$1/10) Offers modern bikes with gears. Located next door to the Restaurante la Casa

de Don Tomás. (Many private homestay owners also rent bikes for similar prices.)

Also rents motos for USD$25 per day.

Cubanacán TOURS
(☑48-79-63-93; Salvador Cisneros No 63c; ☺9am-7pm Mon-Sat) Cubanacán organizes perennially popular day trips to Cayo Levisa (USD$47), Cayo Jutías (USD$15), Gran Caverna de Santo Tomás (USD$20) and a bike and canopy tour (USD$33). Official park hikes leave from here daily (USD$10).

🛏 Sleeping

Viñales is like a giant hotel. Practically every house rents private rooms, giving you at least – oh – 600 to choose from. Most are of a decent standard offering family-style lodging in a large village-like setting with breakfast available for USD$5 extra. Two of the settlement's hotels are situated on higher ground between 2km and 3km outside Viñales village. Both have to-die-for views.

★Casa Daniela CASA PARTICULAR $
(☑48-69-55-01; casadaniela@nauta.cu; Carretera a Pinar del Río; r USD$25-30; ❄🅿❄🛏) Run by a former doctor and nurse, who must have had formidable bedside manners if their hospitality in this surgically clean place is anything to judge by. The sunny yellow Daniela has expanded into a sizable residence without losing its local intimacy. There are six rooms, a super pool, a giant roof terrace and a shady yard.

Casa Papo y Niulvys CASA PARTICULAR $
(☑48-69-67-14; papoyniulvys@gmail.com; Rafael Trejo No 18a; r USD$30-35; 🅿❄❄) One of the few houses in Viñales with a front garden, this place gives you room to swing on a hammock as well as rock on a rocking chair on the front porch. Rooms are small but recently decorated in a modern style. It's a dreamily tranquil spot with a wraparound porch. Book well ahead – it gets busy.

Villa El Cafetal CASA PARTICULAR $
(☑48-69-50-37, 5-331-1752; edgar21@nauta.cu; Adela Azcuy Final; r USD$25; 🅿❄❄) The son of the owners of this foliage-draped house on the edge of town is an expert on climbing, meaning there's a shed stacked with equipment – and the best climbs in Viñales are on their doorstep. Ensconced in a resplendent garden that cultivates its own coffee (served at breakfast), you can practically taste the mountain air as you swing on the hammock.

The two rooms are simple but effective, the setting is sublime and climbing escapades can be organized here from around USD$30 per day.

Villa Los Reyes CASA PARTICULAR $
(☑48-79-33-17; http://villalosreyes.com; Salvador Cisneros No 206c; s/d/tr USD$25/30/35; 🅿❄@❄❄) Yoan Reyes has put huge efforts into shaping his fabulous house, which now has five modern bedrooms (some with king-sized beds), a round pool, a well-tended garden (plus vegetable patch) and a bridge-like structure linking two separate roof terraces. You're on the edge of the countryside here and the family can organize all number of excursions into the green domain.

Ridel & Claribel CASA PARTICULAR $
(☑48-69-51-27; ridel326@gmail.com; Salvador Cisneros B No 203c; r USD$25-30; ❄❄) Simple but effective homestay run by a doctor-dentist couple that exhibits all of the essentials for a delightful Viñales stay. Tick off relaxing rocking chairs, huge fruity breakfasts, a roof terrace with views over the tobacco fields and highly congenial hosts who, despite their professional qualifications, are proud *guajiros* (country folk) at heart. The house is tucked away behind the town market.

Casa Haydée Chiroles CASA PARTICULAR $
(☑5-254-8921; casahaydee@nauta.cu; Rafael Trejo No 139; r USD$25-30; ❄❄) With six rooms split between two adjacent houses and a lovely lush communal back patio where you can contemplate the stars on your *sillón* (rocking chair), this house reflects all the best attributes of Viñales. Rooms are simple but effective, there's a mini-library-book-exchange, and breakfasts are laid out buffet style. Best of all, the hosts are super courteous.

Villa El Niño CASA PARTICULAR $
(☑48-69-66-66; casaelninoalexander@nauta.cu; Adela Azcuy No 9; r USD$25; ❄) Lovely green abode with multiple terraces and swing-chairs on Calle Adela Azcuy away from the noise of main drag Salvador Cisneros. It offers four small but adequate rooms and plenty of chill-out space.

Casa Nenita CASA PARTICULAR $
(☑48-79-60-04; emiliadiaz2000@yahoo.es; Salvador Cisneros Internal No 1; r USD$35-40; 🅿❄❄❄) Nenita's has quietly become one of Cuba's top private homestays. While its out-of-center location might deter some,

the eight rooms are above par and, when augmented by the amazing restaurant, pool and roof terrace, give you a luxurious launchpad from which to explore. Nenita's battered fish has even featured in recipe books.

Casa Jean-Pierre
CASA PARTICULAR $

(📱 48-79-33-34; cnr Celso Maragoto & Salvador Cisneros; r USD$25-30; 🅿 ❄ 🛜) Jean-Pierre's recently renovated house is a smart, spotless and central option. There are four rooms, one smaller in size (USD$25) and a large upper room with its private terrace. The place is run by JP, owner of local tapas bar Tres Jotas, and all guests are offered a free cocktail-making class in his restaurant. Entry is from the side street.

Casa El Balcón
Mignelys & Juanito
CASA PARTICULAR $

(📱 48-69-67-25; elbalcon2005@yahoo.es; Rafael Trejo No 48a, 2nd fl; r USD$25-35; ❄) Situated a block south of the plaza, El Balcón has four modern private rooms upstairs (there is another house for rent below), a street-facing balcony and a huge roof terrace where fine food is served. Friendly owners Mignelys and Juanito speak English and can organize all number of rustic activities.

Hostal Doña Hilda
CASA PARTICULAR $

(📱 48-79-60-53; riveraanaflavia@gmail.com; Carretera a Pinar del Río No 4 Km 25; r USD$25-30; ❄) One of the first houses in town on the road from Pinar del Río, Hilda's house has three rooms with porches and rockers. This unpretentious place is classic Viñales – just like the perennially smiling hostess – with divine food. The mojitos are among Cuba's very best. Ask here about dance classes.

Hotel La Ermita
HOTEL $$

(📱 48-79-64-11; Carretera de La Ermita Km 1.5; s/d incl breakfast USD$60/96; 🅿 ❄ 🛜) La Ermita takes Viñales' top hotel honors for architecture, interior furnishings and all-round service. The views over town rooftops and haystack hills are equally award-worthy. The upper-floor rooms housed in handsome two-story colonial edifices overlook the misty valley. Extracurricular attractions include an excellent pool, tennis courts, a shop, horseback riding and massage.

Hotel Central
BOUTIQUE HOTEL $$

(📱 48-69-58-15; www.cubanacan.cu; Salvador Cisneros, cnr Ceferino Fernández; s/d incl breakfast USD$72/96; ❄ 🛜) Viñales' first new hotel in decades has added a different dimension in a town chock-a-block with homely casas particulares (private homestays). If you are craving space, privacy and elegance without compromising the town's rustic spirit, this might be your bag. Large rooms are colored with bottle greens and rust reds, and are equipped with coffee machines, irons and umbrellas.

The lovely porch has a bar and strong wi-fi, if you don't mind sharing it with practically everyone else in town.

★ Hotel Los Jazmines
HOTEL $$$

(📱 48-79-64-11; Carretera a Pinar del Río; s/d incl breakfast USD$88/138; 🅿 ❄ 🛜) Prepare yourself! The vista from this pastel-pink colonial-style hotel is one of the best in Cuba. Open the shutters of your classic valley-facing room and drink in the shimmering sight of magnificent *mogotes* (limestone monoliths), red oxen-plowed fields and palm-frond-covered tobacco-drying houses. Although the facilities are long overdue a refurbishment, the location is unrivaled and there's a gloriously inviting swimming pool.

Handy extras include an international medical clinic, a massage room and a small shop/market. The setting comes at a cost: bus tours stop off here almost hourly, thus eroding some of the ethereal ambience.

🍴 Eating

Viñales' restaurant scene has responded to the recent spike in tourist numbers with aplomb. Country-style *cerdo asado* (whole roast pig) is the traditional dish, with trimmings of rice, beans and root vegetables. Seek it out. Elsewhere, tapas and Italian rule the roost.

Restaurant La Berenjena
VEGETARIAN $

(📱 5-254-9269; Mariana Grajales, btwn Salvador Cisneros & Rafael Trejo; mains USD$4-7; ⊘ 10am-10pm; 🚲) 🍴 A commendable attempt to fill a void in Cuba's food market – ie vegetarianism – La Berenjena inhabits a smart two-story house with an awning-covered terrace out front. This is a genuine ecorestaurant plying fruit shakes, vegetable lasagna, crepes, soups and a few meat dishes for those who can't be swayed.

Furthermore it uses recycled rainwater, makes its own honey and uses ingredients from its own vegetable garden.

La Esquinita
FAST FOOD **$**

(cnr Rafael Trejo & Adela Azcuy; mains USD$4; ⊙10am-11pm) Born as a quick walk-up cafe several years back, the 'little corner' has grown bigger as the service has become concurrently slower. No matter: it's still a good place for simple sandwiches and – even better – Viñales' finest desert: hot chocolate-filled churros.

Cocinita del Medio
CUBAN **$**

(Salvador Cisneros, btwn Celso Maragoto & Adela Azcuy; mains USD$3-8; ⊙noon-11pm) A radical rethink a couple of years ago has transformed Cocinita from a family dining room serving salt-of-the-earth Viñales staples to a chicer cafe plying Cuban dishes plus an augmented menu of pizzas, pasta and tapas. The staples are still pretty good (and cheap), the pizzas less so. Top marks to the generous slices of cake.

★ Tres Jotas
TAPAS **$$**

(☑5-331-1658; Salvador Cisneros No 45; tapas USD$2-6; ⊙8am-2am) One of the best restaurants in Cuba outside Havana, Tres Jotas is Viñales' original tapas bar that has since been copied by all and sundry. Its inviting polished-wood interior is the perfect place to unwind after a day in the countryside, with classy cocktails, taste-exploding tapas, and boards piled high with cured ham and manchego cheese.

For something more dinner-worthy, don't leave before you've tasted the signature slow-cooked lamb stewed in red wine – not a tapa this one, but a real feast.

The sociable manager Jean-Pierre is a perfect host, always on hand to ensure the atmosphere is nothing less than electric. He is backed up by a team of highly professional staff who offer sharp but highly discreet service.

★ El Olivo
MEDITERRANEAN **$$**

(www.olivovinalescuba.com; Salvador Cisneros No 89; pasta USD$5-10; ⊙noon-11pm; ☑) Viñales' most popular restaurant, as the happy buzz of conversation will testify, serves tremendous lasagna and pasta dishes, backed up by other Med classics such as duck *à l'orange*. The salads topped with goat's cheese and dried fruits are spectacular, while the joker in the pack is the rabbit dressed with herbs in a dark chocolate sauce.

The secret? Olivo is a genuine farm-to-table affair. Most of what you eat here

VALLE DEL SILENCIO

When you've had your fill of the big-city therapist, decamp to Viñales and book a vacation in the Valle del Silencio for an alternative cure. This is the park's gentlest, least explored and – arguably – most picturesque valley, where the lion's share of the municipality's tobacco is grown. It gets its name from... well, sit on a rocking chair on a rustic porch at sunset at one of the valley's beautiful rustic *fincas* (farms) and you'll soon deduce how it got its name. Golden silence.

You can go it alone in the valley or hitch up with an organized excursion. Yoan and Yarelis Reyes at Villa Los Reyes (p183) in Viñales arrange a sublime sunset trip that ends in a beautiful eco-farm where you can banter with local farmers and share life-changing views of the sun's orb slipping behind the *mogotes* (limestone monoliths).

comes from its own farm (p180), 3km up the road. If you liked what you ate, go and see where it came from.

Cubar
INTERNATIONAL **$$**

(☑5-364-2791; Salvador Cisneros No 55; mains USD$7-22; ⊙9am-midnight, to 2am Fri & Sat) A sophisticated entry into Viñales' overcrowded dining scene, Cubar hits all the right notes with a smart dark-wood interior advertising the joys of Cuban rum and a menu that touts Cuban food colored with Italian and Spanish inflections. Expect fine tastes and creative presentation in dishes such as rabbit cacciatore, grilled octopus and a zesty lobster spaghetti.

Cubar is the sort of place where you'll feel hunger pangs for every plate that flies past your table (oh those burgers!). Moreover, it emits a classy aura with fresh flowers on the bar, romantic candles on the tables and extra virgin olive oil with which to dress your avocado salad.

Balcón del Valle
CUBAN **$$**

(Carretera a Pinar del Río; mains USD$8; ⊙noon-midnight) With three deftly constructed wooden decks overhanging a panorama of tobacco fields, drying houses and craggy *mogotes* (limestone monoliths), 'Balcony of the Valley' has food that stands up to its sensational views. The unwritten menu includes half a dozen mains, all prepared country-style with copious trimmings. It's 3km outside Viñales toward Hotel Los Jazmines.

La Cuenca INTERNATIONAL **$$**
(☑48-69-69-68; Salvador Cisneros No 97, cnr Adela Azcuy; mains USD$5-12; ⊙11am-10:30pm) Looking less rustic than some of its Viñales brethren, La Cuenca's narrow covered terrace and funky black-and-white interior are rather tempting. The food is all over the map, from Spanish tapas to rack of lamb, although some dishes (rabbit with chocolate) seem to mimic some of its nearby competitors. If you're not lingering long, the coffee and cocktails are famously good.

☆ Entertainment

Viñales is a place for tranquility and the appreciation of nature, and doesn't swing too loud – or too late. That said, there are a couple of places that host traditional local bands and some new-ish tapas bars that stay open until the small hours.

WAYS OF ESCAPE: CIMARRÓNES & PALENQUES

The inhuman slave system that blighted Cuba for nearly four centuries between 1513 and 1886 drove many slaves to hatch risky escape plans in pursuit of their freedom. In Cuba, escaped enslaved people were known as *cimarrónes* and the loosely organized free communities they formed were called *palenques*. *Palenques* were usually set up in inaccessible mountainous regions, often in caves, where small collectives of runaways would hide and sometimes plot rebellion against their former masters. In the early days of slavery, fugitive African slaves sometimes teamed up with surviving bands of indigenous Taínos, particularly in the Oriente; and it was not uncommon for competing African tribes to unite in informal alliances in their bid to stay free. Hidden away in the mountains of the Sierra Maestra or the caves of Viñales, the *cimarrónes* cultivated small plots of land where they grew maize and root vegetables, kept animals in dusty corrals and preserved food in underground stores. Always on guard, they stockpiled basic armaments in order to defend themselves from their nemesis, the feared *rancheadores* (slave-hunters). Gangs of *rancheadores* regularly hunted down escaped slaves with firearms and trained dogs, and penalties for being caught were brutal. Foot amputation was the norm, but castration for men and breast removal for women was not unheard of.

Evidence suggests that since *palenques* in Cuba were small compared to Maroon settlements elsewhere in the Caribbean, *cimarrónes* usually elected for flight over a fight. One of Cuba's best documented *palenques*, El Portillo, located in the Sierra Maestra was broken up in 1747 by slave-hunters who captured 11 of the 21 *cimarrónes* living there. Testimonies from their later trial claim that most of the Portillo slaves had been on the run for between 10 and 25 years.

After a bloody slave rebellion broke out in Haiti in 1791, Cuba's paranoid slave owners, fearing a repeat performance in their own colony, stepped up actions against *cimarrónes*. In 1796 official militia groups were organized to hunt them down and destroy *palenques*, but while they were able to stifle large-scale rebellions, small groups of *cimarrónes* managed to hold out right up until 1886.

One of the only testimonies from a runaway slave was recorded by of Esteban Montejo. Born in 1860, Montejo escaped from a sugar plantation in the Villa Clara area in the late 1870s and lived as a fugitive in a bat-infested cave near Remedios until the abolition of slavery in 1886. In 1963 Montejo, then aged 103, related his story to Cuban ethnographer Miguel Barnet, who published the account in the fascinating book *Biografía de un cimarrón* (Biography of a Runaway Slave).

Remnants of *palenques* have been unearthed all over Cuba, with over 25 archaeological sites found in the Pinar del Río region alone. The Palenque de los Cimarrones in the Cueva de San Miguel (p188) near Viñales has a small 'museum' with basic information on how runaway slave communities were organized.

Centro Cultural
Polo Montañez
LIVE MUSIC

(cnr Salvador Cisneros & Joaquin Pérez; after 9pm USD$1; ⊙music 9pm-2am) Named for the late Pinar del Río resident-turned-*guajiro* (country folk) hero and legendary folk singer Polo Montañez, this open-to-the-elements patio off the main plaza is a bar-restaurant with a full-blown stage that hits the higher gears after 9pm.

Patio del Decimista
LIVE MUSIC

(Salvador Cisneros No 102; ⊙music from 7pm) The ebullient and long-standing Patio del Decimista serves up live music, cold beers, snacks and rummy cocktails.

🛍 Shopping

Mercado de Artesanía
ARTS & CRAFTS

(Joaquin Pérez; ⊙10am-7pm) This private-enterprise market sells Cuba-themed arts and crafts, and sets up in Calle Joaquin Pérez every day.

Los Vegueros
CIGARS, RUM

(☑48-79-60-80; Salvador Cisneros No 57; ⊙9am-7pm) A hot selection of cigars – with a roller often in residence – and rum too.

ℹ️ Information

INTERNET ACCESS

Etecsa Telepunto (Ceferino Fernández No 3; internet per hour USD$1; ⊙8:30am-6pm, to 5pm Sun) Three terminals in a tiny office; it also sells cards for wi-fi.

The main square has good wi-fi reception.

MEDICAL

Farmacia Internacional (☑48-79-64-11; Hotel Los Jazmines, Carretera a Pinar del Río; ⊙8am-8pm) Pharmacy in Hotel Los Jazmines. There's also a medical clinic here.

Policlinico (☑48-79-33-48; Salvador Cisneros interior)

MONEY

Banks in Viñales have long queues. Arrive early or consider changing money in Pinar del Río.

Banco de Crédito y Comercio (Salvador Cisneros No 58; ⊙8am-noon & 1:30-3pm Mon-Fri, 8am-11am Sat) Has two ATMs.

Cadeca (cnr Salvador Cisneros & Adela Azcuy; ⊙8:30am-4pm Mon-Sat) Quickest service.

TOURIST INFORMATION

Infotur (Salvador Cisneros No 63b; ⊙9am-6pm)

Most casas particulares (private homestays) have an abundance of information on the area and can organize excursions at short notice.

ℹ️ Getting There & Away

BUS

The well-ordered **Víazul ticket office** (Salvador Cisneros No 63a; ⊙8am-noon & 1-3pm) is opposite the main square in the same building as Cubataxi. Two daily Víazul buses (www.viazul. com) depart from here for Havana (USD$12, 3¼ hours). There's also one daily bus to Cienfuegos (USD$32, eight hours) and Trinidad (USD$37, 9½ hours), usually leaving early in the morning. All buses stop at Pinar del Río (USD$6, 30 minutes).

Conectando buses run by Cubanacán (p183), and departing from outside the Cubanacán office, have daily transfers to Havana, Trinidad and Cienfuegos. Book a day ahead. Prices are the same as Víazul.

Daily transfer buses run to Cayo Levisa (USD$47, including lunch and boat transfer) and Cayo Jutías (USD$15).

For María la Gorda, you'll need to negotiate a *colectivo* (shared taxi); expect to pay USD$35 per person if full.

CAR & MOTORCYCLE

To reach Viñales from the south, take the long and winding road from Pinar del Río; the roads from the north coast are not as sinuous, but due to their condition are way more time-consuming. The remote mountain road from the Península de Guanahacabibes through Guane and Pons is one of Cuba's most spectacular routes. Allow a lot of travel time.

Car hire can be arranged at **Cubacar** (☑48-79-60-60; Salvador Cisneros No 63c; ⊙9am-7pm) in the Cubanacán office (if cars are available).

Mopeds can be rented for USD$26 a day at the Bike Rental Point (p182) next to Restaurante la Casa de Don Tomás.

TAXI

Víazul buses are often fully booked days in advance. The solution? A *colectivo* (shared taxi). These can be booked at the office that **Cubataxi** (☑48-79-31-95; Salvador Cisneros No 63a) shares with Víazul or at your casa particular (private homestay). Prices per person, if taxis are full (four people), are Havana (USD$20), Varadero (USD$30), Cienfuegos (USD$35) and Trinidad (USD$40).

ℹ️ Getting Around

The Viñales Bus Tour is a hop-on/hop-off minibus that runs nine times a day between the valley's spread-out sites. Starting and finishing in the town plaza, the whole circuit takes 65 minutes, with the first bus leaving at 9am and the last at 4:50pm. There are 18 stops along the route, which runs from Hotel Los Jazmines to Hotel Rancho San Vicente, and all are clearly marked with route maps and timetables. All-day tickets cost USD$5 and can be purchased on the bus.

Parque Nacional Viñales

Parque Nacional Viñales' extraordinary cultural landscape covers 150 sq km and supports a population of 25,000 people. A mosaic of settlements studded with *mogotes* (limestone monoliths) grows coffee, tobacco, sugarcane, oranges, avocados and bananas on some of the oldest, most tradition-steeped landscapes in Cuba.

◉ Sights

Los Aquáticos   VILLAGE

🚶 A kilometer beyond the turnoff to Dos Hermanas and the Mural de la Prehistoria, a dirt road twists up to the mountain community of Los Aquáticos, founded in 1943 by followers of visionary Antoñica Izquierdo, who discovered the healing power of water when the campesinos (farmers) of this area had no access to conventional medicine. They colonized the mountain slopes and two families still live there. It's accessible only by horse or on foot. Most of Viñales' casas particulares (private homestays) can organize tours.

You can also go it alone. Although no signs mark the path, there are plenty of homesteads en route where you can ask the way. From the main road follow a dirt road for approximately 400m before branching left and heading cross-country. You should be able to pick out a blue house halfway up the mountain ahead of you. This is your goal. Once there, you can admire the view, procure grown-on-site coffee and chat to the amiable owners about the water cure. After your visit, you can make a loop by returning via Campismo Dos Hermanas and the Mural de la Prehistoria cliff paintings; it's a wonderfully scenic route (the complete Los Aquáticos–Dos Hermanas circuit totals 6km from the main highway).

Mural de la Prehistoria   PUBLIC ART

(incl drink USD$3; ⊙9am-6pm) A 120m-long painting, 4km west of Viñales village on the side of Mogote Pita. Leovigildo González Morillo, a follower of Mexican artist Diego Rivera, designed it in 1961 (the idea was hatched by Celia Sánchez, Alicia Alonso and Antonio Núñez Jiménez). On a cliff at the foot of the 617m-high Sierra de Viñales, the highest portion of the Sierra de los Órganos, this massive mural took 18 people four years to complete.

The huge snail, dinosaurs, sea monsters and humans on the cliff symbolize the theory of evolution and are either impressively psychedelic or monumentally horrific, depending on your viewpoint. You don't really have to get up close to appreciate the artwork, but the admission fee is waived if you take the overpriced, USD$15 lunch at the on-site **restaurant** (set lunch USD$15; ⊙8am-7pm). Horses are usually available here (USD$5 per hour) for various excursions.

Gran Caverna de Santo Tomás   CAVE

(USD$15; ⊙9am-3pm) Welcome to Cuba's largest cave system and the second largest on the American continent. There are over 46km of galleries on eight levels, with a 1km section accessible to visitors. There's no artificial lighting, but headlamps are provided for the 90-minute guided tour. Highlights include bats, stalagmites and stalactites, underground pools, interesting rock formations and a replica of an ancient indigenous mural.

Wear suitable shoes and be aware that the cave requires some steep climbs and scrambling over slippery rocks. Most people visit the cave on an organized trip from Viñales (USD$28).

Cueva del Indio   CAVE

(USD$5; ⊙9am-5:30pm; 🚗) In a pretty nook 5.5km north of Viñales village, this cave is very popular with tourists. An ancient indigenous dwelling, the cave was rediscovered in 1920. After a short 200m walk, you're transferred to a motor boat to ply the final 400m along an underground river. The cave is electrically lit and the experience underwhelming. Exit through the gift shop. Good for kids.

Cueva de San Miguel   CAVE

(incl drink USD$3; ⊙9am-5:30pm) This is a small cave at the jaws of the Valle de San Vicente, with the cave entrance serving as a bar/nightspot. Your entrance fee gets you into a gaping cave that engulfs you for a brief, kind-of-absorbing 10-minute tour before dumping you a tad cynically in the Palenque de los Cimarrones restaurant on the other side. In both cave and restaurant are a few scant objects relating to runaway slave culture and the *palenque* (settlement) that resided here.

Proyecto Raíces   SCULPTURE

(☑5-274-9007; Carretera al Moncada Km 6; USD$3; ⊙dawn-dusk) 🚶 Immersed in the

CLIMBING IN VIÑALES

You don't need to be Reinhold Messner to recognize the unique climbing potential of Viñales, Cuba's mini-Yosemite. Sprinkled with steep-sided *mogotes* (limestone monoliths) and blessed with whole photo-albums' worth of natural vistas, climbers from around the world have been coming here for over two decades to indulge in a sport that has struggled to gain official recognition from the Cuban government.

In typical Cuban style, climbing in Viñales occupies a gray area: it's not openly recognized by the authorities, yet plenty of people do it without consequence. As a tourist, it's unlikely you'll face any problems, instead it's the local guides who need to be more careful about watching their backs.

Consequently, Viñales' climbing remains very much a word-of-mouth affair. There's little visible on-the-ground information save for a couple of climbing areas sketched onto a map at the national park office. If you are keen to get up onto a rock face, your first points of reference should be the comprehensive website of Cuba Climbing (www.cubaclimbing.com), along with the book *Cuba Climbing* by Aníbal Fernández and Armando Menocal (currently out of print, but available secondhand). Once on the ground, the best nexus for climbers are the casas of Oscar Jaime Rodríguez and Villa El Cafetal (p183) in Viñales. Ask any locals for directions to either.

Viñales has numerous well-known climbing routes, including the infamous 'Wasp Factory,' and a handful of skillful Cuban guides, but there's no proper equipment rental (bring your own or borrow from the locals). Safety is another issue. With no official safety procedures in place, everything you do is at your own risk. For this reason, Viñales is best suited to climbers who know the ropes as opposed to beginners looking to learn. That said, there are some very good and experienced Cuban guides, plenty of local enthusiasm and epic scenery.

foothills of Viñales' *mogotes* (limestone monoliths) lies a bucolic manifestation of all that is best about this region given unique form by local sculptor Noel Díaz Galart. The disparate 'complex' named Raíces (roots) over which Galart presides contains several *miradores* (lookouts), a rustic restaurant suspended above a lake, and numerous serpentine paths dotted with the sculptor's wooden carvings, many of them exhibiting supernatural elements. It's a great place to unwind, stroll and admire the view.

From the *miradores*, see if you can spot Martí Yacente, an outline on the mountaintops that is said to resemble the profile of a supine José Martí.

El Memorial 'Los Malagones' MONUMENT
(USD$1; ☉9am-5pm) Los Malagones, from the community of El Moncada, was the first rural militia in Cuba. It comprised 12 men who rooted out a counterrevolutionary band from the nearby mountains in 1959. A mausoleum and memorial fountain inaugurated in 1999 contains niches dedicated to the 12 militiamen (all but one are now dead).

It is crowned by a stone re-creation of their leader, Leandro Rodríguez Malagón, copied from a famous photo by Raúl

Corrales. The water features are designed to replicate (with unerring accuracy) the sound of machine-gun fire. A tiny museum is on-site.

🏃 Activities

Cycling

Despite the sometimes hilly terrain, Viñales is one of the best places in Cuba to cycle (most roads follow the valleys and are relatively flat). Traffic on the roads is still light, and the scenery is a conveyor belt of natural beauty. Many casas particulares (private homestays) now offer cheap bike rentals (around USD$10 per day). Some also offer bike tours. Ask around.

Hiking

The Parque Nacional Viñales offers around 15 official hiking routes and maps are displayed at the visitor center. It is best to go with a guide as signposting is terrible. Prices for guides are around USD$10 per person but depend on distance and group size.

You can arrange hikes at the park's visitor center (p191) or at the Museo Municipal (p181) in Viñales. Guided hikes leave from the museum twice a day at 8:45am and 2:30pm.

Aside from the park guides, almost every casa particular (private homestay) in Viñales will be able to hook you up with a private guide who can pretty much custom-build any trip you want. Eternally popular is the loop around the **Valle de Palmarito**, which starts and ends in the village and takes in a coffee plantation, tobacco house and the Cueva de Palmarito where swimming by torchlight is possible.

Other favorites are the hikes to Los Aquáticos and the Valle del Silencio.

★**Coco Solo & Palmarito Mogotes** HIKING
This walk starts on a spur road about 100m south of the entrance to La Ermita hotel and progresses for 8km, taking in the Valle del Silencio, the Coco Solo and Palmarito *mogotes* (limestone monoliths), and the Mural de la Prehistoria. There are good views and ample opportunities to discover the local flora and fauna, including a visit to a tobacco farm.

It returns you to the main road back to Viñales.

San Vicente/Ancón HIKING
The trail around the more remote Valle Ancón enables you to check out still-functioning coffee communities in a valley surrounded by *mogotes* (limestone monoliths). It's an 8km loop.

Tradiciones Campesinas HIKING
Starting just east of Hotel Los Jazmines, this bucolic 8.5km loop ushers you up through woods to a hilltop *mirador* (lookout) and returns you via typically delightful tobacco-plantation scenery.

Cueva El Cable HIKING
A 3.5km hike into a local cave typical of Viñales' karst topography. It starts in the Valle de San Vicente near the Cueva del Indio (p188).

Maravillas de Viñales HIKING
A 5km loop beginning 1km northeast of El Moncada and 13km from the Dos Hermanas turnoff, this hike takes in endemic plants, orchids and the biggest leaf-cutter ant hive in Cuba (so they say).

Horseback Riding
The lush hills and valleys around town lend themselves to horseback riding, particularly the Valle de Palmarito and the route to Los Aquáticos. Most casas particulares (private homestays) can hook you up with a guide for around USD$5 per hour. Riding a horse

will mean you see more in a shorter space of time. It's particularly useful in the wet season (April to October) when the trails can be muddy.

Zip Lining

Canopy Tour ADVENTURE SPORTS
(☑5-398-8975; Carretera al Moncada, Km 6; per person USD$8; ⊙9am-5pm) Around 6km west of town, you'll encounter one of only three canopy tours in Cuba, a fairly modest set of lines (total distance 1000m, maximum height 35m), but fun all the same and highly economical to boot. Book beforehand at the Cubanacán (p183) office in town, or just turn up and wait for the next departure.

🛏 Sleeping

Campismo Dos Hermanas CAMPISMO $
(Cubamar; ☑48-79-32-23; www.campismopop ular.cu; Mogote Dos Hermanas; d/tr USD$23/32; P🏊) Trapped between the sheer-sided jaws of two *mogotes* (limestone monoliths), and in view of the Mural de la Prehistoria, is one of Cubamar's best international campismos (cheap rustic accommodations). Bonuses include a restaurant, pool, geological museum, horseback riding and nearby hiking trails. The only incongruity is the loud music that spoils the tranquil ambience.

Hotel Rancho San Vicente HOTEL $$
(☑48-79-62-01; Carretera a Esperanza Km 33; s/d USD$60/96; P🌂🛜🏊) After Viñales' two spectacularly located hotels, you probably thought it couldn't get any better, but Rancho San Vicente comes close as far as setting is concerned. Situated 8km north of the village, this bucolic scattering of cabins is nestled in a grove amid trees and birdsong. The rooms are a different matter, however, with some older cabins succumbing to mold.

A better bet is the more modern 22-room extension block located on the opposite (west) side of the road. There are two pools and a restaurant, plus a spa with massage facility on-site. Birdwatching walks can be organized too.

🍴 Eating

La Carreta MEDITERRANEAN $$
(☑5-331-1658; Carretera a Esperanza Km 36; mains USD$10-15; ⊙10am-5pm) A *carreta* is a simple oxen-drawn cart, but there's nothing basic about how this restaurant transports you up its steep steps and into the privileged pantheons of wonderful Cuban food laced with subtle Mediterranean influences. The

classics? Lamb stewed in a red-wine sauce, or fresh crayfish from the Ancón River. It's 2km north of Hotel Rancho San Vicente.

Finca San Vicente   CUBAN $$
(Carretera a Esperanza Km 32½; mains USD$11; ⊘10am-4:30pm) A large, but reasonable rural restaurant typical of the Viñales area, Finca San Vicente serves a slap-up USD$10 lunch. If there are enough people, it serves whole roast pork with all the trimmings. It's ever popular with tour buses.

❶ Information

The park is administered through the highly informative **Parque Nacional Viñales Visitors Center** (☑ 48-79-61-44; Carretera a Pinar del Río Km 22; ⊘8am-6pm), located 3km south of the town of Viñales. Inside, colorful displays (in Spanish and English) map out the park's main features. Hiking information and guides are also on hand.

THE NORTHERN COAST

Cayo Jutías

Pinar del Río's most discovered 'undiscovered' beach is the diminutive blanket of sand that adorns the northern coast of Cayo Jutías, a mangrove-covered key situated approximately 65km northwest of Viñales and attached to the mainland by a short *pedraplén* (causeway). Jutías – named for its indigenous tree rats – vies with Cayo Levisa to the east for the title of the province's most idyllic beach, and while the latter might be prettier, the former has no overnight accommodations and thus commands greater tranquility.

The cayo's access road starts about 4km west of Santa Lucía. Ten minutes after crossing the causeway the **Faro de Cayo Jutías** appears; this metal lighthouse was built by the US in 1902 and makes for an interesting walk along the abutting mangrove-studded sands. The road kinks sharp left to culminate at the main Jutías beach, caressed by crystal-clear water, 12.5km from the coastal highway.

Jutías has a small nautical center that rents out kayaks for USD$1 per hour, runs snorkeling trips for USD$12 and other boat trips for USD$10 to USD$25. Beyond the initial arc of sand, the beach continues for 3km; you can hike barefoot through the mangroves. Beware the mosquitoes in the summer!

If you're looking for something to eat, the open-sided **Restaurante Cayo Jutías** (mains USD$7-10; ⊘10am-5:30pm) right on the beach specializes in local seafood.

❶ Getting There & Away

Daily transfer buses from Viñales cost USD$15 and will give you six hours at the beach. Alternatively you can organize a *colectivo* (shared taxi) through your casa particular (private homestay) or use your own wheels. The pretty drive takes you through Minas de Matahambre and rolling pine-clad hills, but the road is in a terrible state.

Puerto Esperanza

POP 7000

Becalmed at the end of a long, bumpy road, the fishing village of Puerto Esperanza (Port of Hope), 6km north of San Cayetano and 25km north of Viñales, isn't sleepy so much as veritably slumbering. The clocks haven't worked here since...oh...1951. According to town lore, the giant mango trees lining the entry road were planted by enslaved people in the 1800s. A long pier pointing out into the bay, a favored perch for catatonic fishers, is tempting for a jump into the ocean.

Puerto Esperanza has a loyal following of ultra-independent travelers who are keen to see a side of Cuba where few foreigners care to tread. Rich in money it isn't. Rich in wild off-the-cuff experiences it is. Come here to spin with local cyclists through craggy hills and end up on an unkempt beach fishing for your dinner.

If you want to stay the night, the charismatic Teresa runs **Casa Teresa Hernández Martínez** (☑48-79-37-03; Calle 4 No 7; r incl breakfast USD$25) and is as colorful as her six bright and clean rooms furnished in lurid pink, blue and green. She also runs a private restaurant in a jungle-like garden out back, where fish (seafood plate CUC$10) and lobster headline the menu. Local activities from cycling trips to horseback riding can be arranged here.

❶ Getting There & Away

You'll need your own wheels to get to Puerto Esperanza – two or four. There's a handy Servi-Cupet gas station at San Cayetano. The road on to Cayo Jutías deteriorates to dirt outside San Cayetano: expect a throbbing backside if you're on a bike or moped.

Cayo Levisa

More frequented than nearby Cayo Jutías, and perhaps more splendid, Cayo Levisa sports a beach-bungalow-style hotel, a basic restaurant and a fully equipped diving center, yet still manages to feel relatively isolated. Separation from the mainland obviously helps. Unlike other Cuban keys, there's no causeway here, and visitors must make the 35-minute journey by boat from Palma Rubia. It's a worthwhile trip: 3km of sugar-white sand and sapphire waters earmark Cayo Levisa as Pinar del Río's best beach. American writer Ernest Hemingway first 'discovered' the area, part of the Archipiélago de los Colorados, in the early 1940s after he set up a fishing camp on Cayo Paraíso, a smaller coral island 10km to the east. These days Levisa attracts up to 100 visitors daily as well as 50-plus hotel guests. While you won't feel like an errant Robinson Crusoe here, you should find time (and space) for plenty of rest and relaxation.

🏃 Activities

Levisa has a small marina offering scuba diving for USD$40 per immersion, including gear and transport to the dive site. There are 14 dive sites peppered off the coast. These include the popular La Corona de San Carlos (San Carlos' Crown), the formation of which allows divers to get close to marine life unobserved, and Mogotes de Viñales, so called for its towering coral formations, which are said to bear a likeness to the *mogotes* (limestone montoliths) outside Viñales. La Cadena Misteriosa (Mysterious Chain) is a shallow reef where some of the most colorful fish hereabouts – including barracudas and rays – can be seen. Snorkeling plus gear costs USD$12 and a sunset cruise goes for the same price. Kayaking and aqua biking are also possible.

🛏 Sleeping & Eating

Casa Mario & Antonia CASA PARTICULAR $
(☎ 5-228-3067; Palma Rubia; r USD$25) Ideal for resort-phobes or people who miss the last boat to the key, Mario and Antonia's place is a simple and rustic place where genuine Cuban hospitality makes up for any lack of modern appliances. The small, simple house has four bedrooms for rent, great food and a quiet bucolic setting. The boat dock is a five-minute walk away.

Hotel Cayo Levisa HOTEL $$$
(☎ 48-75-65-01; www.hotelcayolevisa-cuba.com; s/d incl meals USD$114/190; ✱) With an idyllic tropical beach just outside your front door, you won't worry about the outdated *cabañas* (cabins) and dull food choices here. Expanded to a 60-room capacity several years back, the Levisa's newer wooden cabins (with bathrooms) are an improvement on the old concrete blocks. Service has pulled its socks up too. Book ahead: it's isolated but popular.

Restaurant Paraíso CUBAN $$
(Cayo Levisa; buffet incl in day-trip tickets; ⊙ 7am-10pm) Your only dining option on Cayo Levisa is this restaurant at the Hotel Cayo Levisa. A buffet lunch is usually included for day-trippers. The food isn't legendary, but it'll keep you going till dinnertime.

ℹ️ Getting There & Away

Most day-trippers visit Cayo Levisa on organized tours from Viñales (USD$47 including bus, ferry, lunch and a drink). Buses depart Viñales daily at 8am and are timed to coincide with the ferry.

The dock for embarkations to Cayo Levisa is around 21km northeast of La Palma and 40km west of Bahía Honda. Take the turnoff to Mirian and proceed 4km through a large banana plantation to reach the coastguard station at Palma Rubia, where there is a snack bar (10am to 6pm) and the departure **dock** for the island. The Cayo Levisa boat leaves daily at 10am, 2pm and 6pm, and returns at 9am, 12:30pm and 5pm. It costs USD$35 per person roundtrip (including boat, three drinks and buffet lunch). Should you miss the boat, you may be able to hire a water taxi for an extra USD$10.

From the Cayo Levisa dock you cross the mangroves on a wooden walkway to the Hotel Cayo Levisa and the gorgeous beach along the island's north side.

SAN DIEGO DE LOS BAÑOS & AROUND

San Diego de los Baños

POP 6300

Sitting 130km southwest of Havana, this nondescript town just north of the Carretera Central is popularly considered the country's best spa location. Its medicinal waters were supposedly 'discovered' in the early colonial period when a sick slave stumbled upon a sulfurous spring, took a revitalizing bath and was miraculously cured. Thanks to its proximity to Havana,

San Diego's fame spread quickly and a permanent spa was established in 1891. During the early 20th century American tourists flocked here, leading to the development of the current hotel-bathhouse complex in the early 1950s.

Despite numerous possibilities for tourism, San Diego's scruffy bathhouse with its creepy sanatorium feel isn't everyone's cup of tea. More alluring is the attractive natural region to the west known as the Sierra de Güira, an area replete with pine, mahogany and cedar forests. It's a favorite spot for birdwatchers.

◉ Sights & Activities

Balneario San Diego   HOT SPRINGS
(baths USD$8; ⊘ 8am-5pm) Thermal pools, hot springs, recuperation center; there are many terms to describe San Diego's famous bathhouse, but 'spa' isn't one of them. Whatever you do, don't come here expecting fluffy towels, fancy facials and the alluring whiff of eucalyptus oil. Reopened in 2015 after a lengthy closure, the famous *balneario* (bathhouse) still looks more like a semi-abandoned hospital than a Roman bathhouse. Nevertheless, baths in thermal waters (30°C to 40°C), along with massages and acupuncture are all available.

Perennially popular with Cubans undergoing courses of medical treatment, the bathhouse is open to all-comers yet only receives the odd curious tourist. Prepare for an all-pervading stench of sulfur.

Julio César Hernández   BIRDWATCHING
(☑ 5-248-6631; carpeta@mirador.sandiego.co.cu) Birdwatching and trekking trips into Parque la Güira with qualified guide Julio César Hernández can be organized at Hotel Mirador. You'll need your own wheels. Possible feathered sightings include the bee hummingbird, the Cuban pygmy owl and the Cuban soltaire. It's one of the best birding spots in Cuba.

⌂ Sleeping

Hotel Mirador   HOTEL $$
(☑ 48-77-83-38; Calle 23 Final; s/d incl breakfast USD$38/58/80; ❘P❘❘❘❘) The Mirador is a low-key stop-off. Predating the revolution by five years, the hotel was built in 1954 to accommodate spa-seekers headed for the adjacent Balneario San Diego. Well-tended terraced gardens slope up to simple, slightly dated rooms that look for the most part onto balconies with garden and *balneario* (bathhouse) views.

Downstairs there's a pleasant swimming pool and an outdoor grill that does whole roast pig on a spit. There's also a proper restaurant *con una vista* (with a view) inside, serving Cuban cuisine. It's popular with cycling groups, birdwatchers and holidaying Cubans in the summer.

❶ Getting There & Away

The area is only accessible by car or bicycle.

The town is on a kink in the Carretera Central and around 10km north of the Autopista. There's a Servi-Cupet gas station at the entrance to San Diego de los Baños from Havana.

A taxi from Havana will cost about USD$60, from Viñales about USD$25.

Sierra de Güira

With rough roads and precious few accommodations, the untamed Sierra de Güira, a medley of limestone karst cliffs and swooping pockets of forest west of San Diego de los Baños, is off the tourist radar. This didn't prevent it becoming a retreat for the revolution's most renowned figures in the past and, to this day, a host of rare birdlife.

◉ Sights

Hacienda Cortina   HISTORIC SITE
(USD$5; ⊘ dawn-dusk) A grand crenelated entry gate a few kilometers west of San Diego de los Baños announces the surreal, long-abandoned grounds of Hacienda Cortina. The brainchild of wealthy lawyer José Manuel Cortina, this rich-man's-fantasy-made-reality was built as a giant park during the 1920s and 1930s, with Cortina plonking a stately home in its midst. After nigh-on a century of neglect, in 2014 refurbishment money arrived out of the blue and the hacienda has been partially restored.

There's a lot to take in at this tropical pleasure dome, although most of it is yet to be fully appreciated by foreign visitors (most passers-by are Cuban). A driveway from the grandiose entrance leads up to a cluster of attractively restored buildings, including a restaurant, swimming pool and hotel (Cubans only). From here a staircase leads down through a French-style garden adorned with colorful buds and statues of Carrera marble. Beyond lie the ruins of Cortina's erstwhile mansion, partially restored and incorporating another open-air bar-restaurant.

On either side, the extensive plant-rich grounds spread out to incorporate an artificial boating lake, several ornamental bridges, plus Japanese and Chinese gardens complete with pagodas. It's a spirit-lifting and beautiful domain and would be even more so if the various eating joints didn't insist on playing ear-splitting music.

The hacienda grounds fan out beyond into the wild 25,000-hectare Parque la Güira.

Cueva de los Portales   CAVE
(USD\$2; ☺8am-5pm) During the October 1962 Cuban Missile Crisis, Ernesto 'Che' Guevara transferred the headquarters of the Western Army to this vast and spectacular cave, 11km west of Parque la Güira and 16km north of Entronque de Herradura on the Carretera Central. The cave is set in a beautiful remote area among steep-sided vine-covered *mogotes* (limestone monoliths) and was declared a national monument in the 1980s.

Within the cavemouth, a small outdoor museum exhibits Che's roughshod artifacts including his bed and the table where he played chess (while the rest of the world stood at the brink of nuclear Armageddon). Three other caves called El Espejo, El Salvador and Cueva Oscura are further up the hillside. This area is brilliant birdwatching turf: birding tours can be arranged at San Diego de los Baños' Hotel Mirador (p193), or you can ask staff at the cave entrance. There's a good campismo (cheap, rustic accommodations; Cuban guests only) outside the cave with a bar-restaurant open to all-comers. You'll need your own wheels to get here.

ⓘ Getting There & Away

The area is only accessible by car.

The road across the mountains from San Diego de los Baños to the Cueva de los Portales is beautiful, but narrow and bumpy. The approach from Entronque de Herradura is an easier drive. There's a Servi-Cupet gas station at the entrance to San Diego de los Baños from Havana.

PINAR DEL RÍO AREA

Pinar del Río

POP 143,000

Surrounded by beautiful verdant countryside and enriched by its proximity to the world's best tobacco-growing terrain, the city of Pinar del Río emits a strange energy, exacerbated by its famous *jineteros* (touts), who can abrade the most thick-skinned traveler. As a result, the place probably has more detractors than fans, especially since the bucolic hassle-free paradise of Viñales is so close by. But a stopover here needn't be purgatorial. There's some weirdly interesting architecture, and a hot, frenetic after-dark scene. Plus, if you're serious about your smokes, you've just arrived in cigar-central.

Despite this, Pinar often feels like a city in the slow lane, an urban backwater that has become the butt of countless jokes about the supposedly easy-to-fool *guajiros* (country folk), who are sometimes portrayed as simple-minded hicks. Not so. Check out the local art, for starters, or pop by during the July Carnaval.

◉ Sights

Palacio de los
Matrimonios   HISTORIC BUILDING
(Martí, btwn Rafael Morales & Plaza de la Independencia) Wow! West on Martí, the grand neoclassical facades give way to this gushingly opulent wedding venue dating from 1924, with its huge mirrors, chandeliers and plentiful artwork, much of it Chinese in origin. In secular Cuba, weddings are often held in government-run 'palaces' rather than churches. If you're lucky, you may spy a ceremony in action. If not, the guard will usually let you have a look around for a small tip.

Casa Taller Pedro Pablo Oliva   GALLERY
(www.pedropablooliva.com; Martí No 160, Plaza de la Independencia; ☺hours vary) FREE The Plaza de la Independencia is the hub of the art scene. First and foremost, on the northwest side, is the workshop-gallery of renowned Cuban artist Pedro Pablo Oliva (b 1949). The key point of the gallery is to promote and encourage artistic talent in Pinar del Río; several local artists have work displayed. Ring the bell if you want to browse.

Fábrica de Tabacos
Francisco Donatien   FACTORY
(Antonio Maceo Oeste No 157; USD\$5; ☺9am-1:30pm Mon-Fri) If you're tracking the full story of tobacco from plant to cigar then this is the inevitable end-point – the factory where they skillfully roll them by hand. Smaller than Havana's Partagás factory, it's possible to get a more intimate insight here, though the foibles are the same – robotic guides, rushed tours and the nagging notion that it's all a bit voyeuristic.

Teatro José Jacinto Milanés THEATER
(☑ 48-75-38-71; Martí Este No 60, btwn Colón & Isabel Rubio) Often included in a set of seven classic 19th-century Cuban provincial theaters, the 540-seat Milanés dates from 1845, making it one of Cuba's oldest. It was refurbished in the early 2000s and, with its three-tiered auditorium, antique seats, and Spanish-style patio and cafe, is well worth a look. Check the noticeboard for upcoming performances.

Museo de Historia Natural MUSEUM
(Martí Este No 202; USD$1, camera USD$1; ⏱ 9am-5pm, to 1pm Sun) A mad but magnificent neo-Gothic-meets-Moorish-meets-Hindu-meets-Byzantium mansion built by local doctor and world traveler Francisco Guasch in 1914. Once you've got over the shock of the whimsical exterior (gargoyles, turrets and sculpted seahorses), the decrepit exhibits inside will slow your pulse right down again. The giant stone dinosaur in the garden is fun though.

Fábrica de Bebidas Casa Garay FACTORY
(Isabel Rubio Sur No 189, btwn Ceferino Fernández & Frank País; USD$1; ⏱ 9am-3:30pm Mon-Fri, to 12:30pm Sat) Workers here use a secret recipe to distill sweet and dry versions of the city's signature liquor, Guayabita del Pinar guava brandy. Whistle-stop 15-minute multilingual tours of what is essentially a one-machine factory are topped off with a taste of the brew in the sampling room. There's a shop adjacent.

Catedral de San Rosendo CHURCH
(Antonio Maceo Este No 3) The city's understated cathedral is four blocks southeast of the cigar factory. It dates from 1883 and its exterior seems to change color every couple of years. As with most Cuban churches, the interior is often closed. Get a peek during Sunday-morning service.

Museo Provincial de Historia MUSEUM
(Martí Este No 58, btwn Colón & Isabel Rubio; USD$1; ⏱ 8am-10pm Tue-Sat, to noon Sun) A museum collecting the history of the province from pre-Columbian times to the present, including Enrique Jorrín ephemera (Jorrín was the creator of the *chachachá*). It's browse-worthy, if not particularly riveting.

🛏 Sleeping

Casa Colonial La Nonna CASA PARTICULAR $
(☑ 48-77-43-35; Máximo Gómez No 161, btwn Rafael Ferro & Ciprián Valdés; r USD$20-25; ❋ 🛜) Classic Pinar house (Tuscan pillars holding up a shady front porch) with four rooms spread over a couple of floors, the Nonna (an Italian influence?) is full of lovely nooks and crannies and serves great food, often barbecued by chef/owner Moro who rents another apartment over by the bus station. Best digs in the city.

Terra Mar 1910 CASA PARTICULAR $
(☑ 48-75-58-42; Martí No 140, btwn Rafael Morales & González Coro; s/d/q USD$35/40/60; ❋ 🛜) Right on Pinar del Río's main street, this place is run by a Cuban who has lived in Brussels (hence the Belgian flag outside). There are six rooms and a restaurant spread around an attractive colonial residence. One room has a king-sized bed; another has a huge hot tub/bath. They're good, if a little overpriced.

Pensión El Moro CASA PARTICULAR $
(☑ 48-77-43-35; moro75@nauta.cu; Adela Azcuy No 46, btwn Colón & Ciprián Valdés; r USD$20-25; ❋) Two bright little apartments - one down, one up - opposite the Víazul bus station. The inviting kitchen with its breakfast bar is shared between both. The upper room is ultimately best, as it's right alongside a roof terrace. English spoken.

Hotel Vueltabajo HOTEL $$
(☑ 48-75-93-81; cnr Martí & Rafael Morales; s/d incl breakfast USD$86/97; ❋) A colonial throwback with high ceilings and striped Parisian window awnings, this dustily atmospheric hotel has rooms so spacious the furniture struggles to fill them. Old-fashioned shutters open onto the street, and downstairs there's a fairly average bar-restaurant.

🍴 Eating

El Mesón 1995 CUBAN $
(☑ 48-75-28-67; Martí Este 205; meals USD$4-6; ⏱ noon-midnight) Long-standing *paladar* (privately owned restaurant) serving up liberal helpings of simple *comida criolla* (Creole food), heavy on the rice and beans, with plenty of Cuban company. Try a piña colada served in a hollowed-out pineapple.

El Gallardo CUBAN $
(☑ 48-77-84-92; Martí Este 207; CUP$40-125; ⏱ 8am-11:30pm; ❋) A rather lavish entrance leads back to a more typical *ranchón* (rustic, opened-sided restaurant) eating area. Good food, particularly the fish, and a long menu mainly highlighting Cuban classics with less illustrious Italian inflections including pizza.

Pinar del Río

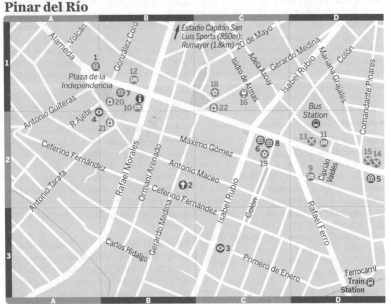

Pinar del Río

Sights
1 Casa Taller Pedro Pablo Oliva	A1
2 Catedral de San Rosendo	B2
3 Fábrica de Bebidas Casa Garay	C3
4 Fábrica de Tabacos Francisco Donatien	A2
5 Museo de Historia Natural	D2
6 Museo Provincial de Historia	C2
7 Palacio de los Matrimonios	B1
8 Teatro José Jacinto Milanés	C2

Sleeping
9 Casa Colonial La Nonna	D2
10 Hotel Vueltabajo	B1
11 Pensión El Moro	D2
12 Terra Mar 1910	B1

Eating
13 Café Ortuzar	D2
14 El Gallardo	D2
15 El Mesón 1995	D2

Drinking & Nightlife
16 Café Pinar	C1
17 Disco Azul	E2

Entertainment
18 Casa de la Música 'La Sitiera'	C1
19 La Piscuala	C2

Shopping
20 Casa del Habano	B1
21 La Casa del Ron	B2
22 La Colosal	C1

★ **Café Ortuzar**   CUBAN, INTERNATIONAL $$

(Martí 127; mains USD$4-9; ⊗11:30am-midnight; ❋) Before you write off Pinar del Río as an itchy nexus for bored Cuban men peddling fake cigars, make sure you slurp a coffee in this salubrious streetside cafe or, even better, gravitate inside to the elegant air-conditioned dining room. Herein abstract pictures of the province's famous *guajiros* watch on while you sample Peruvian *lomo saltado* (stir-fried beef) or chocolate-orange martinis. Pinar del Río uncultured? We think not.

🍷 Drinking & Nightlife

Café Pinar   LIVE MUSIC

(Gerardo Medina Norte No 34; cover USD$3; ⊗8:30am-3am) This spot gets the local youth vote and is also the best place to meet other travelers (not abundant in this town). Situated on a lively stretch of Calle Gerardo Medina, it features bands playing at night on the open patio, and light menu items such as pasta, chicken and sandwiches are available during the day. Mondays and Saturdays are the best nights.

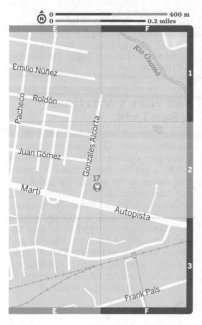

N 0 — 400 m
0 — 0.2 miles

Rumayor CABARET

(48-76-30-51; Carretera a Viñales Km 1; cover USD$5; noon-midnight) Reports vary on the nocturnal action at this state-run restaurant and entertainment center on the edge of the city. There's so-so food during the day and a rather rugged nighttime disco from Tuesday through Sunday heating up around 10pm-ish. The kitschy Sunday cabaret ain't half bad.

Shopping

Casa del Habano CIGARS

(Antonio Maceo Oeste No 162; 9am-5pm Mon-Sat) Opposite the Fábrica de Tabacos Francisco Donatien tobacco factory, this store is one of the better outlets of this popular government cigar chain, with a patio bar, an air-conditioned shop and a smoking room.

La Casa del Ron ARTS & CRAFTS, RUM

(Antonio Maceo Oeste No 151; 9am-4:30pm, to 1pm Sat & Sun) Near the Fábrica de Tabacos Francisco Donatien, sells souvenirs, CDs and T-shirts, plus plenty of the strong stuff.

Disco Azul CLUB

(Martí Final & Autopista; USD$5; from 10pm Tue-Sun) A drab hotel, but a kicking disco – this glittery nightclub in Hotel Pinar del Río, on the edge of town coming from the Autopista, is the city's most popular, loved by locals, despised by hotel guests.

Entertainment

La Piscuala CULTURAL CENTER

(cnr Martí & Colón) Peaceful patio alongside the Teatro José Jacinto Milanés. Check the schedule posted outside for nightly cultural activities.

Estadio Capitán San Luis Sports SPECTATOR SPORT

(48-75-38-95; Herryman, btwn Rafael Morales & San Luis; CUP$1; matches 7pm Tue-Thu & Sat, 4pm Sun Oct-Apr) From October to April, exciting baseball games happen at this stadium on the north side of town. Pinar del Río is one of Cuba's better teams. Pop by in the evenings to see the players going through a training session.

Casa de la Música 'La Sitiera' LIVE MUSIC

(Gerardo Medina Norte No 21; USD$1; concerts nightly at 9pm) After warming up at nearby Café Pinar, many revelers cross the street for more live music here.

La Colosal ARTS & CRAFTS

(cnr Martí & Gerardo Medina; 9am-4:30pm Mon-Fri, 8:30am-3:30pm Sat) An interesting, if dusty, selection of regional handicrafts run by the BFC (Cuban cultural agency), although revenue goes almost exclusively to the government rather than the makers themselves.

Information

SAFE TRAVEL

For a relatively untouristed city Pinar del Río has plenty of *jinteros* (touts). The majority are young men who hang around Calle Martí, offering everything from *paladar* (privately owned restaurant) meals to 'guided tours' of tobacco plantations. Most will back off at your first or second '*no me moleste, por favor*,' but bolder ones have been known to mount bicycles and accost tourist cars when they stop at traffic lights. Although they're generally nonaggressive, it's best to be firmly polite from the outset and not invite further attention.

MEDICAL SERVICES

Farmacia Internacional (cnr Martí Final & Autopista; 8am-11pm) In the Hotel Pinar del Río

Hospital Provincial León Cuervo Rubio (78-75-44-43; Carretera Central) Located 2km north of town.

MONEY

Banco de Crédito y Comercio (Martí, btwn Medina & Arenado; ⊘8:30am-3:30pm Mon-Fri) ATMs.

Cadeca (Martí No 46; ⊘8:30am-4pm Mon-Fri) Fewer queues compared to Viñales.

TOURIST INFORMATION

Cubanacán (☑48-77-01-04, 48-75-01-78; Martí No 109, cnr Colón; ⊘8am-6pm) Come here to arrange tours of local tobacco plantations and find out about the so-called 'Ruta del Tabaco.' It also arranges tickets for Conectando buses (a back-up for Víazul).

Infotur (☑48-72-86-16; Hotel Vueltabajo, cnr Martí & Rafael Morales; ⊘9am-6pm Mon-Fri, to noon Sat) One of the city's most helpful sources of information.

❶ Getting There & Away

BUS

The city's **bus station** (Adela Azcuy, btwn Colón & Comandante Pinares) is conveniently close to the center. Pinar del Río is on the Víazul (www.viazul.com) network, with all services to Havana and destinations east originating in Viñales. There are two daily departures to Havana (USD$11, 2½ hours) and one to Trinidad (USD$36, nine hours) via Cienfuegos (USD$31, 7½ hours). The later Havana bus also stops in Las Terrazas. In the opposite direction, three daily buses go to Viñales (USD$6, 45 minutes).

Conectando buses running most days offer services to Havana and Viñales. You'll need to book ahead with Cubanacán; ask here about other transfers to Cayo Levisa, Cayo Jutías and María la Gorda.

TAXI

Private taxis hanging around outside the bus station will offer prices all the way to Havana. It's worth considering if you can find someone to share the fare with.

TRAIN

Theoretically there are alternate-day services to Havana from the **train station** (cnr Ferrocarril & Comandante Pinares Sur), but you won't find any printed timetables and the painfully slow train is for masochists only. The line also extends west from Pinar to its terminus at Guane, but again, no timetables.

❶ Getting Around

Cubacar (☑48-75-93-81; Hotel Vueltabajo, cnr Martí & Rafael Morales; ⊘9am-5pm) has an office at Hotel Vueltabajo. Mopeds can be rented from Cubanacán.

Servicentro Oro Negro (Carretera Central) is opposite the Hospital Provincial on the Carretera Central. There's another on Rafael Morales Sur at the south entrance to town.

Horse-drawn carts (CUP$1) on Isabel Rubio near Adela Azcuy go to the Hospital Provincial and out onto the Carretera Central. Bici-taxis cost CUP$5 around town.

San Juan y Martínez & San Luis

Viñales might attract the lion's share of Cuba's tobacco tourists, but it is the verdant San Luis region, southwest of the provincial capital Pinar del Río, that nurtures the plants that end up in the world's best cigars. For true aficionados, the pancake-flat farming terrain around the smart town of San Juan y Martínez is the place to visit, the heart of the heartland where tending tobacco has long been both an economic mainstay and a traditional way of life. The Cuban tourist ministry has recently started to promote the area as the 'Ruta del Tabaco' and several tobacco farms are now open to visitors.

◉ Sights

Vega Quemado del Rubi   FARM
(☑5-820-3839; Comunidad de Obeso; tours USD$2; ⊘9am-5pm) 🖉 The tobacco farm of Hector Luis Prieto currently produces the 'Champagne' of Cuban cigars and invites visitors to find out exactly how they're nurtured. Prieto is Cuba's youngest-ever winner of the prestigious Hombre Habano award, given annually to the nation's best tobacco producer, and his 6-hectare farm, which rears around 250,000 tobacco plants a year, offers detailed tours in English, French and Spanish.

But that's just half of it. At Prieto's wonderfully relaxing farm you can also go horseback riding, sit down for lunch, partake in a bit of cigar–rum pairing or even stay over in one of two wooden cabins (USD$45 to USD$50 per night). In the true spirit of eco-endeavor, the farm also allows volunteers to partake in agricultural work, which becomes more interesting during the tobacco growing season between November and February.

Finca El Pinar
(Robaina Tobacco Plantation)   FARM
(☑48-79-74-70; USD$2; ⊘9am-5pm) The famous Robaina *vegas* (fields), in the rich Vuelta Abajo region southwest of Pinar del Río, have been growing quality tobacco since 1845, but it wasn't until 1997 that a brand

of cigars known as Vegas Robaina was first launched to wide international acclaim. The former owner Alejandro Robaina, who made the brand so famous, died in April 2010. But the show must go on, and does at the plantation today. It's been open to outside visitors for some years.

With some deft navigational skills, you can roll up to the farm and get the lowdown on the tobacco-making process from delicate plant to aromatic wrapper: tours are 25 minutes long.

To get there, take the Carretera Central southwest out of Pinar del Río for 12km, turn left toward San Luis and left again after approximately 3km at the Robaina sign. This rougher track continues for 1.5km to the farm. Do not hire a *jintero* (tout) to lead you, as they often take you to the wrong farm. Tours are available every day. The tobacco-growing season runs from November to February, and this is obviously the best time to visit. Plants only reach an impressive height from December.

Rancho la Guabina RANCH
(☑ 48-75-76-16; Carretera de Luis Lazo Km 9.5) A former Spanish farm spread over 1000 hectares of pasture, forest and wetlands, the Rancho la Guabina is a jack of all trades and a master of at least one. You can partake in horseback riding here, go boating on a lake or enjoy a scrumptious Cuban barbecue. The big drawcard for most, though, is the fantastic horse shows.

❶ Getting There & Away

Your own wheels are the best bet in this area. If you're visiting the tobacco plantations, taxis can easily be organized in Viñales or Pinar del Río. Inquire at Cubataxi (p187) in Viñales.

Península de Guanahacabibes

As the island narrows at its western end, you fall upon the low-lying and ecologically rich Península de Guanahacabibes. One of Cuba's most isolated enclaves, it once provided shelter for its earliest inhabitants, the Guanahatabeys. A two-hour drive from Pinar del Río, this region lacks major tourist infrastructure, meaning it feels far more isolated than it is. There are two reasons to come here: a national park (also a Unesco Biosphere Reserve) and an international-standard diving center at María la Gorda.

Although the park border straddles the tiny community of La Fe, the reserve entrance is at La Bajada.

It's a 120km round trip to Cuba's western-most point from La Bajada. The lonesome Cabo de San Antonio is populated by a solitary lighthouse (Faro Roncali), the Gaviota Marina and Villa Cabo San Antonio. Abutting the hotel is Playa las Tumbas, Cuba's most isolated beach, where you can swim.

Parque Nacional Península de Guanahacabibes

If you want to see Cuba how Columbus must have seen it, come to the Península de Guanahacabibes, the flat and deceptively narrow finger of land that points toward Mexico on the island's western tip. Protected by a national park and a Unesco Biosphere Reserve, this place is practically virgin territory. Picture miles of limestone karst guarded by iguanas, lagoons full of petrified trees and sun-bathing crocodiles, rare birds fluttering through veritable forests of palm trees, and storm-lashed beaches where even Robinson Crusoe would have felt lonely.

In summer sea turtles come ashore at night to lay their eggs (the only part of mainland Cuba where this happens), while April sees swarms of *cangrejos colorados* (red-and-yellow crabs) crawling across the peninsula's rough central road only to be unceremoniously crushed under the tires of passing cars. The area is also thought to shelter important archaeological sites relating to the pre-Columbian Guanahatabey people.

◉ Sights

★ **Playa las Tumbas** BEACH
If they gave out Academy Awards for Cuban beaches, Las Tumbas might just win, edging out Playa Sirena on Cayo Largo del Sur (too many tourists) and Playa Pilar on Cayo Guillermo (blemished by an ugly hotel). It's certainly the nation's most isolated beach, 60km from the nearest population and backed only by a quiet 16-room hotel.

Faro Roncali LIGHTHOUSE
On the far western tip of Cuba sits the nation's oldest lighthouse, which was constructed by enslaved people and Chinese laborers in 1849. It was named after the then governor of Cuba, the Spaniard, Federico Roncali Ceruti.

TURTLE-WATCHING

Guanahacabibes is still a park in tentative development, but it includes turtle-monitoring opportunities among its limited stash of organized excursions. The turtle program has been running since 1998 under the direction of environmental researchers and with involvement from the local population (primarily schoolchildren). In recent years, outsiders have been allowed to participate. Approximately 1500 nesting green turtles lay their eggs on over half a dozen of the peninsula's south-facing beaches between June and August, and willing participants are invited to observe, monitor and aid in the process. To take part, inquire in advance at the visitor center (see next page). Tours (USD$15 per person) take place nightly between 10pm and 2am in season, and there are observation shelters at Playa La Barca, the main turtle-watching beach. The release of baby turtles begins in mid-September.

Activities

Centro Internacional de Buceo   DIVING
(📞 48-77-13-06; María la Gorda) Diving is María la Gorda's raison d'être and the prime reason people come to Cuba's western tip. The nerve center is this well-run base next to the eponymous hotel at the Marina Gaviota. Good visibility and sheltered offshore reefs are highlights, plus the proximity of the 32 dive sites to the shore.

Couple this with the largest formation of black coral in the archipelago and you've got a recipe for arguably Cuba's best diving reefs outside the Isla de la Juventud.

A dive here costs USD$35 (night dive USD$40), plus USD$10 for equipment. The center offers a full CMAS (Confédération Mondiale des Activités Subaquatiques; World Underwater Activities Federation) scuba certification course (USD$365, four days) and snorkelers can hop on the dive boat for USD$12.

Among the 50 identified dive sites in the vicinity, divers are shown El Valle de Coral Negro, a 100m-long black-coral wall, and El Salón de María, a cave 20m deep containing feather stars and brilliantly colored corals. The concentrations of migratory fish can be incredible. The furthest entry is only 30 minutes by boat from shore.

Tours

It's a long drive from Pinar del Río to the national park entrance, so to avoid disappointment, phone ahead and reserve a guide for park activities through the visitor center.

The park currently offers seven different excursions, four of them added in 2019. Most involve some hiking. Independent travelers with a reservation at Villa Cabo San Antonio are also granted access.

★ **Cabo de San Antonio Excursion**   WILDLIFE
(guide USD$15) The five-hour tour to Cuba's isolated and practically virgin western tip at Cabo de San Antonio is superb. Along the way you'll see jungles of palms, deserted beaches, iguanas, crocodiles (if you're lucky), *cenotes* (sinkholes) and petrified forests. The responsibility is yours to supply transport and sufficient gas, water and food, so you'll need a taxi or your own wheels.

During most of the 120km round trip through the Parque Nacional Península de Guanahacabibes, you'll have dark, rough *diente de perro* (dog's teeth) rock on one side and the brilliant blue sea on the other. Iguanas will lumber for cover as you approach and you might spy small deer and *jutías* (tree rats), plus lots of birds. Beyond the lighthouse is deserted Playa las Tumbas, where you'll have time to swim should you desire. Thanks to the upgraded road surface, any hire car can make this trip. The five-hour excursion costs USD$15 per person, plus the USD$80 or so you'll need for car hire. (There's car rental at Hotel María la Gorda.) Besides the beaches and exotic flora, there's a chance to see crocodiles, explore a bat-ridden cave and climb a wooden *mirador* (lookout) to spy Cuba's north *and* south coasts. Near Playa La Barca, a recently wrecked ship adds romance to the proceedings.

Caminata El Tesoro de María   HIKING
(guided hike USD$15) An offering from the park authorities since 2019, this four-hour coastal walk starts from the Hotel María la Gorda and heads toward the Cabo Corrientes headland amid wild coastal scenery. The birdwatching potential is immense and the surrounding seas are full of shipwrecks and – allegedly – lost treasure.

Del Bosque al Mar — HIKING
(guided hike USD$10) Leaving from near the Estación Ecológica Guanahacabibes, this 1.5km trail highlights the diversity of the national park, passing through at least four different ecosystems including semi-deciduous forest and swampland. Birdlife is abundant, especially in the morning, and flora includes ferns and orchids. The hike ends with a dip in a crystal-clear *cenote* (sinkhole).

Cueva las Perlas — HIKING
(guided hike USD$12) The three-hour 3km round-trip trek to the 'pearl cave' traverses deciduous woodland replete with a wide variety of birds, including *tocororos* (Cuban trogon), *zunzuncitos* and woodpeckers. You'll clock evidence of former indigenous occupants en route. In the cave itself you can spy (and hear) screech owls: it's a multi-gallery cavern with a lake, of which 300m is accessible to hikers.

🛌 Sleeping

Villa Azul — CASA PARTICULAR $
(☑48-75-10-17; La Bajada; r USD$20-25; ✳) La Bajada is a one-street village facing the surf where practically all of the dozen or so houses rent out rooms. This one is easy to find (it's blue and there's a sign) and is a decent alternative to Hotel María la Gorda, inside the national park. There are two simple rooms with air-con and an on-site restaurant cooking up local fish. The park entrance is 500m away.

Hotel María la Gorda — HOTEL $$
(☑48-77-81-31; www.hotelmarialagorda-cuba.com; Bahía de Corrientes; s/d incl breakfast USD$63/80; P✳@☎) This is among Cuba's remotest hotels, and the isolation has its advantages. The adjoining palm-fringed beach is pretty (if a little rocky), but most people come here to dive; reefs and vertical drop-offs beckon just 200m from the hotel. María la Gorda (literally 'Maria the Fatso') is on the Bahía de Corrientes, 150km southwest of Pinar del Río.

Room-wise you get a choice of three beach-hugging pink-concrete, motel-type buildings or, further back, either attractive white two-floor apartment blocks or rustic wooden cabins connected by walkways. Far from being a posh resort, María la Gorda is an easygoing place where hammocks are strung between palm trees, cold beers are sipped at sunset and dive talk continues into the small hours.

There are two restaurants and a beach bar. Opinions on the food vary, though it's overpriced for what you get. A small shop sells water and basic provisions, and there's a handy medical clinic. There's a USD$5.50 charge to nonguests for visiting Hotel María la Gorda and its adjoining 5km beach.

Villa Cabo San Antonio — CABIN $$
(☑48-75-76-55; Playa las Tumbas; r incl breakfast USD$118; P✳) A 16-villa complex on the almost-virgin Península de Guanahacabibes behind idyllic Playa las Tumbas, set 3km beyond the Faro Roncali (Roncali Lighthouse) and 4km shy of the Gaviota Marina. The detached wooden villas are attractive from the outside although a little dated within and the restaurant (your only eating option for 60km) is – ahem – modest.

You really get splendid isolation here, which is ideal for some, but less alluring for others who don't have a get-out clause when they tire of the food – and mosquitoes.

ℹ Information
It's advisable to phone the **visitor center** (☑48-75-03-66; lmarquez@vega.enf.cu; La Bajada; ◷9am-9pm) at La Bajada to arrange park activities before showing up at the park entrance, as limited resources mean staff are often unable to arrange impromptu guided tours.

The center has interpretive displays on the local flora and fauna. French, English and Italian are spoken. You can arrange to meet guides here for all activities except diving, which is organized from Hotel María la Gorda. Just beyond the visitor center, the road splits, with the left branch going south to María la Gorda (14km along a paved coastal road) and the right branch heading west toward the end of the peninsula.

ℹ Getting There & Away
BUS
Transfer buses (return USD$35) between Viñales and María la Gorda are sporadic and depend on demand. Ask ahead at Cubanacán (p183) in Viñales or Infotur (p198) in Pinar del Río. Otherwise, you can organize a *colectivo* (shared taxi) at the same agencies or at your casa particular (private homestay).

CAR
Via Gaviota (☑48-77-81-31; Hotel María la Gorda) theoretically offers car hire from around USD$80 per day for a small car. However, cars are often in short supply. At last visit there were none available.

The road into the national park has recently been upgraded and is passable in a normal car.

Parque Libertad (p221), Matanzas
NORDWAND/SHUTTERSTOCK ©

Varadero & Matanzas Province

With a name translating as 'massacres,' Matanzas Province conceals an appropriately tumultuous past beneath its modern-day reputation for glam all-inclusive holidays. In the 17th century pillaging pirates ravaged the region's prized north coast, while three centuries later, more invaders grappled ashore in the Bahía de Cochinos (Bay of Pigs) under the dreamy notion that they were about to liberate the nation.

The Bahía de Cochinos attracts more divers than mercenaries these days, while sunbathers rather than pirates invade the northern beaches of Varadero, the vast Caribbean resort and lucrative economic 'cash cow' that stretches 21km along the sandy Península de Hicacos.

Providing a weird juxtaposition are the scruffy cities of Matanzas and Cárdenas. Tourists may be scant in these parts, but soulful, only-in-Cuba experiences are surprisingly abundant.

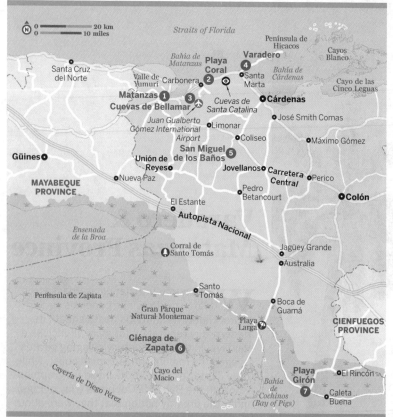

Varadero & Matanzas Province Highlights

1 **Matanzas** (p220)
Unlocking the buried secrets of the long-neglected but rapidly re-emerging 'Athens of Cuba.'

2 **Playa Coral** (p219)
Indulging in a rare opportunity to dive and snorkel from the shore at this north-coast beach.

3 **Cuevas de Bellamar** (p219) Delving into Cuba's

deepest cave system just outside Matanzas.

4 **Varadero** (p205)
Finding your own private nirvana on the sandy expanses of Cuba's longest beach.

5 **San Miguel de los Baños** (p229) Admiring forgotten grandeur in long abandoned bathhouses.

6 **Ciénaga de Zapata** (p233) Exploring the vast, varied vegetation zones in one of Cuba's last true wildernesses.

7 **Playa Girón** (p235)
Discovering the plunging drop-offs and colorful coral walls of Cuba's most accessible dive zone.

NORTHERN MATANZAS

Home to Cuba's largest resort area (Varadero) and one of its biggest ports (Matanzas), the northern coastline is also Matanzas Province's main population center and a hub for industry and commerce. Despite this, the overriding feel is distinctly green, and

most of the region is undulating farmland – think a cross between North American prairie and the UK's Norfolk Broads – occasionally rupturing into lush, dramatic valleys like the Valle de Yumurí, or sinking into enigmatic caves such as the giant Cuevas de Bellamar.

Varadero

POP 27,000

Varadero, located on the sinuous 20km-long Hicacos Peninsula, stands at the vanguard of Cuba's most important industry – tourism. As the largest resort in the Caribbean, it guards a huge, unsubtle and constantly evolving stash of hotels (over 60), shops, water activities and poolside entertainment; its trump card, however, is its beach, an uninterrupted 21km stretch of blond sand that is undoubtedly one of the Caribbean's finest. While these large, tourist-friendly mega-resorts may be essential to the national economy, they offer little in the way of unique Cuban experiences.

Most Varadero tourists buy their vacation packages overseas and are content to enjoy a week or two of beach sloth without ever leaving the all-inclusiveness of their resort. For independent travelers not over-enamored with manufactured 'paradises,' Varadero also has a small Cuban town at its southwestern entrance complete with casas particulares (rooms in private homes), private restaurants and free access to that magnificent beach.

◉ Sights

For art and history, Varadero is the wrong place; nevertheless, there are a couple of sights worth checking out if the beach life starts to bore you.

Varadero town's two adjacent central squares, **Parque de las 8000 Taquillas** (sporting a small subterranean shopping center) and **Parque Central**, are disappointingly bland, save for a somewhat out-of-place colonial-style church, **Iglesia de Santa Elvira** (Map p210; cnr Av 1 & Calle 47), one block east.

Mansión Xanadú   NOTABLE BUILDING

(Map p206; cnr Av las Américas & Autopista Sur) Everything east of Varadero's small stone water tower (it looks like an old Spanish fort, but was built in the 1930s) once belonged to the Du Pont family. Here the millionaire American entrepreneur, Irenée, built the three-story Mansión Xanadú. It's now a small hotel perched on a bluff in the middle of Varadero's 18-hole golf course. The mahogany Mirador bar on the top floor is conducive for sipping sunset cocktails.

Marina Gaviota   MARINA

(Map p206) At the peninsula's eastern tip, state-run Gaviota's impressive marina, built in the early 2010s, encompasses a wide malecón (main street), luxury apartments and the ultra-posh Hotel Marina Varadero (p212) with designer shops and restaurants, and the popular Sala de la Música (p215) music venue. Cubans come from miles around to marvel: it's a little bit more of Florida that's found its way across the water and the only marina in Cuba worthy of international rating.

Parque Josone   PARK

(Map p210; cnr Av 1 & Calle 58; ◷ 9am-midnight; ⊛) If you're set on sightseeing in Varadero, ensconce yourself in this pretty green oasis. These landscaped gardens date back to 1940 and take their name from the former owners, José Fermín Iturrioz y Llaguno and his wife Onelia, who owned the Arechabala (p227) rum distillery in nearby Cárdenas and built a neoclassical mansion here: the Retiro Josone.

Expropriated after the revolution, the mansion became a guesthouse for visiting foreign dignitaries. The park is now a public space for the enjoyment of all – you may see Cuban girls celebrate their *quinceañeras* (15th-birthday celebrations) here. Josone's expansive, shady grounds feature a lake with rowboats (per person per hour USD$0.50) and water-bikes (per hour USD$5), atmospheric eateries, resident geese, myriad tree species and a minitrain (ride USD$1). There's a public swimming pool (USD$2) in the south of the park and sometimes an odd ostrich lurking nearby.

Cueva de Ambrosio   CAVE

(Map p206; Autopista Sur; USD$5; ◷ 9am-4:30pm) For something completely different in Varadero's tourist circus, decamp to this large cave 500m beyond the Club Amigo Varadero on the Autopista Sur. It's known for its 47 pre-Columbian drawings, discovered in a recess in 1961 and thought to be around 2000 years old. The black-and-red drawings feature the same concentric circles seen in similar paintings on the Isla de la Juventud, perhaps a form of solar calendar. You'll be given a torch at the entrance and told to mind the bats!

Reserva Ecológica Varahicacos   PARK

(Map p206; USD$5; ◷ 9am-5pm) The Varahicacos is about all that's left of the 'wild' Hicacos Peninsula: hotel developers have been chomping away at its edges for years. There are three underwhelming trails here which, despite their tameness, attract an entry fee. The highlight is the **Cueva de Musulmanes**

Varadero Hotel Zone

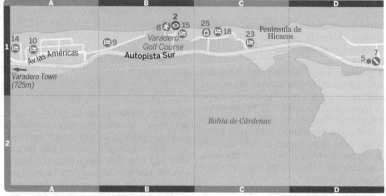

Varadero Hotel Zone

with its 2500-year-old human remains, followed by the giant cactus called **El Patriarca** (separate USD$2 entrance fee) accessed from a different road near the eponymous hotel (p212).

🏃 Activities

Diving & Snorkeling

Varadero is home to one good dive center, Barracuda (p207), which retains three separate offices, although, this being tourist-ville, the prices are double those in the Bahía de Cochinos on Matanzas Province's south coast. Additionally, all of the 21 dive sites around the Península de Hicacos require a boat transfer of approximately one hour. Highlights include reefs, caverns and a Russian patrol boat sunk for diving purposes in 1997. The nearest shore diving is 20km west at Playa Coral (p219). The centers also offer day excursions to superior sites at the Bahía de Cochinos (p236; two immersions with transfer USD$85) – or you could bus it there yourself and dive unrushed with local instructors, including an overnight stay at a local casa (homestay) for just a fraction more.

Note that when the weather is inclement on the north coast, divers are often bused over to more sheltered Bahía de Cochinos in the south.

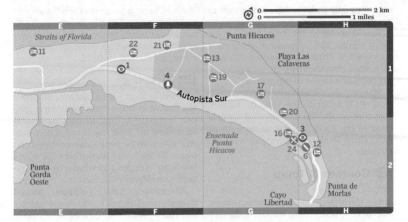

Barracuda Scuba Diving Center
DIVING

(Map p216; ☑ 45-61-34-81; Av Kawama btwn Calles 2 & 3; ☺ 11am-7pm) Varadero's top scuba facility is the mega-friendly, multilingual Barracuda. Diving costs USD$50 per dive with equipment, cave diving is USD$80 and night diving costs USD$65. Packages of multiple dives work out cheaper.

Barracuda conducts introductory resort courses for USD$70, and American Canadian Underwater Certificate (ACUC) courses starting at USD$250, plus many advanced courses. Snorkeling at Playa Coral (p219) with guide is USD$39. Barracuda also has offices at Marina Chapelin and a booth on Av 1 and Calle 59. On Thurdays, the center runs trips to the Caribbean coast in a minibus (90-minute drive) for wall-diving off Playa Girón; this costs a very reasonable USD$85 for two dives including transport.

Marina Gaviota
DIVING

(Map p206; ☑ 45-66-77-55, 45-66-47-22; Autopista Sur Final; ☺ 9am-4pm) At the eastern end of Autopista Sur, Varadero's largest marina is one of several places on the peninsula where you can organize water activities including diving and fishing.

Marlin Marina Chapelín
(Aquaworld) Diving Center
DIVING

(Map p206; ☑ 45-66-88-71; Autopista Sur Km 12; ☺ 9am-5pm) At the Marlin Marina Chapelín, Aquaworld organizes diving/snorkeling trips. Prices are USD$50 per immersion.

Fishing

Fishing can be organized at Varadero's marinas or at the all-inclusive hotels. You'll usually need a minimum of four people. Prices are pretty generic.

Marina Dársena
BOATING, FISHING

(☑ 45-66-80-60; www.nauticamarlin.com; Vía Blanca Km 31) Located just off the west end of the Hicacos Peninsula on the Vía Blanca, the Dársena offers fishing trips and catamaran excursions.

Kiteboarding

Varadero has good conditions for kiteboarding and the sport has become popular over the last five years, with several operators setting up at various points along the beach. You can organize lessons (one/two hours USD$45/80) and board rental (one/two hours USD$35/50) through the dive outfit Barracuda (p207).

Golf

Varadero Golf Club
GOLF

(Map p206; ☑ 45-66-77-88; www.varaderogolfclub.com; Mansión Xanadú; green fees with carts & clubs USD$130; ☺ 7am-7pm) The uncrowded, well-landscaped and remarkably attractive Varadero Golf Club is Cuba's first and (as yet) only fully fledged 18-hole course (par 72). The original nine holes created by the Du Ponts are between Hotel Bella Costa and Du Pont's Mansión Xanadú; another nine holes added in 1998 flank the southern side of the three Meliá resorts.

Bookings for the course are made through the Caddy House next to the Mansión Xanadú (p212) (now a cozy hotel with free, unlimited tee time). Bizarrely, golf carts are mandatory.

Other Activities

There are sailboards available for rent at various points along the public beach (per hour USD$10), plus small catamarans, banana boats, sea kayaks etc. The upmarket resorts usually include these water toys in the all-inclusive price.

Tour desks at all the main hotels churn out a regular diet of nautical or sporting activities and arrange organized sightseeing excursions from Varadero. They are perennially popular with the all-inclusive set.

Standard days trips include sunset cruises, a 4WD safari to the Valle de Yumurí, boat trips on the Río Canímar and a whole range of bus tours to places as far away as Santa Clara, Trinidad, Viñales and, of course, Havana.

Courses & Tours

ABC Academia de
Arte y Cultura   DANCING, LANGUAGE
(Map p210; ☑ 45-61-25-06; cnr Av 1 & Calle 34; ☺ 9am-6:30pm) Organized through Paradiso, a state-run cultural agency, this center offers lessons in dance and percussion. One-off two-hour classes cost USD$15 or you can organize packages of up to 12 lessons. They also run a unique trip called 'Be a Cuban for One Day', which takes groups to the ultra-green Finca Coincidencia (p229) to learn about pottery, farming and sowing the seeds of sustainability.

Boat Adventure   BOATING
(Map p206; ☑ 45-66-84-40; 1-/2-person boat USD$65/85; ☺ 9am-5pm) This two-hour guided trip, leaving from a separate dock next to the Marlin Marina Chapelín, is a speedy sortie through the adjacent mangroves on two-person self-drive motorboats to view myriad forms of wildlife, including curious crocs. Bookings for all these watery excursions can also be made at most of the big hotels (for cheaper rates).

Gaviota   TOURS
(Map p216; ☑ 45-66-78-64; Calle 13, btwn Avs 2 & 3; ☺ 9am-5pm Mon-Fri) This operator has a desk in most of the all-inclusive hotels and a folder listing around 40 different day excursions, including catamaran cruises (USD$109) and a Tour de Azúcar (sugarcane tour; USD$39) visiting a disused sugar mill. Ever popular is the jeep safari to the Valle de Yumurí near Matanzas (USD$81).

Marlin Marina Chapelín
(Aquaworld)   BOATING
(Map p206; ☑ 45-66-75-50; www.nauticamarlin. com; Autopista Sur Km 12; ☺ 8am-4pm) Aquaworld Marina Chapelín organizes Varadero's nautical highlight in the popularity stakes: the Seafari Cayo Blanco (USD$75) from Marina Chapelín to nearby Cayo Blanco and its idyllic beach. The trip includes an open bar, lobster lunch, two snorkeling stops, live music and hotel transfers. Sunset cruises are a more economical USD$25.

Sleeping

Varadero is huge – there are over 60 hotels and almost as many casas particulares (private homestays). Want to hunt down that bargain room? Book ahead and concentrate your efforts on the peninsula's southwest end where all the casas particulares lie, where hotels are cheaper and where the town retains a semblance of Cuban life.

All-inclusive hotel packages booked through travel agents in your home country will almost always have differing (cheaper) rates to their published rack rates.

★ Beny's House   CASA PARTICULAR $
(Map p210; ☑ 45-61-17-00; www.benyhouse.com; Calle 55, btwn Avs 1 & 2; r incl breakfast USD$45; ☐ ❄) Why would you want to blow hundreds of dollars on an all-inclusive when you can pay USD$45 a night to stay at Beny's house? It's within spitting distance of the beach and you can converse with one of Varadero's great characters.

There's everything you need here: landscaped garden, patio, three smart rooms with queen-size beds and flat-screen TVs, restaurant specializing in fish, and – best of all – Beny himself.

Casa Mary y Ángel   CASA PARTICULAR $
(Map p210; ☑ 45-61-23-83; www.casamaryyangel. com; Calle 43 No 4309, btwn Avs 1 & 2; d/tr USD$35/40; ❄) The array of shady terraces at this leading private homestay option will have hotels hereabouts looking enviously over their shoulders – as will the three gleaming, well-appointed rooms. Breakfast will run to several courses, and to several hours if the rich, strong coffee has anything to do with it. Best of all are the hosts – warm, welcoming and full of local info.

Papo's House   CASA PARTICULAR $
(Map p210; ☑ 45-61-26-40; papomoreno89@yahoo. es; Calle 55 No 114, btwn Avs 1 & 2; r USD$35-40; ☐ ❄) A treat of a house, Papo's is modest on the outside but surprisingly elegant within with antique Louis XV furniture – and that includes in the bedrooms. It has a strong following among French travelers. and is right next to Parque Josone. The beach is a 100m dash away and there's a wi-fi hotspot on the adjacent street.

Hostal Sol RyA
CASA PARTICULAR **$**

(Map p210; ☎ 45-61-29-25; rafael.g@nauta.cu; Calle 36 No 117, btwn Av 1 & Autopista; USD$35-40; ❋) Handy little homestay right next to the Vía-zul bus station with one independent apartment (with bunk beds and ideal for families) and another normal double room. Rooms have all mod cons and there's plenty of local information on hand.

Casa Menocal
CASA PARTICULAR **$**

(Map p216; ☎ 45-61-31-64; vmoralesmenocal1@gmail.com; Calle 14 No 1, cnr Callejón del Mar; r USD$35-55; ❋) Traditional gray-stone Vara-dero house right on a dreamy slice of beach. Five rooms with roof beams and traditional 1940s feel. Book ahead.

Dormiendo en las Olas
CASA PARTICULAR **$**

(Map p210; ☎ 45-61-23-63, 5-268-8195; mi63@nauta.cu; cnr Av de la Playa & Calle 43; r USD$50; P ❋) 'Sleeping in the waves' is how the name of this beach-fronting house translates and you almost are – at least, you're far closer to them than you would be at most all-inclusives. The rooms themselves are clean, but unexceptional: the real beauty is that the back terrace here leads straight out onto a prime stretch of Cuba's finest beach.

Casa Betty y Jorge
CASA PARTICULAR **$**

(Map p216; ☎ 45-61-25-53; Calle 31 No 108a; r USD$30-35; ❋ 🛜) Two rooms, one with its own neat little breakfast bar, front a peaceful private courtyard below, whilst up and round the corner, Betty will cook for you (inside or on the upper terrace) and Jorge will chinwag with you (in English if you like) about the peaks and pitfalls of the Varadero hospitality trade.

Hotel Acuazul
HOTEL **$**

(Map p216; ☎ 45-66-71-32; Av 1, btwn Calles 13 & 14; r incl breakfast USD$30; ❋ @ 🛜 ⛳) Not fussy? Then head for this all-inclusive at the west end of the peninsula, whose architecture is a little Russian and where the ambience is more Cuban than international. If the buffet gets boring (and it will), there are plenty of private restaurants nearby. Bring earplugs if you don't like ear-splitting reggaeton music.

Starfish Las Palmas
HOTEL **$$**

(Map p210; ☎ 45-66-70-40; www.starfishresorts.com; Calle 60, btwn Avs 1 & 2; s/d incl breakfast USD$90/120; P ❋ 🛜) This Starfish hotel is different from other 21st-century Varadero accommodations. It's not an all-inclusive, it's not a casa particular (private homestay); rather it's a kind of budget motel-standard hotel spread over several buildings in the eastern part of town.

★ Royalton Hicacos Resort
RESORT **$$$**

(Map p206; ☎ 45-66-88-44, 45-66-88-51; www.royaltonresorts.com; Punta Hicacos; ste all-inclusive USD$420; P ❋ @ ⛳) Wood and thatch combined with vast public areas with babbling

---

VARADERO'S HOTELS IN A NUTSHELL

Varadero's confusingly large Hotel Zone can, for simplicity's sake, be broken into four broad segments.

The accommodations in the spread-out Cuban town (Varadero town) at the west end of the peninsula consist of older budget hotels wedged in among the shops, banks, bars and vintage beach houses. Since 2011, town residents have been able to legally rent out rooms to foreigners and over 30 casas particulares (rooms in private homes) have now taken root.

The section from Calle 64 northeast to the golf course (p207) is punctuated by a thin strip of hodgepodge architecture, from kitschy Holiday Camp to bloc-style Soviet-esque. Selling cheap packages to mainly foreign tourists, many of these hotels are already looking dated after only three or four decades in operation.

East of the Mansión Xanadú (p205) is a cluster of large single-structure hotels with impressive lobbies and multiple stories, built mostly in the early 1990s. The tallest is the spectacular 14-story Blau Varadero (p211), designed to resemble an Aztec pyramid.

The nearer you get to the east end of the peninsula, the more it starts to look like a Florida suburb. Contemporary Cuban all-inclusive resorts favor detached one-to-three-story blocks that are laid out like mini-towns and spread over multiple acres. Most of these sprawling resorts have been built since 2000 and it is here that you'll find Varadero's largest (the 1025-room Memories Varadero (p212)) and most exclusive (Blau Marina Palace's Planta Real; p211) accommodations, although every year brings tidings of new resorts opening with new never-seen-before attributes.

Varadero Town – East

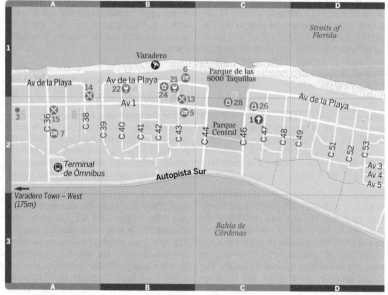

Varadero Town – East

water features lend a mellifluous air to this undeniable slice of Varadero luxury run by the Canadian Sunwing Group's Blue Diamond subsidiary. Bedrooms (nay *suites*) with king-sized beds are done up in sunny yellows and oranges, and staff are expert in advanced forms of towel-folding origami.

Paradisus Varadero   RESORT **$$$**
(Map p206; 📞 45-66-87-00; www.meliacuba.com; Autopista Sur; s/d USD$325/525; 🅿 ❄ @ 🛜 🌊) The five-star Paradisus has fairly recently carved a campus out of what's left of Varadero's fallow land and renovated its original complex. They join a third wing – the

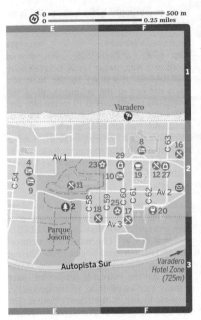

adults-only Royal Service suites (an interesting oxymoron in steadfastly republican Cuba). The whole place is open-plan with tasteful architecture directing views toward a wide beach backed by perfectly manicured lawns shaded by palms.

Paradisus Princesa del Mar   RESORT $$$
(Map p206; ☎45-66-72-00; www.meliacuba. com; Carretera las Morlas Km 19.5; s/d all-inclusive USD$325/465; P☀@☎☳) With a big asking price, you're going to have high expectations of this adults-only Meliá resort. Despite its size (630 rooms), it's certainly heavy on the romantic theme with luxury beds around the pool, a big spa complex and plenty of honeymooners strolling around contentedly hand in hand. It's certainly *paradisus* (paradise) for some.

Fiesta Americana   RESORT $$$
(Map p206; ☎45-66-99-66; www.fiestamericana. com; Autopista Sur Final; s/d all-inclusive USD$276/356; P☀@☎☳) Always one of Varadero's more salubrious offerings, this attractive low-rise resort at the end of the peninsula has recently changed brands from Spanish-run Blau to Mexican-run Fiesta Americana. Owners aside, the beach is close by and the facilities seem to have an extra gloss here, from the light fittings to the fountains.

Meliá Varadero   RESORT $$$
(Map p206; ☎45-66-70-13; Carretera las Morlas; s/d all-inclusive USD$283/405; P☀@☎☳) Twice as big as its sister hotel Meliá Las Américas, and happy to cater to families, the 490-room Meliá Varadero immediately impresses with its cylindrical vine-draped lobby and vivid pillars painted by Cuban artists. Perched on a small rocky promontory, the beach is set to one side and offers plenty of shade. Unlike many of its Varadero brethren it offers guests free bike use.

Blau Varadero   RESORT $$$
(Map p206; ☎45-66-75-45; Carretera de las Morlas Km 15; s/d all-inclusive USD$228/375; P☀@☎☳) Suspend your judgment on Varadero's tallest and most architecturally unsubtle resort. Trying hard to imitate an Aztec pyramid from the outside (why?), the interior is nothing short of spectacular: a 14-story enclosed courtyard embellished by hundreds of hanging plants, some falling for over 80m. Huge rooms are surgically clean and the higher ones have the best views in Varadero.

Meliá Las Américas   RESORT $$$
(Map p206; ☎45-66-76-00; Autopista Sur Km 7; s/d all-inclusive USD$313/450; P☀@☎☳) The smaller, more grown-up alternative to the Meliá Marina Varadero (p212) next door, Las Américas has a no-kids policy, a nice slice of palm-tree-embellished beach and elegant white arches. With 225 rooms, it's too large to be intimate, though there's a more refined ambience here than in the other resort giants nearby.

Meliá Internacional   RESORT $$$
(Map p206; ☎45-62-31-00; www.melia.com; Av las Américas Km 1; s/d USD$323/465; ☀@☎☳) Varadero's erstwhile art deco hotel, the Continental was regrettably knocked down a couple of years ago to make way for this high-rise giant. Granted, it's a Meliá and suitably luxurious, but it somehow lacks the intimacy and architectural panache of its predecessor. A replacement cabaret venue (Varadero's wannabe 'Tropicana') is being built on the campus and was due to open in 2021.

Sol Palmeras   RESORT $$$
(Map p206; ☎45-66-70-09; www.meliacuba. com; Carretera de las Morlas; s/d all-inclusive USD$207/306; P☀@☎☳) Part of the Meliá group's cheaper 'Sol' brand, this 3½-star dates from 1990. While the architecture doesn't exactly take your breath away, the hotel has received regular renovations, keeping the common areas looking buffed and

VARADERO & MATANZAS PROVINCE VARADERO

modern. The revamped family bungalows are particularly handsome. Repeat visitors (and there are many) regularly applaud the excellent service here.

La Ocean Varadero El Patriarca   RESORT $$$
(Map p206; 45-66-81-66; www.oceanvaradero. com; Autopista Sur Km 18; s/d USD$365/441; P✳@🛜🏊) Named for a nearby giant cactus that the hotel developers mercifully didn't bulldoze, the Patriarca has some worthy quirks. The room units are wooden rather than concrete, there's a lovely intimate almost Moorish patio beside the lobby, and poolside 'entertainers' keep a lower profile than elsewhere. Then there's the beach – pure bliss!

Meliá Marina Varadero   RESORT $$$
(Map p206; 45-66-73-30; www.meliacuba.com; Autopista Sur Final; s/d all-inclusive from USD$252/ 375; P✳@🛜🏊) No, that's not a beached cruise liner, but a five-star Meliá! Part of the plushly redeveloped Marina Gaviota (p205), this has several key advantages over its competitors up at this eastern end of the peninsula: gleaming marina views, plus access to a host of restaurants and shops within the marina complex that makes the stay that little bit more varied than at the other all-inclusives.

The caveat? There's no beach here (a walkway over the road connects you to one, however) and reports on the rooms vary, but if you can't make it to Miami, this is as close as you'll get in Cuba.

Mansión Xanadú   RESORT $$$
(Map p206; 45-66-73-88; www.varaderogolfclub. com; cnr Av las Américas & Autopista Sur; d USD$145; P✳@🛜) Varadero's most intimate lodging is in the grand former residence of US chemical-entrepreneur Irenée Du Pont, where eight fairly simple art deco–era rooms tempt guests. Rates include breakfast, three-course dinner and unlimited green fees at the adjacent golf course (p207). The house was being gradually renovated at last visit but remained open.

Meliá Península Varadero   RESORT $$$
(Map p206; 45-66-88-00; www.meliacuba.com; r/all-inclusive from USD$190/270; P✳@🛜🏊) Giant chess set, thatched beach parasols, swim-up pool bar; it's all here at the 4½-star Península (one of 11 Meliás in Varadero). In case you get them mixed up, this one's got a mock-up Cuban castle plonked randomly aside its pool (for variation?). Elsewhere, a

lavish plant-draped lobby leads to 581 comfortable if plain rooms.

Memories Varadero   RESORT $$$
(Map p206; 45-66-70-09; www.memories resorts.com; Autopista Sur Km 18; s/d all-inclusive USD$208/340; P✳@🛜) By the time you reach the end of the peninsula, all of the strung-out resorts appear to merge into one – this one. The Memories (not to be confused with the nearby Grand Memories) is an identikit of a humongous beach hotel: a mini-town with 1035 rooms, multiple restaurants, wall-to-wall entertainment and lots of sunburned Europeans whizzing around on golf carts.

Be Live Experience Tuxpán   RESORT $$$
(Map p206; 45-66-75-60; www.belivehotels.com; Av las Américas Km 2; s/d all-inclusive from USD$112/ 152; P✳@🛜🏊) Concrete-block architecture and palm-fringed beaches make jarring bedfellows that are all too common in Varadero. But the Tuxpán is famous for other reasons, such as its disco, La Bamba (p215), purportedly one of the resort's hottest. For those not enamored with the concrete jungle architectonics, the beautiful beach is never far away.

Hotel Club Kawama   RESORT $$$
(Map p216; 45-61-44-16; www.gran-caribe.cu; cnr Av 1 & Calle 1; s/d all-inclusive from USD$94/147; P✳@🛜🏊) A venerable old 1930s hacienda-style building, the sprawling Kawama was the first of the 60-plus hotels to inhabit this once-deserted peninsula more than 70 years ago. The service struggles here and facilities are a bit haggard despite sporadic renovations, but optimists will still detect some silver linings in the 235 colorful rooms, which blend artfully into the sliver of beach at Varadero's western extremity.

Hotel Starfish Cuatro Palmas   RESORT $$$
(Map p210; 45-66-70-40; Av 1, btwn Calles 60 & 62; r all-inclusive from USD$140; P✳@🛜🏊) One wonders if this former personal residence of dictator Fulgencio Batista would still appeal to his opulent taste. The first of what could be termed the big all-inclusive resorts as you head east has succumbed to tourist kitsch in recent years, though it's still close enough to town for getting around on foot. The beach is adjacent, though you may need earplugs.

Be Live Experience Varadero   RESORT $$$
(Map p206; 45-66-82-80; www.belivehotels. com; Av las Américas Km 2; all-inclusive villas from

USD$220; P❄@☎) Settling for a could-do-better 'C' grade, Be Live looks suspiciously like the airport you just left to come here (right down to the observation tower), but inside feels more like a 1970s holiday camp. A multitude of villas range from two to six bedrooms, while the architecture looks like it was thrown together by a hyperactive five-year-old on *Minecraft*.

🍴 Eating

Atlantida   INTERNATIONAL $
(☑ 5-834-9508; Av 1 btwn Calles 6 & 7, Santa Marta; USD$3-9; ☉ 7am-4am) Like most restaurants in the busy crossroads of Santa Marta, Atlantida is set up mainly for Cubans, but has recently garnered a good reputation among tourists suffering from resort buffet fatigue. The lure? Well-executed but economical dishes that run the gamut from lobster down to *camarones* (spicy prawn) enchiladas. Good piña coladas too!

Terrasita's Café   BREAKFAST $
(Map p216; ☑ 45-61-25-14; Av 1 No 2806, btwn Calles 28 & 29; breakfast USD$2-5; ☉ 8am-2pm Mon-Sat) Varadero town has traditionally been a little light on breakfast options, so all hail this engagingly modest joint almost hidden behind greenery on arterial Av 1. For less than USD$5 you can enjoy eggs, coffee, juice and a plate piled high with the Caribbean's juiciest fruit. The fast, friendly service and congenial beach-shack ambience add to the flavor.

★ Salsa Suárez   INTERNATIONAL $$
(Map p216; ☑ 45-61-41-94; www.salsasuarezvaradero.com; Calle 31 No 103, btwn Avs 1 & 3; mains USD$8-12; ☉ 10:30am-11pm; ☑) With possibly the most all-encompassing menu of Varadero's private restaurants, Salsa Suárez impresses with its salubrious greenery-covered patio and ultra-professional never-miss-a-beat service. Food influences are all over the map (tapas, quesadillas, risotto, sushi and good old Cuban lobster), but it's consistently good, right down to the details – complimentary bread baskets and excellent Italian-style coffee. Good wine list too.

Restaurante La Barbacoa   STEAK $$
(Map p210; ☑ 45-66-77-95; cnr Calle 64 & Av 1; steaks USD$11-20; ☉ noon-11pm) Varadero's best state-run restaurant is a steakhouse that serves relatively cheap steak and lobster in an old-world decor (stag's heads, horsey paraphernalia), staffed by very straight-faced waitstaff.

Paladar Nonna Tina   ITALIAN $$
(Map p210; ☑ 45-61-24-50; www.paladar-nonna tina.it; Calle 38, btwn Av 1 & Av de la Playa; pizza & pasta USD$6-10; ☉ noon-11pm Tue-Sun; ☑🖢) Veteran Cuba visitors will remember an era when the word 'pasta' was a euphemism for 'mush.' But times have changed and, thanks to inspired restaurants such as Italian-owned Nonna Tina, the term 'al dente' is no longer an untranslatable foreign term. You'll find proof in this restaurant's pretty front garden where traveling Italophiles enjoy wood-fired thin-crust pizza, pesto linguine and proper cappuccinos.

La Rampa   CUBAN $$
(Map p210; ☑ 45-60-24-14; Calle 43, btwn Av 1 & Av de la Playa; mains USD$4.50-14; ☉ noon-11pm) A modest private place that's family-run and rightly lauded for its decent food. Seating is half inside and half out. The lobster tails are recommended (and amazingly cheap).

La Vaca Rosada   SEAFOOD $$
(Map p216; ☑ 45-61-23-07; Calle 21, btwn Avs 1 & 2; mains USD$8-23; ☉ 6:30-11:45pm Tue-Sun) If it's not raining, the 'pink cow' is worth an evening of your time. The place is set on an atmospheric rooftop terrace and serves surf and turf dishes, with international cameos from sushi, ceviche, spring rolls and good old thin-crust pizza.

La Fondue   SWISS $$
(Map p210; cnr Av 1, btwn Calles 62 & 63; mains USD$7-18; ☉ noon-midnight) Locals rate this fondue-focused restaurant as one of the best state-run joints in town, but, while it's a welcome change from rice and beans, it's not quite up to Swiss standards in cheese quality. Nonetheless, the little hot cauldrons of melted *queso* (cheese) can make a worthwhile away-day from the hotel buffet.

Dante   ITALIAN $$
(Map p210; ☑ 45-66-77-38; Parque Josone; mains USD$7-15; ☉ noon-10:30pm) Going strong since 1993, Dante takes its name from an entrepreneurial chef who continues to rustle up good Italian fare to complement the serene lakeside setting in Parque Josone. Starters include bruschette and beef carpaccio, mains move onto pizza, lasagne and cannelloni, and, waiting in the wings, polite waitstaff guard one of Varadero's most impressive wine stashes.

Restaurante Esquina Cuba   CUBAN $$
(Map p210; cnr Av 1 & Calle 36; mains USD$7-22; ☉ noon-11pm) This place was one-time

favorite of Buena Vista Social Club luminary Compay Segundo, and the man obviously had taste. All dishes, including the pork special, come with lashings of beans, rice and plantain chips under the gaze of the great Cuban ephemera that line the walls – and the resident American car.

★ **Varadero 60** INTERNATIONAL **$$$**
(Map p210; ☑ 45-61-39-86; cnr Calle 60 & Av 3; mains USD$10-20; ☺ noon-midnight) Rivaling anything Varadero's five-star resorts can cough up, this 'five-star' fine-dining establishment exudes an aura of refinement not seen since Benny Moré twirled his cane. Lobster and *solomillo* (steak) are the house specialties, but everything from the bread basket to the quality cigars and rums is top-notch here. The charcoal-grilled whole fish is definitely worth the investment. And let's not forget the waitstaff. In over two decades of repeat visits to Cuba, we've rarely seen such impeccable service.

Waco's Club INTERNATIONAL **$$$**
(Map p210; ☑ 5-297-1408, 45-61-21-26; Av 3, btwn Calles 58 & 59; mains USD$12-28; ☺ noon-11pm; ☝) Travelers rate this sequestered-away spot, which was once Varadero's Club Náutico. The restaurant is clearly aiming high with its impressive international menu (nothing as wacko as you might think with a name like this, but all well presented and flavorsome) and refined upstairs dining terrace. The specialty is the lobster done numerous ways, including *langosta Varadero* (flambéed in rum).

Kike-Kcho SEAFOOD **$$$**
(Map p206; ☑ 45-66-41-15; Marina Gaviota, Autopista Sur Final; mains USD$15-30; ☺ noon-11pm) A posh 'floating' restaurant in the Marina Gaviota, state-run Kike-Kcho pushes its lobster, which is caught locally and stored on-site meaning it's ultra-fresh. It's backed up by all number of other fish species – cod, tuna, hake, eels, you name it. Granted, it has a great location, but the place is often empty and the food somehow lacks the 'soul' of Varadero's privately run places.

🍷 Drinking & Nightlife

★ **Cafeccino** CAFE, BAKERY
(Av 1 btwn J & I, Santa Marta; ☺ 6am-midnight) The best coffee in Cuba outside Havana is ignored by most of Varadero's tourists simply because they don't know about it. The reason: this open-all-hours cafe-bakery is in Santa Marta, the small settlement at the southwest end of the peninsula. Cafeccino is also notable for its cakes – served by the slice or whole.

The sweet union of cappuccino and *tres leches* cake, enjoyed on a funky stool as the hubbub of Cuban life pulsates around you, is a marriage made in heaven.

Factoria Varadero
43 Cervecería CRAFT BEER
(Map p210; Calle 43, cnr Av de la Playa; ☺ 12:30pm-midnight) Specializing in large, super-chilled jars of house-brewed beer served a drunken stumble from the beach, La Factoria is related to a similar well-established brewpub in Havana (p130). There are three varieties of *cerveza* (beer) on offer: *claro* (light and citrusy), *oscuro* (stronger and darker) and *negro* (more like a stout), none of them as hop-heavy as craft beers in other countries, but at USD$2 a liter, who's complaining?

Casa del Chocolate CAFE
(Map p210; Av 1, btwn Calles 61 & 62; ☺ 10:30am-11:45pm) Cafe specializing in hot or cold mugs of Baracoan chocolate, a concoction that manages to taste both sweet and bitter at the same time. There's inside and outside seating, and assorted confectionery sold from a small counter within. Bypass the meager food offerings and stick to the sweet stuff.

La Bodeguita del Medio BAR
(Map p210; Av de la Playa, btwn Calles 40 & 41; ☺ 10:30am-11:30pm) In recent years, Varadero has sprouted a copy of Hemingway's favorite Havana dive bar, aka La Bodeguita del Medio, a cool place where musicians strum in the courtyard and punters add graffiti to the walls inside while sipping afternoon mojitos. The question is – can you *really* successfully make a boho dive bar into a chain?

La Isabelica Casa del Café COFFEE
(Map p206; Marina Gaviota, Autopista Sur Final; snacks/sweets from USD$2; ☺ 9am-11pm) In the Miami-esque Marina Gaviota at the eastern end of the peninsula, you get a Miami-esque cafe. The Isabelica tries to impress Starbucks-starved tourists with its Ikea-like sofas and coffee-growing scenes on the walls. A full menu runs from lattes to *café helado* with condensed milk. There's also an attractive selection of cakes and air-con the temperature of ice cream.

Calle 62 BAR
(Map p210; cnr Av 1 & Calle 62; ☺ 8am-2am) Set in the transition zone between old and new Varadero, this simple snack bar attracts clientele from both ends. It's good for a cheese

SANTA MARTA

Santa Marta is an incorporated locality of Varadero situated close to the southwestern end of the Hicacos Peninsula and bisected by the main road between Matanzas and Cárdenas. For many years it was little more than a crossroads for *colectivos* (shared taxis) and rusty old buses taking Cuban workers to Varadero's all-inclusive hotels (a purpose it still serves), but in recent times the 'town' has sprouted a handful of bars, restaurants and cafes good enough to lure in foreign vacationers suffering from resort buffet fatigue.

Two perfect spots to absorb the organized chaos of horse-drawn carts, bicycles and old American cars that characterize this busy nexus are Atlantida (p213), an excellent perch for seafood and cocktails, and Cafeccino (p214), serving the best cakes and coffee in Cuba outside Havana.

Santa Marta is a 1km walk from the southwestern end of Varadero town. Cross the bridge over the Laguna de Paso Malo and veer left.

sandwich during the day, and the ambience becomes feistier after dark with cheap cocktails and live salsa music going on until midnight.

Discoteca Havana Club   CLUB
(Map p210; cnr Av 3 & Calle 62; USD$10; ◷10:30pm-3am) Near the Centro Comercial Copey. Expect big, boisterous (young) crowds and plenty of male posturing.

Bar Mirador   BAR
(Map p206; Mansión Xanadú, Av las Américas; USD$2; ◷11am-midnight) On the top floor of Mansión Xanadú (p212), the dark-wood Bar Mirador is Varadero's ultimate romantic hangout where happy hour conveniently coincides with sunset cocktails.

Discoteca la Bamba   CLUB
(Map p206; Hotel Tuxpán, Av las Américas Km 2; USD$10; ◷10pm-4am) Varadero's most modern video disco is at Hotel Tuxpán (p212), in eastern Varadero. It plays mostly Latin music and is considered 'hot.'

☆ Entertainment

★ Beatles Bar-Restaurant   LIVE MUSIC
(Map p210; cnr Av 1 & Calle 59; ◷1pm-1am) A *roquero's* (Cuban rock fan's) delight on the edge of Parque Josone, honoring the previously banned Beatles in a bar that evokes the decidedly un-Cuban swinging spirit of the 1960s. Simple food and beer are served but the real draw is the live rock 'n' roll kicking off alfresco at 10pm most nights. Varadero's best night out.

Sala de la Música la Marina   LIVE MUSIC
(Map p206; Marina Gaviota, Autopista Sur Final; USD$10-15; ◷10pm-late) A cool-vibe place at the Marina Gaviota complex that's

(obviously) heavy with tourists. Most nights it's a disco with a live DJ. On Saturdays it usually has a live band – top-notch Cuban rock duo Buena Fe were recent guests. It's pleasantly modern with white lounge sofas and an upstairs terrace with marina views.

Casa de la Música   LIVE MUSIC
(Map p210; cnr Av de la Playa & Calle 42; USD$10; ◷10:30pm-3am Wed-Sun) Aping its two popular Havana namesakes, this place has some quality live acts and a definitive Cuban feel. It's in town and attracts a local crowd.

Centro Cultural Comparsita CULTURAL CENTER
(Map p210; Calle 60, btwn Avs 2 & 3; USD$1-5; ◷10pm-3am) An ARTex cultural center on the edge of Varadero town, offering concerts, shows, dancing, karaoke and plenty of local flavor. Check the current schedule taped on the door.

🛍 Shopping

Casa del Ron   ALCOHOL
(Map p210; cnr Av 1 & Calle 63; ◷9am-7pm, to 1pm Sun) The best selection of rum in Varadero as well as tasting opportunities in a venerable old building that acts as a small museum. It gives a through-the-ages look at Cuba's spirited relationship with the drink, including a beautiful scale model of Matanzas' Santa Elena distillery to admire as you sup.

Casa del Habano   CIGARS
(Map p216; Av de la Playa, btwn Calles 31 & 32; ◷9am-6pm) *The* place for cigars: this place has top-quality merchandise from humidors to perfume, and helpful service. There's also a small bar-tasting room and a small grocery shop abutting a quiet slice of beach. It's all encased in a typical wooden Varadero beach house.

Varadero Town – West

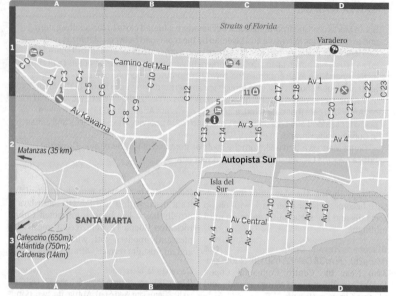

Varadero Town – West

🟢 Activities, Courses & Tours

1	Barracuda Scuba Diving Center	A2
2	Gaviota	C2

🛏 Sleeping

3	Casa Betty y Jorge	F2
4	Casa Menocal	C1
5	Hotel Acuazul	C2
6	Hotel Club Kawama	A1

❌ Eating

7	La Vaca Rosada	D1
8	Salsa Suárez	F2
9	Terrasita's Café	F1

🛍 Shopping

10	Casa del Habano	F1
11	Gran Parque de la Artesanía	C1

La Casa BOOKS, MUSIC
(Map p210; cnr Av 1 & Calle 59; ⏰9am-7pm) A retail outlet of Havana's famous Casa de las Américas, this place sells art, postcards and those old pre-internet-age throwbacks – books!

Gran Parque de la Artesanía MARKET
(Map p216; Av 1, btwn Calles 15 & 16; ⏰9am-7pm) The largest of several open-air artisans markets lining Primera Avenida, with private vendors selling mainly Cuba-themed crafts.

Galería de Arte Varadero ART
(Map p210; Av 1, btwn Calle 59 & Calle 60; ⏰9am-7pm) Antique jewelry, museum-quality silver and glass, paintings and other heirlooms from Varadero's bygone bourgeois days are sold here. As most items are of patrimonial importance, everything is already conveniently tagged with export permission.

Taller de Cerámica Artística ARTS & CRAFTS
(Map p210; Av 1, btwn Calles 59 & 60; ⏰9am-7pm) Buy fine artistic pottery made on the premises. Most items are in the USD$200 to USD$250 range.

ARTex 'La Epoca' GIFTS & SOUVENIRS
(Map p210; Av 1, btwn Calles 46 & 47; ⏰9am-8pm) Showcases CDs, T-shirts, musical instruments and more. There's a handicraft market next door.

Centro Comercial Hicacos SHOPPING CENTER
(Map p210; Parque de las 8000 Taquillas; ⏰10am-10pm) Varadero town's modern subterranean mall in Parque de las 8000 Taquillas is small by American standards, but has the basics including souvenirs, cigars, a spa/gym and a small market.

Plaza América SHOPPING CENTER
(Map p206; Autopista Sur Km 7; ⏰10am-8:30pm) Built in 1997, and already looking dated, Cuba's first bona fide shopping mall is one

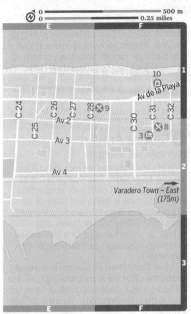

0 —————————— 500 m
0 —————————— 0.25 miles

Varadero Town – East (175m)

of Varadero's less-inspired architectural creations, though it serves its purpose. Useful outlets include a pharmacy, bank, a music store, fashion stores, three average restaurants and various souvenir shops.

ⓘ Information

SAFE TRAVEL

Crime-wise, Varadero's dangers are minimal. Aside from getting drunk at the all-inclusive bar and tripping over your bath mat on the way to the toilet, you haven't got too much to worry about.

Out on the beach, a red flag means no swimming allowed, due to the undertow or some other danger. A blue jellyfish known as the Portuguese man-of-war, most common in summer, can produce a bad reaction. Wash the stung area with vinegar and seek medical help if the pain becomes intense. Theft of unguarded shoes, sunglasses and towels is routine along this beach.

INTERNET ACCESS

Most of Varadero's hotels and many casas particulares (private homestays) have internet access. Buy your internet card at hotel receptions or at the **Etecsa Telepunto** (cnr Av 1 & Calle 30; ⊙8:30am-7pm).

There's a wi-fi hot spot on Calle 54.

MEDICAL SERVICES

Most of the large resort hotels have medical clinics that can provide free, basic first aid.

Clínica Internacional Servimed (⊉45-66-77-11; cnr Av 1 & Calle 61; ⊙24hr) Also has a 24-hour **pharmacy** (⊉45-66-80-42; cnr Av 1 & Calle 61; ⊙24hr).

Novafarma (⊉45-61-44-70; Av Kawama, cnr Calle 4; ⊙9am-9pm) At the west end of the peninsula near Hotel Club Kawama.

There's another pharmacy in the Plaza América.

MONEY

If you change money at your hotel front desk, you'll sacrifice 1% more than at a bank.

Banco de Ahorro Popular (Calle 36, btwn Av 1 & Autopista Sur; ⊙8:30am-4pm Mon-Fri) ATM.

Banco de Crédito y Comercio (Av 1 btwn Calles 35 & 36; ⊙9am-7pm, to 5pm Sat & Sun) ATM.

Banco Financiero Internacional (Autopista Sur Km 7; ⊙9am-noon & 1-6pm Mon-Fri, 9am-6pm Sat & Sun) Money exchange in Plaza América in the Hotel Zone.

Cadeca (Parque de los 8000 Taquillas; ⊙8:30am-6pm, to noon Sun)

POST

Many of the larger Varadero hotels have branch post offices.

Post Office (Map p210; Calle 62, cnr Av 2; ⊙10am-6pm Mon-Fri)

TOURIST INFORMATION

Every all-inclusive hotel in Varadero has a tourist-info desk.

Cubatur (⊉45-66-72-16; cnr Av 1 & Calle 33; ⊙8:30am-6pm) Reserves hotel rooms nationally, and organizes bus transfers to Havana hotels and excursions. Can act as a general information point, too.

Infotur (Map p216; ⊉45-66-29-61; cnr Av 1 & Calle 13; ⊙8:30am-4pm) Main office is next to Hotel Acuazul, but it has a desk in most large resorts.

ⓘ Getting There & Away

AIR

Juan Gualberto Gómez International Airport (VRA; ⊉45-61-30-16, 45-24-70-15) is 20km from central Varadero toward Matanzas and another 6km off the main highway. Airlines here include Blue Panorama (Milan), American Airlines (Miami), plus Air Transat, Air Canada, Sunwing and WestJet from various Canadian cities. The check-in time at Varadero is 90 minutes before flight time.

BUS

The **Terminal de Ómnibus** (Map p210; cnr Calle 36 & Autopista Sur) has daily air-con Víazul (www.viazul.com) buses to a few destinations. Warning: they fill up fast. Book ahead!

Destination	Cost (USD$)	Duration (hr)	Frequency (daily)
Havana	10	3	4
Santa Clara	11	3	2
Santiago de Cuba	49	15¼	1
Trinidad	20	6¼	1
Viñales	22	7¼	1

All five daily Havana buses stop at Matanzas (USD$6, one hour) and Juan Gualberto Gómez International Airport (p217; USD$6, 25 minutes).

The Trinidad bus stops in Cienfuegos (USD$16, 4½ hours). The Santiago bus also stops in Santa Clara (USD$11, 3¼ hours), Sancti Spíritus (USD$17, five hours), Ciego de Ávila (USD$19, 6¼ hours), Camagüey (USD$25, eight hours), Las Tunas (USD$33, 10 hours), Holguín (USD$38, 11¼ hours) and Bayamo (USD$41, 13 hours).

For Cárdenas, you can go on local bus 236 (USD$1), which departs every hour or so from next to a small tunnel marked Ómnibus de Cárdenas outside Varadero's main bus station. Don't rely on being able to buy tickets for non-Víazul buses from Varadero to destinations in Matanzas Province and beyond: the official line is tourists can't take them, and tourists in Varadero are generally recognizable from Cubans. With decent Spanish you could get lucky.

Cubanacán's Conectando runs a handy bus service between hotels in Varadero and hotels in Havana (bookable through hotel receptions). There's also a daily service between Varadero and Trinidad via Cienfuegos. Prices are similar to Víazul. Book tickets at least a day in advance through Infotur (p217).

CAR

There are car-rental offices in practically every hotel in Varadero, and prices are pretty generic between different makes and models. Once you've factored in fuel and insurance, a standard car will cost you approximately USD$75 to USD$85 a day.

Aside from the hotel reps, you can try the **Cubacar** (☑ 45-66-81-96; cnr Av 1 btwn Calles 21 & 22; ☺ 9am-5pm) office in town or car rental offices at the airport (p217).

Take note – there is a shortage of rental cars in Cuba, so book in advance and be prepared to wait a little, even if you have a reservation.

There's a Servi-Cupet gas station on the Autopista Sur at **Calle 17** (cnr Autopista Sur & Calle 17; ☺ 24hr), and another at **Calle 54** (Autopista Sur & Calle 54).

If heading to Havana, you'll have to pay the USD$2 toll at the booth on Vía Blanca upon leaving.

TAXI

With Víazul buses (www.viazul.com) in high demand, colectivo (shared) taxis are picking up the slack. You can book one by asking at your casa particular (private homestay), or hanging around at the Víazul bus station (p217). There are usually other passengers seeking lifts when fully booked buses are due to leave, so you can club together. A full colectivo (four people) will charge between USD$20 to USD$25 to Havana.

❶ Getting Around

TO/FROM THE AIRPORT

Varadero and Matanzas are each about 20km from the spur road to Juan Gualberto Gómez International Airport (p217); it's another 6km from the highway to the airport terminal. A tourist taxi from the airport to Varadero/Matanzas costs about USD$35/30 and takes around half an hour. Or you can arrange for a (cheaper) pickup through most casas particulares (private homestays).

All four Víazul (www.viazul.com) buses bound for Havana call at the airport, arriving in Havana 2¾ hours later. Tickets cost USD$10. Three buses go in the other direction to Varadero (USD$6, 25 minutes).

BICYCLE

Bikes are an excellent way of getting off the Hicacos Peninsula and discovering a little of the Cuba outside. Rentals are available at most of the all-inclusive resorts, and bikes are usually lent as part of the package. Some casas particulares (private homestays) will be able to rent (or lend) you basic bicycles. Ask around.

BUS

Varadero Beach Tour (all-day/night-bus tickets USD$5/3; ☺ 9am-9pm & 11pm-4am) is a handy open-top double-decker tourist bus with 45 hop-on/hop-off stops linking all the resorts and shopping malls along the length of the peninsula. It utilizes well-marked stops with route and distance information. Buy tickets on the bus itself.

A gimmicky toy train connects the three large Meliá resorts.

Local buses 47 and 48 run from Calle 64 to Santa Marta, south of Varadero on the Autopista Sur; bus 220 runs from Santa Marta to the far-eastern end of the peninsula. There are no fixed schedules. Fares are small change. You can also utilize bus 236 to and from Cárdenas, which runs the length of the peninsula.

HORSE CARTS

A state-owned horse-and-cart trip around Varadero costs around USD$10 for a full two-hour tour – plenty of time to see the sights.

TAXI

Metered tourist taxis in Varadero charge a USD$1 starting fee plus USD$1 per kilometer (same tariff day and night). Coco-taxis (*coquitos* or *huevitos* in Spanish) charge less with no starting fee. A taxi to Cárdenas/Havana (15 minutes/2¼ hours) will be about USD$20/85 one way. Taxis hang around all the main hotels and the bus station (p217), or you can phone **Cuba Taxi** (☏45-61-05-55).

Cheap *máquinas* (old American cars used as shared taxis) leave from the main road in Santa Marta to Cárdenas (USD$1) and Matanzas (USD$2). If you're versed in the Cuban *mecanica* (way of doing things), you'll work out where to find them.

Varadero to Matanzas

The 40-minute drive along the wide, smooth 36km sweep of the Vía Blanca Hwy, heading between the cities of Matanzas and Varadero, passes many of northern Matanzas' most magnificent sights: subterranean swimming holes, superb snorkeling and boat trips on hidden rivers. You could spend the best part of a day lingering for aquatic diversions at the Río Canímar and Playa Coral, and there's even a cabaret venue for evening entertainment.

◉ Sights & Activities

Parque Turístico Río Canímar   RIVER

(☉8am-4:30pm; 🚻) Boat trips on the Río Canímar, 8km east of Matanzas, are a truly magical experience. Gnarly mangroves dip their jungle-like branches into the ebbing water and a warm haze caresses the regal palm trees as your boat slides 12km upstream from the Vía Blanca bridge to a riverside *ranchón* (rustic, opened-sided restaurant) called 'La Arboleda,' where you can have lunch and go horseback riding or kayak the river's headwaters.

Four-person self-drive motor boats (first hour USD$35, each additional hour USD$15) can be rented to get upstream or you can take a larger launch if there are enough people (USD$25 per person). The rental point is on the east side of the river by the Vía Blanca bridge, where there's also a bar and indigenous dancing performances. It takes roughly 30 minutes to reach La Arboleda with a motor boat and one hour in the larger boat.

Most Varadero hotels have tour agencies offering this trip as part of a 'Jeep Tour.'

Playa Coral   BEACH

Your closest bet for shore snorkeling in the Varadero area is Playa Coral, on the old coastal road, about 3km off the Vía Blanca, halfway between Matanzas and Varadero. You can snorkel solo from the beach, but it's far better (and safer) to enter from the Flora y Fauna Reserve (8am to 5pm), 400m east. Professional Ecotur provide guides to take you out to the reef 150m offshore (40 minutes, USD$5).

There are a reported 300 species of fish here and visibility is a decent 15m to 20m. Diving is on offer, too (immersion USD$39), but must be organized beforehand through Barracuda (p207) in Varadero.

The flora and fauna reserve also incorporates the **Laguna de Maya** (🅿🚻), 2km inland from Playa Coral, with a couple of trails and some boating activities. Ask about packages in Varadero's hotels. The Flora y Fauna center has a bar and masseuse.

Most of the coast hereabouts is a graywhite coral shelf, but there are beaches just west of Playa Coral.

Cuevas de Bellamar   CAVE

(☏45-25-35-38, 45-26-16-83; USD$10, camera USD$5; ☉9am-5pm; 🅿🚻) Cuba's oldest tourist attraction, according to local propaganda, lies 5km southeast of Matanzas and is 300,000 years old. There are 2500m of caves here, discovered in 1861 by a Chinese workman in the employ of Don Manuel Santos Parga. The entrance is through a small museum, and a 45-minute Cuevas de Bellamar visit leaves almost hourly starting at 9:30am. The caves on show include a vast 12m stalagmite and an underground stream; cave walls glitter eerily with crystals.

Well-maintained, well-lit paths mean it's easy for kids to imbibe the stupendous geology, too. Outside the Cuevas de Bellamar are two restaurants and a playground.

It's 5km from central Matanzas – you can walk, take a taxi or hop on bus 12 from Plaza Libertad (p226).

Cueva de Saturno   CAVE

(☏45-25-32-72, 45-25-38-33; USD$5; ☉8am-6pm) The freshwater Cueva de Saturno, 1km south of the Vía Blanca by the road to Varadero's international airport, is a highly popular (ie crowded) subterranean cave with a pool billed as a snorkeling and/or swimming spot. The water's about 20°C and the maximum depth is 22m, though there are shallower parts. There's a snack bar and equipment rental post on-site. Arrive early if you want to avoid the Varadero tour groups.

Castillo del Morrillo
CASTLE, MUSEUM

(USD$1; ⊙9am-5pm Tue-Sun) On the western side of the Río Canímar bridge, 8km east of Matanzas, a road runs 1km down to a cove presided over by the four guns of this yellow-painted castle. The castle (1720) is now a museum dedicated to the student leader Antonio Guiteras Holmes (1906–35), who founded the revolutionary group Joven Cuba (Young Cuba) in 1934.

☆ Entertainment

Tropicana Matanzas
CABARET

(☎45-26-53-80; Carretera Matanzas-Varadero Km 5; USD$35; ⊙9pm-2am Tue & Thu) Capitalizing on its success in Havana and Santiago de Cuba, the famous Tropicana cabaret has a branch 8km east of Matanzas, next to the Hotel Canimao. While following the same entertaining formula of lights, feathers, flesh and frivolity as its Havana equivalent, it's less flamboyant and less reliable. Phone ahead for show times.

❶ Getting There & Away

To access the sights between Varadero and Matanzas, you'll need a taxi, your own car or a bicycle (the terrain is pretty flat). Alternatively, take a tour from Varadero: several of the sights (including the Cuevas de Bellamar, Cueva de Saturno and Parque Turístico Río Canímar) are usually incorporated.

Matanzas

POP 140,000

Matanzas is awakening! After nearly 60 years festering beneath the stormy waters of Cuba's fickle economy, the city is slowly being brought back to the surface piece by piece. The recent reconstruction – an avant-garde art street, a freshly painted central square, and a smattering of attractive restaurants and hotels – is still in its early stages, but, given time, could restore this sleeping giant into the cultural colossus it once was.

Go back a few generations and Matanzas was the epitome of elegance and eloquence. During the 18th and 19th centuries, the city developed a gigantic literary and musical heritage that earned it the moniker the 'Athens of Cuba.' Two pivotal Cuban musical forms, *danzón* (ballroom) and rumba, were hatched here, along with various religions of African origin.

While the aura of decay still fogs the picture, Matanzas' riches are quietly re-appearing. You just need a bit of patience to disentangle them.

◎ Sights

★ Taller-Galería Lolo
GALLERY

(☎45-26-08-54; www.osmanybetancourt.com; Calle 97, cnr Calle 288; ⊙hours vary) Imagine. You're tramping through Matanzas' tatty streets wondering whether the 'Athens of Cuba' moniker is just a local joke when you stumble upon this industrious artist's collective down by the river, guarded by epic surreal sculptures seemingly made out of bits of a salvaged ship. Inside you plunge, for plenty more artistic apparitions from the cutting edge of Matanzas' cultural custodians.

Lolo is Osmany Betancourt Falcon who, with his sharp-witted, mysterious, sometimes disquieting art, is putting Matanzas back where it should be – alongside Havana on the cultural map.

★ Iglesia de Monserrate
CHURCH

(Calle 306) For a mappable view of mildewed Matanzas on one side and the broccoli-green Valle de Yumurí on the other, climb 1.5km northeast of the center up Calle 306 to this renovated church dating from 1875. The lofty bastion perched high above the city was built by colonists from Catalonia in Spain, as a symbol of their regional power.

The lookout near here has a couple of *ranchónes* (rustic, opened-sided restaurants), good for skull-splitting music and basic refreshments. Come in the early morning, however, and the views offer a whole new perspective on this deceptively beautiful city.

Galería-Taller El Garabato
GALLERY

(Calle 97, btwn Calles 288 & 282; ⊙hours vary) **FREE** The workspace and gallery of local painter Adrián Socorro is fortuitously located next to Taller-Galería Lolo, inviting you to witness a double-whammy of chin-scratching art. You can watch, chat with the artist, and purchase Socorro's work right from the source. Some of his more affordable creations are painted onto old vinyl records.

Plaza de la Vigía
SQUARE

The original Plaza de Armas still remains as Plaza de la Vigía (literally 'lookout place'), a reference to the threat from piracy and smuggling that Matanzas' first settlers faced. This diminutive square was where Matanzas was founded in the late 17th century and numerous historical buildings still stand guard.

Teatro Sauto · THEATER
(☑ 45-24-27-21; Plaza de la Vigía) The defining symbol of the city according to Mexican painter (and admirer) Diego Rivera, the Teatro Sauto (1863) on Plaza de la Vigía's south side is one of Cuba's finest theaters and famous for its superb acoustics. The lobby is graced by marble Greek goddesses and the ceiling in the main hall bears paintings of the muses.

Three balconies enclose this 775-seat theater, which features a floor that can be raised to convert the auditorium into a ballroom. The original theater curtain is a painting of Matanzas' very own Puente de la Concordia, and notables like Russian dancer Anna Pavlova have performed here. At the time of research the theater was due to re-open after a long restoration.

Catedral de San Carlos Borromeo · CHURCH
(Calle 282, btwn Calles 83 & 85; ⊙ 8am-noon & 3-5pm, to noon Sun) Standing back from the disorganized melee of Calle 83 behind shady Plaza de la Iglesia is Matanzas' main church, a neoclassical structure with two unequal towers founded in 1693 (although the existing building dates from the 1730s). Despite being made a cathedral in 1912, the church suffered terribly from years of neglect in the 20th century. It reopened in 2016 after eight years of renovation. The interior is relatively plain, but handsome, and is once again a hub of local life.

Puente Calixto García · BRIDGE
If you've only got time to see *one* bridge (there are 21 in total) in Cuba's celebrated 'city of bridges,' gravitate toward this impressive steel structure built in 1899, spanning the Río San Juan with its kayaks floating lazily by. Just south is a distinctive Che Mural while the northern side leads directly into Plaza de la Vigía.

Museo Farmacéutico · MUSEUM
(Calle 83 No 4951; USD$3; ⊙ 10am-5pm, to 4pm Sun) Museo Farmacéutico is one of Matanzas' showcase sights. Founded in 1882 by the Triolett family, the pharmacy was the first of its type in Latin America and still looks much as it did in the 1880s. The fine displays include all the bottles, instruments and suchlike used in the trade. The obligatory guided tour will explain the rest.

Parque Libertad · SQUARE
A few blocks directly west of Plaza de la Vigía is Parque Libertad, the anchor of Matanzas' cultural life and home to several of the city's most stimulating sights, including a 'liberty' statue depicting an open-armed woman, her wrists bearing broken chains, and a bronze statue (1909) of José Martí.

Museo Palacio de Junco · MUSEUM
(cnr Calles 83 & 272; USD$2; ⊙ 10:30am-3:30pm Mon-Fri, 1-5pm Sat) This double-arched edifice on the Plaza de la Vigía showcases the full sweep of Matanzas' history from pirate incursions to the cruel reign of slavery. There's a huge statue of unpopular Spanish king Ferdinand VII on a side patio, made in Italy in the 1830s.

Iglesia de San Pedro Apóstol · CHURCH
(cnr Calles 57 & 270, Versalles) Dominating the scruffy Versalles neighborhood is this fine neoclassical church, which was refurbished inside and out in the mid-2010s. The interior is bright with cream-colored arches but little ornamentation.

Cuartel de Bomberos · MUSEUM
(Plaza de la Vigía; ⊙ 9am-4pm Mon-Sat) FREE This unique firefighting museum occupies a still-working fire station and is staffed by friendly volunteers who'll show you around lovingly polished vintage engines, provide a potted history of Cuba's *bomberos* (firefighters) and point out a world map decorated with badges left by visiting firefighters (Canada is well represented).

Castillo de San Severino · FORT
(Av del Muelle; USD$2; ⊙ 10am-7pm Tue-Sat, 9am-noon Sun) Northeast of Versalles lies this formidable bastion, built by the Spanish in 1735 as part of Cuba's defensive ring. It was tested early on by the British; during their 1762 invasion, they mercilessly bombarded it. Rebuilt in the 1770s, it became an offloading point for enslaved people. Later, Cuban patriots were imprisoned within the walls – and sometimes executed. San Severino remained a prison until the 1970s and in more recent times has become the modest slavery-themed Museo de la Ruta de los Esclavos.

The castle itself has great views of the Bahía de Matanzas, but could offer a lot more to inspire curious visitors.

Matanzas

☆☆☆ Festivals & Events

Festival del Bailador Rumbero   MUSIC

(☉ Oct) During the 10 days following October 10, Matanzas rediscovers its rumba roots with talented local musicians. Events enliven the Teatro Sauto and a small park outside Museo Histórico Provincial. The festival coincides with the anniversary of the city's founding (October 12), a multiday party that includes celebrations of luminaries who have made this great city what it is.

🛏 Sleeping

★ Hostal Azul   CASA PARTICULAR $

(☏ 45-24-24-49; hostalazul.cu@gmail.com; Calle 83 No 29012, btwn Calles 290 & 292; r USD$25-30; ❋ 🐾) 🏍 With a front door large enough to ride a stagecoach through, this handsome blue house dating from the 1890s has original tiled floors, an antique wooden spiral staircase and four castle-sized rooms set around a spacious alfresco patio.

Hotel Río San Juan   HOTEL $

(www.islazul.cu; Calle 282 No 8503, btwn Calles 85 & 91; s/d USD$38/40; ❋ 🐾) Gone are the days when hotel rooms in Matanzas were luxuries you had to be 50 years old to remember. Tying in with the city's recent beautification, this hotel run by Cuba's cheaper Islazul brand looks anything but cheap inside. There's a lovely mahogany bar, color-refracting stained glass and smart rooms which, though dark, are enlivened by bright photo graphics.

Villa Soñada   CASA PARTICULAR $

(☏ 45-24-27-61; mandy_rent_habitaciones@yahoo.com; Calle 290 No 6701, cnr Santa Isabel; r USD$25-30; ❋) The aptly named 'villa of dreams,' set four blocks north of Matanzas' main square, has an attractive facade topped by a huge terrace guarded by sculpted lions. Rooms are modern, with glass bricks, lots of space (one has two levels), minibars and super-slick bathrooms. Inside and out, there

Matanzas

are plenty of nooks to relax. Breakfasts are fabulous and plentiful.

Hostal Río CASA PARTICULAR $
(☑45-24-30-41; hostalrio.cu@gmail.com; Calle 91 No 29018, btwn Calles 290 & 292; r USD$25-30; ❄) This house is owned by the parents of Joel, star of nearby Hostal Azul; the overriding color here is *amarillo* (yellow) rather than Joel's *azul* (blue). There are two comfortable rooms with high ceilings in colonial digs. Meals are served at Hostal Azul two blocks away.

Evelio & Isel CASA PARTICULAR $
(☑45-24-30-90; evelioisel@yahoo.es; Calle 79 No 28201, btwn Calles 282 & 288; r USD$20-25; 🅿❄) Rooms at this 2nd-floor apartment have TV, security boxes and balconies, plus there's underground parking. Exceedingly helpful owner Evelio is a fount of knowledge about the Matanzas music scene.

Hostal Alma CASA PARTICULAR $
(☑45-29-08-57; hostalalma63@gmail.com; Calle 83 No 29008, btwn Calles 290 & 292; r USD$25-30; ❄) A house with *mucha alma* (a lot of soul), Mayra's place has Seville-invoking *azulejos* (tiles), relaxing rocking chairs, and rainbow *vitrales* (stained-glass windows) that refract colored light across the tiled floors. You can enjoy a welcome cocktail on one of its two colossal terraces while surveying Matanzas'

semi-ruined rooftops. There are three comfortable rooms.

Hotel Velazco HOTEL $$
(☑45-25-38-80; Calle 79, btwn Calles 290 & 288; s/d incl breakfast USD$55/70; ❄@🛜) This lovely period hotel harks back to the early years of the Cuban Republic – the original 1902 fin-de-siècle style blends seamlessly with the horses, carts and antediluvian autos in the square outside. A beautiful mahogany bar lures you in; 17 elegant rooms (with flat-screen TVs and wi-fi) encourage you to stay.

Hotel Louvre BOUTIQUE HOTEL $$
(☑45-24-40-74; Calle 83, btwn 288 & 290; s/d incl breakfast USD$55/70; ❄🛜) Inhabiting an enchanting perch on Matanzas' main square, the Louvre is a new rendition of an old hotel that remained closed for over a decade before reopening in 2019. The decor and rooms closely mirror the Hotel Velazco across the square. The hotel was founded in 1879 and has been at its current location since the early 20th century.

🍴 Eating

⭐ **El Chiquirrín** INTERNATIONAL $
(☑45-24-38-77; Calle Laborde No 27013; mains USD$3-7; ⏱12:30-11pm Tue-Sun) A pianist plays on a baby grand, chefs work artistically behind a glass partition in the kitchen, and a

VARADERO & MATANZAS PROVINCE MATANZAS

CALLE NARVÁEZ: MATANZAS' ART STREET

The self-proclaimed 'Athens of Cuba' is quietly stirring after a lengthy slumber and its artistry burns brightest on Calle Narváez (aka Calle 97), a riverside esplanade lined with dynamic art-cafes and punctuated with some mind-bending Cuban sculpture. Within a short 200m stroll you'll encounter an emaciated pig atop a squashed balloon, a post-modern rendering of the crucifixion, and a bust of José Martí with a sword clasped between his teeth. Ground zero for the innovators is the peerless Taller-Galería Lolo (p220), Matanzas' mastermind of trailblazing ideas and bizarre inventions, but plenty more galleries, workshops and art-cafes have sprung up in the last couple of years. Check out Galería-Taller El Garabato (p220), the artistic sanctuary of local painter Adrián Socorro; Artys (see below), a bar-cum-art-center near the Puente Calixto García and Helados Pompón (see below), a gallery that also happens to sell ice cream. After decades in the doldrums and several years of encouraging noises, Matanzas is officially back.

waiter carves Chateaubriand at your table. New York? Paris? No, the former culinary wasteland of Matanzas. A testament to how things have changed in Cuba is this charming restaurant facing the bay in the city's Versalles quarter.

Restaurant-Galería Esa Talla
TAPAS $

(☑ 5-357-6931; Calle 97, btwn Calles 282 & 272; tapas USD$5-7; ☺ noon-1am) An exclamation mark of artistic genius down by the river, the Talla could be your best bet for food among the newer crop of bars and galleries hereabouts. There are fine meat skewers, snack-sized pizzas and well-constructed quesadillas, which you can enjoy alfresco sitting on painted packing cases in Calle Narváez.

Amelia del Mar
CUBAN, INTERNATIONAL $

(☑ 45-26-16-53; Via Blanca No 22014, Playa; mains USD$5-7; ☺ noon-2am, closed Wed) Amelia del Mar brings tongue-in-cheek creativity to standard Cuban 'international' food through flashy presentation and then serves the concept in a neat open-air patio doubling as a lively bar. Dishes here have playful names that translate to the likes of 'blue meteorite,' 'white-bodied lady' and 'unearthed corpses,' but what's in them is class – chicken fajitas, tropical fish and huge paellas.

La Fettuccine
ITALIAN $

(☑ 5-412-2553; Calle 83 No 29018, btwn Calles 290 & 292; mains USD$2-3; ☺ 1-8:30pm, closed Thu) Small is beautiful. With three tables squeezed into a space the size of an entry vestibule and the day's menu chalked onto a blackboard, Fettuccine is not a good place to host your high-school reunion. However, the Italian-themed food (homemade and industrial pasta with various sauces and flatbread-style pizza) has many local plaudits.

Cremería Helados Pompón
ICE CREAM $

(Calle 97, btwn Calles 282 & 272; ice cream from USD$2; ☺ 2pm-midnight Tue-Thu, to 1am Fri-Sun) Another artistic surprise on awakening Calle Narváez (aka Calle 97), Pompón is an ice cream–biased cafe that doubles as an art gallery, workshop and crossroads for hot new ideas exchanged over chilly cones.

Restaurante Romántico San Severino
INTERNATIONAL $

(Calle 290, btwn Calles 279 & 283; mains USD$5-7; ☺ 6-11pm) A bit of old-world ambience in Parque Libertad, the Romántico is a 1st-floor perch up a steep flight of stairs with good park views if you can bag a balcony seat. The interior is scattered with colonial relics, the clientele is mainly Matanzeros and the food is above average, especially the shrimp-stuffed fish fillets.

🍸 Drinking & Nightlife

Matanzas doesn't visibly rock in the evening, but you can sometimes uncover something interesting. Parque Libertad is a good starting point, while Calle Narváez is the hottest new spot.

★ Galería-Bar Artys
BAR

(☑ 5-278-4660; Calle 97, btwn Calles 280 & 272; ☺ 10am-2am, to 3am Fri-Sun) Matanzas has recently made a giant leap into a new artistic domain, thanks largely to places like this smart cafe-cum-art-collective on riverside Calle Narváez that plies tacos, pizzas and small tapas, but is particularly good for drinks, including an epic iced lemonade.

Not surprisingly, the walls are lined with fabulous art, most of it courtesy of the imaginative owners, including a superbly sinister rendering of an Abakuá devil.

Café Mambo Jambo CAFE

(Calle 85 No 27414; ⊙10:30am-6pm) Hardworking little private cafe full of antique radios and old album covers that serves strong coffee, *frapuccinos* and basic snacks. Clientele is a mix of arty students and old ladies fresh from a makeover at the local hairdressers.

Kaiser Bistro Kuba BAR

(Calle 83, btwn Calles 292 & 290; ⊙11am-2am) Dark, coolly air-conditioned and rather swish for Matanzas, this small, mod bar has tables that light up to show old city landmarks. Cocktails are incredible, ditto the espresso. For the peckish there are ham and cheese tasting platters. The crowd's mostly Cuban and there's live music several nights per week.

ACAA CAFE

(Asociación Cubana de Artistas y Artesanos; Calle 85, btwn Calles 280 & 282; ⊙10am-late) What begins as an old-school art-supplies shop and exhibition venue leads back into a courtyard reminiscent of bohemian Paris, where artsy culture vultures sit around slurping strong coffee and conversing animatedly. A rooftop bar gets going after dark, often with live music as an accompaniment.

Taberna Plaza la Vigía BAR

(cnr Plaza de la Vigía & Calle 85; snacks USD$2-3; ⊙11am-11pm) Rum and draft beer rule the menu, while old-timers and young students make up the clientele in this old, stripped-down bar, a dusty relic in an otherwise grand building. The ultimate anti-Varadero escape.

Ruinas de Matasiete BAR

(cnr Vía Blanca & Calle 101; ⊙10am-10pm, club 10pm-2am) The city's famed drinking hole is a frenetic place housed in the ruins of a 19th-century, bay-facing warehouse. Drinks and grilled meats are served on an open-air terrace. In recent years, it has become a favored gay venue and is the nearest of its kind to Varadero. There's usually live music 9pm Friday to Sunday (cover charge USD$3).

★ Entertainment

★ **Sala de Conciertos**

José White CONCERT VENUE

(☑45-26-70-32; Calle 79, btwn Calles 290 & 288) Restoration of this 1876 building abutting Hotel Velazco (p223) was completed in 2014 and every inch, flourish and cornicing of its former glory is well worth a lingering look. Fitting for a building that formerly hosted the city symphony orchestra, classical music makes up the majority of its performances, although there is also that made-in-Matanzas dance *danzón* (ballroom dance) performed here.

The concert hall melds modern and traditional and is first-class. A courtyard bar with a huge tile mural complements proceedings.

Rumba al Pie de la Ceiba DANCE

(Calle 282, cnr Calle 85) Where else would you want to see live rumba but in its crucible city (Matanzas) underneath a ceiba tree (considered sacred in the Santería religion) being performed by local aficionados? Hit the small square on the corner of Calles 282 and 85 (aka Medio) on Saturdays at 10pm and watch the magic unfold.

Estadio Victoria de Girón SPECTATOR SPORT

(Av Martín Dihigo) From October to April, baseball games take place at this stadium, home of beloved local team the Cocodrilos. It's 1km southwest of the market (p226).

🛍 Shopping

Ediciones Vigía BOOKS

(Plaza de la Vigía, cnr Calle 91; ⊙9am-5pm Mon-Sat) To the southwest of Plaza de la Vigía this unique book publisher, founded in 1985, produces high-quality handmade paper and 1st-edition books on a variety of topics. The books are typed, stenciled and pasted in editions of 200 copies. Visitors are welcome in the Dickensian workshop where they can purchase beautiful numbered and signed copies (USD$5 to USD$40).

ℹ Information

INTERNET ACCESS

Etecsa Telepunto (cnr Calles 83 & 282; per hour USD$1.50; ⊙8:30am-7:30pm) sells phone and internet cards.

There's wi-fi in the park outside the cathedral (p221) and in Parque Libertad (p221).

MEDICAL SERVICES

Servimed (☑45-25-31-70; Hospital Faustino Pérez, Carretera Central Km 101; ⊙24hr) Clinic by hospital, just southwest of Matanzas.

MONEY

Banco de Crédito y Comercio (Calle 85 No 28604 btwn Calles 286 & 288; ⊙9am-5pm) ATM.

Cadeca (Calle 85, btwn Calles 280 & 282; ⊙8:30am-8pm Mon-Sat, 9am-6pm Sun)

TOURIST INFORMATION

Infotur (Calle 85, cnr 288; ⊕8:30am-5:30pm Mon-Fri, to 3pm Sat) For the rundown on caves, rumba and Matanzas' emerging art scene.

ℹ Getting There & Away

AIR

Matanzas is connected to the outside world through Juan Gualberto Gómez International Airport (p217), aka Varadero airport, 20km east of town.

BUS

All buses to Matanzas, long distance and provincial, use the **National Bus Station** (cnr Calles 131 & 272, Pueblo Nuevo), in the old train station south of the Río San Juan.

Matanzas has decent connections, although for destinations like Cienfuegos and Trinidad you need to change at Varadero, taking the first Varadero bus of the day then waiting for the afternoon Varadero–Trinidad bus.

Víazul (www.viazul.com) has four daily departures to Havana (USD$7, two hours). There are also four departures to Varadero (USD$6, one hour), all of which call at the airport (p217) (USD$6, 25 minutes).

CAR

The nearest car rental to the center is **Cubacar** (☑45-25-32-46; cnr Calles 127 & 204, Playa) in the Playa neighborhood.

TAXI

Taxis hang around the bus station and in Parque Libertad (p221). For a *colectivo* (shared taxi) to destinations south and east, you might be better off heading to Varadero bus station (p217) and looking for a ride-share there.

Cheaper *máquinas* (old American cars used as shared taxis) to Varadero (USD$2) and Havana (USD$5) stop on the **Carretera Nacional** behind the Teatro Sauto.

TRAIN

Matanzas has two train stations. The main **train station** (☑45-29-16-45; Calle 181) is in Miret, at the southern edge of the city. This is the terminal for Cuba's main west–east railway line. Eight of Cuba's newer trains service the city. Tren 1 goes to Santiago de Cuba (USD$62, 13 hours) every other day via Santa Clara (USD$16, three hours), Ciego de Ávila (USD$28, 5½ hours), Camagüey (USD$37, 7½ hours) and Las Tunas (USD$46, 9½ hours). Tren 2 runs in the opposite direction to Havana (USD$10, two hours) also on alternate days. There are additional trains to and from Holguín (USD$54, 12 hours) every three days, Bayamo (USD$52, 13 hours) and Manzanillo (USD$56, 15¼) every three days, and Guantána-mo (USD$66, 15 hours) every three days. Check at the station beforehand to find out exactly which days the trains are running.

When it's working, the Hershey train runs from Matanzas' **Hershey Train Station** (☑45-24-48-05; cnr Calles 55 & 67, Versalles), an easy 15-minute walk from Parque Libertad, to Casablanca station in Havana (USD$2.80, four hours) via Canasí, Jibacoa (for Playa Jibacoa), Hershey (for Jardines de Hershey) and Guanabo. There are no printed timetables and service was suspended at last visit due to maintenance issues. Inquiries about reopening were greeted with sarcastic sighs.

ℹ Getting Around

Bus 12 links Plaza Libertad with the Cuevas de Bellamar and the Iglesia de Monserrate.

The **Oro Negro gas station** (cnr Calles 129 & 210) is 4km outside central Matanzas on the Varadero road. If you're driving to Varadero, you will pay a USD$2 highway toll between Boca de Camarioca and Santa Marta (no toll between Matanzas and the airport).

Bici-taxis congregate next to the **Mercado la Plaza** (cnr Calles 97 & 298) and can take you to most of the city's destinations for one to two Cuban pesos. A taxi to Juan Gualberto Gómez International Airport (p217) should cost USD$25 to USD$30 (20 minutes).

Cárdenas

POP 81,000

Bereft of the bright lights of Varadero or the rejuvenated cultural legacy of Matanzas, Cárdenas can appear downright shabby. Punctuated by threadbare buildings and surviving with horse-drawn carts as its primary means of transportation, the city glimmers like a sepia-toned photo from another era. Yet, this is where the majority of Varadero's waitstaff, front-desk clerks and taxi drivers call home.

It's not all dereliction. Search a trio of interesting museums in the main square (the primary reason to visit the city) and you'll discover that Cárdenas has played an episodic role in Cuban history. In 1850 Venezuelan adventurer Narciso López and a ragtag army of American mercenaries raised the Cuban flag here for the first time, in a vain attempt to free the colony from its Spanish colonizers. Other history-making inhabitants have included revolutionary student leader José Antonio Echeverría and the Arechabala rum family, the original crafters of Havana Club.

ABAKUÁ

A secret all-male society, a language understood only by initiates, a close-knit network of masonic-like lodges, and the symbolic use of the African leopard to denote power: the mysterious rites of Abakuá read like a Cuban *Da Vinci Code*.

In a country not short on foggy religious practices, Abakuá is perhaps the least understood. It's a complicated mixture of initiations, dances, chants and ceremonial drumming that testifies to the remarkable survival of African culture in Cuba since the slave era.

Not to be confused with Santería or other syncretized African religions, Abakuá's traditions were brought to Cuba by enslaved Efik people from the Calabar region of southeastern Nigeria in the 18th and 19th centuries. With practitioners organizing themselves into *juegos* (lodges), the first of which was formed in the Havana suburb of Regla in 1836, Abakuá acted as a kind of African mutual aid society made up primarily of black dock workers whose main goal was to help buy their tribal brethren out of slavery.

In the early days, Abakuá lodges were necessarily anti-slavery and anti-colonialist, and were suppressed by the Spanish. Nonetheless, by the 1860s the lodges were increasingly admitting white members and finding that their strength lay in their secretiveness and invisibility.

Today, there are thought to be over 100 Abakuá lodges in Cuba, some up to 600-strong, based primarily in Havana, Matanzas and Cárdenas (the practice never penetrated central or eastern Cuba). Initiates are known as *ñáñigos* and their intensely secret ceremonies take place in a temple known as a *famba*. Although detailed information about the brotherhood is scant, Abakuá is well known to the outside world for its masked dancers called *Ireme* (devils) who showcase their skills in various annual carnivals and were instrumental in the development of the *guaguancó* style of rumba. Cuba's great abstract artist, Wilfredo Lam, used Abakuá masks in his paintings, and composer Amadeo Roldán incorporated its rhythms into classical music.

While there is a strong spiritual and religious element to the brotherhood (forest deities and the leopard symbol are important), it differs from the more widespread Santería religion in that it does not hide its deities behind Catholic saints. Cuban anthropologist Fernando Ortíz Fernández once referred to Abakuá societies as a form of 'African masonry' while other researchers have suggested it acts like a separate state within the Cuban nation with its owns laws and language. The casual Cuban word *'asere'* (meaning 'mate') is actually derived from the Abakuá term for 'ritual brother.'

◉ Sights

★ **Museo Oscar María de Rojas**   MUSEUM
(cnr Av 4 & Calle 13; USD$5; ⊘9am-6pm, to 1pm Sun) Cuba's second-oldest museum (after the Museo Bacardí in Santiago) offers a selection of weird artifacts, including a strangulation chair from 1830, a face mask of Napoleon, the tail of Antonio Maceo's horse, Cuba's largest collection of snails and, last but by no means least, some preserved fleas – yes fleas – from 1912.

The museum is set in a lovely colonial building and was getting a well-earned refurbishment at last visit (throughout which it remained open).

Plaza Molocoff   HISTORIC BUILDING
(cnr Av 3 Oeste & Calle 12) In a city of lost glories, Plaza Molocoff is one of the grandest yet most disfigured sights. This whimsical two-story cast-iron market hall with a glittery 16m-high silver dome was built in 1859 and once served as the city vegetable market. These days it lies temporarily abandoned crying out for a face-lift, though you can still detect its erstwhile elegance.

Museo de Batalla de Ideas   MUSEUM
(Av 6, btwn Calles 11 & 12; USD$2; ⊘9am-5pm Tue-Sat, to noon Sun) The newest of Cárdenas' three museums offers a keenly curated if propaganda-heavy overview of the history of US–Cuban relations inspired by the case of Elián González, a boy from Cárdenas whose mother, stepfather and 11 others drowned attempting to enter the US by boat in 1999. The museum is the solid form of Castro's resulting *batalla de ideas* (battle of ideas) with the US government.

The displays' themes naturally center round the eight months during which Cuba and the US debated the custody of Elián – but they also include bits of a US plane shot down during the Bay of Pigs invasion, discussions on the quality of the Cuban education system and a courtyard containing busts of anti-imperialists who died for the revolutionary cause. Anchoring the show is the original cast of a statue of José Martí holding a child that now stands on Havana's Malecón.

Arechabala Rum Factory FACTORY
(cnr Calle 2 & Av 13) To the northwest of the center of Cárdenas, in the industrial zone, is this famous rum factory founded in 1878 by Spanish immigrant José Arechabala. Arechabala concocted Havana Club, Cuba's second most iconic rum (after Bacardí), until the family business was requisitioned by the Cuban government in 1959. Arechabala left for the US, but failed to register the Havana Club trademark, which was picked up by the Cuban government in 1976.

Arechabala (and its international partner Bacardí) were entangled in a long trademark dispute with the Cuban government and partner Pernod Ricard over the rights to sell Havana Club in the US, an argument that has yet to be fully rectified. The factory still operates but is now called the José Antonio Echeverría Distillery. No tours are available.

Flagpole Monument MONUMENT
(cnr Av Céspedes & Calle 2) No, not just any old flagpole. Follow Av Céspedes past Catedral de la Inmaculada Concepción to its northern end and you will see *this* flagpole is attached to a monument and commemorates the first raising of the Cuban flag on May 19, 1850.

Catedral de la Inmaculada Concepción CHURCH
(Av Céspedes, btwn Calles 8 & 9) Cárdenas' twin-towered cathedral was built in 1846, though it looks older. The main ecclesiastical building of Cárdenas, it is noted for its stained glass and fronted by what is purportedly the oldest statue of Christopher Columbus in the western hemisphere. Opening times for the cathedral are sporadic. Your best bet for a peep is during Sunday Mass.

Dating from 1862, the statue outside of Cristóbal Colón, as he's known in Cuba, stands rather authoritatively with his face fixed in a thoughtful frown and a globe (and usually some bird shit) resting at his feet.

The cathedral and statue stand in Parque Colón, five blocks north of Parque Echeverría.

Museo Casa Natal de José Antonio Echeverría MUSEUM
(Av 4 Este No 560; USD$2; ⊙10am-5pm Tue-Sat, 9am-1pm Sun) This museum with temperamental opening times was where student leader José Antonio Echeverría was born in 1932. Echeverría, a rebel leader not dissimilar to Fidel Castro, led a a botched assassination attempt on Batista in Havana's Presidential Palace in 1957. He was subsequently slain by the state police, but elevated to a national hero after Castro took power in 1959. The house collects family artifacts, historical testimonies, and display's Echeverría's pink 1954 Chrysler in the courtyard.

🛏 Sleeping

Down the road Varadero flaunts 60 hotels (and counting). Here in humble Cárdenas there are precisely zero. Fortunately, Cárdenas sports a couple of good (if notoriously hard-to-find) casas particulares (private homestays).

Hostal Ida CASA PARTICULAR $
(✆45-52-15-59; ida83@nauta.cu; Calle 13, btwn Avs 13 & 15; d/apt USD$25/35; P❄) Don't let the tatty street setting put you off here. Inside are two comfortable doubles and a plush apartment with private entrance, garage, salubrious living room/kitchenette, and a decadently furnished bedroom/bathroom that might have floated over from a decent Varadero hotel. There's a communal terrace to boot and ample breakfasts (USD$5) can be procured.

Ricardo Domínguez CASA PARTICULAR $
(✆5-289-4431; yaniamaria82@nauta.cu; cnr Av 31 & Calle 12; r USD$35; P❄) Ricardo's place is 1.5km northwest of Parque Echeverría and worth tracking down. The spick-and-span white terracotta-roofed house is cocooned within a large, leafy garden and seemingly just plucked from one of Miami's more tasteful suburbs. Three rooms available.

🍴 Eating

★Don Qko CUBAN $
(✆45-52-45-72; Av Céspedes No 1000, cnr Calle 21; mains USD$3-8; ⊙noon-11pm, closed Tue) Don Qko is a well-executed and quietly sophisticated restaurant hidden in Cárdenas, otherwise tatty street grid that serves classic Cuban dishes in a sprawling mini oasis. It includes a cafe, restaurant, pool and fern-filled patio. It's primarily frequented

by in-the-know Cubans, but Varadero tour groups have started to discover it.

Plan B ICE CREAM $
(Calle 12, btwn Avs 4 & 6; ice cream USD$0.50-2; ◷11am-11pm) Make Plan B your plan A when visiting Cárdenas – particularly if you're in the mood for ice cream. This diminutive place with five tables rustles up superb ice-cream desserts dispatched out of a hidden back room. Try a *batido* (milkshake) in one of eight flavors, a generous *tres gracias* (three scoops) or a mountainous *turquino* (named after Cuba's highest peak).

The air-con is as cold as the ice cream.

Studio 55 CAFE $
(Calle 12, btwn Avs 4 & 6; light snacks USD$1-2; ◷noon-10pm Mon-Thu, to midnight Fri & Sat) Industrial-film-themed private cafe in Cárdenas' main square that's a bit hip and very local. Grab a pew amid the metal sculptures and rescued movie spotlights and settle down with a Cuban-style burger, a fruit shake or some random tapas. Nothing on the menu costs more than USD$2.

Restaurant Don Ramón INTERNATIONAL $
(Av 4, btwn Calles 12 & 3; mains USD$6-8; ◷noon-10:30pm; ✦) Overlooking Parque Echeverría, the lovely Don Ramón woos you with its old-style colonial charm. For a varied sit-down meal, there's nowhere better in Cárdenas. Elect for the *ropa vieja* (shredded beef) over the various attempts at Italian-style pizza and pasta.

❶ Information

INTERNET ACCESS

Etecsa Telepunto (cnr Av Céspedes & Calle 12; per hour USD$1; ◷8:30am-7pm) Telephone and internet access.

Parque Echeverría is also a wi-fi hot spot.

MEDICAL

Centro Médico Sub Acuática (☑45-52-21-14; Carretera a Varadero Km 2; per hour USD$80; ◷8am-4pm Mon-Sat, doctors on-call 24hour) Two kilometers northwest on the road to Varadero at Hospital Julio M Aristegui; has a Soviet recompression chamber dating from 1981.

Novafarma (☑45-52-20-36; Calle 12 No 60 btwn Avs 3 & 5; ◷8am-6pm) Reasonably well-stocked pharmacy opposite Plaza Molocoff.

MONEY

Banco de Crédito y Comercio (Calle 9 btwn Avs 1 & 3)

Cadeca (cnr Av 1 Oeste & Calle 12; ◷8:30am-8pm Mon-Sat, 9am-6pm Sun)

❶ Getting There & Away

It's simplest to go to Varadero to get onward bus connections, because whilst the Varadero–Santiago de Cuba Víazul bus (www.viazul.com) does pass through, it doesn't officially stop here. Varadero also has many more daily bus services to places such as Trinidad and Havana.

Máquinas (old American cars used as shared taxis) pass along Calle 13 toward Varadero (USD$1). Flag one down. An 'official' yellow taxi for the same journey costs USD$15 to USD$20 (15 minutes).

❶ Getting Around

Coches (horse carriages) are how one gets around Cárdenas. The main route is northeast on Av Céspedes from the **bus station** (cnr Av Céspedes & Calle 22) and then northwest on Calle 13 to the hospital, passing the stop of bus 236 (to Varadero) on the way. Pay with your smallest USD$ coin.

The **Servi-Cupet gas station** (cnr Calle 13 & Av 31 Oeste) is opposite an old Spanish fort on the northwest side of town, on the road to Varadero.

When asking for directions, beware that Cárdenas residents often use the old street names rather than the newer street-naming system (numbered *calles* and *avenidas*). Double-check if uncertain.

San Miguel de los Baños

Nestled in the interior of Matanzas Province amid rolling hills and vivid splashes of bougainvillea, San Miguel de los Baños is an atmospheric spa town that once rivaled Havana for opulence. Once, that is. Flourishing briefly as a destination for wealthy folk seeking the soothing medicinal waters that were 'discovered' here in the early 20th century, San Miguel saw a smattering of lavish neoclassical villas shoot up; they still line the town's arterial Av de Abril today. But the boom times didn't last. Just prior to the revolution, pollution from a local sugar mill infiltrated the water supply and the resort quickly faded from prominence. Now it's an architectural time capsule scattered with gorgeous ruins that resemble Miss Havisham's boarded-up mansion in Charles Dickens' *Great Expectations*.

◉ Sights

Aside from its strikingly ruined Gran Hotel and a climbable hill punctuated with overgrown Stations of the Cross, San Miguel has plenty of other tumbledown real estate to admire, from handsome clapboard houses to decrepit neoclassical villas.

★ **Gran Hotel & Balneario** RUINS

A gorgeous ruin lying truly abandoned in the middle of small-town Cuba that's heavy with atmosphere and still shines (despite the mildew) with a perceptible beauty. Between the 1920s and 1950s, this grand building functioned as an expensive bathhouse and hotel. These days it hosts birds' nests, weeds and – who knows? – the ghosts of guests past.

There's no entry fee and barely any other visitors. Just slip inside and enjoy the magic on your own while you still can.

★ **Finca Coincidencia** FARM

(☑ 45-81-39-23; Carretera Central, btwn Coliseo & Jovellanos) ✔ FREE Enhance your taste for bucolic provincial life away from the razzmatazz of Matanzas Province's north coast at this ecological farm 14km northeast of San Miguel de los Baños and 6km east of Colesio on the Carretera Central. Chill in the grounds replete with mango and guava trees, participate in ceramics classes and look around gardens where 83 types of plants are cultivated.

The owner, Héctor Correa, is an ecological genius who grows practically everything he consumes. He also maintains a small ceramics workshop and has constructed a quirky sculpture garden amid the mango trees – pride of place goes to the life-sized Charlie Chaplin. For those seeking total rural immersion, accommodations (☑ 5-245-2892; Carretera Central, btwn Coliseo & Jovellanos; r USD$25; P ❋) ✔ and meals (around USD$10) are also available.

Loma de Jacán HILL

Looming above San Miguel de los Baños are the steep slopes of Loma de Jacán, a glowering hill with 448 steps embellished by faded murals of the Stations of the Cross. When you reach the small chapel on top you can drink in the town's best views with the added satisfaction that you are standing at the highest point in the province. The views are tremendous.

❶ Getting There & Away

To get to San Miguel de los Baños, follow Rte 101 from Cárdenas to Colesio where you cross the Carretera Central; the town is situated a further 8km to the southwest of Colesio. A taxi from Cárdenas (25 minutes) should cost USD$20 to USD$25 – bargain hard.

For cyclists, it makes for a pleasant day-ride from Cárdenas (42km out-and-back) or, if you're fit, Varadero town (80km out-and-back).

PENÍNSULA DE ZAPATA

POP 10,000

A vast, virtually uninhabited swampy wilderness spanning the entirety of southern Matanzas, the 4520-sq-km Península de Zapata quickens the pulses of wildlife-watchers and divers alike with the country's most important bird species and some of the most magical offshore reef diving secreted in its humid embrace. Most of the peninsula is a protected zone, safeguarded nationally as the Gran Parque Natural Montemar, and internationally as the Ciénaga de Zapata Unesco Biosphere Reserve.

The sugar-mill town of Australia in the northeast of the peninsula marks the main access point to the park. Just south of here is one of the region's big tourist money-spinners, the cheesy yet oddly compelling Boca de Guamá, a reconstructed Taíno village.

The road hits the coast at Playa Larga, home to the peninsula's best beaches, at the head of the Bahía de Cochinos (Bay of Pigs) where propaganda billboards still laud Cuba's historic victory over the *Yanquis* in 1961.

Central Australia

No, you haven't just arrived Down Under. About 1.5km south of the Autopista Nacional, on the way to Boca de Guamá, is the large disused Central Australia sugar mill, originally built in 1862, now home to a small museum, along with a rather absurd rural 'farm.' It's a viable lunch stop on the way to Playa Girón or Cienfuegos.

The concrete memorials lining the road to the Bahía de Cochinos mark the spots where defenders were killed in 1961.

During the 1961 Bay of Pigs invasion, Fidel Castro had his headquarters in the former office of this sugar mill, but since 2001 the building has been devoted to a small revolutionary museum (USD$1; ⊙ 9am-5pm Tue-Sat). You can see the desk and phone from where Fidel commanded his forces, along with other associated memorabilia. Outside is the wreck of an invading aircraft shot down by Fidel's troops.

The sugar mill, founded in 1862, was considered revolutionary long before 1961. In 1869 it became the first mill in western Cuba to join the independence cause, four months after Céspedes' Grito de Yara. It ultimately freed its own enslaved people in 1883, three years before slavery was abolished in Cuba.

THE US AND THE BAY OF PIGS

What the Cubans call Playa Girón, the rest of the world has come to know as the Bay of Pigs 'fiasco,' a disastrous attempt by the Kennedy administration to invade Cuba and overthrow Fidel Castro.

Conceived in 1959 by the Eisenhower administration and headed up by deputy director of the CIA, Richard Bissell, the plan to initiate a program of covert action against the Castro regime was given official sanction on March 17, 1960. There was but one proviso: no US troops were to be used in combat.

The CIA modeled their operation on the 1954 overthrow of the left-leaning government of Jacobo Árbenz in Guatemala. However, by the time President Kennedy was briefed on the proceedings in November 1960, the project had mushroomed into a full-scale invasion backed by a 1400-strong force of CIA-trained Cuban exiles and financed with a military budget of US$13 million.

Activated on April 15, 1961, the invasion was a disaster from start to finish. Intending to wipe out the Cuban Air Force on the ground, US planes painted in Cuban Air Force colors (and flown by Cuban-exile pilots) missed most of their intended targets. Castro, who had been forewarned of the plans, had scrambled his air force the previous week. Hence, when the invaders landed at Playa Girón two days later, Cuban Sea Furies (light aircraft) were able to promptly sink two of the US supply ships and leave a force of 1400 men stranded on the beach.

To add insult to injury, a countrywide Cuban rebellion that had been much touted by the CIA never materialized. Meanwhile a vacillating Kennedy told Bissell he would not provide the marooned exile soldiers with US air cover.

Abandoned on the beaches, without supplies or military back-up, the invaders were doomed. There were 114 killed in skirmishes and a further 1189 captured. The prisoners were returned to the US a year later in return for US$53 million worth of food and medicine.

The Bay of Pigs failed due to a multitude of factors. First, the CIA had overestimated the depth of Kennedy's personal commitment and had made similarly inaccurate assumptions about the strength of the fragmented anti-Castro movement inside Cuba. Second, Kennedy himself, adamant all along that a low-key landing should be made, had chosen a site on an exposed strip of beach close to the Zapata swamps. Third, no one had given enough credit to the political and military know-how of Fidel Castro or to the extent to which the Cuban Intelligence Service had infiltrated the CIA's supposedly covert operation.

The consequences for the US were far-reaching. 'Socialism or death!' a defiant Castro proclaimed at a funeral service for seven Cuban 'martyrs' on April 16, 1961. The revolution had swung irrevocably toward the Soviet Union.

The museum and its monuments act as a twin to the much better Museo de Playa Girón (p236).

A favorite with Guamá-bound tour buses, **Pío Cuá** (Carretera de Playa Larga Km 8; meals USD$8-20; ⊙11am-5pm; P) is set up for big groups, but retains fancy decor with lots of stained glass. Prawn, lobster and chicken meals are reasonably good, but not spectacular. It's 8km from the Autopista Nacional turnoff, heading south from Australia.

❶ Getting There & Away

Your transport options when coming to Central Australia are the daily Víazul (www.viazul.com) buses to Havana and Cienfuegos/Trinidad. With an engaging smile, Víazul drivers running the Autopista Nacional route between Havana and the

east will stop at the **La Finquita** (☑ 45-91-32-24; Autopista Nacional Km 142; ⊙ 9am-5pm Mon-Sat, 8am-noon Sun) information center, plonking you around 2km from Jagüey Grande (north) and Australia (south). (Note that you'll probably be charged the Playa Larga fare to La Finquita.)

Short of Víazul, you'll need your own wheels or a taxi.

Boca de Guamá

Boca de Guamá may be a tourist creation, but as resorts around here go it's among the more imaginative. Situated about halfway between the Autopista Nacional at Jagüey Grande and the famous Bahía de Cochinos, it takes its name from native Taíno chief Guamá, who made a last stand against the

Spanish in 1532 (in Baracoa). The big attraction is the boat trip through mangrove-lined waterways and across Laguna del Tesoro (Treasure Lake) to a 'recreation' of a Taíno village. Fidel once holidayed here and had a hand in developing the Taíno theme. You'll struggle to draw parallels with pre-Columbian Cuba, however: raucous tour groups and even louder reggaeton music welcome your voyage back in time. Arranged around the dock the boats depart from are a cluster of restaurants, expensive snack bars and a crocodile farm. The palm-dotted grounds make a pleasant break from the surrounding swampy heat.

◎ Sights

Laguna del Tesoro LAKE
This lake is 5km east of Boca de Guamá via the Canal de la Laguna, accessible only by boat. On the far (east) side of the 92-sq-km body of water is a tourist resort named Villa Guamá, built to resemble a Taíno village, on a dozen small islands.

A sculpture park next to the mock village has 32 life-size figures of Taíno villagers in a variety of idealized poses. The lake is called 'Treasure Lake' due to a legend about some treasure the Taíno supposedly threw into the water just prior to the Spanish conquest (not dissimilar to South American El Dorado legends). The lake is stocked with largemouth bass, so fishers frequently convene.

Criadero de Cocodrilos CROCODILE FARM
(☑45-91-56-66; Carretera a Playa Larga; adult/child incl drink USD$5/3; ⊙9:30am-5pm) ∅ This highly successful crocodile-breeding facility, run by the Ministerio de la Industria Pesquera, straddles the road as you come into Boca de Guamá from the Autopista. On the right-hand side of the road is the actual breeding facility (tours available), which is more interesting if you want to learn a little about the reptilian beasts. On the left, next to the Guamá boat launch, is a kind of mini-zoo where you can watch a daily feeding show.

Two species of crocodiles are raised here: the native and endangered *Crocodylus rhombifer* (*cocodrilo* in Spanish, or Cuban crocodile), and the *Crocodylus acutus* (*caimán* in Spanish), which is found throughout the tropical Americas.

Prior to the establishment of this program in 1962 (considered the first environmental protection act undertaken by the revolutionary government), these two species of marsh-dwelling crocodiles were almost extinct.

The breeding has been so successful that in the adjacent Boca de Guamá complex you can buy stuffed baby crocodiles or dine, legally, on crocodile steak.

If you buy anything made from crocodile leather at Boca de Guamá, be sure to ask for an invoice (for the customs authorities) proving that the material came from a crocodile farm and not wild crocodiles. A less controversial purchase would be one from the site's **Taller de Cerámica** (⊙9am-6pm Mon-Sat).

⌇ Sleeping & Eating

Villa Guamá CABIN $$
(☑45-91-55-51; r half-board USD$60; ✳✳) This place was built in 1963 on the east side of the Laguna del Tesoro, about 8km from Boca de Guamá by boat (cars can be left at the crocodile farm; USD$1). The 50 thatched *cabañas* (cabins) with bath and TV are on piles over the shallow waters.

The six small islands bearing the units are connected by wooden footbridges to other islands with a bar, cafe, overpriced restaurant and a swimming pool containing chlorinated lake water. Breakfast and dinner are included in the room price; the 20-minute ferry transfer (adult/child USD$12/6) isn't.

ⓘ PENINSULA SHUTTLE SERVICE

Complementing the Havana–Cienfuegos–Trinidad Víazul bus (www.viazul.com), which runs through the Zapata Peninsula – but with a history of altering (or canceling) its schedule – there is a twice-daily hop-on/hop-off shuttle bus linking all of the area's key sights. The service starts at Hotel Playa Girón at 8:30am, heads out to Caleta Buena and then back past Punta Perdiz, Cueva de los Peces and Hotel Playa Larga to Boca de Guamá at 10am. The shuttle then leaves Boca de Guamá at 11am for the reverse journey. The service is repeated in the afternoon with departure times of 2pm from Hotel Playa Girón and 4pm from Boca de Guamá. A ticket for the day costs USD$3 per person.

Schedules are subject to change, so check when you arrive in the destination.

Restaurante El Colibrí CUBAN **$$**
(set meals USD$12-15; ☺9:30am-5pm; ℗) Basic restaurant at the boat dock for Villa Guamá, frequented by swarms of tourists bused in from Varadero. The house specialty is crocodile steak made using the locally (and legally) farmed reptiles.

❶ Getting There & Away

The daily Havana–Cienfuegos–Trinidad Víazul (www.viazul.com) bus runs through the Zapata Peninsula; ask the driver if he will leave you at the Boca de Guamá ferry dock. It's not an official stop so you'll probably have to pay Playa Larga fares.

You can also travel on the daily hop-on/hop-off shuttle bus (USD$3 per day) between Boca de Guamá and all points south to Caleta Buena (total time 2½ hours). It stops in the car park by the ferry dock.

Otherwise, it's your own wheels all the way.

❶ Getting Around

A passenger ferry (adult/child USD$12/6, 20 minutes) departs Boca de Guamá for Villa Guamá – across Laguna del Tesoro – four times a day. Speedboats depart more frequently and whisk you across to the pseudo-indigenous village in just 10 minutes any time during the day for USD$12 per person round trip (with 40 minutes' waiting time at Villa Guamá, two-person minimum). In the morning you can allow yourself more time on the island by going one way by launch and returning by ferry.

Gran Parque Natural Montemar

The largest *ciénaga* (swamp) in the Caribbean, Ciénaga de Zapata is protected on multiple levels as the Gran Parque Natural Montemar, a Unesco Biosphere Reserve and a Ramsar Convention Site. Herein lies one of Cuba's most diverse ecosystems, a steamy mix of wildlife-rich wetlands and briny salt flats. Crowded onto a vast, practically uninhabited peninsula (essentially two swamps divided by a rocky central tract) are 14 different vegetation formations including mangroves, wood, dry wood, cactus, savannah, selva and semideciduous. The extensive salt pans and marshes make Zapata the best birdwatching spot in Cuba, as well as a haven for crocodiles, and an excellent spot for catch-and-release fishing.

The main industry today is tourism, and ecotourists are arriving in increasing numbers to take advantage of several expertly led excursions. Access is only possible with a guide.

❶ INSECT REPELLENT

Insect repellent is absolutely essential on the peninsula and while Cuban repellent is available locally, it's like wasabi on sushi for the ravenous buggers here.

🏃 Activities

There are seven main excursions into Gran Parque Natural Montemar, with a focus on birdwatching. Itineraries are flexible.

Transport is not usually laid on and is best to arrange beforehand.

Activities and transport options can be discussed at Playa Larga's **National Park Office** (☎45-98-72-49; ☺8am-4:30pm) or La Finquita (p231), at the Playa Larga turnoff on the Autopista Nacional.

Birdwatching

The park is *the* place to come to see *zunzuncitos* (bee hummingbirds), Cuban emerald hummingbirds, cormorants, cranes, ducks, flamingos, hawks, herons, ibis, owls, parrots, partridges and *tocororos* (Cuba's national bird, the Cuba trogon). Numerous migratory birds from North America winter here, making November to April prime birdwatching season.

★**Reserva de Bermejas** BIRDWATCHING
(per person USD$15) This is, arguably, Cuba's best birding trip, which takes you with a qualified park ornithologist around the Reserva de Bermejas. Here, it is possible to see an astounding 21 of Cuba's 28 endemic bird species including the prized *ferminia* (Zapata wren), *cabrerito de la ciénaga* (Zapata sparrow) and *gallinuela de Santo Tomás* (Zapata rail). Inquire at the National Park Office or ask around Playa Larga for a private guide. Reserve four hours for the 3km walk.

Transport to and from the reserve from the Playa Larga park office should cost between USD$40 and USD$45 plus waiting time.

Laguna de las Salinas BIRDWATCHING
(per person USD$15) One of the most popular excursions. Large numbers of migratory waterfowl can be seen here from November to April: picture 10,000 pink flamingos at a time, plus 190 other feathered species. The road to Las Salinas passes through forest, swamps and lagoons (where aquatic birds can be observed). Guides (and vehicle) are mandatory to explore the refuge.

The 22km trip lasts over four hours.

Cayo Venado is an optional extension of the Las Salinas excursion (two hours extra), where you'll be transported by boat to said cayo for a lowdown on the exotic fauna and the birdlife that call it home.

Book a day in advance through the National Park Office (p233). A car and driver costs around USD$35 extra.

Chino Zapata
BIRDWATCHING

(☑ 5-253-9004, 45-98-75-45; www.cubabirdguide.com; per person USD$10-20) Garnering a reputation as the Zapata Peninsula's most knowledgeable resident ornithologist, Orestes Martínez (aka 'El Chino') is one of Cuba's top bird guides. His personalized ornithological forays into the area are highly rewarding. He runs a casa particular (private homestay) near Playa Larga.

Santo Tomás
OUTDOORS

(per person USD$20) This trip, available December through April, begins 30km west of Playa Larga in the Gran Parque's only real settlement (Santo Tomás) and proceeds along a tributary of the Hatiguanico – walking or boating, depending on water levels. It's a good option for birdwatchers.

Río Hatiguanico
BIRDWATCHING

(per person USD$15) Switching from land to boat, this three-hour 14km river trip runs through the densely forested northwestern part of the peninsula. You'll have to dodge branches at some points, while at others the river opens out into a wide delta-like estuary. Birdlife is abundant and you may also see turtles and crocodiles. You need independent transport to cover the 90km to the start point.

Fishing

Aspiring fishers can arrange fly-fishing from canoes or (due to the shallowness of the water) on foot at either Las Salinas (p233) or Río Hatiguanico. Ask at La Finquita (p231) or just turn up if you have your own gear. Between them the two locations offer Cuba's best angling: Las Salinas has excellent fishing; Río Hatiguanico is great for tarpon. *Palometa*, *sábalo* (prochilos) and *robalo* (snook), as well as bonefish, also thrive.

Hiking

Sendero Enigma de las Rocas
HIKING

(per person USD$15) Excellent park guides and an abundance of wildlife and ecosystems make this 2km hike a kind of *Blue Planet* documentary in miniature. In a fascinating

three hours you'll likely see snakes, screech owls, bats, crocodiles and an array of birdlife. At the turnaround point you'll be invited to jump off a modestly high cliff into a refreshing *cenote* (sinkhole).

The trip starts in the village of Playa Girón, from where you'll be escorted in a horse and cart for 4km to the start point. Between May and October, bring plenty of repellent as the mosquitoes are brutal.

Excursions can be booked through the National Park Office (p233) and at most of Playa Girón's casas particulares.

ℹ Information

The National Park Office (p233) for Gran Parque Natural Montemar is on the northern edge of Playa Larga and can arrange guided trips, but not the vehicles to do them in. The Playa Larga or Girón hotels can also arrange tours, as can many of the casas particulares (private homestays) in the village of Caletón by Playa Larga.

ℹ Getting There & Away

Public transport to Gran Parque Natural Montemar only runs as far as Playa Larga: to see anything of the *ciénaga* (swamp) proper you'll need to come here as part of a tour, or with your own wheels.

When available, cars can be rented from **Cubacar** (☑ 45-98-41-26; Villa Playa Girón; ☉ 9am-5pm) in Playa Girón. Chauffeur-driven 4WDs usually congregate opposite the National Park Office (p233) in the mornings.

Playa Larga

Playa Larga, several kilometers south of Boca de Guamá at the head of the Bahía de Cochinos (Bay of Pigs), was one of two beaches invaded by US-backed exiles on April 17, 1961 (although Playa Girón, 35km further south, saw far bigger landings). Nowadays, it's the best base for exploring the Zapata Peninsula, Cuba's largest wilderness area, and is also known for its diving (although Playa Girón makes a better base for the latter activity). There's a cheapish resort here, a scuba-diving center, and a liberal smattering of casas particulares (private homestays) in the adjacent village of Caletón, which also sports a lovely palm-fringed beach.

🏃 Activities

Club Octopus International Diving Center
DIVING

(☑ 45-98-72-25, 45-98-72-94) The Club Octopus International Diving Center is 200m west of Villa Playa Larga. Most of the actual dive sites are further south in and around Playa Girón. From USD$25 for one immersion.

Sleeping & Eating

There's a dowdy **hotel** (☑ 45-98-72-94; s/d incl breakfast USD$67/100; P ✳ ☎) abutting Playa Larga, but you're far better off heading to one of the dozens of friendly casas particulares in the adjacent village of Caletón. Unlike Playa Girón, further down the coast, Caletón's casas are practically on the beach.

Several good restaurants have popped up in Caletón in recent years. Most of them are *ranchónes* specializing in seafood (including local crab) and rum-based cocktails.

Casa Kirenia   CASA PARTICULAR $
(☑ 45-98-73-68; kirenia800320.roque@nauta.cu; r USD$25-30; P ✳ ☎) OK, it's not abutting the beach, but the modernity, cleanliness and attention to detail at this bright orange house make up for the short walk. Three spotless rooms are light, with plenty of space to spread out, there's excellent food and drink, and the hosts are extremely welcoming (and can help organize local nature activities).

Casa Zuleida & Viñola   CASA PARTICULAR $
(☑ 45-98-75-99; r with/without sea view USD$45/35; ✳) Reap the benefits of being right on the beach at this place in rambling Caletón. Five rooms (a couple with sea views) cater for all your basic needs, but you'll probably spend more time on the beach-facing patio admiring swaying palms and tangerine sunsets.

Hostal Enrique   CASA PARTICULAR $
(☑ 45-98-74-25; enriqueplayalarga@gmail.com; r USD$25-40; ✳) Located smack in the middle of the village of Caletón is this humongous place with 14 rooms, all with private bathrooms. There's a dining area (serving large portions of food), a rooftop terrace and a path from the back garden leading to the often-deserted Caletón beach. Enrique can help arrange diving and birdwatching at distinctly cheaper prices than the hotels hereabouts.

Getting There & Away

There's a thrice-daily Víazul (www.viazul.com) bus from Havana that heads onto Playa Girón (USD$6, 30 minutes), Cienfuegos (USD$7, two hours) and Trinidad (USD$12, 2¾ hours). It stops at the main road junction, 400m west of the Villa Playa Larga. There's only one daily bus in the opposite direction toward Havana (USD$13, 2½ hours), and another to Varadero (USD$10, 2½ hours). Note: buses are usually full. Book in advance, preferably at the ticket office in Playa Girón.

Bahía de Cochinos

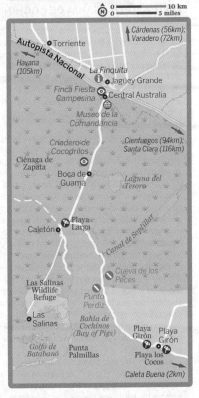

Playa Girón

The sandy arc of Playa Girón nestles peacefully on the eastern side of the infamous Bahía de Cochinos (Bay of Pigs), backed by one of those gloriously old-fashioned Cuban villages where everyone knows everyone else. Notorious as the place where the Cold War almost got hot, the beach is actually named for a French pirate, Gilbert Girón, who met his end here by decapitation in the early 1600s at the hands of embittered locals. In April 1961 it was the scene of another botched raid, the ill-fated, CIA-sponsored invasion that tried to land on these remote sandy beaches in one of modern history's classic David-and-Goliath struggles. Lest we forget, there are still plenty of propaganda-spouting billboards dotted around rehashing the 'Yanqui defeat.'

These days Girón, with its clear Caribbean waters and precipitous offshore drop-off, is one of the best places in Cuba to go diving and snorkeling.

DON'T MISS

DIVING IN THE BAHÍA DE COCHINOS

While the Isla de la Juventud and María la Gorda head most Cuban divers' wish lists, the Bahía de Cochinos has some equally impressive sub-aquatic action. The diving spectacle is courtesy of a huge underwater drop-off running 30m to 40m offshore for over 30km from Playa Larga down to Playa Girón, a fantastic natural feature that has created a 300m-high coral-encrusted wall with amazing swim-throughs, caves, gorgonians and marine life. Even better, the proximity of this wall to the coastline means that the region's 30-plus dive sites can be easily accessed without a boat – you just glide out from the shore. Good south-coast visibility stretches from 30m to 40m and there is a handful of wrecks scattered around.

Organizationally, **Playa Girón** is well set up with highly professional instructors bivouacked at five different locations along the coast. Generic dive prices (immersion USD$25, night dive USD$35, five dives USD$100 or open-water course USD$365) are some of the cheapest in Cuba. Snorkeling is USD$5 per hour.

The **International Scuba Center** (📞 45-98-41-10, 45-98-41-18; Villa Playa Girón), at Villa Playa Girón, is the main diving headquarters here, but you can also organize dives from casas particulares (private homestays). Casa Julio y Lidia (see next page) and Casa Ivette y Ronel in Playa Girón are both run by passionate divers.

A special diver's bus picks up tourists at locations in Playa Girón every morning and heads to **Playa el Tanque**, the best nearby dive spot, on the Playa Larga road: particularly good for learners because you start off in shallow water.

Eight kilometers southeast of Playa Girón is **Caleta Buena** (USD$15; ⊙9:30am-4pm), a lovely sheltered cove perfect for snorkeling and kitted out with another diving office. Black coral ridges protect several sinkholes and underwater caves teeming with the oddly shaped sponges for which the area is renowned: a great opportunity for speleo-scuba diving! Because saltwater meets freshwater, fish here are different from other sites. Admission to the beach is USD$15 and includes an all-you-can-eat lunch buffet and open bar. Beach chairs and thatched umbrellas are spread along the rocky shoreline. Snorkel gear is USD$3.

More underwater treasures can be seen at the **Cueva de los Peces** (⊙8am-5pm), a *cenote* (sinkhole) about 70m deep on the inland side of the road, almost exactly midway between Playa Larga and Playa Girón. There are lots of bright, tropical fish, plus you can explore back into the darker, spookier parts of the *cenote* with snorkel/dive gear (bring torches). There's a handy restaurant and an on-site dive outfit.

Just beyond the Cueva de los Peces is **Punta Perdiz** (incl lunch USD$15; ⊙10am-5pm), another phenomenal snorkeling/scuba-diving spot with the wreck of a US landing craft (scuttled during the Bay of Pigs invasion) to explore. The shallow water is gemstone-blue here and there's good snorkeling right from the shore. There's a smaller on-site diving concession. Nonwater-based activities include volleyball and chances to play the amiable custodians at dominoes. Beware the swarms of mosquitoes and *libélulas* (enormous dragonflies).

👁 Sights

Museo de Playa Girón　　　MUSEUM
(USD$2, camera USD$1; ⊙8am-5pm) This exceedingly well-kept museum evokes a tangible sense of the history of the famous Cold War episode that unfolded within rifle-firing distance of this spot in 1961. Sitting halfway down the access road to the Villa Playa Girón, it offers two rooms of artifacts from the Bay of Pigs skirmish plus numerous photos with (some) bilingual captions.

The mural of victims and their personal items is harrowing and the tactical genius of the Cuban forces comes through in the graphic depictions of how the battle unfolded. A British Hawker Sea Fury aircraft used by the Cuban Air Force is parked outside the museum along with a couple of Russian tanks used in the battle.

🏃 Activities

All things considered Girón could offer the best diving in Cuba. The reasons? Well, a) it's relatively close to Havana; b) most of the dives are directly offshore and don't need boat transfers; c) at USD$25 an immersion, the diving is cheap; d) water clarity is excellent; and e) there's a plenitude of good diving instructors, many of whom also rent rooms.

Girón is also a good place to learn to dive. Besides good instructors, initiation courses for beginners in the ocean only cost USD$35 (including one immersion). Beginner dives take you to a depth of between 7m and 10m.

🛏 Sleeping & Eating

Aside from Villa Playa Girón (a so-so hotel popular with the diving fraternity), the small settlement of Playa Girón is awash with superb private houses – practically every house in the village now rents rooms and many throw in useful extras like free bikes and snorkel masks.

★ Casa Julio y Lidia CASA PARTICULAR $
(🖉45-98-41-35; lidia.aguero@nauta.cu; r USD$30; 🅿❄) Owner Julio is the most experienced dive instructor hereabouts, meaning his modern house with three plush rooms is a useful option for divers. The huge rooms are equipped with some of the most comfortable beds and softest sheets in Cuba. The food is spectacular. It's the second house on the left as you're entering Playa Girón from the west.

★ Hostal Luis CASA PARTICULAR $
(🖉45-98-42-58; hostalluis@yahoo.es; r incl breakfast USD$30; 🅿❄) The second house on the road to Cienfuegos is Playa Girón's premier casa, and arguably one of Cuba's best. Set back from the road with two stone lions guarding the gate, Luis and his wife offer eight spotless rooms meticulously cleaned daily and adorned with fresh flowers. Breakfast is a feast and super-professional staff can help organize local activities.

Casa Ivette y Ronel CASA PARTICULAR $
(🖉45-98-41-29; ivette.marquez@nauta.cu; r USD$25-30; 🅿❄🛜) The first house on the left (if entering Playa Girón from the west), Ivette and Ronel's benefits from having a casa-owner-cum-dive-master at the helm. There are five rooms and a small animal farm out back with *jutías* (tree rats) and crocs. The use of bicycles and snorkel masks is included in the room rate – both pretty useful in these parts.

KS Abella CASA PARTICULAR $
(🖉45-98-43-83; r USD$25-30; ❄) Host Ricardo is a former chef at Villa Playa Girón, now trying out his seafood specialties on his casa

guests. The two-bedroom abode (with roof terrace) is the impressive brightly painted bungalow a few houses up the Cienfuegos road from the junction with the road to Playa Larga. Ricardo speaks fluent English.

Villa Playa Girón RESORT $$
(🖉45-98-41-10; s/d all-inclusive USD$52/80; 🅿❄🛜) On a beach imbued with historical significance lies this pretty mediocre hotel. The preserve of divers and holidaying Cubans these days, the villa has clean, basic rooms that are often a long walk from the main block. The beach is a 50m dash away, though its allure has been spoiled somewhat by the construction of a giant wave-breaking wall.

★ Girón Especial CUBAN $
(🖉5-867-1085; mains USD$4-7; ⊘10am-10:30pm) The best in a quartet of private places in Playa Girón, this family-run joint, known colloquially as Carlito's, serves what might be the cheapest lobster in Cuba – USD$7 for a generous portion served with mini-mountains of rice, root veg and salad. Crab, dorado and prawns also available. Served under a thatched shade behind a one-story family home.

ℹ Information

There's a **Cadeca** (⊘8:30am-noon & 12:30-4pm Mon-Fri, 8:30-11:30am Sat) bank opposite the Museo de Playa Girón, but no ATM.

ℹ Getting There & Away

There are two daily Víazul (www.viazul.com) buses to Havana (USD$13, 3¼ hours), three departures to Cienfuegos (USD$7, 1½ hours) and one to Varadero (USD$10, three hours). Book at least a day in advance. The **bus stop** and ticket office are opposite the Museo de Playa Girón.

ℹ Getting Around

BICYCLE

Many of the local casas particulares (private homestays) rent (or lend) basic bikes; they're perfectly adequate for the Playa Girón area's flat roads and a great way to link with the various beaches and dive sites, most of which are less than 10km away.

CAR & MOTORCYCLE

Cubacar (p234) has a car-rental office on the approach road to Villa Playa Girón, but is often lacking automobiles. Alternatively, you can hire a moped for USD$25 per day.

East of Caleta Buena, the coastal road toward Cienfuegos is not passable in a normal car; backtrack and take the inland road via Rodas.

1. Playa Varadero 2. Playa Sirena 3. Playa Larga 4. Playa Maguana

Cuba's Best Beaches

Playa Varadero

Measuring 21km end-to-end and consisting of an unbroken ribbon of soft white sand, the beach at Varadero (p205) might just qualify as one of the best in the world. Granted, giant all-inclusive resorts have laid claim to a lot of it, but there's still a broad public section abutting Varadero town at its southwestern end.

Playa Sirena

Lapped by the protected waters of the Caribbean off Cuba's south coast, the Sirena (p173) – one in a trio of interconnected beaches on Cayo Largo del Sur – is wide enough to host a football match and soft enough to make a bed on. For refreshment, there's a humble thatched bar-restaurant but, mercifully, no hotels.

Playa Las Tumbas

Hate resorts? Need splendid isolation? Come to Las Tumbas (p199) on Cuba's western tip, protected inside the Guanahacabibes National Park and located 100km from the nearest town. Your only company: crabs and the odd sand flea.

Playa Larga

Something of an unsung bijou on Cuba's southern underbelly, Larga (p234) is abutted by a ramshackle Cuban village offering a medley of homestays, barbecued beach-shack food and a big dollop of local ambience. There's good swimming, ample palm trees and fine wildlife-watching nearby.

Playa Maguana

Way out east, just north of the magic realist town of Baracoa, Maguana (p453) is a paradisaical beach washed by choppy seas where locals roll in with their old American cars and beat boxes for a slice of weekend action. Join the party.

AT A GLANCE

POPULATION
407,000

HIGHEST POINT
Pico de San Juan:
1156m

BEST THEATER
Teatro Tomás Terry
(p253)

**BEST
ARCHITECTURAL
RESTORATION**
Palacio Barón Balbín
(p248)

**BEST WATERSIDE
RESTAURANT**
Restaurante Villa
Lagarto (p251)

WHEN TO GO

Nov–Apr
High season with
relatively cooler
temperatures and
less rain. Beach
lovers and divers hit
the Caribbean coast.

May–Jul
Low season when
mostly locals go on
holiday.

Aug–Oct
Wet-season road
conditions make
travel tougher at
El Nicho. Expect
fewer tourists and
cheaper hotel rates.

El Nicho (p257)
RPHSTOCK/SHUTTERSTOCK ©

Cienfuegos Province

B *ienvenue* (welcome) to Cienfuegos, Cuba's Gallic heart, which sits in the shadow of the crinkled Sierra del Escambray like a displaced île-de-France on Cuba's untamed southern coastline. The French, rather than the Spanish, were the colonizing force in this region, arriving in 1819 and bringing with them the ideas of the European Enlightenment, which they incorporated into their fledgling neoclassical city: the result today is a debonair collection of squares, boulevards and erstwhile mansions.

Beyond the city, the coast is surprisingly underdeveloped, a mini-rainbow of emerald greens and iridescent blues, flecked with coves, caves and coral reefs.

Though ostensibly Francophile and white, Cienfuegos' once-muted African 'soul' gained a mouthpiece in the 1940s with local-born Mambo king Benny Moré and in the Catholic-Yoruba Santería brotherhoods, which still preserve their slave-era traditions in the town of Palmira.

INCLUDES

Cienfuegos Province Highlights

1 Palacio Ferrer (p243)
Viewing the grand eclectic
architecture in Unesco-listed
Cienfuegos from one of its
finest buildings.

2 Palacio de Valle
(p244) Enjoying a perfect
sundowner in an Arabian
Nights palace in Punta
Gorda, the ultimate
expression of Cuban
eclecticism.

3 El Nicho (p257)
Escaping to the jungle-like
landscapes of the Sierra del
Escambray to cool down
underneath an invigorating
waterfall.

4 Palmira (p251) Tracking
the legends of the Santería
religion in this unlikely Afro-
Cuban outpost.

**5 Jardín Botánico
de Cienfuegos** (p246)
Beholding the astounding

collection of plants and trees
at Cuba's oldest botanical
garden.

**6 Castillo de Nuestra
Señora de los Ángeles de
Jagua** (p246) Visiting one of
the only military bastions on
Cuba's south coast.

7 Laguna Guanaroca
(p245) Spotting pink
flamingos and pelicans at
this little-visited protected
area.

History

The first settlers in the Cienfuegos area were
Taínos, who called their fledgling principal-
ity Cacicazgo de Jagua – a native term for
'beauty.' In 1494 Columbus surveyed the
Bahía de Cienfuegos (Cuba's third-largest
bay, with a surface area of 88 sq km) on his
second voyage to the New World, and 14
years later Sebastián de Ocampo stopped by
during his pioneering circumnavigation of
the island. He liked the bay so much he built
a house there.

The pirates followed the explorers: during
the 16th and 17th centuries buccaneering
raids got so bad the Spanish built a bayside
fort, the imposing Castillo de Jagua – one of
the most important military structures in
Cuba.

Cienfuegos

POP 150,500

Cienfuegos has a good pedigree. Immortal-
ized in a song by local musical legend Benny
Moré as the city he liked the best, the so-
called 'Pearl of the South' has long seduced
travelers from Cuba and beyond with its
enlightened French airs and dreamy waterside setting. If Cuba has a Paris, this is most
definitely it.

Arranged around the country's most spectacular natural bay, Cienfuegos is a nautical
city founded in 1819 by French émigrés,
whose homogeneous grid of elegant neoclassical architecture earned it a Unesco
World Heritage site listing in 2005. Geo-
graphically, the city is split into two distinct

parts: the colonnaded central zone with its stately 'Prado' boulevard and salubrious main square, and Punta Gorda, a thin knife of land slicing into the bay crowned with a clutch of outrageously eclectic palaces built by the moneyed classes in the 1920s.

History

Cienfuegos was founded in 1819 by a pioneering French émigré from Louisiana named Don Louis D'Clouet. Sponsoring a scheme to increase the population of whites on the island, D'Clouet invited 40 families from New Orleans and Philadelphia, and Bordeaux in France to establish a fledgling settlement known initially as Fernandina de Jagua. Despite having their initial camp destroyed by a hurricane in 1821, the unperturbed French settlers rebuilt their homes and – suspicious, perhaps, that their first name had brought them bad luck – rechristened the city Cienfuegos after the then governor of Cuba.

With the arrival of the railway in 1850 and the drift west of Cuban sugar growers after the War of Independence (1868–78), Cienfuegos' fortunes blossomed, and local merchants pumped their wealth into a dazzling array of eclectic architecture that harked back to the neoclassicism of their French forefathers.

D-day in Cienfuegos' history came on September 5, 1957, when officers at the local naval base staged a revolt against the Batista dictatorship. The uprising was brutally crushed, but it sealed the city's revered place in revolutionary history.

Modern-day Cienfuegos retains a plusher look than many of its urban counterparts. This is partly due to the investment of much-needed Unesco money into the city, as well as its growing industrial clout and its position as a cruise port that (briefly) welcomed ships from the United States.

◉ Sights

◉ Historic Center

Elegant Paseo del Prado (Calle 37), stretching from the Río el Inglés in the north to Punta Gorda in the south, is the longest street of its kind in Cuba and a great place to see *cienfuegueños* going about their daily business. The boulevard is a veritable smorgasbord of fine neoclassical buildings and pastel-painted columns.

★ Teatro Tomás Terry   THEATER
(Map p248; ☑ 43-51-33-61, 43-55-17-72; Av 56 No 270, btwn Calles 27 & 29; tours USD$2; ⊙9am-6pm) Sharing French and Italian influences, this theater on the northern side of Parque José Martí is grand from the outside (look for the gold-leafed mosaics on the front facade), but even grander within. Built between 1887 and 1889 to honor Venezuelan industrialist Tomás Terry, the 950-seat auditorium is embellished with Carrara marble, hand-carved Cuban hardwoods and whimsical ceiling frescoes.

In 1895 the theater opened with a performance of Verdi's *Aida* and it has witnessed numerous landmarks in Cuban music, as well as performances by the likes of Enrico Caruso and Anna Pavlova, and pulsates with plays and concerts still.

Palacio Ferrer – Museo de las Artes   MUSEUM
(Map p248; Calle 25 No 5401; USD$3; ⊙10am-5:30pm Tue-Sat) FREE On the western side of Parque José Martí, this riveting neoclassical building (1918) was lovingly restored in time for Cienfuegos' 200th anniversary in 2019. Inside art exhibits compete with expensive furnishings spearheaded by Italian marble floors and – most noticeably – a rooftop cupola equipped with a wrought-iron staircase, which you can climb for city and water views.

Other exhibits inside the museum include stories about the house's former owners, its distinguished guests (including opera singer Enrico Caruso) and other Cienfuegos residents such as Benny Moré.

Malecón   WATERFRONT
Keep heading south on Paseo del Prado and the street becomes the Malecón as it cuts alongside one of the world's finest natural bays, offering exquisite vistas. Like all waterside drives (Havana's being the archetype), this area comes alive in the evening when poets come to muse and couples to canoodle.

Statue of Benny Moré   MONUMENT
(Map p248; cnr Av 54 & Calle 37) Before you hit the Malecón, at the intersection of Av 54 and Paseo del Prado you can pay your respects to this life-sized likeness of the Cienfuegos-born musician with his trademark cane.

Cementerio la Reina   CEMETERY
(☑43-52-15-89; cnr Av 50 & Calle 7; ⊙8am-5pm) FREE A listed national monument, the city's oldest cemetery was founded in 1837 and

is lined with the graves of Spanish soldiers who died in the Wars of Independence. This is the only cemetery in Cuba where bodies are interred above ground (in the walls), due to the high groundwater levels. It's an evocative place if you're into graveyards (tours are available). Look for the marble statue called Bella Durmiente: a tribute to a 24-year-old woman who died in 1907 of a broken heart.

Approach is via the slum-like Av 50: a long, hot walk or horse-cart ride passing a sorry-looking collection of trains in the so-called Parque de Locomotivas en route.

Arco de Triunfo   LANDMARK
(Map p248; Calle 25, btwn Avs 56 & 54) Prepare yourself: it's smaller than the one in Paris, but the Arch of Triumph on the western edge of Cienfuegos' serene central park catapults the plaza into the unique category: there is no other construction of its kind in Cuba. Dedicated to Cuban independence, the Francophile monument ushers you through its gilded gateway toward a marble statue of revolutionary and philosopher José Martí.

Palacio de Gobierno   HISTORIC BUILDING
(Map p248; Av 54, btwn Calles 27 & 29) Most of Parque José Martí's south side is dominated by this grandiose, silvery-gray building where the provincial government (Poder Popular Provincial) operates. The palace doesn't allow visitors, but you can steal a look at the palatial main staircase through the front door. It's in wonderful condition. From the outside the giant dome and thick frontal columns are magnificent, even by Cienfuegos standards.

Catedral de la Purísima
Concepción Church   CHURCH
(Map p248; Av 56 No 2902; ☺7am-noon Mon-Fri) On the eastern side of Parque José Martí, Cienfuegos' cathedral dates from 1869 and is distinguished by its French stained-glass windows in an otherwise austere interior that has long been awaiting a thorough restoration. Chinese writing discovered on columns is thought to date from the 1870s.

Colegio San Lorenzo   HISTORIC BUILDING
(Map p248; cnr Av 56 & Calle 29) On the east side of Teatro Café Tomás, this building with its striking colonnaded facade was constructed during the 1920s with funds left by wealthy city patron Nicolás Salvador Acea, whose name also graces one of the city's cemeteries. You can admire it from the outside only.

Casa del Fundador   HISTORIC BUILDING
(Map p248; cnr Calle 29 & Av 54) On the southeastern corner of Parque José Martí stands the city's oldest building, once the residence of city founder Louis D'Clouet and now a souvenir store. El Bulevar (p254), Cienfuegos' quintessential shopping street, heads east from here to link up with Paseo del Prado.

Museo Histórico Naval Nacional   MUSEUM
(Map p248; cnr Av 60 & Calle 21; ☺9am-4:30pm Tue-Sun) **FREE** Close to the railway tracks, five blocks northwest of Parque José Martí, is this crenelated blue and white museum, dating from 1933. It's housed in the former headquarters of the Distrito Naval del Sur, and is approached by a wide drive flanked with armaments dating from different eras. It was here in September 1957 that a group of sailors and civilians staged an unsuccessful uprising against the Batista government. The revolt is the central theme of the modest museum.

Museo Provincial   MUSEUM
(Map p248; cnr Av 54 & Calle 27; USD$2; ☺10am-6pm Tue-Sat, 9am-1pm Sun) Poorly presented, slightly grubby museum on the south side of Parque José Martí that proffers a microcosm of Cienfuegos' history including a few indigenous artifacts. Other random exhibits include frilly furnishings of refined 19th-century French-Cuban society, all of which could do with a more regular appointment with the duster. The once grand upstairs rooms were undergoing restoration at last visit.

◉ Punta Gorda

When the Malecón sea wall runs out, you will know you have landed in Punta Gorda, Cienfuegos' old upper-class neighborhood, characterized by its bright clapboard homes and turreted palaces. Highlighting a 1920s penchant for grandiosity are the cupola-topped Palacio Azul (now the Hostal Palacio Azul) and the Club Cienfuegos, once an exclusive yacht club and now a slightly less exclusive restaurant and activity center. Nearby, an inventive Parque de Esculturas (Map p245; Calle 37 & Av 6) throws some innovative modern sculpture into the mix.

Palacio de Valle   HISTORIC BUILDING
(Map p245; Calle 37, btwn Avs 0 & 2; ☺9:30am-11pm) Just when you thought Cienfuegos' eclectic architecture couldn't get any more

Punta Gorda

Punta Gorda

◉ Sights
1 Centro Recreativo la Punta	A4
2 Palacio de Valle	A3
3 Parque de Esculturas	A3

⊙ Activities, Courses & Tours
4 Marlin Marina Cienfuegos	A3

⊟ Sleeping
5 Ángel y Isabel	A4
6 Casa los Delfines	A4
7 Casa Verde	A3
8 Hostal Palacio Azul	A2
9 Hotel Jagua	A3
10 Perla del Mar	A3
11 Villa Lagarto – Maylin & Tony	A4
12 Vista Al Mar	A3

⊗ Eating
13 Club Cienfuegos	A2
El Marinero	(see 13)
14 Finca del Mar	A1
Palacio de Valle	(see 2)
Restaurante Café Cienfuegos	(see 13)
Restaurante Villa Lagarto	(see 11)

⊙ Drinking & Nightlife
Bar la Terraza	(see 13)

⊕ Entertainment
15 Estadio 5 de Septiembre	B1

eclectic, you reach the southern end of Punta Gorda where, with a sharp intake of breath, you'll stumble upon the impossible-to-classify Palacio de Valle. Built in 1917 by Acisclo del Valle Blanco, a wealthy Spaniard from Asturias, the structure resembles an outrageously ornate Moroccan casbah, but draws on a mad mix of Gothic, Byzantine, *mudéjar* and baroque influences.

Batista planned to convert this colorful riot of tiles, turrets and stucco into a casino, until the Cuban Revolution sent the gamblers back to Vegas. Today it's an (aspiring) upscale restaurant with an inviting terrace bar and plenty of architectural details to admire.

Centro Recreativo la Punta   PARK

(Map p245; ⊙ 9am-10pm, to midnight Sat) Lovers come to watch the sunset amid sea-framed greenery at the gazebo on the extreme southern tip of this park. The bar is also popular with local police officers.

◉ Outside Town

Necrópolis Tomás Acea   CEMETERY

(☑ 43-52-52-57; Av 5 de Septiembre; USD$1; ⊙ 8am-5pm) Perhaps the finest Cuban cemetery outside Havana and Santiago, the Acea is classed as a 'garden cemetery' and is entered through a huge neoclassical pavilion (1926) flanked by 64 Doric columns modeled on the Parthenon in Greece. This cemetery contains a monument to the marine martyrs who died during the abortive 1957 Cienfuegos naval uprising. It's 2km east of the city center along Av 5 de Septiembre.

Laguna Guanaroca   LAKE

(☑ 43-54-81-17; incl tour USD$10; ⊙ 8am-3pm) ✏ Laguna Guanaroca is a mangrove-rimmed saline lake southeast of Cienfuegos. It's second only to Las Salinas on the Península de Zapata as a bird magnet, and is Cienfuegos Province's only *area protegida* (natural protected area). Trails lead to a viewing platform where flamingos, pelicans and *tocororos* (trogons; Cuba's national bird) are regular visitors.

WORTH A TRIP

CASTILLO DE NUESTRA SEÑORA DE LOS ÁNGELES DE JAGUA

Predating the city of Cienfuegos by nearly a century, this **fort** (USD$5; ⊘9am-5pm), to the west of the mouth of Bahía de Cienfuegos, was designed by José Tontete in 1738 and completed in 1745. At the time it was the third most important fortress in Cuba, after those of Havana and Santiago de Cuba.

Extensive renovation in 2010 gave the castle the makeover it sorely needed. In addition to a cracking view of the bay, the castle has a basic museum spread over three levels showcasing its history in a detailed timeline along with old cannons, armaments and engravings. Captions are in Spanish.

Passenger ferries to and from the castle ply the waters to Cienfuegos (CUC$1, 50 minutes) at least daily, leaving Cienfuegos at 8am and 1pm and returning at 10am and 3pm. Another ferry leaves every 30 minutes or so to a landing (p256) just below the Hotel Pasacaballo in Rancho Luna (CUC$0.50, five minutes).

Nestled on a headland below the Jagua fort, **El Pescador** (☑5-312-7736; Jagua; mains USD$8-15; ⊘10am-6pm) is the only eating option for castle visitors. Staff will meet you off the boat, but throw your cynicism aside and take their sales patter seriously. The lightly seasoned seafood served inside an airy, if slightly scruffy, covered terrace surrounded by buoys and fishing nets is perfecto.

Plant life includes pear, lemon and avocado trees, as well as the *güira*, the fruit used to make maracas. Tours take around two hours and include a short hike and a boat trip to the far side of the lake. Arrive early to maximize your chances of seeing a variety of birds.

The reserve entrance is 12km from Cienfuegos, off the Rancho Luna road on the cut-through to Pepito Tey. A taxi there and back with a wait costs around USD$15.

Jardín Botánico de Cienfuegos GARDENS
(Circuito Sur Km 15; USD$2.50; ⊘8am-5pm) 🅿
The 94-hectare botanic garden, 17km east of Cienfuegos, is Cuba's oldest, established in 1901. (Decades later the botanical garden in Havana used its seedlings to found its own green space.) The garden houses 2000 species of trees, including 23 types of bamboo, 65 types of fig and 150 different palms. It was founded by US sugar baron Edwin F Atkins, who initially intended to use it to study different varieties of sugarcane, but instead began planting exotic tropical trees.

You can explore the gardens independently or with a multilingual free guide. If you reserve ahead, you can also partake in a special 7am birdwatching excursion.

To reach the gardens, you'll need your own wheels or a taxi (around USD$20 return with a wait). The cheapest method is to go with an organized excursion; Cubanacán (p255) in Cienfuegos runs trips for USD$10. Drivers coming from Cienfuegos

should turn right (south) at the junction to Pepito Tey.

Juragua Nuclear Power Plant LANDMARK
Across the bay from Cienfuegos with its dome clearly visible from the city is the infamous, but never completed, Juragua nuclear power plant, a planned joint venture between Cuba and the Soviet Union that was conceived in 1976 and incorporated the ominous disused apartment blocks of the adjacent Ciudad Nuclear. Only 288km from the Florida Keys, construction met with strong opposition from the US and was abandoned following the collapse of communism in the former Eastern Bloc. Foreigners can't visit.

🏃 Activities

Marlin Marina Cienfuegos FISHING, SAILING
(Map p245; ☑43-55-16-99; http://nauticamarlin.tur.cu/en; Calle 35, btwn Avs 6 & 8; ⊘11am-8:45pm) Hook up with this 36-berth marina a few blocks north of Hotel Jagua to arrange local bay excursions (USD$12 to USD$16), including a Castillo de Jagua tour and a sunset cruise. You can also book through Cubatur (p255) or Cubanacán (p255).

Hotel La Unión Swimming Pool SWIMMING
(Map p248; cnr Calle 31 & Av 54; nonguest pool access USD$10) Even if you're a nonguest, you can use the beautiful Italianate pool at Hotel La Unión and its adjacent bar. The access fee includes USD$7 worth of food and drink.

✿ Festivals & Events

Benny Moré International Music Festival MUSIC

(☉Dec) This festival remembers the province's biggest all-time hero, singer Benny Moré. In recent years, it has been held annually in December, both in town and in nearby Santa Isabel de las Lajas.

🛏 Sleeping

In contrast to other Cuban cities, where the state-run hotels are often a joke, Cienfuegos has at least five good ones ranging from re-imagined colonial to slickly modern. The casas particulares (rooms in private homes) are equally fitting of the refined bayside setting. Those at Punta Gorda are more removed, generally more atmospheric and pricier.

🏛 Historic Center

★ **Bella Perla Marina** CASA PARTICULAR $

(Map p248; ☑ 43-51-89-91; bellaperlamarina@ yahoo.es; Calle 39 No 5818, cnr Av 60; r/ste USD$30/70; P❋@) Long popular for its city-center location and warm hospitality, Bella Perla is what you might call a 'boutique' private homestay. The house, with two standard rooms and a super-modern rooftop suite, has taken on fortress-like dimensions in recent years with a gorgeous plant-filled terrace crowning everything. Antique beds mix with romantic art and refined chandeliers and a full-sized billiards table.

Owner Waldo is a lover of antiques, old vinyl record players and plenty of facts and figures about the city he likes the best (Cienfuegos).

Hostal Amigos de Barceló CASA PARTICULAR $

(Map p248; ☑ 43-52-53-85; mailebarcelo@yahoo. es; Ave 56A No 4116, btwn Calles 41 & 43; r USD$25-30; ❋🛜) A once tiny house in a Cienfuegos backstreet that has been radically refurbished to include six super-modern rooms and a rooftop terrace bar that might have been flown over from Miami. What hasn't changed is the charm of hostess Mailé who is always wearing a smile and will endeavor to make your stay extra special.

Casa las Golondrinas CASA PARTICULAR $

(Map p248; ☑ 43-51-57-88; drvictor61@yahoo.es; Calle 39, btwn Avs 58 & 60; r USD$25-30; ❋🛜) Run by Dr Victor and his wife, this is a gorgeous renovated colonial house with three

ample rooms. There's a lot of TLC in the restoration, from the colonnaded front room to the long, plant-bedecked roof terrace where guests can relax with food and/or cocktails. The owners also rent good hybrid bikes with gears (USD$15 per day).

Hostal Colonial Pepe & Isabel CASA PARTICULAR $

(Map p248; ☑ 43-51-82-76; hostalcolonialisapepe@ gmail.com; Av 52 No 4318, btwn Calles 43 & 45; r USD$25-35; ❋) Charismatic ex-teacher Pepe greets you with *mucho gusto* at his deceptively large colonial house, which incorporates five modern rooms set around two long, narrow upstairs and downstairs terraces. Each room has a queen bed and an extra pull-down single bed. Two come with an additional living room or kitchen space.

The style is elegant Cienfuegos meets art deco with some modern touches thrown in. The hosts are friendliness personified.

Hostal La Cascada CASA PARTICULAR $

(Map p248; ☑ 43-51-67-39; Calle 39 No 4616, btwn Avs 46 & 48; r USD$25; ❋🛜) Classic family-run place where you can enjoy a welcome cocktail in the lounge, partake in substantial home-cooked breakfasts on the back patio and relax in small but perfectly adequate rooms maintained by ever-smiling hosts. There's reliable wi-fi and a fast laundry service.

Casa Amigos del Mundo CASA PARTICULAR $

(Map p248; ☑ 43-55-55-34; Av 60, btwn Calles 33 & 35; r USD$25; ❋🛜) You'll be *amigos* two sips into your fruity 'welcome drink' at this lovely place with two ground-floor rooms set a long way back from the road here, making them some of the quietest in central Cienfuegos. You can also chill on a secluded patio or inviting roof terrace.

Casa de la Amistad CASA PARTICULAR $

(Map p248; ☑ 43-51-61-43; casaamistad@corre ocuba.cu; Av 56 No 2927, btwn Calles 29 & 31; r USD$25; P❋) Friendship's the word in this venerable colonial house stuffed full of family heirlooms just off Parque José Martí. The senior owners have been renting for eons and have welcomed travelers from all over the world. There are two well-kept rooms, a lovely roof terrace and several resident cats.

Claudio & Ileana CASA PARTICULAR $

(Map p248; ☑ 43-51-97-74; Av 54 No 4121, btwn Calles 41 & 43; r USD$25-30; ❋🛜) At this hospitable house, you'll be looked after by two

Central Cienfuegos

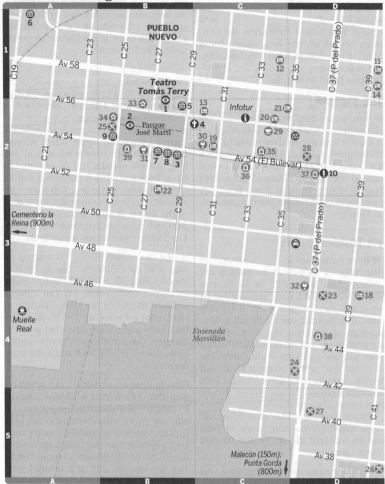

doctors who run a highly polished operation with two bedrooms, air-con units, wi-fi, roof terrace and bags of local information on tap. The bus station and the Unesco-listed city center are both walking distance.

⭐ **Palacio Barón Balbín**   CASA PARTICULAR $$
(Map p248; ☎43-59-60-76; www.hotelpalacio baronbalbin.com; Av 52 No 2706, btwn Calles 27 & 29; r USD$60-80; ❄️🌐) If you've always wanted to stay in a *palacio*, then this incredible melange of baroque and eclecticism built by an Italian architect for a Spanish businessman in 1912 will more than suffice. The house and its five bedrooms are lavishly dec-

orated, yet faithful to the building's original decor, brimming with frescoes, marble, intricate stucco and twisted columns.

You could write a book about the finer details spearheaded by stately bedheads, flamboyant chandeliers, Grecian columns and decorative French furnishings. Some bathrooms even retain their original claw-footed tubs, while the roof terrace, reached by a wrought-iron spiral staircase, is one of the highest points in the city. The meticulous restoration work undertaken by the owners recently claimed second prize in a Cuba-wide competition won by the Palacio del Segundo Cabo (p70) in Havana.

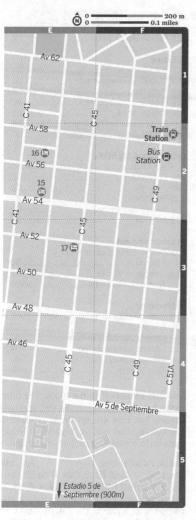

✳@🛜🏊) Barcelona, Naples, Paris? There are echoes of all these cities in this plush, colonial-style hotel with its European aspirations and splendid Italianate pool, fit for a Roman emperor. Tucked away in a maze of marble pillars, antique furnishings and two tranquil inner courtyards are 46 well-furnished rooms with balconies either overlooking the street or a mosaic-lined patio.

You'll also find a gym, hot tub and local art gallery. Service is refreshingly efficient: there's a well-regarded roof terrace that showcases live salsa in the evenings. Breakfast is served in the 1869 restaurant (Map p248; cnr Av 54 & Calle 31; mains USD$10; ☺7:30-9am, noon-2pm & 7-9:45pm).

Hotel Meliá San Carlos HOTEL $$$
(Map p248; ☎43-87-51-00; www.melia.com; Av 56, btwn Calles 33 & 35; s/d USD$193/276; ✳🛜🏊) Providing competition for the long-established Hotel La Unión, this refurbished 1925-era hotel is under the tutelage of the Spanish Meliá chain. While the façade is classic early-20th-century Cienfuegos, the interior flouts more modern lines emboldened with a few historic touches.

The 56 large rooms are spread over six floors and guests can use the pool at the nearby Unión for no charge.

🛏 Punta Gorda

Ángel y Isabel CASA PARTICULAR $
(Map p245; ☎43-51-15-19; Calle 35 No 24, btwn Av 0 & Litoral; r USD$40-50; ✳🛜) Location, location, location. Ángel and Isabel's place is one of many architecturally accomplished abodes on the coveted mansion-studded final stretch of Punta Gorda. At the back of the turreted main house are three rooms facing onto a patio that abuts the bay. It even has its own private little boat dock. Bliss.

Vista Al Mar CASA PARTICULAR $
(Map p245; ☎43-51-83-78; www.vistaalmarcuba.com; Calle 37 No 210, btwn Avs 2 & 4; r USD$25-30; P✳🛜) It really is a *vista al mar* (sea view) – in fact, this highly professional place has even got its own private scoop of beach out back with plunge pool and hammocks. The two rooms have been regularly upgraded, meaning they're clean and modern.

Casa los Delfines CASA PARTICULAR $$
(Map p245; ☎43-52-04-58; Calle 35 No 4e; r USD$50; P✳🛜) Right at the southern tip of Punta Gorda, Casa los Delfines (the dolphins) enjoys all of the benefits of this

Lagarto Ciudad CASA PARTICULAR $$
(Map p248; ☎43-52-23-09; www.lagartociudad.com; Calle 35 No 5607, btwn Avs 56 & 58; r incl breakfast USD$60; ✳@🛜) A classic, eclectic Cienfuegos building dating from the 1920s and stuffed with all the city's calling cards: columns, antique beds, tiled floors, *vitrales* (stained-glass windows) and chandeliers. Name another place where you can get all this for USD$60! The food is good too, and English is spoken. Book online.

⭐**Hotel La Unión** HISTORIC HOTEL $$$
(Map p248; ☎43-55-10-20; www.hotellaunion-cuba.com; cnr Calle 31 & Av 54; s/d USD$182/261;

Central Cienfuegos

idyllic strip, backing directly onto the calm, shallow bay with the Sierra del Escambray beckoning in the distance. The two rooms with minibars are cozy and light-filled, not that you'll be spending much time in them in this setting. Cocktails on the terrace are obligatory.

Villa Lagarto –
Maylin & Tony   CASA PARTICULAR $$
(Map p245; ☑43-51-99-66; villalagartocuba@gmail.com; Calle 35 No 4b, btwn Avs 0 & Litoral; r incl breakfast USD$60; ❋🛜🞉) Established as one of Cienfuegos' leading restaurants, the Lagarto also rents out three rooms cocooned on a delightful terrace, all with king-sized beds, hammocks and glinting views of the bay. While the bayside setting is magnificent, the restaurant gets busy. If it's intimacy and privacy you're after, look elsewhere.

Perla del Mar   BOUTIQUE HOTEL $$$
(Map p245; ☑43-55-10-03; Calle 37, btwn Avs 0 & 2; s/d USD$208/307; ❋@🛜) Opened in the 2010s, Perla del Mar takes the 'historical boutique' hotel theme of the nearby Palacio

Azul and updates it to the 1950s. The nine rooms have a sleek modernist feel, and two alfresco hot tubs are invitingly positioned overlooking the bay. A feature staircase leads up to a made-for-sunbathing terrace.

Hostal Palacio Azul   HOTEL $$$
(Map p245; ☑43-58-28-28; Calle 37 No 201, btwn Avs 12 & 14; s/d USD$208/307; 🅿❋@🛜) A palace posing as a hotel rather than a hotel posing as a palace, the Palacio Azul was one of the first big buildings to grace Punta Gorda on its construction in 1921. Its seven renovated rooms are named after flowers and sparkle with plenty of prerevolutionary character. You'll find an intimate on-site restaurant called El Chelo and a graceful rooftop cupola with splendid views.

Casa Verde   BOUTIQUE HOTEL $$$
(Map p245; ☑43-55-10-03; Calle 37, btwn Avs 0 & 2; s/d USD$208/307; 🅿❋🛜🞉) Casa Verde (yes, it's bottle green from the facade down to the bedspreads) has eight lovely rooms, tall ceilings, gorgeous original tile work and a restaurant overlooking an enclosed pool

that captures a small square of the Bahia de Cienfuegos.

Hotel Jagua
HOTEL **$$$**

(Map p245; ☑ 43-55-10-03; Calle 37 No 1, btwn Avs 0 & 2; s/d USD$172/247; ⓟ✱@🛜🏊) It's not clear what Batista's brother had in mind when he erected this modern concrete giant on Punta Gorda in the 1950s, though making money was probably the prime motivation. Still, the Jagua is a jolly good hotel – airy and surprisingly plush with modern common areas hung with revolving avant-garde art. Upper rooms (there are seven floors) are best.

🍴 Eating

Cienfuegos has some truly memorable dining options, both in setting and food, particularly on Punta Gorda. Not surprisingly, the food has occasional French inflections.

El Louvre Studio Café
CAFE **$**

(Map p248; ☑ 5-895-3839; Calle 25, btwn Avs 54 & 56; snacks USD$2-4; ⏰9am-10pm) At last, a bar in French-accented Cienfuegos that wouldn't look out of place in Paris. The Louvre serves the best coffee in town backed up by well-stuffed baguette-style sandwiches and some neat sweet snacks. Both the location (right on the main square) and the urban bistro ambience enhance the overall flavor.

Restaurante Las Mamparas
INTERNATIONAL **$**

(Map p248; ☑ 43-51-89-92; Calle 37 No 4004, btwn Avs 40 & 42; mains USD$3-6; ⏰noon-10:30pm) The usually busy Mamparas is named for the antique swing doors found in Cuba's colonial houses. There aren't many in evidence here, but the ambience is nice and the food is hearty – mainly Cuban-biased with lashings of rice and beans.

⭐ Doña Nora
INTERNATIONAL **$$**

(Map p248; ☑ 43-52-33-31; Calle 37, btwn Avs 42 & 44; mains USD$6-10; ⏰noon-11pm) Arguably the best of the town's private restaurants, Nora's inhabits a 1st-floor suite and balcony in a typical neoclassical edifice on the Prado. Tying in with the decor, the menu leans toward French with dishes like rabbit in a white wine sauce. Service is highly polished, and a resident saxophonist keeps the mood jazzy most nights.

Paladar Aché
SEAFOOD **$$**

(Map p248; ☑ 43-52-61-73; Av 38, btwn Calles 41 & 43; mains USD$8-12; ⏰noon-10:30pm Mon-Sat) One of only two surviving private restau-

---

OFF THE BEATEN TRACK

PALMIRA

If you're interested in Santería and its affiliated mysteries, stop by Palmira, 8km north of Cienfuegos, a town famous for its Santería *cabildos* (brotherhoods), including the societies of Cristo, San Roque and Santa Barbara. A brief exposé of their raison d'être can be found at the **Museo Municipal de Palmira** (☑43-54-45-33; Villuendas No 41; USD$1; ⏰10am-6pm Tue-Sat, to 1pm Sun) on the main plaza. Cultural agency Paradiso (p255) in Cienfuegos sometimes runs guided tours here, with the opportunity to experience live musical performances. Palmira's main religious festivals are held in early December.

rants from the austere 1990s, Aché has taken on the newer opposition and kept abreast of the pack. Interesting decor includes a fruit-tree-shaded garden with statuettes and rockers and a spectacular mural of Cienfuegos' architectural icons. Spit-roasted pork headlines the comprehensive menu.

Casa Prado Restaurante
INTERNATIONAL **$$**

(Map p248; ☑ 5-262-3858; www.casapradorestaurant.com; Calle 37 No 4626, btwn Avs 46 & 48; mains USD$4-11; ⏰11:30am-10:30pm) A highly economical Cienfuegos restaurant serves what is perhaps the largest and quickest seafood paella you'll see in Cuba. It has a couple of air-conditioned, if windowless, rooms downstairs, plus a roof terrace with occasional live music. Ring the bell on the Prado to get in.

Palacio de Valle
SEAFOOD **$$**

(Map p245; cnr Calle 37 & Av 2; mains USD$7-12; ⏰10am-10pm) The food doesn't have as many decorative flourishes as the eclectic architecture, but the setting is unique and it would be a shame to miss it. Seafood dominates the menu downstairs; if you aren't enthralled, use the rooftop bar here for a pre-dinner cocktail or post-dinner cigar.

Restaurante Villa Lagarto
INTERNATIONAL **$$$**

(Map p245; ☑ 43-51-99-66; Calle 35 No 4b, btwn Av 0 & Litoral; mains USD$10-18; ⏰noon-11pm) The truly wondrous bayside setting at Lagarto (the lizard) is emulated by the food and made even more memorable by some of the fastest yet most discreet service you'll see in Cuba. With its excellent fricassee chicken,

CIENFUEGOS' FRENCH-INFLUENCED ARCHITECTURE

The elegant bayside city of Cienfuegos is Cuba's most Gallic corner. Its innate Frenchness is best exemplified not in its cuisine, where rice and beans still hold sway, but in its harmonious neoclassical architecture. With its wide, paved streets laid out in an almost perfect grid, Cienfuegos' enlightened 19th-century settlers sought to quash slums, promote hygiene and maximize public space using a system of urban planning later adopted by Baron Haussmann in Paris in the 1850s and '60s. Porches, pillars and columns are the city's most arresting architectural features. They're best seen on the 'Prado,' a broad Parisian-style avenue that runs north–south for over 3km, embellished with neat lines of colonnaded facades painted in an array of pastel colors.

Although founded by French émigrés in 1819, most of Cienfuegos' surviving neoclassical buildings date from between 1850 and 1910. By the early 20th century, eclectic features had begun to seep into the architecture. One of the first to break the mold was the Palacio Ferrer in Parque José Martí, built in 1917, whose uncharacteristically decorative cupola started a craze for eye-catching rooftop lookouts.

The flamboyance continued in the 1920s and '30s on the upscale Punta Gorda Peninsula, where filthy-rich sugar merchants invested their profits in ever more ostentatious mansions, turning the neighborhood into a mini-Miami. You can track the evolution as you head south on Calle 37 past the regal Palacio Azul and the wedding-cake Club Cienfuegos to the baroque-meets-Moorish Palacio de Valle, possibly Cuba's most riotously eclectic building.

Cienfuegos' city center was declared a World Heritage site by Unesco in 2005 for both the beauty of its architecture and the progressiveness of its urban planning, which was considered revolutionary in 19th-century Latin America. Money has since gone into livening up the main square, Parque José Martí and its environs, where various interpretive signboards pinpoint the most important buildings.

roast pork and stewed rabbit, Lagarto is at the vanguard of Cuba's flourishing private dining sector and could hold its own in Miami – easily!

Te Quedarás
INTERNATIONAL $$$

(Map p248; ☑ 5-826-1283; Av 54, btwn Calles 35 & 37; mains USD$10-18; ☺ noon-midnight) *Te quedarás* means 'you will stay,' and you probably will if you can bag a seat on the small, narrow wrought-iron balcony overlooking El Bulevar. Sip a shaved-ice daiquiri as the live band breaks into something by Benny Moré (such as 'Te Quedarás,' which was one of his more popular songs).

The restaurant is something of a shrine to Moré, and it has a lovely ambience with a mahogany bar, mambo-era black-and-white photos and those elegant Cienfuegos columns. The food is almost secondary, but it delivers, especially the prawns.

Finca del Mar
SEAFOOD $$$

(Map p245; Calle 35, btwn Avs 18 & 20; mains USD$10-20; ☺ noon-midnight) A fine restaurant by any yardstick in terms of service and food (seafood, including lobster and octopus, is the specialty), which is good, but a little pricey – meaning it's more of a tourist

domain than a place to meet Cubans. That said, you can't fault the ambience: a walled garden near the water with palm trees and a gentle musical accompaniment.

Club Cienfuegos
SEAFOOD $$$

(Map p245; ☑ 43-51-28-91; Calle 37, btwn Avs 10 & 12; set meals USD$20; ☺ noon-10:30pm) When in Cienfuegos, it's practically obligatory to go to Club Cienfuegos, if not for the cuisine (it's state-run) then for the wedding-cake architecture, sunset views and bygone yacht-club ambience.

That said, there are plenty of food options here: Bar la Terraza for cocktails and beer; El Marinero (Map p245; snacks USD$3-7; ☺ noon-3pm), a smart sea-level establishment for snacks and light lunches; and the top-floor Restaurante Café Cienfuegos (Map p245; mains USD$12-17; ☺ 6-10pm), a more refined, adventurous place where the steak or paella almost emulate the food in a private restaurant.

♥ Drinking & Nightlife

Cienfuegos has a pretty suave drinking scene and many of its bars are close to the water. Excellent drinking perches (especially at sunset) can be found at Club Cienfuegos and the upstairs bar of the Palacio de Valle.

Bar la Terraza   BAR

(Map p245; Calle 37, btwn Avs 10 & 12; ⊙11am-10pm, to 2am Sat) At ye olde yacht club, this bar is great for cocktails and beer. Sunsets are sublime.

Teatro Café Terry   CAFE

(Map p248; Av 56 No 2703, btwn Calles 27 & 29; entry after 10pm USD$2; ⊙9am-midnight) Cafe, souvenir stall and nightly music venue, this small space wedged between the Teatro Tomás Terry and the neoclassical Colegio San Lorenzo is the most atmospheric place to flop down and observe the morning exercisers in Parque José Martí. The side patio, covered by a canopy of flowers, reveals its true personality in the evenings, with great live music ranging from *trova* (traditional poetic singing) to jazz.

Bar Terrazas   BAR

(Map p248; cnr Av 54 & Calle 31; ⊙10am-midnight) Re-create the dignified days of old with a mojito upstairs at the Hotel La Unión; live salsa music usually kicks off around 10pm.

Cubita Café   CAFE

(Map p248; Av 56, btwn Calles 33 & 35; ⊙8am-10pm) Strong, thick coffee for trained Cuban palates, or weak lattes for those reared on Starbucks, plus some ultra-sweet cakes.

El Palatino   BAR

(Map p248; Av 54 No 2514, btwn Calles 25 & 27; ⊙noon-midnight) Liquid lunches were invented with El Palatino in mind – a dark-wood bar set in one of the city's oldest buildings on the southern side of Parque José Martí. Impromptu jazz sets sometimes erupt, but prepare to be hit up for payment at the end of song number three.

El Benny   CLUB

(Map p248; Av 54 No 2907, btwn Calles 29 & 31; per couple USD$8; ⊙10pm-3am Tue-Sun) It's difficult to say what the Barbarian of Rhythm, Benny Moré, would have made of this disco-club named in his honor. Bring your dancing shoes, stock up on the rum and Cokes, and come prepared for music that's more techno than mambo.

Tropisur   CLUB

(Map p248; cnr Calle 37 & Av 48; USD$2; ⊙from 9:30pm Thu-Sun) A fiesty open-air venue on the Prado with a traditional Cuban vibe. Known for its cabaret.

☆ Entertainment

Teatro Tomás Terry   LIVE MUSIC, THEATER

(Map p248; ☑ 43-55-17-72, 43-51-33-61; Av 56 No 270, btwn Calles 27 & 29; ⊙box office 11am-3pm) Best theater in Cuba? The Tomás Terry is certainly a contender. The building is worth a visit in its own right, but you'll really get to appreciate this architectural showpiece if you come for a concert or play; the box office also opens 90 minutes before show time.

Centro Cultural
de las Artes Benny Moré   LIVE PERFORMANCE

(Map p248; Av 56, btwn Calles 25 & 27; ⊙10am-11pm) A state-run cultural center with a bar and dancing space within. A noticeboard out front displays what's showing on any given night, though it's mostly traditional music – *son*, jazz, *trova* (traditional poetic singing). Thursdays at 8pm is a weekly homage to *boleros* (traditional ballads).

Jardines de Uneac   LIVE MUSIC

(Map p248; Calle 25 No 5413, btwn Avs 54 & 56; USD$2; ⊙10am-2am) Uneac's a good bet in any Cuban city for live music in laid-back environs. Here it's quite possibly Cienfuegos' best venue, with an outdoor patio hosting Afro-Cuban *peñas* (musical performances), *trova* and top local bands such as the perennially popular Los Novo, two brothers who perform on Sunday nights at the so-called 'Trova de Guardia.'

Estadio 5 de Septiembre   SPECTATOR SPORT

(Map p245; ☑ 43-51-36-44; Av 20, btwn Calles 45 & 51A) From October to April the provincial baseball team – nicknamed Los Elefantes – plays matches here. Its best-ever national series finish was fourth in 1979.

🛍 Shopping

Most of Cienfuegos' shops hug the main drag Av 54 (known colloquially as El Bulevar), which mixes souvenir outlets with traditional shops selling cheap goods in the local currency. A few more esoteric private shops have recently sprung up on Calle 37 (Paseo del Prado).

★ Librería 'La Fernandina'   BOOKS, VINTAGE

(Map p248; ☑ 43-51-70-37; Calle 37 No 4404, btwn Avs 44 & 46; ⊙9am-1pm & 8-10:30pm) Fabulous private bookshop selling literary tomes as well as retro magazines, 1950s curiosities and other pieces of sunken treasure.

Tienda Terry
GIFTS & SOUVENIRS

(Map p248; Av 56 No 270, btwn Calles 27 & 29; ⊙9am-6pm) A good bet for bongos, books and Che Guevara T-shirts.

Casa del Habano 'El Embajador'
CIGARS

(Map p248; cnr Av 54 & Calle 33; ⊙9am-5:30pm Mon-Sat) Offering frigid air-conditioning and hazy views of puffing cigar aficionados, this is where you come for the city's best smokes. Rum and coffee play second and third fiddle.

Maroya Gallery
ARTS & CRAFTS

(Map p248; Av 54, btwn Calles 25 & 27; ⊙9am-5:30pm, to 1pm Sun) Gallery run by Cuban cultural agency that sells folk art. There's usually a small bookstall set up in the street outside.

El Bulevar
STREET

(Map p248; Av 54) The best traffic-free stretch runs from Calle 37 (Paseo del Prado) to Parque José Martí, full of shops of all shapes and sizes.

Librería Dionisio San Román
BOOKS

(Map p248; Av 54 No 3526, cnr Calle 37; ⊙9am-5:30pm Mon-Sat) Well-stocked, modern bookstore with a handful of English tomes. Has poetry readings on the fourth Thursday of every month at 3pm.

❶ Information

INTERNET ACCESS

Hotel La Unión and Parque Martí are popular wi-fi hot spots.

Etecsa Telepunto (Calle 31 No 5402, btwn Avs 54 & 56; per hour USD$1; ⊙8:30am-7pm) Buy scratch cards here.

BENNY MORÉ: PRINCE OF MAMBO & BARBARIAN OF RHYTHM

No one singer encapsulates the gamut of Cuban music more eloquently than Bartolomé 'Benny' Moré. A great-great-grandson of a king of the Congo, Moré was born in the small village of Santa Isabel de las Lajas in Cienfuegos Province in 1919. He gravitated to Havana in 1936, where he earned a precarious living selling damaged fruit on the streets. In the evenings, he played and sang in the smoky bars and restaurants of Habana Vieja's tough dockside neighborhood, where he made just enough money to get by.

His first big break came in 1943 when his velvety voice and pitch-perfect delivery won him first prize in a local radio singing competition and landed him a regular job as lead vocalist for a Havana-based mariachi band called the Cauto Quartet.

His meteoric rise was confirmed two years later when, while singing at a regular gig in Havana's El Temple bar, he was spotted by Siro Rodríguez of the famed Trío Matamoros, then Cuba's biggest son-bolero band. Rodríguez was so impressed that he asked Moré to join the band as lead vocalist for an imminent tour of Mexico. In the late 1940s, Mexico City was a proverbial Hollywood for young Spanish-speaking Cuban performers. Moré was signed up by RCA records and his fame spread rapidly.

Moré returned to Cuba in 1950 a star, and was quickly baptized the Prince of Mambo and the Barbarian of Rhythm. In the ensuing years, he invented a brand-new hybrid sound called batanga and put together his own 40-piece backing orchestra, the Banda Gigante. With the Banda, Moré toured Venezuela, Jamaica, Mexico and the US, culminating in a performance at the 1957 Oscars ceremony. But, the singer's real passion was always Cuba. Legend has it that whenever Benny performed in Havana's Centro Gallego, hundreds of people would fill the surrounding parks and streets to hear him sing.

With his multitextured voice and signature scale-sliding glissando, Moré's real talent lay in his ability to adapt and seemingly switch genres at will. As comfortable with a tear-jerking bolero as he was with a hip-gyrating rumba, Moré could convey tenderness, exuberance, emotion and soul, all in the space of five tantalizing minutes. Although he couldn't read music, Moré composed many of his most famous numbers, including 'Bonito y sabroso' and the big hit 'Que bueno baila usted.' When he died in 1963, more than 100,000 people attended his funeral. No one in Cuba has yet been able to fill his shoes.

Moré fans can follow his legend in the settlement of Santa Isabel de las Lajas, a few kilometers west of Cruces on the Cienfuegos–Santa Clara road, where there's a small museum and a cemetery containing his tomb. Paradiso (p255) in Cienfuegos sometimes run trips here.

MONEY

Banco de Crédito y Comercio (Bandec; cnr Av 56 & Calle 31; ☺9am-5pm Mon-Fri) Has ATMs.

Cadeca (Av 56 No 3316, btwn Calles 33 & 35; ☺8:30am-4pm, to noon Sun) Change cash for convertibles or Cuban pesos.

POST

Post office (Map p248; Av 56 No 3514, btwn Calles 35 & 37; ☺9am-5pm Mon-Fri)

TOURIST INFORMATION

Cubanacán (☑43-55-16-80; Av 54, btwn Calles 29 & 31) First stop for organized excursions.

Cubatur (☑43-55-12-42; Calle 37 No 5399, btwn Avs 54 & 56; ☺9am-6pm Mon-Sat) Organizes excursions.

Infotur (Map p248; ☑43-51-46-53; Calle 56 No 3117, btwn Avs 31 & 33; ☺9am-6pm) Maps and brochures.

Paradiso (☑43-51-18-79; Av 54 No 3301, btwn Calles 33 & 35; ☺9am-6pm Mon-Sat) Cultural tours of the local city and surrounds including to Palmira and San Isabel de las Lajas.

❶ Getting There & Away

AIR

Jaime González Airport (CFG; ☑43-55-22-35; Carretera a Caonao Km 3), 5km northeast of Cienfuegos, receives seasonal international flights from Canada with **Sunwing Airlines** (www.sunwing.ca). There are no connections to Havana.

BUS

Cienfuegos' **bus station** (Map p248; ☑43-51-81-14, 43-51-57-20; Calle 49, btwn Avs 56 & 58) is relatively well organized by Cuban standards. **Víazul** (www.viazul.com) has an office on the lower level (down the stairs and left) that issues tickets; for local buses to Rancho Luna, Santa Isabel de las Lajas and Palmira for USD$1-ish, plus other destinations, check the blackboard on the lower level.

Víazul buses serve the following destinations. Check its website for updates.

Destination	Cost (USD$)	Duration (hr)	Frequency (daily)
Cayo Santa María	16	4¼	1
Havana	20	5	3
Trinidad	6	1½	5
Varadero	16	5	2
Playa Girón	7	1½	3

Varadero buses also call at Santa Clara (USD$6, 1½ hours). The Cayo Santa María bus calls at Santa Clara, Remedios and Caibarién.

To reach other destinations, you have to connect in Trinidad or Havana. Note that when heading to Trinidad from Cienfuegos, buses originating further west may be full.

❶ Getting Around

BOAT

A 120-passenger ferry runs to the Castillo de Jagua (USD$1, 50 minutes) from the **Muelle Real** (Map p248; cnr Av 46 & Calle 25). Take note – this is a Cuban commuter boat, not a sunset cruise. Check at the port for current schedules. It's supposed to run at 8am and 1pm. A smaller ferry (USD$0.50, 10 minutes) makes the short jump across the harbor mouth between the *castillo* and Rancho Luna's Hotel Pasacaballo. Last departure from the *castillo* is 8pm.

BICYCLE

Cienfuegos is a great cycling city with a strong sporting culture, and bikes are a good way to connect with the spread-out sights in Punta Gorda or even as far south as Rancho Luna. For quality European bike rentals contact Casa las Golondrinas (p247).

CAR

Cubacar (Hotel Jagua, Calle 37, btwn Avs 0 & 2; ☺9am-5pm) rents mostly manual-transmission cars and has an office opposite Hotel Jagua.

The **Servi-Cupet gas station** (cnr Calle 37 & Av 16) is in Punta Gorda. There's another station 5km northeast of Hotel Rancho Luna.

HORSE CARTS

Horse carts and bici-taxis ply Calle 37, charging Cubans one peso a ride and foreigners USD$1 (you may have to bargain). It's a pleasant way to travel between town, Punta Gorda and the two outlying cemeteries.

TAXI

There are plenty of cabs in Cienfuegos. Most hang around outside Hotel Jagua and Hotel La Unión and the bus station. Bici-taxis patrol the Malecón and will ferry you to/from Punta Gorda for about USD$3. Negotiate. A taxi to the airport from downtown should cost USD$6. Check the **Cubat-axi** (Map p248; ☑43-55-11-72; Av 50, btwn Calles 35 & 37) office for latest prices.

Rancho Luna

Rancho Luna is a diminutive beach resort 18km south of Cienfuegos, close to the jaws of Bahía de Cienfuegos. It has two midrange, low-key hotel complexes, plus a scattering of casas particulares (private homestays) on the approach road to the Hotel Faro Luna. Protected by a coral reef, the coast has good snorkeling. The beach isn't

Varadero-standard sand; then again, it isn't Varadero-standard noise or incessant development, either.

Activities

Besides sunbathing or viewing the *faro* (lighthouse), the main activity here is diving organized through the dive center beside Hotel Faro Luna.

Dive Center
DIVING

(43-54-80-40; Carretera Pasacaballos Km 18; dives from USD$35, open-water certification USD$365) This dive center next door to the Hotel Faro Luna visits 30 sites within a 20-minute boat ride. There are caves, profuse marine life and dazzling coral gardens (dubbed Notre Dame by divers for their sheer, vast beauty). From November to February harmless whale sharks frequent these waters.

Other underwater sights include six sunken ships and remnants of a transmission cable once linking Cuba with Spain and laid by the Brits in 1895.

Courses

Academia Cienfuegos
LANGUAGE

(www.formationcuba.com; Carretera Faro Luna) This Canadian-run Spanish-language school is one of the best in Cuba, running courses for one or two weeks from a base in the Hotel Faro Luna, with cultural activities offered too. See website for prices.

Sleeping

Rancho Luna has two hotels – one is all-inclusive and both are reasonably priced. Even better value for money are the half-dozen or so casas particulares (rooms in private homes) that line the approach road to Hotel Faro Luna.

★ Casa Larabi
CASA PARTICULAR $

(43-54-81-99; casa.larabi1@gmail.com; Carretera Faro Luna; r USD$35;) Possibly the most whimsical house in the whole province, the impossible-to-miss Larabi – painted turquoise, purple and pink (it works) – jumps out at you on the approach road to the Hotel Faro Luna. Inside is a riot of museum-worthy antique furniture and botanical-garden-worthy plants. The icing on the cake: a wonderful pink terrace with sea views.

Hotel Rancho Luna
RESORT $$

(43-54-80-12; Carretera Rancho Luna Km 18; s/d all-inclusive USD$75/120) Rancho Luna might not offer Varadero levels of comfort and a good refurb wouldn't go amiss, but it has a loyal following among budget-conscious travelers (especially Canadians), many of whom have been coming here for years. The advantages over more expensive north-coast resorts? It's quiet and there's a beautiful Unesco-listed city 15 minutes away. Daily free shuttles head into town.

Hotel Faro Luna
RESORT $$

(43-54-80-30; Carretera Faro Luna; s/d incl breakfast USD$80/120;) The dark horse of Cuba's south coast, Faro Luna is a refreshingly unpretentious place and one of only two hotels to grace what is possibly Cuba's most un-resort-like resort area. Unlike neighboring Hotel Rancho Luna, the Faro doesn't offer all-inclusive packages and hugs a rocky headland rather than a beach, but the in-house restaurant does passable dinners enhanced by the setting.

There's a dive center next door.

Hotel Pasacaballo
HOTEL $$

(43-59-28-22; Carretera Pasacaballos Km 22; s/d incl breakfast USD$45/80;) A strong contender for Cuba's 'ugliest hotel,' the Pasacaballo looks like it got catapulted over from a Moscow housing estate in the mid-1970s. Worn-out bedrooms are outdated if clean, while communal areas exhibit a spacious bar, a restaurant, a pool and pool tables – though given that there's nothing else around for miles, even this dazzling array of entertainment may prove insufficient.

The best strip of beach is a 4km hike away, the city of Cienfuegos a 25km drive.

Getting There & Away

Theoretically, there are half-a-dozen local buses daily from Cienfuegos, but this is Cuba – prepare for waits and chalked-up schedules. The Jagua ferry runs from the dock (Carretera Pasacaballos Km 22) directly below Hotel Pasacaballo several times daily; more sporadic is the boat from Castillo de Jagua back to Cienfuegos (which runs between all three points, departing from the Jagua dock at 10am and 3pm only at the time of research). Most reliable is a taxi; a one-way fare to Cienfuegos should cost around USD$10 – taxis wait outside Hotel La Unión (p249) or the bus station. Bargain hard.

The two local hotels lay on a daily free shuttle to and from Cienfuegos.

An even better way to get here is zipping along from Cienfuegos on a bicycle. Rent one at Casa las Golondrinas (p247) in the city.

El Nicho

While Cienfuegos Province's share of the verdant Sierra del Escambray is extensive (and includes the range's highest summit, 1156m Pico de San Juan), access is limited to a small protected area around **El Nicho** (USD$10; ⊙ 8am-5pm), an outlying segment of the Parque Natural Topes de Collantes.

El Nicho is the name of a refreshing **waterfall** on the Río Hanabanilla, reached by a short trail that passes two natural pools (where you can swim). Just beyond the falls is a *mirador* (lookout) offering views over lush mountains and the distant Embalse Hanabanilla.

The beautiful road to El Nicho via Cumanayagua is legendary for its twists and turns. *'Tienes mas curvas de la carretera por Cumanayagua'* (you have more curves than the road to Cumanayagua) is supposedly a compliment to *chicas* (girls) hereabouts. The falls make a popular and worthwhile day trip from Cienfuegos, but don't expect to have the place to yourself.

❶ Getting There & Away

There's no reliable public transportation to El Nicho. Hiring a taxi in Cienfuegos (about USD$50 round trip with a two-hour wait) is the best bet. Half-day tours can be organized for less through the excellent Cubanacán (p255) in Cienfuegos. Agencies and casas particulares (private homestays) can also organize El Nicho trips with onward transportation to Trinidad.

With your own wheels, you can drive through the mountains on a reasonable road to the Embalse Hanabanilla area in Villa Clara Province.

Caribbean Coast

Heading east toward Trinidad in Sancti Spíritus Province, shadowy views of the Sierra del Escambray loom ever closer until their ruffled foothills almost engulf the coast road, while offshore hidden coral reefs offer excellent diving.

🏃 Activities

Guajimico Diving Center DIVING
(☑ 43-42-06-46; Carretera de Trinidad Km 42) Villa Guajimico has its own dive center with 16 dive sites situated atop an offshore coral ridge nearby. Guajimico means 'place of the fishes' in the language of the indigenous tribes that once lived here, and the dive sites harbor some exotic marine life. All are close

to the shore and six are located in a serene forest-rimmed inlet.

The center competes with Playa Girón for the cheapest diving in Cuba at just USD$25 per immersion.

Hacienda la Vega HORSEBACK RIDING
(Carretera de Trinidad Km 52; per hour USD$6) On the main road, approximately 9km east of Villa Guajimico, this bucolic cattle farm is surrounded by fruit trees and has an attached restaurant serving Cuban staples (USD$5 to USD$10) – a good place to relax in the shade. Unhurried travelers can hire horses and trot down to the nearby beach, Caleta de Castro, where the snorkeling is excellent (BYO gear).

🛏 Sleeping & Eating

Villa Yaguanabo CABIN $$
(☑ 43-54-19-05; Carretera de Trinidad Km 55; s/d incl breakfast USD$59/69; ▣ ❋) Something of an unheralded (if overpriced) place located too close to Trinidad to delay most of the drive-by traffic, Villa Yaguanabo sits on a sublime stretch of coast at the mouth of the Río Yaguanabo. Basic but recently renovated motel-style rooms look out on a quiet swath of tan-colored beach. There's a large pool, plus bar, restaurant and small shop.

Using the surprisingly salubrious hotel as a base, you can catch a boat (USD$3) for a 2km ride upriver to the Valle de Iguanas, where you'll find thermal waters, horseback-riding and a small trail network in the foothills of the verdant Sierra del Escambray.

Villa Guajimico CABIN $$
(☑ 43-42-06-46; Carretera de Trinidad Km 42; s/d USD$41/68; ▣ ❋ ▣) This is one of Cubamar's most luxurious campismos (rustic accommodations). The 51 multi-colored cabins with their idyllic seaside setting have facilities matching most three-star hotels and act as a nexus for scuba divers. Also offered: bike hire, car rental, various catamaran or kayaking options and short hiking trails. Cienfuegos–Trinidad buses pass by. It's also popular with Cubans.

There's a restaurant serving buffet food on-site.

❶ Getting There & Away

Long-distance buses ply this route, but they don't stop at the various points of interest, meaning your best option is a car or taxi using either Trinidad or Cienfuegos as a base.

Conjunto Escultórico Comandante Ernesto Che Guevara (p261), Santa Clara
PAUL MCKINNON/SHUTTERSTOCK ©

Villa Clara Province

Villa Clara is Cuba's weighty anchor, the axis around which everything else spins and the place where the word 'revolution' first imprinted itself in the Cuban consciousness. Che Guevara liberated its capital, Santa Clara, from Batista's corrupt gambling party in 1958 to kick-start the long reign of Fidel Castro. The city remains a veritable shrine to the controversial Argentinian, but it's also a guardian of Cuba's avant-garde (having the nation's only drag show and its main rock festival). Further north, the compact colonial town of Remedios is tranquil for 362 days of the year and ballistic for the other three during its Christmas festival.

The beach-rimmed Cayerías del Norte off Villa Clara's north coast is experiencing Cuba's most drastic contemporary tourist development: 20 resorts have been built here in as many years. Meanwhile, in the deep south, the Escambray Mountains harbor an inviting lake and plenty of little-explored trails.

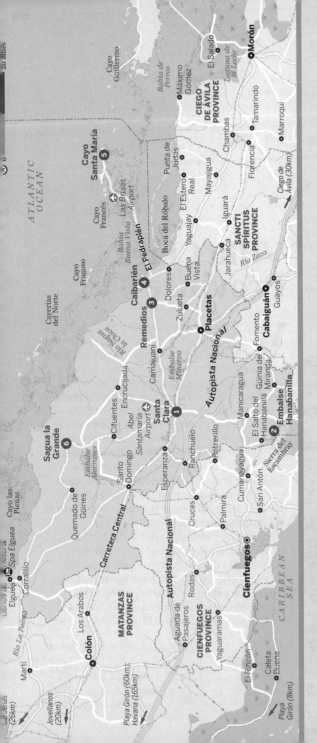

Villa Clara Province Highlights

1 Santa Clara (p261)
Tracing the legend of Ernesto 'Che' Guevara, a trail that ends inevitably at his mausoleum.

2 Embalse Hanabanilla (p269) Hiking the trails, bathing in the pools and soaking up the solitude at this lovely lake surrounded by mountains.

3 Remedios (p271)
People-watching from a plaza cafe in this recently rejuvenated but, as yet, unspoiled colonial town.

4 Caibarién (p273) Seeing what the Villa Clara tourist board forgot to mention in this ramshackle yet heart-warming waterside settlement.

5 Cayo Santa María (p275) Basking on the balmy sands of Playa Las Gaviotas, one of Cayo Santa María's last remaining public-access beaches.

6 Hotel Sagua (p274) Admiring the reconfigured streets of erstwhile sugar giant Sagua La Grande from this exquisitely restored hotel.

History

The Taíno people were the first known inhabitants of the region, but a recreation of a settlement at a hotel outside Santa Clara is their only surviving legacy. Strategically located in the island's geographical center, Villa Clara has historically been a focal point for corsairs, colonizers and revolutionaries vying for political control.

Pirates were a perennial headache in the early colonial years, with the province's first town, Remedios, being moved twice and then abandoned altogether in the late 1600s by a group of families who escaped inland to what is now Santa Clara. Later, the area's demographics were shaken up further by Canary Islanders, who brought their agricultural know-how and distinctive lilting Spanish accents to the tobacco fields of the picturesque Vuelta Arriba region. In December 1958 Ernesto 'Che' Guevara – aided by a motley crew of scruffy *barbudos* (bearded ones) – orchestrated the fall of the city of Santa Clara by derailing an armored train carrying more than 350 government troops and weaponry to the east. The victory rang the death knell for Fulgencio Batista's dictatorship and signaled the triumph of the Cuban Revolution. Santa Clara has been known as 'Che City' ever since, and in 1997 his remains were laid to rest here after being found in Bolivia.

Things have calmed down in recent years, but provincial goings-on continue to keep everyone on the edge of their seats: resort development in the province's north has continued unabated since the 1990s and by the mid-2010s Villa Clara's northern keys had morphed into Cuba's second-largest resort zone after Varadero. Naysayers cite the adjacent Unesco Buenavista Biosphere Reserve and the damage development could wreak on this internationally important marine habitat.

Santa Clara

POP 216,000

Sorry Havana. Santa Clara is Cuba's most revolutionary city – and not just because of its historical obsession with Argentine doctor turned *guerrillero* (guerrilla) Che Guevara. Smack bang in the geographic center of Cuba, this is a city of new trends and insatiable creativity, where an edgy youth culture has been testing the boundaries of Cuba's censorship police for years. Unique Santa Clara offerings include Cuba's only official drag show, a graphic artists' collective that produces satirical political cartoons, and the country's best rock festival: Ciudad Metal. The city's fiery personality has been shaped over time by the presence of the nation's most prestigious university outside Havana, and a long association with Che Guevara, whose liberation of Santa Clara in December 1958 marked the end of the Batista regime. Little cultural revolutions have been erupting here ever since.

◉ Sights

Santa Clara's sights are liberally distributed to the north, east and west of Parque Vidal. All are within walking distance, with the big Che sight, Conjunto Escultórico Comandante Ernesto Che Guevara, 2km from the center.

★ Conjunto Escultórico Comandante Ernesto Che Guevara
MAUSOLEUM, MUSEUM

(Plaza de la Revolución; ◷9:30am-4pm Tue-Sun) **FREE** The end point of many a Che pilgrimage, this monument, mausoleum and museum complex is 2km west of Parque Vidal (via Rafael Tristá on Av de los Desfiles), near the Víazul bus station. Even if you don't care for the Argentine guerrilla for whom many reserve an almost religious reverence, there's poignancy in the vast square that spans both sides of a wide avenue, guarded by a bronze statue of El Che atop a 16m-high pedestal.

The statue was erected in 1987 to mark the 20th anniversary of Guevara's murder in Bolivia, and can be viewed any time. Accessed from behind the statue, the respectful mausoleum contains 38 stone-carved niches dedicated to the other guerrillas killed in the failed Bolivian revolution. In 1997 the remains of 17 of them, including Guevara, were recovered from a secret mass grave in Bolivia and reburied in this memorial. Fidel Castro lit the eternal flame on October 17, 1997. The adjacent museum houses the details and ephemera of Che's life and death.

The best way to get to the monument is a 15-minute walk, or by hopping on a horse carriage on Calle Marta Abreu outside the cathedral for a couple of Cuban pesos.

Parque Vidal
SQUARE

(Map p262) A veritable alfresco theater named for Colonel Leoncio Vidal y Caro, who was killed here on March 23, 1896, Parque Vidal was encircled by twin sidewalks during the colonial era, with a fence separating blacks and whites. Scars of more recent division are evident on the facade of mint-green

Santa Clara

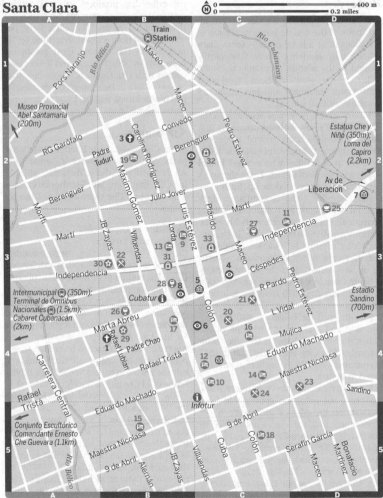

Hotel Santa Clara Libre on the park's west side: it's pockmarked by bullet holes from the 1958 battle for the city between Guevara and Batista's government troops.

Today all the colors of Cuba's cultural rainbow mix in one of the nation's busiest and most vibrant urban spaces, with old men in *guayabera* shirts smoking cigars on the shaded benches and young kids getting pulled around in carriages led by goats. Find time to contemplate the **statues** of local philanthropist Marta Abreu and the emblematic *El niño de la bota* (Boy with a Boot), a long-standing city symbol. Since 1902 the municipal orchestra has played rousing music in the park bandstand at 8pm every Thursday and Sunday.

Museo Provincial Abel Santamaría MUSEUM
(☏ 42-20-30-41; USD$1; ⊗ 8:30am-5pm Mon-Fri, to noon Sat) Not actually a memorial to Señor Santamaría (Fidel's right-hand man at Moncada), but rather a small provincial museum quartered in former military barracks where Batista's troops surrendered to Che Guevara on January 1, 1959. The comprehensive and well-labeled displays (Spanish only) make good use of photos and cover the full trajectory of Santa Clara's often exciting history. On the ground floor there's a less interesting collection of stuffed animals.

Santa Clara

Catedral de las Santas Hermanas de Santa Clara de Asís   CATHEDRAL

(Map p262; Marta Abreu) Three blocks west of Parque Vidal, Santa Clara's cathedral was constructed amid huge controversy in 1923 after the demolition of the city's original church in the main park. It contains a fantastic collection of stained-glass windows, some notable art deco influences and a mythical white statue of Mother Mary known (unofficially) as La Virgen de la Charca (Virgin of the Pond). The statue was discovered in a ditch in the 1980s, having mysteriously disappeared shortly after the cathedral's consecration in 1954. It returned to grace the cathedral in 1995.

Sitio-Museo Acción Contra El Tren Blindado   MUSEUM

(Map p262; USD$1; ◷8:30am-5pm Tue-Sat, 9am-1pm Sun) History was made at the site of this small boxcar museum on December 29, 1958, when Ernesto 'Che' Guevara and a band of 18 rifle-wielding revolutionaries barely out of their teens derailed an armored train using a borrowed bulldozer and home-made Molotov cocktails.

The battle lasted 90 minutes and improbably pulled the rug out from under the Batista dictatorship, ushering in 50 years of Fidel Castro. The museum – east on Independencia, just over the river – marks the spot where the train derailed and ejected its 350 heavily armed government troops. The celebrated bulldozer is mounted on its own plinth at the entrance.

Fábrica de Tabacos Constantino Pérez Carrodegua   FACTORY

(Map p262; Maceo No 181, btwn Julio Jover & Berenguer; USD$4; ◷9-11am & 1-3pm Mon-Fri) Santa Clara's tobacco factory, one of Cuba's best, makes a quality range of Montecristos, Partagás and Romeo y Julieta cigars. Tours here are lo-fi compared to those in Havana, and so the experience is a lot more interesting and less rushed. Buy tickets in advance at the Cubatur (p269) office. Beware, opening times can be erratic. Across the street is La Veguita (p268), the factory's diminutive but comprehensively stocked sales outlet.

Teatro la Caridad   THEATER, HISTORIC BUILDING

(Map p262; cnr Marta Abreu & Máximo Gómez) Many are deceived by the relatively austere neoclassical facade, but toss USD$1 to whoever is manning the door and you'll serendipitously discover why the 1885 Teatro la Caridad is one of the three great provincial theaters of the colonial era.

The ornate interior is almost identical to the Tomás Terry in Cienfuegos and the Sauto in Matanzas: three tiers, a U-shaped auditorium and decadent marble statues. The rich ceiling fresco by Camilo Zalaya provides the pièce de résistance.

CHE GUEVARA

Few 20th-century figures have successfully divided public opinion as deeply as Ernesto Guevara de la Serna, whose remains are now interred in a mausoleum (p261) in Santa Clara. Better known to his friends (and enemies) as El Che, he has been revered as an enduring symbol of Third World freedom and celebrated as the hero of the Sierra Maestra – and yet he was once the most wanted man on the CIA hit list.

So who was this handsome yet often misunderstood Argentine physician turned *guerrillero* (guerrilla) who not only started a rebellion in rural Cuba, but also sparked a revolution in worldwide T-shirt design?

Born in Rosario, Argentina, in June 1928 to a bourgeois family of Irish-Spanish descent, Guevara was a delicate and sickly child who developed asthma at the age of two. It was an early desire to overcome this debilitating illness that instilled in the young Ernesto a willpower that would dramatically set him apart from other people.

A pugnacious competitor in his youth, Ernesto earned the name 'Fuser' at school for his combative nature on the rugby field. Graduating from the University of Buenos Aires in 1953 with a medical degree, he shunned a conventional medical career in favor of a cross-continental motorcycling odyssey, accompanied by his old friend and colleague Alberto Granado. Their nomadic wanderings – well documented in a series of posthumously published diaries – would open Ernesto's eyes to the grinding poverty and stark political injustices all too common in 1950s Latin America.

By the time Guevara arrived in Guatemala in 1954 on the eve of a US-backed coup against Jacobo Arbenz' leftist government, he was enthusiastically devouring the works of Marx and nurturing a deep-rooted hatred of the US. Deported to Mexico for his pro-Arbenz activities in 1955, Guevara fell in with a group of Cubans that included Moncada veteran Raúl Castro. Impressed by the Argentine's sharp intellect and never-failing political convictions, Raúl – a long-standing Communist Party member himself – decided to introduce Che to his charismatic brother, Fidel.

The meeting between the two men at Maria Antonia's house in Mexico City in June 1955 lasted 10 hours and ultimately changed the course of history. Rarely had two characters needed each other as much as the hot-headed Castro and the calmer, more ideologically polished Che. Both were favored children from large families, and both shunned the quiet life to fight courageously for a revolutionary cause. Similarly, both men had little to gain and much to throw away by abandoning professional careers for what most would have regarded as narrow-minded folly.

In December 1956 Che left for Cuba on the *Granma* yacht, joining the rebels as the group medic. One of only 12 or so of the original 82 rebel soldiers to survive the catastrophic landing at Las Coloradas, he proved himself to be a brave and intrepid fighter who led by example and quickly won the trust of his less reckless Cuban comrades. As a result Castro rewarded him with the rank of Comandante in July 1957, and in December 1958 Che repaid Fidel's faith when he masterminded the battle of Santa Clara, an action that effectively sealed a historic revolutionary victory.

Guevara was granted Cuban citizenship in February 1959 and soon assumed a leading role in Cuba's economic reforms as president of the National Bank and minister of industry. His insatiable work ethic and regular appearance at enthusiastically organized volunteer worker weekends quickly saw him cast as the living embodiment of Cuba's 'New Man.'

But the honeymoon wasn't to last. Disappearing from the Cuban political scene in 1965 amid many rumors and myths, Guevara eventually materialized again in Bolivia in late 1966 at the head of a small band of Cuban *guerrilleros*. After the successful ambush of a Bolivian detachment in March 1967, he issued a call for 'two, three, many Vietnams' in the Americas. Such bold proclamations could only prove his undoing. On October 8, 1967, Guevara was captured by the Bolivian army. Following consultations between the army and military leaders in La Paz and Washington, DC, he was shot the next day in front of US advisers. His remains were eventually returned to Cuba in 1997.

Museo de Artes Decorativas MUSEUM
(Map p262; Parque Vidal No 27; USD$2; 9am-5pm Mon & Wed-Fri, 3-6pm Sat & Sun) Something of a sleeping beauty on Parque Vidal, this 18th-century mansion turned museum is packed with period furniture from a whole

gamut of styles that seem to ape Cuba's architectural heritage. Look for baroque desks, art nouveau mirrors, art deco furniture and Veláquez' epic *Rendición de Brega* (Surrender of Brega), reproduced on a china plate. Live chamber music adds to the romanticism in the evenings.

Iglesia de Nuestra
Señora del Carmen CHURCH

(Map p262; Carolina Rodríguez) The city's oldest church is five blocks north of Parque Vidal. It was built in 1748, with a tower added in 1846. During the War of Independence it stood in as a jail for Cuban patriots. A modern cylindrical monument facing the church commemorates the spot where Santa Clara was founded in 1689 by a dozen or so refugee families from Remedios.

Estatua Che y Niño MONUMENT

(Av Liberación) Far more intimate and intricate a monument than its big brother on the other side of town, this statue in front of the Oficina de la Provincia (PCC) four blocks east of Tren Blindado shows El Che with a baby (symbolizing the next generation) on his shoulder. Looking closer you'll see smaller sculptures incorporated into the revolutionary's uniform depicting junctures in his life, including likenesses of the 38 men killed with Guevara in Bolivia concealed within the belt buckle.

Loma del Capiro LANDMARK

Two blocks east of the Estatua Che y niño, a road to the right leads to Santa Clara's best lookout, the distinctive Loma del Capiro. The crest is marked by two flags and a series of stakes supporting the metallic but recognizable face of, you've guessed it, Che Guevara. The hill was a crucial vantage point for his forces during the 1958 liberation of Santa Clara.

✷✷ Festivals & Events

Santa Clara's renegade annual offerings include Miss Trasvesti, a Miss World–type event with transvestite contestants in March, and November's Ciudad Metal (☺late Nov), when headbanging to the country's leading rock acts happens at various venues citywide.

🛏 Sleeping

It's not always obvious from street level, but Santa Clara has some of the best casas particulares (rooms in private homes) in Cuba, many of them hidden away in rambling colonial abodes.

The city now counts half a dozen hotels, two of them several kilometers outside the city. Some of the newer ones are rather good.

★Hostal Florida Terrace CASA PARTICULAR $

(Map p262; ☑42-22-15-80; www.hostalflorida-center.com; Maestra Nicolasa No 59, btwn Maceo & Colón; r USD$30-35; P❋☀) This finely decorated hotel-like place is affiliated with Restaurant Florida Center (p267) across the road and has more floors (four) than most private homestays have rooms. The smart colonial decor has art deco echoes, offering plenty to admire, and the eight rooms with antique beds are top drawer. It has an upstairs bar and *mirador* (lookout) with some of Santa Clara's best views.

★Hostal Familia
Sarmiento CASA PARTICULAR $

(Map p262; ☑42-20-35-10; www.santaclarahostel.com; Lorda No 56, btwn Martí & Independencia; r USD$25-35; ❋☀) The Sarmiento offers three well-appointed rooms in an attractive Cuban home in the center of town. Recently renovated bedrooms feature rain showers, graded light settings and Nespresso coffee machines.

Casa Mercy 1938 CASA PARTICULAR $

(Map p262; ☑42-21-69-41; casamercy@gmail.com; Independencia No 253, btwn Estévez & Gutiérrez; r USD$30-35; ❋☀) The name might hark back to another age, but this wonderful house has been restored to include modern comforts. The details are spectacular: an art deco–neocolonial hybrid anchored by a Seville-style fountain that sets off the central patio. The house is diligently staffed by friendly multilingual owners and comes with two large rooms and plenty of communal space – including that patio.

La Casona Jover CASA PARTICULAR $

(Map p262; ☑42-20-44-58; almiqui2009@yahoo.es; Colón No 167, btwn 9 de Abril & Serafín García; r USD$30-35; ❋) The Jover is classic Santa Clara, hiding a minipalace behind a prosaic facade. Five large colonial rooms line a terrace stuffed with a profusion of plants and a tempting plunge pool.

Authentica Pérgola CASA PARTICULAR $

(Map p262; ☑42-20-86-86; carmen64@yahoo.es; Luis Estévez No 61, btwn Independencia & Martí; r USD$30; ❋☀) The Pérgola is set around an Alhambra-esque patio draped in greenery and crowned by a fountain, from where several large rooms lead off. Pretty much everything here is antique, including in the bedrooms. It's better than the town museum. There's a beautiful roof-terrace restaurant open to all called La Aldaba.

Olga Rivera Gómez
CASA PARTICULAR $

(Map p262; ✆42-21-17-11; Evangelista Yanes No 20, btwn Máximo Gómez & Carolina Rodríguez; r USD$25-30; ❄) Another of those fascinating Santa Clara casas, this one is art deco on the outside and a wonderful mix of styles within. There's a fabulous roof terrace where guests are spoiled with vistas of Santa Clara's prettiest church, plus two rooms, a fecund patio and columns with capitals.

Hostal Marilin & Familia
CASA PARTICULAR $

(Map p262; ✆42-20-76-55; marilin1103@gmail.com; 116 Maestra Nicolasa, btwn Alemán & JB Zayas; r USD$25-30; ❄🕸) A charming cornerstone of Santa Clara's accommodations scene with three bedrooms (one big enough for families), a leafy back courtyard, a front terrace and an executive cigar-smoking lounge. Owner Marilin is an experienced cigar expert and knows all about the nuances of Cohibas, Montecristos et al.

Hostal Alba
CASA PARTICULAR $

(Map p262; ✆42-29-41-08; wilfredo.alba@yahoo.com; Eduardo Machado No 7, btwn Cuba & Colón; r USD$30-35; ❄) This architectural stunner with lovely antique beds, original tile work and a patio serves amazing breakfasts and is just one block from the main square. The congenial owner, Wilfredo, is chef at the superb Restaurant Florida Center – enough said!

Casa de Mercy
CASA PARTICULAR $

(Map p262; ✆42-21-69-41; casamecy@gmail.com; Eduardo Machado No 4, btwn Cuba & Colón; r USD$25-35; ❄🕸) There are two rooms with private bathrooms available in this friendly family house, which has two terraces, a dining room and a tempting cocktail menu. English, French and Italian are spoken by the engaging hosts, Moreno and Mercy.

Hotel Central
BOUTIQUE HOTEL $$

(Map p262; ✆42-20-15-85; www.cubanacan.cu; Parque Vidal; s/d incl breakfast USD$56/102; ❄@🕸) Of the dozen or so state-run boutique hotels that have opened over the last few years, this is one of the best, courtesy of its Parque Vidal location, colonial furnishings and attractive streetside bar that sits opposite Santa Clara's energetic square.

Downside? All but two of the rooms face the inner courtyard, meaning they lack natural light, but with motivated young staff and

plenty of communal areas to escape to, it's a small price to pay.

Villa Los Caneyes
HOTEL $$

(✆42-20-45-13; cnr Av de los Eucaliptos & Circunvalación de Santa Clara; s/d incl breakfast USD$59/90; P❄@🕸) Long popular with tour groups, this out-of-town option should be a serious consideration, particularly if you like peace and quiet. A mock-indigenous village, Los Caneyes has 95 thatched *bohíos* (bungalows) in suitably verdant grounds replete with abundant birdlife, good on-site restaurant, pool, well-stocked bar and souvenir shop. It's 3km from Santa Clara and well away from the urban racket.

Hotel América
HOTEL $$$

(Map p262; ✆42-20-15-85; www.cubanacan.cu; Mujica, btwn Colón & Maceo; s/d USD$102/164; ❄@🕸) Sandwiched into the city core, the 27-room América is still young enough to have kept its opening shine, although it can't quite claim a 'boutique' moniker. Though modern, it incorporates some designer details and finds space for a decent bar (open to nonguests) and a small outdoor pool.

✗ Eating

For a city of Santa Clara's clout, dining options are below average, though there are exceptions. The best places – as always – are usually within, or attached to, casas particulares (private homestays).

Bodeguita del Medio
CUBAN $

(Map p262; ✆42-21-54-34; Vidal No 1, btwn Colón & Maceo; mains USD$3-7; ⊙11am-11pm; ❄) A love child of Havana's original Bodeguita (p129), this carefully branded 'dive' bar has a couple of advantages over its big-city mentor: 1. Hemingway never came here, meaning the signature mojitos only cost USD$2; and 2. it's free of space-hogging tour groups.

However, despite the graffiti-covered streetside bar where *son*-playing musical trios roam, we're recommending this place for its food served in an air-conditioned restaurant out back. Waited on by keen young guys dressed in *guayabera* shirts, you'll be served generous meals of *comida criolla* (Creole food). The deep, rich *picadillo* (spicy minced beef) is highly recommended.

El Alba
CUBAN $

(Map p262; ✆42-20-39-35; cnr Maceo & R Pardo; CUP$3-8; ⊙noon-11pm) The Alba has had a bit of a rethink of late: the interior has been enlarged and they've toned down the Melaíto cartoons (p268) on the walls (mercifully a few good ones remain). The Cuban-meets-Italian food is still pretty tasty and comes in large portions.

El Gobernador
CUBAN $

(Map p262; cnr Independencia & JB Zayas; mains USD$3-8; ⊗11am-5pm & 7-11:30pm) With the more recent competition from independents, state-run places have to perform better, and this one certainly has had a go. In a glamorous former state office furnished in somber colonial splendor and hung with original artwork, El Gobernador's food was never going to *quite* live up to the ambience. Eschew the pasta and stick to the Cuban dishes.

Panadería Doña Neli
BAKERY $

(Map p262; cnr Maceo Sur & 9 de Abril; bread/snacks around USD$1; ⊗7am-6pm) This staunchly Cuban bakery amid austere shopfronts on Calle Maceo has plenty of tables in an adjacent cafe where you can relax with a piece of aromatic fruit cake and a frothy cappuccino.

★ Restaurant
Florida Center
CUBAN, FUSION $$

(Map p262; ☑42-20-81-61; Maestra Nicolasa No 56, btwn Colón & Maceo; mains USD$10-15; ⊗6:30-9:30pm) The Florida has been Santa Clara's best restaurant for at least a decade. The food is as good as the experience. Diners eat in a colonial, plant-festooned, candlelit courtyard full of interesting antiques. Ever-present owner Ángel is the perfect host, advising on the profusion of dishes in French, English, Italian and Spanish. The menu is simple but classic Cuban. The highlight: lobster with prawns in a 'secret' tomato sauce.

La Aldaba
CUBAN $$

(Map p262; ☑42-20-86-86; Luis Estévez No 61, btwn Independencia & Martí; mains USD$12-20; ⊗11:30am-11pm) The rooftop restaurant in the Authentica Pérgola casa particular is a great place to repose, preferably in the evening, amid potted ferns and in the company of chefs who know how to prepare good Cuban dishes with a few zings (eg curried chicken).

🍷 Drinking & Nightlife

Thanks to its large student population, Santa Clara has some of Cuba's best nightlife outside Havana – and it's not just the usual suspects. The city has an established gay scene and a strong contingent of *roqueros* (rock musicians). Most of the nightlife is on or around Parque Vidal, although there are a couple of outlying strongholds, including a cabaret venue.

★ La Marquesina
BAR

(Map p262; Parque Vidal, btwn Máximo Gómez & Lorda; ⊗9am-1am) You can chinwag and neck a cold bottled beer with locals of all types in this legendary dive bar under the porches of the equally legendary Teatro la Caridad on the corner of Parque Vidal. The clientele is a potpourri of Santa Clara life – students, cigar-factory workers, off-duty taxi drivers and the odd bewildered tourist. Live music (and dancing) erupts regularly.

Cafe-Museo Revolución
CAFE

(Map p262; Independencia No 313; ⊗9am-11pm; 🛜) You say you want a revolution... Well, Santa Clara's a good place to start. It's already had one, successfully ignited by Che Guevara in 1958. This cafe-museum pays homage to Cuba's revolutionary past with photos, old uniforms and other ephemera lovingly curated by the Spanish owner. The house coffee, served with syrup, meringue, milk and a shot of rum, is pretty revolutionary too.

Cuba 'n' Roll
BAR

(Map p262; ☑5-366-7007; JB Zayas, btwn Marta Abreu & Callejón de los Ángeles; ⊗noon-midnight) Situated close enough to Club Mejunje to absorb some of its edgy atmosphere, this small dive is a great place to get smashed with the locals.

Santa Rosalia
BAR

(Map p262; Máximo Gómez, btwn Independencia & Marta Abreu; ⊗11am-2am) The Santa Rosalia styles itself as a state-run *complejo* (complex); there's a restaurant, a bar and a music venue on-site. We're recommending it for the latter (although the food isn't bad by state standards, you can eat far better in Santa Clara). The colonial building is a joy and the patio out back is large and atmospheric after dusk. Live bands kick off at 10pm-ish.

El Bar Club Boulevard
CLUB

(Map p262; Independencia No 2, btwn Maceo & Pedro Estévez; USD$2; ⊗10pm-2am Mon-Sat) This meet-the-locals cocktail lounge has live bands and dancing, plus the odd comedy show. It generally gets swinging around 11pm.

☆ Entertainment

★ Club Mejunje
LIVE MUSIC

(Map p262; Marta Abreu No 107; ⊗4pm-1am Tue-Sun; 📶) Urban graffiti, children's theater, LGBTQ-friendly performances, old crooners belting out *boleros*, tourists dancing salsa. You've heard about 'something for everyone,' but this is ridiculous. Welcome to Club

LOCAL KNOWLEDGE

MELAÍTO – SATIRE & STREET ART

While socialism in Cuba hasn't always been a bundle of laughs, the revolution didn't snuff out political humor completely – at least not in Santa Clara, home of *Melaíto*, a periodical that, for over 50 years, has provided a pulpit for some of Cuba's best caricaturists and graphic artists. Founded in 1968 as a lighthearted propaganda supplement to support the upcoming 'Zafra de Diez Millones' (10-million-tonne sugar harvest), the magazine was named after one of its early characters, a hapless Chinese-Cuban cane-cutter called Melaíto. With the sugar harvest over, the magazine worked hard to build on its new-found popularity, tackling more general political themes with satire and wit. By the 1970s it had become a regular monthly supplement to the local Villa Clara newspaper, *Vanguardia*, a position it holds to this day thanks primarily to the talent of its humorists, cartoonists and artists, who are some of the finest in Cuba.

In the last few years, *Melaíto* has widened its reach to include the internet and street art. The magazine's distinctive cartoons regularly pop up in public spaces in Santa Clara, where they serve to lift local spirits. The cartoons change regularly, but you can usually find the newest and most topical murals on or around the **Vanguardia office** (Map p262; Céspedes cnr Placido) one block east of Parque Vidal.

Mejunje, set in the ruins of an old roofless building given over to sprouting greenery. It's a local – nay, national – institution, famous for many things, not least Cuba's oldest official drag show (every Saturday night).

Cabaret Cubanacán CABARET
(Carretera Central, btwn Caridad & Venecia; cover USD$5; ⊙10am-3pm Wed-Sun) This slightly-out-of-town cabaret venue has a late-night disco preceded by a Cuban-style singing and dancing 'show' at weekends. It's one of Santa Cara's suaver nights out.

La Casa de la Ciudad ARTS CENTER
(Map p262; ☑42-20-55-93; cnr Independencia & JB Zayas; ⊙8am-9pm) The pulse of the city's progressive cultural life, hosting art expositions, *Noches del Danzón* (traditional dance nights), a film museum and impromptu music events – an all-female choir was performing at last visit.

Estadio Sandino SPECTATOR SPORT
(9 de Abril Final) From October to April, you can catch baseball games in this stadium east of the center via Calle 9 de Abril. Villa Clara, nicknamed Las Naranjas (the Oranges) for their team strip, are one of Cuba's better baseball teams and were last national series champions in 2013.

🛍 Shopping

Boulevard STREET
(Map p262; Calle Independencia) Calle Independencia between JB Zayas and Maceo is the pedestrianized 'Boulevard', full of shoppers during the day and bar-hoppers at night.

La Veguita CIGARS, RUM
(Map p262; ☑42-20-89-52; Maceo No 176a, btwn Julio Jover & Berenguer; ⊙9am-7pm Mon-Sat, 11am-4pm Sun) Sales outlet for Fábrica de Tabacos Constantino Pérez Carrodegua that is staffed by a friendly team of cigar experts.

Las Arcadas GIFTS & SOUVENIRS
(Map p262; Independencia, btwn Luis Estévez & Plácido; ⊙9am-5pm, to noon Sun) On Santa Clara's pedestrianized 'Boulevard,' this AR-Tex outlet sells handicrafts and the usual souvenirs, including plenty of the obligatory Che Guevara T-shirts and mugs.

ℹ Information

INTERNET ACCESS

Etecsa Telepunto (Marta Abreu No 55, btwn Máximo Gómez & Villuendas; internet per hour USD$1; ⊙8:30am-7pm) Eight internet terminals and three phone cabins.

Parque Vidal Wi-fi hot spot.

MEDICAL

Farmacia Internacional (Colón, cnr Maestra Nicolasa; ⊙8:30am-8pm Mon-Sat) Centrally located pharmacy with all the basics.

Hospital Arnaldo Milián Castro (☑42-46049; btwn Circunvalación & Av 26 de Julio) Southeast of the city center. It's the best option for foreigners; often called Hospital Nuevo.

MONEY

Banco Popular de Ahorro (cnr Cuba & Maestra Nicolasa; ⊙8am-3pm Mon-Fri, to 11am Sat) Has an ATM.

Cadeca (cnr Rafael Tristá & Cuba; ⊙8:30am-7pm Mon-Sat, 9am-6pm Sun) On the corner of the main square, this is the best place to change money. Long opening hours.

POST

Post Office (Map p262; Colón No 10, btwn Machado & Parque Vidal; ⊙8am-6pm, to noon Sun)

TOURIST INFORMATION

Cubanacán (☑ 42-20-51-89; Colón, cnr Maestra Nicolasa; ⊙8am-8pm Mon-Sat) Also has a desk in Hotel Central.

Cubatur (Map p262; ☑ 42-20-89-80; Marta Abreu No 10, btwn Máximo Gómez & Villuendas; ⊙9am-noon & 1-8pm) Book tobacco-factory tours here.

Infotur (Map p262; ☑ 42-20-13-52; Cuba No 68, btwn Machado & Maestra Nicolasa; ⊙8:30am-5pm Mon-Sat) Handy maps and brochures in multiple languages.

❶ Getting There & Away

AIR

Located 12km northeast of Santa Clara, **Abel Santamaría Airport** (☑ 42-22-75-25; off Rte 311) receives numerous weekly flights from Montreal and Toronto, a Copa Airlines flight to Panama City, and regular connections to the US (Miami and Fort Lauderdale), Mexico and the Bahamas. It is now the country's third-most-important airport. There are no flights to Havana.

BUS

The **Terminal de Ómnibus Nacionales** (☑ 42-20-34-70; Carretera Central, cnr Oquendo), which is also the bus station for **Víazul** (www.viazul.com), is 2.5km west of the center, out on the Carretera Central toward Matanzas, 500m north of the Che monument. Tickets for air-conditioned Víazul buses are sold at a special 'foreigners' ticket window at the station entrance.

Destination	Cost (USD$)	Duration (hr)	Frequency (daily)
Cayo Santa María	13	2½	1
Havana	18	4	3
Santiago de Cuba	33	12½	4
Trinidad	8	3½	2
Varadero	11	3¼	2

The Santiago de Cuba bus travels via Sancti Spíritus (USD$6, 1¼ hours), Ciego de Ávila (USD$9, 2½ hours), Camagüey (USD$15, 4½ hours), Holguín (USD$26, 7¾ hours) and Bayamo (USD$26, 9¼ hours).

The Cayo Santa María bus also stops in Remedios (USD$7, one hour) and Caibarién (USD$7, 1¼ hours).

The **intermunicipal bus station** (Carretera Central), west of the center via Calle Marta Abreu, has cheap local buses to Remedios, Caibarién and Manicaragua (for Embalse Hanabanilla). Trans-

port could be by bus or truck, gets overcrowded and isn't reliable.

Private homestay owners usually know schedules, or will find them out on your behalf.

TAXI

Colectivos (shared taxis) hang around the Terminal de Ómnibus Nacionales to drum up custom for the journey to Havana. The best time to catch them is just before the scheduled Víazul departures. They'll whisk you to addresses in Central Havana (USD$30, three hours), Varadero (USD$25, 3¼ hours) and Trinidad (2¼ hours, USD$20), but they only leave when full (four people).

TRAIN

The **train station** (Parque de los Mártires) is straight up Luis Estévez from Parque Vidal on the north side of town.

Santa Clara is on Cuba's main west–east railway line. Eight of Cuba's trains service the town. Tren 1 goes to Santiago de Cuba (USD$47, 10 hours) every other day via Ciego de Ávila (USD$12, 2½ hours), Camagüey (USD$21, 4½ hours) and Las Tunas (USD$30, 6½ hours). Tren 2 runs in the opposite direction to Matanzas (USD$16, three hours) and Havana (USD$25, five hours) also on alternate days. There are additional trains to and from Holguín (USD$38, nine hours) every three days, Bayamo (USD$36, 10 hours) and Manzanillo (USD$41, 12¼ hours) every three days, and Guantánamo (USD$51, 12 hours) every three days.

Check at the station beforehand to find out exactly which days the trains are running.

❶ Getting Around

Horse carriages congregate outside the cathedral on Marta Abreu and will angle for USD$1 per ride. Bici-taxis (from the northwest of the park) cost the same. Taxis from the center to the Terminal de Ómnibus Nacionales/airport cost USD$3/15.

CAR

Cars can be rented from **Cubacar** (☑ 42-21-81-77; Marta Abreu, btwn JB Zayas & Alemán; ⊙9am-5pm), which has offices in town, and **Rex** (☑ 42-22-22-44; ⊙8:30am-5:30pm), which has an office at the airport. Availability is often limited unless you reserve in advance.

There's a **gas station** (cnr Carretera Central & Calle 9 de Abril) southwest of the city center.

Embalse Hanabanilla

Embalse Hanabanilla, Villa Clara's main gateway to the Sierra del Escambray, is a 36-sq-km reservoir nestled prettily amid traditional farms and broccoli-toned hills. The glittering lake is fjord-like and comes stocked with a famed supply of record-breaking bass.

Fishers, boaters and nature lovers are well catered for, with several excursions and some rewarding seldom-trodden hikes available. The area is best accessed by boat from the Hotel Hanabanilla on the reservoir's northwestern shore. Curiously overlooked by foreign tourists, the area is mainly the domain of holidaying Cubans.

🏃 Activities

Boat Trips

Boats ferry passengers over to Casa del Campesino, which offers coffee, fresh fruit and a taste of bucolic Cuban life (with lunch if desired). Another popular boat trip is to the Río Negro Restaurant, perched atop a steep stone staircase overlooking the lakeshore, 50 minutes away. You can enjoy *comida criolla* surrounded by nature, and hike 920m up to a *mirador*. Another 2km by boat from the Río Negro is a tiny quay; disembark for the 1km hike to the Arroyo Trinitario waterfall, where you can swim. A couple of other trails lead off from here. Depending on duration and passenger numbers, return trips will be USD$10 to USD$20 per person.

A lesser-known seasonal boat trip runs to the spectacular El Nicho waterfall (p257) in Cienfuegos Province, via the southwestern arm of the lake. Bank on USD$35 return.

You can organize these activities at the Hotel Hanabanilla or book a day excursion (around USD$33 from Santa Clara; USD$69 from Cayo Santa María). Outside the hotel gates, licensed private guides offer all the above trips for cheaper prices.

Fishing

Whopping 9kg largemouth bass have been caught on the lake, and fishing trips can be organized at the hotel: or with private guides outside. For two people with a guide, prices start at USD$50 for four hours. December to March is the best season.

Hiking

The Sierra del Escambray is riddled with walking trails. The most accessible and well-publicized routes emanate out of Topes de Collantes in Sancti Spíritus Province and are well traipsed by tourists based in nearby Trinidad. Far less crowded are the trails that surround Embalse Hanabanilla in Villa Clara Province, most of which require a boat transfer from the Hotel Hanabanilla. The hotel has more information on the trails and a (very) rough relief map stuck on the wall. Private guides wait outside the hotel.

La Colicambiada A 9km out-and-back trail to a *mirador* atop a forested hill passing an isolated farmer's house on the way. It starts near the Río Negro, utilizing the same trailhead as La Montaña por Dentro.

La Montaña por Dentro A 17km hike connecting Embalse Hanabanilla to El Nicho waterfall on the Cienfuegos side of the Sierra del Escambray. It's signposted from the boat dock at Río Negro, but get a guide as it's poorly marked.

Un Reto a Loma Atahalaya A 12km all-encompassing walk starting from near the Hotel Hanabanilla that incorporates a climb up the 700m-high Loma Atahalaya, a waterfall and a local *campesino* (farmer) house. It finishes at La Cueva de Brollo.

🛏 Sleeping & Eating

Body-swerve the rather drab restaurant in the Hotel Hanabanilla and enjoy some full-on rustic cooking at the Casa del Campesino (lunch USD$8; ⊙11am-3pm) atop a small hill overlooking the lake. There's another country-style restaurant at Río Negro (mains USD$5-6; ⊙9am-5pm), the starting point for most of the area's hikes.

Hotel Hanabanilla   HOTEL $$
(📞42-20-84-61; Salto de Hanabanilla; s/d USD$62/72; 🅿❄🛁) Another page from the utilitarian school of Cuban architecture that blemished many a beauty spot in the 1970s, the 125-room Hanabanilla has attempted regular refurbs in the years since, though none have fully eradicated its incongruous ugliness. However, closer inspection reveals reasonable facilities inside, including an à la carte restaurant, a swimming pool, a vista-laden bar and lake-facing rooms with small balconies.

Peaceful during the week but packed with mainly Cuban guests at weekends, it is your only option for miles and the best base for lakeside activities. To get here from Manicaragua, proceed west on route 152 for 13km. Turn left at a junction (the hotel is signposted) and follow the road 10km to the hotel.

ℹ Getting There & Away

The chalked-up bus schedule in Santa Clara advertises daily buses to Manicaragua (but check ahead). Theoretically, there are buses from Manicaragua on to Embalse Hanabanilla, but the only practical access is by car, bike or moped. Taxi drivers in Santa Clara will energetically offer the trip (about USD$50 one way). Negotiate hard if you want the driver to wait while you participate in excursions.

Remedios

POP 46,000

A small, tranquil town that goes berserk every Christmas Eve in a cacophonous firework festival known as Las Parrandas, Remedios is one of Cuba's lesser-glimpsed colonial highlights. Some historical sources claim it is Cuba's second-oldest settlement, although it is officially listed at number eight. It proudly celebrated its quincentennial in 2015. The anniversary transformed Remedios from a slightly scruffy stopover on the way to Cayo Santa María into a mini Trinidad replete with handsome boutique hotels, a beautifully restored central square (Plaza Martí) and several decent eating joints. However, the bulk of Cuba's culture-seeking tourists have yet to cotton on to Remedios' glorious rebirth. Come now before they find out.

◉ Sights

Remedios is the only city in Cuba with two churches on its main square. Since the 500th anniversary celebrations in 2015, the place has been reborn as its former elegant self: the once-tatty colonial buildings haven't sparkled this brightly since – oh – 1850.

★ Parroquia de San Juan Bautista de Remedios   CHURCH
(Map p272; Camilo Cienfuegos No 20; by donation; ⊙9am-noon & 2-5pm Mon-Sat) One of the island's most interesting and oldest ecclesiastical buildings, Remedios' main church dates from around 1550, although much of the current structure is the result of extensive 18th-century renovations. The wooden ceiling was once the hull of a boat, while the gold-leaf high altar is carved from Cuban cedar in classic baroque style. The church's main curiosity is a rare carving of a pregnant Inmaculada concepción made in Seville, Spain. Other important statues include San Salvador (north side) and Carmen (south side), depicting the two neighborhood patrons represented in the town's Las Parrandas festival. The statue of the Virgen del Cobre (Cuba's patron saint) is the second oldest in Cuba after the Santiago original.

Entrance to the church is through the small rear door. Get one of the assistants to show you around, as its precious artifacts deserve a full explanation.

Museo de las Parrandas Remedianas   MUSEUM
(Map p272; Alejandro del Río No 74; USD$1; ⊙9am-6pm Tue-Sat) Visiting this museum two blocks

off Parque Martí is no substitute for the real-life revelry of Remedios' firework-driven Las Parrandas, but what the hell? It maintains a photo gallery that usually recaps the previous year's festival along with historical information on the tradition, including scale models of floats and depictions of how the fireworks are made. Enthusiastic guides will show you around when available, but beware of temperamental opening times.

Iglesia de Nuestra Señora del Buen Viaje   CHURCH
(Map p272; Alejandro del Río No 66) On Parque Martí, the 18th-century Iglesia de Nuestra Señora del Buen Viaje has a striking bell tower. It is named after a statue of the Virgin Mary taken there by sailors in 1600.

Museo de Música Alejandro García Caturla   MUSEUM
(Map p272; Parque Martí No 5; ⊙9am-5pm Tue-Sat) Between the churches in the main square is the former house of Alejandro García Caturla, a Cuban composer and musician who lived here from 1920 until his murder in 1940. Caturla was a pioneer who integrated Afro-Cuban rhythms into classical music and also served as a lawyer and judge. The house hosts occasional impromptu concerts as well as this small museum.

★ Festivals & Events

Las Parrandas   CARNIVAL
(⊙Dec) Small-town Remedios ignites (quite literally) one of Cuba's biggest festivals a few days before Christmas with revelries culminating on December 24. The town divides into two competing camps in a street 'battle' of colorful floats, illuminations and fireworks. It's a show to behold – if very noisy and crowded. Book well ahead for accommodations.

⎙ Sleeping & Eating

Despite its other attributes, Remedios has rather a light coating of private restaurants. Fortunately, many of the casas particulares (private homestays) also serve excellent food. There are a couple of government bars that ply snacks in pleasant nooks and the hotels are all equipped with food service.

★ 'Villa Colonial' – Frank & Arelys   CASA PARTICULAR $
(Map p272; ☑42-39-62-74; www.cubavillacolonial.com; Maceo No 43, cnr Av General Carrillo; r USD$25-30; ❈@☞) Frank and Arelys' wonderful colonial house is their pride and joy

Remedios Ⓝ 0 ———— 100 m

Remedios

◎ Top Sights
1 Parroquia de San Juan
   Bautista de Remedios B3

◎ Sights
2 Iglesia de Nuestra Señora
   del Buen Viaje B1
3 Museo de las Parrandas
   Remedianas A1
4 Museo de Música Alejandro
   García Caturla B2

⊜ Sleeping
5 Hostal Camino del Príncipe B2
6 Hostal Casa Richard B4
7 Hostal La Estancia B3
8 Hotel Barcelona A3
9 La Paloma A2
10 'Villa Colonial' – Frank &
   Arelys B4

⊗ Eating
11 La Piramide A1

◉ Drinking & Nightlife
12 Driver's Bar B3
13 El Louvre A2
14 Taberna de los 7 Juanas A2

◉ Entertainment
15 Centro Cultural las
   Leyendas A3

⊜ Shopping
16 Tres Reyes A2

– and it shows. The six independent rooms have their own entrance, private bathroom, dining area (with stocked fridge), and living room with massive windows protected by iron *rejas* (bars) and adorned with decorative *mamparas* (swing doors).

Hostal Casa Richard   CASA PARTICULAR $
(Map p272; ☑5-294-0285, 42-39-66-49; hostal-casarichard@gmail.com; Maceo No 52, btwn Av General Carrillo & Fe del Valle; r USD$25-30; ❋☎) Long-term renters with four rooms that include plenty of extras (hairdryers, soaps, umbrellas). The rooms open onto a lovely uncluttered patio (unless you count the lush avocado tree), complete with the essential rocking chairs. Owner Richard is extremely obliging and a great source of local knowledge. If his place is full, he can recommend another family house nearby.

Hostal La Estancia   CASA PARTICULAR $
(Map p272; ☑42-39-55-82; www.laestanciahostal. com; Camilo Cienfuegos 34, btwn Av General Carrillo

& José Peña; r USD$30; ❋) This house dating from 1849 has myriad museum-worthy furnishings, attractive beamed ceilings, a fancy drawing room with a piano, and three big rooms surrounding a small largely decorative pool. The patio hosts one of Remedios' best private restaurants.

La Paloma   CASA PARTICULAR $
(Map p272; ☑42-39-54-90; Parque Martí No 4; r USD$25; ℗❋☎) Sharing prime frontage on Remedios' main square along with four of the town's historic hotels, the rooms in this private home date from 1875 and share antique trimmings, tile work and furnishings that would be worth zillions anywhere else.

★**Hostal Camino
del Príncipe**   BOUTIQUE HOTEL $$
(Map p272; ☑42-39-51-44; Camilo Cienfuegos No 9, btwn Montaiván & Alejandro del Río; s/d USD$55/80; ❋☎) A mark of Remedios' recent progression, this hotel with its elegant white pillars holding up a handsome terracotta facade is

one of Cuba's best boutique offerings. Loaded with the kind of low-key charm the town is famous for, it successfully melds modern comfort with old-world glory.

Hotel Barcelona
BOUTIQUE HOTEL $$

(Map p272; ☑42-39-51-44; José Peña No 67; s/d USD$50/80; ❄) The mint-green Barcelona instantly impresses with its stained glass, wooden lattice and noble arches. Its 34 rooms wrap around three floors of a glorious vine-draped internal courtyard. No expense is spared throughout. There is also an atmospheric restaurant.

La Piramide
CUBAN $$

(Map p272; ☑42-39-54-21; Andrés del Río No 9; 3-course meals USD$10-13; ⊙10:30am-2:30pm & 6:30-10:30pm, closed Tue) Remedios doesn't have many private restaurants, making this 1st-floor haven of good taste especially welcome. Three-course meals such as surf and turf *brochetas* (shish kebabs) come with bread, coffee and all the trimmings.

🍷 Drinking & Nightlife

Driver's Bar
BAR

(Map p272; José Peña No 61, cnr Camilo Cienfuegos; ⊙10am-midnight) Once a dive, the Driver's has lifted itself into posher territory. A local artist has given it a throwback 1950s feel with a strong focus on automobiles. Vintage-car enthusiasts and the local bici-taxi drivers tend to congregate here, meaning the prices are cheap and the atmosphere authentically Cuban.

Taberna de los 7 Juanas
BAR

(Map p272; Parque Martí, cnr Máximo Gómez; ⊙10am-midnight) Remedios' 500th anniversary bequeathed the city many good things, not least this colonial-style place across the square from long-standing default bar, El Louvre (which probably benefits from the competition). The service is sharp, the location sublime and the beer plentiful. It even has its own wine cellar.

El Louvre
CAFE, BAR

(Map p272; Máximo Gómez No 122; ⊙7:30am-midnight) With a gravitational pull on Remedios' scattering of tourists, El Louvre is, so locals proclaim, the oldest bar in the country, in continuous service since 1866 – and who are *you* to argue? The bar was good enough for Spanish poet Federico García Lorca, who heads the list of famous former patrons. It does basic food too.

⭐ Entertainment

Centro Cultural las Leyendas
CULTURAL CENTER

(Map p272; Máximo Gómez, btwn Margalí & Independencia) Under the shady arcades in the main square, 'Legends' is an ARTex cultural center with music till 1am from Wednesday to Saturday.

🛍 Shopping

Tres Reyes
CIGARS

(Map p272; cnr Máximo Gómez & Margali; ⊙9am-5pm) Heavily air-conditioned cigar shop selling Cuba's best smokes along with coffee, rum, local honey and other souvenirs. The servers are generally pretty knowledgeable about their wares and a *torcedor* (cigar roller) is often present.

ℹ Getting There & Away

BUS

The **bus station** (Av Cespedes, btwn Margalí & La Fragua) is on the southern side of town at the beginning of the 45km road to Santa Clara.

There's one daily Víazul bus (www.viazul.com) to Cayo Santa María (USD$6, 1½ hours) via Caibarién, and one in the other direction calling at Santa Clara (USD$7, 1¼ hours), Cienfuegos (USD$11, three hours) and Trinidad (USD$14, 4¼ hours).

TAXI

A taxi from the bus station to Caibarién will cost roughly USD$5; to Santa Clara or Cayo Santa María the fare is USD$30 to USD$35. Bici-taxis run from the bus station to Parque Martí for small change.

Caibarién

POP 32,500

Hit hard by Hurricane Irma in 2017, Caibarién is a town in recovery. Since the piers slumped into the sea and the provincial sugar mills closed down several decades ago, the town's economic foundations have shifted to tourism (one old sugar mill is now a museum). Although there are few sights in the town itself, the settlement supplies most of the staff for Cayo Santa María's all-inclusive resorts.

Caibarién is also famous for its *cangrejo* (crab), the best in Cuba, and crackling December Las Parrandas festival, allegedly second only to Remedios' in explosiveness.

For those keen to catch a glimpse of the keys and their beaches without shelling out the expensive all-inclusive prices, Caibarién makes a cheap and friendly alternative base.

SAGUA LA GRANDE

Off the beaten path since the brakes were put on Cuba's sugar industry in the 1930s, the erstwhile sugar town of Sagua La Grande is currently enjoying a mini revival. The renaissance reflects recent efforts by the Cuban government to invest in the Villa Clara settlement after it was listed as a 'national monument' in 2011. With plans to develop the virgin keys on the nearby coast with all-inclusive resorts, Sagua's lure as a historical draw for tourists could soon thrust it further into the limelight.

For the time being, the place remains deliciously sleepy – part contemporary Cuban reality, part primped and painted recreation of its affluent past.

Bar a few noisy games of dominoes, there's not much to break the reverie in central Plaza Martí. With its elegant streetlamps and attractive neoclassical facades, the square is anchored by the Iglesia de Purísima Concepción, the fourth incarnation of a church first built here in 1796, 16 years before the town itself was founded. Rising beside the church is the exquisite four-story Hotel Sagua (42-66-55-66; Ribalta btwn Martí & Balton; s/d USD$35/50;), surely one of Cuba's finest historic accommodations. First opened in 1925 (Spanish poet Federico Lorca was an early guest), it reopened in 2017 after a long hiatus. Other distractions in the square include the Café Real (Martí btwn Céspedes & Ribalta; 8am-10pm), a ruby-colored meeting point for caffeine-fueled gossip, and the Galería Wifredo Lam (Martíi cnr Céspedes; noon-8pm Tue-Fri, 8am-noon & 2-6pm Sat, 2-6pm Sun) FREE, a small exhibition space for local art. Lam, arguably Cuba's greatest painter, was born in Sagua in 1902 and many of his abstract works reflect aspects of the local sugar industry.

Sagua is 53km north of Santa Clara, but currently has no reliable public transport. Rent a car or taxi and be sure to pay a visit to the Puente El Triunfo (1905) on arrival, an iron truss bridge that crosses the lazy Sagua River on the northeast side of town.

Towards Remedios, 3km past the crab statue, lies the former sugar mill (decommissioned in 1998), which is now Museo de Agroindustria Azucarero Marcelo Salado (42-36-32-86; Carretera Caibarién-Remedios Km 3.5; USD$3, with train ride USD$9; 9am-4pm Mon-Sat) FREE. Of the four preserved sugar mills in Cuba, it's probably the best. On the campus, you'll find potted histories of slave culture, the sugar industry, and pre-diesel locomotives. There's a video of Cuba's sugar industry models of figures toiling to harvest the product and lots of original machinery. A guide talks you through the process and dispatches gratis *guarapo* (sugarcane juice).

An added bonus is the extensive collection of locomotives – the place is also known as the Museo de Vapor (Museum of Steam) – featuring Latin America's largest steam engine, and there are daily rides in a 1904 American steam train to Remedios (mechanics permitting).

Positioning itself as an all-in-one Caibarién stop, Casa Pocurull (5-251-0763; Calle 10 No 1106; mains USD$4-15; 7am-11pm;) is a three-pronged business consisting of a streetside cafe (enjoy cheap sandwiches, fruit shakes and burgers), a bright patio restaurant (reasonable seafood dishes for around CUC$15) and three classic Cuban

rooms for rent with high ceilings, large beds and wi-fi (CUC$25 per night).

ℹ Getting There & Away

National carrier Víazul (www.viazul.com) has one daily bus to Cayo Santa María (USD$6, 1¼ hours), departing at 12:05pm. In the other direction there's one daily bus that stops in Remedios (USD$3, 10 minutes), Santa Clara (USD$7, 1½ hours) and Cienfuegos (USD$11, three hours), before terminating in Trinidad (USD$14, 4½ hours). It departs Caibarién at 3pm from outside the **Servi-Cupet gas station** at the entrance to town.

Several local buses a day go to Remedios, Santa Clara and Yaguajay from Caibarién's old blue-and-white **bus and train station** (Calle 6) on the western side of town.

Cayerías del Norte

Cuba's newest tourist project splays across a scattered archipelago of pancake-flat keys off the north coast of Villa Clara Province. While avoiding some of the architectural hideousness of other Cuban resorts, development here is wide-reaching and rapid, and sits a little awkwardly alongside the Buenavista Unesco Biosphere Reserve, which it abuts. The keys were uninhabited wilderness until 1998 when the first hotel went up. Recently the almost identical all-inclusive resorts support a clientele that's predominantly Canadian. Located on three different keys – Cayo las Brujas, Cayo Ensenachos and Cayo Santa María – linked by an impressive 48km causeway called El Pedraplén, the enclave aims at the luxury end of the market.

For day-trippers, the Cayerías have retained two slivers of public-access beach, with water activities, and a (very) small wildlife refuge. Resorts sell day-use passes from around USD$70.

Sights & Activities

Every hotel offers the same organized activities for the same prices, all administered by state-run Gaviota. Most are water-based, including diving, snorkeling and fishing. Jeep safaris head to the mainland daily, and there are also tours of Remedios and Santa Clara. For a DIY experience, there are several tame walking trails in the Refugio de Fauna Cayo Santa María (Map p276).

Playa Las Gaviotas   BEACH
(Map p276; Cayo Santa María; USD$4) One of the few beaches left on Cayo Santa María not connected to a resort, Playa Las Gaviotas is located inside a nature reserve at the far east of the island. Pay your entry fee in the car park and follow a 700m trail to the beach, which has an offshore reef but little shade since a recent hurricane blew away most of the trees.

Marina Gaviota   WATER SPORTS
(Map p276; 42-35-00-13; Cayo las Brujas) Most water-based activities are funneled through the hotels, but you can also arrange them directly at the marina on Cayo las Brujas. Highlights include a day-long catamaran cruise with snorkeling (USD$89 to USD$100), and deep-sea fishing (USD$305 for four people). Diving to one of 24 offshore sites is also offered (USD$45/65 for one/two immersions).

La Bolera   BOWLING
(Map p276; per person USD$5; ⊙10am-2am) There's a modern bowling alley with an adjacent bar and pool tables in Plaza La Estrella. Dead in the day, the balls roll faster in the evenings.

Sleeping

The cayos have 20 (and counting) all-inclusive resorts, most of them on Cayo Santa María. All the resorts offer comfortable accommodations in two- or three-story buildings spread over expansive grounds. All have pools and gyms; most have tennis courts. Five, including the plush Meliá Buenavista, are adults only. Gaviota, a company owned by the Cuban government, runs the whole show.

Villa las Brujas   HOTEL, RESORT $$
(Map p276; 42-35-01-99; www.gaviota-grupo.com; Cayo las Brujas; s/d incl breakfast USD$70/86; P ❄ @) Atop a small, relatively untamed headland crowned by a statue of a *bruja* (witch), Villa las Brujas is the cayerías' oldest (1999), smallest and most modest resort. If you can't abide sprawling all-inclusives, you may well love this quiet non-manicured place situated amid tangled mangroves and evoking the air of a tropical *Wuthering Heights* when a cold front blows in.

★ Meliá Buenavista   RESORT $$$
(Map p276; 42-35-07-00; www.meliacuba.com; Punta Madruguilla, Cayo Santa María; s/d all-inclusive USD$360/450; ❄ @ 🛜 🏊) Small really is beautiful at the Buenavista, where 105 rooms (a baby by cayo standards) are located apart from the other hotels at the western end of Cayo Santa María where, on a quiet sunset-facing beach, wine is brought to you by obliging butlers. Welcome to a veritable romantic heaven (no kids allowed).

★ Iberostar Ensenachos   RESORT $$$
(Map p276; 42-35-03-00; www.iberostar.com; Cayo Ensenachos; s/d all-inclusive USD$250/380; ❄ @ 🛜 🏊) A top-end paradise reminiscent of a Maldives private-island getaway, this is the only hotel on tiny Cayo Ensenachos and bags two of Cuba's best beaches (Playas Ensenachos and Mégano). One portion of the hotel is adults only. Refined decor, with Alhambra-esque fountains and attractive natural foliage. Guests are accommodated in pretty 20-unit blocks; each unit has its own private concierge.

Royalton Cayo Santa María   RESORT $$$
(Map p276; 42-35-09-00; www.royaltonresorts.com; Cayo Santa María; s/d all-inclusive USD$245/340; ❄ @ 🛜 🏊) The favorite of many on the cayos, the Royalton lays on the romantic theme pretty strong with lots of lace-curtain four-poster sunbeds around a terraced infinity pool. It is relatively small (122 rooms), adults only and popular with the Canadian honeymoon set.

Ocean Casa del Mar   RESORT $$$
(Map p276; 42-35-08-50; www.oceanhotels.net; Cayo Santa María; s/d all-inclusive USD$150/221; ❄ @ 🛜 🏊) Run by the Spanish H10 chain, the Ocean, with its gleaming modern

Cayo Santa María Area

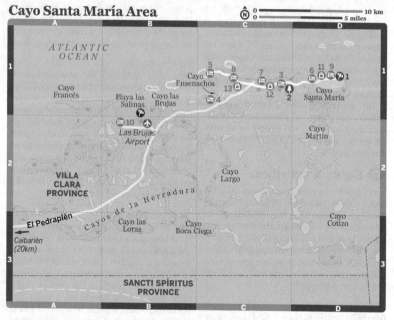

Cayo Santa María Area

three-story blocks, resembles a plush Miami suburb. There are some interesting touches like retro tiles in the lobby, heavy drapes and wooden (as opposed to plastic) sun-loungers, but with a clientele that's almost exclusively Canadian, you're more likely to end up discussing ice hockey than José Martí's poems.

Valentín Perla Blanca   RESORT **$$$**
(Map p276; 42-35-06-21; www.valentin hotels.com; Cayo Santa María; s/d all-inclusive USD$216/288; ❄@🛜⊠) The resort furthest east on the cayo is the adults-only Valentín, a 1020-room mini-town that is split into two areas, one reserved for tranquility

seekers and the other for the party set. Sparkling rooms are hosted in white three-story apartment-style blocks and the overall look is clean-lined minimalist with sharp color accents. Procure a map at reception for navigation.

Sol Cayo Santa María   RESORT **$$$**
(Map p276; 42-35-02-00; www.meliacuba. com; Cayo Santa María; s/d all-inclusive from USD$167/238; ❄@🛜⊠) The Sol was the first resort to grace this then virgin key in 2001 (it has since been joined by 15 more) and remains its lowest ranked by star-rating (3½ stars). The advantages? Reasonable prices

married with a few old-school quirks including rocking chairs on terraces, leafy grounds, and wooden buildings embellished with latticework and brown balustrades.

Golden Tulip Aguas Claras   RESORT $$$
(Map p276; ☑ 42-35-00-16; Cayo Santa María; r all-inclusive from USD$320; ❄@🛜🏊) Open since 2013, this massive 846-room hotel, currently managed by the French Louvre Group, has already changed its name twice. What hasn't changed is the Fuego y Hielo restaurant, one of the sleekest resort eateries hereabouts; the romantically inclined may appreciate the private dining in the middle of the three-level pool.

🍴 Eating

The cayos are an all-inclusive zone. Most people eat exclusively in their hotels.

Plaza La Estrella and Pueblo Las Dunas on Cayo Santa María have several restaurants each where visitors not staying in the resorts (and vacationers sick of the buffet food) can dine.

Farallón Restaurant   INTERNATIONAL $$
(Map p276; Villa las Brujas; mains USD$6-12; ⊙noon-3pm & 7-10:30pm) If you buy a day pass to enjoy Playas Las Salinas, you'll be eating in the strategically located if gastronomically mediocre Farallón, perched like a bird's nest overlooking the blissful beach. It's part of the Villa las Brujas and nonguests can enjoy lunch with use of beach, bathrooms and parking for USD$15.

☆ Entertainment

Jazz Bar   LIVE MUSIC
(Map p276; Plaza La Estrella; ⊙8pm-2am) If you get sick of Kyle from Kitchener, Ontario, hogging the karaoke machine, head over to this jazz bar in the Plaza La Estrella shopping center for momentary solace.

🛍 Shopping

Plaza Las Dunas   SHOPPING CENTER
(Map p276) One of three 'toy town' shopping centers on the cayos, this one comes complete with fake Spanish galleon, fake lighthouse and fake town square. Granted, it isn't ugly and the shops might come in handy if you've forgotten your swimming gear or sunglasses, but there's something faintly Vegaslike about the atmosphere (or lack of it).

Las Terrazas del Atardecer   SHOPPING CENTER
(Map p276; Cayo Santa María) The newest of the three shopping/entertainment centers on Cayo Santa María, this one has its own beach – although you're supposed to pay USD$5 to use it. There's also the obligatory bowling alley, multiple shops and a good ocean-facing cocktail bar called Chachachá's.

Plaza La Estrella   SHOPPING CENTER
(Map p276; Cayo Santa María; ⊙9am-7:30pm) Welcome to a Cuban town full of...Canadians. It's hard to know what to make of this mock colonial village with its imitation Manaca Iznaga tower and phony plaza surrounded by shops, a bowling alley, spa-gymnasium and restaurants designed for the resort crowds. Think of it as a curious anomaly that's easier on the eye than your average North American shopping mall.

ⓘ Getting There & Away

AIR

Las Brujas Airport (Map p276; ☑ 42-35-00-09) has occasional charter flights to Havana with Aerogaviota. However, most tourists arrive at Abel Santamaría Airport (p269) near Santa Clara and transfer from there.

BUS

Víazul (www.viazul.com) has a daily bus to and from Trinidad (USD$20, 5¾ hours) that also stops in Caibarién (USD$6, 1¼ hours), Remedios (USD$6, 1½ hours) and Santa Clara (USD$13, three hours). Once on the cayos, it stops at most of the hotels. Check at your accommodations for exact arrival/departure times.

CAR & MOTORCYCLE

For those not on package tours with airport pickups, access is by rental car, moped or taxi. From Cayo Santa María it is 56km to Caibarién, 65km to Remedios and 110km to Santa Clara. The causeway is accessed from Caibarién and there's a toll booth (USD$2 each way), where you'll need to show your passport/visa.

There's a Servicentro gas station opposite Las Brujas Airport.

TAXI

The one-way fares from Caibarién/Remedios/Santa Clara by taxi are approximately USD$30/35/75 to Cayo Santa María (depending on which hotel you're aiming for). Bargain hard – particularly if you want to get a return fare with waiting time.

ⓘ Getting Around

Panoramic Bus Tour is a double-decker open-topped hop-on, hop-off bus that links all the hotels between Cayo las Brujas and Cayo Santa María hotels several times daily. A daily pass costs USD$2.

AT A GLANCE

POPULATION
465,931

OLDEST COLONIAL CITY
Trinidad: 1514

BEST MUSEUM
Museo Nacional
Camilo Cienfuegos
(p303)

BEST HIKE
Sendero 'Centinelas
del Río Melodioso'
(p294)

BEST WINE
Vista Gourmet
(p287)

WHEN TO GO

Nov–Apr
Peak season when
the town is busy
with visitors. The
popular Semana de
la Cultura Trinitaria
takes place during
the second week of
January.

May–Oct
May is a good time
to visit this province,
as you can avoid
both the crowds and
bad weather during
the quiet off-season.

Trinidad (p281)
ANTON_IVANOV/SHUTTERSTOCK ©

Trinidad & Sancti Spíritus Province

This small province is Cuba at its loveliest, and it also guards a precious chunk of the country's fantastical historical legacy. Sancti Spíritus Province boasts nature worth exploring. The best beach on Cuba's underwhelming south coast, Playa Ancón, is a stunner. And then there are mountains. Outside Trinidad, the haunting Escambray offers outstanding hiking on a network of picturesque trails.

A postcard come alive, Trinidad is one of the most intact colonial towns in the Americas, with red-tile roofs, cobblestone streets and pastel houses with castle-sized colonial doors. Its underdog rival, the city of Sancti Spíritus, offers a more intangible, crumbling allure. In 2014 both celebrated their 500th anniversaries to much fanfare and an invigorated shine on their finest architecture.

But there's even more: a surprisingly varied cache of oft-overlooked curiosities, including lightly trodden eco-parks, a seminal museum dedicated to guerrilla icon Camilo Cienfuegos, and the Unesco-protected Bahía de Buenavista.

Sancti Spíritus Province Highlights

1 **Trinidad** (p281) Visiting museums and basking in the colonial comfort of well-heeled restaurants.

2 **Valle de los Ingenios** (p296) Climbing the tower at the Manaca Iznaga for a killer view of the Unesco-listed sites throughout this lush valley.

3 **Sancti Spíritus** (p296) Strolling without an itinerary around this city's renovated colonial streets.

4 **Jobo Rosado** (p303) Exploring the woodlands, waterfalls and war history in this rich reserve.

5 **Playa Ancón** (p291) Renting a house in La Boca to enjoy the sunset hours on the sands of this popular beach.

6 **Salto del Caburní** (p294) Hiking to a frigid natural bathing pool and diving in.

7 **Centro Ecuestre Diana** (p284) Horseback riding and visiting the cowboy-cool countryside around Trinidad.

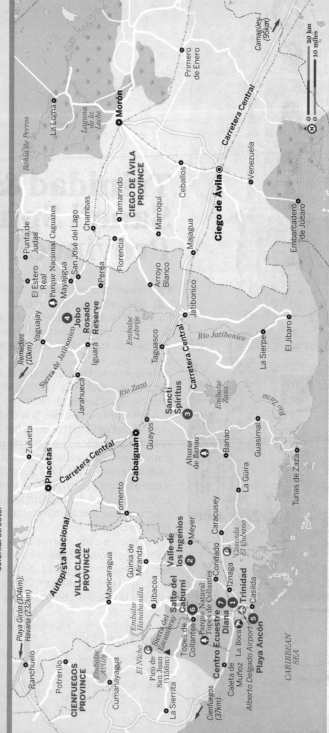

Trinidad

🕿 41 / POP 76,885

Trinidad is one of a kind, a perfectly preserved Spanish-colonial settlement where the clocks stopped in 1850 and – apart from a zombie invasion of tourists – have yet to restart. Huge sugar fortunes amassed in the nearby Valle de los Ingenios during the early 19th century created the illustrious colonial-style mansions bedecked with Italian frescoes, Wedgwood china and French chandeliers.

Declared a World Heritage site by Unesco in 1988, Cuba's oldest and most enchanting 'outdoor museum' attracts busloads of visitors. Yet the cobblestone streets, replete with leather-faced *guajiros* (country folk), snorting donkeys and melodic troubadours, retain a quiet air. Come nightfall, the live-music scene is particularly good.

Trinidad is also surrounded by sparkling natural attractions. Twelve kilometers south lies platinum-blond Playa Ancón, the best beach of Cuba's southern coast. Looming 18km to the north, the purple-hued shadows of the Sierra del Escambray (Escambray Mountains) offer a lush adventure playground with hiking trails and waterfalls.

History

In 1514 conquistador Diego Velázquez de Cuéllar founded La Villa de la Santísima Trinidad on Cuba's south coast, the island's third settlement after Baracoa and Bayamo. In 1518 Velázquez' former secretary, Hernán Cortés, passed through the town recruiting mercenaries for his all-conquering expedition to Mexico, and the settlement was all but emptied of its inhabitants. Over the ensuing 60 years, it was left to a smattering of the local Taíno people to keep the ailing economy alive through a mixture of farming, cattle-rearing and a little outside trade.

Reduced to a small rural backwater by the 17th century and cut off from the colonial authorities in Havana by dire communications, Trinidad became a haven for pirates and smugglers who conducted a lucrative illegal slave trade with British-controlled Jamaica.

Things began to change in the early 19th century when the town became the capital of the Departamento Central, and hundreds of French refugees fleeing a slave rebellion in Haiti arrived, setting up more than 50 small sugar mills in the nearby Valle de los Ingenios. Sugar soon replaced leather and salted beef as the region's most important

product; by the mid-19th century, the area around Trinidad was producing a third of Cuba's sugar.

The boom ended rather abruptly during the Independence Wars, when the surrounding sugar plantations were devastated by fire and fighting. The industry never fully recovered. By the late 19th century, the focus of the sugar trade had shifted to Cienfuegos and Matanzas provinces, and Trinidad slipped into an economic coma.

The tourist renaissance began in the 1950s, when President Batista passed a preservation law that recognized the town's historical value. In 1965 the town was declared a national monument, and in 1988 it became a Unesco World Heritage site.

◉ Sights

In Trinidad, all roads lead to **Plaza Mayor** (Map p282), the town's remarkably peaceful main square, located at the heart of the *casco histórico* (old town) and ringed by a quartet of impressive buildings.

★**Museo Histórico Municipal** MUSEUM
(Map p282; 🕿 4199-4460; Simón Bolívar No 423; USD$2; ⊙ 9am-5pm Sat-Thu) Just off Plaza Mayor, this grandiose mansion, Trinidad's main museum, belonged to the Borrell family from 1827 to 1830. Later it passed to a German planter named Kanter, or Cantero, for whom it's now named. The run-down exhibits could use a full makeover, but the city panoramas from the tower, reached by rickety stairs, is worth the price of admission alone.

Reputedly, Dr Justo Cantero acquired vast sugar estates by poisoning an old slave trader and marrying his widow, who also suffered an untimely death. Cantero's ill-gotten wealth is well displayed in the stylish neoclassical decoration of the rooms. Visit before 11am, when the tour buses start rolling in.

**Iglesia Parroquial
de la Santísima Trinidad** CHURCH
(Map p282; ⊙ 11am-12:30pm Mon-Sat) Despite its unremarkable facade, this church on the northeastern side of Plaza Mayor graces countless Trinidad postcards. Rebuilt in 1892 on the site of a church destroyed in a storm, it mixes 20th-century touch-ups with artifacts dating to the 18th century, such as the venerated Christ of the True Cross (1713), second altar from the front to the left.

Plaza Santa Ana PLAZA
(Camilo Cienfuegos; ⊙ 11am-10pm) Located on the eponymous square, which delineates

Trinidad

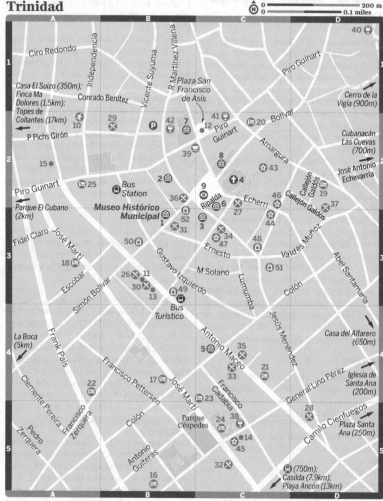

Trinidad's northeastern reaches, is a former Spanish prison (1844) that has been converted into the Plaza Santa Ana tourist center. The complex includes an art gallery, handicraft market, ceramics shop, bar and restaurant.

Museo Romántico MUSEUM
(Map p282; ☎4199-4363; Echerri No 52; USD$2; ☺9am-5pm Tue-Sun) The ground floor of the glittering Palacio Brunet was built in 1740, and the upstairs was added in 1808. In 1974 the mansion was converted into a museum with 19th-century furnishings, a fine collection of china and various other period pieces.

Pushy museum staff may materialize out of the shadows for a tip.

The shop adjacent has a good selection of photos and books in English.

Museo de Arquitectura Trinitaria MUSEUM
(Map p282; ☎4199-3208; Ripalda No 83; USD$1; ☺9am-5pm Sat-Thu) A public display of wealth sits on the southeastern side of Plaza Mayor in a museum showcasing upper-class domestic architecture of the 18th and 19th centuries. Housed in buildings erected in 1738 and 1785 and joined in 1819, the museum was once the residence of the wealthy Iznaga family.

Trinidad

Maqueta de Trinidad　　　　　MUSEUM
(Map p282; ☑4199-4308; cnr Colón & Maceo; USD$1; ⊙9am-5pm Tue-Sat, to 1pm Sun) Opened in 2014 and encased in the beautifully restored Casa Frias, this scale model of Trinidad's *casco histórico* displays amazing attention to detail (try to pick out your casa particular – private homestay). A resident guide will fill you in on what's what with a conductor-like stick. Also offers city tours in English and Spanish (USD$5).

Casa Templo de Santería Yemayá　MUSEUM
(Map p282; Rubén Martínez Villena No 59, btwn Simón Bolívar & Piro Guinart; ⊙hours vary) **FREE**
You will need some luck to find this religious center in action. While no Santería museum can replicate the ethereal experience of Regla de Ocha (also known as Santería, Cuba's main religion of African origin), this house tries with a Santería altar to Yemayá, goddess of the sea, laden with myriad offerings of fruit, water and stones.

The house is presided over by *santeros* (priests), who'll emerge from the back patio and surprise you with some well-rehearsed tourist spiel. On the goddess's anniversary, March 19, ceremonies are performed day and night.

**Museo Nacional de la
Lucha Contra Bandidos**　　　　MUSEUM
(Map p282; ☑4199-4121; Echerri No 59; USD$1; ⊙9am-5pm Tue-Sun) The most recognizable building in Trinidad, this dilapidated pastel-yellow bell tower occupies the former convent of San Francisco de Asís. Since 1986 it's been a museum with photos, maps, weapons and objects relating to the struggle against the various counterrevolutionary bands that took a leaf out of Fidel's book and operated illicitly out of the Sierra del Escambray between 1960 and 1965.

The fuselage of a US U-2 spy plane shot down over Cuba is also on display. You can climb the bell tower for good views.

TRINIDAD'S COLONIAL ARCHITECTURE

Trinidad is one of the best-preserved colonial towns in the Americas. Most of its remarkably homogeneous architecture dates from the early 19th century when Trinidad's sugar industry reached its zenith. Typical Trinidad houses are large one-story buildings with terracotta-tiled roofs held up by wooden beams. Unlike in Havana, the huge front doors usually open directly into a main room rather than a vestibule. Other typical Trinidadian features include large glass-less windows fronted with wooden (or iron) bars, wall frescoes, verandas, and balconies with wooden balustrades raised above the street. Larger Trinidad houses have *mudéjar*-style courtyards with trademark *aljibes* (storage wells).

Galería de Arte Benito Ortiz   GALLERY
(Map p282; cnr Rubén Martínez Villena & Simón Bolívar; ⊙9am-4:30pm Mon-Sat) **FREE** On the southeastern side of Plaza Mayor, the 19th-century Palacio Ortiz houses an art gallery. It's worth a look for its quality local art, particularly the embroidery, pottery and jewelry. There's also a pleasant courtyard.

🏃 Activities

Ride a bike to one of Cuba's outstanding beaches, work up a sweat on a couple of DIY hikes, or get a different perspective astride a horse.

When booking an excursion in the region, check that transportation is included. It's not included with snorkel and dive trips.

★ Centro Ecuestre Diana   HORSEBACK RIDING
(Map p282; Independencia No 39, btwn Girón & Benítez; riding USD$26) Among the barrage of offers you'll hear in Trinidad are those for horseback rides. Booking on the street is discouraged, as you won't know the condition of the (sometimes neglected or mistreated) horses. Rest assured that with this outfit, you will enjoy a safe ride on a healthy, mild-mannered and well-cared-for horse. Book a day before at the address listed; rides depart at 9am.

Rides meander into the Valle de los Ingenios, though not as far as the historical sugar sites. There's a lunch stop (not included in the price) and an opportunity to swim in a small waterfall-fed pool.

Parque El Cubano   HIKING
(USD$10) This pleasant spot within a protected park consists of a *ranchón* (farm-style restaurant) serving *pez gato* (catfish) from the on-site fish farm. Take the **Huellas de la História trail** (3.6km) to the refreshing **Javira Waterfall**. With a stop for lunch in the *ranchón*, it can make an excellent day trip.

Cubatur (p290) leads trips with motorized transportation, or you can hire a taxi from Trinidad (USD$30 round trip).

The hike to El Cubano from Trinidad is approximately 16km. Go west out of town on the Cienfuegos road. Pass the 'Welcome to Trinidad' sign and cross a bridge over the Río Guaurabo. A track on your left leads back under the bridge and up a narrow, poorly paved road for 5km to Parque el Cubano.

Cerro de la Vigía   HIKING
For a good workout and broad vistas of Trinidad, the Valle de los Ingenios and the Caribbean littoral, walk up Simón Bolívar between the Iglesia Parroquial and the Museo Romántico to the destroyed 18th-century hermitage, part of a former Spanish military hospital turned luxury hotel. From here it's 30 minutes further up the hill to the radio transmitter (180m).

🎓 Courses

Las Ruinas del Teatro Brunet   DANCING
(Map p282; Antonio Maceo No 461, btwn Simón Bolívar & Zerquera; lessons per hour from USD$5) The roofless ruins of an 1840-vintage theater are now an entertainment space where you can take drumming and dance lessons (inquire within for times).

Paradiso   MUSIC
(Map p282; General Lino Pérez No 306, Casa ARTex; ⊙8am-5pm Mon-Sat, to noon Sun) This tour desk in Casa Fischer has some interesting courses, including salsa, percussion, Spanish and cultural topics such as Cuban architecture and Afro-Cuban culture. These courses last four hours and are taught by cultural specialists. They also offer the best-priced tours of the area, including the Valle de los Ingenios and Trinitopes waterfall (USD$15). A city night tour travels via horse-drawn carriage (USD$20).

👉 Tours

With its sketchy public transportation and steep road gradients making cycling arduous, it's easiest to visit the extensive natural park of Topes de Collantes on a day tour from Trinidad.

Trinidad Travels
TOURS

(Map p282; ☑ 5-282-3726; www.trinidadtravels. com; Antonio Maceo No 613a) One of the best private guides is English- and Italian-speaking Reinier at Trinidad Travels. He leads all kinds of excursions, including hiking in the Sierra del Escambray and horseback riding in the nearby countryside, as well as Spanish lessons. This is a safe, reputable outfit with healthy horses. He's based at Casa de Victor (p286).

Free Walking Tour
WALKING

(Map p282; Parque San Francisco de Asís; ⊙10am & 4pm) A cool bunch of multilingual Cubans lead free two-hour walking tours of Trinidad, daily at 10am and 4pm. This is an excellent way to familiarize yourself with the city, giving insight into historical background and local tips. Meet up at Parque San Francisco de Asís, the little plaza across from the Museo Nacional de la Lucha Contra Bandidos (p283). Tip your guide!

Ecotur
TOURS

(Map p282; ☑ 4199-8416; Simón Bolívar No 424) While this permanent office is under renovation, there's a desk in Mesón del Regidor restaurant (p287). It has excursions to Trinitopes by jeep (full day USD$50), a tour to a waterfall and easy hiking in Guanayara (USD$55) and a waterfall safari to El Nicho (USD$65) in Cienfuegos Province.

✨ Festivals & Events

Fiestas Sanjuanera
FIESTA

(⊙late Jun) Trinidad's second big annual shindig takes place around June 24 and is the height of Trinidad-style revelry. This local carnival features buoyant parade floats, costumes, a carnival queen, games and displays of horsemanship – all fueled with plenty of rum and live music.

Semana de la Cultura Trinitaria
CULTURAL

(Trinidad Culture Week; ⊙mid-Jan) This popular festival takes place during the second week of January and coincides with the city's feted anniversary. Trinidad, already bursting with color and music, turns up the volume with folkloric dance and music performances as well as art exhibitions throughout the city.

Semana Santa
RELIGIOUS

(Holy Week; ⊙Mar or Apr) Semana Santa is important in Trinidad, and on Good Friday thousands of people form a procession through the center.

🛏 Sleeping

Almost every house seems to be a casa particular. Arriving by bus or walking the streets with luggage, you'll be besieged by *jineteros* (hustlers) working for commissions, or by casa owners. Take your time and shop around.

A boutique five-star hotel, Pansea Trinidad, is due to open soon. The much-stalled project will integrate part of Ermita de Nuestra Señora de la Candelaria de la Popa, the ruins of a mid-18th-century church, into the hotel.

Casa Muñoz – Julio & Rosa
CASA PARTICULAR $

(Map p282; ☑ 4199-3673; www.trinidadphoto. com; José Martí No 401, cnr Escobar; d/tr/apt USD$40/45/50; P ❄ 🛜) A stunning colonial home with courteous, English-speaking assistance. There are three huge rooms and a two-level apartment. Book early as it's insanely popular with licensed US people-to-people groups. Julio is an accomplished photographer offering courses and tours (USD$25) on documentary photography, religion and life in Cuba's new economic reality.

Casa Particular El Arcangel
CASA PARTICULAR $

(Map p282; ☑ 5-299-2187, 5-277-0439; arcangel migueltvc@gmail.com; Amargura No 11; r USD$35) The attractive, shaded porch beckons from the cobbled street, and it only gets better from there: terra-cotta floors, white stucco walls, wood-beamed ceilings and the most inclusive, welcoming atmosphere of a true home. Strongly evocative of Mexico, this refuge contains two spotless guest rooms complemented by a spiral staircase to an inviting rooftop oasis with nooks for lounging.

Nelson Fernández Rodríguez
CASA PARTICULAR $

(Map p282; ☑ 4199-3849; www.hostalcasanelson trinidad.com; Piro Guinart No 226, btwn Antonio Maceo & Gustavo Izquierdo; r USD$30; ❄) Nelson's place above the lovely Restaurant El Dorado (p287) bears all the hallmarks of a fine Trinidadian homestay – lush patio, romantic terrace and Unesco-standard colonial splendor. Four rooms are available, as well as two across the street (run by the same family).

El Rústico
CASA PARTICULAR $

(Map p282; ☑ 4199-3024; Amargura No 54a, btwn Piro Guinart & Simón Bolívar; s/d/tr USD$25/30/35; ❄) These upstairs rooms above El Criollo restaurant (guests get discounts) are a pleasant, breezy surprise, with attractive, immaculate spaces and hair dryers in the bathrooms. The roof terrace is a nice bonus. It's one cobbled block from Plaza Mayor.

Hostal José & Fatima
CASA PARTICULAR $

(Map p282; 4199-6682; hostaljoseyfatima@gmail.com; Zerquera No 159, btwn Frank País & Pettersen; r USD$35; ❄🛜) Highly popular casa with five rooms and colonial trimmings, including a terrace. The helpful hosts can hook you up with many local activities. There's also an adorable dachshund keen on dog lovers.

Casa Gil Lemes
CASA PARTICULAR $

(Map p282; 5-807-0367, 4199-3142; carlosgl3142@yahoo.es; José Martí No 263, btwn Colón & Zerquera; s/d USD$30/40; ❄) This gorgeous casa was one of Trinidad's first, listed in Lonely Planet's 1st-edition *Cuba* guidebook in 1997. Marvel at the noble arches, religious statues and a classic patio with fountain, real hummingbirds and sea serpents. The family only books one room, so snap it up if it's available. Email directly for best rates; English spoken.

Hostal Colina
CASA PARTICULAR $

(Map p282; 4199-2319; Antonio Maceo No 374, btwn General Lino Pérez & Colón; r USD$30; ❄) A homey place that leaves you struggling for superlatives. Although the house dates from the 1830s, it has a definitive modern touch, giving you the feeling of being in a plush Mexican hacienda. Four pastel-yellow rooms surround a patio where you can sit at the wooden bar and catch mangoes and avocados as they fall from the trees.

Casa de Victor
CASA PARTICULAR $

(Map p282; 4199-6444; hostalsandra@yahoo.es; Antonio Maceo No 613a; r USD$25; ❄) Handy to the bus station, Victor's place has three rooms with TV, air-conditioning and private bathrooms. The best are upstairs. Guests share spacious open-air terraces decorated with potted plants. The location is surprisingly quiet, with a tall wall of recycled ceramic pots circling the garden.

BOOKING SERVICE

Trinidad Rent (5-290-0810, 4199-3673; www.trinidadrent.com) is an online English-language booking service with photos that curates some of the best casas in Trinidad. You can reserve the room of your choosing. Handy if you don't want to deal with cash. It can also book tours.

Casa de Aracely
CASA PARTICULAR $

(Map p282; 4199-3558; General Lino Pérez No 207, btwn Frank País & Miguel Calzada; r USD$30; ❄🛜) Had enough of the colonial splendor? Head away from the tourist frenzy to General Lino Pérez, where Aracely rents two upstairs rooms with a private entrance, a very quiet flower-bedecked patio and a splendid roof terrace.

★Casa El Suizo
CASA PARTICULAR $$

(5-377-2812; P Pichs Girón No 22; d USD$50; P❄) Away from the hustle of the center and handily located for excursions by the Trinidad–Cienfuegos road, this spacious lodging feels more like an inn, with five large rooms each featuring private terraces. Installations are relatively new, with safe and hair dryer. English and German are spoken. The only downside is longer walking distances from central attractions.

Finca Ma Dolores
HOTEL $$

(4199-6481; Km 1.5, Carretera de Cienfuegos; s/d USD$45/67, s/d cabin USD$53/75; P❄🏊) Trinidad goes rustic with the out-of-town Finca Ma Dolores, 1.5km west on the road to Cienfuegos and Topes de Collantes. It's equipped with hotel-style rooms and cabins. Cabins are the better option; try for one with a porch overlooking the Río Guaurabo.

★Iberostar Grand Hotel
BOUTIQUE HOTEL $$$

(Map p282; 4199-6070; www.iberostar.com; cnr José Martí & General Lino Pérez; d incl breakfast from USD$400; ❄@🛜) Start in the fern-filled tiled lobby and browse the courtyard surrounded by three floors of rooms in a remodeled 19th-century colonial. The five-star Grand oozes luxury. Forget the standard all-inclusive tourist formula. Instead there's privacy, refinement and an appreciation for local history. Details shine from a cool cigar bar to 36 rooms with designer toiletries, in-room minibars, safes and coffeemakers.

Cubanacán Las Cuevas
HOTEL $$$

(4199-6133; reservas@cuevas.co.cu; Finca Santa Ana; s/d incl breakfast USD$90/130; P❄🏊) Perched on a hill above town, Las Cuevas serves a steady stream of bus tours. While the setting is lush, the rooms – arranged in scattered two-storied units – are a little less memorable, as is the breakfast. There's value added with the swimming pool, well-maintained gardens and panoramic views.

Hotel La Ronda
BOUTIQUE HOTEL $$$

(Map p282; 4199-8538; José Martí No 242, btwn General Lino Pérez & Colón; s/d USD$143/170;

✳@🛜🖼) Steps from Parque Céspedes, this boutique hotel is part of the upscale Estancia chain, with prices to match. Guests enjoy flat-screen TVs and swan-shaped towels in rooms. A modernist fountain, art nouveau photos and *bolero* lyrics on display add individualistic flair, but rooms can be on the small side, overlooking an interior patio without exterior windows.

🍴 Eating

Trinidad is a Cuban culinary oasis in terms of variety and creativity.

Restaurante Mimi
CUBAN $
(Map p282; ☑ 5-338-5230; Antonio Maceo No 397a; meals USD$2.50-9; ⊗ 11am-11pm; 🛜) Simple, hearty Cuban food and the usual Italian suspects emerge from this kitchen, all made with love and served at reasonable prices. Mains are preceded by bread and pumpkin soup, and cocktails go for a shocking USD$1.50. A cheese *tortilla* (omelet) or pizza runs USD$2.50, while the seafood pasta (USD$9) is as extravagant as it gets. Cozy and familial.

Paraito
FAST FOOD $
(Map p282; ☑ 4199-2347; José Martí No 181b, btwn General Lino Pérez & Camilo Cienfuegos; mains USD$3-10; ⊗ 11am-9pm) Here's a rarity for Trinidad: a no-frills eatery with stand-up tables filled by locals engaged in quick-fire gossip. The fried rice is good, or opt for a plate of shrimp and rice. You can order from either menu: the one in USD$ features more elaborate dishes and the wall menu in *moneda nacional* features cheap fast food.

Mesón del Regidor
FAST FOOD $
(Map p282; Simón Bolívar No 424; mains USD$5-15; ⊗ 10am-10pm) A cafe-restaurant with a friendly ambience and a revolving lineup of local musicians, including the best *trovadores* (traditional singer-songwriters), who'll drop by during the day and serenade you with a song over grilled-cheese sandwiches and *café con leche* (coffee with milk). Savor the surprise.

★La Redacción Cuba
INTERNATIONAL $$
(Map p282; ☑ 4199-4593; www.laredaccioncuba. com; Antonio Maceo No 463; mains USD$8-10; 🍽) Contrasting its colonial style with a cleverly titled menu and excellent service, this French-run offering provides a dose of comfort for travelers with culinary homesickness. Think huge lamb burgers with sweet-potato fries, pasta tossed with lobster and herbs, and appealing vegetarian options. For solo travelers, there's a huge shared table in the center conducive to making friends. Otherwise, reserve ahead.

★Vista Gourmet
CUBAN $$
(Map p282; ☑ 4199-6700; Callejón de Galdos No 2f; mains USD$13; ⊗ noon-midnight; 🍽) A slick private option perched on a lovely terrace above Trinidad's red-tiled rooftops – enjoy unobstructed 360-degree views from the top terrace. Run by the charismatic sommelier Bolo, its extensive selection of wines have climatized storage. Hungry diners will love the appetizer and dessert buffet. Tender *lechón asado* (roast pork) and fresh lobster are both recommended.

★Restaurante San José
CUBAN $$
(Map p282; ☑ 4199-4702; Antonio Maceo No 382; mains USD$6-15; ⊗ noon-10pm) Word is out on this handsome restaurant serving fresh grilled snapper, sweet potato fries and frozen limeade. It's among the town's best. Servers weave between gleaming furniture and crowded tables. Come early if you don't want to wait.

★Sol Ananda
INTERNATIONAL $$
(Map p282; ☑ 4199-8281; Rubén Martínez Villena No 45, cnr Simón Bolívar; mains USD$9-18; ⊗ 11am-11pm; 🍽) Fine 18th-century china, grandfather clocks and even an antique bed: Sol Ananda in Trinidad's Plaza Mayor is, on first impression, more museum than restaurant. Situated in one of the town's oldest houses (dating from 1750), it tackles an ambitious cross-section of global food from traditional Cuban (excellent lamb *ropa vieja*) to South Asian (fish kofta and samosas). Good vegetarian options.

Restaurant El Dorado
INTERNATIONAL $$
(Map p282; ☑ 4199-3849; Piro Guinart No 226, btwn Antonio Maceo & Izquierdo; meals USD$6-12; ⊗ noon-midnight) An exquisite colonial house, meticulously polished period furniture and highly courteous waitstaff. Food is not always consistent, but you can look forward to beef strips, well-seasoned fish and grilled turkey, rounded off with some professional touches such as a complimentary bread basket and starters.

Guitarra Mia
CUBAN $$
(Map p282; ☑ 4199-3452; Jesús Menéndez No 19, btwn Camilo Cienfuegos & General Lino Pérez; mains USD$10-15; ⊗ 12:30-11pm) Drift a few blocks from the *centro histórico* and crowds disperse without any measurable drop in

Trinidad Area

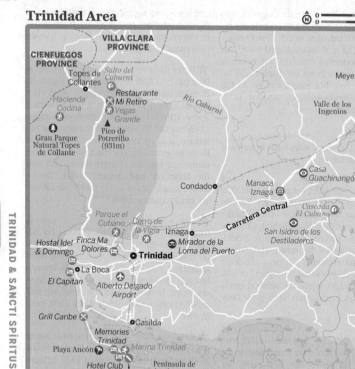

food quality. Music is the theme in this interesting nook, never short of a quintet or passing troubadour. From the menu, the *tostones* (plantain pan-fried in oil) stuffed with minced crab linger longest in the memory.

La Ceiba   CUBAN $$
(Map p282; P Pichs Girón No 263; meals USD$12-24; ⊙ noon-11pm) Set in a back patio under a giant ceiba tree, this upscale cafe specializes in *pollo meloso* (chicken in honey and lemon sauce). Order Trinidad's favorite cocktail, the *canchánchara* (a lemony rum drink), in ceramic cups and bask in the tranquility. Service is hovering but attentive, and the setting can't be beat. Mains include sides, salad and fruit plate.

Cubita Restaurant   INTERNATIONAL $$
(Map p282; ☑ 5-430-6376; Antonio Maceo No 471; mains USD$8-15; ⊙ 11am-midnight) Setting Cubita apart from Trinidad's other higher-end restaurants is the complimentary amuse-bouche commencing the dining experience.

This is where its uniqueness ends, as its offerings are attractively presented but decidedly underwhelming for the cost. It's run by Trinidad's famous ceramic-makers, and the service is attentive.

Restaurante Plaza Mayor   CARIBBEAN $$
(Map p282; cnr Rubén Martínez Villena & Zerquera; dishes USD$3-8; ⊙ noon-11pm) Trinidad's best government-run restaurant courtesy of its on-again/off-again lunchtime buffet, which ought to fill you up until dinnertime.

★ Esquerra   CUBAN $$$
(Map p282; ☑ 4199-3434; Zerquera No 464; mains USD$8-18; ⊙ noon-11pm) With a prime location on the cobblestone plaza, this elegant restaurant serves well-prepared Cuban fare. It differs from the competition with specialty flavors – spicy *criollo* tomato sauce, meunière and Catalan sauces that give a boost to fish or pork. Shrimp cocktail is a standout, as is service. There's also a nice intimate courtyard option.

Drinking & Nightlife

★ Taberna La Botija   BAR
(Map p282; cnr Amargura & Piro Guinart; ⊙24hr)
While other restaurants send their waitstaff
out into the street to fish for customers, La
Botija crams half the town into its lively corner bar without even trying. The key: a warm
talk-to-your-neighbor atmosphere, cold beer
served in ceramic mugs and the best house
band in Trinidad (think jazz meets soul over
a violin). The food ain't bad either.

Café Don Pepe   CAFE
(Map p282; ☑4199-3573; cnr Piro Guinart & Rubén
Martínez Villena; ⊙8am-11pm) In an adorable
colonial courtyard decorated with modern
graffiti, the best coffee in Trinidad is served
in ceramic mugs with a square of Baracoan
chocolate.

Disco Ayala   CLUB
(La Cueva; Map p282; USD$1-5; ⊙10pm-3am) Lo-
cated in an actual cave, this frenetic disco
heats up (literally – there's little air circulation down there) around midnight. Entry
includes one drink; it's a good mix of locals and tourists. To get there, follow Calle
Bolívar from Plaza Mayor up to the Ermita
de Nuestra Señora de la Candelaria de la
Popa. It's 100m further along on your left.

Taberna La Canchánchara   BAR
(Map p282; cnr Rubén Martínez Villena & Ciro Re-
dondo; ⊙10am-midnight) This place is famous
for its eponymous house cocktail made from
rum, honey, lemon and water. Local musicians regularly drop by for off-the-cuff jam
sessions, and it's not unusual for the *can-
chánchara*-inebriated crowd to break into
spontaneous dancing. Note that hours can
be sporadic.

Bar Floridita   BAR
(Map p282; ☑4199-6304; General Lino Pérez
No 313; ⊙24hr) A cheap state-run copy of
Havana's much-hyped Hemingway bar, although this one peddles its daiquiris for a
reasonable price. A life-sized statue of the
revered writer props up the bar.

☆ Entertainment

Get ready for the best Cuban nightlife outside Havana.

★ Casa de la Música   LIVE MUSIC
(Map p282; Echerri; cover USD$2) One of Trini-
dad's (and Cuba's) classic venues, this casa
is an alfresco affair that congregates on
the sweeping staircase beside the Iglesia

Parroquial off Plaza Mayor. A good mix of
tourists and locals take in the 10pm salsa
show here. Alternatively, full-on salsa concerts are held in the casa's rear courtyard
(also accessible from Amargura).

★ Casa de la Trova   LIVE MUSIC
(Map p282; Echerri No 29; USD$1; ⊙9pm-2am)
Trinidad's spirited casa retains its earthy
essence despite the high package-tourist-to-
Cuban ratio. Local musicians to look out for
here are Semillas del Son, Santa Palabra and
the town's best *trovador* (traditional singer-
songwriter), Israel Moreno.

Rincon de la Salsa   LIVE MUSIC
(Map p282; ☑5-391-0245; Zerquera, btwn Rubén
Martínez Villena & Ernesto; cover USD$2; ⊙10pm-
2am) A fun live-music venue aimed at those
practicing their salsa steps. It can also connect travelers to dance teachers for private
lessons during the daytime.

Palenque de los Congos Reales   LIVE MUSIC
(Map p282; cnr Echerri & Jesús Menéndez; cover
USD$1) A must for rumba fans, this open
patio on Trinidad's music alley has an eclectic menu incorporating salsa, *son* (Cuban
popular music) and *trova* (traditional poetic singing). The highlight, however, is the
10pm rumba drumming with soulful African
rhythms and energetic fire-eating dancers.

Casa Fischer   ARTS CENTER
(ARTex; Map p282; General Lino Pérez No 312, btwn
José Martí & Francisco Cadabia; show USD$1) The
local ARTex patio cranks up at 10pm with
a salsa orchestra (on Tuesday, Wednesday,
Thursday, Saturday and Sunday) or a folklore show (Friday). If you're early, kill time at
the art gallery (free) and chat to the staff at
the on-site Paradiso office about salsa lessons
and other courses.

Shopping

Galería La Paulet   ART
(Map p282; Simón Bolívar No 411) Interesting
selection of probing, mainly abstract art by
local artists.

Casa del Habano   CIGARS
(Map p282; cnr Antonio Maceo & Zerquera;
⊙9am-7pm) Dodge the street hustlers and
satisfy your alcoholic (rum) and tobacco
vices here.

Arts & Crafts Market   MARKET
(Map p282; Jesús Menéndez; ⊙9am-6pm) This
open-air market in front of the Casa de la
Trova is the place to buy souvenirs, especially

> ### ℹ TALL TALES
>
> Trinidad's *jineteros* (hustlers) are becoming increasingly sophisticated and meddlesome for locals and tourists alike. Touts on bikes besiege travelers fresh off the buses, or divert rental cars entering the city, with tall tales about how the traveler's chosen casa particular (private homestay) is full or out of business. They have even been known to assume the identities of real casa owners to lure travelers elsewhere.
>
> If you have prebooked your casa particular, make sure you agree to meet the casa owner *inside* the house in question. If you haven't, feel free to stroll the streets unmolested and make your own choice.
>
> Arriving with a *jinetero* in tow will not only add at least USD\$5 to your room rate, but will also exacerbate a problem that has left many of Trinidad's honest casa owners unfairly out of pocket.

textiles and crochet work. Avoid buying black coral or turtle-shell items, made from endangered species, plus they cannot be brought in to many countries.

Casa del Alfarero CERAMICS
(☑ 4199-3146; Andrés Berro No 51, btwn Pepito Tey & Abel Santamaría; ⊙ 8am-noon & 2-5pm Mon-Fri) **FREE** Trinidad is known for its pottery. In this large factory, teams of workers make trademark Trinidad ceramics from local clay using a traditional potter's wheel. You can watch them at work and buy the finished product.

Tienda Amelia Peláez GIFTS & SOUVENIRS
(FCBC – Fondo Cubano de Bienes Culturales; Map p282; Simón Bolívar No 418; ⊙ 9am-6pm Mon-Sat, to noon Sun) Just down from Plaza Mayor, this government store has a good selection of Cuban handicrafts and regular souvenirs.

Taller Instrumentos Musicales MUSICAL INSTRUMENTS
(Map p282; cnr Jesús Menéndez & Valdés Muñoz) Musical instruments are made here and sold in the adjacent shop.

ℹ Information

SAFE TRAVEL

Theft, though still relatively uncommon, is not unheard of in Trinidad. Incidents usually occur late at night when travelers have had a few drinks. To avoid being a potential target for thieves, make sure that you are alert and on your guard, particularly when returning to your hotel or casa after a night out. A little bit of caution can go a long way.

INTERNET ACCESS

There's public wi-fi in Plaza Mayor and on the steps leading to the Casa de la Música, as well as at Parque Céspedes.

Dulcinea (Antonio Maceo No 473; internet per hour USD\$4.50; ⊙ 9am-8:30pm) Couple of terminals on the corner of Simón Bolívar.

Etecsa Telepunto (cnr General Lino Pérez & Pettersen; internet per hour USD\$1.50; ⊙ 8:30am-7pm) Modern, if slow, computer terminals.

MEDICAL SERVICES

Trinidad has a hospital and pharmacy services.

General Hospital (☑ 4199-4012, 4199-3201; Antonio Maceo No 55) Southeast of the city center.

Servimed Clínica Internacional Cubanacán (☑ 4199-6492, 4199-6240; General Lino Pérez No 103, cnr Anastasio Cárdenas; ⊙ 24hr) There is an on-site pharmacy selling products in convertibles.

MONEY

There are banking services and a currency-exchange house.

Banco de Crédito y Comercio (José Martí No 264; ⊙ 9am-3pm Mon-Fri) Has an ATM.

Cadeca (Antonio Maceo, btwn Camilo Cienfuegos & General Lino Pérez; ⊙ 8:30am-5pm) Money changers.

TOURIST INFORMATION

The agencies in Trinidad usually have a line – try to go early.

Cubatur (☑ 4199-6314; Antonio Maceo No 447, btwn Zerquera & Colón; ⊙ 8am-8pm) Good for general tourist information, plus hotel bookings and excursions. Goes to the Valle de los Ingenios (USD\$35) and Salto del Caburní in Topes de Collante (USD\$30). Snorkeling excursions go to Cayo Iguanas (USD\$45) and Cayo Blanco (USD\$50). State taxis congregate outside.

Infotur (☑ 4299-8258; Izquierdo No 112; ⊙ 9am-5pm) Useful for general information on the town, its surroundings and Sancti Spíritus Province.

ℹ Getting There & Away

BUS

The centrally located **bus station** (Map p282; Piro Guinart No 224) has buses for nationals and the more reliable Víazul service aimed at foreign travelers. The **Víazul ticket office** (☑ 4199-4448; www.viazul.com; ☺ 8:30am-4pm) is further back in the station.

With Víazul, Varadero departures can deposit you in Jagüey Grande (USD$15, three hours) with stops on request in Jovellanos, Colesio and Cárdenas. The Santiago de Cuba departure goes through Sancti Spíritus (USD$6, 1½ hours), Ciego de Ávila (USD$9, 2¾ hours), Camagüey (USD$15, 5¼ hours), Las Tunas (USD$22, 7½ hours), Holguín (USD$26, nine hours) and Bayamo (USD$26, 10½ hours).

The Cubanacán Conectando tourist shuttle service has direct links daily with Havana (USD$25). There's no office. Inquire at Infotur (p290).

VÍAZUL DEPARTURES FROM TRINIDAD

Destination	Cost (USD$)	Duration (hr)	Frequency (daily)
Cienfuegos	6	1½	6
Havana	25	6	3
Santa Clara	8	3	2
Santiago de Cuba	33	12½	1
Varadero	20	6½	2

ⓘ Getting Around

BICYCLE

Casas particulares can help organize bike rentals with a local. Just don't expect the latest Shimano gears. Trinidad to Playa Ancón is a pleasant and flat 30-minute ride; Trinidad to Topes de Collantes is akin to a tough stage in the Tour de France.

BUS

Trinidad has a handy hop-on, hop-off tourist-oriented minibus, **Bus Turístico** (Map p282; Antonio Maceo; all-day ticket USD$5), similar to Havana's and Viñales', linking its outlying sights.

CAR & MOTORCYCLE

The rental agencies at the Playa Ancón hotels rent cars and mopeds (USD$25 per day).
Cubacar (☑ 4199-6633; General Lino Pérez, btwn Francisco Cadabia & Antonio Maceo; per day USD$70) rents cars and scooters.

The Oro Negro gas station is at the entrance to Trinidad from Sancti Spíritus, 1km east of Plaza Santa Ana. The **Cupet-Cimex gas station** (☺ 24hr), 500m south of Trinidad on the road to Casilda, has an El Rápido snack bar attached.

Guarded parking is available in certain areas around the *casco histórico*. Ask at your hotel or casa particular, where staff can arrange it.

HORSE CARTS

Horse carts leave for Casilda from Paseo Agramonte at the southern end of town.

TAXI

State-owned taxis tend to congregate outside the Cubatur office on Antonio Maceo. A cab to Sancti Spíritus (70km) should cost approximately USD$40.
Taxi Cuba (☑ 4199-8080) Official taxi. Round-trip services to area attractions require some negotiation depending on wait times.

Playa Ancón

A ribbon of white beach on Sancti Spíritus' iridescent Caribbean shoreline, Playa Ancón is often considered the finest arc of sand on Cuba's south coast. The beach has three all-inclusive hotels and a well-equipped marina with catamaran trips to nearby coral keys. While it can't compete with the north-coast giants of Varadero, Cayo Coco and Guardalavaca, Ancón has one trump card: Trinidad, Latin America's sparkling colonial diamond, lies just 12km to the north.

Between Playa Ancón and Trinidad lies half-forgotten La Boca, a small fishing village at the mouth of the Río Guaurabo with a pebbly beach shaded by flowering acacias. If you like lazy rocking-chair tranquility, fresh lobster, raspberry-ripple sunsets and bantering in Spanish with the local fishers, it's bliss.

The one paved road crosses a tidal flat teeming with birdlife visible in the early morning. Be warned: sand fleas are famously ferocious at sunrise and sunset.

🏃 Activities

Marina Trinidad   BOATING

(☑ 4199-6205; www.nauticamarlin.com; half-day deep-sea fishing USD$300; ☺ 8am-5pm) Romantic types might want to check out the sunset cruise, enthusiastically recommended by readers. The marina runs an all-day snorkeling-and-beach tour to Cayo Iguanas. Travel agencies in Trinidad also sell these tours with 24 hours' notice. A four-hour deep-sea fishing tour includes transportation, gear and guide. The marina is a few hundred meters north of Hotel Club Amigo Ancón (p292).

Cayo Blanco International Dive Center   DIVING

(Marina Trinidad; single dive/open-water course USD$34/339; ☺ 8am-5pm) Diving out of the marina, Cayo Blanco International Dive Center offers single/multiple dive packages as well as open-water courses. Cayo Blanco, a reef islet 25km southeast of Playa Ancón,

CYCLING FROM TRINIDAD TO PLAYA ANCÓN

Cycling to Playa Ancón is a great outdoor adventure, and once there you can snorkel, catch some rays or casually storm the nearby resort swimming pool or ping-pong table. The most scenic route, via the small seaside village of La Boca (16km one way), involves some rolling hills of varying steepness; bring plenty of water.

has 22 marked scuba sites where you'll see black coral and bountiful marine life. To reserve, head to the desk inside Hotel Club Amigo Ancón nearby.

Windward Islands
Cruising Company   BOATING
(www.caribbean-adventure.com; Marina Trinidad) This company charters crewed and bareboat monohulls and catamarans out of the Marina Trinidad to the Jardines de la Reina and the Archipiélago de los Canarreos. You can sail with or without guides, on a partial package or an all-inclusive tour. Make inquiries via the contact details on the website.

✷ Festivals & Events

Fiesta de Santa Elena   RELIGIOUS
(Casilda; ☉ Aug 17) On August 17, the Fiesta de Santa Elena engulfs little Casilda, an old fishing port 6km due south of Trinidad. The friendly village comes alive with feasting, competitions, horse races and loads of rum.

🍴 Sleeping & Eating

Ancón's hotels offer all-inclusive rates. On our visit, construction was happening on a new Meliá resort, which promises to be the most high-end offering on the beach. Budget travelers can consider a homestay in the seaside village of La Boca.

Dine at the one restaurant at the beach, in your casa particular or at the all-inclusive resorts.

Hostal Idel & Domingo   CASA PARTICULAR $
(☎ 4199-8634; Av del Mar No 9, La Boca; r USD$30; P ❄) The queen of kitsch, Idel is a lovely grandma offering simple rooms. This is La Boca life personified, with rockers and hammocks on a wraparound porch within sight of the sea, and two simple rooms with all

you need (fan, air-conditioning, fridge and double bed) to keep you *muy contente*.

Villa Río y Mar   CASA PARTICULAR $
(☎ 5-277-0912; www.villarioymar.com; San José No 65, La Boca; r USD$30-40; P ❄) Right at the boca (mouth) of La Boca where the river meets the sea, you'll find this two-story yellow casa off the main road. The rooms upstairs give out on to a lovely tiled veranda, and it's a short walk to the water. The casa owners speak some English.

★ El Capitan   CASA PARTICULAR $$
(☎ 4198-4355; captaincasanovatrinidad@yahoo.es; Playa Boca No 82; d/tr incl breakfast USD$60/70; ❄🛜) With true B&B style, this modern beach house provides a great escape. Owners Yile and Maikel have four smart guest rooms, each with refrigerator and safe, facing a terrace where breakfast is served. There's also a sprawling seafront garden with shade – prime relaxation territory. Budget travelers can ask for the room without sea view and save USD$15.

Hotel Club Amigo Ancón   RESORT $$
(☎ 4199-6120, 4199-6129; asubdirector@brisastdad.co.cu; s/d/tr all-inclusive USD$73/109/149; P ❄ @ 🛜 🏊) Built during Cuba's 30-year flirtation with Soviet architectonics, the Ancón wouldn't win any beauty contests. Indeed, this steamship-shaped seven-story concrete pile contrasts with the natural beauty of Ancón beach. Installations are tired, and food gets bad reports. Some like the lack of pretension and low prices; others, like Groucho Marx, suspect a club that would have them as a member.

Memories Trinidad del Mar   RESORT $$$
(☎ 4199-6500; reserva5@brisastdad.co.cu; s/d all-inclusive USD$115/184; P ❄ @ 🛜 🏊) Although a kitschy attempt to recreate Trinidad in a resort environment, Memories wins kudos for rejecting monolithic architecture in favor of low-rise colonial-style villas. A recent change in ownership brought significant upgrades to the property and its staff, making it a lovely choice for a resort stay. The swath of beach is stunning, and the sauna, gym and tennis courts are handy.

Grill Caribe   CARIBBEAN $$
(meals USD$5-23; ☉ 8am-8pm) On a lovely beach, this open-air restaurant serves fresh seafood, with the daily menu displayed on a chalkboard. Strict vegetarians will be disappointed here. It's a great sunset spot.

ⓘ Getting There & Away

From Trinidad, you can get here in less than 15 minutes by car or an hour-plus on a bike. A shuttle bus run by Transtur links Ancón to Trinidad four times daily each way (USD$5). Otherwise, it's a pleasant bike ride or a cheap taxi to the beach (USD$8) or La Boca (USD$5).

Valle de los Ingenios

Trinidad's immense wealth was garnered not in the town itself, but in a verdant valley 8km to the east. The Valle de los Ingenios (or Valle de San Luís) still contains the ruins of dozens of 19th-century sugar mills, including warehouses, milling machinery, slave quarters, manor houses and a fully functioning steam train. Most of the mills were destroyed during the War of Independence and the Spanish–Cuban–American War, when the focus of sugar-growing in Cuba shifted west to Matanzas.

Though some sugar is still grown here, the valley is more famous today for its status as a Unesco World Heritage site. Backed by the shadowy sentinels of the Sierra del Escambray, the pastoral fields, royal palms and peeling colonial ruins are timelessly beautiful.

◉ Sights

San Isidro de los Destiladeros   HISTORIC SITE
(USD$1; ⊙9am-5pm) After lengthy excavations, the ruins of this once grand sugar mill are accessible to the public. Dating from the early 1830s and sophisticated for its time, the mill belongs to the pre-industrial age and functioned primarily with slave labor. After ceasing production in 1890, the main buildings – a hacienda, a three-story bell tower, slave quarters and some cisterns – fell into ruin. Admission includes an informative tour in one of several languages, providing better insight than at other sites in the valley.

Renovation is ongoing and has been criticized by some who think the ruins should have been left as, well, ruins. San Isidro is accessed by branching right off the Trinidad–Sancti Spíritus road, 10km east of Trinidad. It's a further 2km from there.

Mirador de la Loma del Puerto   VIEWPOINT
Six kilometers east of Trinidad on the road to Sancti Spíritus, this 192m-high lookout provides the best eagle-eye view of the valley with – if you're lucky – a steam train chugging through its midst. This being Cuba, there's also a bar.

Manaca Iznaga   MUSEUM
(tower USD$1; ⊙9am-4pm) Founded in 1750, this important estate is the focal point of the valley. It was purchased in 1795 by Pedro Iznaga, who became one of Cuba's wealthiest men through slave trafficking. Next to the hacienda, a 44m-high tower was used to watch the enslaved people – the bell in front of the house served to summon them. It's 16km northeast of Trinidad.

Today you can climb to the top of the tower for pretty views, followed by a reasonable lunch (from noon to 2:30pm) in the restaurant-bar in Iznaga's former colonial mansion. Don't miss the huge sugar press out back.

Casa Guachinango   LANDMARK
(⊙9am-5pm) Three kilometers beyond the Manaca Iznaga museum, on the valley's inland road, is an old hacienda built by Don Mariano Borrell toward the end of the 18th century. The building now houses a restaurant. Río Ay is just below, and the surrounding landscape is truly wonderful. Horseback riding can be arranged.

To get to Casa Guachinango, take the paved road to the right, just beyond the second bridge you pass as you come from Manaca Iznaga.

Sitio Guáimaro   LANDMARK
(USD$1; ⊙7am-7pm) Seven kilometers east of the Manaca Iznaga turnoff, travel for another 2km south and you'll find the former estate of Don Mariano Borrell, a wealthy early-19th-century sugar merchant. The seven stone arches on the facade lead to frescoed rooms, now a restaurant featuring a *traipiche*, an old-fashioned press for sugarcane juice.

🏃 Activities

Horseback riding trips can be arranged in Trinidad.

Valle de los Ingenios Train   RAIL
(cnr Lino Pérez & Cárdenas; adult/child USD$15/12; ⊙from 9:10am) One of the only pleasurable train journeys you can take in Cuba chugs through the green hills of Valle de los Ingenios. Sip a *canchánchara* while getting serenaded on a slow-rolling open-air car. The train stops for about an hour each at Manaca Iznaga and a retired sugar mill (USD$1).

Buy tickets the morning of your trip at Trinidad's train station southeast of the center. Trains depart at 9:30am if there are at least 20 passengers, returning around 2:30pm. Show up at 9:10am to buy tickets in the little blue building facing the train tracks.

❶ Getting There & Away

For a chilled-out slow travel experience, hop the Valle de los Ingenios train (p293) from Trinidad. If you're short on time or the forecast calls for rain, a taxi can take you to all the sights (USD$30 to USD$40 round trip with wait).

Topes de Collantes

ELEV 771M

The **Sierra del Escambray** is Cuba's second-largest mountain range. The beautiful crenelated hills are rich in flora and surprisingly isolated. With the best network of hiking trails in Cuba, these jungle-clad forests harbor vines, ferns and eye-catching epiphytes.

In late 1958 Che Guevara camped here on his way to Santa Clara. Almost three years later, CIA-sponsored counterrevolutionary groups operated a cat-and-mouse guerrilla campaign from the same vantage point.

Not strictly a national park, Topes is a heavily protected 200-sq-km area straddling three provinces. The umbrella park contains Parque Altiplano, Parque Codina, Parque Guanayara and Parque El Cubano. A fifth enclave, El Nicho in Cienfuegos Province, is administered by the park authority.

The park name comes from its largest settlement, a 1937 health resort founded by dictator Fulgencio Batista for his sick wife. A tuberculosis sanatorium turned health 'resort' began construction in the late '30s and opened in 1954.

◉ Sights

Museo de Arte Cubano Contemporáneo   MUSEUM
(Carretera Principal; USD$2; ⊘8am-8pm) Believe it or not, Topes de Collantes' monstrous sanatorium once harbored a veritable Louvre of Cuban art, containing works by Cuban masters such as Tomás Sánchez and Rubén Torres Llorca. Raiding the old collection in 2008 inspired provincial officials to open this infinitely more attractive museum, which displays more than 70 works in six *salas* (rooms) spread over three floors. The museum is on the main approach road from Trinidad, just before the hotels.

Plaza de las Memorias   MUSEUM
(⊘8am-5pm) **FREE** Topes' token museum is this quaint little display housed in three small wooden abodes just down from the Casa Museo del Café. It tells the history of the settlement and its resident hotels.

Casa Museo del Café   MUSEUM
(⊘7am-7pm) Coffee has been grown in the Sierra del Escambray for more than two centuries. In this small rustic cafe you can fill in the gaps on its boom-bust history while sipping the aromatic local brew called Cristal Mountain. Just up the road, stroll through Jardín de Variedades del Café, a garden with 25 varieties of coffee plants.

🏃 Activities

Hiking

Topes has the best network of hiking trails in Cuba. Wear good, sturdy shoes. A recent relaxation in park rules means you can now tackle most of them solo, although you'll need wheels to reach some of the trailheads.

★**Sendero 'Centinelas del Río Melodioso'**   HIKING
(USD$10, tour incl lunch USD$47) The least accessible but the most rewarding hike by far from Topes de Collantes is this 6km round-trip hike in Parque Guanayara. The trail begins in cool, moist coffee plantations and descends steeply to **El Rocío** waterfall, where you can enjoy a bracing shower. Following the course of the Río Melodioso, pass another inviting waterfall and swimming pool, **Poza del Venado**, before emerging into the gardens of **Casa La Gallega**, a traditional rural hacienda.

Normally, a light lunch can be organized at the hacienda, and camping is sometimes permitted in the lush grounds. It's 15km from the Centro de Visitantes along a series of steep and heavily rutted tracks. Logistics aren't easy. Organize this excursion with a guide from the Centro de Visitantes, or as part of a tour from Trinidad with Cubatur.

★**Salto del Caburní**   HIKING
(USD$10) The classic Topes hike, easily accessed on foot from the hotels, goes to this 62m waterfall that cascades over rocks into cool swimming holes before plunging into a chasm where macho locals dare each other to jump. Be warned: at the height of the dry season (March to May) there may be low water levels.

The entry fee is collected at the toll gate to Villa Caburní, just down the hill from the

Kurhotel near the Centro de Visitantes (it's a long approach on foot). Allow an hour down and 1½ hours back up for this 5km (round trip) hike. Some slopes are steep and can be slippery after rain.

★ **Sendero La Batata** HIKING
(USD$10) This 6km out-and-back trail to a small cave containing an underground river starts at a parking sign just downhill from Casa Museo del Café. When you reach another highway, go around the right side of the concrete embankment and down the hill. Keep straight or right after this point (avoid trails to the left). Allow an hour each way.

Gruta Nengoa HIKING
(USD$10) A recently developed 2.6km trail centered on a grotto and 12m-high waterfall with some good opportunities for birdwatching and swimming. The trailhead is located 16km from Topes, just south of the village of Cuatro Vientos.

Hacienda Codina HIKING
(USD$10) From Hacienda Codina, the **Sendero de Alfombra Mágica** is a 1.2km circular trail through orchid and bamboo gardens and past the Cueva del Altar. There are also mud baths, a restaurant and a scenic viewpoint. It's 8km from Topes by a rough road (the 4km 4WD track begins on a hilltop 3km down the road toward Cienfuegos and Manicaragua).

Alternatively, hike La Batata trail and continue 1.5km past the cave to arrive at the hacienda. Ask for directions at the Centro de Visitantes first and hire a guide.

Sendero Jardín del Gigante HIKING
(USD$10) Those pressed for time can get a taste of Topes' ecosystems with this ideal 1.2km ramble. It starts at the Plaza de las Memorias and finishes just downhill in the Parque La Represa on the Río Vega Grande. En route you can count 300 species of trees and ferns, including the largest *caoba* (mahogany) tree in Cuba.

The small restaurant at the entrance to the garden is in a villa built by Fulgencio Batista's wife, whose love for the area inspired her husband to build the Topes resort.

Vegas Grande HIKING
(USD$10) This 2km waterfall trail begins at the apartment blocks known as Reparto El Chorrito on the southern side of Topes de Collantes, near the entrance to the resort as you arrive from Trinidad. Allow a couple of hours to hike and enjoy a refreshing dip in

the gorgeous aquamarine pool. It's possible to continue to the Salto del Caburní with a guide.

🛏 Sleeping

Villa Caburní CABIN **$$**
(☎ 4254-0330; per person incl breakfast USD$50; 🅿 ❄) It's all about location, in this case, a verdant park setting. With 29 Swiss-chalet-style cabins (some under renovation), all with solar panels, this is a screaming good deal. Each has hot water and refrigerator. Breakfast is served in a dated on-site bar-cafeteria. It sits just behind the Centro de Visitantes.

Hotel Los Helechos HOTEL **$$**
(☎ 4254-0330; s/d incl breakfast USD$51/64; 🅿 ❄ ☷) Never 100% at home in its verdant natural surroundings, this clumsy chocolate-box building with wicker furnishings and holiday-camp-style villas still looks a bit awkward. Not helping matters are the unattractive indoor pool, poky steam baths (if they're working), journeyman restaurant and kitschy local disco (in a natural park of all places!).

🍴 Eating & Drinking

Bar-Restaurante Gran Nena CUBAN **$**
(☎ 4254-0338; Carretera Principal; mains USD$4-6; ⏰ 10am-9pm) An ambient setting where Cuban food that's just OK is served (slowly) under a traditional open-sided sitting area. Bananas, papayas, avocados, oranges and peaches all grow abundantly in the adjacent sloping garden, and you can follow a trail through them to a hidden cave.

Restaurante Mi Retiro CARIBBEAN **$$**
(Carretera de Trinidad; meals USD$6-9; ⏰ 8am-11pm) Situated 3km back down the road to Trinidad, Restaurante Mi Retiro does fair-to-middling *comida criolla* (Creole food) served against a backdrop of forested hillsides accompanied by occasional cowbell.

El Mirador BAR
(Carretera de Trinidad; ⏰ dawn-dusk) A simple bar with stunning views halfway up the ascent road between Trinidad and Topes de Collantes.

ℹ Information

Centro de Visitantes (⏰ 8am-5pm) Near the sundial at the entrance to the hotel complexes. The best place to procure maps, guides and trail info.

❶ Getting There & Away

Without a car, it's very difficult to get to Topes de Collantes and harder still to get around to the various trailheads. Your best bet is a taxi (USD$40 to USD$60 return with a wait), an excursion from Trinidad (from USD$35) or a rental car.

The road between Trinidad and Topes de Collantes is paved but very steep. It's slippery when wet.

For drivers, a spectacular 44km road continues right over the mountains from Topes de Collantes to Manicaragua via Jibacoa (occasionally closed, so check in Trinidad before setting out). It's also possible to drive to/from Cienfuegos via Sierrita on a partly paved, partly gravel road (4WD only).

Alturas de Banao

Still well off the radar, this ecological reserve hides a little-explored stash of mountains, waterfalls, forest and steep limestone cliffs. In the Guamuhaya mountain range, the reserve's highest peak is 842m. Foothills are replete with rivers, abundant plant life (including epiphyte cacti) and the ruins of a handful of pioneering 19th-century farmhouses.

The park headquarters is at Jarico, 3.5km up a beaten track leading off the Sancti Spíritus–Trinidad road. It incorporates a ranchón-style restaurant, visitors center and chalet with eight double rooms.

Within shouting distance is the Cascada Bella waterfall and a natural swimming pool. From Jarico, the 6km La Sabina trail leads to an eponymous biostation and La Sabina Chalet. Guided day hikes (USD$3) are charged separately from entry to the reserve.

Ecotur (p285) in Trinidad can organize overnight and day trips (CUC$30), which include lunch and a donkey ride, hiking and swimming in a natural pool.

A ranchón-style restaurant attached to La Sabina Chalet (per person incl breakfast & dinner USD$30) is the only dining option in the reserve. The chalet offers overnight accommodation and food in eight double rooms. A stay covers trail fees.

❶ Getting There & Away

Tours do not include transportation. You can take a taxi from Trinidad (USD$50 round trip).

Sancti Spíritus

📞 41 / POP 108,482

In any other country, this attractive colonial city would be a cultural tour de force. But cocooned inside illustrious Sancti Spíritus Province, second fiddle to Trinidad, visitors barely give it a glance. For many, therein lies the attraction. Sancti Spíritus is Trinidad without the touts. You can dine, listen to *boleros* on the plaza or search for a casa particular without hassle.

Founded in 1514 as one of the seven original villas of Diego Velázquez, Sancti Spíritus was moved to its present site on the Río Yayabo in 1522. Yet audacious corsairs continued to loot the town until well into the 1660s.

Sancti Spíritus has made its contributions. It concocted the dapper *guayabera*, Latin America's favorite men's shirt, cultivated *guayaba* (guava) fruit and built a quaint humpbacked bridge reminiscent of Yorkshire, England. The city underwent intense beautification in 2014 to celebrate its 500th anniversary.

◉ Sights

The main streets north and south of the Av de los Mártires and Calle M Solano axis get an appropriate north/south suffix.

★ **Casa de la Guayabera**   MUSEUM
(Map p297; 📞 4132-2205; guayabera@hero.cult.cu; San Miguel No 60; USD$1; ⊙10am-5pm Tue-Sun) The favored uniform of South American strongman presidents and blushing grooms at Mexican beach weddings, the *guayabera* shirt was purportedly 'invented' in Sancti Spíritus by the wives of agricultural workers who sewed the trademark pockets into the garments so that their men could safely store their tools and packed lunches. This museum honors the iconic shirts, displaying *guayaberas* worn by Hugo Chávez, Gabriel Garcia Márquez and Fidel.

The complex, set on a lovely riverside patio in front of the city's famous packhorse bridge, also has a bar and lovely garden where public social and cultural events take place after hours on Fridays and Saturdays. Those wishing to order a *guayabera* must wait two days for its completion.

★ **Puente Yayabo**   LANDMARK
(Map p297) Looking like something out of an English country village, this quintuple-arched bridge is Sancti Spíritus' signature sight. Built by the Spanish in 1815, it carries traffic across the Río Yayabo and is now a national monument. For the best view (and a mirror-like reflection) hit the outdoor terrace at the Taberna Yayabo (p300).

It's flanked by cobblestone streets – the most arresting is narrow Calle Llano, where

Sancti Spíritus

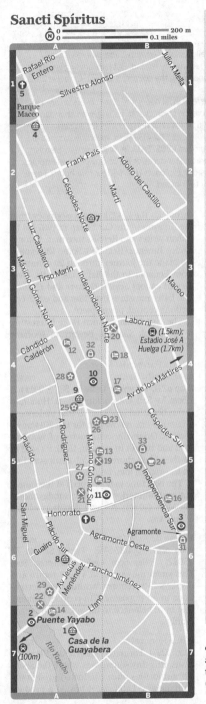

N 0 —————— 200 m
0 —————— 0.1 miles

old ladies peddle live chickens door to door, and neighbors gossip noisily in front of pastel houses. Also worth a wander are Calle Guairo and Calle San Miguel.

EMBALSE ZAZA

Freshwater fishing is not a pastime traditionally associated with Cuba, where visiting fishers brave the high seas in pursuit of the Hemingway legend. But lake angling is widely practiced in several constructed reservoirs, including the country's largest, Embalse Zaza, 11km outside Sancti Spíritus.

Created in the early 1970s by damming several local rivers, the Zaza covers an area of 113 sq km. Currently, nearly 50% of the reservoir is given over to fishing, with abundant stocks of largemouth bass (weighing up to 8kg) providing rich pickings for anglers.

Excursions are run out of the adjacent Hotel Zaza (☑ 4132-7015; ypuerta@islazulssp.tur. cu; Km 5.5, Finca San Jose, Lago Zaza; s/d incl breakfast USD$25/33; P ✹ ✺), an ugly blemish on the landscape even by the cheap and cheerful standards of 1970s Soviet architectonics. Stay in Sancti Spíritus and get a taxi out. A fishing trip costs USD$40 for four hours. There are also trips to the Río Agabama, on the way to Trinidad.

Centro de Interpretación de la Ciudad
CULTURAL CENTRE

(Map p297; Independencia Sur No 67; ⊙10am-7pm Tue-Sat, to noon Sun) Featuring a requisite scale model of the city, this interpretive center also has photographs of the 2014 excavation of the former convent under what is now Parque Serafín Sánchez. Cruise by to check their signboard for local cultural events or live music during your visit.

Parque Serafín Sánchez
SQUARE

(Map p297) While not Cuba's shadiest or most atmospheric square, pretty Serafín Sánchez is full of understated Sancti Spíritus elegance. Metal chairs laid out inside the pedestrianized central domain are usually commandeered by cigar-smoking grandpas and flirty young couples with their sights set on some ebullient local nightlife.

There's plenty to whet the appetite on the square's south side, where the stately Casa de la Cultura (p301) often exports its music on to the street. Next door the columned Hellenic beauty that today serves as the Biblioteca Provincial Rubén Martínez Villena (Map p297; ☑ 4132-7717; Máximo Gómez Norte No 1; ⊙8am-5pm Mon-Thu, 8am-5pm & 7-10pm Fri, 8am-4pm & 7-10pm Sat, 9am-1pm Sun) was built originally in 1929 by the Progress Society.

The magnolia-colored grande dame on the square's northern side is the former La Perla hotel, which lay rotting and unused for years before being turned into a three-level government-run shopping center.

Fundación de la Naturaleza y El Hombre
MUSEUM

(Map p297; ☑ 4132-8342; Cruz Pérez No 1; donation USD$2; ⊙10am-5pm Mon-Fri) Replicating its equally diminutive namesake in Miramar, Havana, this museum on Parque Maceo chronicles the 17,422km canoe odyssey from the Amazon to the Caribbean in 1987 led by Cuban writer and Renaissance man Antonio Nuñez Jiménez (1923–98). Some 432 explorers made the journey through 20 countries, from Ecuador to the Bahamas, in the twin dugout canoes *Simón Bolívar* and *Hatuey*. The latter measures over 13m and is the collection's central, prized piece.

The visit is made much more interesting if you speak Spanish. Beware of sporadic opening hours.

Iglesia Parroquial Mayor del Espíritu Santo
CHURCH

(Map p297; Agramonte Oeste No 58; ⊙9-11am & 2-5pm Tue-Sat) Overlooking Plaza Honorato is this beautiful blue church that underwent a Lazarus-like renovation for the 2014 anniversary. Originally constructed of wood in 1522 and rebuilt in stone in 1680, it's said to be the oldest church in Cuba still standing on its original foundations.

The best time to take a peek at the simple but soulful interior is during Sunday morning Mass (10am). A small donation will go a long way.

Museo de Arte Colonial
MUSEUM

(Map p297; ☑ 4132-5455; Plácido Sur No 74; USD$2; ⊙9am-5pm Tue-Sat, 8am-noon Sun) This small museum had a 2012 refurb and displays 19th-century furniture and decorations in an imposing 17th-century building that once belonged to the sugar-rich Iznaga family.

Plaza Honorato
SQUARE

(Map p297) Formerly known as Plaza de Jesús, this tiny square was where the Spanish authorities once conducted grisly public hangings. Later on, it hosted a produce market, and scruffy peso stalls still line the small connecting lane to the east. The north side of the square is now occupied by a boutique hotel.

Museo Provincial MUSEUM
(Map p297; ☑ 4132-7435; Máximo Gómez Norte No 3; USD$1; ☺ 9am-5pm Tue-Sun) One of those Cuban museums where the collection logs the history of Sancti Spíritus. It also includes a dusty stash of ephemera that comprises English china, cruel slave artifacts, and the inevitable revolutionary M-26-7 (July 26 Movement) paraphernalia.

Iglesia de Nuestra Señora de la Caridad CHURCH
(Map p297; Céspedes Norte No 207) Across from the Fundación de la Naturaleza y El Hombre is the city's second church, the recipient of a handsome 2014 paint job. Its internal arches are a favored nesting spot for Cuban sparrows, who seem unfazed by the church interior's continuing state of disrepair.

Museo Casa Natal de Serafín Sánchez MUSEUM
(Map p297; ☑ 4132-7791; Céspedes Norte No 112; USD$1; ☺ 9am-5pm Tue-Sat) Serafín Sánchez was a local patriot who took part in both Wars of Independence and went down fighting in November 1896. The museum cataloguing his heroics is good for a 20-minute browse.

🛏 Sleeping

Sancti Spíritus' gracious boutique sleeping establishments are branded as Encanto hotels, belonging to the Cubanacán chain. They are complemented by a handful of pleasant casas particulares.

🛏 City Center

⭐**Hostal Paraíso** CASA PARTICULAR $
(Map p297; ☑ 4133-4658; Máximo Gómez Sur No 11, btwn Honorato & M Solano; r USD$25; ❄🤶) The best budget option in town, this central colonial draped in ferns is home to a nice family with a puttering dachshund. Try for one of the two outstanding rooms on the breezy roof deck. The house dates from 1838, with huge bathrooms, powerful showers and uplifting greenery.

Hostal Yayabo CASA PARTICULAR $
(Map p297; ☑ 5-353-0070; liosmany.gomez@nauta.cu; Jesús Menéndez No 109; r USD$25; 🤶) Nuris and her young family host guests in

their riverside home. There's a motorcycle in the living room and a bubblegum-pink bedroom with satin bedspread that would be the envy of any Barbie princess. Guests can cook, and there's a riverside terrace.

Estrella González Obregón CASA PARTICULAR $
(Map p297; ☑ 4132-7927; Máximo Gómez Norte No 26; r USD$15-25; ❄) Don't be surprised if you're invited for a coffee before you even state your business. At this friendly family home, there are two spacious rooms and some cooking facilities. It's ideal for families. Enjoy the roof terrace with good views of the Escambray Mountains. Offers discounts for longer stays.

'Los Richards' – Ricardo Rodríguez CASA PARTICULAR $
(Map p297; ☑ 4132-2656; gisel.rios@nauta.cu; Independencia Norte No 28 altos; r USD$25-30; ❄🤶🤶) A dark stairway off the main square gives way to a clean 2nd-floor apartment with soaring ceilings, vintage tiled floors and airy if aged colonial grace. The two front rooms are enormous; the back two are quieter. A shared front room opens to the fabulous wrought-iron protected balconies overlooking the theatrics of the plaza.

⭐**Hotel del Rijo** BOUTIQUE HOTEL $$$
(Map p297; ☑ 4132-8588; rperurena@islazulssp.tur.cu; Honorato del Castillo No 12; s/d incl breakfast USD$102/122; ❄@🤶) Even committed casa particular fans will have trouble resisting this meticulously restored 1818 mansion situated on quiet (until the Casa de la Trova opens) Plaza Honorato. Sixteen huge, plush rooms – many with plaza-facing balconies – are equipped with everything a romance-seeking Cuba-phile could wish for, including satellite TV, complimentary shampoos and chunky colonial furnishings.

Hotel Don Florencio BOUTIQUE HOTEL $$$
(Map p297; ☑ 4132-8306; rperurena@islazulssp.tur.cu; Independencia Sur No 63; s/d USD$102/122; ❄@🤶) Sancti Spíritus doesn't often get one over on Trinidad, but it does have a better collection of hotels. This beauty has bright spaces, antique furnishings and two inviting Jacuzzis in the cool central patio. Service can be a little lax. It's popular with tour groups.

Hotel Plaza BOUTIQUE HOTEL $$$
(Map p297; ☑ 4132-7102; rperurena@islazulssp.tur.cu; Independencia Norte No 1; s/d incl breakfast USD$102/122; ❄@🤶) On the edge of Parque Serafín Sánchez, this is courtside seating to great people-watching. Public spaces, such

as the romantic patio bar, shine. Rooms are large and spread over two stories, with fluffy bathrobes, an in-room safe and chunky furnishings. Popular with tour groups.

🛌 North of the City

There are two very agreeable hotels along Carretera Central as you head north; either one is a good choice if the city center is full or you're merely passing through. Zaza, 5km to the east, attracts fishers.

Villa Los Laureles   HOTEL $$
(☑ 4136-1016; dperez@islazulssp.tur.co.cu; Km 383, Carretera Central; s/d USD$66/76; 🅿 ❋ @ 🛜 🏊) Not content to rest on them, Los Laureles lines its laurel trees up along a shady entrance drive that beckons visitors into a surprisingly classy Islazul hotel on the fringes of the city.

Villa Rancho Hatuey   HOTEL $$
(☑ 4136-1315; gniubo@islazulssp.tur.co.cu; Km 384, Carretera Central; s/d USD$76/85; 🅿 ❋ @ 🛜 🏊) A veritable Islazul gem accessible from the southbound lane of Carretera Central. Rancho Hatuey spreads 76 rooms in two-story cabins across expansive landscaped grounds set back from the road. Catch some rays around the swimming pool or grab a bite in the on-site restaurant while observing Canadian bus groups and Communist Party officials from Havana mingling in awkward juxtaposition.

🍴 Eating

Never rated highly for its private restaurants, Sancti Spíritus has a couple of good ones since privatization laws were relaxed. The state sector has some equally strong contenders.

Dulce Crema   ICE CREAM $
(Map p297; cnr Independencia Norte & Laborní; ice cream USD$1-2; ☺8am-10pm) What, no Coppelia? Dulce Crema is Sancti Spíritus' long-standing provincial stand-in and is actually – ahem – better. Alternatively, hang around long enough in Parque Serafín Sánchez and a DIY ice-cream man will turn up with his ice-cream maker powered by a washing machine motor.

Al Medio Restaurante   CUBAN $
(Map p297; www.restaurantealmedio.com; Máximo Gómez No 15 Sur; mains USD$2.75-7.25; ☺11am-11:45pm) Serving a variety of quality Cuban food and Cuban-style Italian favorites, Al Medio offers excellent value on classics like *ropa vieja* (shredded beef) and mojitos alike. The brick-and-stucco dining room has a casually refined feel, enhanced by its friendly staff.

Mesón de la Plaza   SPANISH $
(Map p297; Máximo Gómez Sur No 34; mains USD$4-8.50; ☺noon-3pm & 6-10pm) Long a solid option, this state-run restaurant occupies a 19th-century mansion that once belonged to a rich Spanish tycoon. You can tuck into classic Spanish staples such as *potaje de garbanzos* (chickpeas with pork) and some chewable beef while appetizing music drifts in from the Casa de la Trova next door.

★ Taberna Yayabo   SPANISH $$
(Map p297; ☑ 4183-7552; Jesús Menéndez No 106; meals USD$6-12; ☺9am-10:45pm) With an excellent riverside location, wine cellar and wonderful service, there's reason to linger at this pleasant state-run restaurant. Sure, you might be bombarded by a steady stream of '80s hits, but there are also tapas such as serrano ham carved on-site and cheeses – items not easily found on the island. The resident sommelier brims over with enthusiasm.

Restaurante La Fuente   INTERNATIONAL $$
(Map p297; Honorato No 12; meals USD$6-9; ☺7am-11pm) Quiet colonial ambience in the impressive central courtyard of the Hotel del Rijo or on the lovely terrace. Choose from an international menu with filet mignon and chicken in white-wine sauce or a sandwich menu. Service is good, and there is a notable selection of desserts, drinks and coffee.

🍸 Drinking & Nightlife

★ Cafe Colga'o   CAFE
(Map p297; ☑ 5-433-6237; Independencia Sur No 9c; ☺4pm-midnight Fri-Wed) It doesn't get more underground than this Cuban-Italian cafe with its easy-to-miss sign. Follow a staircase to this 9th-floor apartment sporting tiny tables with floor cushions and balcony views. It's filled with local youth grooving to an eclectic music mix, sipping espresso drinks and eating cheap sandwiches sold in *moneda nacional*. Costing mere cents, the coffee flan is outstanding.

Café ARTex   CLUB
(Map p297; M Solano; USD$1-3; ☺10am-10pm Mon-Thu, noon-midnight Fri-Sun) On an upper floor on Parque Serafín Sánchez, this place has more of a nightclub feel than the usual ARTex patio. It offers dancing, live music

and karaoke nightly, and a Sunday matinee at 2pm. Thursday is reggaeton (Cuban hip-hop) night, and the cafe also hosts comedy. Clientele is mainly under 25.

☆ Entertainment

★ Uneac
LIVE MUSIC

(Map p297; Independencia Sur No 10) There are friendly nods as you enter, handshakes offered by people you've never met, and a starry-eyed crooner on stage blowing kisses to his girlfriend(s) in the audience. Uneac concerts always feel more like family gatherings than organized cultural events, and Sancti Spíritus' is one of the nicest 'families' you'll meet.

★ Casa de la Trova
Miguel Companioni
LIVE MUSIC

(Map p297; Máximo Gómez Sur No 26; USD$1; ⏰9pm-midnight Sun-Wed, to 1am Thu-Sat) Another of Cuba's famous trova (traditional poetic singing) houses, this kicking folk-music venue in a colonial building off Plaza Honorato is on a par with anything in Trinidad. But here the crowds are 90% local and 10% tourist.

Casa de la Cultura
LIVE MUSIC

(Map p297; ☑4132-3772; M Solano No 11) Numerous cultural events that at weekends spill out into the street and render the pavement impassable. It's situated on the southwest corner of Parque Serafín Sánchez.

Teatro Principal
THEATER

(Map p297; ☑4132-5755; Jesús Menéndez No 102) This landmark 1876 architectural icon next to the Puente Yayabo still shines after a comprehensive clean-up. It has weekend matinees (at 10am) with kids' theater. The sun-bleached cobbled streets that lead uphill toward the city center are some of the settlement's oldest.

Cine Conrado Benítez
CINEMA

(Map p297; ☑4132-5327; Máximo Gómez Norte No 13) Of the city's two main cinemas, this is your best bet for a decent movie (some in English with Spanish subtitles).

🛍 Shopping

The city's revived shopping street, Calle Independencia Sur (known colloquially as the 'boulevard'), is traffic-free and lined with statues, sculptures and myriad curiosity shops. Check out the opulent Colonia Española building, once a whites-only gentlemen's club, now a mini department store.

The agropecuario (vegetable market) is unusually located right in the city center.

A flea market inhabits Calle Honorato just off Independencia and all around are vendutas (small private shops or stalls), illustrating the recent economic relaxation.

La Colonia
DEPARTMENT STORE

(Map p297; cnr Independencia Sur & Agramonte; ⏰9am-4pm) Mini department store housed in one of the city's finest colonial buildings.

La Perla
SHOPPING CENTER

(Map p297; ☑4132-8171; Parque Serafín Sánchez; ⏰9am-4pm) Three levels of austerity-busting shopping behind a beautifully restored magnolia colonial edifice on Parque Serafín Sánchez.

Librería Julio Antonio Mella
BOOKS

(Map p297; Independencia Sur No 29; ⏰8am-5pm Mon-Sat) Revolutionary (mainly in Spanish) reading material for erudite travelers in a store opposite the post office.

ℹ Information

INTERNET ACCESS

There's wi-fi on the plaza and in all hotels.

Etecsa Telepunto (Independencia Sur No 14; internet per hour USD$1.50; ⏰8:30am-7pm) Two rarely busy computer terminals, plus wi-fi scratchcards for sale.

MEDICAL SERVICES

Farmacia Especial (☑4132-4130; Independencia Norte No 123; ⏰24hr) Pharmacy on Parque Maceo.

Hospital Provincial Camilo Cienfuegos (☑4133-8001; Bartolomé Masó No 128; ⏰24hr) It's 500m north of Plaza de la Revolución.

Policlínico Los Olivos (☑4132-6362; Circunvalación Olivos No 1) Hospital near the bus station. Will treat foreigners in an emergency.

MONEY

There are plenty of ATMs and a money-exchange office.

Banco Financiero Internacional (☑4132-8447; Independencia Sur No 2; ⏰9am-3pm Mon-Fri) On Parque Serafín Sánchez.

Cadeca (☑4133-6184; Independencia Sur No 31; ⏰9am-5pm Mon-Sat) Lose your youth in this bank's line.

TOURIST INFORMATION

Cubatur (☑4132-8518; Máximo Gómez Norte No 7; ⏰9am-5pm Mon-Sat) On Parque Serafín Sánchez. Sells hotel reservations but not excursions.

NORTH COAST NIRVANA

Northern Sancti Spíritus province is one of Cuba's most heavily protected areas, dominated by the 313-sq-km **Buenavista Unesco Biosphere Reserve**. It's also a Ramsar Convention Site (important wetlands area).

The nucleus is Parque Nacional Caguanes (see next page), consisting of the sinuous Caguanes Peninsula, the Guayabera swamps and 10 tiny islets known as Cayos de Piedra.

Beyond its unusual karst formations, the park has 75 caves and a pristine ecosystem with manatees, flamingos and the world's only freshwater cave sponge. So far 263 pictographs have been discovered in 40 different archaeological sites, made by the indigenous people who once frequented this area.

The area has had landmark environmental success in recent years. Pollution in Bahía de Buenavista from inefficient sugar mills had driven numerous bird species away from Caguanes by the late 1990s. The closure of the mills in 2002, coupled with efforts on the part of park authorities, has seen many species return.

❶ Getting There & Away

BUS

The provincial **bus station** (Carretera Central) is 2km east of town. Punctual and air-conditioned Víazul buses (www.viazul.com) serve numerous destinations.

Five daily departures for Santiago de Cuba also stop in Ciego de Ávila, Camagüey, Las Tunas and Bayamo. Five daily Havana buses stop at Santa Clara. The link to Trinidad leaves at a sleep-reducing 6am.

VÍAZUL DEPARTURES FROM SANCTI SPÍRITUS

Destination	Cost (USD$)	Duration (hr)	Frequency (daily)
Santiago de Cuba	28	10	4
Ciego de Ávila	6	1¼	4
Camagüey	10	3	4
Bayamo	21	7	4
Havana	23	5	2
Santa Clara	6	1¼	3
Trinidad	6	1¼	1

TAXI

Trucks (USD$1) to Trinidad, Jatibonico and elsewhere depart from the bus station. A state taxi to Trinidad will cost you around USD$40.

TRAIN

There are two train stations serving Sancti Spíritus. For Havana use the main **train station** (☑ 4132-7914; Jesús Menéndez No 92; ☺ tickets 7am-2pm Mon-Sat), southwest of the Puente Yayabo, an easy 10-minute walk from the city center.

Points east are served out of Guayos, 15km north of Sancti Spíritus, including Holguín (8½ hours), Santiago de Cuba (10¼ hours) and Bayamo (8¼ hours). If you're on the Havana–Santiago de Cuba cross-country express and going to Sancti Spíritus or Trinidad, get off at Guayos.

The ticket office at the Sancti Spíritus train station can sell you tickets for trains departing Guayos, but you must find your own way to the Guayos train station (USD$10 in a taxi).

❶ Getting Around

Horse carts on Carretera Central, opposite the bus station, run to Parque Serafín Sánchez when full (CUP$1). Bici-taxis gather at the corner of Laborni and Céspedes Norte.

CAR

Parking in Parque Serafín Sánchez is relatively safe. Ask in hotels Rijo and Plaza, and they will often find a man to stand guard overnight for USD$1 to USD$3.

There is a **Cubacar** (☑ 4132-8533; Máximo Gómez No 9; ☺ 9am-4pm) car rental booth on the northeast corner of Parque Serafín Sánchez.

A **Cupet-Cimex gas station** (Carretera Central) is 1.5km north of Villa Los Laureles, toward Santa Clara.

Northern Sancti Spíritus

For every 1000 tourists who visit Trinidad, a small handful get to see the province's narrow northern corridor, which runs between Remedios, in Villa Clara, and Morón, in Ciego de Ávila.

The landscape is comprised of karstic uplands characterized by caves and covered in semi-deciduous woodland, juxtaposed with a flat, ecologically valuable coastal plain protected in the hard-to-visit but worthwhile Parque Nacional Caguanes.

◉ Sights

★ Museo Nacional
Camilo Cienfuegos   MUSEUM
(☑ 4155-2689; Yaguajay; USD$1; ⊘ 8am-4pm
Tue-Fri & Sun, to 6pm Sat) This excellent museum was opened in 1989 and is eerily reminiscent of the Che Guevara monument in
Santa Clara. Camilo fought a crucial battle
in this town on the eve of the revolution's
triumph, taking control of a local military
barracks (now the Hospital Docente General, opposite the museum).

The museum is directly below a modernist plaza embellished with a 5m-high
statue of *El Señor de la Vanguardia* (Man
at the Vanguard). It contains an extremely
well-curated display of Cienfuegos' life in-
termingled with facts and mementos from
the revolutionary struggle. A replica of the
small tank 'Dragon I,' converted from a trac-
tor for use in the battle, stands in front of
the hospital. Out back the Mausoleo de los
Mártires del Frente Norte de las Villas is
dedicated to the soldiers who died in the
skirmish.

★ Jobo Rosado   NATURE RESERVE
This 40-sq-km managed-resource area is
still little-explored by independent travelers, although organized groups come here.
Organize guided hikes through Ecotur or at
Villa San José del Lago. Highlights include
La Solapa de Genaro, a 1km hike through
tropical savanna to a gorgeous set of waterfalls and swimming holes. The Cueva de
Valdés walk (800m) goes through semi-deciduous woodland to a cave.

A longer hike heads 8km to Chalet Los
Álamos, the house of an erstwhile sugar
plantation near the village of Meneses.

The reserve includes the Sierra de Meneses y Cueto, a hill range running across
the north of the province that acts as a buff-
er zone for the heavily protected Bahía de
Buenavista.

As in the Sierra Maestra, history is intertwined with the ecology here. General
Máximo Gomez battled through these hills
during the Spanish–Cuban–American War.
In 1958 Camilo Cienfuegos' rebel army (Column No 2) pitched their final command
post here. An imaginative monument by
sculptor José Delarra marks the spot.

You'll need a taxi or your own wheels to
get to Jobo Rosado.

Parque Nacional Caguanes   NATURE RESERVE
Strict conservation measures mean public
access to Parque Nacional Caguanes with its
caves, aboriginal remains and flamingos is
limited but not impossible. There is a basic
biological station on the coast accessible by
a rough road due north of Mayajigua but,
rather than just turn up, your best bet is to
check details first at the Villa San José del
Lago or with Ecotur (p285), which has a
handy public office in Trinidad.

The one advertised excursion is Las Maravillas que Atesora Caguanes (2½ hours),
which incorporates a path to the Humboldt,
Ramos and Los Chivos caves and a boat trip
around the Cayos de Piedra.

Rancho Querete   FARM
(⊘ 9am-4pm Tue-Sun) The nexus for the Jobo
Rosado Reserve is just off the main road
a few kilometers east of Yaguajay and is
equipped with a bar-restaurant, natural
swimming hole, biological station and
small 'zoo' (roosters mainly). Guided hikes
(USD$5) can be organized here.

🛏 Sleeping

Villa San José del Lago   HOTEL $
(☑ 4154-6108; www.islazul.cu; Antonio Guiteras,
Mayajigua; d incl breakfast/meals USD$20/45;
P ❋ ☲) Once popular with vacationing
Americans, this novel spa is just outside
Mayajigua. The tiny rooms are set in a variety of two-story villas, nestled beside a small
palm-fringed lake with pedal boats and two
resident flamingos. It's famous for its thermal waters (32°C), first used by injured
slaves in the 19th century, now for holidaying Cubans.

The 67 rooms are no-frills, but the setting,
wedged between the Sierra de Jatibonico
and Parque Nacional Caguanes, is magnificent and makes a good base for some of
Cuba's lesser-known excursions. There's a
restaurant and snack bar on-site.

ℹ Information

Ecotur (☑ 4155-4930; Pedro Díaz No 54,
Yaguajay) The best information portal for the
region, one block north of the Caibarién–Morón
road in Yaguajay.

ℹ Getting There & Away

A Víazul bus used to ply this northern route, but
it wasn't running at last visit, meaning you're on
your own with a bike, hire car or taxi.

TRINIDAD & SANCTI SPÍRITUS PROVINCE NORTHERN SANCTI SPÍRITUS

AT A GLANCE

POPULATION
435,006

OLDEST CITY
Morón: 1543

**BEST CASA
PARTICULAR**
Alojamiento Maité
(p311)

**BEST KID'S
ACTIVITY**
Rocarena (p315)

BEST SEAFOOD
Lenny's Lobster
Shack (p317)

WHEN TO GO

Nov–Mar
Beachgoers
descend on the
cayos for drier
weather that,
while cool by
Cuban standards,
is still pleasantly
warm. Head for
the countryside in
November for the
Fiesta de los Bandas
Rojo y Azul

Apr–Oct
Morón's Aquatic
Carnival kicks off in
September in the
Laguna de la Leche.

Kiteboarding, Cayo Guillermo (p318)
CLWPHOTO/SHUTTERSTOCK ©

Ciego de Ávila Province

Diminutive Ciego de Ávila's famously decisive moment came during the late-19th-century Cuban Wars of Independence: it became the site of an impressive fortified wall, the Trocha, built to keep out rebellious eastern armies from the prosperous west. Today, the province continues to be the cultural divide between Cuba's Oriente and Occidente. Most tourists come here for the ambitious post–Special Period resort development of Cayo Coco and Cayo Guillermo. The brilliant tropical pearls that once seduced Ernest Hemingway have had their glorious beaches spruced up and daubed with over a dozen exclusive resorts.

Away from the tourist hordes, the province has been harboring intriguing secrets for more than a century. Various non-Spanish immigrants first arrsived here in the 19th century from Haiti, Jamaica, the Dominican Republic and Barbados, bringing with them myriad cultural rites still practiced in cricket matches in Baraguá, folk-dancing in Majagua and explosive fireworks in Chambas.

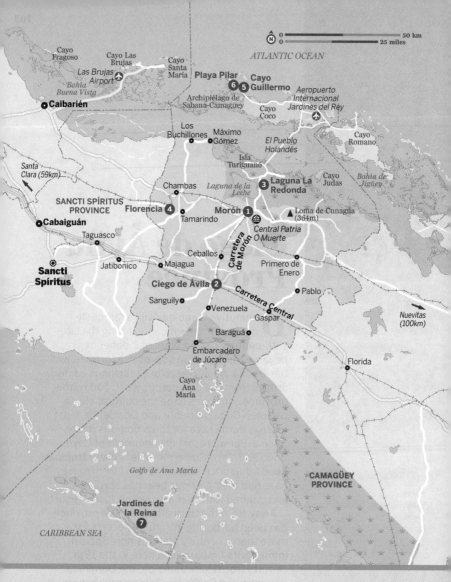

Ciego de Ávila Province Highlights

1 Morón (p311) Staying in a private homestay in this hard-working town for an alternative view.

2 Parque de la Ciudad (p307) Marveling at how waste ground got transformed into Ciego de Ávila's interesting city park.

3 Laguna La Redonda (p313) Taking the controls

of a speedboat through the mangrove-fringed channels of this freshwater lake.

4 Florencia (p313) Taking to the hills on horseback in the bucolic paths and lanes of northern Ciego.

5 Cayo Guillermo (p318) Following in the wake of 'Papa' Hemingway and taking to the waters of the Gulf

Stream for deep-sea fishing or kiteboarding.

6 Playa Pilar (p318) Finding out if this is really the finest beach in Cuba.

7 Jardines de la Reina (p314) Exploring the clear seas of Cuba's finest diving archipelago from a floating hotel.

History

The remnants of a Taíno settlement in the region, Los Buchillones (p314), constitute the most complete pre-Columbian remains in the Greater Antilles. The province got its present name from merchant Jacomé de Ávila, who was granted an *encomienda* (enslaved indigenous workforce) in San Antonio de la Palma in 1538. A small *ciego* (clearing) on Ávila's estate was put aside as a resting place for tired travelers, and it quickly became a burgeoning settlement.

Throughout the 16th and 17th centuries, the northern keys provided a refuge for pirates fresh from lucrative raids on cities such as Havana. During the 19th century, the area was infamous for its 68km-long Morón–Júcaro defensive wall: constructed to prevent marauding Mambís (19th-century rebels) from forging a passage west. Come the 1930s, Señor Hemingway became the region's most celebrated holidaymaker: Papa (Ernesto) fished and even tracked German submarines in the waters off Cayo Guillermo. Thousands more foreign visitors followed, particularly after the mega-hotel construction on the cayos that began in the early 1990s.

Ciego de Ávila

📞 33 / POP 119,859

Orgullo (pride) surges through Ciego de Ávila in improbably large doses for a settlement of such diminutive stature. But proud or not, Ciego isn't one of Cuba's more interesting provincial capitals, although its colonnaded streets are attractive enough. Founded in 1840, the city grew up originally in the 1860s and '70s as a military town behind the defensive Morón–Júcaro (Trocha) line; it later became an important processing center for the region's lucrative sugarcane and pineapple crops (the pineapple is the local mascot). Ciego's inhabitants refer to their city as 'the city of porches,' a reference to the ornate colonnaded house-fronts that characterize the center.

Famous *avileños* include Cuban pop-art exponent Raúl Martínez and local socialite Ángela Hernández, the rich widow of Señor Jiménez who helped finance many of the city's early 20th-century neoclassical buildings, including the Teatro Principal.

Ciego has a successful baseball team, having won the national series thrice since 2012.

◉ Sights

Ciego de Ávila has done its best to ensure it waylays you, with an attractive pedestrianized boulevard, appealing parks and museums that promote a relatively low-key history in an interesting and relevant way.

★ **Parque de la Ciudad**   PARK

(🏞) The once scrubby wasteland between Hotel Ciego de Ávila (p309) and the city center, on the northwestern edge of town, is now a vast park featuring an artificial lake, the Embalse La Turbina, with boating available, children's playgrounds and good eateries. With its offbeat attractions and amiable understatedness, it's one of Cuba's most interesting urban regeneration projects.

It's also testimony to the wonders achievable with scrap: old steam trains have been dusted off in homage to Ciego's transport history; there are impressive *artes plásticos* (art pieces) including an elephant statue fashioned from old car parts; and, among the eating possibilities, an old Aerocaribbean aircraft converted into a restaurant.

The lake fills a hole left by an old quarry that used to provide stone for the Trocha defensive wall in the 1860s and the Carretera Central in the 1920s.

★ **Museo Provincial Simón Reyes**   MUSEUM

(cnr Honorato del Castillo & Máximo Gómez; USD$1; ⊙ 9am-5pm Tue-Fri, 8:30am-4:30pm Sat, 8:30am-noon Sun) One of Cuba's best-presented municipal museums, this mustard-yellow building with a typical *avileño* porch is well worth a visit. Riveting exhibits include a scale model of La Trocha, detailed information on Afro-Cuban culture and religion, and explanations on the province's rich collection of traditional festivals. There are also indigenous artifacts from the nearby Los Buchillones archaeological site (p314).

Museo de Artes Decorativas   MUSEUM

(cnr Independencia & Marcial Gómez; USD$1; ⊙ 9am-5pm Mon-Thu, 1-9pm Sat, 9am-noon Sun) Cuba's most beautiful beds? Not in Varadero, nor in one of the island's classic colonial stop-offs, but downstairs at this modest museum. The thoughtful collection contains items from a bygone age, such as a working Victrola (Benny Moré serenades your visit) and antique pocket watches. Up top, the exhibits impress with ornate oriental art: check the striking Chinese screen.

Parque Martí   SQUARE

All Ciego roads lead to this textbook colonial park laid out in 1877 in honor of then king of Spain, Alfonso XII, but renamed in the early 20th century for newly martyred Cuban national hero, José Martí.

Ciego de Ávila

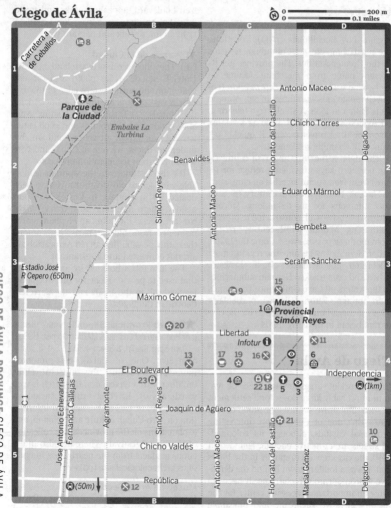

Centro de Promoción
Cultural Guiarte
GALLERY

(Independencia No 65; ⊙8am-9pm Tue-Fri & Sun, to 11pm Sat) **FREE** This gallery has works by Raúl Martínez, Cuba's king of pop art, on permanent display, alongside works by other local artists.

★ Festivals & Events

Fiesta de los Bandos Rojo y Azul   FIESTA
(⊙early Nov) In the town of Majagua, 16 miles west of Ciego de Ávila, this lively festival celebrates campesino culture with a procession, traditional dance and music played on traditional instruments such as the *tres* and marimbas. Groups participate in friendly dance and music competitions.

Noches Avileñas   STREET CARNIVAL
(⊙Sat) For total spontaneity, hit Ciego's streets on a Saturday night for the wonderful Noches Avileñas, when music and temporary food stands set up in the streets around various venues, including Parque Martí (p307).

✉ Sleeping

★**Villa Jabón Candado**   CASA PARTICULAR $
(☑3322-5854;   villajaboncandado@gmail.com; Chicho Valdés No 51, btwn Abraham Delgado & Narciso López; r USD$20-25; Ⓟ✳) Tired cyclists and

Ciego de Ávila

drivers, look no further: here's a bright-pink corner haven with a carport that's easy to find, with owners who have accrued years of experience in the trade. The two rooms are clean and homey, with the upstairs (balcony and kitchen included) being the best, and breakfast spreads are substantial.

María Luisa Muñoz Álvarez CASA PARTICULAR $
(☑ 3320-8649, 5-239-3995; Máximo Gómez No 74, btwn Honorato del Castillo & Antonio Maceo; r USD$25; P❄) Two clean rooms off a long corridor culminating in a patio equals textbook private-rental standard, with no real quirks. It's only a block from the center. The family also runs an equally comfortable casa just two doors down.

Hotel Ciego de Ávila HOTEL $
(☑ 3322-8013; Km 1.5, Carretera a de Ceballos; s/d incl breakfast USD$40/50; P❄@☎❄) Where have all the tourists gone? Cayo Coco probably, leaving this Islazul staple the domain of Cuban sports teams and workers on government-sponsored vacation time. Located 2km from the city center and overlooking Parque de la Ciudad, it has standard rooms, a noisy pool area and boring breakfasts. The staff are friendly, if generally unhelpful.

✕ Eating

Fonda La Cubana CUBAN $
(☑ 3326-6186; Honorato del Castillo No 34, cnr Máximo Gómez; mains USD$2.50-5; ☉ noon-10pm) An atmospheric, open-air corner joint known forever as 'La Fonda' and now a government-run affair, this is a great lunch spot to

watch street life go by before or after a visit to the provincial museum.

El Camarote INTERNATIONAL $
(República No 183, btwn Simón Reyes & Agramonte; mains USD$2-4; ☉ 6:30-11pm) Pop into this modest little place three blocks from the Carretera Central for pizza, tacos, spaghetti or the house special: grilled fish topped with prawns, bechamel and – er – cheese.

El Flotante CUBAN $
(Parque de la Ciudad; mains CUP$25-150; ☉ noon-10pm Wed-Mon) The *restaurante flotante* (floating restaurant) is raised on stilts above the waters of Embalse La Turbina in Parque de la Ciudad, Ciego's commendable urban-regeneration project. It sells basic, but not bad, Cuban nosh in pesos. The setting is lovely.

Solaris FUSION $
(☑ 3322-3424; Doce Plantas Bldg, cnr Honorato del Castillo & Libertad; mains USD$3-8; ☉ 11am-11pm; ❄) City-center joint on the 12th floor of the rather ugly Doce Plantas building on the western side of Parque Martí. Excellent city views, with a terrace and a *parrillada* (barbecue). Cordon bleu (chicken stuffed with ham and cheese), which it refers to as 'Gordon Bleu,' headlines the menu.

El Colonial CUBAN $
(☑ 3322-3595; Independencia No 110, btwn Simón Reyes & Antonio Maceo; meals CUP$50-150; ☉ noon-4pm & 7-11pm Tue-Sun) Who needs fancy food when you're eating in the city's most atmospheric colonial building? A neat Wild West–style saloon bar opens onto a colonnaded patio behind.

Don Ávila
CARIBBEAN $$

(Marcial Gómez, cnr Libertad; mains USD$1-6; ⊙11am-11pm; ✦) Plaza-abutting Don Ávila impresses with its regal ambience, on-site cigar outlet, old-gents-style bar, typically friendly *avileño* service and cheap prices.

🍷 Drinking & Nightlife

Piña Colada
BAR

(cnr Independencia & Honorato del Castillo; ⊙3pm-2am) Proudly mixing Caribbean cocktails with Antarctic air-con since 2011.

La Fontana
CAFE

(cnr Independencia & Antonio Maceo; ⊙6am-2pm & 3-11pm) Ciego's long-standing coffee institution has seen better days. Still if you just want a *cafecito* with no ceremony, milk, take-out cup or wi-fi, it can probably oblige.

El Batanga
CLUB

(Km 1.5, Carretera a de Ceballos, Hotel Ciego de Ávila; per couple USD$3; ⊙10pm-2am) Party with the locals into the wee hours at Hotel Ciego de Ávila's rowdy disco.

☆ Entertainment

Teatro Principal
THEATER

(cnr Joaquín de Agüero & Honorato del Castillo) One block south of Parque Martí (p307), the grand Teatro Principal more than compensates for the park's lack of illustrious edifices. Built in 1927 with help from local financier Ángela Hernández de Jiménez, it purportedly has the island's best (theatrical) acoustics. Check the poster board for performances.

Estadio José R Cepero
SPECTATOR SPORT

(Máximo Gómez) From October to April, baseball games take place to the northwest of Ciego's center. The town's Tigres have experienced a dramatic turnaround in fortune of late and are one of Cuba's best teams.

Casa de la Trova
Miguel Ángel Luna
LIVE MUSIC

(Libertad No 130; ⊙noon-6pm & 9pm-1am Tue-Sun) In the dice-roll of traditional musical entertainment, Ciego's *trova* (national poetic singing) house scores a magic six with polished Thursday night regional *trovadores* in a pleasant colonial setting.

Casa de la Cultura
ARTS CENTER

(Independencia No 76, btwn Antonio Maceo & Honorato del Castillo; ⊙hours vary) Dodge the slumbering receptionist, and all sorts of capers take place here, including a Wednesday *danzón* (ballroom dance) club and weekly *folklórico* (traditional Latin American dance).

🛍 Shopping

La Época
GIFTS & SOUVENIRS

(Independencia, btwn Antonio Maceo & Honorato del Castillo; ⊙9am-5pm Mon-Sat) This is an ARTex souvenir store rather than the well-known Cuban department store. It's on two levels selling everything from arty parasols to Cuban flags.

Librería Juan A Márquez
BOOKS

(Independencia Oeste No 153, cnr Simón Reyes; ⊙9am-5pm Mon-Fri, to noon Sat) Revolutionary tomes for ardent lefties.

ℹ Information

INTERNET ACCESS

Etecsa Telepunto (Joaquín de Agüero No 62; internet per hour USD$1.50; ⊙8:30am-7pm) sells internet cards, and Parque Martí (p307) has a wi-fi hot spot.

MEDICAL SERVICES

General Hospital (☎3322-4015; Máximo Gómez No 257, btwn Onelio Hernández & Cuarta)

MONEY

Banco de Crédito y Comercio (Bandec; ☎3322-3002; Independencia No 71; ⊙8am-5:30pm Mon-Fri)

Banco Financiero Internacional (cnr Honorato del Castillo & Joaquín de Agüero Oeste; ⊙9am-3pm Mon-Fri)

Cadeca (Independencia Oeste No 118, btwn Antonio Maceo & Simón Reyes; ⊙8:30am-12:30pm)

TOURIST INFORMATION

Infotur (☎3320-9109; Doce Plantas Bldg, cnr Honorato del Castillo & Libertad; ⊙9am-noon & 1-6pm) Possibly Cuba's friendliest, most informative Infotur office.

ℹ Getting There & Away

BUS

The **bus station** (www.viazul.com; Carretera Central), about 1.5km east of Ciego de Ávila center, has multiple daily Víazul services.

Destination	Cost (USD$)	Duration (hr)	Frequency (daily)
Havana	27	6½	5
Santiago de Cuba	24	8½	5
Trinidad	9	2¾	1
Varadero	19	6½	1

Santiago de Cuba buses also stop at Camagüey (USD$6, two hours), Las Tunas (USD$13, four

CIEGO DE ÁVILA PROVINCE CIEGO DE ÁVILA

hours), Holguín (USD$17, 5¼ hours) and Bayamo (USD$17, six hours). Havana buses also stop at Sancti Spíritus (USD$6, 1¼ hours) and Santa Clara (USD$9, 2½ hours). Book ahead online or in person at the terminal.

TAXI
The common procedure when a Víazul bus is full is to hang around outside the bus station and wait for a *colectivo* (shared taxi). More often than not, you'll find other travelers with a similar conundrum. Up to four people can share a Cubataxi; the going rate is around USD$0.55 per kilometer.

ⓘ Getting Around

CAR & MOTORCYCLE
The **Carretera a Morón gas station** (Carretera a Morón) is just before the bypass road, northeast of the town center. The **Oro Negro gas station** (Carretera Central) is near the bus station.

Rex (Hotel Ciego de Ávila, Carretera a de Ceballos; ⊙ 8:30am-7:30pm) can help with vehicle and moped rental.

TAXI
A one-way taxi to Morón is USD$15 to USD$20 (40 minutes); to Cayo Coco, it's USD$60 (1¾ hours); and on to Cayo Guillermo, it costs USD$80 (2¼ hours).

Morón

✔ 33 / POP 70,126

Despite its slightly removed position 35km north of Cuba's arterial Carretera Central, Morón remains an important travel nexus (thanks to its railway) and acts as a viable base camp for people not enamored with resort-heaving Cayo Coco.

Founded in 1543, three centuries before provincial capital Ciego de Ávila, Morón is known island-wide as the Ciudad del Gallo (City of the Cockerel), for a 'cocky' bullying official in the colonial era who eventually got his comeuppance. The city has architecture to match its years, with more, better-preserved examples of those Ciego de Ávila column-flanked facades.

The city itself is easygoing and compact, and its inhabitants are more likely to flash you a curious smile than to try to sell you anything. Many independent travelers love it for this breathing room.

◉ Sights

Terminal de Ferrocarriles   NOTABLE BUILDING
(Train Station; Narciso López) Morón has long been central Cuba's main railway crossroads and exhibits the most elegant railway station

outside Havana. Built in 1923, the building's edifice is neocolonial, though inside the busy ticket hall hides a more streamlined art deco look. Equally eye-catching is the stained-glass skylight.

Museo Caonabo   MUSEUM
(Martí No 374, btwn Cervantes & Antuña; USD$1; ⊙ 9am-5pm Mon-Sat, 8am-noon Sun) In among the teeming sidewalks and peeling colonnades, this well-laid-out museum of history and archaeology is housed in Morón's former bank, an impressive neoclassical building dating from 1919.

Central Patria o Muerte   HISTORIC SITE
(Patria; incl tour USD$3; ⊙ 8am-5pm) Cuba's sugar industry is preserved at this huge, rusting ex-sugar mill founded in 1914 in the village of Patria, 3km south of Morón. Guides explain the sugar-milling process from slave times to the factory's decommissioning in 2001. For an extra USD$4, a 1920 Philadelphia-made Baldwin steam train can take you on a 5km ride through cane fields to Rancho Palma, a bucolic **farm** (Km 7, Carretera a Bolivia; mains USD$4-6; ⊙ noon-4pm; **P**) with a bar-restaurant where you can sample *guarapo* (pressed cane juice).

⭐ Festivals & Events

Morón Aquatic Carnival   FIESTA
(⊙ Sep) Takes the typical Cuban carnival frivolity and transposes it onto the water – at Laguna de la Leche (p313) near Morón. Floats on boats, plus more merriment on the lakeshore for landlubbers. Usually held in September.

🛏 Sleeping

While it's not a tourist town per se, Morón has plenty of casas particulares to make up for its lack of hotels and offers a perfect alternative base for those not drawn to the all-inclusive scene on the northern cayos.

⭐ Alojamiento Maité   CASA PARTICULAR $
(✔ 3350-4181; alojamientomaite@gmail.com; Luz Caballero No 40b, btwn Libertad & Agramonte; r USD$25-30; **P ✱ @ 🛜 ⛱**) Surely one of the most professionally run casas in Cuba, Maité's place is reason alone to visit Morón. Relax by the small pool, on the breezy roof terrace or in one of the large well-appointed rooms equipped with complimentary bathroom bags, well-stocked minibars (with wine) and starched white sheets (changed daily).

Alojamiento

Vista al Parque   CASA PARTICULAR $

(☑ 3350-4181; alojamientovistaalparque@gmail.com; Luz Caballero No 49d, btwn Libertad & Agramonte; r USD$25-30; P✷@) There's comfort and independence in this lovely pale-blue house with three rooms (two of them apartments) with a couple of terraces and views across the well-tended park. It's run by Idolka (who speaks some English) and is affiliated with Alojamiento Maité, opposite, where guests can take breakfast.

La Casona de Morón   HISTORIC HOTEL $

(☑ 3350-2236; Colón No 41; s/d USD$34/45; P✷✷) Ostensibly scruffy, Morón is a town of many secrets and here's one of them – a beautiful yellow-and-white plantation house with a two-level wraparound porch made into a small hotel. There are eight simple rooms, attractive colonial embellishments and a lovely outside pool in shady grounds.

✗ Eating

Doña Neli Dulcería   BAKERY $

(Serafín Sánchez No 86, btwn Narciso López & Martí; snacks USD$1-2; ☉ 8am-4pm) On the self-catering front, there's the dependable Doña Neli Dulcería for bread and pastries.

★Restaurante
Maité La Qbana   INTERNATIONAL $$

(☑ 3350-4181; Luz Caballero No 40b, btwn Libertad & Agramonte; mains USD$10-15; ☉ noon-11pm; ✐) Maité is a highly creative cook whose dishes, prepared with *mucho amor*, will leave you wondering why insipid all-inclusive buffets ever got so popular. Prepare for abundant appetizers, fine wines and cocktails, homemade cakes and paella that has visiting *valencianos* reminiscing about their homeland. Reservations highly recommended.

Don Papa   CUBAN $$

(☑ 5-268-9428; Enrique Varona No 56, btwn Calles 5 & 6; mains USD$6-9; ☉ noon-midnight) Despite being draped with international flags, Don Papa is 100% *cubano*. The food here is simply delicious and also abundant. Meat, fish and lobster come with lashings of root vegetables, plantains, rice and beans, and there's a 'side order' of live music. It's a modest place in a backstreet stapled to the side of an average Morón house.

🍷 Drinking & Nightlife

The antithesis of the Cayo Coco resorts, Morón's after-dark scene is 99% local. Want an insight into what average Cubans do on

their weekends off? Grab a Bucanero beer and pull up a stool.

Discoteca Morón   CLUB

(Hotel Morón, Av Tarafa; ☉ 10pm-late) Young, raucous entertainment-seekers test the patience of sleep-deprived paying guests at the Hotel Morón.

☆ Entertainment

Casa de la Trova Pablo Bernal   LIVE MUSIC

(Martí No 169; ☉ 8-11pm) Vibrant alfresco music house with Wednesday comedy night.

ℹ Information

INTERNET ACCESS

You'll find internet at Morón's **Etecsa** (cnr Martí & Céspedes; per hour USD$1.50; ☉ 8:30am-7:30pm), and the park outside is a wi-fi hot spot.

MONEY

There are several ATMs on the main street, Calle Martí. **Cadeca** (cnr Martí & Gonzalo Arena; ☉ 9am-4:40pm Mon-Sat, to noon Sun) has money-changing facilities.

TOURIST INFORMATION

Information on Lagunas de la Leche and La Redonda can be procured at **Cubatur** (Martí No 169; ☉ 9am-5pm) in the Casa de la Trova. It is also possible to arrange tours to Florencia.

ℹ Getting There & Away

BUS

Morón is, somewhat unfairly, a transport conundrum with no Víazul bus connections. The nearest buses stop in the city of Ciego de Ávila, from where a taxi should cost around USD$12 to USD$15 (40 minutes).

Morón's **bus station** (Martí No 12) is a block back toward the center (north) from the train station, though its local buses are sadly not a lot of good for travelers.

TRAIN

Morón was once an important rail terminus, and the glorious **train station** (Narciso López) is legendary, but the trains aren't (late, unreliable and in poor state of repair). There are supposedly three to four daily trains to Ciego de Ávila (USD$1, one hour) where you can pick up services on Cuba's main Havana–Santiago line (or a bus). There are also connections to Camagüey (USD$3, four hours, daily) and Santa Clara (USD$4, six hours, every other day).

ℹ Getting Around

The roads from Morón northwest to Caibarién (112km) and southeast to Nuevitas (168km) are good. Rental cars are in short supply, and it pays to reserve a vehicle several days ahead of when you need it: try **Cubacar** (☑ 3350-2230; Hotel Morón, Av Tarafa; ⊗ 9am-5pm). The **Cupet-Cimex gas station** (Carretera a Ciego de Ávila; ⊗ 24hr) is one block south of Hotel Morón.

For taxis, ask your casa particular owner or try outside the train station. Bank on paying around USD$0.55 per kilometer for out-of-town journeys.

Around Morón

Laguna de la Leche & Laguna La Redonda

Aquatic action creates significant waves at these two large natural lakes just north of Morón, where fish are abundant and you can hire your own motorboat to make a splash in the mangroves. Both lakes offer food, fishing trips and various boating options. Smaller Redonda is on the Cayo Coco day-trip circuit and has better tourist infrastructure. Closer to Morón, the expansive Laguna de la Leche guards a more local scene.

◉ Sights

★**Laguna La Redonda**   LAKE
(⊗ 9am-5pm) Anglers, listen up: 12km north of Morón, off the Cayo Coco road, this mangrove-rimmed, 4-sq-km lake has the island's best square-kilometer density of bass and trout. Four hours of fishing costs USD$70. Speedboat trips (USD$7) take in narrow, foliage-covered tributaries – as close to the Amazon as the province comes. You'll even be allowed to take the wheel if you want!

Not a fishing fanatic? Rock up at the decent, rustic bar-restaurant just for a drink or fish meal with a lake view.

Laguna de la Leche   LAKE
Laguna de la Leche (Milk Lake), named for its reflective underwater lime deposits, is Cuba's largest natural lake (66 sq km). Its water content is a mixture of fresh and salt water, and anglers flock here to hook the abundant stocks of carp, tarpon, snook and tilapia. Guided fishing trips (USD$70 for four hours) can be arranged at the main southern shore entrance.

For a little more, you can keep your catch and cook it on a mobile barbecue aboard a ship. Nonfishing boat excursions (USD$20 for 45 minutes) are also available.

The lake is also the venue for the annual Morón Aquatic Carnival (p311).

✖ Eating

Restaurant Laguna La Redonda   SEAFOOD $
(mains USD$4-8; ⊗ 10am-5pm) This restaurant at the entrance to Laguna La Redonda is good for *comida criolla* or a drink with a lake view. Try the house specialty, a fillet of fish called *calentico*.

La Atarraya   SEAFOOD $
(mains USD$1-7; ⊗ noon-6pm) Raised on stilts in a clapboard building off the southern shoreline of Laguna de la Leche, you'll find one of Cuba's best local fish restaurants. The insanely cheap menu is headlined by *paella valenciana* and *pescado monteroro* (fish fillet with ham and cheese).

Pescado Frito   SEAFOOD $
(mains CUP$50-200; ⊗ noon-6pm) You'll need a small boat to row you across the canal at the jaws of Laguna de la Leche to this simple open-faced restaurant specializing in locally caught tilapia fish.

☆ Entertainment

Cabaret Cueva   CABARET
(Laguna de la Leche; ⊗ 10pm-late Thu-Sun) Locals willingly hitch, walk or carpool to make the 6km trip from Morón to this cabaret, held in a cave on the southern shores of Laguna de la Leche.

❶ Getting There & Away

Laguna La Redonda, 12km north of Morón on the road to Cayo Coco, is accessed via a signposted spur road; it's 500m from the main road to the boat dock. The 6km entry road for Laguna de la Leche starts just north of Morón's **Parque Agramonte** – it's a long but not unpleasant walk along a quiet road, or you can hail a taxi (USD$2; five minutes).

Florencia

☑ 33 / POP 18,910

Ringed by gentle hills, the somnolent town of Florencia was named for Florence in Italy – early settlers claimed the surrounding countryside reminded them of Tuscany. In the early 1990s, the Cuban government constructed a hydroelectric dam, the Liberación de Florencia, on the Río Chambas, and the resulting lake has created an unexpectedly beautiful juxtaposition of water and greenery. With its low-key rural activities and nearby nature reserve at Boquerón, Florencia makes an excellent day trip from Morón.

JARDINES DE LA REINA

The uninhabited Jardines de la Reina is a 120km-long mangrove forest and coral-island system 80km off the south coast of Ciego de Ávila Province and 120km north of the Cayman Islands. The marine park measures 3800 sq km and is virgin territory left more or less untouched since the time of Columbus. It's the best place to dive in Cuba (nay, the Caribbean), but it's strictly limited to fewer than 3000 divers per year on half-a-dozen live-aboard boats.

The flora consists of palm trees, pines, sea grapes and mangroves, while the fauna – aside from tree rats and iguanas – includes an interesting variety of resident birds, including ospreys, pelicans, spoonbills and egrets. Below the waves the main attraction is sharks (whale and hammerhead), and this, along with the pristine coral and the unequaled clarity of the water, is what draws divers from all over the world.

Getting to the Jardines is not easy – or cheap. The only way in is on a diving excursion with the Italian-run Avalon (www.cubandivingcenters.com). One-week dive packages, which include equipment, seven nights of accommodation, guide, park license, 12 dives and food and drink, start from USD$3600. Ask for a quote via the website and book well in advance. Another company, Windward Islands Cruising Company (www.windward-islands.net), incorporates the western tip of the archipelago into its one-week Cuba cruises.

◉ Sights

La Presa de Florencia   LAKE
(⊗10am-5pm) The Florencia area's focal point is an artificial lake called La Presa de Florencia, formed when a dam was built on the Río Chambas in 1991. The lake and its surrounding hills are unexpectedly beautiful and little visited by non-Cubans.

Los Buchillones   ARCHAEOLOGICAL SITE
Tucked away on Ciego de Ávila Province's northwest coastline, this significant archaeological site was originally excavated during the 1980s after fisherfolk began discovering implements such as ax handles and needles in the surrounding swamps. The mud at the bottom of the shallow lagoon preserved these Taíno artifacts so well that the site has yielded the most significant stash of pre-Columbian relics anywhere in the Greater Antilles.

Los Buchillones had been the location of a sizable Taíno settlement of 40 to 50 houses, predating European arrival in the region. Everything from *cemíes* (Taíno deities to gods of rain, cassava and the like) to canoes to house structures have been recovered from the excavation site, most of which remains a waterlogged work in progress.

🏃 Activities

There are two trips that can be organized in the Florencia area. The first is a horse ride and hike in the hills surrounding the lake to a tobacco-growing farm, followed by a boat ride to the lake's sole island with its rustic restaurant for lunch, relaxation and kayaking. The other is a horse ride and hike in the nearby Boquerón nature reserve following the course of the Río Jatibonico where you can swim and explore some caves. To organize either excursion, it's best to call La Esquinita cafe in advance. Prices start at USD$12 per person.

🍴 Eating & Drinking

Restaurante Presa de Florencia   CUBAN **$**
(mains USD$3.50-5; ⊗9am-5pm) A traditional open-sided restaurant under a thatched shelter on a small island in the middle of the Florencia reservoir. It serves straight-up Cuban food using whatever ingredients are available that day. Price is usually included in excursion packages, which can be organized in either Cubatur (p312) in Morón or La Esquinita in Florencia.

La Esquinita   CAFE
(✆3355-9294; cnr Martí & Agramonte; ⊗9am-8pm) A small cafe on the corner of Florencia's main street that's good for a cola or a juice, La Esquinita is also where you can organize local excursions including horse-riding and hiking in the hills around La Presa de Florencia and the nearby Boquerón nature reserve. Prices start at USD$12 per person.

❶ Getting There & Away

There are no regular public transportation options to Florencia beyond the local trucks and buses that run on sketchy schedules. Your best bet is to use a rental car or to hire a taxi in Morón (approximate cost one way USD$25, one hour).

Cayo Coco

Situated in the Archipiélago de Sabana-Camagüey, or the Jardines del Rey (King's Gardens) as travel brochures prefer to call it, Cayo Coco is Cuba's fourth-largest island, a 370-sq-km beach-rimmed key that is unashamedly dedicated to tourism. The area north of the Bahía de Perros (Bay of Dogs) was uninhabited before 1992, when the first hotel – the Cojímar – went up on adjoining Cayo Guillermo. The bulldozers haven't stopped buzzing since.

Cayo Coco largely resembles Cayo Santa María to the west (which it predates), although the latter is now larger in terms of hotel capacity and star-rating. Since 1988, the island has been connected to the mainland by a 27km causeway slicing across the Bahía de Perros. There are also causeways from Cayo Coco to Cayo Guillermo in the west and to Cayo Romano in the east, as well as an international airport.

◉ Sights

Cayo Paredón Grande   ISLAND
East of Cayo Coco, a road crosses over to Cayo Romano (technically Camagüey Province) and turns north to Cayo Paredón Grande and **Faro Diego Velázquez**, a 52m lighthouse dating from 1859. This area has a couple of isolated beaches, including much-lauded Playa Los Pinos, and is good for fishing. Get there soon! Its first hotel is in development.

🏃 Activities & Tours

There's no lack of day excursions available from the main hotel information desks, which are usually staffed by Cubatur or Cubanacán representatives. Highlights include a catamaran cruise (USD$79), a motorboat tour to Cayo Guillermo (USD$46), and a flamingo-spotting tour or a jaunt out to Cayo Mortero – via the fabulous snorkeling spot of Grunt Hole – for downtime with cold beer and fresh fish (USD$30).

Rocarena   CLIMBING
(☑ 3330-2129; Av de los Hoteles; USD$5-16; ⊙ 9am-9pm; 🚼) This rather ingeniously designed climbing extravaganza, created mainly for kids and teens although adults can partake, has tons of pulleys, tightropes, swings, climbing walls and a mini bungee jump.

Ecotur   TOURS
(☑ 3330-8163; Hotel Sol Cayo Coco; ⊙ 9am-5pm) Ecotur's office in the Hotel Sol Cayo Coco can

help arrange visits to the **Loma de Cunagua** (USD$5; ⊙ 9am-4pm), a protected flora and fauna reserve harboring a *ranchón*-style restaurant, a small network of trails and excellent birdwatching opportunities. The guides are experts in the natural environment of the area and can help you navigate around the reserve's unsignposted trails rich with flora and birdlife.

Centro Internacional
de Buceo Blue Diving   DIVING
(☑ 3330-8179, 3330-8180; Pullman Cayo Coco) On the beach inside the Pullman Cayo Coco resort. Dives cost from USD$45 for one immersion, and an introductory course in the swimming pool costs USD$70, including one open-water dive. The diving area stretches for more than 10km mainly to the east, and there are six certified instructors with the capacity for 30 divers per day.

Marina Gaviota Aguas Tranquilas   FISHING
(☑ 3330-1011) Cayo Coco's main marina is on the south-facing shore past the turnoff for the Pullman Cayo Coco and offers deep-sea fishing outings (USD$310 per four hours).

🛏 Sleeping

Cayo Coco is an all-inclusive zone with all of the resorts enjoying direct beach access. Facilities vary from three- to five-star, but are fairly generic. There is no Cuban settlement on the island and thus no private homestays for rent. The best bet for indie travelers is the rustic but cheap Sitio La Güira.

Sitio La Güira   HUT $
(☑ 3330-1208; hut USD$25; ❄) 🍴 Backpackers aren't well catered for on Cuba's resort islands, except perhaps at this imitation of an erstwhile charcoal-burner's camp. Four pseudo-rustic *bohíos* (thatched huts) with private bathrooms and air-con (to dissuade the mosquitoes, which are no joke) are available for rent. A *ranchón*-style restaurant and bar are on-site. Best for those with their own wheels, as it's fairly isolated.

★ Pullman Cayo Coco   RESORT $$$
(☑ 3330-4400; www.accorhotels.com; s/d all-inclusive from USD$230/302; 🅿❄@🛜🌊) This sleek five-star opened in December 2015 and was rebuilt after a gutting by Hurricane Irma. Having bagged a large slice of once tranquil Playa Las Coloradas, it's a stylish if somewhat characterless Accor property with a family section and another for adults only. Service, creative food, beach and decent wi-fi are all superb.

Cayo Coco & Cayo Guillermo

Cayo Coco & Cayo Guillermo

⊚ **Sights**
1 Cayo Paredón Grande F2
2 Playa Pilar A1

⊕ **Activities, Courses & Tours**
Boat Adventure ....(see 16)
Centro Internacional de Buceo
Blue Diving...................................(see 11)
3 Centro Internacional de Buceo Coco
Diving A1
Ecotur ....(see 11)
Havana Kiteboarding Club ....(see 7)
4 Marina Gaviota Aguas Tranquilas D2
Marina Marlin Cayo Guillermo .....(see 16)
5 Rocarena D2

⊝ **Sleeping**
6 Colonial Cayo Coco D2
7 Gran Caribe Club Cayo Guillermo A1
8 Gran Muthu Imperial A1

9 Hotel Tryp Cayo Coco D2
10 Iberostar Daiquirí A1
11 Meliá Cayo Coco...................................D2
12 Meliá Jardines del Rey D2
13 Memories Flamenco Beach Resort......D2
14 Pullman Cayo Coco D2
15 Sitio La Güira C2
16 Villa Gregorio A1

⊗ **Eating**
17 Lenny's Lobster Shack..........................D1
Ranchón Flamingo ....(see 12)
18 Ranchón Las Coloradas E2
19 Ranchón Playa Pilar A1

⊕ **Entertainment**
20 La Cueva del Jabalí...............................D2

⊝ **Shopping**
Plaza Los Flamencos ....(see 12)

CIEGO DE ÁVILA PROVINCE CAYO COCO

★ **Meliá Cayo Coco** RESORT $$$
(☑ 3330-1180; www.meliacuba.com; s/d all-inclusive from USD$239/284; P ✳ @ ☎ ☀) This intimate resort on Playa Las Coloradas is everything you'd expect from Spain's Meliá chain. For a luxury twist, try staying in one of the elegant white bungalows perched on stilts in a lagoon. Prices are high, but the Meliá is unashamedly classy, and a 'no kids' policy enhances the tranquility.

★ **Colonial Cayo Coco** RESORT $$$
(☑ 3330-1311; www.hotelescubanacan.com; s/d all-inclusive from USD$90/180; P ✳ @ ☎ ☀) Spanish-colonial villas with attractively tiled public areas lend the Colonial a refined air, as if you've landed in a village rather than another standard, unadorned Cuban all-inclusive. This was the island's first hotel when it opened in 1993, and it remains a lot more charming than many of its younger siblings.

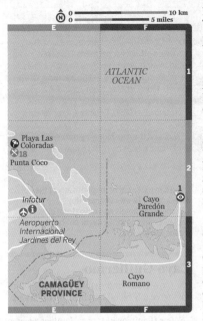

ATLANTIC
OCEAN

Playa Las
Coloradas
18
Punta Coco

Infotur
Aeropuerto
Internacional
Jardines del Rey

CAMAGÜEY
PROVINCE

Cayo
Paredón
Grande

Cayo
Romano

Meliá Jardines del Rey
RESORT $$$

(☎3330-4300; www.meliacuba.com; s/d all-inclusive from USD$182/261; P✳@🛜≋) The big kahuna of Cuba resorts (1176 rooms), this five-star place, which opened in 2014, constitutes a small town with golf carts to get around, maps to aid navigation and more restaurants than the nearby city of Morón. Common areas feature earthy woods and Ikea-like minimalism, while rooms are punctuated with some welcome color accents.

Memories Flamenco Beach Resort
HOTEL $$$

(☎3330-4100; www.memoriesresorts.com; s/d all-inclusive from USD$76/135; P✳@🛜≋) Opened in 2011 and equipped with 624 decent-sized rooms (still looking fairly shiny) in 10 gabled three-floor villas arranged around two pools (one with a swim-up bar). There's an attractive Asian restaurant and all the usual bells and whistles (gym, beauty parlor, kids' club etc), although for some reason it only gets 4½ stars.

Hotel Tryp Cayo Coco
RESORT $$$

(☎3330-1300; www.meliacuba.com; s/d all-inclusive USD$123/177; P✳@🛜≋) The family choice. Tryp is a quintessential all-inclusive with a meandering pool, myriad bars and nightly tourist shows. Facilities are good, although overzealous poolside 'entertainers'

lend the place a holiday-camp feel at times. The 500-plus rooms are big, with balconies and huge beds, although finishes are a little worn. The four-star rating is generous.

🍴 Eating

Amid the ubiquitous as-much-as-you-can-eat hotel buffets in Cayo Coco, there are a few indie restaurants, mainly fronting the beaches.

★Ranchón Flamingo
CARIBBEAN $

(Playa Los Flamencos; mains USD$4-10; ⊙10am-7:30pm; P) Eat exquisite seafood, drink cold beer, swim, sunbathe, drink more beer... you get the picture. The Flamingo guards a small scoop of public beach in the shadow of the resorts.

★Lenny's Lobster Shack
SEAFOOD $$

(Ranchón Playa Prohibida; mains USD$7-15; ⊙10am-7:30pm) Named unofficially after a Canadian tourist and regular patron, Lenny's is a beautiful open-sided thatched rondavel on hotel-free Playa Prohibida, famed for one dish – the lobster, prawn and fish medley, USD$15 (!) well-spent. The house band, Coco Indio, is usually augmented by several passing diners.

Ranchón Las Coloradas
CARIBBEAN $$

(Playa Las Coloradas; mains USD $7-12; ⊙9am-4pm) Seafood in a paradisaical beachside setting, but hotel construction nearby has recently dented the 'paradisaical' tag. As with most indie restaurants on the cayo, it's set under an opened-sided thatched canopy with seafood headlining the menu.

☆ Entertainment

La Cueva del Jabalí
CABARET

(USD$5; ⊙10:30pm-2am Tue-Thu) This natural cave is the only non-all-inclusive entertainment venue in Cayo Coco, although 95% of the audience will be 'all-inclusivers.' It features a slightly cheesy cabaret show.

🛍 Shopping

Plaza Los Flamencos
SHOPPING CENTER

Shopping plaza just outside the entrance to the Meliá Jardines del Rey with souvenir and clothes shops, a bowling alley and a spa open to all visitors.

ℹ Information

MEDICAL SERVICES

Clínica Internacional Cayo Coco (☎3330-2191; ⊙24hr) provides medical treatment 24/7.

KITEBOARDING

You'll glimpse many multicolored sails as you approach Cayo Guillermo before anything else comes into focus. The latest craze, kiteboarding, has taken off all over northern Cuba, but many experts claim this small isle has the best combo of wind, waves and kite-friendly hotels.

Several operators are based here, including the Italian-run **Havana Kiteboarding Club** (☑ 5-671-0109; www.havanakiteboarding.com; ⊗ 8:45am-6:45pm Oct-May, 10am-7pm Jul & Aug), which operates out of the Gran Caribe Club Cayo Guillermo. A basic kiteboarding lesson costs around USD$150, and weekly courses start around USD$650. Equipment rental runs USD$60 for the first hour and USD$400 for a week.

The main launch point for boarders is Playa el Paso, and the most kite-friendly hotels are the Gran Caribe and Sol Cayo Guillermo. Both of these places have large lawns that are ideal for laying out your equipment.

MONEY

All of Cayo Coco's resorts have money exchanges. Rates are marginally better than the bank.

Banco Financiero Internacional (Rotunda, 4 Caminos; ⊗ 8:30am-5pm Mon-Sat)

TOURIST INFORMATION

Infotur (☑ 3330-9109; www.infotur.cu; ⊗ 8:30am-5pm) has a helpful office at the airport, as well as desks at the main hotels. Ciego de Ávila's Infotur office (p310) has bundles of information on Cayo Coco, too.

❶ Getting There & Away

International flights regularly service Cayo Coco, but getting here by land is nigh on impossible without a car, taxi or bike.

AIR

Cayo Coco's **Aeropuerto Internacional Jardines del Rey** (☑ 3330-9165) can process 1.2 million visitors annually. Weekly flights arrive from Canada, the UK, Portugal, Argentina and more. There's a daily service to and from Havana (about USD$110; three hours with stop), usually via Holguín, on Cubana (www.cubana.cu).

TAXI

A taxi to Cayo Coco from Morón will cost about USD$50 (one hour) and USD$70 (1¾ hours) from Ciego de Ávila. You pay a USD$2 fee to enter the causeway and may need to show your passport.

❶ Getting Around

Getting around both Cayo Coco and Cayo Guillermo has become infinitely easier since the introduction of a **Transtur** hop-on, hop-off, open-topped double-decker bus. The service varies according to season, but expect a minimum service of two buses per day in either direction, with six scheduled for peak times. The bus runs east–west between Pullman Cayo Coco and Playa Pilar, stopping at all Cayo Coco and Cayo Guillermo hotels. An all-day pass costs USD$5. The full journey takes 50 minutes with stops.

You can rent a car or moped in any of the hotels with Cubacar (www.cubacar.info).

Some of the hotels also have (free) bicycles available, although they might not be Tour de France worthy.

Cayo Guillermo

Ah, Cayo Guillermo: haunt of pink flamingos, agreeably blond beaches and Cuba's second-most famous Ernesto after Mr Guevara – Señor Hemingway. It was Hemingway who initiated Guillermo's early publicity drive, describing it radiantly in his posthumously published Cuban novel *Islands in the Stream* (1970). Development of the northern keys took off here in 1993 when the first of six all-inclusive resorts, Villa Cojímar, received its formative guests. Long a prized deep-sea fishing spot, 13-sq-km Guillermo has recently morphed into Cuba's most prized kiteboarding spot thanks to its stiff north-coast winds. The mangroves off the south coast remain home to pink flamingos and pelicans, and there's a tremendous diversity of tropical fish and crustaceans on the Atlantic reef.

Would Hemingway like it today? Probably not. Notwithstanding, three statues of the laconic writer, who once revered Guillermo for its solitude and fishing, guard the entry bridge.

◉ Sights & Activities

Playa Pilar   BEACH

This much sought-after strip of sand is regularly touted as Cuba's (and the Caribbean's) best beach, courtesy of its diamond-dust white sand and rugged 15m-high sand dunes (the largest of their kind in the Caribbean). However, the recent construction of a huge four-story resort within sight of the beach has made a massive dent in its splendor. What was once special now seems ordinary.

Resort development aside, the sea at Pilar is warm, shallow and loaded with snorkeling possibilities. One kilometer away across a calm channel lies the shimmering sands of Cayo Media Luna, a one-time beach escape of Fulgencio Batista. There are excursions to the key (USD$25), plus kayaks and aquatic bikes for rent, all arranged at the small office (open 9am to 3pm) along the sand from the rustic beach restaurant, Ranchón Playa Pilar (mains USD$12-18; ◷10am-4:30pm).

The hop-on, hop-off bus from Cayo Coco stops at Playa Pilar six times daily in either direction during peak season (two to four times otherwise). And yes, the beach is named after Hemingway's fishing boat, *Pilar*.

Marina Marlin Cayo Guillermo   FISHING
(☎3330-1515, 3330-1737; www.nauticamarlin.com) On the right of the causeway as you arrive from Cayo Coco, this 36-berth marina is one of Cuba's certified international entry ports. You can organize deep-sea fishing in Hemingway's former playground on large boats that troll 5km to 13km offshore. Prices start at USD$310 per half-day for four people.

Centro Internacional de Buceo Coco Diving   DIVING
(☎3330-1620; www.amazingcocodiving.com) Based at the Meliá Cayo Guillermo, Coco Diving offers multilingual (four languages) dives from USD$45 for one immersion.

👉 Tours

Boat Adventure   BOATING
(2hr boat trip adult/child USD$46/23) This popular activity has its own separate dock on the left-hand side of the causeway as you enter Guillermo. The two-hour motorboat trip takes you through the key's natural mangrove channels.

🛏 Sleeping & Eating

If you're not staying and eating in one of the all-inclusives in Cayo Guillermo, your options are limited to a couple of beachfront restaurants set under thatched canopies close to the sand.

Villa Gregorio   HOTEL $
(☎3330-1611; d incl breakfast USD$25; P❄☀) A budget hotel, aimed as much at Cubans as foreigners, is an unusual occurrence in these parts. The Gregorio, named for Hemingway's old fishing partner, sits next to the marina at the entrance to Cayo Guillermo and offers a small selection of simple but smart rooms set around a small, if sometimes noisy, pool.

★ **Iberostar Daiquirí**   HOTEL $$$
(☎3330-1650; www.iberostar.com; s/d all-inclusive from USD$121/177; P❄☀) Plenty of shade, a lily pond and a curtain of water cascading in front of the pool bar add up to make the Daiquirí as unpretentious and appealing as ever. The 312 rooms are encased in attractive colonial-style apartment blocks that actually show some architectural imagination, and the thin slice of paradisiacal beach is straight out of the brochure.

Gran Muthu Imperial   RESORT $$$
(☎3331-0400; www.muthuhotels.com; s/d all-inclusive from USD$175/190; P❄🛜☀) It may not be the newest kid on the block by the time you read this, but the Gran Muthu Imperial is an attractive choice for adults only. While the architecture and color scheme are reminiscent of the '80s, the property has a feeling of grown-up tranquility. Multiple attractive pools, professional service and a variety of cuisine set it apart.

Gran Caribe Club Cayo Guillermo   HOTEL $$$
(☎3330-1712; www.clubcayoguillermo.com; s/d all-inclusive USD$107/187; P❄@🛜☀) This three-star, economically priced resort is the oldest hotel on the Sabana-Camagüey archipelago (opened in 1993) and has had more name changes than the British royal family. It comprises a low-key collection of salmon-colored bungalows in a quiet beachside location. Part of the hotel is block-booked by tour groups; the rest is increasingly popular with kiteboarders who lay out their kites under the palm trees on the resort's lush lawns. Lessons and board hire can be organized here.

ⓘ Information

You can exchange money in all Cayo Guillermo hotels at slightly poorer rates than those offered by banks.

ⓘ Getting There & Away

BUS

The hop-on, hop-off bus carries people to and from Cayo Coco, stopping at all Cayo Guillermo hotels and terminating at Playa Pilar. An all-day ticket costs USD$5. The bus runs five to six times a day in either direction. A taxi between Cayos Guillermo and Coco should cost USD$10 to USD$15 (25 minutes).

For onward transportation from Cayo Coco, you'll need your own wheels or a taxi.

CAR

Cars can be hired at any of Cayo Guillermo's hotels.

CIEGO DE ÁVILA PROVINCE CAYO GUILLERMO

ROSTISLAV AGEEV/SHUTTERSTOCK ©

1. Statue of José Martí (p86) This historic statue in Havana's Parque Central was the first of thousands built in Cuba of the independence hero.

2. Ruins of the Iglesia de Santa Ana Located in the preserved Spanish colonial settlement of Trinidad (p281).

3. Iglesia de Nuestra Corazón de Sagrado Jesús (p329) This historic church in Camagüey has ornate stained glass, decorative ironwork and arches.

4. Havana (p63) There are hundreds of buildings of historical importance, from intricate baroque to glitzy art deco, in Habana Vieja (p67).

3

AT A GLANCE

POPULATION
767,138

LAND AREA
15,386 sq km -
Cuba's largest
province.

BEST CHURCH
Iglesia de Nuestra
Señora de la Merced
(p329)

BEST GALLERY
Casa de Arte Jover
(p325)

**BEST BOUTIQUE
HOTEL**
El Marqués (p333)

WHEN TO GO

Feb–May
For outdoor
enthusiasts, March
is prime time for
viewing migratory
birds passing
through the little-
developed northern
keys.

Jun–Jan
At Playa Santa
Lucía, divers can
watch the amazing
underwater shark-
feeding show during
these months.
Beware, it's hot a
stormy from June to
late October.

Café Ciudad (p333), Camagüey
FOTOS593/SHUTTERSTOCK ©

Camagüey Province

Neither Occidente nor Oriente, Camagüey is Cuba's provincial contrarian, a region that likes to go its own way in political and cultural matters – and usually does – defying expectations in Havana and Santiago. These seeds were sown in the colonial era, when Camagüey's preference for cattle ranching over sugarcane meant less reliance on the labor of enslaved people and more enthusiasm to eliminate the whole system.

Today Cuba's largest province is a pastoral landscape of grazing cattle, lazy old sugar mill towns and, in the south, a few low-but-lovely hill ranges. It's flanked by Cuba's two largest archipelagos: Sabana-Camagüey in the north and Jardines de la Reina in the south, both almost virgin in places, though development is already underway in the keys to the north.

With its alluring architecture, illustrious citizens of note and cosmopolitan air, the staunchly Catholic capital of Camagüey is the star attraction.

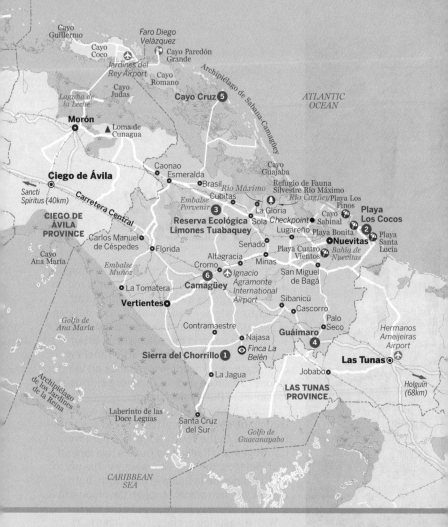

Camagüey Province Highlights

1 Sierra del Chorrillo (p337) Retreating into these verdant hills harboring rare birdlife and petrified forests.

2 Playa Los Cocos (p341) Swimming off the white-sand beach and soaking up the culture of the tiny village of La Boca.

3 Reserva Ecológica Limones Tuabaquey (p337) Checking out the caves, craters and natural gorge of one of Cuba's newest reserves.

4 Guáimaro (p334) Making a history stop in the city of emancipation, where Cuba's first constitution was signed.

5 Cayo Cruz (p338) Fly-fishing for tarpon and bonefish in the shallow flats off the key.

6 Camagüey heritage (p325) Walking the winding streets of the city to visit artists' studios, explore intricate churches and soak up vibrant local life.

Camagüey

POP 331,139

Cuba's third-largest city is easily the suavest and most sophisticated after Havana. The arts shine bright here, and it's also the bastion of the Catholic Church on the island. Well known for going their own way in times of crisis, its resilient citizens are called *agramontinos* by other Cubans, after local First War of Independence hero Ignacio Agramonte, coauthor of the Guáimaro constitution and courageous leader of Cuba's finest cavalry brigade.

Camagüey's pastel colonials and warren-like streets are inspiring. Get lost for a day or two exploring hidden plazas, baroque churches, riveting galleries and congenial bars and restaurants.

In 2008 Camagüey's well-preserved historical center was made Cuba's ninth Unesco World Heritage site, and in 2014 the city celebrated its quincentennial. A unique motif you'll notice around the city are its *tinajones*, large clay pots used to store water, for which Camagüey is famed.

History

Founded in February 1514 as one of Diego Velázquez' hallowed seven 'villas,' Santa María del Puerto Príncipe was originally established on the coast near present-day Nuevitas. A series of bloody rebellions by the local Taíno people caused the site of the city to be moved twice in the early 16th century. Its present spot was established in 1528. Its name was changed to Camagüey in 1903, in honor of the camagua tree from which all life is descended according to indigenous legend.

Despite continued attacks by corsairs, Camagüey developed quickly in the 1600s with an economy based on sugar production and cattle-rearing. Acute water shortages in the area forced the townsfolk to make *tinajones* (clay pots) to collect rainwater. Even today Camagüey is known as the city of *tinajones* – the pots now ornamental.

Besides swashbuckling independence hero Ignacio Agramonte, Camagüey has produced several personalities of note, including poet and patriot Nicolás Guillén and eminent doctor Carlos J Finlay, the man largely responsible for discovering the causes of yellow fever. In 1959 the prosperous citizens quickly fell foul of the Castro revolutionaries when local military commander Huber Matos (Fidel's one-time ally) accused El Líder Máximo of burying the revolution. He was duly arrested and later thrown in prison.

Loyally Catholic, Camagüey welcomed Pope John Paul II in 1998 and in 2008 hosted the beatification of Cuba's first saint, 'Father of the Poor' Fray José Olallo, who aided the wounded of both sides in the 1868–78 War of Independence. In 2014 the city was comprehensively renovated (and given four new hotels) in honor of its quincentennial.

Sights

Camagüey's peculiar street pattern was designed to confuse pillaging invaders and provide cover for its long-suffering residents (or so legend has it). As a result, Camagüey's sinuous streets and narrow winding alleys are more reminiscent of a Moroccan medina than the geometric grids of Lima or Mexico City.

City Center

★**Casa de Arte Jover** GALLERY
(Map p326; ☑3229-2305; Martí No 154, btwn Independencia & Cisneros; ⊙9am-noon & 3-5pm Mon-Sat) FREE Camagüey is home to two of Cuba's most creative and prodigious contemporary painters, Joel Jover and his wife Ileana Sánchez. Their magnificent home in Plaza Agramonte functions as a gallery and piece of art in its own right, with a slew of original pieces, resident chihuahuas and delightfully kitschy antiques on show. Guests can browse and purchase high-quality original art.

The artists also keep a studio and showroom, the **Estudio-Galería Jover** (Map p326; Ramón Pinto No 109; ⊙9am-noon & 3-5pm Mon-Sat) FREE, in Plaza San Juan de Dios.

★**Museo Provincial Ignacio Agramonte** MUSEUM
(Map p326; ☑3228-2425; Av de los Mártires No 2; USD$2; ⊙9am-5pm Tue-Fri, to 4pm Sat, to 1pm Sun) Named (like half of Camagüey) after the exalted local War of Independence hero, this cavernous museum, just north of the train station, is in a Spanish cavalry barracks dating from 1848. There's some impressive artwork upstairs, including much by Camagüey locals, as well as antique furniture and old family heirlooms.

The art collection features both 19th- and early 20th-century art such as the haunting work of *camagüeyano* Fidelio Ponce and

Camagüey

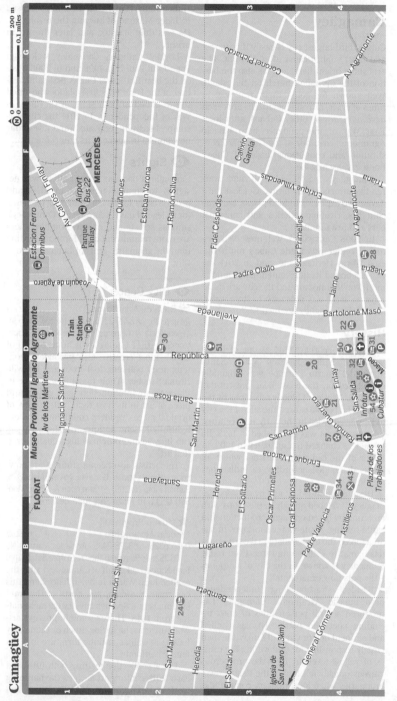

0 200 m
0 0.1 miles

FLORAT

LAS MERCEDES

Estacion Ferro Omnibus

Av Carlos J Finlay

Airport Bus 22

Parque Finlay

Joaquín de Agüero

Museo Provincial Ignacio Agramonte
3

Train Station

Av de los Mártires

Ignacio Sánchez

J Ramón Silva

San Martín

Heredia

Santayana

El Solitario

Oscar Primelles

Gral Espinosa

Padre Valencia

Astilleros

Lugareño

Bembeta

General Gómez

Iglesia de San Lázaro (1.3km)

24

Quiñones

Esteban Varona

J Ramón Silva

Fidel Céspedes

Padre Olallo

Avellaneda

República

Santa Rosa

San Martín

Heredia

El Solitario

San Ramón

Enrique J Varona

Ramón Guerrero

Coronel Pichardo

Av Agramonte

Calixto García

Enrique Villuendas

Oscar Primelles

Jaime

Bartolomé Masó

Alegría

Triana

Av Agramonte

Finlay

Sin Salida

Maceo

Plaza de los Trabajadores

30

51

59

20

21

57

58

34

43

50

22

12

31

32

55

54

11

28

Infotur

Cubatur

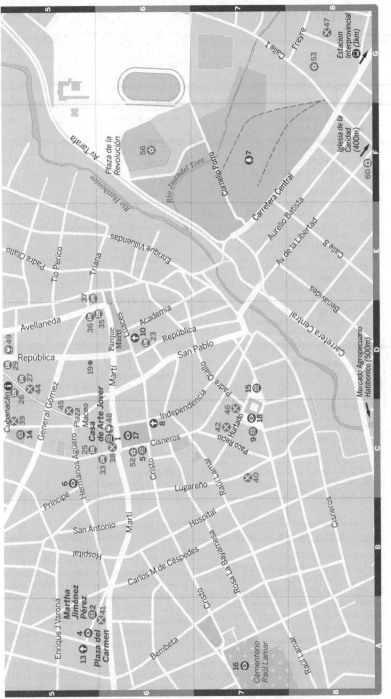

CAMAGÜEY PROVINCE CAMAGÜEY

Camagüey

artes plasticos (modern art) by nationally renowned figures like Alfredo Sosabravo.

Plaza San Juan de Dios SQUARE
(Map p326; cnr San Juan de Dios & Ramón Pinto) Looking more Mexican than Cuban (Mexico was capital of New Spain so the colonial architecture was often superior), Plaza San Juan de Dios is Camagüey's most picturesque and beautifully preserved corner. Its eastern aspect is dominated by the Museo de San Juan de Dios, formerly a hospital. Worthwhile restaurants lurk behind the square's arresting blue, yellow and pink building facades.

Parque Ignacio Agramonte SQUARE
(Map p326; cnr Martí & Independencia) Camagüey's most dazzling square in the heart of the city invites relaxation with rings of marble benches and an equestrian statue (c 1950) of Camagüey's precocious War of Independence hero, Agramonte. Stop by at 6pm to watch local youth in white campesino garb solemnly lowering the flag with great pomp, accompanied by a speaker blasting out the national anthem.

Casa de la Diversidad MUSEUM
(Map p326; ☎ 3229-2598; Cisneros No 150; USD$1; ⊙10am-6pm Mon-Fri, 9am-9pm Sat, 8am-noon

Sun) Impossible to miss thanks to its eclectic facade (a mix of Moorish and neoclassical elements), this museum's best exhibit is the building itself. Four exhibition rooms dedicated to slavery, costumes, art and architecture are explored relatively quickly, but it's worth savoring the ornate lobby with soaring pillars. Pride of place, however, goes to the toilets (yes, toilets!) where intricate frescos have been uncovered. The ladies' is the most ornate.

Museo de San Juan de Dios   MUSEUM
(Map p326; Plaza San Juan de Dios; USD$2; ⊙9am-5pm Tue-Sat, to 1pm Sun) Housed in a former hospital administered by Father José Olallo, the friar who became Cuba's first saint, the museum chronicles Camagüey's history and exhibits some local paintings. Its front cloister dates from 1728 and a unique triangular rear patio with Moorish touches was built in 1840. Ceasing to function as a hospital in 1902, it served as a teachers' college, a refuge during the 1932 cyclone and the Centro Provincial de Patrimonio, responsible for restoring local monuments.

**Iglesia de Nuestra
Señora de la Merced**   CHURCH
(Map p326; Plaza de los Trabajadores) Dating from 1748, this is arguably Camagüey's most impressive colonial church. Its history is imbued with legend. Local myth tells of a miraculous figure that floated from the watery depths here in 1601, and it has been a spot of worship ever since. The active convent in the attached cloister is distinguished by its two-level arched interior, spooky catacombs and the dazzling Santo Sepulcro, a solid silver coffin.

**Catedral de Nuestra
Señora de la Candelaria**   CHURCH
(Map p326; Cisneros No 168) Any exploration of Camagüey's religious history should begin at its most important church, named for the city's patron saint. Rebuilt in the 19th century on the site of an earlier chapel dating from 1530, the cathedral was fully restored with funds raised from Pope John Paul II's 1998 visit. While not Camagüey's most eye-catching church, it is noted for its noble Christ statue that sits atop a craning bell tower.

**Iglesia de Nuestra
Señora de la Soledad**   CHURCH
(Map p326; cnr República & Av Agramonte) Gleaming after a much-lauded 2007 renovation, this massive baroque structure dates from 1779. Its picturesque cream-and-terracotta tower actually predates the rest of the church. It's an eye-catching landmark on the city skyline, and inside there are ornate baroque frescoes and the hallowed font where patriotic hero Ignacio Agramonte was baptized in 1841.

**Iglesia de Nuestra
Corazón de Sagrado Jesús**   CHURCH
(Map p326; cnr República & Luaces) One of Cuba's rare neo-Gothic churches beautifies Parque Martí, a few blocks east of Parque Ignacio Agramonte. The triple-spired Iglesia de Nuestra Corazón de Sagrado Jesús is technically from an architectural subgenre called Catalan Gothic and dazzles with its ornate stained glass, decorative ironwork and pointed arches.

**Centro de Interpretacion
de la Ciudad**   ARCHITECTURE
(La Maqueta; Map p326; ☑3222-1235; Martí; USD$1; ⊙9am-6pm Mon-Sat, to 1pm Sun) Cuba loves its *maquetas* (scale models), and Camagüey is no exception. This one offers a good overview of the twisting streets of the city.

**Casa Natal de
Nicolás Guillén**   CULTURAL CENTER
(Map p326; Hermanos Agüero No 58; ⊙9am-5pm Tue-Sat) FREE This modest house gives visitors a small insight into Cuba's late national poet and his books. It doubles as the Instituto Superior de Arte, where local students come to study music.

◉ West of the City Center

★Plaza del Carmen   SQUARE
(Map p326; Hermanos Agüero, btwn Honda & Carmen) Around 600m west of the frenzy of República sits another sublimely beautiful square, one less visited than the central plazas. It's backed on the eastern side by the masterful Iglesia de Nuestra Señora del Carmen, one of the prettiest city churches.

More than a decade ago Plaza del Carmen was a ruin, but it's now restored to a state better than the original. The cobbled central space has been infused with giant *tinajones* (clay pots), atmospheric street lamps and unique life-sized sculptures of *camagüeyanos* going about their daily business (reading newspapers and gossiping, mostly).

★Martha Jiménez Pérez   GALLERY
(Map p326; ☑3225-7559; www.martha-jimenez.com; Martí No 282, btwn Carmen & Honda;

8am-8pm) **FREE** In Cuba's ceramics capital, the studio-gallery of Martha Jiménez Pérez shows the work of one of Cuba's greatest living artists. See everything from pots to paintings being produced here. The studio overlooks Pérez' magnum opus, Plaza del Carmen's alfresco statue of three gossiping women entitled *Chismosas* (gossipers). The *chismosas* also feature in many of her paintings inside. Her accessible sense of humor is embodied in the fountain in the tiny patio garden out back.

Necropolis de Camagüey   CEMETERY
(Map p326; Plaza del Cristo; 7am-6pm) This sea of elaborate, lop-sided, bleached-white Gothic tombs makes up Cuba's most underrated cemetery, secreting the resting place of Camagüey-born independence hero Ignacio Agramonte, among others. It might not quite have the clout of Havana's Cementerio Colón but isn't too far behind in its roll call of famous incumbents.

Agramonte lies halfway down the second avenue on the left after the entrance (the blue-painted tomb). Harder to find are the tombs of Camagüey freedom-fighters Tomás Betancourt or Salvador Cisneros Betancourt (one-time president of Cuba); show up for tours that depart from the entrance behind Iglesia de San Cristo de Buen Viaje.

**Iglesia de Nuestra
Señora del Carmen**   CHURCH
(Map p326; Plaza del Carmen) This twin-towered baroque beauty dates from 1825. Its former convent, Monasterio de las Ursalinas, is a sturdy arched colonial building with a pretty cloistered courtyard that once provided shelter for victims of the furious 1932 hurricane. Today it serves as the offices of the City Historian.

North of the City Center

**Museo Casa Natal
de Ignacio Agramonte**   MUSEUM
(Map p326; 3228-2425; Av Agramonte No 459; USD$2; 9am-5pm Tue-Fri, to 4pm Sat, to 1pm Sun) The birthplace of independence hero Ignacio Agramonte (1841–73), the cattle rancher who led the Camagüey area's revolt against Spain. The house – an elegant colonial building in its own right – tells of the oft-overlooked role of Camagüey and Agramonte in the First War of Independence. The hero's gun is one of his few personal possessions displayed.

In July 1869, rebel forces under Agramonte bombarded Camagüey. Four years later he was killed in action at the young age of 32. Cuban folk singer Silvio Rodríguez lionized this hero, nicknamed 'El Mayor' (the major), on his album *Días y flores*. It's opposite Iglesia de Nuestra Señora de la Merced, on the corner of Independencia.

South & East of the City Center

Lago de los Sueños   PARK
The so-called 'lake of dreams' is as an out-of-town escape from Camagüey's urban maze. It uses the same inventive (if slightly kitschy) methodology employed by a similar venture in Ciego de Ávila. The bizarre pièce de résistance is an ice-cream parlor encased in the fuselage of an old Soviet plane. Runner up is the antediluvian train-carriage-turned-restaurant.

Elsewhere, you can enjoy the lake, go for a boat ride or even stroll along a specially constructed *malecón* (main street). There are copious places to eat.

Casino Campestre   PARK
(Map p326; Carretera Central) Cuba's largest urban park sits across the Río Hatibonico from the old town, and was laid out in 1860. There are shaded benches, a baseball stadium, concerts and activities. On a traffic island near the park entrance, there's a monument dedicated to Mariano Barberán and Joaquín Collar, Spaniards who made the first nonstop flight between Seville, Spain, and Camagüey, Cuba, in 1933. The pair made the crossing in their plane Cuatro Vientos, but tragically the plane disappeared when flying to Mexico a week later. Ubiquitous bici-taxis are on hand to pedal you around.

Mercado Agropecuario Hatibonico   MARKET
(Carretera Central; 7am-6pm) If you visit just one market in Cuba, make it this muddy one. Beside the murky Río Hatibonico just off the Carretera Central, and characterized by its *pregones* (singsong, often comic, offering of wares) ringing through the stalls, this is a classic example of Cuban-style free enterprise juxtaposed with cheaper but lower-quality government stalls.

The best section to visit is the *herberos* (purveyors of herbs, potions and secret elixirs); also visit the plant nursery where Cubans can buy dwarf mango trees and various ornamental plants. Keep a tight hold on your money belt.

CINEMA STREET

Cinema Street aka *La Calle de los Cines* is one of the most inspired and creative of Camagüey's 2014 renovation projects organized to tie in with the 500th anniversary of the city's founding. The idea – to turn a short stretch of Calle Agramonte between the Iglesia de la Soledad and the Plaza de los Trabajadores into a homage to the big screen – makes perfect historical sense. The street has long been known for its cinemas and *sala-videos* (video rooms). Cine Casablanca and Cine Encanto opened in the 1940s and '50s, while the *sala-video* Nuevo Mundo dates from 1985. The latter was the first video room of its type in Cuba, a country where few families could afford home video-recorders in the '80s.

By the 2000s, the cinemas and *salas*, like much of Camagüey's once glittering cityscape, had fallen into a serious state of disrepair. Enter Camagüey's City Historian's Office with a bold artistic plan. In common with most restoration projects in Cuba, progress on Cinema Street has been slow but concise, paying meticulous attention to detail. By the end of 2014, Cine Casablanca (Map p326; ☑ 3229-2244; Av Agramonte No 428) had reopened as a three-screen multiplex; Cine El Circuito (Map p326; ☑ 3225-6543; Av Agramonte) had become a fount of video-art (the on-site Galería Pixel shows revolving documentary films; while the former *sala-video* Nuevo Mundo had become a film studies center offering expos, courses, documentaries and information.

Almost all of the other businesses in the street carry film themes. A local women's hairdresser is called La Ciudad de las Mujeres after a 1980 Fellini movie. The great Italian director is also honored in the nearby Cafetería La Dolce Vita. Next door, Coffee Arábiga has a more daring moniker. It is named after a controversial 1968 documentary film by Nicolás Guillén Landrián, nephew of the famed *camagüeyano* poet Nicolás Guillén. The film *Coffee Arábiga* gained notoriety in the '60s for its subtle artistic protest. In it, Guillén played the intro to The Beatles' song 'The Fool on the Hill' over news footage of Fidel Castro. The film was censored, and Guillén was later imprisoned before fleeing Cuba in 1989.

The nexus of Calle Agramonte and Plaza de los Trabajadores is the site of Camagüey's first cinema, now a salubrious restaurant called La Isabella (p334) where diners recline in directors' chairs beneath iconic film posters and enjoy Italian food. Arrive early and you might be able to bag Fellini's or Tomas Gutiérrez Alea's much-sought-after pews.

Iglesia de la Caridad　CHURCH
(cnr Av de la Libertad & Sociedad Patriótica) On the southeastern edge of the city, this church was originally constructed as a chapel in the 18th century. It got a couple of 20th-century renovations (in 1930 and 1945) and has a fine silver altar (c 1730) and image of the Virgin de la Caridad del Cobre, complete with an embossment of Cuba's national flower, *la mariposa* (white jasmine).

☞ Tours

★ **Camaguax Tours**　TOURS
(Map p326; ☑ 3228-7364, 5-864-2328; www.camaguax.com/en; República No 155, Apt 7 (altos); ⊘ 8:30am-5:30pm) A private agency with English- and French-speaking guides and myriad quality offerings throughout the province with a cultural or adventure focus. Hits include a city tour, sugarcane-farm visits, hiking and caving. There are excursions to Sierra del Chorrillo, Reserva Ecológica Limones Tuabaquey and Río Máximo. Uses

4WD vehicles for rough roads and has overnight options.

Ecotur　TOURS
(Map p326; ☑ 3224-4957; República No 278; ⊘ 8am-noon & 1-4:30pm Mon-Sat) Can arrange excursions to Finca La Belén (p338) in the Sierra del Chorrillo and Reserva Ecológica Limones Tuabaquey. Read the fine print as you book since some outings don't include transport. The office is inside the Complejo Turístico Bambú.

✹ Festivals & Events

San Juan Camagüeyano　CARNIVAL
(⊘ Jun 24-29) The annual carnival includes dancers, floats and African roots music.

Festival Nacional de Teatro　PERFORMING ARTS
(⊘ late Sep-early Oct) Camagüey showcases the best that Cuban theater has to offer at the Festival Nacional de Teatro (National Theater Festival).

🛏 Sleeping

The city has experienced a boom in boutique hotels, with a clutch of attractive colonial-style accommodations.

★ Los Vitrales   CASA PARTICULAR $

(Emma Barreto & Rafael Requejo; Map p326; ☎3229-5866, 5-294-2522; requejobarreto@gmail.com; Avellaneda No 3, btwn General Gómez & Martí; r USD$30; [P] ❄) A former convent, this enormous, painstakingly restored colonial house sports broad arches, high ceilings and dozens of antiques. The helpful owner Rafael is an architect, and it shows. Three rooms with good water pressure are arranged around a shady patio draped in lush gardens that are a highlight. There are over-the-top breakfasts and dinners with special orders available (vegetarians welcome).

Touts often lead guests astray to another 'Vitrales' – be sure to call ahead for taxi pickup and confirm your reservation a day ahead.

La China House   CASA PARTICULAR $

(Map p326; ☎3228-3028, 5-465-9240; houselachina@gmail.com; Padre Valencia No 57 (altos); r USD$25; ❄) In front of the Teatro Principal, this impeccably kept 2nd-story apartment features modern art and colonial style. There are two rooms with leather headboards, TV and electric showers. Friendly host Misleydi offers dinner and can arrange massages and salsa and guitar classes. Some English spoken.

Natural Caribe   CASA PARTICULAR $

(Map p326; ☎3229-1417, 5-276-7598; requejoarias@nauta.cu; Avellaneda No 8; r USD$25-30; ❄) 🐟 Tropical minimalism sets the tone for this sleek renovated colonial. Cleverly designed by a local architect, it wouldn't look out of place in a Miami loft strewn with ferns. Breakfasts are large. To top it all off, there's an expansive roof terrace bedecked with lights and places to lounge, making it an excellent retreat in the evenings.

Casa Láncara   CASA PARTICULAR $

(Map p326; ☎3228-3187; aledino@nauta.cu; Avellaneda No 160; r USD$30; ❄🔊) A dose of Seville with beautiful blue-and-yellow azulejos (tiles), this welcoming colonial is overseen by Andalusian fanatic Alejandro and his wife, Dinorah. The two rooms are hung with original local art, and there's a roof terrace all within spitting distance of the Soledad church.

Maria Eugenia Requejo   CASA PARTICULAR $

(Map p326; ☎3225-8670; Avellaneda No 3a; r USD$30; ❄🔊) An offshoot of Los Vitrales run by the daughter of the owner, this ultramodern apartment is good for families or those who want some privacy.

Casa Los Helechos   CASA PARTICULAR $

(Map p326; ☎5-231-1897, 3229-4868; v.manuel@nauta.cu; República No 68; r USD$30; ❄) *Helechos* means 'ferns,' and plenty occupy the long interior patio of this pleasant colonial house. There's one sizable room with two beds and its own private open-air kitchen, perfect for families.

Casa Yaneva   CASA PARTICULAR $

(Map p326; ☎3229-7931; www.casayaneva.com; San Martin No 763; r USD$25-30; ❄🔊) A gleaming option that's a bit of a walk from the center, perhaps best for those with a rental car. Eva knows tourism and provides three very clean and secure rooms with safe and refrigerator. There's also an interior patio. Rooms also available at two outlying houses nearby, all of which enjoy breakfast at the main casa.

Hostal Angelito   CASA PARTICULAR $

(Map p326; ☎3229-8271; Maceo No 62 (altos); r USD$25; [P]❄) Angelito jokes that he's the cozier, cheaper alternative to the Gran Hotel in front. Climb the stairs to this 2nd-floor accommodation with small, modest rooms off a large terrace. Hang out sipping a cocktail or take breakfast among the plants. It's an affable family home and very central.

Casa Alba Ferraz   CASA PARTICULAR $

(Map p326; ☎3228-3081; jose.collot5477@gmail.com; Ramón Guerrero No 106; r USD$20-30; ❄) A home with lovely multigenerational hosts. Two rooms open onto a grand colonial courtyard bedecked with plants. There's a roof terrace, and the host, Alba, can arrange dance and guitar lessons for guests. Alba can also arrange a taxi pickup from the bus station or airport.

Hostal de Carmencita   CASA PARTICULAR $

(Map p326; ☎3229-6930, 5-251-2468; cysabel@nauta.cu; Av Agramonte No 259, btwn Padre Olallo & Alegría; r USD$20-25; [P]❄) On a narrow, traffic-choked street, this home features two well-equipped self-contained rooms with ample privacy on the top floor. There are two lovely terraces and a tight-fitting garage (a rarity in central Camagüey).

★**Hotel La Avellanada**   BOUTIQUE HOTEL **$$$**
(Map p326; ☑3224-4958; ventas@ehoteles.cmg.
tur.cu; República No 226; s/d USD$115/140; ❋ @)
Named for a notable 19th-century Cuban
woman writer, this ground-floor hotel (part
of the E hotel brand managed by Cuba-
nacán) emanates class. The colonial has
a large interior patio lined with columns,
patterned tiles and a portrait of Gertrudis
herself, famed for her stories of love, femi-
nist stance and antislavery messages. Rooms
feature a safe, minibar, TV and big windows.
If you want to splurge, book the fabulous
minisuite.

★**El Marqués**   BOUTIQUE HOTEL **$$$**
(Map p326; ☑3224-4937; ventas@ehoteles.
cmg.tur.cu; Cisneros No 222; s/d incl breakfast
USD$120/160; ❋ @ ⬢) Simply lovely, this
six-room colonial (an E hotel) is a treasure
trove of character. Rooms shoot off a central
courtyard with wrought-iron furniture, each
door guarded by a Martha Jiménez Pérez
sculpture on a pedestal. Bedrooms feature satellite TV, safe and air-conditioning.
There's period furniture, and the place is
quiet throughout. Also features a small bar
with 24-hour service and hot tub.

★**Hotel Camino
de Hierro**   BOUTIQUE HOTEL **$$$**
(Map p326; ☑3228-4264; ventas@ehoteles.cmg.
tur.cu; Plaza de la Solidaridad; s/d USD$115/140;
❋ @ ⬢) Among the best of Camagüey's bou-
tique hotels (another E hotel), it occupies an
attractive city-center building that was once
an office for the Cuban *ferrocarril* (railway),
hence the railway theme. There's also lovely
colonial furniture and romantic balconies.
Guests enjoy a 24-hour bar and a pleasant
patio privy to all the downtown action.

Hotel Sevillana   BOUTIQUE HOTEL **$$$**
(Map p326; ☑3224-4937; Cisneros, btwn Her-
manos Agüero & Martí; s/d USD$120/160; ❋ @)
In a gorgeous 1920s mansion (yet another
E hotel) decked with stained glass and chandeliers. Great spaces include a huge courtyard with a spurting fountain and a rooftop
terrace with hot tubs. Compared to all this,
rooms are less impressive, though adequate.
There's a small on-site restaurant, too.

Hotel Santa María   BOUTIQUE HOTEL **$$$**
(Map p326; ☑3224-4944; cnr Av Agramonte
& República; s/d incl breakfast USD$120/160;
❋ @ ⬢) Camagüey's mothership of boutique
Estancia hotels, the Santa María has elegant
common areas depicting scenes of Camagüey

and sculptures by Martha Jiménez Pérez.
It's also the most frayed of the bunch. The
31 rooms come equipped with safe, TV and
minibar; suites feature claw-foot tubs, and
one room offers wheelchair access. The roof
garden restaurant has good views.

Gran Hotel   HOTEL **$$$**
(Map p326; ☑3229-2093; Maceo No 67, btwn Av
Agramonte & General Gómez; s/d incl breakfast
from USD$111/164; ❋ @ ⬢) This time-warped,
city center hotel classic dates from 1939. A
haughty prerevolutionary atmosphere stalks
the 72 clean rooms reached by a marble
staircase or ancient lift with cap-doffing attendants. There are bird's-eye, citywide views
from the 5th-floor restaurant and gorgeous
rooftop bar. A piano bar is accessed through
the lobby, and an elegant renaissance-style
swimming pool shimmers out back.

Hotel Colón   HOTEL **$$$**
(Map p326; ☑3225-1520; República No 472, cnr
José Ramón Silva; s/d incl breakfast USD$108/132;
❋) This central mainstay has been outshone
by newer offerings. The classic mahogany
bar, tile walls and a stained-glass portrait of
Christopher Columbus over the lobby door
imbue a mixed colonial and *fin-de-siècle*
feel, although rooms are mostly tiny. The bar
is a favorite of older tourists courting their
young Cuban dates.

✖ **Eating**

Camagüey has an abundance of elegant,
high-quality private restaurants.

Restaurante Carmen   CUBAN **$**
(Map p326; ☑3228-7902; Maceo No 6; mains
USD$2-12; ◷11am-1:30pm, 2-4:30pm, 5-7:30pm &
8-11pm; ❋) With a Siberian chill thanks to
hyperactive air-conditioning, this popular
restaurant on the pedestrian stretch of Ma-
ceo brims with locals at midday. Most come
for the cheap lunch specials – get yours early
because they usually run out. It's consistent,
with a diverse menu that ranges from sand-
wiches to stewed meat with rice.

Café Ciudad   CAFE **$**
(Map p326; ☑3225-8412; Plaza Agramonte, cnr
Martí & Cisneros; snacks USD$2-5; ◷9am-11pm;
⬢) Camagüey has made Agramonte-like ef-
forts to carve culinary quality into its histor-
ical inheritance. This lovely plaza-hugging
colonial cafe melds grandiosity with great
service, emulating anything in Havana Vieja.
Try the *jamón serrano* (cured ham) or savor
a superb *café con leche* under the louvers.

334

OFF THE BEATEN TRACK

GUÁIMARO, THE CITY OF EMANCIPATION

Guáimaro would be just another nameless Cuban town if it wasn't for the famous Guái-maro Assembly of April 1869, which approved the first Cuban constitution and called for the emancipation of enslaved people. The assembly elected Carlos Manuel de Céspedes as president.

If you are a history buff, stop here. The events of 1869 are commemorated by a large monument erected in 1940 in **Parque Constitución** (Guáimaro). Around the base of the monument are bronze plaques with likenesses of José Martí, Máximo Gómez, Carlos Manuel de Céspedes, Ignacio Agramonte, Calixto García and Antonio Maceo, the stars of Cuban independence. The park also contains the mausoleum of Cuba's first – and possibly greatest – heroine, Ana Betancourt (1832–1901) from Camagüey, who fought for women's emancipation alongside the abolition of slavery during the First War of Independence. Also be sure to stop at the **Museo Histórico** (Constitución 85 btwn Libertad & Máximo Gómez, Guáimaro; USD$1; ☺9am-5pm Mon-Fri), with a couple of rooms given over to art and history.

Guáimaro is on the Carretera Central between Camagüey and Las Tunas. A number of Víazul (www.viazul.com) buses pass through daily. Speak to the driver if you want to get off.

The picture occupying one wall shows the exact continuation of the old street.

Restaurante La Isabella   ITALIAN $
(Map p326; ☎3224-2925; cnr Av Agramonte & Independencia; mains USD$5-7; ☺11am-4pm & 6:30-10pm) This hip restaurant was opened during a visit by delegates from Gibara's iconic film festival, Festival Internacional del Cine Pobre, in 2008. Blending Italian-style food with a maverick movie-themed decor, the restaurant occupies the site of Ca-magüey's first-ever cinema.

Cremería 1514   ICE CREAM $
(El Lago de los Sueños; ice cream USD$0.50; ☺10am-10pm) Prize for the oddest instal-lation in the lakeside park, Cremería 1514 serves up ice cream in the fuselage of an old Soviet plane – a 1960s Antonov A26.

Restaurante Italiano Santa Teresa ITALIAN $
(Map p326; ☎3229-7108; Av de la Victoria No 12, btwn Padre Carmelo & Freyre; meals USD$3-7; ☺noon-midnight) An Italian feast-in-wait-ing. Divine pizza, great ice cream and more-than-passable espresso on the patio definitely make this a spot to savor.

Café Cubita   CAFE $
(Map p326; cnr Independencia & Av Agramonte; snacks USD$1-3; ☺24hr) Just off Plaza de los Trabajadores, Cubita is alfresco and lively. And it really does stay open all hours, offer-ing cold beer and 3am ropa vieja (shredded beef and vegetables in a tomato salsa).

Gran Hotel Snack Bar   FAST FOOD $
(Map p326; Maceo No 67, btwn Av Agramonte & Gen-eral Gómez; snacks USD$1-4; ☺9am-11pm) Has

coffee, sandwiches, chicken and ice cream. The hamburgers (when available) are good and the atmosphere is 1950s retro.

Panadería Doña Neli   BAKERY $
(Map p326; ☎3229-6493; Maceo No 60; snacks USD$2; ☺8am-10pm) For bread and delicate cakes, try this particularly well-stocked bak-ery, opposite the Gran Hotel.

★ Casa Austria   EUROPEAN $$
(Map p326; ☎3228-5580; Lugareño No 121, btwn Raúl Lamar & Matías Varona; meals USD$4-13; ☺11:30am-11:30pm; ﹡) Locals line up for stru-del and decadent cakes at this Austrian-run cafe. After so much comida criolla, travelers embrace the international menu featuring chicken cordon bleu, schnitzel and garban-zos stewed in tomato sauce with bacon. It's all good. The setting, stuffed with heavy co-lonial furniture, is a bit claustrophobic, but there's also patio dining.

★ El Paso   INTERNATIONAL $$
(Map p326; ☎3227-4321; Hermanos Agüero No 261, btwn Carmen & Honda; meals USD$5-10; ☺9am-11pm) Finally, a private restaurant with all-day hours, plus a funky interior and an enviable Plaza del Carmen location. There's flavorful ropa vieja (spiced shredded beef), heaping bowls of arroz con pollo a la chor-rillana (chicken, rice, prunes and peppers in a ceramic bowl). Try pan patato for dessert – consisting of cassava and coconut. Good happy-hour deals from 2pm to 8pm.

★ Mesón del Príncipe   CUBAN $$
(Map p326; ☎5-240-4598; Astilleros No 7; meals USD$8-12; ☺noon-midnight) This elegant

CAMAGÜEY PROVINCE CAMAGÜEY

restaurant offers an affordable fine-dining experience in a typically refined Camagüeyan residence. It is places like this that have put Camagüey at the cutting edge of Cuba's new culinary revolution – a notch above Santiago. Bonus: tit doesn't use straws – a laudable, sustainable novelty.

Restaurante de los Tres Reyes
CARIBBEAN $$

(Map p326; ☑ 3228-6812; Plaza San Juan de Dios No 16; meals USD$8-12; ☉10am-10pm) A handsome, state-run place set in beautiful colonial digs on Plaza San Juan de Dios that sells mainly chicken dishes. Ruminate on Camagüey life by one of the giant iron-grilled windows out front or enjoy greater privacy on a plant-bedecked interior patio.

Gran Hotel
INTERNATIONAL $$

(Map p326; Maceo No 67, btwn Av Agramonte & General Gómez; meals USD$6-14; ☉6-11pm) A 5th-floor restaurant with superb city views and a rather nice buffet; get here early to watch the sun set over the church towers.

La Campana de Toledo
CARIBBEAN $$

(Map p326; Plaza San Juan de Dios No 18; meals USD$7-12; ☉10am-10pm) Offering *comida criolla* (creole food), this classic Camagüey eatery has colonial digs, a shady patio and a serenading quartet.

🍸 Drinking & Nightlife

Maybe it's the pirate past, but Camagüey has great tavern-style drinking houses.

Gran Hotel Bar Terraza
BAR

(Map p326; Maceo No 67, btwn Av Agramonte & General Gómez; ☉1pm-2am) The aesthete's choice. At the top of the Gran Hotel, its cocktail maestro will prepare mojitos and daiquiris while you gaze at the city's premier vista – all Camagüey laid bare before you. Duck below to the swimming pool for the bizarrely addictive water ballet shows, happening several times weekly at 9:15pm.

Bar Yesterday
BAR

(Map p326; ☑ 3224-4943; República No 222; ☉noon-midnight Mon-Fri, to 1am Sat & Sun) This Beatles-themed bar has a large inner patio and life-sized bronze sculptures of the fab four. Locals come for snacks and chilly brews.

Bodegón Don Cayetano
BAR

(Map p326; ☑ 3229-1961; República No 79; ☉noon-11pm) This casual Spanish-style

taverna, nestled beneath Iglesia de Nuestra Señora de la Soledad, is best used as a drinking option. There's a decent wine collection but better food elsewhere. Tables spill into the adjacent alley.

Bar El Cambio
BAR

(Map p326; cnr Independencia & Martí; ☉7am-late) The Hunter S Thompson choice. A dive bar with graffiti-splattered walls and interestingly named cocktails, this place consists of one room, four tables and bags of atmosphere.

Taberna Bucanero
BAR

(Map p326; ☑ 3225-3413; cnr República & Fidel Céspedes; ☉24hr) The beer drinker's choice. Fake pirate figures and Bucanero beer on tap characterize this swashbuckling tavern, faintly reminiscent of a British pub.

☆ Entertainment

★ Teatro Principal
THEATER

(Map p326; ☑ 3229-3048; Padre Valencia No 64; USD$5-10; ☉shows 8:30pm Fri & Sat, 5pm Sun) If a show's on, go! Second only to Havana in its ballet credentials, the Camagüey Ballet Company, founded in 1971 by Fernando Alonso (ex-husband of number-one Cuban dancing diva Alicia Alonso), is internationally renowned, and performances are the talk of the town. Also of interest is the wonderful theater building of 1850 vintage, bedizened with majestic chandeliers and stained glass.

Casa de la Trova Patricio Ballagas
LIVE MUSIC

(Map p326; ☑ 3229-1357; Cisneros No 171, btwn Marti & Cristo; USD$3; ☉7pm-1am) An ornate entrance hall gives way to an atmospheric patio where old crooners sing and young couples *chachachá*. One of Cuba's best *trova* (traditional poetic singing) houses, where regular tourist traffic doesn't detract from the old-world authenticity. Tuesday's a good night for traditional music. Cover includes one drink.

Centro Cultural Caribe
CABARET

(Map p326; ☑ 3229-8112; cnr Narciso Montreal (Calle 1) & Freyre; USD$3-6; ☉10pm-2am, to 4am Fri & Sat) Some say it's the best cabaret outside Havana, and at this price, who's arguing? Book your seat (from the box office on the same day) and pull up a pew for an eyeful of feathers and a few frocks. There's a trousers-and-shirt dress code.

CAMAGÜEY PROVINCE CAMAGÜEY

Estadio Cándido González   SPECTATOR SPORT
(Map p326; ☑3229-3140; Av Tarafa; ◎games 7:15pm Oct-Apr) Baseball games are held at this stadium alongside Casino Campestre. Team Camagüey, known as the Alfareros (the Ceramicists), have long been underdogs, but recent seasons have seen them winning more games.

Sala Teatro José Luis Tasende   THEATER
(Map p326; ☑3229-2164; Ramón Guerrero No 51; ◎shows 9pm Fri & Sat, ticket sales 9am-4pm) For serious live theater, head to this venue, which has quality Spanish-language performances.

🛍 Shopping

Calle Maceo is Camagüey's top shopping street, with a number of souvenir shops, bookstores and department stores on an attractive pedestrian boulevard.

Fondo Cubano
Bienes Culturales   ARTS & CRAFTS
(Map p326; Av de la Libertad No 112; ◎8am-6pm Mon-Sat) Sells all kinds of artifacts in a pleasantly nontouristy setting.

ARTex Souvenir   GIFTS & SOUVENIRS
(Map p326; República No 381; ◎10am-6pm Mon-Sat, 9am-1pm Sun) Che T-shirts, mini-*tinajones*, Che key rings, Che mugs. Get the picture? Also a decent selection of Cuban CDs.

ⓘ Information

SAFE TRAVEL
Camagüey's hardworking *jineteros* (touts) are experts at making a buck off tourists. Many travelers have been offered help finding their casa particular, only to later realize they have been led to a different house (usually with less-desirable facilities). Or someone outside your reserved house will tell you it's under renovation or closed. Ring the bell to be sure.

Try to book accommodations in advance, ideally arranging a pickup from the station or airport. Particularly at these places, be wary of strangers approaching and offering 'services' (eg to be your guide). Bici-taxis at the bus station can be particularly predatory.

INTERNET ACCESS
There's public wi-fi (with scratchcard-code access) at Parque Ignacio Agramonte and between Plaza Los Trabajadores and Iglesia de Nuestra Señora de la Soledad. Visitors can buy a scratch card for wi-fi at Etecsa Telepunto (☑3225-1559; República No 453, btwn San Martín & José Ramón Silva; internet per hour USD$1.50; ◎8:30am-7pm).

MEDICAL SERVICES
Hospitals **Policlínico José Martí** (☑3229-7810; Luaces No 1; ◎24hr) and **Policlínico Integral Rodolfo Ramirez Esquival** (☑3228-1481; cnr Ignacio Sánchez & Joaquín de Agüero) will treat foreigners in an emergency.

MONEY
Bank services and money changers are plentiful.
Banco de Crédito y Comercio (☑3229-2531; cnr Av Agramonte & Cisneros; ◎9am-3pm Mon-Fri) Has an ATM.

Banco Financiero Internacional (☑3229-4846; Independencia No 21, btwn Hermanos Agüero & Martí; ◎9am-3pm Mon-Fri) Has an ATM.

Cadeca (☑3229-5220; República No 84, btwn Oscar Primelles & El Solitario; ◎8:30am-8pm Mon-Sat, 9am-6pm Sun)

TOURIST INFORMATION
There are plenty of tour agencies in the city.
Cubanacán (Map p326; ☑3228-7879; Maceo No 67, Gran Hotel) The best place for information in the city center.

Cubatur (Map p326; ☑3225-4786; Av Agramonte 446, btwn República & Independencia) Can book hotels in Playa Santa Lucía.

Infotur (Map p326; ☑3225-6794; www.facebook.com/camaguey.travel; Av Agramonte; ◎8:30am-5:30pm) Helpful information office hidden in a gallery near Casablanca cinema.

ⓘ Getting There & Away

AIR
Air Transat (www.airtransat.com) and Sunwing (www.sunwing.ca) fly in the all-inclusive crowd to **Ignacio Agramonte International Airport** (☑3226-7202; Km 7, Carretera Nuevitas) from Toronto, who are hastily bussed off to Playa Santa Lucía. There's also a weekly **Cubana** (☑3229-1338; www.cubana.cu; Republica No 400, btwn Callejon de Correa & Céspedes; ◎8:15am-4pm Mon-Sat) flight to Havana on Monday mornings.

BUS & TRUCK
The **Estacion Ferro Omnibus** (Map p326) is near the train station and has trucks to regional destinations (CUP$20) including Playa Santa Lucía. Arrive at 5am to be ensured a spot for beach-bound trucks.

Long-distance Víazul buses depart from the **Estacion Interprovincial** (☑3227-0396; www.viazul.com; Carretera Central), 3km southeast of the center.

Passenger trucks (charging tourists around USD$1) to Las Tunas, Ciego de Ávila and nearby towns also leave from this station. Arriving before 9am will greatly increase your chances of having a spot.

WORTH A TRIP

RESERVA ECOLÓGICA LIMONES TUABAQUEY

One of Cuba's newest reserves, Reserva Ecológica Limones Tuabaquey (USD$6) is made up of heavily wooded uplands, occupying the Sierra de Cubitas in northern Camagüey Province. The star attraction is Cuba's most important indigenous art: pre-Columbian cave paintings at Cueva Pichardo and Cueva María Teresa. Its Hoyo de Bonet is a unique 300m-wide, 90m-deep natural karstic depression covered in vegetation with a cool, humid microclimate with trippy giant ferns. The rich birdlife includes an abundance of tocororos and cartacubas known to produce a symphony of birdsong.

Paths fan out to caves, craters and a narrow natural gorge called the Paso de los Paredones, with sheer 40m-high walls. Historical infamy is recalled nearby: a post marks the spot where, in February 1869, a group of *mambises* (19th-century Cuban independence fighters) successfully saw off a Spanish attack.

Walking on the trails is permitted with a guide only. Guided tours of the reserve (CUC$37 per person including transport and lunch) can be arranged at Ecotur (p331) or with private agencies in Camagüey. There is a visitor center, plus cabin accommodation.

The reserve lies approximately 35km north of the city of Camagüey on the main (bumpy) road between Morón and Nuevitas. The turnoff is near the village of Cubitas.

VÍAZUL BUS DEPARTURES FROM CAMAGÜEY

Destination	Cost (USD$)	Duration (hr)	Frequency (daily)
Havana	33	9	5
Holguín	11	3	5
Santiago de Cuba	18	6½	5
Trinidad	15	4½	1
Varadero	25	8¼	1

TAXI

A taxi to Playa Santa Lucía should cost around USD$50 to USD$60 one way: bargain hard.

A taxi between the center and the airport should cost around CUC$10 from town, but you can try to bargain the price down. **Airport Bus 22** (Map p326; Parque Finlay; CUP$1) runs from Parque Finlay (opposite the regional bus station Estacion Ferro Omnibus) to the airport every 30 minutes on weekdays and hourly on weekends.

TRAIN

The revamped **train station** (☑ 3228-4766; cnr Avellaneda & Av Carlos J Finlay) is more conveniently located than the bus station, though its service isn't quite as convenient. Every other day the train leaves for Santiago at 1:25am and departs for Havana three times a week.

Schedules change frequently: check at the station a couple of days before you intend to travel. Slower *coche motor* (cross-island) trains also serve the Havana–Santiago route, stopping at places such as Matanzas and Ciego de Ávila.

Going east, there are daily services to Las Tunas, Manzanillo and Bayamo. Heading north, there are (theoretically) four daily trains to Nuevitas and four to Morón.

ℹ Getting Around

BICI-TAXI

Bicycle taxis are found around most of the city's squares, with the main contingent in Plaza de los Trabajadores. They pedal hard in city humidity – USD$1 or USD$2 fare is more than fair.

CAR

Driving in Camagüey's narrow one-way streets is a sport akin to underground street racing. Experts only! Car rental prices start around USD$70 a day plus gas, depending on the make of car and hire duration. Try **Cubacar** (☑ 3229-7472; www.transturcarrental.com; Casino Campestre).

Guarded parking (USD$2 for 24 hours) is available for those brave enough to attempt Camagüey's maze in a car. Ask at your hotel or casa particular for details.

There are two **Cupet-Cimex gas stations** (Carretera Central; ⊗24hr) near Av de la Libertad.

HORSE CART

Horse carts shuttle along a fixed route (USD$1) between the regional bus station and the train station. You may have to change carts at Casino Campestre, near the river. Use discretion and choose drivers whose horses look healthy and well treated.

Sierra del Chorrillo

This protected area 36km southeast of Camagüey contains three low hill ranges: the Sierra del Chorrillo, the Sierra del Najasa and the Guaicanámar (highest point: 324m). Visitors access the area through Finca La Belén, a ranch turned nature reserve with a zoo, petrified forest and excellent birdwatching.

◉ Sights & Activities

Treks around the reserve can be arranged by 4WD or on horseback, and there are two guided walks. Most popular is the flat **Sendero de las Aves** (1.8km) with a cornucopia of birdlife. Sendero Santa Gertrudis (4.5km) includes a cave.

Nestled in grassy uplands, **Finca La Belén** (USD$6; Sendero de las Aves hike USD$7) was built by a Peruvian architect during WWII. It is now run as a nature reserve by Ecotur. It's one of the best places in Cuba to view rare bird species such as the Cuban parakeet, the giant kingbird and the Antillean palm swift. Another curiosity is a three-million-year-old petrified forest spread over 1 hectare. Also roaming the landscape are non-indigenous animals such as zebras, deer, bulls and horses.

Visitors can hike Sendero de las Aves for a fee. To find the petrified forest, drive several kilometers past the ranch entrance to the road junction and bear right to reach a dead end at a factory. There's a large fossilized tree nearby.

Within the ranch, simple and countrified **Hotel Finca La Belén** (☑ 3224-4957; s/d all-inclusive USD$40/55; ❄ ✾) includes a swimming pool, restaurant, TV lounge and clean, air-conditioned rooms. Glorious landscapes are a stroll away. Reserve via Ecotur (p331) in Camagüey.

❶ Getting There & Away

Tours from Camagüey visit the area. Otherwise, you can come by rental car. Drive 24km east of Camagüey on Carretera Central and then 30km southeast following signs to Najasa. If approaching from Las Tunas, another potholed road to Najasa branches south off the Carretera Central in Sibanicú. The ranch is 8km beyond Najasa along a rutted road. Alternatively, negotiate a rate with a taxi in Camagüey.

Cayo Sabinal

Though slated for development, Cayo Sabinal is still virgin territory in part. The 30km-long coral key with marshes is favored by flamingos and iguanas. The land cover is mainly flat and characterized by marshland

CAYOS & CAUSEWAYS

In any other country, the necklace of beach-embellished cayos (keys) that lies between Cayo Coco and Playa Santa Lucía would have been requisitioned by the biggest, richest hotel chains. But in Cuba, because of a mix of economic austerity and nitpicking government bureaucracy, they are largely untouched, though hotels are in the works for several cayos.

In-the-know fishers ply the waters out as far as Cayo Cruz. The flats, lagoons and estuaries off Camagüey's north coast are fly-fishing heaven (bonefish, permit and tarpon are concentrated in a designated fishing area of just under 350 sq km that's invariably deserted). The fishing season runs from November to August, and no commercial fishing is allowed.

Rough causeways and roads were built across Camagüey's cayos in the late 1980s in preparation for Cuba's next big tourist project – a plan that, because of the Special Period economic meltdown, never got off the ground. Instead, the islands and their unblemished waters have remained the preserve of in-the-know fisherfolk, resolute birdwatchers and those in search of splendid solitude. Running west to east are Cayo Paredón Grande, home to the checkered lighthouse Faro Diego Velázquez, a sultry beach and bevies of day-trippers from Cayo Coco; Cayo Romano, Cuba's third-largest island and a haven for flamingos, mangroves and blood-thirsty mosquitoes; Cayo Guajaba, an untouched roadless wilderness; and Cayo Sabinal, which has a rough road and a trio of unblemished beaches, plus an old Spanish fort and lighthouse. Tucked away to the north is 800m-long Cayo Confites, where a 21-year-old Fidel Castro hid out in 1947 in preparation for an abortive plot to overthrow the dictatorial regime of Rafael Trujillo in the Dominican Republic (Fidel jumped ship in the Bay of Nipe and swam 15km to shore carrying his weapon).

You'll need a sturdy car or a bike to penetrate these potholed northern wildernesses. Entry points to Cayo Romano are from Cayo Coco, or Brasil in northwestern Camagüey Province. Cayo Cruz is accessed via a causeway from Cayo Romano. Cayo Sabinal is linked to the mainland by a small causeway northwest of Nuevitas. There are police checkpoints, so you'll need your passport.

and lagoons. The fauna consists of tree rats, wild boar and a large variety of butterflies. It's astoundingly beautiful.

◉ Sights

Playa Bonita   BEACH
Of Cayo Sabinal's 30km of beaches, this one has top billing. It's frequented by daily catamaran excursions from Playa Santa Lucía offering lunch at a rustic *ranchón* (open-sided restaurant).

Fuerte San Hilario   FORT
Cayo Sabinal has quite some history for a wilderness area. Following repeated pirate attacks in the 17th and 18th centuries, the Spanish built a fort here (1831) to keep marauding corsairs at bay. The fort later became a prison and, in 1875, witnessed the only Carlist uprising (a counter-revolutionary movement in Spain that opposed the reigning monarchy) in Cuba – ever.

Faro Colón   LIGHTHOUSE
(Punta Maternillo) Erected in 1848, Faro Colón is one of the oldest lighthouses still operating on the Cuban archipelago. As a result of various naval battles fought in the area during the colonial era, a couple of Spanish shipwrecks – *Nuestra Señora de Alta Gracia* and the *Pizarro* – rest in shallow waters nearby, providing great fodder for divers.

❶ Getting There & Away

There is a dirt road to the key. The 2km causeway linking the key to the mainland was the first of its kind constructed in Cuba and the most environmentally destructive.

Access Cayo Sabinal via a catamaran tour from Playa Santa Lucía that visits Playa Bonita. Trips run most days and include transfers and lunch. Book through the Playa Santa Lucía hotels.

Playa Santa Lucía

With 20km of golden sand, this beach competes with Varadero as Cuba's longest. Travelers generally come here to dive the north coast's best and most accessible coral reef, lying just a few kilometers offshore. Another highlight is the beach itself – a tropical idyll, most of it still deserted – though it collects seaweed even in the radius of the hotels. This isolated resort strip has seen better days, with many hotels sporting a cheap holiday-camp feel.

The swimming, snorkeling and diving are exceptional, however, and the four all-inclusive resorts are well-priced for snowbirds. In peak season, the clientele is primarily Canadian. The flat surroundings feature flamingos, scrubby bushes and the odd grazing cow. Backed by wetlands, mosquitoes can be a huge annoyance, particularly at dusk. Prepare accordingly.

🏃 Activities
Boating

★ Catamaran to Playa Bonita   BOATING
(adult/child USD$72/36) Fulfill your deserted-island fantasy traveling on a 14-passenger catamaran to remote Playa Bonita on Cayo Sabinal. Included is a 45-minute snorkel session and lunch with an open bar. It departs Playa Santa Lucía at 9:30am and returns at 4:20pm. Bring plenty of sunscreen.

Book the trip through Marlin, which has aquatic activity centers in every hotel.

Diving

Playa Santa Lucía is a diving destination extraordinaire and the world's second-longest coral reef after Australia's Great Barrier Reef.

The 35 scuba sites take in six Poseidon ridges, the Cueva Honda dive site, shipwrecks, and abundant marine life, including several types of rays at the entrance to the Bahía de Nuevitas. A much-promoted highlight is the hand-feeding of 3m-long bull sharks from June to January.

Hotels can organize other water activities, including kayaking, deep-sea fishing and kitesurfing (the last from November to April).

**Centro Internacional
de Buceo Shark's Friends**   DIVING
(✆ 3236-5182; www.nauticamarlin.com; Av Tararaco; shark feeds USD$69, dives from USD$45) Shark's Friends has gotten mixed reviews concerning equipment and safety protocols; experienced divers can judge for themselves; novices might opt to dive elsewhere. Dive masters speak English, French, German and Italian. The center, on the beach between Brisas Santa Lucía and Gran Club Santa Lucía, offers dives, open-water certification and shark feeds (best November through January). It also has snorkeling excursions.

🛏 Sleeping & Eating

The small hotel strip begins 6km northwest of the roundabout at the entrance to Santa Lucía. The four big ones are Cubanacán resorts whose star ratings and quality decrease as you head northwest. Because of

Playa Santa Lucía

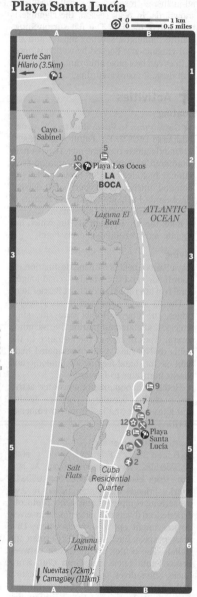

Fuerte San Hilario (3.5km)

Cayo Sabinel

Playa Los Cocos
LA BOCA

Laguna El Real

ATLANTIC OCEAN

Playa Santa Lucía

Salt Flats

Cuba Residential Quarter

Laguna Daniel

Nuevitas (72km); Camagüey (111km)

Islazul Tararaco   HOTEL $
(📞3233-6310; s/d USD$33/36; ❄) Bargain hunters can thank Changó for the strip's oldest hotel (it actually predates the revolution). Every room has a little patio and is within stone-chucking distance of the beach. With a semi-abandoned, Lynchian air, you won't be harassed with forced entertainment.

Club Amigo Caracol   RESORT $$
(📞3233-6302; s/d all-inclusive USD$63/100; P❄@🛜🏊) Sleek remodeled rooms with comfortable beds and Caribbean colors give style points to this resort. The kids' program makes it the beach's family favorite, and staff here are the most winsome in Santa Lucía. Choose your room wisely: shows on the central stage could keep you up unwillingly, and not all in-room safes work.

Gran Club Santa Lucía   RESORT $$
(📞3233-6109; s/d all-inclusive USD$77/115; P❄@🛜🏊) Gran Club is one of the better options on the hotel strip, with 249 colorfully painted rooms in well-maintained two-story blocks. It's the most sceney club of the lot, with Discoteca La Jungla drawing a more party-centric crowd.

Club Amigo Mayanabo   RESORT $$
(📞3236-5168; s/d all-inclusive USD$80/90; P❄@🛜🏊) Doing a good impersonation

Playa Santa Lucía's size and isolation, it's good to book a room beforehand.

Casas particulares can be found in the village of La Concha, located southeast of the hotels. Here, the beaches are inferior but often deserted.

of a tacky postwar British holiday camp, the Mayanabo has seen better days – a long time ago. But if budget's your prime consideration, it's cheap and right on the beach.

Brisas Santa Lucía
RESORT $$$

(☎3233-6317; aloja@brisas.stl.tur.cu; s/d/tr all-inclusive USD$143/190/193; P✳@☎☀) With 412 rooms in several three-story buildings, Brisas covers a monstrous 11 hectares. It has the strip's top rating and comes with an overly jaunty holiday camp atmosphere of pool entertainers and special kids' programming.

Restaurante Luna Mar
SEAFOOD $$

(mains USD$7-20; ⊗noon-9pm) This place, flush up against the beach and wedged between Gran Club Santa Lucía and Club Amigo Caracol, offers a seafood menu in an easy-to-reach setting.

☆ Entertainment

Mar Verde Centro Cultural
LIVE MUSIC

(☎3233-6205; Mar Verde Centro Comercial; USD$1; ⊗10pm-3am) Has a pleasant patio bar and a cabaret with live music nightly.

🔒 Shopping

Mar Verde Centro Comercial
MALL

This strip mall between the Gran Club Santa Lucía and Club Amigo Caracol has an ARTex store, a bookstore and a couple of government-run Caracol outlets selling Che Guevara T-shirts, rum, cigars and the like.

ℹ Information

MEDICAL SERVICES
There's a **clinic** (☎3233-6370; Ignacio Residencial No 14) in the Cuban residential quarter east of the hotels.

MONEY
Cadeca (Mar Verde Centro Comercial; ⊗9am-4pm)

TOURIST INFORMATION
For tour agencies, Cubanacán, which owns four of the five hotels here, is well represented with a desk in each hotel. There's a good Cubatur office just outside Gran Club Santa Lucía.

ℹ Getting There & Away

A taxi from Camagüey (USD$50 to USD$60 one way) is your most comfortable option for getting to Playa Santa Lucía. Budget travelers can hop a *camioneta* (truck; USD$1) outside the Camagüey train station; arrive by 5:30am.

Rent cars or mopeds via Cubacar, which has desks in all the hotels. A Cupet-Cimex gas station is at the southeastern end of the strip, near the access road from Camagüey. Another large gas station is just south of Brisas Santa Lucía.

Playa Los Cocos

This comma of beach at the end of 20km-long Playa Santa Lucía, 7km from the hotels at the mouth of the Bahía de Nuevitas, is a stunner, with yellow-white sand and iridescent jade water. Sometimes flocks of pink flamingos are visible in Laguna el Real behind this beach. The small Cuban settlement here is known as La Boca. This is a fine swimming spot, with views of the Faro Colón (lighthouse) on Cayo Sabinal, but beware of tidal currents further out. Avoid swimming on the ocean-facing beaches where there are sea urchins.

🛌 Sleeping & Eating

★Point of Pilots
CASA PARTICULAR $

(☎5-544-8821, 5-341-4660; robertobasulto@ nauta.cu; La Boca No 16; r USD$20-25) A stone's throw from the water, this marine-blue house on a sandy alley has the world's nicest hosts. There are three shipshape rooms, one very small, and an upstairs terrace.

Casa Betty
CASA PARTICULAR $

(☎5-219-0126; La Boca No 38a; r USD$20-25) Basic but well-located and renovated, this seafront cottage has two rooms right over the water. The savory smells wafting from the tiny kitchen reveal its secondary purpose – as a *paladar*. You can get seafood at all hours here, not such a good sign for lodgers but great for hungry beachgoers.

★El Bucanero
SEAFOOD $$

(☎3236-5226; meals USD$8-12; ⊗10am-10pm) With a prime beach setting, this thatched seafood hut is in its own class. Call it simple and fresh. The house special of lobster and prawns is enhanced immeasurably by the setting. There are also deck chairs for rent, and with fresh coconut juice and cold beer at the ready, it's not a bad spot.

ℹ Getting There & Away

A horse and carriage from the Santa Lucía hotels to Playa Los Cocos is USD$20 round trip plus the wait.

You can also walk it, jog it or bike it (free gearless but adequate bikes are available at all the resorts). It's 12km by road and 8km by the coast – at the time of writing, the coastal route was only passable on foot.

AT A GLANCE

POPULATION
535,335

CUBAN NATIONAL BASEBALL LEAGUE WINS
One - in 2019

BEST SEAFOOD
El Bodegón de Polo (p350)

BEST CASA PARTICULAR
Hostal Melina (p345)

BEST CUBAN CUISINE
La Negra (p347)

WHEN TO GO

Jun–Oct
Avoid the wettest months when more than 160mm of average precipitation inundates the streets.

Nov–May
Cooler months preferred by foreign visitors. The National Sculpture Exhibition, an event befitting the so-called 'City of Sculptures,' happens in February.

Memorial Vicente García (p345), Las Tunas
ROBERTO MACHADO NOA/LIGHTROCKET VIA GETTY IMAGES ©

Las Tunas Province

M ost travelers say hello and goodbye to Las Tunas Province in the time that it takes to drive across it on the Carretera Central – one hour on a good day. But, hang on a second! With laid-back, leather-skinned cowboys and poetic country singers, the province is known for daredevil rodeos and Saturday night street parties. Here barnstorming entertainment is served up at the drop of a sombrero.

Although historically associated with the Oriente, Las Tunas Province shares many attributes with Camagüey in the west. The flat grassy fields of the interior are punctuated with sugar mills and cattle ranches, while the beaches on the north coast remain wild and lightly touristed by Varadero standards.

In this low-key land of the understated and underrated, accidental visitors can enjoy the small-town charms of the provincial capital, or head north to beaches off the old mill town Puerto Padre where serenity rules.

INCLUDES

Las Tunas Province Highlights

❶ **Parque 26 de Julio**
(p348) Checking out the
Cuban version of the lasso-
wielding cowboy in this
fairground hosting Las Tunas's
celebrated rodeo twice a year.

❷ **Playa La Herradura**
(p351) Enjoying this unkempt

village beach while nary
a resort spoils its tranquil
sands.

❸ **Puerto Padre** (p349)
Lingering awhile in this
friendly, unpretentious and
out-on-a-limb seaside town.

❹ **Jornada Cucalambeana**

(p345) Rolling into El Cornito
in June to experience some
country crooning at the
music festival.

❺ **Punta Covarrubias**
(p350) Diving in a dozen sites
with largely undiscovered
reefs off this pristine beach.

History

The settlement of Las Tunas was founded in
1759 but wasn't given the title of 'city' until
1853. In 1876 Cuban General Vicente García
briefly captured the city during the War of
Independence, but repeated Spanish successes in the area soon led the colonizers
to rename it La Victória de Las Tunas. During the Spanish–Cuban–American War, the
Spanish burned Las Tunas to the ground, but
the Mambís fought back, and in 1897 General
Calixto García forced the local Spanish garrison to surrender in a pivotal Cuban victory.

Las Tunas became a provincial capital in
1976 during Cuba's postrevolutionary geographic reorganization.

Las Tunas

📞 31 / POP 211,596

La Victória de Las Tunas (as it's officially
known) is a sleepy agricultural town anoint-
ed provincial capital. It has long held a sleazy
reputation for being the Oriente's capital of

sex tourism. But thanks to good private lodg-
ings, welcoming locals and a handy location
on Cuba's arterial Carretera Central, handfuls
of road-weary travelers drop by and are pleasantly surprised. Missing here are the touts
that exasperate tourists in other destinations.
It's a window into real provincial life.

Referred to as the 'city of sculptures,' Las
Tunas is certainly no Florence. But what it
lacks in grandiosity it makes up for in small-
town quirks. You can see an authentic country rodeo, admire a statue of a two-headed
Taíno chief, go wild at one of the city's riotous
Saturday night street parties or wax lyrical at
the weird and witty Jornada Cucalambeana,
Cuba's leading country-music festival.

⊙ Sights

**Museo Memorial
Mártires de Barbados**   MUSEUM
(Map p346; Lucas Ortíz No 344; ⊙10am-6pm
Mon-Sat) **FREE** Las Tunas' most evocative
sight is in the former home of Carlos Leyva
González, an Olympic fencer killed in the

nation's worst terrorist atrocity: the bombing of a Cubana airliner in 1976. Individual photos of victims of the attack line the museum walls, providing poignant reminders of the fated airplane.

On October 6, 1976, Cubana de Aviación Flight 455, on its way back to Havana from Guyana, took off after a stopover in Barbados' Seawell airport. Nine minutes after clearing the runway, two bombs went off in the cabin's rear toilet causing the plane to crash into the Atlantic Ocean. All 73 people on board – 57 of whom were Cuban – were killed. The toll included the entire Cuban fencing team fresh from a clean sweep of gold medals at the Central American Championships. At the time, the tragedy of Flight 455 was the worst ever terrorist attack in the western hemisphere.

Memorial Vicente García   MUSEUM
(Map p346; ☑3134-5164; Vicente García No 7; USD$1; ☺9am-5pm Tue-Sat, 8am-2pm Sun) A colonial-era structure near the eponymous park that commemorates Las Tunas' great War of Independence hero who captured the town from the Spanish in 1876 and torched it 21 years later when the colonizers sought to reclaim it. The building was once García's house, but only a small exposed section of floor tiles remains from the original structure.

The museum's four rooms are best navigated with a guide who'll fill in the many historical gaps.

Museo Provincial
General Vicente García   MUSEUM
(Map p346; ☑3134-5164; cnr Francisco Varona & Ángel de la Guardia; USD$1; ☺8am-12:30pm & 1-4:30pm Wed-Fri, noon-8pm Sat, 8am-noon Sun) Housed in the royal blue town hall with a clock mounted on the front facade, the provincial museum documents local *tunero* history. A member of staff will happily lead you through the exhibits.

El Cornito   FOREST
(Km 8, Carretera Central; ☺9am-5pm) The bamboo woods around Motel El Cornito, about 6km outside town, offer a welcome, shady diversion from the scorching city bustle. You'll find *ranchón*-style restaurants (favoring the usual booming reggaeton music), the site of the old farmhouse of great Las Tunas poet Juan Cristóbal Nápoles Fajardo (aka El Cucalambé) and a reservoir.

Back toward the main road, there's a zoo, a fun park and a motocross circuit. A taxi here costs USD$5 to USD$7 round trip.

✹ Festivals & Events

★ Jornada Cucalambeana   MUSIC
(☺Jun) Cuba's biggest celebration of country music, where local lyricists impress each other with their 10-line *décima* verses. It happens in June, just outside Las Tunas, by Motel El Cornito.

Fundación de la Ciudad   FIESTA
(☺Sep 26) Flames, fireworks, torchlight parades and historical reenactments of native son General Vicente García's heroics in 1876 are part of the moving Fundación de la Ciudad festival held every September 26. García famously said he would see Las Tunas 'burnt rather than enslaved.' They were heated words, and the people of Las Tunas haven't forgotten them.

In all, Las Tunas was burned three time during the wars of independence for, far from being a backwater, in the revolutionary days of the mid-19th century, the city was considered key to controlling the entire Oriente.

Festival Internacional
de Magia Ánfora   CULTURAL
(☺Nov) Pro magicians from Europe, the US and Latin America are drawn to this passionate magic festival held in the provincial capital each November.

⎙ Sleeping

★ Hostal Melina   CASA PARTICULAR $
(Map p346; ☑3134-3503; Frank País No 55; r USD$25; ℗❄) With a warm welcome, this 1970s home sparkles with care. Of the four guest rooms in total, the two in back offer ample privacy and space, with flat-screen TVs and refrigerators. There's also a private covered patio and roof deck, and breakfasts are huge.

★ Mayra Busto Méndez   CASA PARTICULAR $
(Map p346; ☑5-271-3084, 3134-4205; mayra. busto@nauta.cu; Hirán Durañona No 16, btwn Frank País & Lucas Ortíz; r USD$25; ℗❄) A very helpful and secure casa particular with personalized attention. The sheen coming off the furnishings in this immaculate bungalow might dazzle you. There are two guest rooms, one enormous, and updated bathrooms. To find it, let the taxi know that it's a dead-end street (*calle sin salida*).

Las Tunas

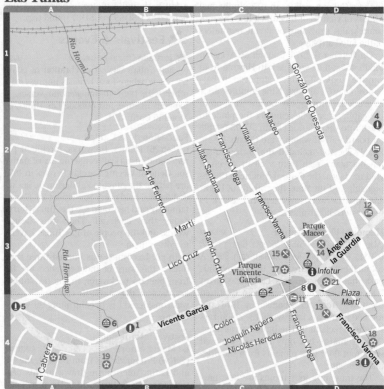

Casa Mayra   CASA PARTICULAR **$**
(Map p346; ☏ 3134-3878; kyl@itu.sld.cu; Lico Cruz No 93, btwn Villalón & Juan Gualberto Gómez; r USD$25; ✳️🛜) With sleek, modern design that's a rare find in Cuba, this second-story home with two spacious rooms is a welcome addition. There's original art on the walls, bold colors and an excellent roof terrace.

Motel El Cornito   CABIN **$**
(☏ 3138-1815; Km 8, Carretera Central; r USD$31) A Cuban-oriented place located in bamboo woods near the site of El Cucalambé's old farm. The Jornada Cucalambeana country-music festival takes place here. Some 60 cabins, verging between basic breeze block-style and decent chalets, are scattered through the woods. Phone ahead.

Hotel Cadillac   HOTEL **$$**
(Map p346; ☏ 3137-2791; cnr Ángel de la Guardia & Francisco Vega; s/d incl breakfast USD$72/86; ✳️🛜) A Las Tunas hotel that doesn't give you flashbacks to the Khrushchev and Brezhnev years. Opened in 2009, this rehabilitated, centrally located 1940s building features eight rooms, including a lovely corner suite, with safe and minibar. There are flat-screen TVs, up-to-the-minute bathrooms and a dash of old-fashioned pre-revolutionary class. Out front is the lively Cadillac Snack Bar (p348).

✕ Eating & Drinking

Las Tunas has an abundance of Italian restaurants for a city of its size. The local culinary claim to fame around these parts is *caldosa kike y marina,* a stew of meat and root vegetables with banana: it's even been sung about. Ask around.

There is nightlife in this sleepy town, but the pickup scene of older tourists with young escorts can make it unappealing.

★Caché   INTERNATIONAL **$**
(Map p346; ☏ 3199-5557; Francisco Varona, btwn Nicolás Heredia & Joaquín Agüera; sandwiches

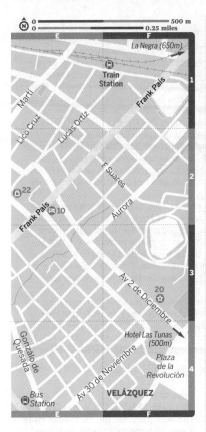

N
0 ——— 500 m
0 ——— 0.25 miles

La Negra (650m)

Train Station

Frank País

Martí

Lico Cruz

Lucas Ortiz

F Suárez

Aurora

Frank País

22

10

Av 2 de Diciembre

20

Hotel Las Tunas (500m)

Gonzálo de Quesada

Av 30 de Noviembre

Plaza de la Revolución

Bus Station

VELÁZQUEZ

Las Tunas

& burgers USD$3-11; ☺noon-2am) Proof that things are changing in Cuba, this swanky cocktail bar/cafe/restaurant attempts to bring the taste of Miami to Las Tunas. The dimly lit, air-conditioned interior is dressed to impress with leather seats, dexterous cocktail waiters and a menu heavy with deluxe burgers and club sandwiches. Locals favor the tasty fried *croquetas*.

La Patrona CUBAN $

(Map p346; ☏3134-0511; Custodio Orive No 94; meals USD$3-4; ☺11am-11pm) A largely local place with highly reasonable prices and equally reasonable food. The mains are primarily *comida criollla* (Creole food), but it also does cheap eggs and pasta.

Restaurante La Bodeguita INTERNATIONAL $

(Map p346; ☏3137-1536; Francisco Varona No 293; meals USD$5; ☺noon-11pm) A Palmares state-run joint, meaning that it's a better bet than the usual peso parlors and is likely to be open when others are not. You'll get checkered tablecloths, a limited wine list and what the Cuban government calls 'international cuisine' – read spaghetti and pizza. Try the chicken breast with mushroom sauce.

★La Negra CUBAN $$

(☏5-845-9237, 3139-8148; Israel Santos No 41; mains USD$5-12; ☺11am-11pm) Among provincial Cuba's best eats, this private home with a leafy courtyard serves up stunning Cuban classics. Crisp plantain shavings, fragrant pork stir-fry (*fajita de cerdo*) and shrimp *criollo,* served with a creamy tomato sauce, do not disappoint. Though the founding chef has left the building, his brother carries on the family business. It's a short taxi ride from downtown.

SCULPTURE VULTURES

Las Tunas has an eclectic, sometimes eccentric collection of urban sculptures, more than 150 of them in fact, dating back to a pioneering sculpture expo that was held in the city in 1974. For a small but precocious precis of the town's new young talent, check out the Galería Taller Escultura Rita Longa (see next page).

Las Tunas' most important and emblematic statue is Rita Longa's La Fuente de las Antilles (Map p346; Vicente García). First unveiled in 1977, it was elemental in reviving Cuba's sculpturing traditions and making Las Tunas its HQ. The sculpture comprises a huge fountain filled with elaborate interwoven figures symbolizing the emergence of the Greater Antilles' indigenous people from the Caribbean Sea. Cuba is represented by an *India dormida* (sleeping Taíno woman). The work reawakened interest in indigenous-themed art in Cuba and has spawned other complex sculptures, such as Mestizaje (Map p346; Francisco Varona), a multifaced representation of Cuba's mixed races in the Parque de la India near the bus station.

In the central hub of Plaza Martí is another Longa work, an inventive bronze statue (Map p346) of the 'apostle of Cuban independence,' José Martí, which doubles as a solar clock. It was opened in 1995 to commemorate the 100th anniversary of Martí's death.

Elsewhere in town you'll find sculptures with revolutionary themes. The 8m-high abstract Monumento Al Trabajo (Map p346; cnr Carretera Central & Martí) by José Peláez pays cubist homage to Cuban workers, while the pencil-like Monumento a Alfabetización (Map p346; Lico Cruz) marks the 1961 act passed in Las Tunas to stamp out illiteracy.

Further afield, the Janus-inspired Cacique Maniabo y Jibacoa is a two-headed Taíno chief looking in opposite directions, which dominates the surroundings at the rustic Motel El Cornito 6km west of town. Also at El Cornito is the Columna Taina, a kind of native totem pole, along with Las Tunas' newest sculpture, the Cornito Al Toro (2013), a legendary bull made out of metal and cement that guards the approach road to the complex looking down from a giant pedestal.

Cadillac Snack Bar CAFE
(Map p346; cnr Ángel de la Guardia & Francisco Vega; ⊙9am-11pm) This offshoot of the Hotel Cadillac (p346) has tables on a terrace overlooking the Plaza Martí action and serves decent cappuccinos.

☆ Entertainment

★ **Parque 26 de Julio** RODEO
(Map p346; Vicente García; ⊙9am-6pm Sat & Sun) FREE Located in the park where Vicente García bends into Av 1 de Mayo. Every weekend sees a farmers market, music, food stalls and kids' activities, but the key times to visit are in summer and winter (exact dates vary) for its biannual rodeos, complete with displays of riding and roping skills, bucking broncos and Cuban county fair vibes.

Teatro Tunas THEATER
(Map p346; ☑3134-5010; cnr Francisco Varona & Joaquín Agüera) This theater shows quality movies and some of Cuba's best touring entertainment including flamenco, ballet and plays.

Casa de la Cultura ARTS CENTER
(Map p346; ☑3134-3500; Vicente García No 8) The best place for the traditional cultural events with concerts, poetry and dance. The action spills out into the street on weekend nights.

Discoteca Luanda DANCE
(Map p346; ☑3134-8678; Francisco Varona, btwn Lora & Menocal; USD$3; ⊙11pm-3am Mon-Sat, 3-8pm Sun) Get your groove on with reggaeton, salsa and pop at this disco. There's a matinee program on Sundays.

Sala Polivalente STADIUM
(Map p346; ☑3134-7135; Av 2 de Diciembre) An indoor arena hosting sporting events near Hotel Las Tunas (☑3134-5014; Av 2 de Diciembre; s/d USD$62/72; P ❋ 🛜 ❄).

Cabaret El Taíno CABARET
(Map p346; ☑3134-3823; cnr Vicente García & A Cabrera; per couple USD$1; ⊙9pm-2am Tue-Sun) This large thatched venue at the west entrance to town has the standard feathers, salsa and pasties show on Saturdays and Sundays.

🛍 Shopping

Galería Taller Escultura Rita Longa ART
(Map p346; ☑3134-2969; cnr Villalón & Lucas Ortíz; ⊙9am-5pm Mon-Sat) The small gallery pulls together some fine local work for perusal or purchase.

**Fondo Cubano de
Bienes Culturales** ARTS & CRAFTS
(Map p346; ☑3134-6983; cnr Ángel de la Guardia & Francisco Varona; ⊙9am-noon & 1:30-5pm Mon-Fri, 8:30am-noon Sat) This store sells fine artwork, ceramics and embroidered items opposite the main square.

ℹ Information

INTERNET ACCESS
There are many Etecsa branches in the city center.
Etecsa Telepunto (☑3134-6554; Francisco Vega, btwn Vicente García & Lucas Ortíz; internet per hour USD$1.50; ⊙8:30am-7pm) Spanking modern air-conditioned haven on the shopping boulevard.

MEDICAL SERVICES
Casas particulares can help visitors get home doctor visits.
Hospital Che Guevara (☑3134-5012; cnr Avs CJ Finlay & 2 de Diciembre) A kilometer from the highway exit toward Holguín.

MONEY
ATMs are easy to find.
Banco Financiero Internacional (☑3134-6202; cnr Vicente García & 24 de Febrero; ⊙9am-3pm Mon-Fri)
Cadeca (☑3134-6382; Colón No 141; ⊙9am-6pm Mon-Sat, to noon Sun) Money changing.

TOURIST INFORMATION
Infotur (Map p346; ☑3137-2717; infotur@tunas.infotur.tur.cu; Francisco Varona No 298; ⊙8:15am-4:15pm Mon-Fri & alternate Sat) One of the friendliest information offices in Cuba.
Ecotur (☑3134-2073; Av 2 de Diciembre, Hotel Las Tunas; ⊙9am-4:30pm Mon-Fri, to noon Sat) Visit Ecotur to book excursions to Monte Cabaniguan (USD$20), though you will also need a separate 4WD transfer.

ℹ Getting There & Away

BUS
The main **bus station** (Map p346; Francisco Varona) is 1km southeast of the main square. Víazul buses (www.viazul.com) have daily departures; tickets are sold by the *jefe de turno* (shift manager). Get tickets one hour early or days before during high season.

Havana-bound buses stop at Camagüey (USD$7, two hours), Ciego de Ávila (USD$13, four hours), Sancti Spíritus (USD$17, 5½ to six hours) and Santa Clara (USD$22, seven hours). Service to Holguín (USD$6, 70 minutes) departs five times daily.

Santiago buses stop at Bayamo (USD$6, 1½ hours). To get to Guantánamo or Baracoa, you have to connect through Santiago de Cuba.

VÍAZUL DEPARTURES FROM LAS TUNAS

Destina-tion	Cost (USD$)	Duration (hr)	Frequency (daily)
Havana	39	11	5
Trinidad	22	7	1
Varadero	33	10½	1
Santiago	11	5	5

TRAIN
The **train station** (☑3134-8146; Tony Alomá, btwn Martí and Lucas Ortíz) is near Estadio Julio Antonio Mella on the northeast side of town. See the *jefe de turno* for tickets and double-check locally for the latest train schedules, which change somewhat frequently. Trains to Havana (via Camagüey and Santa Clara) leave every four days, as do trains to Santiago. There are daily services to Camagüey and Holguín.

TRUCK
Passenger trucks to other parts of the province, including Puerto Padre, pick up passengers on the main street near the train station, with the last departure before 2pm.

ℹ Getting Around

Taxis hang around outside the bus station, Hotel Las Tunas and the main square. Horse carts run along Frank País near the baseball stadium to the town center; they cost CUP$10.

For car and scooter rentals, try **Cubacar** (☑3134-6899; cnr Ángel de la Guardia & Maceo; ⊙8am-5pm Mon-Fri, to noon Sat) at Hotel Las Tunas. An **Oro Negro gas station** (cnr Francisco Varona & Lora) is a block west of the bus station. A **Cupet-Cimex gas station** (Carretera Central; ⊙24hr) is at the exit from Las Tunas toward Camagüey.

Puerto Padre

☑31 / POP 91,879

Languishing in a half-forgotten corner of Cuba's least spectacular province, it's hard to believe that Puerto Padre – or the 'city of mills' as it is locally known – was once the largest sugar port on the planet. But for die-hard travelers the wanton abandonment inspires a wistful sense of curiosity.

LAS TUNAS PROVINCE PUNTA COVARRUBIAS

MONTE CABANIGUAN

This fauna refuge just south of the municipality of Jobabo on the alluvial plains of the Río Cauto is a vital nesting ground for aquatic birds such as flamingos, the endangered Cuban parakeet and the Cuban tree-duck. The swamps are also the largest nesting ground for the American crocodile (*Cocodrilo acutus*) in Latin America. The area is protected internationally as a Ramsar wetlands zone. Ecotur runs short boat trips here for aspiring twitchers.

Blessed with a Las Ramblas–style boulevard, a miniature *malecón* (main street) and a scrawny, forlorn statue of Don Quixote beneath a weathered windmill that has registered one too many hurricanes, the town is the sort of place where you stop to ask the way at lunchtime and end up, a couple of hours later, tucking into fresh lobster at a bayside restaurant.

◉ Sights

Fuerte de la Loma FORT
(☑ 3151-5224; Av Libertad; USD$1; ☺ 9am-4pm Tue-Sat) This fort at the top of the sloping Av Libertad, also known as the Salcedo Castle, is testimony to Puerto Padre's former strategic importance. There's a small military museum with temperamental opening hours.

**Museo Fernando García
Grave de Peralta** MUSEUM
(☑ 3151-5308; Yara No 45, btwn Av Libertad & Martí; USD$1; ☺ 9am-4pm Tue-Sat) Lashed regularly by hurricanes, the municipal museum – when it's not being renovated – contains the usual round of fallen revolutionaries, stuffed animals and antiques. Look out for the antique record players.

🍃 Courses

Silverio Cuevas Vargas DANCING
(☑ 5-326-6639; silcuevas@nauta.cu; Mártires de la Herradura No 109; per hour USD$10) Salsa, rumba and popular Cuban dances: years of rigid Teutonic form will limber up under Silverio's warm tutelage. Classes are usually one-on-one and can even be held in Las Tunas. His house is across from the taxi area.

🛏 Sleeping & Eating

La Casita Iraida CASA PARTICULAR $
(☑ 5-546-6455, 3151-5172; iraida30@nauta.com.cu; Vicente García No 1; r USD$20-25) With a prime seafront location on a dead-end corner, this friendly casa has three upstairs rooms, all with balconies overlooking the sea. It's a short walk to the boulevard and steps from Puerto Padre's pleasantly low-key *malecón*.

★ El Bodegón de Polo CUBAN $
(☑ 3151-2357; Lenin No 54, btwn 24 de Febrero & Ameijeira; meals USD$2-5; ☺ 10am-10pm) Keen-to-please local restaurant serving delicacies such as crab, octopus and swordfish on a breezy upstairs terrace. The best deal in town and friendly to boot.

Paladar Villa Odalis CREOLE $
(☑ 5-284-1719; Cuba, btwn 24 de Febrero & Martí; mains CUP$25-150; ☺ 9am-11pm) With a plant-festooned patio and quiet downtown location, the offerings at this local spot skew toward seafood specialties. Spaghetti, mutton, pork and the Cuban favorite chicken 'Gordon Blue' round out the menu.

☆ Entertainment

Casa de la Cultura ARTS CENTER
(☑ 3151-5463; Parque de la Independencia; ☺ hours vary) In sleepy Puerto Padre, your best bet for catching musical performances or other nighttime cultural activities is at the municipal culture house.

1913 Ballroom DANCE
(☑ 3151-6897; Jesús Menéndez, btwn 24 de Febrero & Ameijeira; ☺ hours vary) Have a drink or bite to eat and work up a sweat dancing at this downtown venue.

❶ Getting There & Away

The 52km between Las Tunas and Puerto Padre are well paved. Puerto Padre is best accessed by truck (CUP$10), leaving from Las Tunas train station, or with your own wheels. A taxi from the provincial capital should cost approximately USD$30.

Punta Covarrubias

Punta Covarrubias has a spotless sandy beach. It's a haven for scuba diving off the beaten path.

Scuba diving at the coral reef 1.5km offshore is the highlight. Packages of two dives per day start at CUC$45 at the Marina Covarrubias. There are 12 dive sites here.

Self-sufficient travelers can turn in to the beach at the *mirador* (a tower with fantastic panoramic views), 200m before the hotel, or procure a hotel day-pass for CUC$25.

Las Tunas Province's only all-inclusive resort is also one of the island's most isolated, its highlight being scuba diving at the coral reef 1.5km offshore. Sitting aside the blue-green Atlantic, the Brisas Covarrubias (☑3151-5530; s/d all-inclusive USD$41/82; P❋@☎❋) has 122 comfortable rooms in cabin-blocks, with one for disabled guests.

ℹ️ Getting There & Away

Almost all guests arrive on all-inclusive tours and are bused in from Frank País Airport in Holguín, 115km to the southeast. It's very secluded.

The road from Puerto Padre to Playa Covarrubias is a dream, having been repaved post–Hurricane Irma. West to Manatí and Playa Santa Lucía is not quite as pristine.

You may find a taxi in Las Tunas (one way USD$45, plus USD$10 per hour to wait).

Playas La Herradura, La Llanita & Las Bocas

This wild string of northern beaches hugs the Atlantic coast. Come to read, relax and lose yourself in the vivid colors of traditional Cuban life.

From Puerto Padre it's 30km to the rustic Playa La Herradura. Enjoy this delicious scoop of golden sand with no resort in sight. In this attractive small town, everyone knows everyone.

Continue west 11km to Playa La Llanita. There's a long, straight beach, and the water is somewhat shallow. The sand here is softer and whiter than in La Herradura, but the beach lies on an unprotected bend, and there's sometimes a vicious chop.

Just 1km beyond, Playa Las Bocas marks the end of the road with a few houses, a convenience store and open-air bar. You can usually catch a local ferry to El Socucho (USD$1) to continue to Puerto Padre.

🛏️ Sleeping & Eating

⭐ **Villa Carolina**   CASA PARTICULAR $
(☑5-238-7272; giuseppetesta@nauta.cu; Casa No 99, Playa La Herradura; r USD$20-25; ❋) On the way into town look for this yellow two-story home of a lovely Cuban-Italian couple. The rooms are all upstairs along a long shaded terrace with rockers and sea views. There are three rooms, all impeccable, with refrigerators and TV. Meals are extra and worth paying for, especially when it comes to the homemade pasta.

Casa Reinold   CASA PARTICULAR $
(☑3154-7124, 5-493-8396; Playa La Llanita; r USD$25; ❋) Let's be clear. There is little else to do here than dig your feet into the white sand and watch the lapping surf. For some, that will be enough. This beachfront electric-pink house has two average rooms for rent, electric showers and meals when you want them. There are two Adirondack chairs alongside a sea-grape tree and shallow waters. The location is just at the entrance to La Llanita, to the right of a fork in the road.

Villa Rocio   CASA PARTICULAR $
(☑5-277-3921; odaisimf@nauta.cu; Casa No 185, Playa La Herradura; r USD$25) Close to the beach with three guest rooms and good food. At the time of our visit the house was undergoing major renovation to add a second story.

Restaurante Roberto   SEAFOOD $$
(☑3154-7126; Playa Las Bocas; mains USD$3-12; ⏰hours vary; ❋) A coral wall surrounds this small home courtyard with a couple of open-air tables and friendly service. The shady patio is pleasant, but there's no sea view. Seafood is offered at all hours, and there are also a couple of dark rooms for rent.

ℹ️ Getting There & Away

There are trucks (CUP$3) that can take you as far as Puerto Padre from Las Tunas. From Puerto Padre, other trucks (CUP$2) make the trip. It's much easier to get up this way from Holguín, changing at the town of Velasco.

Driving is the best shot, though after Puerto Padre the road can be in poor condition. Taxis from Puerto Padre cost USD$20, or more because of road conditions. Taxis from Las Tunas to the beaches cost USD$61 to USD$66, depending on the distance.

AT A GLANCE

POPULATION
1,027,249

**HIGHEST
WATERFALL**
Salto del Guayabo
(p376): 127m

BEST HOTEL
Hotel Ordoño (p367)

**BEST ADULTS-
ONLY RESORT**
Paradisus Río de Oro
(p369)

BEST ARTS CENTER
Uneac (p362)

WHEN TO GO

Dec–Mar
Guardalavaca and
Playa Pesquero
resorts are at
their best during
the prime tourist
season.

Apr–Jun
The city of Holguín
shows off its
religious spirit
during the Romerías
de Mayo in early
May.

Jul–Nov
To miss the peak
storm period,
avoid the hurricane
season.

Holguín Province

I n this beautiful hill-studded hinterland, Cuba's contradictions are magnified. For the visitor, rich landscapes range from the pine-scented mountains of the Sierra del Cristal to the palm-fringed beaches around Guardalavaca. Holguín's beauty was first spied by Christopher Columbus, who by most accounts docked near Gibara in October 1492 where he was met by a group of curious Taíno natives. The Taínos didn't survive the ensuing Spanish colonization, though fragments of their legacy can be reconstructed in Holguín Province, which contains more pre-Columbian archaeological sites than anywhere else in Cuba.

Perhaps something in the water breeds extremes. Fulgencio Batista and his ideological opposite Fidel Castro were both reared in this province, as were dissident writers Reinaldo Arenas and Guillermo Infante. There's plenty of contrast in settings as well: the inherent Cuban-ness of Gibara contrasts sharply with the tourist swank of resort-complex Guardalavaca.

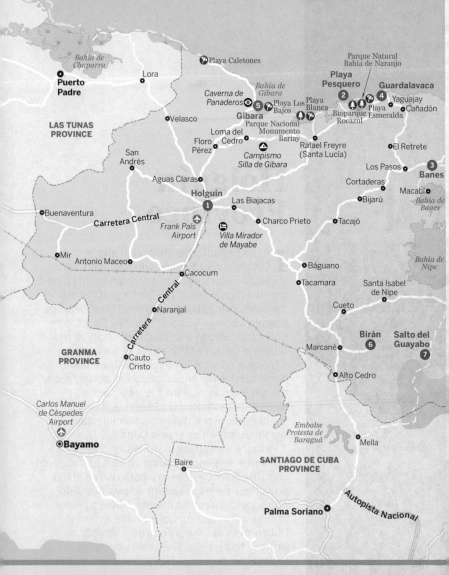

Holguín Province Highlights

1 Loma de la Cruz (p356) Seeing Holguín spread out like a map beneath you from the heights of this city peak.

2 Playa Pesquero (p368) Reveling in luxuriant beach time at one of several plush resorts.

3 Banes (p375) Pedaling leisurely through bucolic villages to this quintessential *holguiñero* town.

4 Museo Chorro de Maita (p371) Discovering Taíno treasures in one of Cuba's most important archaeological sites in Guardalavaca.

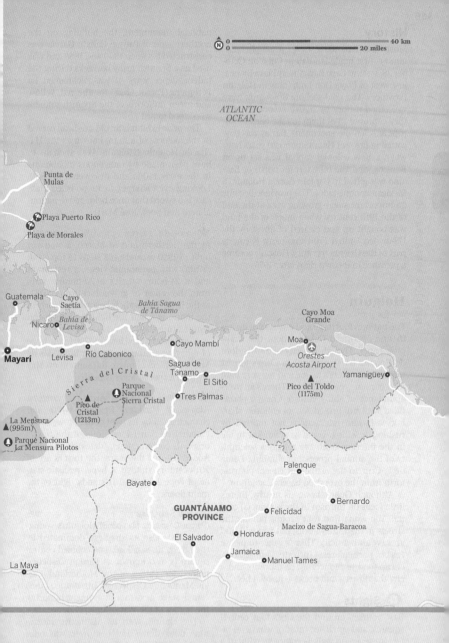

ATLANTIC
OCEAN

Punta de
Mulas

Playa Puerto Rico
Playa de Morales

Guatemala   Cayo
Saetía   *Bahía Sagua*
Nicaro   *Bahía de*   *de Tánamo*   Cayo Moa
        Levisa   Grande
Mayarí   Levisa   Río Cabonico   Cayo Mambí   Moa
                    Orestes
            Sagua de   *Acosta Airport*
    S i e r r a   d e l   C r i s t a l   Tánamo   El Sitio   Yamanigüey
            Parque   Pico del Toldo
        Pico de   Nacional   Tres Palmas   (1175m)
        Cristal   Sierra Cristal
        (1213m)
La Mensura
(995m)
Parque Nacional
La Mensura Pilotos

                        Palenque

        Bayate   Bernardo

        GUANTÁNAMO   Felicidad
        PROVINCE   Macizo de Sagua-Baracoa
    El Salvador   Honduras

La Maya   Jamaica
                Manuel Tames

⑤ **Gibara** (p364) Relaxing
in gorgeous colonial
accommodations in this
enigmatic seaside town.

⑥ **Museo Conjunto
Histórico de Birán** (p365)
Peeping behind the scenes of
the Castro family compound
while touring Fidel's childhood
home in Birán.

⑦ **Salto del Guayabo**
(p376) Gazing upon a
spectacular waterfall in Cuba's
little Switzerland.

History

Most historians agree that Christopher Columbus first made landfall in Cuba on October 28, 1492, at Cayo Bariay near Playa Blanca, just west of Playa Don Lino (now in Holguín Province). The gold-seeking Spaniards were welcomed ashore by native *seborucos*, and they captured 13 of them to take back to Europe as scientific 'specimens.' Bariay was boycotted in favor of Guantánamo 20 years later when a new colonial capital was set up in Baracoa, and the hilly terrain north of Bayamo was gifted to Captain García Holguín, a Mexican conquistador. The province became an important sugar-growing area at the end of the 19th century when much of the land was bought up and cleared of forest by the US-owned United Fruit Company. Formerly part of the Oriente territory, Holguín became a province in its own right after 1975.

Holguín

POP 356,322

The nation's fourth-largest city serves up authentic provincial Cuba without the wrapping paper. Though the city of San Isidoro de Holguín barely features in Cuba's tourist master plan, there's magic and mystery here for a certain type of traveler. There's an overabundance of shiny vintage Chevys, plazas filled with uniformed school children sharing wi-fi, and interactions not marred by rushing or selling. Use it as a window to life in the interior: from the religious solemnity of the annual procession climbing Loma de la Cruz to the exuberant cheers pouring forth from the oversized baseball stadium.

Although Guardalavaca is nearby, there's little focus on tourism in the provincial capital. You won't find tour groups milling the streets in migratory herds, but you will find an easy authenticity. There's eager-to-please casas particulares (private homestays), cheap food in pioneering restaurants and a city that loves – and brews – its own beer.

◉ Sights

Base yourself around the city's four central squares, and you'll see most of what's on offer. However, no walk is complete without a climb up the emblematic Loma de la Cruz – a little off the grid, but well worth the detour.

★**Museo de Historia Provincial**   MUSEUM
(Map p358; ☑ 2446-3395; Frexes No 198; USD$1; ⊙8am-4:30pm Tue-Sat, to noon Sun) Now a national monument, the building on the northern side of Parque Calixto García was constructed between 1860 and 1868 and was used as a Spanish army barracks during the independence wars. It was nicknamed La Periquera (Parrot Cage) for the red, yellow and green uniforms of the Spanish soldiers who stood guard.

The prize exhibit is an old axe-head carved in the likeness of a man, known as the Hacha de Holguín (Holguín Axe), thought to have been made by indigenous inhabitants in the early 1400s and discovered in 1860. Looking even sharper in its polished glass case is a sword that once belonged to national hero and poet, José Martí.

★**Loma de la Cruz**   LANDMARK
At the northern end of Maceo, a stairway built in 1950 ascends 465 steps to top a hill (275m) with panoramic views, a restaurant and a 24-hour bar. It's a 20-minute walk from the center or go via bici-taxi (USD$1) to the base. This walk is best tackled early in the morning when the light is pristine and temperature cooler.

A cross was raised here in 1790 in the hope of relieving a drought. During Romerías de Mayo, devotees climb to the summit on May 3 where a special Mass is held.

★**Catedral de San Isidoro**   CATHEDRAL
(Map p358; Manduley) Dazzling white and characterized by its twin domed towers, the Catedral de San Isidoro, one of the town's original constructions, dates from 1720. Added to over the years, the towers are of 20th-century vintage. A hyper-realistic statue of Pope John Paul II stands right of the main doors.

Parque San José   PARK
(Parque Céspedes; Map p358) Holguín's youngest park is also its shadiest, dominated by the Iglesia de San José. The cobbled central square is also known as Parque Céspedes, named for 'Father of the Motherland' Carlos Manuel de Céspedes – his statue stands center stage next to a monument honoring the heroes of the War of Independence.

The church, with its distinctive mezzanine floor, dome and belltower, was once used by the Independistas as a lookout tower. Locals still refer to the park by its old name, San José, or as Parque Infantil.

Parque Peralta   SQUARE
(Parque de las Flores; Map p358) This square is named for General Julio Grave de Peralta

(1834–72), who led an uprising against Spain from Holguín in October 1868. His marble statue (1916) faces the imposing Catedral de San Isidoro. On the western side of the park is the **Mural de Origen**, depicting the development of Holguín and of Cuba from indigenous times to the end of slavery.

Plaza de la Marqueta SQUARE
(Map p358) Laid out in 1848, rebuilt in 1918 and renovated only recently, this gleaming square is dominated by bronze busts and an impressive covered marketplace housing a cafe and artisan stalls. Running along the north and south sides of the plaza are myriad shops selling music, crafts and cigars.

Parque Calixto García SQUARE
(Map p358) This wide, expansive square is more about atmosphere than architecture. It was laid out in 1719 as the original Plaza de Armas and served for many years as the town's meeting point and marketplace. The centerpiece today is a 1912 statue of General Calixto García, where you'll find a mixture of old sages, baseball naysayers and teenagers on the prowl.

In the southwestern corner is the **Centro de Arte** (Map p358; ☑ 2442-2392; Maceo No 180; ☻ 9am-4pm Mon-Sat) **FREE**, a gallery for temporary exhibitions that shares space with **Biblioteca Alex Urquiola** (Map p358; ☑ 2446-2562; Maceo No 178; ☻ 8am-9pm Mon-Sat), named after a local revolutionary and housing Holguín's biggest book collection.

Museo de Historia Natural MUSEUM
(Map p358; ☑ 2442-3935; Maceo No 129, btwn Parques Calixto García & Peralta; USD$1; ☻ 9am-noon & 12:30-5pm Tue-Sat, 9am-noon Sun) You'll find more stuffed animals here than in a New York toy store – everything from the world's smallest frog to the world's tiniest hummingbird. There's also a big collection of the unique yellow polymita seashells found on Cuba's far-east coastline. To be frank, the building, guarded by two stone lions, is more impressive than what's inside.

Casa Natal de Calixto García MUSEUM
(Map p358; ☑ 2442-5610; Miró No 147; USD$1; ☻ 9am-5pm Tue-Sat) To learn more about the militaristic deeds of Holguín's local hero, head to this house situated two blocks east of the namesake park. The hugely underestimated García – who stole the cities of Las Tunas, Holguín and Bayamo from Spanish control between 1896 and 1898 – was born here in 1839.

This small collection gives a reasonable overview of his life: military maps, old uniforms and even a spoon he ate with on the campaign trail in 1885.

Fábrica de Órganos FACTORY
(Carretera de Gibara No 301; ☻ 8am-4pm Mon-Fri) **FREE** Visitors can tour the only mechanical music-organ factory in Cuba. This small factory produces about six organs a year, as well as guitars and other instruments. A good organ costs between US$10,000 and US$28,000. Eight professional organ groups exist in Holguín (including the Familia Cuayo, based at the factory): if you're lucky, you can hear one playing on Parque Céspedes on Thursday afternoon or Sunday morning.

Plaza de la Revolución SQUARE
(Map p360) Holguín is a city most *fiel* (faithful) and its bombastic revolutionary plaza, east of the center, is a huge monument to the heroes of Cuban independence, bearing quotations from José Martí and Fidel Castro. Massive rallies are held here every May 1 (Labor Day). The **tomb of Calixto García** (Map p360; Plaza de la Revolución), containing his ashes, is also here, as is a smaller monument to García's mother.

Galería Holguín GALLERY
(Map p358; Manduley No 137; ☻ 8am-10pm Thu-Sun, to 6pm Tue & Wed) **FREE** Situated in a colonial building, the Galería Holguín displays a revolving cache of good local art.

✦ Festivals & Events

Romerías de Mayo RELIGIOUS
(☻ early May) Holguín's big annual pilgrimage is held the first week of May: devotees climb Loma de la Cruz for a special Mass. The whole city turns out to follow the procession from the Catedral de San Isidoro, a custom dating back to the 1790s. In recent times, the parade has become livelier with arty contributions from the Hermanos Saíz youth organization.

Carnaval FIESTA
(☻ mid-Aug) Holguín's annual shindig happens in the third weekend of August, with outdoor concerts and copious amounts of dancing, roast pork and potent potables.

★ Fiesta de la Cultura Iberoamericana MUSIC
(www.casadeiberoamerica.cu; ☻ late Oct) Musicians from all over Latin America and beyond take over the city for a week of concerts

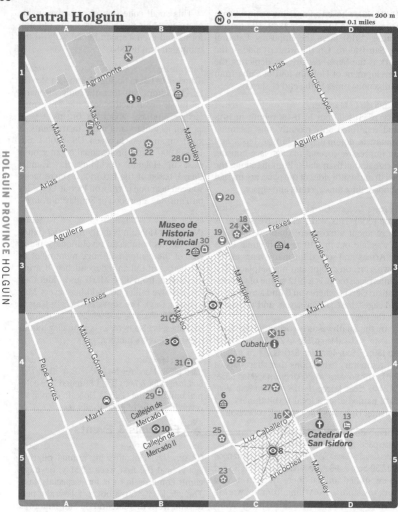

Central Holguín

(many free) in venues throughout the city. Some big Cuban acts play, too. Forty countries and diverse genres are represented. There are also workshops for musicians and a nod to the arts and dance.

💤 Sleeping

Palma Casa Enrique   CASA PARTICULAR **$**
(Map p360; ☏ 2442-4683; lapalmaenrique@nauta.cu; Maceo No 52a, btwn Urbano & Línea; r USD$25; ✽) Resembling a little piece of Florida, this smart, detached neocolonial with requisite palm tree dates from 1945. It sits in the shadow of the Loma de la Cruz, a calm location worth the minor inconvenience.

Two spacious guest rooms occupy their own wing of the house, offering ample privacy. Enrique and Mayda are thoughtful and deeply knowledgeable hosts.

Check out the skilled artwork of Enrique's son: a terracotta bust of Che Guevara in the living room next to an unusual 3m-long canvas copy of Da Vinci's *The Last Supper* with St John as a woman.

Villa Liba   CASA PARTICULAR **$**
(Map p360; ☏ 2442-3823, 5-289-6931; villaliba@nauta.cu; Maceo No 46, cnr Calle 18; s/d USD$25/30; ✽) The *alma* (soul) bubbles over at this smart bungalow evoking a 1950s

Central Holguín

North American suburb. At the center are welcoming hosts: Jorge is a modern-day Pablo Neruda with whimsical anecdotes aplenty on Holguín life; and Mariela is an accomplished massage and Reiki specialist offering on-site treatments (USD$25). It's worth dining in. Meals (USD$4 to USD$8), including vegetarian fare, have a Lebanese flair.

Villa Janeth CASA PARTICULAR **$**
(Map p360; ☎5-314-0313, 2442-9331; filihlg@infomed.sld.cu; Cables No 105 (altos); r USD$20-25; ❋) With great spaces, Janeth's clean, spacious house is a solid choice. Guests have the run of a full floor with balcony. There's classic Cuban style: one princess pink room and another featuring a king-sized bed with a leather headboard. There's kitchen use, TV and electric showers. She's also a welcoming host.

Casa Don Diego CASA PARTICULAR **$**
(Map p358; ☎5-226-9047, 5-326-9362; diego10@nauta.cu; Arias No 167, btwn Manduley & Maceo; r incl breakfast USD$25; ❋) While the initial welcome might be tepid, this central colonial is decent value. It's prettier inside than out, with wonderful spiral staircases. There are four rooms with high ceilings, a pleasant rooftop terrace and a prime Parque San José location.

Villa Mirador de Mayabe HOTEL **$$**
(☎2442-2160; director@mayabe.islazul.tur.cu; Km 8, Alturas de Mayabe; s/d/ste USD$69/81/102; ❒❋❂❅) Cresting the Loma de Mayabe, 10km southeast of Holguín, this large hilltop compound includes adorable bungalows tucked into lush grounds. The views, taking in vast mango plantations, are especially good from the pool. For families, it's a welcome retreat. Pastel bungalows are small but pleasant, but the thatched restaurant is unremarkable.

Hotel Esmeralda BOUTIQUE HOTEL **$$**
(Map p358; ☎2447-4301; Maceo, btwn Agramonte & Arias; r USD$44-62; ❋❅) With only four rooms, this petite boutique hotel – part of the high-end Encanto chain – sits prettily alongside Parque San José. While super central and full of colonial charm, it does not provide breakfast, as there's no kitchen on the premises. It does have a small bar, where you can procure coffee.

Hotel Pernik HOTEL **$$**
(Map p360; ☎2448-1011; cnr Avs Jorge Dimitrov & XX Aniversario; s/d incl breakfast USD$40/65; ❒❋@❅❂) The nearest conventional hotel to the city center is a dose of Soviet-inspired '70s nostalgia. Its dour reputation is partially offset by edgy art by local artists. The breakfast buffet is plentiful, and there's

Holguín

an information office, Cadeca (money exchange) and internet cafe. However, the hotel suffers from the usual foibles of interminable renovations and blaring late-night music.

★ **Hotel Caballeriza** BOUTIQUE HOTEL **$$$**
(Map p358; ☏2442-9191; www.hotelescubanacan.com; Miró No 203; s/d incl breakfast USD$100/130; ❄️🛜) A renovated 1846 mansion that's seen it all. After the original owner went bankrupt, it was turned into stables. Now it sports contemporary interiors with a grand colonial facade and a gloriously over-the-top horse theme. The grand entrance features a lobby bar and restaurant. Branching off a central courtyard, big rooms have 19th-century decor and flat-screen TVs.

There's 24-hour reception, attentive service and money-changing services. It's part of the elite Encanto hotel line represented by Cubanacán.

🍴 Eating

Restaurante-Bar San José CUBAN **$**
(Map p358; ☏2442-4877; Agramonte No 188; meals USD$3-9; ⏰noon-11pm) A hub of locals slap-bang in the central square (Parque San José) with mismatched paint and uniformed servers. The menu is nothing fancy, but this is where you come for *comida criolla* (Creole food).

Cremería Guamá ICE CREAM **$**
(Map p358; ☏2446-2622; cnr Luz Caballero & Manduley; ice cream USD$1; ⏰10am-10:45pm) Havana's famous ice-cream parlor. Lose an hour underneath the striped red-and-white awning overlooking pedestrianized Calle Manduley and enjoy peso treats alfresco.

Cafetería Cristal FAST FOOD **$**
(Map p358; ☏2442-1041; Edificio Pico de Cristal, cnr Manduley & Martí; snacks USD$1-3; ⏰24hr) Typical of such cafes across Latin America: Cristal's reliable and affordable

Holguín

Cuba's best offerings. Guests tuck into thick steaks as if it were their last day on earth. There's also tender grilled octopus with garlic sauce, lovely chocolate *torta* (cake) and an extensive wine and liquor menu. Courteous service to boot. The restaurant is filled with locals and travelers alike. Come early or reserve.

Restaurante Maragato
CUBAN $$
(Map p360; ☑ 5-246-6802; Carbó, btwn Garayalde & Agramonte; mains USD$4-11; ⊙noon-11pm) Worth getting off the beaten path for, this easygoing restaurant does *comida criolla* (Creole food) with style. It also has the best cocktail bar in town, thanks to the barman owner. Dine on grilled meats, tender lamb shanks, yams and fresh salad.

Ranchón Los Almendros
PARRILLA $$
(Map p360; ☑ 2442-9652; José A Cardet No 68f, btwn Calles 12 & 14; mains USD$10-12; ⊙10am-11pm) With excellent smoked meats with copious trimmings, *tostones* (fried plantain) and huge stuffed peppers filled with *ropa vieja* (shredded beef), this restaurant is worth the little bit extra it costs. Located near Loma de la Cruz, it doesn't look much from the outside but rest assured – inside is a different story.

Salón 1720
CARIBBEAN $$
(Map p358; ☑ 2446-8150; Frexes No 190, cnr Miró; meals USD$6-9; ⊙noon-10:30pm) A painstakingly restored wedding cake mansion with a full social atmosphere. Tuck into paella or

chicken meals are dished up by formal waiters whose elegance prepares you for cuisine far superior to what you end up getting. The air-conditioning replicates a frigid day in Toronto. Perch on the outside terrace with the surprisingly great house coffee and soak up Holguín life.

Taberna Pancho
CARIBBEAN $
(Map p360; Av Jorge Dimitrov; meals USD$3-5; ⊙noon-10pm) This bar-restaurant inspired by the Mirador de Mayabe's famous beer-drinking donkey has echoes of a Spanish tavern, done up in dark wood. The menu includes actual chorizo (unusual in Cuba) and draft Mayabe beer comes in proper frosted glasses.

★1910 Restaurante & Bar
INTERNATIONAL $$
(Map p360; ☑ 2442-3994; www.1910restaurante bar.com; Mártires No 143, btwn Aricochea & Cables; meals USD$8-11; ⊙10am-midnight) Count this elegant wood-trimmed colonial among

LOCAL KNOWLEDGE

BEER CITY

The large **Fábrica de la Cervezería Bucanero** on the outskirts of the city produces the nation's three most popular beers, including the best beer in Cuba. Cuba's most ubiquitous brand is Cristal (4.9% alcohol by volume), a light brew perennially popular with tourists looking to extinguish the heat of a long afternoon in the sunlounger. Some opt for the stronger, darker Bucanero whose 'Fuerte' variety rings in at 5.4%. Even stronger and maltier is Bucanero 'Max' at a respectable 6.5%. Rarely seen in tourist resorts is 'Mayabe,' a clear, light golden pilsner that registers at 4%.

chicken stuffed with vegetables and cheese; there are even complimentary crackers. In the same colonial-style complex, there's a cigar shop, bar, boutique, car rental and a terrace with nighttime music. Check out the wall plaques that give interesting insights into Holguín's history.

Drinking & Nightlife

Casa de la Música CLUB
(Map p358; ☎ 2442-9561; cnr Frexes & Manduley; ⊗9pm-3am Tue-Sun) There's a young, trendy vibe at this place on Parque Calixto García. If you can't dance, stay static sinking beers on the adjacent Terraza Bucanero (entry via Calle Manduley).

Bar Terraza BAR
(Map p358; Frexes, btwn Manduley & Miró; ⊗8pm-1am) Perched above Salón 1720, this is the city's poshest spot. Cocktails are in order as you drink in the views over Parque Calixto García (p357) while listening to live music.

Terraza del Pernik CLUB
(Map p360; ☎ 2448-1011; Hotel Pernik, cnr Avs Jorge Dimitrov & XX Aniversario; guest/nonguest USD$2/4; ⊗10pm-2am Tue-Sun) Holguín's premier disco at Hotel Pernik. If you're staying there, the music will visit you – in your room – like it or not, until 1am.

Disco Cristal CLUB
(Map p358; ☎ 2442-1041; 3rd fl, Edificio Pico de Cristal, Manduley No 199; USD$1; ⊗9pm-2am) A nexus for Holguín's skilled dancers (most of whom are young, cool and determined to have a good time), this place is insanely popular at weekends when you'll find lots

of inspiration for the salsa/rap/reggaeton (Cuban hip-hop) repertoire.

Taberna Mayabe BAR
(Map p358; Manduley, btwn Aguilera & Frexes; ⊗noon-6pm & 8-11pm Tue-Sun) A grotty tavern on pedestrian-only Manduley, where wooden tables and ceramic mugs create a hearty olden days atmosphere. Solo travelers elicit more than one sideways glance. Best for pairs or groups. The eponymous local brew is served.

Cafeteria La Begonia BAR
(Map p358; ☎ 2446-8586; Maceo No 176; ⊗8am-7pm & 7:45pm-5am; ☎) Sells drinks and snacks (USD$1 to USD$4) beneath flowering trellises on Parque Calixto García, and it's a relaxed place to meet other travelers. If you don't like rubbery cheese sandwiches, stick to the beer and enjoy the cultural interchange.

☆ Entertainment

★Uneac ARTS CENTER
(Map p358; ☎ 2447-4066; Manduley No 148, btwn Luz Caballero & Martí) There's at least one National Union of Cuban Writers and Artists per province in Cuba, but if you visit only one, make it here. Situated in the lovingly restored Casa de las Moyúas (1845) on car-free Calle Manduley, this friendly establishment offers literary evenings with famous authors, music nights, patio theater (including Lorca) and cultural reviews.

There's an intermittent bar on a gorgeous central patio and an on-site art gallery/studio called La Cochera.

★Teatro Comandante Eddy Suñol THEATER
(Map p358; ☎ 2442-7994; Martí No 111; ☎) Holguín's premier theater is an art deco treat from 1939 on Parque Calixto García. It hosts both the Teatro Lírico Rodrigo Prats and the Ballet Nacional de Cuba, and is renowned both nationally and internationally for its operettas, dance performances and Spanish musicals.

Check here for details of performances by the famous children's theater Alas Buenas and the Orquesta Sinfónica de Holguín (Holguín Symphony Orchestra).

★Casa de la Trova El Guayabero LIVE MUSIC
(Map p358; ☎ 2445-3104; Maceo No 174; ⊗10am-7pm & 9pm-2am Tue-Sun) Old guys in Panama

hats croon under the rafters, and musicians in *guayaberas* (Caribbean dress shirts) blast on trumpets, while ancient couples in their Sunday best map out a perfect *danzón* (traditional Cuban ballroom dance). So timeless, so Holguín.

Salón Benny Moré   LIVE MUSIC
(Map p358; ☑ 2442-3518; cnr Luz Caballero & Maceo; ☺ 2-7pm & 9:30pm-2:30am) Holguín's impressive outdoor music venue is the best place to round off a bar crawl with some live music and dancing.

Jazz Club   JAZZ
(Map p358; cnr Frexes & Manduley; ☺ 2pm-2am) Jams start around 8pm at this jazz venue, weaving their magic for a few hours, and then there's piped music until 2am. There's a sporadically functioning daytime cafe downstairs.

Casa Iberoamericana   LIVE MUSIC
(Map p358; ☑ 2442-7715; www.casadeiberoamerica.cu; Arias No 161; ☺ hours vary) Situated in quieter Parque San José, this paint-peeled place frequently hosts *peñas* (musical performances) and cultural activities.

**Estadio General
Calixto García**   SPECTATOR SPORT
(Map p360; ☑ 2442-2614; Av de los Libertadores; USD$1-2) Mosey on down to this stadium to see Holguín's baseball team, former giant-killers the Perros (dogs), who snatched the national championship from under the noses of the 'big two' in 2002, but haven't barked much since. The stadium also houses a small but interesting sport museum.

**Cominado Deportivo
Henry García Suárez**   SPECTATOR SPORT
(Map p358; ☑ 2446-3487; Maceo; CUP$1; ☺ 8pm Wed & 2pm Sat) You can catch boxing matches at this spit-and-sawdust gym on the western side of Parque Peralta, where three Olympic medalists have trained. If you can pluck up the courage, ask about some (noncontact) training sessions. It's very friendly.

🛍 Shopping

Fondo de Bienes Culturales   ARTS & CRAFTS
(Map p358; ☑ 2442-3782; Frexes No 196; ☺ 9am-5pm Mon-Sat) This state-run shop on Parque Calixto García sells small affordable paintings and similar handicrafts to the private vendor market a few blocks away.

**Bazar – Proyecto
de Desarollo Local**   MARKET
(Map p358; ☑ 2446-1652, 2446-1401; Manduley, btwn Aguilera & Arias; ☺ 9am-6pm Mon-Sat, from noon Sun) Listen for music blasting from the doorway of this private, community-run market that sells jewelry, magic boxes, Cuban art and goat-leather goods. It's the same stuff as the government-run store, but the money goes directly into the pockets of the vendors.

Pentagrama   MUSIC
(Map p358; ☑ 2445-3135; cnr Maceo & Martí; ☺ 8am-noon & 12:30-4:30pm) Official outlet of the Cuban state record company Egrem, selling a small but decent stash of CDs.

El Jigue   BOOKS
(Map p358; ☑ 2646-8521; cnr Martí & Mártires; ☺ 9am-12:30pm & 1-4:45pm) Well-stocked bookstore and souvenir outlet adjacent to Plaza de la Marqueta.

ℹ Information

INTERNET ACCESS
There is a wi-fi hot spot in Parque Calixto García, and **Etecsa Telepunto** (☑ 2447-4067; Martí No 122, btwn Mártires & Máximo Gómez; internet per hour USD$1.50; ☺ 8:30am-7:30pm) sells wi-fi scratch cards.

MEDICAL SERVICES
Holguín has a **city hospital** (☑ 2442-5302; Av VI Lenin) and a designated **pharmacy** (☑ 2442-5790; Maceo No 170; ☺ 8am-10pm Mon-Sat) for foreigners.

MONEY
There are plenty of places to change money in Holguín, including at **Banco de Crédito y Comercio** (☑ 2446-7389; Arias; ☺ 9am-3pm Mon-Fri), **Banco Financiero Internacional** (☑ 2446-8502; Manduley No 167, btwn Frexes & Aguilera; ☺ 9am-3pm Mon-Fri) and **Cadeca** (☑ 2446-8663; Manduley No 205, btwn Martí & Luz Caballero).

TOURIST INFORMATION
A number of agencies near the main plaza, such as **Cubatur** (Map p358; Edificio Pico de Cristal, cnr Manduley & Martí), offer similar services for reservations, tickets and tours.

ℹ Getting There & Away

AIR
Cubana connects Holguín with Havana daily (in theory) – make reservations at the **Cubana office** (☑ 2446-1610; www.cubana.cu; 2nd fl, Edificio Pico de Cristal, cnr Manduley & Martí; ☺ 8am-4pm Mon-Fri) in the city center. A tourist

taxi to the **airport** (☏ 2447-4630) costs USD$15 to USD$20. It's also possible to spend your last night in Bayamo and then catch a taxi for slightly more to Holguín's airport.

If you are considering regional transportation arrangements, note that Holguín's airport is considered the most reliable in eastern Cuba in terms of on-time departures.

BUS

Viazul buses (cnr Carretera Central & Independencia) connect Holguín with longer-distance destinations. An alternative is the **Conectando a Cuba bus** (Map p360) that runs to Havana and Santiago.

A daily bus, run by Transtur, connects to the Guardalavaca resorts (round trip USD$15). It departs from outside the Museo de Historia Provincial (p356) daily at 1pm and comes back from Guardalavaca at 8:30am.

VÍAZUL BUS DEPARTURES FROM HOLGUÍN

Destination	Cost (USD$)	Duration (hr)	Frequency (Daily)
Bayamo	6	1¼	3
Havana	44	12	4
Santiago	11	3½	3
Trinidad	26	7¾	1
Varadero	38	11¼	1

TAXI

Colectivos (shared taxis) run to Gibara (CUP$20) and Puerto Padre in Las Tunas Province from Av Cajigal. Those going to **Guardalavaca** (Map p360) (USD$5) leave from outside Estadio General Calixto García.

Trucks have sporadic departures because they leave when full. From outside **Estadio General Calixto García** (Map p360; Av de los Libertadores), trucks go to Guardalavaca for USD$1 to USD$2.

TRAIN

The newer Havana-bound trains depart from the **train station** (☏ 2442-2331; Vidal Pita No 3) every three days (2nd-/1st-class USD$60/80, 14 hours), with stops in Las Tunas, Camagüey, Ciego de Ávila, Santa Clara and Matanzas. Purchase tickets at the **Ladis Ticket Office** (☏ 2447-4071; Vidal Pita; ⊗ 7:30am-3pm) and always confirm your ticket at least an hour before departure.

❶ Getting Around

BICI-TAXI

Definitely worth a try, the sidecar bici-taxi, resembling a bike with a wheelchair fused on, was invented here. Holguín's ubiquitous bici-taxis charge USD$1 for a short trip, USD$2 for a long one.

CAR

You can rent a car at Cubacar, with branches at Hotel Pernik (p359), **Aeropuerto Frank País** (☏ 2446-8414; Aeropuerto Frank País) and **Cafetería Cristal** (☏ 2446-8559; Edificio Pico de Cristal, cnr Manduley & Martí; ⊗ 8am-9pm).

A **Cupet-Cimex gas station** (Av Cajigal; ⊗ 24hr) is 3km out of town toward Las Tunas; another station is just outside town on the road to Gibara. An **Oro Negro gas station** (Carretera Central) is on the southern edge of town. The road to Gibara is north on Av Cajigal; also take this road and fork left after 5km to reach Playa La Herradura.

TAXI

A **Cubataxi** (Map p358; ☏ 2447-3535; Máximo Gómez, cnr Martí) to Guardalavaca (54km) costs around USD$35. To Gibara, one way should cost no more than USD$20.

Gibara

POP 71,991

Matched only by Baracoa for its wild coastal setting, half-forgotten Gibara, with its faded pastel facades and surging ocean rollers, conspires to seduce you. There's a cultural life here that seems big for a small town. In 2008, Hurricane Ike almost wiped the town off the map. Luckily, it did not.

Situated 33km from Holguín via a scenic road that winds and rolls through villages, Gibara is a small, intimate place receiving a lift from much-needed investment. Unlike nearby Guardalavaca, development here is low key and focused on renovating the town's beautiful but dilapidated architecture. The saddle-shaped Silla de Gibara crag that so captivated Columbus creates a gorgeous backdrop. Nearby is the site of one of Cuba's first wind farms.

◉ Sights

Gibara has seen a small renaissance with government investment aimed at restoring and renovating the city's architecture. Though the specific attractions are few, this is more a town to stroll the streets and absorb the local flavor. There are a couple of decent beaches within striking distance of Gibara.

⭐ **Playa Caletones** BEACH

A lovely little beach 17km northwest of Gibara, this stretch of white sand and azure sea is a favorite of Holguín vacationers. The town is ramshackle, with no services except a rustic restaurant. Ask here about freshwater *pozas* (pools) where you can go

DON'T MISS

CASTRO'S BIRTHPLACE

Fidel Castro Ruz was born on August 13, 1926, at the Finca Las Manacas near the village of Birán, south of Cueto. The sprawling ranch, bought by Fidel's father Ángel in 1915, includes its own workers' village (a cluster of small thatched huts for the mainly Haitian laborers), a cockfighting ring, butcher's shop, post office, store and telegraph. The several large yellow wooden houses surrounded by lush cedars housed the Castro family. Tours are thorough and very worthwhile.

The farm opened as **Museo Conjunto Histórico de Birán** (USD$10, camera/video USD$10/10; ⊙ 9am-3:30pm Tue-Sat, to noon Sun) in 2002, its unassuming name intending to downplay any Castro 'personality cult.' This gaggle of attractive wooden buildings on expansive grounds constitutes a *pueblito* (small town) and makes a fascinating excursion. It appears as a backwater today, but once sat on the camino real, Cuba's main east–west road in colonial times.

Around the various houses, you can see more than a hundred photos, assorted clothes, Fidel's childhood bed and his father's 1918 Ford motorcar. Perhaps most interesting is the schoolhouse where Fidel first studied before moving on to Santiago as an outstanding pupil. Fidel sat in the middle of the front row. There are pictures of young Fidel and Raúl and Fidel's birth certificate, made out in the name of Fidel Casano Castro Ruz.

A cemetery contains the grave of Fidel's and Raúl's father, Ángel, and siblings. The site illustrates, if nothing else, the extent of the inheritance that this hot-headed ex-lawyer gave up when he absconded to the Sierra Maestra for two years, surviving on a diet of crushed crabs and raw horse meat. Finca Las Manacas was the first property to be appropriated by the government after the revolution.

Those who come on their own should bring a detailed map. Otherwise, tour agencies offer it as a day trip from Holguín.

swimming. Get here by bike, taxi (round trip with wait USD$25) or rental car.

Guided **cenote diving** (USD$10), 5km further along, purportedly visits some of Cuba's best cave diving sites. You'll need your own equipment. With crystalline waters, the cave system goes back some 3000m, with water depth about 15m.

On the beachfront road, **Restaurante La Proa** serves up some of Cuba's most delectable fresh seafood on an upstairs terrace overlooking the water.

El Cañonazo MUSEUM
(Map p370; ☑ 5-381-2672; elpatriotaflores@gmail. com; ⊙ hours vary) There's nothing else quite like this in Cuba. Known as the patriot, Miguel Flores has a quirky collection of homemade satire memorabilia featuring the Pope, former US president Barack Obama, 1950s movie stars and others. He is even considering a parody slave auction targeting Cuba's history. Refusing to take sides in politics, he calls all art 'a statement for peace.'

Because hours vary, it's best to call or email ahead of your visit.

Iglesia de San Fulgencio CHURCH
(Map p370; Parque Calixto García; ⊙ 8am-noon & 2-4:30pm Tue-Sun) Built in 1850, this church still gleams from its last renovation. Twin cupolas face Parque Calixto García, and its hushed stately interior is worth a peek.

Caverna de Panaderos CAVE
(Map p370; Independencia; USD$5) This complex cave system with 19 galleries and a lengthy underground trail is close to town at the top end of Calle Independencia. Guides are required as there are no installations or signs here. Go with a qualified local guide who can offer helmets and headlamps. The walk to the cave is 1km. Those who are not too claustrophobic can squeeze into an inner chamber with a lake where you can swim. Reserve at least two hours for the excursion.

Locals have been working arduously to clean up this trail and remove an improvised trash dump from near the entrance, but it's still a work in progress.

Playa Blanca BEACH
(Map p370) Across the bay from Gibara, this small sandy beach begs for bathers. From the Gibara dock, take a local *lancha* (open boat ferry; USD$2) across Bahía de Gibara to Juan Antonio, from where it's 400m on to Playa Blanca. There's a casa particular (p366) but no services, so bring your own picnic.

Parque Calixto García SQUARE
(Map p370) A central plaza lined with weird *robles africanos,* African oaks with large pods. The Statue of Liberty in front commemorates the Spanish–Cuban–American War.

Spanish Fort FORT
(Map p370; Cabada) At the top of Calle Cabada, this crumbling brick Spanish fort with graceful arches provides stunning town and bay views. Continue on this street for 200m to **Restaurante El Mirador** (⊘24hr) for an even better vantage point.

🛶 Activities & Tours

Viñales might be Cuba's climbing capital, but word is spreading about the smaller, no-less-attractive routes on the Silla de Gibara, where there's also hiking and horseback riding.

Silla de Gibara CLIMBING
(Map p370) Silla de Gibara, the saddle-shaped limestone crag 35km southeast of Gibara, has around 20 'mapped' climbing routes on its shadowy north face, best tackled in the cooler months between November and February. With little government support, climbing here is similar to Viñales. Bring your own gear and use a guide.

Jose Corella Varona TOURS
(⌂5-397-9096; joselin54@nauta.cu; city tour USD$5) Professional and friendly, Gibara's resident historian also guides tours on weekends to Caverna de Panaderos (p365) and dives to the cave system near Playa Caletones (p364). He also offers short historic city tours.

Alexis Silva García TOURS
(⌂2484-4458) Local guide for Gibara-based climbing and caving excursions. Find him at the **Museo de Historia Natural** (Map p370; Luz Caballero No 23; USD$1; ⊘8am-noon & 1-5pm Tue-Sat, 1-4pm Mon).

🛏 Sleeping

⭐**Hostal Sol y Mar** CASA PARTICULAR $
(⌂5-240-2164; hostalsolymar.gibara@yahoo.fr; J Peralta No 59; r USD$25; ▣ 🛜) With wonderful sea breezes and romantic sea views, this big yellow waterfront home beats all competition on ambience. The multiple terraces are conducive to privacy. Five rooms are well equipped and modern with electric showers. The young host, who can speak French, English, Dutch and German, and the ladies

running the casa, will make your stay a pleasant one.

⭐**Hostal El Patio** CASA PARTICULAR $
(⌂2484-4269; oceanomg@nauta.cu; José Mora No 19, btwn Cuba & J Agüero; r USD$30; ▣ 🛜) Tucked away behind this high-walled patio are Gibara's coziest digs: a lovely, partially covered, plant-strewn patio leading to airy renovated rooms, one with a private patio and outdoor shower. It has an updated '50s style, white with bright accents, and there's also a rooftop terrace. Mealtimes are magical in this little getaway, and the family is very helpful with local information.

Bayview CASA PARTICULAR $
(Map p370; ⌂5-224-5570; San Antonio, Playa Blanca; r USD$25-30; ▣ 🛜 🛏) Location, location, location. With boat access only, this small house is 900m from Playa Blanca, a comma of white sand blissfully free of development. There are hammocks and the possibility of home-cooked meals (recommended). To get here, take the 10-minute ferry from Gibara. It's not to be confused with the Playa Blanca near Guardalavaca. Reservations only – call Jimmy.

Luz del Norte CASA PARTICULAR $
(⌂5-860-6449; anabeatriziberia@nauta.cu; Donato Mármol No 69; r USD$25; ▣ 🛜) Crafted for the millennial crowd, this cool refurbished home maintains its plank wooden floors with sparse furnishings and trompe l'oeil murals showing vivid sunsets or a Magritte-worthy wall of clouds surrounding an open window. There are five rooms and ample living space, a bit uphill from the action. The host Ana speaks English, and her hotel experience shows in her hospitality.

Hostal Los Hermanos CASA PARTICULAR $
(⌂2484-4542; odalisgg@nauta.cu; Céspedes No 13, btwn Luz Caballero & J Peralta; r USD$20-25; ▣) This casa, with signature Gibara stained glass and baroque colonial splendor, has a bright shared courtyard patio and five big, dark bedrooms behind large old-fashioned wooden doors. The best room is alone upstairs. If it's out of rooms, you might end up next door in an equally lovely home.

Villa Caney CASA PARTICULAR $
(⌂2484-4552; tleticia@nauta.cu; Sartorio No 36, btwn J Peralta & Luz Caballero; r USD$20-25; ▣) There's more stunning Gibara beauty in Villa Caney, captured in a sturdy stone colonial house that withstood the Category 4 force of Hurricane Ike. Two rooms off an impressive

courtyard are large and have private baths. Fantastic meals are served in the *paladar*, also open to nonguests.

★**Hotel Ordoño** HOTEL **$$$**
(☎ 2484-4448; www.iberostar.com; J Peralta, cnr Donato Mármol; s/d incl breakfast USD$90/140; ❈ @ 🖤) Once a general store, this majestic three-story colonial oozes character. The most gracious of the three Iberostar properties in Gibara, it has 27 enormous renovated rooms, particularly on the 3rd floor, some with details like filigree pillars. The lovely roof terrace affords 360-degree views overlooking town, the working waterfront and the sea.

Throw in exemplary service and an ethereal Gibara setting, and you'll feel like Louis XIV kicking back in Versailles (without the guilty conscience). Best hotel in Cuba? Definitely a contender.

Hotel Arsenita BOUTIQUE HOTEL **$$$**
(☎ 2484-4400; www.iberostar.com; General Sartorio; s/d incl breakfast USD$90/140; ❈ @ 🖤) Run by the Iberostar chain, this lovely colonial remodel infuses old-time glamour into staid old Parque Calixto García. There's an elegant three-seat lobby bar with a bow-tied barman mixing daiquiris, a gorgeous wall mural in the vaulted entry and 12 modern rooms with flat-screen TVs.

✖ Eating

★**Cueva Taína** PARRILLA **$**
(☎ 2484-5333; Calle 2da No 131, cnr Carretera & Playa Caletones; dishes USD$6; ☺ noon-midnight Tue-Sun) Gibara's eating scene becomes imaginative with this private place that grows its own herbs to garnish those grilled meats. It even has a small farm. There's a *ranchón*-style part and a more formal restaurant area above. It's at the northern end of town; you can get there by horse cart (USD$2).

Perla del Norte SEAFOOD **$**
(☎ 2484-4542; Céspedes No 18; mains USD$3-11; ☺ 11am-11pm) For above average seafood fare, this 2nd-story restaurant is a godsend. Go for the crab, *camarones enchilados* (shrimp in garlicky-tomato sauce), tasty fried rice and crisp plantain chips. There's some outdoor seating or a chilly dining room. It's ultra-clean and run by the family from Hostal Los Hermanos.

Casa de Los Amigos SEAFOOD **$$**
(☎ 2484-4115; Céspedes No 15, btwn J Peralta & Luz Caballero; meals USD$5-10; ☺ 11am-9pm)

Both casa and private restaurant, this place has an amazing interior patio with frescoes, a gazebo and hand-painted Gibara doors. It rents rooms, but the dining is more notable – a profusion of local fish dishes with ample trimmings.

🍷 Drinking & Nightlife

Absorb small-town life at the ambient local watering hole or at the elegant small bars of the recently refurbished hotels.

Bar La Loja BAR
(☎ 2484-4485; J Agüero; ☺ 9am-midnight Wed-Sun, from 4pm Mon & Tue; 🖤) Another quiver in Gibara's freshly renovated bow, this bar next to the Casa de la Cultura hosts live music on Friday and Sunday nights, but is always a good place to hang with the locals. It also features a wine cave and a huge interior patio.

☆ Entertainment

As in most Cuban seaside towns, the local youth hang around the *malecón* (main street) on weekend evenings. Spontaneous outbreaks of music are likely at any time in and around Parque Calixto García and Parque Colón.

Siglo XX ARTS CENTER
(☎ 2484-5475; Martí; ☺ 8am-11pm Wed-Sun, to 5pm Mon & Tue) A fine cultural center in the main square that hosts live traditional music on a Saturday night and provides taped stuff at other times. The courtyard is a good place to chill with an icy *refresco* on a hot afternoon.

Cine Jiba CINEMA
(☎ 2484-4689; Parque Calixto García) Cuba's international **film festival** (Gibara International Film Festival; www.ficgibara.com; ☺ Jul) hosts most of its cutting-edge movies (some in English) in this small but quirky cinema covered with distinctive art-house movie posters. If you're going to go to the cinema anywhere in Cuba, it should be in Gibara – it's a local rite of passage.

Centro Cultural
Batería Fernando VII ARTS CENTER
(☎ 2481-4471; Plaza del Fuerte; ☺ hours vary) The diminutive Spanish fort hovering above the choppy ocean is today an atmospheric cultural center run by ARTex. It puts on weekend shows and serves food and drink from a sinuous bar-restaurant and disco.

DON'T MISS

GIBARA'S INDIE FILM FEST

There's no red carpet, no paparazzi and no Hollywood stars, but what the Festival Internacional de Cine de Gibara lacks in glitz it makes up for in raw, undiscovered talent. Inaugurated in 2003, the Cine de Gibara was the brainchild of late Cuban director Humberto Solás, who fell in love with this town after shooting his seminal movie *Lucía* here in 1968.

Open to independent filmmakers of limited means, the festival attracts up to US$100,000 in prize money, despite limited advertising. Lasting for seven days, proceedings kick off with a gala in the Cine Jiba (p367) followed by film screenings, art exhibitions and nightly music concerts. The competition is friendly but hotly contested, with prizes used to reward and recognize an eclectic cache of digital movie guerrillas from countries as varied as Iran and the US.

ℹ Information

It's possible to change money at the **Bandec** (☏ 2484-4101; cnr Independencia & J Peralta; ⊗ 9am-3pm Mon-Fri) in town, but more reliable to do so in nearby Holguín.

ℹ Getting There & Away

There are no Víazul buses to Gibara. Travelers can tackle the route with Cuban transport on a truck or *colectivo* (USD$1) from Holguín. The **bus station** (cnr Máximo Gómez & Aguero) is 1km out on the road to Holguín. There are two daily buses (USD$1) in each direction. It's possible to taxi to Holguín airport (USD$40) or Guardalavaca (USD$40).

For drivers heading toward Guardalavaca, the link road from the junction at Floro Pérez is hell at first, but improves just outside Rafael Freyre. There's an Oro Negro gas station at the entrance to town.

To get to Playa Blanca, take the ferry (USD$2) to Juan Antonio and the beach is 400m further. It leaves the dock at 6:30am, 8:30am, 10:10am, 1pm, 3:40pm and 5pm.

Playa Pesquero & Playa Esmeralda

With a luxury Caribbean sheen missing elsewhere on the island, these lesser-known beaches make for one serious getaway. The beach is sublime, with golden sand, shallow, warm water and great opportunities for snorkeling. You won't find a lot of action: besides a small shopping center, there is little to do beyond lounging. Of Holguín's three northern resort areas, Playa Pesquero (Fisher's Beach) is the most high-end. There are four tourist colossi here, including the five-star Hotel Playa Pesquero.

Nearby Playa Esmeralda occupies the middle ground between Guardalavaca's economy and Playa Pesquero's opulence.

Two megaresorts line this superior stretch of beach, 6km to the west of Guardalavaca and accessed by a spur just east of the Cayo Naranjo boat launch.

◉ Sights

Bioparque Rocazul, Parque Nacional Monumento Bariay and Las Guanas at Playa Esmeralda are part of the **Parque Natural Cristóbal Colón**.

Bioparque Rocazul   NATURE RESERVE
(Map p370; ☏ ext 115 2443-3310; ejecutivo.comercial@pncolon.co.cu; Playa Esmeralda; ⊗ 9am-5:30pm; ⊕) Located just off the link road that joins Playa Turquesa with the other Pesquero resorts, this protected park in Parque Natural Cristóbal Colón offers the usual hand-holding array of outdoor activities under the supervision of a nonnegotiable government guide. It's a commendable environmental effort in a major resort area, but the limitations are that it can be a little stifling (and costly).

There are leisurely walking excursions (first hour USD$8, per extra hour USD$2), horseback riding on healthy animals (per hour USD$16) and reef fishing (USD$49). If you plan to stay the whole day, opt for the 'day in the country' package (USD$40). The park is extensive with hills, trails, a (depressing) mini-zoo aimed at kids, and ocean access. You can also overnight in a **cabin** (Map p370; Bioparque Rocazul; r incl 3 meals USD$59). There's a friendly bar at the entrance to the park where you can weigh up the options.

Parque Nacional
Monumento Bariay   HISTORIC SITE
(Map p370; ☏ 2443-0766; Playa Blanca; USD$8; ⊗ 9am-5pm) Ten kilometers west of Playa Pesquero and 3km west of Villa Don Lino is Playa Blanca. Columbus landed somewhere near here in 1492. The meeting of

two cultures is commemorated with a goofy reenactment and through varied sights, including an impressive Hellenic-style monument designed by Holguín artist Caridad Ramos for the 500th anniversary of the landing in 1992.

Other points of interest include an information center, the remains of a 19th-century Spanish fort, three reconstructed Taíno huts and an archaeological museum. It makes a pleasant afternoon's sojourn.

🛌 Sleeping

🛌 Playa Pesquero

Campismo Silla de Gibara CABIN $
(Map p370; ☎2442-2881; Rafael Freyre; s/d USD$18/36; P☀) This campismo (cheap rustic accommodations) sits on sloping ground beneath Gibara's signature saddle-shaped hill. Reached via a rough road between Floro Pérez and Rafael Freyre, it's 35km southeast of Gibara itself and 1.5km off the main road. Come for the views, not the comfort. It's imperative that you book ahead via **Campismo Popular** (Map p358; ☎2446-2492; comercial@hlg.campismopopular.cu; Miró No 183) in Holguín, as foreigners are sometimes turned away.

There's also a cave you can hike to, 1.5km up the hill, and horseback riding is available.

Villa Don Lino CABIN $$
(Map p370; ☎2443-0308; director@donlino.co.cu; Rafael Freyre; s/d from USD$49/78; P☀) The bargain alternative to Playa Pesquero's 'big four,' Don Lino's refurbished wooden *cabañas* are planted right on a diminutive white beach. It makes for a romantic retreat. There's a small pool, nighttime entertainment and an element of Cuban-ness missing in the bigger resorts. Villa Don Lino is 8.5km north of Rafael Freyre along a spur road.

Memories Holguín RESORT $$
(Map p370; ☎2443-3540; www.memoriesresorts. com; Playa Pesquero; s/d all-inclusive from USD$80/ 119; P☀@🛜) Slightly apart from the other resorts on its own clean scoop of beach (known as Playa Yuraguanal), Memories writes the word 'privacy' into its four stars. Otherwise, you're looking at all the usual high-end, all-inclusive givens – meaning most guests are happy to never leave the complex.

★**Hotel Playa Pesquero** RESORT $$$
(Map p370; ☎2443-3530; Playa Pesquero; s/d all-inclusive from USD$136/223; P☀@🛜)

Among Cuba's biggest hotels, Playa Pesquero has 933 rooms taking up prime real estate on a beautiful beach. It was opened by Fidel Castro in 2003, and his speech is displayed in the reception area. Beautifully landscaped grounds over 30 hectares include Italianate fountains, fancy shops, seven restaurants, a spa and acres of swimming pool space linked by zippy golf carts.

Hotel Playa Costa Verde RESORT $$$
(Map p370; ☎2443-0520; reservationsmanager@ playacostaverde.co.cu; Playa Pesquero; s/d all-inclusive USD$110/180; P☀@🛜) Despite the faux veneer, the Costa Verde has top-notch facilities including a Japanese restaurant, a gym, colorful gardens and a lagoon you cross to get to the beach. Run by hotel group Gaviota, the atmosphere is ticky-tacky but far more subdued than the hotels in Guardalavaca proper.

Fiesta Americana Costa Verde RESORT $$$
(Map p370; ☎2443-3510; Playa Pesquero; s/d all-inclusive USD$107/184; P☀🛜) With blocky architecture, this smaller offering turns out to be decent value. Attractive tiled rooms, friendly staff and wi-fi are selling points, although the property could use a little TLC.

🛌 Playa Esmeralda

★**Paradisus Río de Oro** RESORT $$$
(Map p372; ☎2443-0090; www.melia.com; Playa Esmeralda; s/d all-inclusive from USD$265/378; P☀@🛜) You may need a wallet of gold to access the river of gold resort by Meliá. Oft touted as Cuba's best resort, this 356-room resort shines with a five-star pedigree. There's cliffside massage, a Japanese restaurant floating on a koi pond, and garden villas with private pools. Palm groves and thick foliage keep the property protected and private. Adults only.

While it is promoted as an eco-resort, its only sustainable distinction is keeping the property forested. High rollers should bid for the newer luxury area within the compound, featuring only several hundred rooms. Also enticing is the Royal Service Garden Villa Room, with private pool, watchtower, sauna and private entrance – yours for only USD$2287 per night.

Sol Río Luna y Mares Resort RESORT $$$
(Map p372; ☎2443-0030; Playa Esmeralda; s/d all-inclusive from USD$154/202; P☀@🛜) This two-in-one hotel is an amalgamation

Guardalavaca & Playa Pesquero

Guardalavaca & Playa Pesquero

of two resorts, though its presentation is a bit stale. Its main advantages over Guardalavaca are the superior food at the on-site French and Italian restaurants and the truly sublime beach, with beach toys included in the price.

🛍 Shopping

Centro Comercial Playa Pesquero MALL
(Map p370; ⊙9am-11pm Sun-Thu, 24hr Fri & Sat) Mall with fast food, money exchange, shop and bowling alley.

ℹ Getting There & Away

The four resorts of Playa Pesquero are accessible from the main Holguín–Guardalavaca road via a spur road 12km west of Guardalavaca proper. Playa Esmeralda and its two resorts lie at the end of a short spur road 6km west of Guardalavaca. Hotels rent mopeds and bicycles.

A shuttle bus (USD$5) run by Transtur links Playa Pesquero with Playa Esmeralda and Guardalavaca. Departures and returns are spaced two hours apart. There's also a trolley making the rounds of hotel grounds and Guardalavaca.

Taxis, including classic cars and horse carriages, wait outside the resorts. It should cost about USD$10 to Guardalavaca.

Guardalavaca

Guardalavaca is a string of megaresorts draped along a succession of idyllic beaches backed by verdant hills. Before the rows of sunloungers and poolside bingo, Columbus described this stretch of coast as the most beautiful place he ever laid eyes on.

Sheltered turquoise coral reefs teem with aquatic action. More spread out than Varadero and less isolated than Cayo Coco,

Guardalavaca has enduring popularity. There's also long been beach access for Cubans, which helps provide a more local atmosphere.

In the early 20th century, this region was a rural village and important cattle-rearing area (Guardalavaca means 'shelter the cow'). The tourism boom moved into first gear in the late 1970s when local *holguiñero* Fidel Castro inaugurated Guardalavaca's first resort – the sprawling Atlántico – with a quick dip in the hotel pool. The local economy hasn't looked back since.

◉ Sights

★ **Museo Chorro de Maita**   MUSEUM
(Map p370; ☑ 2443-0201; USD$2; ☺ 9am-5pm Tue-Sat, to 1pm Sun) This archaeological-site-based museum protects the remains of an excavated indigenous village and cemetery, including the well-preserved remains of 62 human skeletons and the bones of a barkless dog. The village dates from the early 16th century and is one of nearly 100 archaeological sites in the area. New evidence suggests indigenous people were living here many decades after Columbus' arrival.

Aldea Taína   MUSEUM
(Taíno Village; Map p370; ☑ 2443-0201; USD$5; ☺ 9am-5pm Mon-Sat, to 1pm Sun) The reconstructed Aldea Taína features life-size models of traditional dwellings and inhabitants in a replicated indigenous village with limited interpretive signage. You can usually tag along with lunchtime tour groups for the staged rituals, and there's a restaurant/bar.

🏃 Activities

You can arrange **horseback riding** in Playa Esmeralda or privately: USD$10 per hour is the going rate. Have a look at the horses on offer beforehand and consider riding elsewhere if the animals seem unhealthy or otherwise mistreated.

You can rent **mopeds** at all the hotels for up to USD$27 per day. Some all-inclusive resorts include bicycle use, but the bikes are fairly basic (no gears). The road between Guardalavaca and Playa Esmeralda, and on to Playa Pesquero, is flat and quiet and makes an excellent day excursion. For a bit more sweat, you can make it to Banes and back (66km round trip).

Boat Trips

Many water-based excursions leave from the **Marina Gaviota Puerto de Vita** (Map p370; ☑ 2443-0132) and can be booked through the hotels. There's another newer but smaller marina at **Boca de Samá** (Map p370), 9km east of Guardalavaca and run by Cubanacán.

Aside from the ubiquitous sunset cruise possibilities (USD$60), you can organize deep-sea fishing (up to six people USD$360), and occasional catamaran trips across Bahía de Vita with snorkeling and open bar.

Diving

Guardalavaca has some excellent diving (better than Varadero and up there with Cayo Coco). The reef is 200m out, and there are 32 dive sites, most of which are accessed by boat. Highlights include caves, wrecks, walls and La Corona, a giant coral formation that resembles a crown.

Eagle Ray Marlin Dive Center   DIVING
(Map p372; ☑ 2443-0316; dives from USD$45; ☺ 8:30am-4:30pm Mon-Sat) Guardalavaca beach's one dive center abuts the sand about 300m west of the Club Amigo Atlántico – Guardalavaca. This outfit is suitable for experienced divers who are well versed in safety protocols but not recommended for novices.

Hiking

Las Guanas
Eco-Archaeological Trail   HIKING
(Map p372; USD$3; ☺ 8am-4:30pm) At the end of the Playa Esmeralda road is this self-guided hike, which, at USD$3 for 1km, is quite possibly Cuba's most expensive trail. Walk slowly to get your money's worth! The marked route (with several more kilometers of bushwhacking on fire trails leading to a picturesque bluff with a lighthouse) apparently has 14 endemic plant species. Inauthentic sculptures of indigenous Taínos guard the route.

The bluff was originally touted for hotel development but was saved from the bulldozers by government intervention. A model at the start shows what the hotel would have looked like.

Kitesurfing

Luís Riveron   KITESURFING
(Map p372; ☑ 5-378-4857; luiskitesurf@nauta.cu; lessons per hour USD$50, rental per hour USD$30) Cuba's newest sport has sprouted a private Guardalavaca operator that offers private lessons and board rental. His perch is on the beach of Brisas Guardalavaca (p373).

Guardalavaca

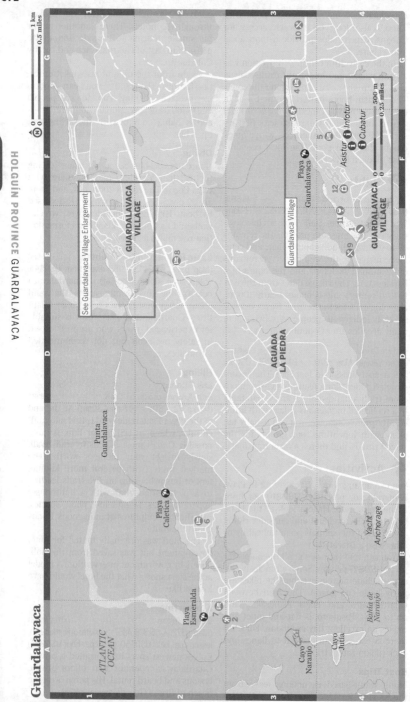

ATLANTIC OCEAN

Punta Guardalavaca

Playa Caletica

Playa Esmeralda

Cayo Naranjo

Cayo Jutía

Bahía de Naranjo

Yacht Anchorage

AGUADA LA PIEDRA

GUARDALAVACA VILLAGE

See Guardalavaca Village Enlargement

Guardalavaca Village

GUARDALAVACA VILLAGE

Playa Guardalavaca

Asistur   Infotur

Cubatur

0   500 m
0   0.25 miles

0   1 km
0   0.5 miles

Guardalavaca

🛏 Sleeping

★ Villa Bely   CASA PARTICULAR $
(Map p372; ☑5-261-4192; villabely@nauta.cu; Los
Posos No 263, Guardalavaca village; r USD$25-30;
🅿❄) The resort alternative, this casa has a
top-floor apartment that's bigger and better
than your average hotel room. It works for
small families, with a tiny balcony and a
lovely sleeping area raised on a dais. There
are two smaller rooms below. It's just opposite the last highway exit from the all-inclusive zone.

Also offers snorkeling equipment and arranges guided horseback riding.

Brisas Guardalavaca   RESORT $$$
(Map p372; ☑2443-0218; Playa Guardalavaca; s/d
all-inclusive USD$110/160; 🅿❄@🛜🏊) Attract-
ing Canadians and trans-Atlantic snowbirds,
this 437-room resort is a package-tour paradise stirring memories of 1970s British holiday camps. Bonuses are huge rooms, floodlit
tennis courts and general lack of pretension.
The setup is a bit reminiscent of a retire-
ment home, with the kitsch never far from
the surface, but it's quieter than nearby offerings and has a decent beach.

Club Amigo Atlántico –
Guardalavaca   RESORT $$$
(Map p372; ☑2443-0121; Playa Guardalavaca;
s/d all-inclusive USD$90/140;   🅿❄@🛜🏊)
As cheap getaways go, this is Guardalavaca's bargain resort offering, but it's not for

particular guests. Cleanliness is not always
paramount in this 600-room village, an
aging mishmash of villas, bungalows and
standard rooms. An extensive kids' activities program makes it popular with families. There are more rocky inlets here than
further down the beach. Inland rooms are
quieter.

This hard-to-fathom resort fused the
former Guardalavaca and Atlántico hotels.
The latter was Guardalavaca's oldest resort,
completed in 1976 and christened by Fidel
Castro with a swim in the pool.

🍴 Eating & Drinking

★ El Ancla   SEAFOOD $$
(Map p372; ☑2443-0381; meals USD$4-20;
🕐noon-9:30pm) On a rocky promontory of
land at the far western end of Guardalavaca
beach, this glass-walled restaurant is a fine
spot to spend a few hours dining and sea
gazing. The 180-degree view is outrageous.
Somehow it didn't get blown away by Hurricane Ike in 2008. Come here for excellent
lobster served on white linen and decent
service.

El Uvero   CUBAN $$
(Map p372; ☑5-239-3571; alexuvero01@gmail.
com; Cuatro Caminos No 3; meals USD$10-18;
🕐11:30am-11:30pm) Four kilometers and a
short taxi ride east of Guardalavaca's main
resort strip, this modest-looking local house
in the village of Cuatro Caminos is well
worth the small effort to get here. Pride
of the menu is the *tres hermanos* (three
brothers) consisting of prawns, lobster and
white fish.

The place is guarded by an uvero (sea
grape tree) as the name implies.

Bar Pirata   BAR
(Map p372; Playa Guardalavaca; 🕐9am-9pm)
Right on the sand at Guardalavaca's liveliest
strip of beach, Pirata is your standard beach
shack with beer, music and enough ingredients to muster up a sand-free sandwich
lunch. It's accessed via the flea market just
west of Club Amigo Atlántico.

🛍 Shopping

Boulevard   MARKET
(Map p372; Playa Guardalavaca; 🕐7am-5pm) This
touristy, open-air handicraft market caters to resort clients from the surrounding
area. Find the usual Che merch, postcards
and beaded jewelry – not much outside the
knick-knack box.

CUBA'S ARCHAEOLOGICAL CAPITAL

Cuba's pre-Columbian history can be traced back over 8000 years, yet it rarely receives more than a passing mention in contemporary history books. Those interested in padding out the details should come to Holguín Province where the region around Banes has the highest concentration of pre-Columbian archaeological sites in the country.

Most archaeological remains unearthed so far in Cuba date from around 1050 to the early 1500s. The Taínos were the third wave of immigrants to reach the isles, in the footsteps of the less sophisticated Guanahatabeys and Siboneys with whom they ultimately coexisted. Primarily peace-loving, they were skilled farmers, weavers, ceramicists and boatbuilders, and their complex society exhibited an organized system of participatory government that was overseen by a series of local *caciques* (chiefs).

Sixty percent of the crops still grown in Cuba today were pioneered by Taíno farmers, who planted cotton to use in hammocks, fishing nets and bags. Adults practiced a form of artificial cranial deformation by flattening the soft skulls of their young children, and groups lived together in villages characterized by their thatched *bohíos* (rustic huts) and *bateys* (communal 'plazas'). A reconstructed Taíno village can be seen at the Aldea Taína (p371) near Guardalavaca. Next door in Museo Chorro de Maita (p371), Cuba's most extensive archaeological site, some of the exhumed skeletons exhibit cranial deformation.

Columbus described the Taínos with terms such as 'gentle,' 'sweet,' 'always laughing' and 'without knowledge of what is evil,' which makes the genocide that he inadvertently unleashed even more horrendous. Estimates vary wildly as to Cuba's indigenous population pre-Columbus, though 100,000 is a good consensus figure. Within 30 years, 90% of the Taínos had been wiped out.

As Taíno villages were built of wood and mud, they left no great towns or temples. Instead, the most important and emblematic artifacts unearthed are of *cemís* or idols, small figurines depicting Taíno deities. *Cemís* were cult objects that represented social status, political power or fertility.

The *hacha del Holguín*, a 600-year-old god-like figure made of peridotite rock, is on display in Holguín's Museo de Historia Provincial (p356). The *ídolo del oro*, a rare 10-karat gold fertility symbol from the 13th century or earlier, is in Banes' Museo Indocubano Bani (p375). The oldest *cemí* found to date in Cuba was discovered near Maisí in Guantánamo Province in the 1910s. Called the Ídolo de Tabaco, it dates from the 10th century and is made of Cuban hardwood. It is currently on display at the Museo Antropológico Montané (p94) in Havana University.

ℹ Information

MEDICAL SERVICES

The **Clínica Internacional de Guardalavaca** (☑ 2443-0312; Segunda No 15; ⊙ 24hr) runs 24 hours. Resorts offer medical services and have limited drugstores.

MONEY

Euros are accepted in all the Guardalavaca, Playa Esmeralda and Pesquero resorts. Additionally, all the big hotels have money-changing facilities, and there's a **Banco Financiero Internacional** (☑ 2443-0217; Centro Comercial Los Flamboyanes; ⊙ 9am-3pm Mon-Fri) in the Centro Comercial Los Flamboyanes.

TOURIST INFORMATION

Find travelers' assistance at **Asistur** (Map p372; ☑ 2443-0148; Centro Comercial Los Flamboyanes; ⊙ 8:30am-5pm Mon-Fri, to noon Sat) and an **Infotur desk** (Map p372; ☑ 2443-0260; Centro Comercial Los Flamboyanes; ⊙ 8am-4pm Mon-Sat) at the Centro Comercial Los Flamboyanes.

Make travel arrangements at the **Cubatur** (Map p372; ☑ 2443-0430; ⊙ 8am-5pm).

ℹ Getting There & Away

Transtur (☑ 2443-0490; comercialhlg@transtur.cu; round trip USD\$15) runs a tourist bus from Guardalavaca to Holguín via Playa Esmeralda and Playa Pesquero once a day.

You can also take a taxi from Guardalavaca to Holguín (one way USD\$25). For radio taxis, call **Cubataxi** (☑ 2443-0139) or **Transgaviota** (☑ 2443-4966). Shared colectivos or *maquinas* – often classic cars – run from Guardalavaca village to Holguín for USD\$5.

ℹ Getting Around

A Transtur shuttle bus (day pass USD\$5) in Guardalavaca links the three beach areas and the Aldea Taína (p371). Theoretically it runs three times a day in either direction, but check at your hotel to see if there are any glitches. Drop-offs include Parque Rocazul, Playa Pesquero, Playa

Costa Verde, Playa Esmeralda hotels, Club Amigo Atlántico – Guardalavaca and Aldea Taína.

Coches de caballos (horse carriages) run between Playa Esmeralda and Guardalavaca, or you can rent a moped (per day USD$25) or bicycle (free at all-inclusives) at the resorts. You can also taxi to Playa Esmeralda or Playa Pesqueros (USD$10).

For car rental, try **Cubacar** (📞 2443-0389; btwn Club Amigo Atlántico & Brisas Guardalavaca; ⊙ 7am-7:45pm). A **Cupet-Cimex gas station** (⊙ 24hr) is situated between Guardalavaca and Playa Esmeralda.

Banes

POP 77,883

The former sugar town of Banes is the site of one of Cuba's oddest historical moments. Cuban president Fulgencio Batista was born here in 1901. Some 47 years later, Fidel Castro and Birta Díaz Balart tied the knot in the local clapboard church of Nuestra Señora de la Caridad. Generous, and surely unsuspecting the groom would one day overthrow him, Batista gave the couple a honeymoon present of US$500.

Founded in 1887, this effervescent company town was a virtual fiefdom of the US-run United Fruit Company until the 1950s. Many of the old American company houses still remain. These days, the sun-streaked streets and squares feature cigar-smoking cronies slamming dominoes and mothers carrying meter-long loaves of bread; in short, everything Cuban that is missing from the all-inclusive resorts.

Thanks to its Taíno museum and the various indigenous sites nestled in the surrounding countryside, Banes is known as the archaeological capital of Cuba.

⊙ Sights

If you're coming from the resorts, Banes' biggest attraction might be enjoying the street life provided by a stroll through town. Don't miss the fine old company houses that once provided homes for the fat cats of United Fruit. Banes is one of those towns with no street signs and locals who don't know street names – they might just walk you where you want to go if you get lost.

⭐**Playa de Morales**   BEACH

One day in the not-too-distant future (after it's been Cancun-ized), we'll all wax nostalgic about this precious strip of sand situated 13km east of Banes along the paved

continuation of Tráfico. For the time being, enjoy whiling away an afternoon in this fishing village, dining with locals and watching the men mend their nets. A few kilometers to the north is the even quieter **Playa Puerto Rico.**

⭐**Museo Indocubano Bani**   MUSEUM

(Map p370; General Marrero No 305; USD$1; ⊙ 9am-5pm Tue-Sat, 8am-noon Sun) This museum's small but rich collection of indigenous artifacts is one of the best on the island. Don't miss the tiny golden fertility idol unearthed near Banes (one of only 20 gold artifacts ever found in Cuba). Excellent guides will enthusiastically show you round. **La Plaza Aborigen** outside has replicas of local cave paintings.

The museum's resident expert, **Luis Quiñones García** (📞 2480-2691; luisq1962@ nauta.cu; tours USD$2), will fill you in on every facet of indigenous culture and local archaeology. He also offers tours of the town.

Iglesia de Nuestra Señora de la Caridad   CHURCH

(Map p370; Parque Martí) On October 12, 1948, Fidel Castro Ruz and Birta Díaz Balart were married in this unusual art deco church in the center of Banes. After their divorce in 1954, Birta remarried and moved to Spain. Through their only child, Fidelito, Fidel has several grandchildren.

Steam Locomotive 964   HISTORIC SITE

(Map p370; Tráfico, El Panchito) Railway enthusiasts shouldn't miss this old steamer built at the HK Porter Locomotive Works in Pittsburgh, Pennsylvania, in 1888, now on display 400m east of the bus station.

🛏 Sleeping

Villa Lao   CASA PARTICULAR $

(📞 2480-3049; Bayamo No 78, btwn José M Heredia & Augusto Blanco; r USD$25; ✲) Shimmering clean, professionally run house with two rooms; grab the upstairs one with its kitchen and plant-laden terrace if possible. It's got a front porch rocker overlooking the central park.

Villa Gilma   CASA PARTICULAR $

(📞 2480-2204; Calle H No 1526, btwn Veguitas & Francisco Franco; r USD$25; ✲) This classic colonial abode stands guard at the entrance to the town center and has one huge room (those ceilings must be 7m high) with private bath and fridge.

Casa 'Las Delicias' CASA PARTICULAR **$**
(☑ 2480-2905; Augusto Blanco No 1107, btwn Bruno Merino & Bayamo; r USD$25; ❀) One spick-and-span room, a private entrance, friendly owners and decent food in the downstairs private restaurant – what more could you ask from tranquil Banes?

✕ Eating

Restaurante Don Carlos CUBAN **$**
(☑ 2480-2176; Veguitas No 1702, cnr Calle H; meals USD$3-8; ☺ noon-10pm) Salt-of-the-earth, meet-the-locals private restaurant where you can discover the other side of Cuba over some pretty decent seafood less than 30 minutes from Guardalavaca's gigantic resorts.

Restaurant El Latino CARIBBEAN **$**
(General Marrero No 710; mains USD$5-8; ☺ 11am-11pm) A long-standing Banes favorite, this state-run place should be newly renovated by the time you visit. With all the usual Creole dishes delivered with a little extra flair and charm, the service is good and the accompanying musicians unusually talented and discreet.

☆ Entertainment

Casa de Cultura ARTS CENTER
(☑ 2480-4658; General Marrero No 320) This venue, housed in the former Casino Español (1926), has a regular Sunday *trova* (traditional poetic song) matinee at 3pm and Saturday *peña del rap* (rap music session) at 9pm. On any given evening, you might find municipal band rehearsals, discos, *son* septets and zen-inducing jazz jams.

❶ Getting There & Away

From the **bus station** (cnr Tráfico & Mulas), there are two daily buses (CUP$1) to Holguín (72km). There are no timetables; check the chalkboards. Trucks (CUP$5) leave Banes for Holguín more frequently.

A taxi from Guardalavaca (33km) will cost around USD$25 one way. If you're fit and adventurous, getting here from Guardalavaca by bicycle is a rare treat through undulating, bucolic terrain. This route can also be tackled by moped.

Sierra del Cristal

Cuba's own 'little Switzerland' is a rugged amalgam of the Sierra del Cristal and the Altiplanicie de Nipe, with two important national parks. Parque Nacional Sierra Cristal, Cuba's oldest, was founded in 1930 and harbors 1213m Pico de Cristal, the province's highest summit. Of more interest to travelers, the piney 53-sq-km Parque Nacional La Mensura, 30km south of Mayarí, protects the island's highest waterfall. Notable for its cool alpine microclimate and 100 or more species of endemic plants, La Mensura offers hiking and horseback riding and accommodation in a Gaviota-run ecolodge. It also hosts a mountain research center run by Academia de Ciencias de Cuba.

Flanking the Sierra del Cristal, the landscape inspired Buena Vista Social Club's hit 'Chan Chan.' Now frequented by aficionados of lead singer Compay Segundo, the route is often dubbed Ruta de Chan Chan.

◎ Sights

★ Salto del Guayabo WATERFALL
(USD$5) At just over 100m in height, Guayabo (15km from the Villa Pinares del Mayarí) is considered the highest waterfall in Cuba. There's a spectacular overlook, and the guided 1.2km hike to its base through fecund tropical forest includes swimming in a natural pool.

Salto de Capiro WATERFALL
A short 2km trail from Villa Pinares del Mayarí brings you to this hidden waterfall in lush forest.

Farallones de Seboruco CAVE
Speleologists may want to ask about trips to these ghostly caves, designated a national monument, which contain aboriginal cave paintings.

🏃 Activities

Most activities can be organized at Villa Pinares del Mayarí or via 4WD excursions from Guardalavaca's or Santiago de Cuba's hotels.

Sendero La Sabina HIKING
(USD$3) A short interpretive trail at the Centro Investigaciones para la Montaña, located 1km from Villa Pinares del Mayarí. Check out the vegetation of eight different ecosystems, including a 150-year-old tree – the 'Ocuje Colorado' – and rare orchids.

Hacienda La Mensura HORSEBACK RIDING
Eight kilometers from Villa Pinares del Mayarí is this breeding center for exotic animals such as antelope. Horseback riding for all levels can be arranged here through Villa Pinares del Mayarí.

🛏 Sleeping

★ **Villa Pinares del Mayarí** CABIN $$
(☎2445-5628; s/d incl breakfast USD$38/55; P❄☀) Ensconced in one of Cuba's largest pine forests, Pinares del Mayarí stands between the Altiplanicie de Nipe and Sierra del Cristal at 600m. Part chalet resort, part mountain retreat, this isolated alpine-style rural hideaway features two- and three-bedroom cabins with hot showers and comfortable beds. There's a large restaurant (mains USD$4 to USD$9), bar, sports court, gym and sublime pool.

El Cupey, a small natural lake, sits 300m away. It's great for an early morning dip. The compound, 30km south of Mayarí on a rough dirt road, is run by Gaviota.

❶ Getting There & Away

The only way to get to Villa Pinares del Mayarí and Parque Nacional La Mensura outside an organized tour is via car, taxi (from Holguín USD$50) or bicycle (if you're adventurous and it's not a Cuban one).

The access road is mostly a rough collection of holes with the odd bit of asphalt thrown in, but it's passable in a hire car if driven with care. You'll need at least 1½ hours to cover the 30km.

Cayo Saetía

East of Mayarí, the road becomes increasingly potholed, and the dusty rural surroundings are progressively more remote. The culmination of this rustic drive is lovely Cayo Saetía, a small, flat, wooded island in Bahía de Nipe that's connected to the mainland by a small bridge. During the 1970s and '80s, this was a favored hunting ground for communist apparatchiks who enjoyed spraying lead into the local wildlife. Now Cayo Saetía is a protected wildlife park with 19 species of exotic animals, including camels, zebras, antelopes, ostriches and deer.

Bisected by grassy meadows and adorned by hidden coves and beaches, it's the closest Cuba gets to an African wildlife reserve. However, it's still run by the military and not overly friendly to visitors – particularly those just out to explore. The gorgeous beach is often commandeered by organized catamaran groups from Guardalavaca.

Villa Cayo Saetía (☎2451-6900; s/d incl breakfast USD$54/82, all-inclusive USD$76/126; ❄), a rustic key resort on a 42-sq-km island at the entrance to Bahía de Nipe, is small, remote and more upmarket than the price suggests. The 12 rooms are split into rustic and standard *cabañas* with a minimal price differential. You'll feel as if you're 1000 miles from anywhere.

The in-house restaurant (mains CUC$5 to CUC$12), **La Güira**, sits decked out Hemingway-style with hunting trophies mounted on the wall like gory art. It's fully in tune with the exotic meats, such as antelope, found on the menu.

❶ Getting There & Away

Road conditions are poor in the final 20km approaching the key (separated by a bridge). Those arriving by car reach a control post 15km off the main road at the bridge; every visitor must pay USD$7 here for access. It's another 8km along a rough, unpaved road to the resort.

If it hasn't been raining, a rental car will make it with care. Don't attempt the drive in rain as the clay surface becomes impossibly slippery. Be warned that without reservations you will be in for a world of harassment by the guards.

From Guardalavaca, there are catamaran day tours (per person USD$120), arranged through travel agencies and resorts.

❶ Getting Around

There are three ways to explore Cayo Saetía, aside from the obvious two-legged sorties from the villa itself. A one-hour 4WD safari costs USD$9 per person, and there are also excursions by horse and boat, arranged directly through the resort.

POPULATION
834,380

HIGHEST POINT
Pico Bayamesa:
1730m

**BEST BOUTIQUE
HOTEL**
Hotel Telégrafo
(p385)

**BEST CARIBBEAN
FOOD**
Restaurante San
Salvador de Bayamo
(p386)

**BEST RURAL
HOTEL**
Villa Santo Domingo
(p390)

WHEN TO GO

Jan–Feb
The beach area of
Marea del Portillo
becomes the warm-
est place in Cuba.
Don't miss the
Incendio de Bayamo
on January 12.

Mar–Apr
The driest times for
hiking the trails, with
bearable nighttime
temperatures.

May–Dec
Low season brings
humid and wet
conditions in the
mountains

Gran Parque Nacional Sierra Maestra (p388)
ALEXANDRE G. ROSA/SHUTTERSTOCK ©

Granma Province

Few parts of the world get named after yachts, which helps explain why in Granma (christened for the boat that delivered Fidel Castro and his bedraggled revolutionaries ashore to kick-start a guerrilla war in 1956) Cuba's *viva la Revolución* spirit burns most fiercely. This is the land where José Martí died and where Granma native Carlos Manuel de Céspedes freed his enslaved people and formally declared Cuban independence for the first time in 1868.

The alluringly isolated countryside helped the revolutionary cause. Road-scarce Granma is one of Cuba's remotest regions, with lofty tropical mountains dense enough to harbor Castro for more than two years in the 1950s.

Its isolation has bred a special brand of Cuban identity. Granma's settlements are esoteric places enlivened with weekly street parties (with outdoor barbecues and archaic hand-operated street organs), and provincial capital Bayamo is among the most tranquil and cleanest places in the archipelago.

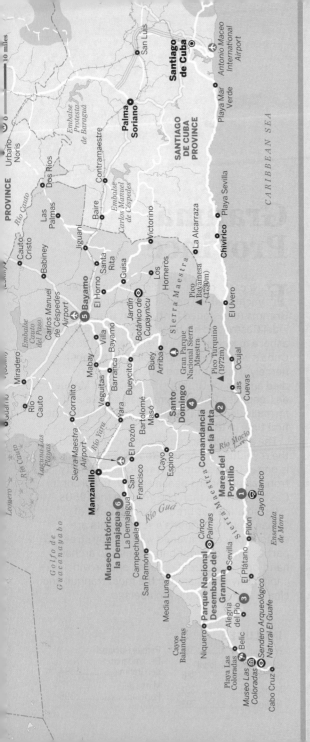

Granma Province Highlights

1 **Marea del Portillo**
(p396) Enjoying one of Cuba's balmiest microclimates in this secluded beach resort.

2 **Comandancia de la Plata** (p388) Trekking up to Fidel's wartime headquarters in Gran Parque Nacional Sierra Maestra.

3 **Parque Nacional Desembarco del Granma** (p394) Exploring marine terraces and archaeological remains.

4 **Santo Domingo** (p389) Getting a dose of mountain air at the bucolic entrance to Gran Parque Nacional Sierra Maestra with horseback riding through the hills or a stroll to a swimming hole.

5 **Fiesta de la Cubanía** (p383) Immersing yourself in the inimitable Bayamo party spirit with pork roast, street organs and a chess game.

6 **Museo Histórico La Demajagua** (p391) Visiting the site where the Cubans uttered their first cry of independence.

History

Stone petroglyphs and remnants of Taíno pottery unearthed in Parque Nacional Desembarco del Granma suggest the existence of native cultures in the Granma region long before the Spanish arrived.

Columbus, during his second voyage, was the first European to explore the area, taking shelter from a storm in the Golfo de Guacanayabo. All other early development schemes came to nothing, and by the 17th century Granma's untamed coast had become the preserve of pirates and corsairs.

On October 10, 1868, sugar-plantation owner Carlos Manuel de Céspedes called for the abolition of slavery from his Demajagua sugar mill near Manzanillo, freed his own enslaved people by example and incited the First War of Independence.

Drama unfolded again in 1895 when the founder of the Cuban Revolutionary Party, José Martí, was killed in Dos Ríos just a month and a half after landing with Máximo Gómez off the coast of Guantánamo to ignite the Spanish–Cuban–American War.

More recent history saw Fidel Castro and 81 rebel soldiers disembark from the yacht *Granma* off the province's coast at Playa Las Coloradas (ironically, the boat that literally launched the revolution – and later gave the province its present name – was purchased from an American, who had named it in honor of his grandmother). Routed by Batista's troops shortly after landing in a sugarcane field at Alegría del Pío, 15 or so survivors managed to escape into the Sierra Maestra, establishing headquarters at Comandancia de la Plata. From there they coordinated the armed struggle, broadcasting their progress and consolidating their support among sympathizers nationwide. After two years of harsh conditions and unprecedented beard growth, the forces of the M-26-7 (July 26 Movement) triumphed in 1959.

Bayamo

POP 159,629

Elegant and old, this relatively hush city spells oasis to the traveler weary of confrontation. Predating both Havana and Santiago, it has been cast for time immemorial as the city that kick-started Cuban independence. Yet self-important it isn't. The *ciudad de los coches* (city of horse carts) is an easygoing, slow-paced, trapped-in-time place, where you're more likely to be quoted literature than sold trinkets. Cuba's balmiest provincial

capital, it resounds to the clip-clop of hooves; nearly half the population use horses for daily travel.

Bayamo has played a sacrificial role in Cuba's convoluted historical development. '*Como España quemó a Sagunto, así Cuba quemó a Bayamo,*' (As the Spanish burnt Sagunto, the Cubans burnt Bayamo) wrote José Martí in the 1890s. While an 1869 arson blaze destroyed many of the city's classic colonial buildings, there are still plenty left. Neither did it undermine Bayamo's intransigent spirit or its long-standing traditions.

History

Founded in 1513 as the second of Diego Velázquez de Cuéllar's seven original villas (after Baracoa), Bayamo's early history was characterized by clashes between the indigenous Taíno people and the incoming colonists. But with the Taíno population devastated by deadly European diseases such as smallpox, the resistance soon fizzled out. By the end of the 16th century, Bayamo had grown rich and was established as the region's most important cattle-ranching and sugarcane-growing center. Frequented by pirates, the town filled its coffers further in the 17th and 18th centuries via a clandestine smuggling ring run out of the nearby port of Manzanillo. Bayamo's new class of merchants and landowners lavishly invested their money in fine houses and expensive overseas education for their offspring.

One such protégé was local lawyer-turned-revolutionary Carlos Manuel de Céspedes, who, defying the traditional colonial will, led an army against his hometown in 1868 in an attempt to wrest control from the conservative Spanish authorities. But the liberation proved short-lived. After the defeat of an ill-prepared rebel army by 3000 regular Spanish troops near the Río Cauto on January 12, 1869, the townspeople – sensing an imminent Spanish reoccupation – set their town on fire rather than see it fall into enemy hands.

Bayamo was also the birthplace of Perucho Figueredo, composer of the Cuban national anthem, which begins, rather patriotically, with the words *Al combate corred, bayameses* (Run to battle, people of Bayamo).

In 2006, Fidel Castro gave his last large-scale public oration in Bayamo's Plaza de la Patria: there to give his annual commemorative 'Triumphs of the Revolution' speech, he was taken ill shortly after and within days handed power over to his brother Raúl.

◉ Sights

★ **Parque Céspedes** SQUARE

(Plaza de la Revolución; Map p384) One of Cuba's leafiest squares, Bayamo's central meeting point is surrounded by pedestrian-only streets, making it a rare and peaceful spot. In addition to its friendly airs and role as the city's best outdoor music venue (orchestras regularly play here), the square is loaded with historical significance.

In 1868 Céspedes proclaimed Cuba's independence for the first time in front of the columned Ayuntamiento (City Hall; Map p384; General García). The square is surrounded by grand monuments and big trees loaded with birdlife at dusk. Facing each other in the center are a bronze statue of Carlos Manuel de Céspedes, hero of the First War of Independence, and a marble bust of Perucho Figueredo, with the lyrics of the Cuban national anthem (which he wrote), carved upon it.

★ **Casa Natal de Carlos Manuel de Céspedes** MUSEUM

(Map p384; Maceo No 57; USD$1; ⊙9am-5pm Tue-Fri, 9am-5pm & 8-10pm Sat, 10am-1:30pm Sun) Birthplace of the 'father of the motherland,' this museum is where Céspedes was born (on April 18, 1819) and spent his first 12 years. Inside, Céspedes memorabilia is complemented by a collection of spectacularly preserved period furniture. It's notable architecturally as Bayamo's only remaining two-story colonial house, one of the few buildings to survive the 1869 fire.

Fabrica de los Coches FACTORY

(☑2341-1644; Prolongación General García No 530; USD$1; ⊙8am-3pm Mon-Fri & every 2nd Sat) It's worth the jaunt to observe the goings-on at Cuba's only handcrafted coche (horse cart) production line. Most horse carts you'll see in Cuba are metal, but these are fashioned in wood and take far longer to produce (up to three months per cart). You'll see horse carts in various stages of completion, meet the workers and be able to buy Bayamo's best souvenir: miniature model horse carts with incredible attention to detail. The big ones cost about 8000 pesos (USD$325) and don't fit quite so well into a suitcase.

Paseo Bayamés AREA

(Calle General García; Map p384) Bayamo's main shopping street was pedestrianized in the 1990s and reconfigured with benches and funky artwork. At its southern end you'll find wax museum Museo de Cera; centrally, there are various public utilities and Cuban-style commerce, including food stalls at night.

Museo de Cera MUSEUM

(Map p384; ☑2342-5421; General García No 261; USD$2; ⊙9am-5pm Tue-Fri, 10am-1pm & 7-10pm Sat, 9am-noon Sun) The tiny Museo de Cera, Bayamo's diminutive version of Madame Tussauds, has convincing waxworks of Cuban personalities such as Polo Montañez, Benny Moré and local hero Carlos Puebla. On a more internationalist note, you'll also find Gabriel García Márquez and Hugo Chávez.

Plaza de la Patria PLAZA

(Av Felino Figueredo) This square is where Fidel Castro gave his final, rousing public speech in July 2006 before being taken ill and stepping down as president. The monument to the Cuban greats here features Carlos Manuel de Céspedes, Antonio Maceo, Máximo Gómez, Perucho Figueredo and, subtly placed left of center, Fidel: it's the only monument he appears on in Cuba.

Parque Chapuzón PARK

(Map p384; Av Amado Estévez) Greenery beckons about a kilometer from Bayamo's center where the Bayamo River has carved a lush belt through the urban grid. Locals come to this blissful spot to water their horses or have a family barbecue. Footpaths and gazebo-shaped stalls selling food and drink embellish the banks but never detract from the all-pervading mood of tranquility.

Capilla de la Dolorosa CHURCH

(Map p384; cnr José Joaquín Palma & Plaza del Himno; donations accepted; ⊙9am-noon & 3-5pm Mon-Fri, 9am-noon Sat) This is the one original section of Bayamo's main church to survive the 1869 fire. It sports a gilded wooden altar.

Catedral de San Salvador de Bayamo CHURCH

(Map p384; ☑2342-2514; José Joaquín Palma No 130) There's been a church on this site since 1514. The current edifice dates from 1740 but was devastated in the 1869 fire, so much of what you see results from building work in 1919. One original section surviving the fire is the Capilla de la Dolorosa (p382) with its gilded wooden altar.

A highlight of the main church is the central arch, which exhibits a mural depicting the blessing of the Cuban flag in front of the revolutionary army on October 20, 1868. Outside, Plaza del Himno Nacional is where the Cuban national anthem, 'La Bayamesa,' was sung for the first time in 1868.

Museo Provincial
MUSEUM

(Map p384; ☑2342-4125; Maceo No 55; USD$5; ⊙8am-5pm Tue-Fri, from 9am Sat, 9am-1pm Sun) Directly next door to Céspedes' ex-home, this provincial museum completes Bayamo's historical trajectory with a yellowing city document dating from 1567 and a rare photo of Bayamo immediately after the fire.

Torre de San Juan Evangelista
RUINS

(Map p384; cnr José Martí & Av Amado Estévez) A church dating from Bayamo's earliest years stood at this busy intersection until it was destroyed in the great fire of 1869. Later, the church's tower served as the entrance to the first cemetery in Cuba, closed in 1919. The cemetery was demolished in 1940, but the tower survived. A monument to local poet José Joaquín Palma (1844–1911) stands in the park diagonally across the street from the tower, and beside the tower is a bronze statue of Francisco Vicente Aguilera (1821–77), who led the independence struggle in Bayamo.

Activities & Tours

Bayamo is known for its cerebral chess players (Céspedes was the Kasparov of his day) and Saturday night street parties, often to the tune of antiquated street organs (imported via Manzanillo). All three are on show at the weekly Fiesta de la Cubanía, one of the island's most authentic street shows – bayamés to its core.

Walking around is extra pleasant since the whole Plaza de la Revolucíon (Parque Céspedes) and the streets surrounding the cathedral are pedestrian only. Horse-and-cart tours can be arranged at Cubanacán (Map p384; Maceo; ⊙9am-noon & 1-4:30pm Mon-Sat). There are good private guided tours operating around Bayamo and, further afield, for Gran Parque Nacional Sierra Maestra.

Academia de Ajedrez
CHESS

(Map p384; ☑2342-9179; José A Saco No 63, btwn General García & Céspedes; ⊙9am-noon, 2-3:30pm & 8-10pm Mon-Fri) Catering to students in school uniforms, the Academia de Ajedrez is the place to go to improve your pawn-king-four technique. Stop by to see if any potential opponents await a friendly game. Pictures of Cuban heroes emblazoned onto the walls of this cerebral institution offer plenty of inspiration.

Anley Rosales Benitez
TOURS

(☑5-292-2209; www.bayamotravelagent.com; Carretera Central No 478) Anley coordinates trips to the Sierra Maestra, which can be difficult to find transport for on your own. Since he

doesn't make all trips personally, confirm bilingual guide services ahead. The highlight tour takes in the revolutionary sites of the 1956–58 years when the rebels were holed up hereabouts, such as the village where Fidel famously played baseball with locals.

Services include everything from day trips to the Jardín Botánico Cupaynicu to Bayamo airport pick up and all-inclusive Comandancia de la Plata excursions (two people USD$115).

Festivals & Events

Fiesta de la Cubanía
FIESTA

(⊙8pm Sat) Bayamo's quintessential nighttime attraction is an ebullient street party, the likes of which are found nowhere else in Cuba. It includes the locally famous pipe organs, whole roast pig, an eye-watering oyster drink called ostiones and – incongruously in the middle of it all – rows of tables laid out diligently with chess sets. Dancing is, of course, de rigueur.

Traditionally the fiesta has been held in Calle Saco close to the main square but, to the chagrin of many locals, it has been moved to a site just outside the center in Plaza de la Fiesta. Check its current status at Infotur (p387).

Incendio de Bayamo
CULTURAL

(⊙Jan 12) The biggest annual event is the Incendio de Bayamo, remembering the city's 1869 burning with live music and theatrical performances in Parque Céspedes, and culminating in fireworks launched from nearby buildings.

Sleeping

Villa La Paz
CASA PARTICULAR $

(Map p384; ☑5-277-3459, 2342-3949; anyoleg 2005@yahoo.es; Coronel J Estrada No 32, btwn William Soler & Av Milanés; r USD$20-25; ❄@✆) Any visitor to Cuba would consider this spotless modern home with attractive renovated rooms great value. Guests have flat-screen TVs, wi-fi and their own separate dining area. While the house is short on outdoor spaces, the indoor ones are extra pleasant, as are the hosts, who speak English and Russian.

Casa Olga
CASA PARTICULAR $

(Map p384; ☑5-495-5954, 2342-3859; olgacr@ nauta.cu; Parada No 16, cnr Martí; r USD$25; ❄✆) With a balcony gazing out on the plaza, these three 2nd-floor rooms couldn't be more central. Olga is a welcoming host who prepares substantial breakfasts. Open your window

Bayamo

N
0 —————————— 200 m
0 —————————— 0.1 miles

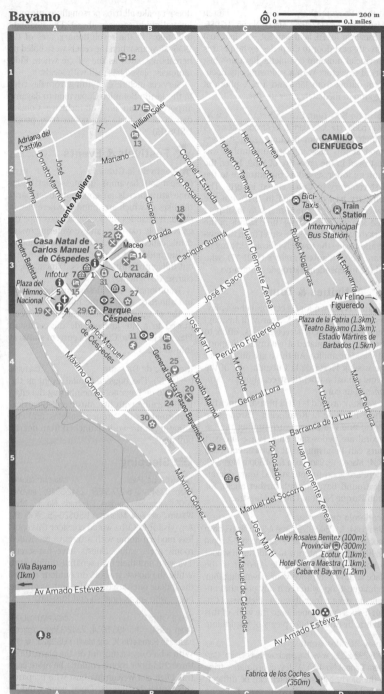

GRANMA PROVINCE BAYAMO

Bayamo

and suave sounds from the Casa de la Trova (situated opposite) waft in.

Casa de la Amistad   CASA PARTICULAR $
(Map p384; ☑ 2342-5769; gabytellez2003@gmail.com; Pío Rosado No 60, btwn Ramíriez & N López; r USD$25; P ❋ @ ☎) Gabriel and Rosa let out two spacious apartments on the upper floor of their pastel-shaded house. Guests have a private entrance, kitchen, sitting area, bedroom and bathroom. They are fine and helpful hosts who speak excellent English, and there's even wi-fi.

Casa Alvaro   CASA PARTICULAR $
(Map p384; ☑ 2342-4861, 5-815-0749; vere55@nauta.com; Vincente Aguilera No 240; r USD$25; ❋) Offers three sizable rooms and breakfasts among Bayamo's best, with divine *bocadillos* (toasted ham and cheese sandwiches) and Spanish tortilla served on a terrace that exudes tranquility despite the busy location.

★ **Hotel Telégrafo**   BOUTIQUE HOTEL $$
(Map p384; ☑ 2342-5510; José A Saco No 275, cnr Mármol; s/d incl breakfast USD$100/115; ❋) A modern rooftop bar, Jacuzzi and bright plant-laden courtyard enhance the colonial bones of the revamped Hotel Telégrafo, making it the most luxurious in town. Equipped with amenities like hairdryers, coffee makers and flat-screen TVs, the 21 rooms themselves feel more antiseptic than the public areas.

Hotel Royalton   HOTEL $$
(Map p384; ☑ 2342-2290; Maceo No 53; s/d USD$90/104; ❋ ☎) Bayamo's most central hotel has 33 rooms upgraded to boutique standard with power showers and flat-screen TVs; there's also a roof terrace. Downstairs an attractive bar complements the reception area with seats spilling out onto a sidewalk terrace overlooking Parque Céspedes. The on-site restaurant is a good eating option.

Hotel Sierra Maestra   HOTEL $$
(☑ 2342-7970; Carretera Central; s/d USD$56/64; P ❋ ☎ ⛱) With a ring of the Soviet '70s about it, the Sierra Maestra hardly merits its three stars, although rooms have had some much-needed attention. Three kilometers from the town center, it's OK for an overnighter. Let the mojitos at the bar be your consolation.

Villa Bayamo   HOTEL $$
(☑ 2342-3102; s/d USD$58/64; P ❋ ⛱) This out-of-town option (it's 3km southwest of the center on the road to Manzanillo) offers a definitive rural feel and a pleasant swimming pool overlooking fields at the back. Has well-appointed rooms and a reasonable restaurant.

JARDÍN BOTÁNICO CUPAYNICU

For a floral appreciation of Bayamo's evergreen hinterland, head to this botanic garden about 16km outside the city off the Guisa road. It's on very few itineraries, so you can have the serene 104 hectares more or less to yourself. There are 74 types of palms, scores of cacti, blooming orchids and sections for endangered and medicinal plants.

The guided tour (Spanish only) gains you access to greenhouses, notable for the showy ornamentals. To get here, take the road to Santiago de Cuba for 6km and turn left at the signposted junction for Guisa. After 10km you'll see the botanic garden sign on the right. From Bayamo, trucks (MN$10) heading in this direction leave from the intermunicipal bus station in front of the train station.

🍴 Eating

There's some unique street food in Bayamo, sold from Calle Saco and Parque Céspedes. Otherwise, you're dealing with mainly local restaurants with prices in Cuban pesos.

El Polinesio   CUBAN **$**
(Map p384; ☑ 2342-2449; Parada No 125, btwn Pío Rosado & Cisneros; meals USD$6-8; ☺ noon-11pm) This longtime staple debuted in the days when private restaurants could only seat 12 people and serve pork and chicken. Today's menu ventures into seafood with wine sauce and chicken with vegetables. What hasn't changed is the venue and the service. Big smiles all round.

La Sevillana   SPANISH **$**
(Map p384; ☑ 2342-1472; General García, btwn General Lora & Perucho Figueredo; mains USD$1-4; ☺ noon-2pm & 6-10pm) Come and see Cuban chefs attempt Spanish cuisine – paella and *garbanzos* (chickpeas). This is a new kind of peso restaurant, with a dress code (no shorts), a door attendant in a suit, and a reservations policy. Press your trousers, brush up on your Spanish, but don't expect *sevillano* creativity.

★ Restaurante San Salvador de Bayamo   CARIBBEAN **$$**
(Map p384; ☑ 2342-6942; Maceo No 107; mains USD$3-9; ☺ noon-11pm) Who isn't in the mood to be serenaded by violins in a splendid colonial place? Thanks to the knowledgeable owner, dishes avoid the obvious to tap into indigenous and buccaneer influences on regional cuisine. Try tortilla with cassava and local cheese or the *cerveza mambisa,* jagua juice fermented in a sugarcane stalk.

★ Meson La Cuchipapa   CUBAN **$$**
(Map p384; ☑ 2341-1992; lacuchipapa@gmail.com; Parada, btwn Mármol & Martí; mains USD$6-10; ☺ 11am-midnight) Real *comida cubana* fashioned on reviving traditions rarely known to visitors. At wooden picnic benches, try cassava bread originally consumed by native Taínos, fragrant bean stews and big portions of regular fare such as smoked pork chops. You can also brave *frutanga,* a cocktail starring the local firewater sweetened with sugarcane crushed by your own hand on an old handcrank mill.

Restaurante Plaza   CUBAN **$$**
(Map p384; ☑ 2342-2290; Maceo No 53, Hotel Royalton; mains USD$6-10; ☺ 7:30am-10:30pm) The Hotel Royalton hosts one of the town's best restaurants; nothing legendary mind you, but with an excellent setting including the option to sit outside overlooking one of Cuba's most pleasant squares. Food is generously labeled 'international' with a strong meat, rice and beans bias. Service is officious on a bad day, quietly polite on a good one.

La Bodega   CARIBBEAN **$$**
(Map p384; ☑ 2342-1011; Plaza del Himno Nacional No 34; meals USD$5-15, cover after 9pm USD$3; ☺ 11am-1am) On Bayamo's main square, head to the rear terrace overlooking Río Bayamo, fringed by a bucolic backdrop worthy of an isolated country villa. Set menus offer pork or *vaca frita* (a kind of shredded beef) with sides and dessert. Try the beef and taste the coffee, or simply relax before the tour groups arrive. Has live music on some afternoons.

🍷 Drinking & Nightlife

Bayamo is one of Cuba's quieter cities on the nightlife front, but live music comes to restaurants and bars. The main hotels have decent bars.

Café Literario Ventana Sur   BAR
(Map p384; Perucho Figueredo No 62; ☺ 10am-midnight) Join the town's poets, artists and musicians imbibing strong coffee and swapping ideas. You'll see them at the alfresco tables strumming their guitars before launching

into spontaneous outbreaks of music – Silvio Rodríguez meets Radiohead.

Bar La Esquina
BAR

(Map p384; ☑ 2342-1731; cnr Mármol & Maceo; ☺ noon-midnight) International cocktails are served in this tiny corner bar replete with plenty of local atmosphere.

Piano Bar
BAR

(Map p384; ☑ 2342-4027; Bartholomé Masó, btwn General García & Mármol; ☺ noon-2am) Ice-cold air-con, starched tablecloths, stern waiters, good live music from piano recitals to *trovadores* (folk singers) and crooners of *musica romantica*. So plush it's sometimes invite-only. Music is daily, except for Mondays.

La Taberna
BAR

(Map p384; General García, btwn José A Saco & Perucho Figueredo; ☺ 10am-10pm) This busy local place on the main shopping street has beer on tap in ceramic mugs and a constant buzz of conversation. Pay in Cuban pesos.

☆ Entertainment

Teatro Bayamo
THEATER

(☑ 2342-5106; cnr Figueredo & Av Maceo, Reparto Jesús Menéndez) Six blocks northeast of the bus station, opposite Plaza de la Patria, lies one of the Oriente's most impressive theaters. Constructed in 1982, the theater was converted into its current function only in 2007. The *vitrales* (stained glass windows) in the lobby are sensational. Performances are usually Wednesday, Saturday or Sunday.

Casa de la Trova
la Bayamesa
TRADITIONAL MUSIC

(Map p384; ☑ 2342-5673; Maceo No 111; USD$1; ☺ 10am-1am) One of Cuba's best *trova* houses, in a lovely colonial building on Maceo. Pictures on the wall display the famous '70s afro of Bayamo-born *trova* king Pablo Milanés. There's no sign outside, but you'll likely follow your ears to find it.

Uneac
ARTS CENTER

(Map p384; ☑ 2342-3670; Céspedes No 158; ☺ hours vary) You can catch heartfelt *boleros* (danceable Cuban ballads)on the flowery patio here in the former home of disgraced first president Tomás Estrada Palma, the man invariably blamed for handing Guantánamo to the *yanquis* (Yankees).

Cine Céspedes
CINEMA

(Map p384; ☑ 2342-4267; Libertad No 4; CUP$5) This cinema is on the western side of Parque Céspedes by the post office. It offers everything from Gutiérrez Alea to the latest Hollywood blockbuster (occasional English-language films with Spanish subtitles).

Casa de la Cultura
ARTS CENTER

(Map p384; ☑ 2342-5917; General García No 15) Wide-ranging cultural events, including art expos, on the east side of Parque Céspedes.

🛍 Shopping

Paseo Bayamés is the main pedestrian shopping street but, with few tourists, stores are mainly aimed at locals.

ARTex
GIFTS & SOUVENIRS

(Map p384; ☑ 2348-7956; General García No 7; ☺ 9am-4:30pm Mon-Sat) The usual mix of Che Guevara T-shirts and bogus Santería dolls in Parque Céspedes.

ⓘ Information

INTERNET ACCESS

There is wi-fi in the Plaza de la Revolucion and the small park in front of the Casa de la Trova.

Buy internet scratch cards at **Etecsa Telepunto** (☑ 2342-8353; General García, btwn Saco & Figueredo; internet per hour USD$1.50; ☺ 8:30am-7pm Mon-Fri, to 11pm Sat) or use the internet terminals; it's rarely busy.

MEDICAL SERVICES

Hospital Carlos Manuel de Céspedes (☑ 2342-5012; Km 1, Carretera Central)

Farmacia Internacional (☑ 2342-9596; General García, btwn Figueredo & General Lora; ☺ 8am-noon & 1-5pm Mon-Sat)

MONEY

There are plenty of ATMs.

Banco de Crédito y Comercio (☑ 2342-6340; cnr General García & Saco; ☺ 8am-4pm Mon-Fri, to 11am Sat) Has an ATM.

Cadeca (☑ 2342-7222; Saco No 101; ☺ 8:30am-4pm Mon-Sat) Has money-changing facilities.

TOURIST INFORMATION

Infotur (Map p384; ☑ 2342-3468; Plaza del Himno Nacional, cnr Joaquín Palma; ☺ 8:30am-noon & 1-5pm Mon-Fri) staff can help flesh out your plans; **Ecotur** (☑ ext 639 2348-7006; Carretera Central, Hotel Sierra Maestra) will assist in manifesting them.

ⓘ Getting There & Away

BUS & TRUCK

The **provincial bus station** (☑ 2342-7482; cnr Carretera Central & Av Felino Figueredo) has Víazul buses (www.viazul.com) to several destinations.

Buses heading west also stop at Las Tunas (USD$6), Camagüey (USD$11), Ciego de Ávila (USD$17), Sancti Spíritus (USD$21) and Santa Clara (USD$26).

Passenger trucks leave from an adjacent terminal for Santiago de Cuba, Holguín, Manzanillo, Pilón and Niquero several times per day. You can truck it to Bartolomé Masó, as close as you can get on public transport to the Sierra Maestra trailhead. Trucks leave when full, and you pay as you board.

The **intermunicipal bus station** (Map p384; ☑ 2342-4040; cnr Saco & Línea), opposite the train station, receives mostly local buses of little use to travelers, although trucks to Guisa leave from here.

VÍAZUL BUS DEPARTURES FROM BAYAMO

Destination	Cost (USD$)	Duration (hr)	Frequency (daily)
Havana	44	13½	3
Holguín	6	1¼	4
Santiago	7	2	5
Trinidad	26	9½	1
Varadero	42	13¼	1

TAXI

Taxis can be procured for hard-to-reach destinations such as Manzanillo (USD$30), Pilón (USD$75) and Niquero (USD$80). Prices are estimates and will depend on the current price of petrol. Nonetheless, it is usually cheaper to reach all these places by taxi than by rental car.

TRAIN

The **train station** (☑ 2342-3056; cnr Saco & Línea) is 1km east of the center. There are three local trains a day to Manzanillo (via Yara). The long-distance Havana–Manzanillo train passes through Bayamo every third day.

❶ Getting Around

Cubataxi (☑ 2342-4313) can supply a taxi to Bayamo airport for USD$5 or to Aeropuerto Frank País in Holguín for USD$35. A taxi to Villa Santo Domingo (the setting-off point for the Alto del Naranjo trailhead for Sierra Maestra hikes) or Comandancia de la Plata will cost approximately USD$35 one way. There's a taxi stand in the south of town near Museo Ñico López.

Cubacar (☑ 2359-7005; Carretera Central, Hotel Sierra Maestra; ⊗ 9am-5pm) rents cars at the Hotel Sierra Maestra.

The **Cupet-Cimex gas station** (Carretera Central) is between Hotel Sierra Maestra and the bus terminal as you arrive from Santiago de Cuba.

The main horse-cart route (CUP$1) runs between the train station and the hospital, via the bus station. **Bici-taxis** (Map p384) (a few pesos a ride) are also useful for getting around town. There's a stand near the train station.

Gran Parque Nacional Sierra Maestra

Comprising a sublime mountainscape of verdant peaks and humid cloud forest, and home to honest, hardworking campesinos (country folk), Gran Parque Nacional Sierra Maestra (USD$15; ⊗ 8am-5pm) is an alluring natural sanctuary that still echoes with the gunshots of Castro's guerrilla campaign of the late 1950s. Situated 40km south of Yara, up a very steep 24km concrete road from Bartolomé Masó, this precipitous, little-trammeled region contains the country's highest peak, Pico Turquino (1972m; just over the border in Santiago de Cuba Province), unlimited birdlife and flora, and the rebels' one-time wartime headquarters, Comandancia de la Plata.

History

History resonates throughout these mountains, the bulk of it linked indelibly to the guerrilla war that raged between December 1956 and December 1958. For the first year of the conflict, Fidel and his growing band of supporters remained on the move, never staying in one place for more than a few days. It was only in early 1958 that the rebels established a permanent base on a ridge in the shadow of Pico Turquino. This headquarters became known as La Plata, and it was from here that Castro drafted many of the early revolutionary laws while he orchestrated the military strikes that finally brought about the ultimate demise of the Batista government.

◉ Sights

★ **Comandancia de la Plata**   LANDMARK
(guided hike incl transportation USD$45, camera USD$5) Topping a crenelated mountain ridge amid thick cloud forest, this pioneering camp was established by Fidel Castro in 1958 after a year on the run. Well-camouflaged and remote, the rebel HQ was chosen for its inaccessibility, and it served its purpose well – Batista's soldiers never found it.

Today it remains much as it was left in the '50s, with 16 wooden buildings providing an evocative reminder of one of the most successful guerrilla campaigns in history. It's easy to appreciate the site's strategic location. The main site, culminating in the Casa de Fidel

Gran Parque Nacional Sierra Maestra

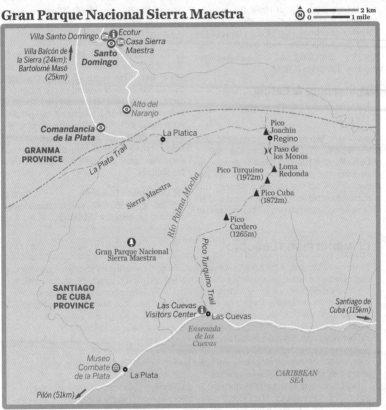

(Fidel's House), is approached via an open space and then a climb through thick trees.

Highlights include the small museum near the beginning of the complex, the masterfully designed Casa de Fidel with its seven concealed escape routes in case the revolution's leaders were discovered, and the steep climb up Radio Rebelde to the radio-communications buildings where the rebels' early broadcasts were aired. The hospital buildings, a wake-up call to the brutality of guerrilla medical care, lie far below along a separate path (positioned here so the injured wouldn't give the camp location away in their agony).

Comandancia de la Plata is controlled by the Centro de Información de Flora y Fauna in Santo Domingo. Aspiring guerrilla-watchers must first hire a guide at the park headquarters and then get transport (or walk) 5km up to Alto del Naranjo and then proceed on foot along a muddy track for the final 4km. You can organize it at the Ecotur (p391) office in Villa Santo Domingo.

★ **Santo Domingo**   VILLAGE

This tiny village nestles in a deep green valley beside the deliciously clean Río Yara. Communally it provides a wonderful slice of peaceful Cuban campesino life that has carried on pretty much unchanged since Fidel and Che prowled these shadowy mountains in the 1950s. If you decide to stick around, you can get a taste of rural socialism at the local school and medical clinic, or ask at Villa Santo Domingo about the tiny village **museum** (admission USD$1; hours vary).

Locals offer horseback riding (USD$10 per hour), pedicure treatments, hikes to natural swimming pools and some classic old firsthand tales from the annals of revolutionary history.

Alto del Naranjo   LANDMARK

All trips into the park begin at the end of the near-vertical, corrugated-concrete access road at Alto del Naranjo (after Villa Santo Domingo the road gains 750 vertical meters in less than 5km). To get there, it's an arduous two-hour walk or zippy ride in a 4WD. There's a wondrous view of the plains of Granma from this 950m-high lookout; otherwise, it's a launching pad for La Plata (3km) and Pico Turquino (13km).

🛏 Sleeping & Eating

Bring your own food. There are no services in the park.

Casa Sierra Maestra   CASA PARTICULAR **$**
(☎ 5-261-0846, 2352-6405; Santo Domingo; r USD$20-30; ❋ 🛜) Rustic heaven! Across the river from the park entrance in Santo Domingo (cross on the stepping stones), this place has four perfectly decent rooms and an atmospheric *ranchón*-style bar-restaurant

(mains USD$4 to USD$8). Chickens cluck, and rural bliss descends.

Villa Balcón de la Sierra   HOTEL **$**
(☎ 2356-5513; s/d incl breakfast USD$36/46; 🅿 ❋ 🛜 ≋) One kilometer south of Bartolomé Masó and 16km north of Santo Domingo, this simple hotel is nestled in the mountain foothills somewhat far for easy park access. A swimming pool and restaurant are perched on a small hill with killer mountain views, while 20 air-conditioned cabins are scattered below. Lovely natural ambience juxtaposed with the usual basic-but-functional Islazul furnishings.

★**Villa Santo Domingo**   HOTEL **$$**
(☎ 2356-5834, 2356-5568; www.villasantodomingo. com; s/d incl breakfast USD$60/80; 🅿 ❋) This

---

CLIMBING PICO TURQUINO

Towering 1972m above the calm Caribbean, Pico Turquino – so named for the turquoise hue that colors its steep upper slopes – is Cuba's highest and most regularly climbed mountain.

Carpeted in lush cloud forest and protected in a 140-sq-km national park, the peak's lofty summit is embellished by a bronze bust of national hero José Martí. In a patriotic test of endurance, the statue was dragged to the top in 1953 by a young Celia Sánchez and her father, Manuel Sánchez Silveira, to mark the centennial of the apostle's birth.

Four years later, Sánchez visited the summit again, this time with a rifle-wielding Fidel Castro in tow to record an interview with American news network CBS. Not long afterwards, the rebel army pitched their permanent headquarters in the mountain's imposing shadow, atop a tree-protected ridge near La Plata.

Best tackled as a through trek from the Santo Domingo (Granma Province) side, the rugged, two- to three-day grind up Turquino starts from Alto del Naranjo above Santo Domingo and ends at Las Cuevas on the Caribbean coast (an out-and-back Alto del Naranjo–Pico Turquino hike is also possible). Guides are mandatory and can be arranged through Flora y Fauna employees at Villa Santo Domingo or at the small hut at Las Cuevas. The cost varies, depending on how many days you take. If you organize it through Ecotur or Cubanacán in Bayamo, bank on USD$68 for two days. You'll also need to stock up on food (dinner and breakfast at the overnight shelters are included but nothing else), warm clothing, candles and a sleeping bag. Even in August it gets cold at the shelters, so be prepared. Water is available along the trail, but it's scarce: carry reserves.

The trail through the mountains from Alto del Naranjo passes the village of La Platica (water), Palma Mocha (campsite), Lima (campsite), Campismo Joachín (shelter and water), El Cojo (shelter), Pico Joachín, Paso de los Monos, Loma Redonda, Pico Turquino (1972m), Pico Cuba (1872m; with shelter and water at 1650m), Pico Cardero (1265m) and La Esmajagua (600m; with basic refreshments) before dropping down to Las Cuevas on the coast. The first two days are spent on the 13km section to Pico Turquino (normally overnighting at Campismo Joachín and/or Pico Cuba shelters), where a prearranged guide takes over and leads you down to Las Cuevas. As with all guide services, tips are in order. Prearranging the second leg from Pico Cuba to Las Cuevas is straightforward and handled by park staff.

These hikes are well coordinated and the guides efficient. The sanest way to begin is by overnighting at Villa Santo Domingo and setting out in the morning (you should enter the park gate by 10am). Transport from Las Cuevas along the coast is sparse, with one scheduled truck on alternate days. Arrange onward transport from Las Cuevas in advance. Approaching from Santo Domingo, you will not (officially) be able to do the Comandancia de la Plata and Pico Turquino hikes the same day, but must stay overnight in the village then begin the Pico Turquino hike the following day.

villa, 24km south of Bartolomé Masó, flanks the gateway to Gran Parque Nacional Sierra Maestra. There are 40 cabins (20 cheaper concrete ones and 20 newer ones in smart wooden buildings) next to the Río Yara. The setting, among cascading mountains and campesino huts, is idyllic and the best jumping-off point for Comandancia de la Plata and Pico Turquino.

ℹ️ Information

Ecotur (☎ 2356-5834; Villa Santo Domingo; ⊘ 8am-noon & 2-5pm) maintains a very handy desk at Villa Santo Domingo. If you want to book in advance, try the offices in Bayamo or Santiago.

The park closes at 4pm, but rangers won't let you pass after mid-morning, so set off early to maximize your visit.

ℹ️ Getting There & Away

There's no public transport from Bartolomé Masó to Alto del Naranjo (and trucks to Bartolomé Masó from Bayamo are infrequent and uncomfortable). A taxi from Bayamo to Villa Santo Domingo should cost around USD$35 one way. Ensure it can take you all the way; the last 7km before Villa Santo Domingo is extremely steep but passable in a (decent) normal car. Returning, the hotel should be able to arrange onward transport for you to Bartolomé Masó, Bayamo or Manzanillo.

A 4WD vehicle with good brakes is necessary to drive the last 5km from Santo Domingo to Alto del Naranjo; it's the steepest road in Cuba with 45% gradients near the top. Powerful 4WDs pass regularly, usually for adventurous tour groups, and you may be able to find a space on board for approximately USD$5 (ask at Villa Santo Domingo). Alternatively, it's a tough but rewarding 5km hike (or a gut-wrenching morning run!).

Manzanillo

POP 127,819

Bayside Manzanillo isn't exactly pretty, but it does find its way under your skin. Hang out in the semiruined central park with its old-fashioned street organs and distinctive neo-Moorish architecture. With bare-bones transport links, few travelers make it here. Off the standard tourist trail, you can see how Cubans have learned to live with decades of austerity.

The city also makes a good base for exploring *espiritismo*, a local syncretization of Catholic and Taíno beliefs, whose rituals and elements are unique to this region of Cuba. The largest *espiritismo* center in Cuba, called Centro La Ville, is located in the area;

arrange a visit through Infotur (☎ 2357-4412; Maceo btwn Merchán & Gómez; ⊘ 8am-5:30pm Mon-Fri).

Manzanillo's famous hand-operated street organs were first imported from France in the early 20th century. The city's musical legacy was solidified further in 1972 with a government-sponsored *nueva trova* festival that culminated in a solidarity march to Playa Las Coloradas.

◎ Sights

★ **Museo Histórico La Demajagua**   MUSEUM
(☎ 5-219-4080; USD$1; ⊘ 8am-5pm Tue-Sat, to 2pm Sun) Ten kilometers south of Manzanillo is the moving sight of the sugar estate of Carlos Manuel de Céspedes, whose outcry, known as Grito de Yara, and the subsequent freeing of his enslaved people on October 10, 1868, marked the opening of Cuba's independence wars. Renovated in 2018 on the 150th anniversary of independence, the small museum has well-organized interpretive displays. Outside, find the Demajagua bell that Céspedes tolled to announce Cuba's (then unofficial) independence, plus remnants of the sugar mill machinery.

In 1947 an as-yet-unknown Fidel Castro 'kidnapped' the bell and took it to Havana in a publicity stunt to protest against the corrupt Cuban government.

Also at La Demajagua are the remains of Céspedes' original *ingenio* (sugar mill) and a poignant monument (with a quote from Castro). To get here, travel south 10km from the Cupet-Cimex gas station in Manzanillo, in the direction of Media Luna, and then another 2.5km off the main road, toward the sea.

Parque Céspedes   SQUARE
Manzanillo's central square is notable for its priceless glorieta (gazebo), an imitation of the Patio de los Leones in Spain's Alhambra, where Moorish mosaics, a scalloped cupola and arabesque columns set off a theme that's replicated elsewhere. Nearby, a permanent statue of Carlos Puebla, Manzanillo's famous homegrown troubadour, sits contemplatively on a bench. Cruise by on Sunday evenings around 8pm, when traditional live music provides the soundtrack for rollerskating kids and dancing oldsters alike.

On the eastern side of Parque Céspedes is Manzanillo's **Museo Histórico Municipal** (☎ 2357-2053; Martí No 226; ⊘ 8am-noon & 2-6pm Tue-Fri, 8am-noon & 6-10pm Sat & Sun) **FREE**, whilst the Iglesia de la Purisma

Concepción is a neoclassical beauty from 1805, with an impressive gilded altarpiece.

Celia Sánchez Monument MONUMENT

Seven blocks southwest of the park lies Manzanillo's most evocative sight. Built in 1990, this terracotta-tiled staircase embellished with colorful ceramic murals runs up Calle Caridad between Martí and Luz Caballero. The birds and flowers on the reliefs represent Sánchez, linchpin of the M-26-7 (July 26 Movement) and longtime aid to Castro, whose visage appears on the central mural near the top of the stairs. It's a moving memorial with excellent views out over the city and bay.

Yara HISTORIC SITE

A small town amid vast fields of sugarcane, Yara is barely mentioned in most travel literature, but several important chapters of Cuban history took place here, marked by monuments and a modest local museum.

Early Spanish colonizers earmarked it as one of their *pueblos indios* (indigenous towns) and a statue of rebel *cacique* (chief) Hatuey in the main square supports claims that the Spanish burned the dissenting Taíno chief here rather than in Baracoa.

The next chapter of Yara's history began on October 11, 1868, when it became the first town to be wrested from Spanish control by rebel forces led by Carlos Manuel de Céspedes. A second monument in the main square recalls this important event and the famous Grito de Yara (Yara Declaration) that followed, in which Céspedes proclaimed Cuba's independence for the first time. Just off the square, the Museo Municipal chronicles Yara's historical legacy along with the town's role as a key supply center during the revolutionary war in the 1950s.

Buses traveling between Manzanillo and Bayamo can stop here.

City Bank of NY Building NOTABLE BUILDING

(cnr Merchán & Dr Codina) For an example of the city's striking architecture, check out the old City Bank of NY building from 1913.

🛏 Sleeping

★ Adrián & Tonia CASA PARTICULAR $

(☑2357-3028; ato700714@gmail.com; Mártires de Vietnam No 49; r USD$20-25; P❋) This fabulous casa would stand out in any city, let alone Manzanillo. The position, on the terracotta staircase to the Celia Sánchez Monument, obviously helps. But Adrián and Tonia have gone beyond the call of duty with a vista-laden terrace, super-friendly staff and four suites that include kitchens (except for the smallest).

Hostal Carlo's CASA PARTICULAR $

(☑2357-2582; hostalcarlos@nauta.cu; Mártires de Vietnam No 182, btwn Figueredo & Masó; r USD$25; ❋) Run by no-nonsense former PE teacher Carlo, this colonial casa is central, comfortable and laissez-faire.

La Roca CASA PARTICULAR $

(Hostal Marcel y Mercy; ☑2357-7980, 5-815-1851; mercyandraca@nauta.cu; Mártires de Vietnam No 68; r USD$25; ❋ 🛜) Climb the Celia Sánchez staircase to this smart multistory home with two guest rooms. Rooms are ample and bright, and there are great city views. The recommended on-site restaurant (mains USD$5 to USD$10) is for guests only.

🍴 Eating & Drinking

Paladar Rancho Luna CUBAN $

(☑2357-3858; José Miguel Gómez No 169; meals USD$3-5; ⊙noon-11pm) The most appealing restaurant in town, even if blaring reggaeton, it's your best option for reasonably priced fare. A decorative, typically Manzanillan facade sets the tone. The food is perfectly good and is enhanced by the friendly service and attractive ambience.

Cayo Confite SEAFOOD $$

(Malecón; mains USD$8; ⊙9am-9pm) Utter simplicity – sit on this shady deck facing the waterfront for whole fried fish served with plantain chips. It's on the edge of town at the far end of the Malecón (boardwalk).

Complejo Costa Azul PARRILLA $$$

(off Av 1ro de Mayo; mains CUP$15-30; ⊙food noon-9:30pm daily, cabaret 8pm-midnight Tue-Sun) Down by the bay is this grillhouse and cabaret in one. It's highly likely neither amenity will blow your mind, but nevertheless, the eating and entertainment are nigh on as good as it gets here. This complex was under renovation on our visit, but slated to reopen.

Bodegón Pinilla BAR

(Martí No 212; ⊙9am-8pm Mon-Thu, to 2am Fri & Sat) This bar on the *peatonal* (pedestrianized section) is a choice spot if you're craving a rum cocktail in a fancier bar setting.

☆ Entertainment

Teatro Manzanillo THEATER

(☑2357-2539; Villuendas, btwn Maceo & Saco; ⊙shows 8pm Fri-Sun) Touring companies such as the Ballet de Camagüey and

---

WORTH A TRIP

MEDIA LUNA

One of a handful of small towns punctuating the swaying sugar fields between Manzanillo and Cabo Cruz, Media Luna is worth a pit stop on the basis of its Celia Sánchez connections. The revolution's 'first lady' was born here in 1920 in a small clapboard house that is now the fastidiously curated Celia Sánchez Museum. (✆2359-3466; Raúl Podio No 111, Media Luna; USD$1; ⏰9am-5pm Mon-Sat, 8am-noon Sun)

If you have time, take a stroll around this quintessential Cuban sugar town dominated by a tall soot-stained mill (now disused) and characteristic clapboard houses decorated with gingerbread embellishments. There is also a lovely *glorieta* (gazebo), almost as outlandish as Manzanillo's. The main park is the place to get a take on the local street theater while supping on quick-melting ice cream.

Danza Contemporánea de Cuba perform at this lovingly restored venue. Built in 1856 and restored in 1926 and again in 2002, this 430-seat beauty is packed with oil paintings, stained glass and original detail.

Casa de la Trova　TRADITIONAL MUSIC
(✆2357-5423; Merchán No 213, cnr Masó; CUP$1) In the spiritual home of *nueva trova* (traditional singing), a renovation of the local *trova* house was long overdue. Pay a visit to this hallowed musical shrine where Carlos Puebla once plucked his strings.

Uneac　ARTS CENTER
(✆2357-2610; cnr Merchán & Concepción) For traditional music, head to this dependable option, which has Saturday and Sunday night *peñas* (performances) and painting expos.

ℹ Information

INTERNET ACCESS

There's a wi-fi signal on the plaza. Purchase wi-fi scratch cards at **Etecsa** (✆2357-8891; cnr Gómez & Dr Codina; internet per hour USD$1.50; ⏰8:30am-7pm).

MONEY

Banks with ATMs are plentiful.
Banco de Crédito y Comercio (✆2357-7125; cnr Merchán & Saco; ⏰9am-3pm Mon-Fri) Has an ATM.
Cadeca (✆2357-7467; Martí No 188; ⏰8:30am-4pm Mon-Sat) Two blocks from the main square. Stock up on Cuban pesos, which will come in handy around here.

ℹ Getting There & Away

AIR

Manzanillo's Sierra Maestra Airport is on the road to Cayo Espino, 8km south of the Cupet-Cimex gas station in Manzanillo. In winter, Sunwing (www.sunwing.ca) flies direct from Toronto and Montreal.

A taxi between the airport and the center of town should cost approximately USD$10, though may be more if you have ordered a taxi from your lodging to wait for your flight.

BUS & TRUCK

The **bus station** (✆2357-2727; Av Rosales) is 2km northeast of the city center. There are no Víazul services. This narrows your options down to *guaguas* (local Cuban buses, CUP$3 for regional destinations) or trucks (no reliable schedules and long queues; CUP$10 to CUP$15 for regional destinations).

Services run several times a day to Yara (20 minutes) and Bayamo (two hours) in the east and Pilón (two hours) and Niquero (1¾ hours) in the south. For the latter destinations, you can also board at the crossroads near the Cupet-Cimex gas station and the hospital, which is also where you'll find the *amarillos* (transport officials).

CAR

There's a sturdy road running through Corralito up into Holguín, making this the quickest exit from Manzanillo toward points north and east.

TRAIN

All services from the **train station** (✆2357-7512) on the north side of town are via Yara and Bayamo. Havana-bound trains depart every third day.

ℹ Getting Around

Horse carts (CUP$2) to the bus station leave from Dr Codina between Plácido and Luz Caballero. Horse carts to the shipyard leave from the bottom of Saco (CUP$6).

Niquero

POP 42,262

A good launchpad for Parque Nacional Desembarco del Granma, Niquero is a small fishing port and sugar town in the isolated southwest corner of Granma. It's dominated by the Roberto Ramírez Delgado sugar mill, built in 1905 and nationalized in 1960.

OFF THE BEATEN TRACK

CINCO PALMAS

At the hamlet of Cinco Palmas, pristine natural landscapes are doused in poignant revolutionary history. This is where Castro's rebels regrouped on December 18, 1956, after their baptism of fire at Alegría de Pío, 28km away. A bronze monument of three *campesinos* who helped the beleaguered rebel army, then down to a dozen men, was erected in 2008. The monument guards the *finca* (farm) of Ramón 'Mongo' Pérez where Castro and others sought shelter. There's also a small, free museum with a 3D map of the hilly terrain.

Cinco Palmas lies 28km southeast of the town of Media Luna along a rough but passable dirt road. Trails from the site lead west to Alegría de Pío and east to Comandancia de la Plata. Ask about guided hikes at Ecotur (p387) in Bayamo.

It is one of the few regional mills still in operation. Like many Granma settlements, Niquero is characterized by its distinctive clapboard houses.

Ostensibly, there isn't much to do in Niquero, but you can explore the town park, where there's a cinema, and visit a small museum. Look out for the monument commemorating the oft-forgotten victims of the *Granma* landing, who were hunted down and killed by Batista's troops in December 1956.

Here's a surprise, and a far-from-unpleasant one. Nestled in Niquero's center, Hotel Niquero (☑ 2359-2367; cnr Martí & Céspedes; s/d USD$28/31; ▣ ⊛ ⊚) is a low-key, out-on-a-limb hotel situated opposite the local sugar factory with substantially sized, amenable rooms with little balconies, though there's a lot of ambient noise from the atrium and street. The affordable on-site restaurant can rustle up a reasonable beef steak with sauce.

ⓘ Getting There & Away

There are buses to Manzanillo several times per day, but no Viazul services.

Parque Nacional Desembarco del Granma

Mixing unique environmental diversity with heavy historical significance, the Parque Nacional Desembarco del Granma (USD$5) consists of 275 sq km of forest, peculiar karst topography and uplifted marine terraces. A shrine to the Cuban Revolution, Castro's stricken leisure yacht *Granma* limped ashore here in December 1956.

This Unesco World Heritage site protects some of the Americas' most pristine coastal cliffs. Of 512 plant species identified thus far, about 60% are endemic, with a dozen found only here. Fauna is equally rich, with 25 species of mollusk, seven species of amphibian,

44 types of reptile, 110 bird species and 13 types of mammal.

In El Guafe, archaeologists have uncovered Cuba's second-most important community of ancient agriculturists and ceramic-makers. Thousand-year-old artifacts include altars, carved stones and earthen vessels along with idols guarding a water goddess inside a ceremonial cave.

There are two main access points: Las Coloradas and the village of Alegría de Pío.

◉ Sights & Activities

★ Alegría de Pío   HISTORIC SITE
(USD$5) Considered hallowed revolutionary ground, this is the spot where Castro's shipwrecked rebels were intercepted by Batista's army in 1956 and forced to split up and flee. It's also the official finishing point for the 18km hike from Las Coloradas following the rebels' route in December 1956. There's guided hiking, birdwatching and exploration of a fascinating cave system. It's accessed via 28km of potholed purgatory from a turnoff in Niquero. Bring plenty of drinking water.

There's a monument in the sugarcane field where the rebels were surprised. It's emblazoned with the names of the fallen and the words '*Nadie se rinde aqui, cojone!*' (No one surrenders here, bollocks!), supposedly shouted by Camilo Cienfuegos and repeated by Juan Almeida as all hell broke loose. A guide will show you around the site, which includes various graves, billboards and a cave where Che Guevara and Juan Almeida hid for two days.

The highlight for outdoors enthusiasts will be the cave system. Morlotte-Fustete is a 2km trail that traverses the spectacular marine terraces (sometimes using wooden ladders) and takes in the Cueva del Fustete – a 5km-long cavern replete with stalagmites and stalactites – and the Hoyo de Morlotte, a 77m deep karstic hole caused by water erosion. El Samuel is a 1.3km trail to the Cueva Espelunca, thought to have been used by indigenous people for religious ceremonies. Boca de Toro is a 6km trail to high cliffs overlooking a river valley and takes in the Farallón de Blanquizal, a beautiful natural lookout.

From here the rebel trail from Las Coloradas continues east to Cinco Palmas and, ultimately, Comendancia La Plata.

Cabo Cruz   VILLAGE

Three kilometers beyond the El Guafe trailhead is a tiny fishing community with skiffs bobbing offshore and sinewy men gutting their catch on the golden beach. The 33m-tall Vargas lighthouse (erected 1871) now belongs to the Cuban military. There are plans to install a diving center to take advantage of incredible diving opportunities nearby.

There's good swimming east of the lighthouse; bring gear as there are no facilities.

Museo Las Coloradas   MUSEUM

(USD$5; ⊙8am-6pm) A large monument just beyond the park gate marks the *Granma's* landing spot. A small museum outlines the routes taken by Castro, Guevara and the others into the Sierra Maestra, and there's a full-scale replica of the *Granma,* which – if you're lucky – a machete-wielding guard will let you climb inside to wonder how 82 men ever managed it.

The entry ticket includes a visit to the simple reconstructed hut of the first campesino to help Fidel after the landing. An enthusiastic guide will also accompany you along a 1.3km path through dense mangroves to the ocean and the spot where the *Granma* ran aground, 70m offshore. The walk provides

AND THEN THERE WERE THREE...

It seemed like an ignominious defeat. Three days after landing in a crippled leisure yacht on Cuba's southeastern coast, Castro's expeditionary force of 82 soldiers had been decimated by Batista's superior army. Some of the rebels had fled, others had been captured and killed. Escaping from the ambush, Castro found himself cowering in a sugarcane field along with two ragged companions: his 'bodyguard,' Universo Sánchez, and diminutive Havana doctor, Faustino Pérez. 'There was a moment when I was commander-in-chief of myself and two others,' said the man who would one day go on to overthrow the Cuban government, thwart a US-sponsored invasion, incite a nuclear standoff and become one of the most enduring political figures of the 20th century.

Hunted by ground troops and bombed from the air by military planes, the trio lay trapped in the cane field for four days and three nights. The hapless Pérez had inadvertently discarded his weapon; Sánchez, meanwhile, had lost his shoes. Wracked by fatigue and plagued by hunger, Fidel continued to do what he always did best. He whispered incessantly to his beleaguered colleagues – about the revolution, about the philosophies of José Martí. Buoyantly he pontificated about how 'all the glory of the world would fit inside a grain of maize.' Sánchez, not unwisely, concluded that his delirious leader had gone crazy and that their grisly fate was sealed – it was just a matter of time.

At night, Fidel – determined not to be caught alive – slept with his rifle cocked against his throat, the safety catch released. One squeeze of the finger and it would have been over. No Cuban Revolution, no Bay of Pigs, no Cuban Missile Crisis.

Fatefully, the moment didn't arrive. With the army concluding that the rebels had been wiped out, the search was called off. Choosing their moment, Fidel and his two companions crept stealthily northeast toward the safety of the Sierra Maestra, sucking on stalks of sugarcane for nutrition.

It was a desperate fight for survival. For a further eight days the rebel army remained a bedraggled trio as the fugitive soldiers dodged army patrols, crawled through sewers and drank their own urine. It wasn't until December 13 that they met up with Guillermo García, a campesino sympathetic to the rebel cause, and a corner was turned.

On December 15 at a safe meeting house, Fidel's brother, Raúl, materialized out of the jungle with three men and four weapons. Castro was ecstatic. Three days later a third exhausted band of eight soldiers – including Che Guevara and Camilo Cienfuegos – turned up, swelling the rebel army to an abject 15.

'We can win this war,' proclaimed an ebullient Fidel to his small band of not-so-merry men. 'We have just begun the fight.'

OFF THE BEATEN TRACK

PILÓN

Pilón is a small, isolated settlement wedged between the Marea del Portillo resorts and the Parque Nacional. With the sugar mill shut down, its reason for being is the **Casa Museo Celia Sánchez Manduley** (☑ 2359-4107; Conrado Benitez No 20; USD$1; ☺ 8am-noon daily, 1-5pm Tue-Thu, 1:30-8pm Fri & Sat), a museum in honor of the revolution's 'first lady' who briefly lived at this address. If you happen here on a Saturday, attend the lively **Sábado de Rumba**, a weekly street party with whole roast pig, shots of rum and plenty of live music. This is your best chance of seeing the popular Cuban dance called the *pilón* (named after the town), which imitates the rhythms of pounding sugar.

The hotels at Marea del Portillo 11km away run a weekly Saturday evening transfer bus to Pilón for USD$5 return. Getting here otherwise will involve a car, long-distance bike or trying your luck with the *amarillos* (transport officials).

---

an experiential feel of just how harsh the conditions were for the food-deprived rebels, who had to slog and hack their way for hours through a veritable wall of mangroves simply to reach dry land.

★ **Sendero Arqueológico Natural El Guafe**   HIKING

About 8km southwest of Las Coloradas is this flat, well-signposted 2km-long trail, the park's headline hike for nature and archaeology. An underground river has created 20 large caverns, one of which contains the famous **Ídolo del Agua**, carved from stalagmites by pre-Columbian indigenous people. Another cavern served as a burial chamber; many were sacred sites. The trail also passes a 500-year-old cactus, and butterflies, 170 different species of birds and multiple orchids could make appearances along the way.

Guides are required but included in the park's USD$5 entry cost. You should allow two hours for the stroll. Bring insect repellent.

The park is flecked with other trails, the best of which is the 30km trek to Alegría de Pío (p394), replicating the journey of the 82 rebels who landed here in 1956.

Sleeping & Eating

Campismo Las Coloradas   CABIN $

(Km 17, Carretera de Niquero; s/d USD$8/12; 🌬) A Category 3 campismo with 28 duplex cabins standing on 500m of murky beach, 5km southwest of Belic, just outside the park. All cabins have air-con and baths, and there's a restaurant, a games hall and watersport rental on-site. Book through **Campismo Popular** (☑ 2342-2425; General García No 112; ☺ 8am-noon & 1-5pm Mon-Fri, 9am-noon Sat) in Bayamo.

Restaurante El Cabo   SEAFOOD $

(Cabo Cruz; meals CUP$75; ☺ 7am-9pm Tue-Sun) The cheapest seafood in Cuba comes straight

out of the Caribbean behind this restaurant that lies in the shadow of the lighthouse.

❶ Getting There & Away

Ten km southwest of Media Luna the road divides, with Pilón 30km to the southeast and Niquero 10km to the southwest. Belic is 16km southwest of Niquero. It's another 6km from Belic to the national park entry gate. The turnoff for Alegría de Pío is just after the Servicentro in Niquero.

If you don't have your own transport, getting here is tough. Irregular buses go as far as the Campismo Las Coloradas daily, and there are equally infrequent trucks from Belic. As a last resort, you can try the *amarillos* (transport officials) in Niquero. The closest gas station is in Niquero.

Marea del Portillo

There's something magical about Marea del Portillo, a tiny south-coast village bordered by two low-key all-inclusive resorts. Wedged into a strip of land between the glistening Caribbean and the cascading Sierra Maestra, it occupies a spot of great natural beauty and history.

The problem for independent travelers is getting here. There is no regular public transport, which means that you may, for the first time, have to take a long-distance taxi or brave sporadic truck transport. Another issue for beach lovers is the sand, which is a light gray color and may disappoint those more attuned to the brilliant whites of Cayo Coco.

The resorts themselves are affordable and well maintained but isolated; the nearest town of any size is lackluster Manzanillo 100km to the north. Real rustic Cuba, however, is right outside the hotel gates.

🏃 Activities

There's plenty to do here, despite the area's apparent isolation. Horseback riding to El

Salto, village tours to Sevilla, Pilón and Mota or jeep tours to El Macio River can be arranged. You can also visit Parque Nacional Desembarco del Granma from here. Book trips at Cubanacán desks in Hotel Marea del Portillo and Hotel Farallón del Caribe.

El Salto HIKING

This lovely DIY 10km out-and-back hike takes you through fields and valleys, a small village, past a lake, across a river and, finally, to El Salto, where there's usually a small waterfall and an inviting swimming hole.

Starting right outside the hotel strip, turn right onto the coast road and then, after approximately 400m, hang left onto an unpaved track just before a bridge. The track eventually joins a road and traverses a dusty, scattered settlement. On the far side of the village a dam rises above you. Rather than take the paved road up the embankment to the left, branch right and, after 200m, pick up a clear path that rises steeply up above the dam and into view of the lake behind. This beautiful path tracks alongside the lake before crossing one of its river feeds on a wooden bridge. Go straight on and uphill here and, when the path forks on the crest, bear right. Heading down into a verdant tranquil valley, pass a *casa de campesino* (the friendly owners keep bees and will give you honey, coffee and a geographical reorientation), cross the river (Río Cilantro) and then follow it upstream to El Salto.

Centro Internacional de Buceo Marea del Portillo DIVING

(✏ 2359-7139; nautica@marea.tur.cu; Hotel Marea del Portillo) Adjacent to Hotel Marea del Portillo, this Cubanacán-run dive center offers affordable scuba diving. For real excitement, dive to the *Cristóbal Colón* wreck (sunk in the 1898 Spanish–Cuban–American War). The open-sea fishing excursion includes bar and lunch. There have been complaints about reliability (the excursions will not leave if the center doesn't have fuel for the boats). Other water excursions include a seafari (with snorkeling), a sunset cruise and a trip to uninhabited Cayo Blanco.

Salto de Guayabito HIKING

Starting in the village of Mata Dos about 20km east of Marea, this hike is normally done as part of an organized day trip from the hotels. Groups – who often embark on horseback – follow the Río Motas 7km upstream to an enchanting waterfall surrounded by rocky cliffs, ferns, cacti and orchids.

🛏 Sleeping

Casas particulares are an interesting alternative to all-inclusive resorts.

Casa Particular
Barbara Mendez CASA PARTICULAR $

(✏ 2359-7162; Marea del Portillo No 14; r USD$30; ❄) For a private option in the tiny village of Marea del Portillo, Barbara lets out three rooms in her apartment that's 200m from the beach. Barbara and her husband are both great cooks.

Hotel Marea del Portillo HOTEL $$

(✏ 2359-7008; s/d/tr all-inclusive USD$45/72/97; P❄@🛜🏊) It's not Cayo Coco, but it barely seems to matter here. In fact, Marea's all-round functionalism and lack of big-resort pretension seem to work well in this traditional corner of Cuba. The 74 rooms are perfectly adequate, the food buffet does a good job and the dark sandy arc of beach is within baseball-pitching distance of your balcony.

★ Hotel Farallón del Caribe HOTEL $$$

(✏ 2359-7082; s/d all-inclusive USD$95/120; ⊗Nov-Apr; P❄@🛜🏊) Perched on a low hill with the Caribbean on one side and the Sierra Maestra on the other, the modern Farallón is the most impressive option in Marea de Portillo. Three-star, all-inclusive facilities are complemented by five-star surroundings. The food is superior to the competition's, and views are great, though it is the furthest resort from the actual beach.

ℹ Getting There & Away

The journey east to Santiago is one of Cuba's most spectacular, but the road quality is awful and regularly affected by the weather. Options are your own car (check ahead regarding road conditions), a taxi (bank on at least USD$160 for Marea to Santiago de Cuba), bicycle (a two- to three-day view-loaded roller coaster) or winging it with 'public transport' (possibly one of Cuba's greatest adventures, but only for the hardy who are not averse to long waits and some hitchhiking).

Warning: the road sees very little traffic and has virtually no facilities and no gas stations (the nearest is in Pilón). Travel with supplies.

ℹ Getting Around

The hotels rent out scooters for approximately USD$25 a day. **Cubacar** (✏ 2359-7005; Hotel Marea del Portillo; ⊗9am-5pm) has a desk at Hotel Marea del Portillo, or you can join in an excursion with Cubanacán. The route to El Salto can be covered on foot.

AT A GLANCE

POPULATION
1,049,256

OLDEST BUILDING
Casa de Diego
Velázquez: 1522

**BEST CASA
PARTICULAR**
Roy's Terrace Inn
(p413)

BEST LIVE JAZZ
Iris Jazz Club (p420)

**BEST ROOF
TERRACE**
Casa Granda Roof
Garden Bar (p419)

WHEN TO GO

Jul–Aug
July is the key
month in Santiago
de Cuba's cultural
calendar with the
Festival del Caribe
and the famous
Carnaval.

Sep–Feb
Starts wet but dries
out by December.

Mar–Jun
Renowned season
for high water
clarity, ensuring
excellent diving
conditions for wreck
diving off the south
coast.

Santiago de Cuba Province

Lovely Santiago. Far from the capital in Cuba's mountainous Oriente region, this perennial hotbed of rebellion and sedition is Cuba's most 'Caribbean' enclave. The difference is invigorating and sometimes overwhelming. Cultural influences here have often come from the east, imported via Haiti, Jamaica, Barbados and Africa. There's a raucous West Indian–style Carnaval and a cache of *folklórico* dance groups that owe as much to French-Haitian culture as they do to Spanish.

As the focus of Spain's new colony in the 16th and early 17th centuries, Santiago de Cuba enjoyed a brief spell as Cuba's capital until it was usurped by Havana in 1607. The subsequent slower pace of development has some distinct advantages. Drive 20km or so along the coast in either direction from the provincial capital and you're on a different planet, one of rugged coves, crashing surf, historical coffee plantations and emerald hills riotous with endemism.

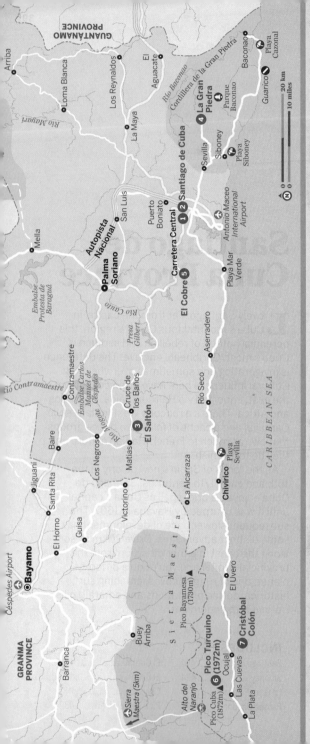

Santiago de Cuba Province Highlights

1 Cementerio Santa Ifigenia (p410) Paying your respects to the nation's heroes at this gorgeous cemetery in Santiago de Cuba.

2 Cuartel Moncada (p405) Taking in the audacity (or folly)

of Castro's 1953 insurrection at this Santiago de Cuba landmark.

3 El Saltón (p430) Making an eco-escape to a luscious mountain getaway.

4 Cafetal La Isabelica (p427) Tracing the history of Cuba's French-inspired coffee culture in La Gran Piedra.

5 El Cobre (p429) Undertaking a pilgrimage with countless believers visiting the

shrine of Cuba's patron saint, La Virgen de la Caridad.

6 Pico Turquino (p432) Standing atop Cuba's highest mountain alongside the bust of José Martí and taking in the gaping panorama.

7 Cristóbal Colón (p432) Diving to the wreck of a Spanish warship off the wild coast near Chivirico.

History

Founded in 1514 by Diego Velázquez de Cuéllar (his bones purportedly lie underneath the cathedral), the city of Santiago de Cuba moved to its present site, on a horseshoe harbor in the lee of the Sierra Maestra, in 1522. Its first mayor was Hernán Cortés – Velázquez' wayward secretary – who departed to explore Mexico in 1518.

Installed as the colony's new capital after the abandonment of Baracoa in 1515, Santiago had a brief renaissance as a center for copper mining. It also served as a disembarkation point for enslaved people arriving from West Africa via Hispaniola. But the boom wasn't to last. In 1556 the Spanish captains-general departed for Havana, and in 1607 the capital was transferred permanently to the west. Raided by pirates and reduced at one point to a small village of only several hundred people, embattled Santiago barely survived the humiliation.

The tide turned in 1655 when Spanish settlers arrived from the nearby colony of Jamaica; their influx grew in the 1790s as French plantation owners escaping a revolt of enslaved people in Haiti settled in the city's Tivolí district. Always one step ahead of the capital in the cultural sphere, Santiago founded the Seminario de San Basilio Magno as an educational establishment in 1722 (six years before the founding of the Universidad de La Habana), and in 1804 the city's top cleric was promoted to the post of archbishop.

In 1898, with Cuba poised to triumph in its long independence struggle, the US intervened in the Spanish–Cuban–American War, landing a flotilla of troops on nearby Daiquirí beach. Decisive land and sea battles of both Wars of Independence were fought in and around Santiago. The first played out on July 1 when a victorious cavalry charge led by Teddy Roosevelt on outlying Loma de San Juan (San Juan Hill) sealed a famous victory. The second ended in a highly one-sided naval battle in Santiago harbor between US and Spanish ships, resulting in the almost total destruction of the Spanish fleet.

A construction boom brought in the first years of the new, quasi-independent Cuban state, but after three successive US military interventions, things started to sour. It was here on July 26, 1953, that Fidel Castro and his companions launched an assault on the Cuartel Moncada (Moncada Barracks). This was the start of a number of events that changed the course of Cuban history. At his trial in Santiago, Castro made his famous *History will Absolve Me* speech, which became the basic platform of the Cuban Revolution.

On November 30, 1956, the people of Santiago de Cuba rose in rebellion against Batista's troops in a futile attempt to distract attention from the landing of Castro's guerrillas on the western shores of Oriente. Although not initially successful, an underground movement led by Frank and Josué País quickly established a secret supply line that ran vital armaments up to the fighters in the Oriente's Sierra Maestra. Despite the murder of the País brothers and many others in 1957–58, the struggle continued unabated. In Santiago de Cuba, Castro first appeared publicly on the evening of January 1, 1959, to declare the triumph of the revolution. All these events have earned Santiago the title 'Hero City of the Republic of Cuba.'

Santiago continued to grow rapidly in the years that followed the revolution, with a construction boom in the 1990s. The city was tarted up again in 2015 to celebrate its quincentennial and became the final resting place of Fidel Castro when his ashes were interred here on December 4, 2016.

Santiago de Cuba

🎵 22 / POP 431,272

Cuba's cultural capital, Santiago is a frenetic, passionate and noisy beauty. Situated closer to Haiti and the Dominican Republic than to Havana, it leans east rather than west, a crucial factor shaping this city's unique identity, steeped in Afro-Caribbean, entrepreneurial and rebel influences.

Trailblazing characters and a resounding sense of historical destiny define it. Diego Velázquez de Cuéllar made Santiago his second capital, Fidel Castro used it to launch his embryonic revolution, Don Facundo Bacardí based his first-ever rum factory here, and nearly every Cuban music genre from salsa to *son* first emanated from these dusty, rhythmic and sensuous streets.

Caught dramatically between the indomitable Sierra Maestra and the azure Caribbean, the colonial *casco histórico* (historical center) retains a time-worn air reminiscent of Salvador in Brazil or forgotten New Orleans. So don't let the hustlers, the speeding Chevys or the clawing heat defeat you. There's untold magic here, too.

◉ Sights

◉ Casco Histórico

★**Museo de Ambiente Histórico Cubano** MUSEUM

(Casa de Diego Velázquez; Map p406; ☑ 2265-2652; Félix Peña No 602; USD$2; ☉ 9am-5pm daily) The oldest house still standing in Cuba, this arresting early colonial abode dating from 1522 was the official residence of the island's first governor, Diego Velázquez. Restored in the late 1960s, the Andalusian-style facade with fine, wooden lattice windows was inaugurated in 1970 as a museum.

The ground floor was originally a trading house and gold foundry, while the upstairs was where Velázquez lived. Today, rooms display period furnishings and decoration from the 16th to 19th centuries. Check the two-way screens, where you could look out without being observed: a Turkish influence (Turkey had a big influence on European style at this time). Visitors are also taken through an adjacent 19th-century neoclassical house.

★**Catedral de Nuestra Señora de la Asunción** CHURCH

(Map p406; Heredia, btwn Félix Peña & General Lacret; ☉ Mass 6:30pm Mon & Wed-Fri, 5pm Sat, 9am & 6:30pm Sun) Santiago's most important church is stunning both inside and out. There has been a cathedral on this site since the city's inception in the 1520s, though a series of pirate raids, earthquakes and dodgy architects put paid to at least three previous incarnations. The present cathedral, characterized by its two neoclassical towers, was completed in 1922; the remains of first colonial governor, Diego Velázquez, are still buried underneath.

The church was restored both inside and out for Santiago's quincentennial in 2015. Expect intricate ceiling frescoes, hand-carved choir stalls and a polished altar honoring the venerated Virgen de la Caridad.

★**Museo Municipal Emilio Bacardí Moreau** MUSEUM

(Map p406; btwn Heredia & Aguilera; USD$2; ☉ 1-5pm Mon, 9am-5pm Tue-Fri, 9am-1pm Sat) Narrow Pío Rosado links Calle Heredia to Calle Aguilera and the fabulous Grecian facade of the Bacardí Museum. Founded in 1899 by the rum-magnate war hero and city mayor, Emilio Bacardí y Moreau (the palatial building was built to spec), the museum is one of Cuba's oldest and most eclectic, with a striking collection of Cuban paintings and some absorbing artifacts amassed from Bacardí's travels.

These include an extensive weapons collection, paintings from the Spanish *costumbrismo* (a 19th-century artistic movement that predates Romanticism) school and the only Egyptian mummy on the island.

Calle José A Saco STREET

(Map p412) A pedestrian-only street stretching from Plaza de Marte to the Paseo Alameda on the waterfront. Heaps of locals browse the shops and restaurants. For extra credit, detour on to pedestrian alley Tamayo Fleites (aka Callejón del Carmen), an ambient three-block stretch between Félix Peña and Pío Rosado, where you'll find stands selling crafts and souvenirs.

Memorial de Vilma Espín Guillois MUSEUM

(Map p406; ☑ 2265-5464; Sánchez Hechavarría No 473; USD$2; ☉ 9am-12:30pm Mon-Sat, 1-5pm Sun) This erstwhile home of Cuba's former 'first lady,' Vilma Espín, the wife of Raúl Castro, and instrumental force in the success of the Cuban Revolution, opened in 2010, three years after her death. This house, where she lived from 1939 to 1959, is packed with lucid snippets of her life.

The daughter of a lawyer to the Bacardí clan, Vilma was first radicalized after a meeting with Frank País in Santiago in 1956. Joining the rebels in the mountains, she went on to found the influential Federation of Cuban Women in 1960.

Calle Heredia STREET

(Map p406) The music never stops on Calle Heredia, Santiago's most sensuous street and also one of its oldest. Melodies waft from the paint-peeled Casa de Cultura Josué País García (p421), where ballroom-dancing pensioners mix with svelte teen rap artists. One door up is Cuba's original Casa de la Trova (p420), a beautiful balconied townhouse redolent of New Orleans' French Quarter. This block is also home to several galleries and shops selling *artesanías* (handicrafts).

Iglesia de San Francisco CHURCH

(Map p406; Juan Bautista Sagarra No 121) This crumbling three-nave, 18th-century ecclesiastical gem is situated three blocks north of Parque Céspedes.

Parque Céspedes PARK

(Map p406) Archetype for romantic Cuban street life, Parque Céspedes is a throbbing kaleidoscope of walking, talking, hustling, flirting, guitar-strumming humanity. Surrounded by colonial architecture, this most ebullient of city squares is a sight to behold day or night. See the bronze bust of Carlos Manuel de Céspedes, who kick-started Cuban independence in 1868, and Cubans enjoying the open wi-fi signal. By publication time, the surrounding streets should be pedestrian-only and the park spiffed up after a renovation.

Plaza de Dolores   SQUARE
(Map p406; cnr Aguilera & Porfirio Valiente) East of Parque Céspedes is the pleasant and shady Plaza de Dolores, a former marketplace now dominated by the 18th-century Iglesia de Nuestra Señora de los Dolores (p421). Many restaurants and cafes flank this square. It's also Santiago's most popular gay cruising spot.

Balcón de Velázquez   VIEWPOINT
(Map p406; cnr Bartolomé Masó & Mariano Corona; donation USD$1) The alfresco Balcón de Velázquez is the site of an old Spanish fort. It offers ethereal views over the terracotta-tiled roofs of the Tivolí neighborhood toward the harbor. If a historian gives you an abbreviated history of the city, it's best to tip.

Museo del Carnaval   MUSEUM
(Map p406; ☎ 2262-6955; Heredia No 303; USD$1; ⏱ 2-5pm Mon, 9am-5pm Tue-Fri & Sun; 2-10pm Sat) A worthwhile museum, this is a quick visit to study the history of Santiago's biggest shindig, the oldest and biggest Carnaval between Río and Mardi Gras. Drop in to see floats, effigies and the occasional *folklórico* dance show on the patio.

Maqueta de la Ciudad   MUSEUM
(Map p406; Mariano Corona No 704; USD$1; ⏱ 9am-5pm Mon-Sat) Cuba is obsessed with scale city models, and Santiago, with this incredibly detailed *maqueta,* is no exception. Interesting historical and architectural information is displayed on illustrated wall panels and you can climb up to a mezzanine gallery for a true vulture's-eye view. For more views, gravitate to the cafe/terrace at the back.

Casa Natal de José
María Heredia y Heredia   MUSEUM
(Map p406; ☎ 2262-5350; Heredia No 260; USD$1; ⏱ 9am-7pm Tue-Sat, to 2pm Sun) A minuscule

---

LA TUMBA FRANCESA

The specter of Haiti, Cuba's Gallic eastern neighbor, loomed large over the isles throughout the late colonial period, especially in the Oriente. The reason? Revolution! Haiti's 1791 rebellion of enslaved people sent thousands of terrified French-Haitian landowners scurrying west to the safer climes of Cuba's eastern mountains, bringing their black enslaved people with them.

As the displaced entrepreneurs set about building sugar mills and coffee plantations in their new home, their indentured enslaved people were put to work on nascent rural estates where they continued to celebrate the music and cultural practices of the land they had left behind. Descended from enslaved people originally brought to Haiti from the French colony of Dahomey (now Benin) in Africa, the centerpiece of Cuban-Haitian culture is a hybrid music and dance style known as *tumba francesa*.

An unusual marriage between 18th-century French ballroom dancing and the frenetic drum rhythms of West Africa, *tumba francesa* is perhaps best described as a kind of Vodou meets Versailles. Picture a trio of drummers accompanied by a chorus of female singers chanting words in a barely decipherable French-African patois. The music provides accompaniment to two key dances. The *masón,* a stately couples' dance that parodies the high society balls of the erstwhile owners of enslaved people wouldn't have looked out of place in the corridors of Louis XIV–era Paris. The *yuba* is a more improvised and athletic dance also partaken by couples. Both are performed by dancers dressed in elegant 19th-century garb: white shirts and colored shawls for men, and wide ankle-length dresses and fans for ladies.

When freed enslaved people started migrating to Cuba's cities from the countryside in the late 1800s, they took their music with them, and *tumba francesa* societies quickly sprang up all over the Oriente. At one time there were more than a hundred such societies.

Today, just three remain: the Santa Catalina de Ricci Pompadour founded in 1902 in the city of Guantánamo, La Caridad de Oriente (Map p412; Pio Rosado No 268) dating from the 1870s in Santiago de Cuba, and the Bejuco de Sagua de Tánamo in Holguín Province. Witnessing a performance is a unique insight into an increasingly rare art. In 2008 the endangered *tumba francesa* was declared an intangible cultural heritage asset by Unesco.

Greater Santiago de Cuba

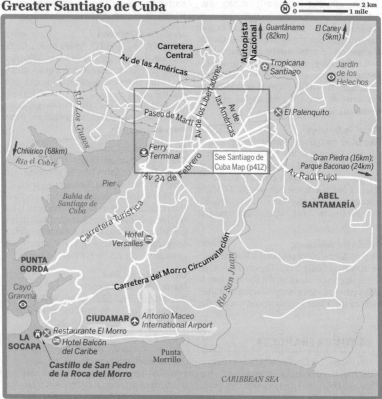

museum illustrating the life of one of Cuba's greatest Romantic poets and the man after whom the street is named, José María Heredia y Heredia (1803–39). Heredia's most notable work, 'Ode to Niagara,' is inscribed outside; it attempts to parallel the beauty of Canada's Niagara Falls with his personal feelings of loss about his homeland. Like many Cuban independence advocates, Heredia was forced into exile, dying in Mexico in 1839.

Plaza de Marte
SQUARE

(Map p406) Guarding the entrance to the *casco histórico,* motorcycle-infested Plaza de Marte formerly served as a macabre 19th-century Spanish parade ground where prisoners were executed publicly for revolutionary activities. Today, the plaza is the city's *esquina caliente* (hot corner), where local baseball fans plot the imminent downfall of Havana's Industriales. The tall column topped with a red cap symbolizes liberty.

Has a public wi-fi signal.

Ayuntamiento
HISTORIC BUILDING

(Map p406; cnr General Lacret & Aguilera) The neoclassical Ayuntamiento was erected in the 1950s using a design from 1783 and was once the site of Hernán Cortés' mayoral office. Fidel Castro appeared on the balcony of the present building on the night of January 2, 1959, trumpeting the revolution's triumph. The edifice was getting thoroughly refurbished on our last visit.

Palacio Provincial
NOTABLE BUILDING

(Poder Popular; Map p406; cnr Pío Rosado & Aguilera) Situated opposite the Bacardí Museum, the equally Hellenic provincial government seat is another building from Cuba's 20th-century neoclassical revival. No public entry is permitted.

North of the Casco Histórico

North of the historic center, Santiago de Cuba turns residential in the Los Hoyos and Sueño neighborhoods.

★**Cuartel Moncada** MUSEUM
(Moncada Barracks; Map p412; ☑2266-1157; Av Moncada; USD$1; ⊘9am-5pm Mon-Sat, 8am-2pm Sun) Santiago's famous Moncada Barracks, a crenelated art deco building completed in 1938, is now synonymous with one of history's greatest failed putsches. Moncada earned immortality on July 26, 1953, when more than 100 revolutionaries led by then little-known Fidel Castro stormed Batista's troops at what was then Cuba's second-most important military garrison.

After the revolution, the barracks, like all others in Cuba, was converted into a school called Ciudad Escolar 26 de Julio, and in 1967 a **museum** (Map p412; USD$2; ⊘9am-5pm Mon-Sat, to 1pm Sun) was installed near gate 3, where the main attack took place. As Batista's soldiers had cemented over the original bullet holes from the attack, the Castro government remade them (this time without guns) years later as a poignant reminder. The museum (one of Cuba's best) contains a scale model of the barracks plus interesting and sometimes grisly artifacts, diagrams and models of the attack, its planning and its aftermath. Most moving, perhaps, are the photographs of the 61 fallen at the end.

The first barracks on this site was constructed by the Spanish in 1859, and actually takes its name after Guillermón Moncada, a War of Independence fighter who was held prisoner here in 1874.

Museo-Casa Natal de Antonio Maceo MUSEUM
(Map p412; ☑2262-3750; Los Maceos No 207; USD$1; ⊘9am-5pm Mon-Sat) This important museum is where the *mulato* general and hero of both Wars of Independence was born, on June 14, 1845, and exhibits highlights of Maceo's life with photos, letters and a tattered flag that was flown in battle. Known as the Bronze Titan in Cuba for his bravery in battle, Maceo was the definitive 'man of action.'

In his 1878 Protest of Baraguá, he rejected any compromise with the colonial authorities and went into exile rather than sell out to the Spanish. Landing at Playa Duaba in 1895, he marched his army as far west as Pinar del Río before being killed in action in 1896.

Parque Histórico Abel Santamaría PARK
(Map p412; cnr General Portuondo & Av de los Libertadores) This is the site of the former Saturnino Lora Civil Hospital, stormed by Abel Santamaría and 60 others on that fateful July day (they were later tortured and killed). On October 16, 1953, Fidel Castro was tried in the Escuela de Enfermeras for leading the Moncada attack. It was here that he made his famous *History will Absolve Me* speech.

The park contains a giant Cubist **fountain**, engraved with the countenances of Abel Santamaría and José Martí, which gushes out a veritable Niagara Falls of water.

Plaza de la Revolución SQUARE
(Map p412) As with all Cuban cities, Santiago has its bombastic Revolution Square. This one's placed strategically at the junction of two sweeping avenues and anchored by an eye-catching **statue** of dedicated city hero (and native son), Antonio Maceo, atop his horse and surrounded by 23 raised machetes. Underneath the giant mound/plinth a small reverential museum contains info on his life. Other notable buildings bordering the square include modern Teatro José María Heredia and the National Bus Station.

Palacio de Justicia LANDMARK
(Map p412; cnr Av de los Libertadores & General Portuondo) On the opposite side of the street to Parque Histórico Abel Santamaría, this court building was taken by fighters led by Raúl Castro during the Moncada attack. They were supposed to provide cover fire to Fidel's group from the rooftop but were never needed. Many of them came back two months later to be tried and sentenced in the court.

Casa Museo de Frank y Josué País MUSEUM
(Map p412; ☑2265-2710; General Banderas No 226; USD$1; ⊘9am-5pm Mon-Sat) Integral to the success of the revolution, the young País brothers organized the underground section of the M-26-7 (26th of July Movement) in Santiago de Cuba until Frank's murder by the police on July 30, 1957. The exhibits in this home-turned-museum tell the story. It's located about five blocks southeast of Museo-Casa Natal de Antonio Maceo .

☉ South of the Casco Histórico

★**Museo de la Lucha Clandestina** MUSEUM
(Map p412; ☑2262-4689; General Jesús Rabí No 1; USD$1; ⊘9am-5pm Tue-Sun) This gorgeous yellow colonial-style building houses a museum detailing the underground struggle against Batista in the 1950s. It's a fascinating, if bloody, story enhanced by far-reaching views from the balcony. The

Casco Histórico Santiago de Cuba

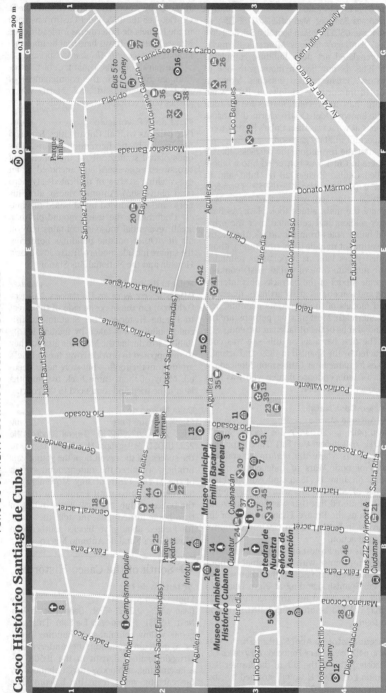

Casco Histórico Santiago de Cuba

museum was a former police station attacked by M-26-7 activists on November 30, 1956, to divert attention from the arrival of the tardy yacht *Granma*, carrying Fidel Castro and 81 others.

It's up the slope from the western end of Diego Palacios.

Parque Alameda   PARK
(Map p412; Av Jesús Menéndez) Below the Tivolí quarter, this narrow park embellishes a dockside promenade opened in 1840 and redesigned in 1893. Refurbishment for the 2015 quincentennial has made it the center of the Malecón (boardwalk) in the style of Havana's, also featuring a playground, palm trees and public wi-fi. The north end features the old **clock tower** (Map p412), *aduana* (customs house) and cigar factory. With smart architecture, sea air and a dash of port-side sketchiness, it's good for a stroll.

Tivolí   AREA
(Map p412) Santiago's old French quarter was first settled by colonists from Haiti in the late 18th and early 19th centuries. Set on a south-facing hillside overlooking the shimmering harbor, its red-tiled roofs and hidden patios are a tranquil haven these days, with old men pushing around dominoes and ebullient kids playing stickball amid pink splashes of bougainvillea.

The century-old **Padre Pico steps** (Map p406; cnr Padre Pico & Diego Palacios), cut into the steepest part of Calle Padre Pico, stand at the neighborhood's gateway.

Museo del Ron   MUSEUM
(Map p412; ☑ 2262-8884; Peralejo No 103; USD$5; ⊙9:30am-4:45pm Mon-Fri) Now housed at the Bacardí Rum Factory, this modern little museum has well-presented exhibits and multilingual guides explaining the history

and manufacture of Cuban rum. Interesting highlights include the actual taxidermied bat that inspired the Bacardí logo, as well as antique machinery used for processing and bottling the sugarcane liquor we know as rum. The end of the tour involves a toast with a shot of *añejo* (tequila).

Bacardí Rum Factory   LANDMARK

(Fábrica de Ron; Map p412; ☑2265-1212; Peralejo No 103; ☺9:30am-4:45pm) While it's not as swanky as its modern Bermuda HQ, the original Bacardí factory, which opened in 1868, oozes history. Spanish-born founder Don Facundo dreamed up the world-famous Bacardí bat symbol after discovering a bat colony in the factory's rafters. The Cuban government continues to make traditional rum here – the signature Ron Caney brand, Ron Santiago and Ron Varadero.

The Bacardí family fled the island post-revolution. In total, the factory knocks out nine million liters of rum a year, 70% of which is exported. There are currently no factory tours, but the Barrita de Ron (p419), a tourist bar attached to the factory, offers rum sales and tastings. A billboard opposite the station announces Santiago's modern battle cry: *Rebelde ayer, hospitalaria hoy, heroica siempre* (Rebellious yesterday, hospitable today, heroic always).

⊙ Vista Alegre

In any other city, Vista Alegre would be a leafy upper-middle-class neighborhood (indeed, it once was); but in revolutionary Cuba the dappled avenues and whimsical early-20th-century architecture are the domain of clinics, cultural centers, government offices, state-run restaurants and a handful of esoteric points of interest.

Palacio de Pioneros   LANDMARK

(Map p412; cnr Av Manduley & Calle 11) This eclectic mansion (built 1906–10) was once the largest and most opulent in Santiago. Since 1974 it has been a developmental center for kids (*pioneros*). In the garden is an old MiG fighter plane on which the younger pioneers play.

Museo de la Imagen   MUSEUM

(Map p412; ☑2264-2234; Calle 8 No 106; USD$1; ☺9am-5pm Mon-Fri, from 2pm Sat & Sun) A short but fascinating journey through the history of Cuban photography from Kodak to Korda, with little CIA spy cameras and lots of old and contemporary photos. The

---

🏃 City Walk
A Walk Through History

START PARQUE ALAMEDA
END CUARTEL MONCADA
LENGTH 2KM; THREE TO FOUR HOURS

Against a backdrop of verdant mountains and a steely blue bay, a walking tour of Santiago's *casco histórico* (historical center) is an obligatory rite of passage for first-time visitors keen to uncover the steamy tropical sensations that make this city tick.

Start beside the bay with your sights set uphill. Parque Alameda inhabits the rundown thoroughfare facing Santiago's not-so-busy port. Most of the excitement lies to the east in a hilly neighborhood colonized by French-Haitians in the early 1800s and baptized ❶ **El Tivolí** (p407). Tivolí is one of Santiago's most picturesque and traffic-lite quarters where red-roofed houses and steep streets retain a time-warped Cuban atmosphere. The neighborhood's only real 'sight' is the ❷ **Museo de la Lucha Clandestina** (p405) reached by following Calle Diego Palacios uphill from the port. From the museum take the famous ❸ **Padre Pico steps** (p407) – a terracotta staircase built into the hillside – downhill to Calle Bartolomé Masó where a right turn will deposit you on the breeze-lapped ❹ **Balcón de Velázquez** (p403), site of an ancient fort. This stupendous view once inspired less calming contemplations; early Spanish colonists used it to look out for meddlesome pirates.

Head east next, avoiding the angry roar of the motorbikes, until you resurface in ❺ **Parque Céspedes** (p402). ❻ **Casa de Diego Velázquez** (p402), with its Moorish fringes and intricate wooden arcades, is believed to be the oldest house still standing in Cuba and anchors the square on its west side. Contrasting impressively on the south side is the mighty, mustard facade of the ❼ **Catedral de Nuestra Señora de la Asunción** (p402). This building has been ransacked, burned, rocked by earthquakes and rebuilt, then remodeled and restored and ransacked again. Statues of Christopher Columbus and Fray Bartolomé de las Casas flank the entrance in ironic juxtaposition.

If you need a break, step out on to the lazy terrace bar at **8 Hotel Casa Granda** (p415) on the southeastern corner of the park. Graham Greene came here in the 1950s on a clandestine mission to interview Fidel Castro. The interview never came off; instead he managed to smuggle a suitcase of clothes up to the rebels in the mountains.

Follow the music as you exit and plunge into the paint-peeled romance of Calle Heredia, Santiago's – and one of Cuba's – most atmospheric streets, which rocks like New Orleans at the height of the jazz era. Its centerpiece is the infamous **9 Casa de la Trova** (p420).

Heading upstream on Heredia, you'll pass street stalls, cigar peddlers, a guy dragging a double bass, and countless motorbikes. That yellowish house on the right with the poem emblazoned on the wall is **10 Casa Natal de José María Heredia y Heredia** (p403), birthplace of one of Cuba's greatest poets. You might find a living scribe in **11 Uneac** (p421), the famous national writers' union a few doors down. Stick your head inside and check out the *cartelera* (culture calendar) advertising the coming week's offerings. Plenty more dead legends are offered up in print in funky **12 Librería La Escalera Eddy Tamayo** (p421), a roguish bookstore across the street.

Cross the street next and stick your nose into the **13 Museo del Carnaval** (p403).

Divert along Pío Rosado one block to Aguilera where you'll be confronted by the sturdy Grecian columns of the **14 Museo Municipal Emilio Bacardí Moreau** (p402). Back outside, narrow Aguilera winds uphill to the shady **15 Plaza de Dolores** (p403), which remains amazingly tranquil, considering the ongoing motorcycle mania. There are benches to relax on underneath the trees while you weigh up if you have enough energy to keep going.

Skip north a block to **16 Calle José A Saco** (p402), a steep pedestrian street with pet shops and *churro* (fried dough) salespeople that will lead you directly east to **17 Plaza de Marte** (p404), the third of the *casco histórico's* pivotal squares and far more manic than the other two.

The walk ends in what is perhaps Santiago's most politically significant site, the art deco **18 Cuartel Moncada** (p405), a one-time military barracks where the first shots of Cuba's Castro-led revolution were fired in 1953. Today it functions more innocuously as a school, but a preserved section at the rear where the short skirmishes between the soldiers and the rebels took place is now one of Cuba's most interesting and poignant museums.

museum also guards a library of rare films and documentaries.

Casa del Caribe
NOTABLE BUILDING

(Map p412; ☑ 2264-2285; Calle 13 No 154; ☺ 9am-5pm Mon-Fri) FREE Founded in 1982 to study Caribbean life, this cultural institution organizes the Festival del Caribe (p412) and the Fiesta del Fuego (p411) every July and also hosts various concert nights. The portal of all things Santería and *folklórico*, this cultural institution can arrange dance lessons in conga, *son* and salsa for USD$10 per hour. Resident staff member Juan Eduardo Castillo can also organize lessons in percussion. Real aficionados can inquire about in-depth courses on Afro-Cuban religions and culture.

Loma de San Juan
MONUMENT

(Map p412; San Juan Hill) Future American president Teddy Roosevelt forged his reputation on this small hillock where, flanked by the immortal rough riders, he supposedly led a fearless cavalry charge against the Spanish to seal a famous US victory. Protected by pleasantly manicured grounds adjacent to the modern-day Motel San Juan, Loma de San Juan marks the spot of the Spanish–Cuban–American War's only land battle (July 1, 1898).

In reality, it is doubtful Roosevelt even mounted his horse in Santiago, while the purportedly clueless Spanish garrison – outnumbered 10 to one – managed to hold off more than 6000 American troops for 24 hours. Cannons, trenches and numerous US monuments, including a bronze rough rider, enhance the classy gardening, while the only acknowledgement of a Cuban presence is the rather understated monument to the unknown Mambís (the name for the 19th-century rebels fighting Spain).

José María Heredia y Heredia Statue
MONUMENT

(Map p412; cnr Av Manduley & Calle 13) The traffic circle at the corner of Av Manduley and Calle 13 contains an impressive marble statue of poet José María Heredia y Heredia.

◉ Around Santiago de Cuba

★ Castillo de San Pedro de la Roca del Morro
FORT

(El Morro; ☑ 2269-1569; USD$5; ☺ 9am-7pm) A Unesco World Heritage site since 1997, the San Pedro fort sits impregnably atop a 60m-high promontory at the entrance to Santiago harbor, 10km southwest of the city.

The stupendous views from the upper terrace take in the wild western ribbon of Santiago's coastline backed by the velvety Sierra Maestra.

Multilingual guides provide invaluable historical background and color; be sure to tip.

The fort was designed in 1587 by famous Italian military engineer Juan Bautista Antonelli (who also designed La Punta and El Morro forts in Havana) to protect Santiago from pillaging pirates who had successfully sacked the city in 1554. Because of financial constraints, the building work didn't start until 1633 (17 years after Antonelli's death), and it carried on sporadically for the next 60 years. In the interim, British privateer Henry Morgan sacked and partially destroyed it.

Finally finished in the early 1700s, El Morro's massive batteries, bastions, magazines and walls got little opportunity to serve their true purpose. With the era of piracy in decline, the fort was converted into a prison in the 1800s, and it stayed that way (bar a brief interlude during the 1898 Spanish–Cuban–American War) until Cuban architect Francisco Prat Puig mustered up a restoration plan in the late 1960s.

Today, the fort hosts the swashbuckling Museo de Piratería, with another room given over to the US-Spanish naval battle that took place in the bay in 1898.

The fort, like Havana, has a cañonazo ceremony (firing of the cannon) each day at sunset when actors dress up in Mambís regalia.

To get to El Morro from the city center, take bus 212 to Ciudamar and walk the final 20 minutes. Alternatively, a round-trip taxi ride from Parque Céspedes with wait should cost no more than USD$25.

★ Cementerio Santa Ifigenia
CEMETERY

(Map p412; Av Crombet; USD$3; ☺ 8am-6pm) Nestled peacefully on the city's western extremity, the Cementerio Santa Ifigenia is second only to Havana's Necrópolis Cristóbal Colón (p88) in its importance and grandiosity. Created in 1868 to accommodate the victims of the War of Independence and a simultaneous yellow-fever outbreak, the Santa Ifigenia includes many great historical figures among its 8000-plus tombs, notably the mausoleum of José Martí and final resting place of Fidel Castro.

Names to look out for include Tomás Estrada Palma (1835–1908), Cuba's now disgraced first president; Emilio Bacardí y Moreau (1844–1922) of the famous rum dynasty; María Grajales, the widow of independence hero Antonio Maceo; and Mariana Grajales, Maceo's mother; 11 of the 31 generals of the independence struggles; the Spanish soldiers who died in the battles of San Juan Hill and Caney; the 'martyrs' of the 1953 Moncada Barracks attack; M-26-7 activists Frank and Josué País; father of Cuban independence, Carlos Manuel de Céspedes (1819–74); and international celebrity-cum-popular-musical-rake, Compay Segundo (1907–2003) of Buena Vista Social Club fame.

Many visitors come to pay homage at the quasi-religious mausoleum to national hero José Martí (1853–95). Erected in 1951 during the Batista era, the imposing hexagonal structure is positioned so that Martí's wooden casket (draped solemnly in a Cuban flag) receives daily shafts of sunlight. This is in response to a comment Martí made in one of his poems that he would like to die not as a traitor in darkness, but with his visage facing the sun. A round-the-clock guard of the mausoleum is changed, amid much pomp and ceremony, every 30 minutes.

Now, the cemetery's most famous resident is a recent arrival, situated alongside his hero, José Martí. After a cross-country procession that re-created the revolutionary's 1959 victory march in reverse, the ashes of Fidel Castro Ruz (1926–2016) were interred here on December 4, 2016. The private ceremony featured a 21-gun salute and no speeches. Castro has famously insisted that he wanted no tributes, statues or honors in his name. This simple monument takes the form of an enormous boulder bearing a plaque with just the name Fidel.

Horse carts go along Av Jesús Menéndez, from Parque Alameda to Cementerio Santa Ifigenia; otherwise, it's a hearty, leg-stretching walk.

Jardín de los Helechos   GARDENS
(✆2260-8335; Carretera de El Caney No 129; USD$3; ⊘9am-5pm Mon-Fri) This peaceful garden is a lush haven of 350 types of ferns and 90 types of orchids. It's the erstwhile private collection of *santiagüero* Manuel Caluff, donated in 1984 to the Academia de Ciencias de Cuba (Cuban Academy of Science), which continues to keep the 3000-sq-meter garden in psychedelic bloom. The center of the garden has an inviting dense copse-cum-sanctuary dotted with benches.

For the orchids, the best time is November to January. Bus 5 (20 centavos) from Plaza de Marte in central Santiago passes this way, or you can hire a taxi. It's 2km from downtown Santiago de Cuba on the road to El Caney.

Cayo Granma   ISLAND
A small, populated key near the jaws of the bay, Cayo Granma is a little fantasy island of red-roofed wooden houses – many of them on stilts above the water – that guard a traditional fishing community. You can hike up to the small whitewashed Iglesia de San Rafael at the key's highest point, or walk around the whole island in 15 minutes.

The best thing about this place, however, is just hanging out and soaking up a bit of the real Cuba. Eat at seafood haven Restaurante El Cayo or the clapboard Palmares restaurant jutting out over the water on the Cayo's far side.

To get to the key, take the regular ferry (leaving every one to 1½ hours) from Punta Gorda just below El Morro fort. The boat stops en route at La Socapa (actually still the mainland; the western jaw of the Bahía de Santiago) where there are decent beaches for swimming.

🌄 Courses & Tours

You can arrange your own tour to out-of-town sights with one of the ubiquitous taxis at Parque Céspedes in front of the cathedral. Ask around for price comparisons.

UniversiTUR   LANGUAGE
(Map p412; ✆2264-3186; www.uo.edu.cu; Universidad de Oriente, cnr Calle L & Ampliación de Terrazas) Arranges Spanish courses. Monthly rates for 60-hour courses (three hours a day, five days a week) start at USD$280.

Ecotur   TOURS
(Map p406; ✆2268-7279; General Lacret No 701a, cnr Heredia) The best bet for guided summit attempts on Pico Turquino.

🎉 Festivals & Events

★Carnaval   CARNIVAL
(⊘Jul) One of the largest and most authentic in the Caribbean, Santiago de Cuba's version of Carnaval lets loose with fantastic costumes, food stalls, and music round the clock. The whole city spills out onto the streets to absorb it.

★Fiesta del Fuego   CULTURAL
(⊘early Jul) The literal firing up for Carnaval, this early-July celebration includes a ceremony where the devil is burned to the glee of huge crowds on the Malecón.

Santiago de Cuba

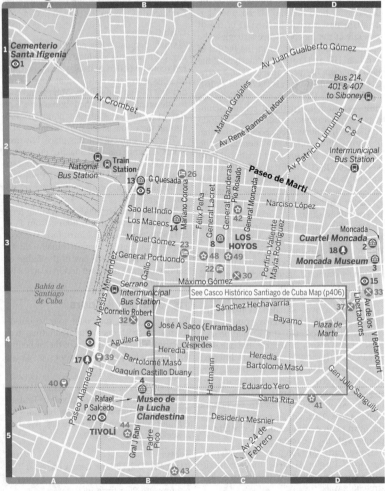

SANTIAGO DE CUBA PROVINCE SANTIAGO DE CUBA

Fiesta de San Juan CULTURAL
(☉ Jun 24) The summer season begins with the Fiesta de San Juan, celebrated with processions and conga dancing by cultural associations called *focos culturales*.

Festival Internacional de la Trova Pepe Sánchez MUSIC
(☉ Mar) Named for the father of *trova*, this festival is well into its sixth decade of celebrating this Cuban musical tradition.

Festival Internacional Matamoros Son MUSIC
(☉ Oct) A tribute to one of Santiago de Cuba's musical greats, Miguel Matamoros, kicks off

in late October with dances, lectures, concerts and workshops. Main venues include the Casa de la Trova (p420) and the Teatro José María Heredia (p421).

Festival Internacional de Coros MUSIC
(☉ Nov) The international choir festival in late November brings in strong international singing groups for some cultural cross-fertilization and spirit-lifting music.

Festival del Caribe CULTURAL
(☉ Jul) Festival of Caribbean culture held in July. Together with the Fiesta del Fuego, it's a warm-up for Carnaval.

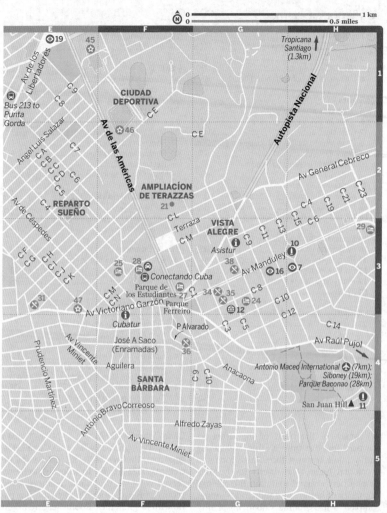

Boleros de Oro   MUSIC
(⊙ Jun) Arrive in mid to late June for this crooner's extravaganza that is replicated in various cities throughout the country.

🛏 Sleeping

With its bounty of colonial casas and grand hotels, Santiago has a room for every type of traveler.

★ **Roy's Terrace Inn**   CASA PARTICULAR **$**
(Map p406; ☑ 2262-0522; roysterraceinn@gmail. com; Diego Palacios No 177, btwn Padre Pico & Mariano Corona; r USD$35; P🌢🛜) From the hanging rooftop garden to wall murals

and impeccable rooms, every fiber gleams. Run by an enthusiastic team of well-traveled Cubans and local mamas who woo you with their warmth and cooking, this spot is tops. Rooms are filled with modern amenities, including TV, hairdryers and information packets. Service – in English, Spanish, French and some German – is a highlight.

Guests are given preference for dinner reservations at the tiny rooftop restaurant. Consider it a must.

★ **Casa Milena**   CASA PARTICULAR **$**
(Map p406; ☑ 5-319-5814, 2262-8822; penelope 1212@nauta.cu; Heredia No 306; r USD$25-30;

Santiago de Cuba

✺) Smack in the heart of the street renowned for live music, this welcoming family home features three huge rooms in a colonial home. The utterly lovely Milena and her husband maintain the colonial simplicity of her great-grandparents' home, complete with genuine Cuban hospitality. It's very clean and central.

★ Casa Terraza Pavo Real CASA PARTICULAR $
(Map p406; ☎2265-8589; juanmarti13@yahoo.es; Santa Rita No 302, cnr Hartmann; r USD$25-30; ✺✸☎) The meticulously maintained family home of Juan Martí has a palatial quality, with a riot of antique furniture, light-filtering *vitrales* (stained-glass windows) and coiled spiral staircases. The crowning glory is a huge Alhambra-esque patio with a sleep-invoking fountain and an expansive roof terrace with exotic orchids. Yet, many might feel at odds with the tropical birds and peacocks in cages. The breakfast spreads are noteworthy.

Casa Colonial 1893 CASA PARTICULAR $
(Map p406; ☎2262-2470; casacolonial1893@gmail.com; Hechavarría No 301, cnr General Lacret; r USD$25-30; ✺) In a lovely, well-preserved colonial, this home features seven rooms gathered around a huge interior patio with original tiles. Rooms feature bright satin bedcovers. Not unusual for casas where renting is important to the household, but still unsettling, the family congregates off to the side, beyond a partial wall in the front room.

Casa Señora Inalvis CASA PARTICULAR $
(Map p412; ☎5-308-8020, 2265-1113; nalvis casado@nauta.cu; Calle 6ta No 660; r USD$25-30; ✺) Located on a convenient corner near Meliá Santiago de Cuba hotel, this cute suburban home has just a couple of rooms and a shady back patio. The host Sra Inalvis is a gem, a former journalist who is unusually helpful and quick to offer fresh juice or coffee.

Casa Nelson & Deisy
CASA PARTICULAR $

(Map p406; ☑ 5-365-8133, 2265-6372; casanelson ydeysi@yahoo.es; Donato Mármol No 476½; r USD$20-25; ✳) Decked in white, this thoroughly modern casa sits in a renovated building in the colonial core. There are three smart rooms and a private terrace. Nelson and Deisy are famous for their cooking, with good vegetarian fare and cocktails to boot. Has very cordial service.

Casa Lola
CASA PARTICULAR $

(Map p412; ☑ 2265-4120; Mariano Corona No 309, btwn General Portuondo & Miguel Gómez; r USD$20-25; ✳) With a large private garden crowned by a gazebo, who needs plaza chill-out time? The young resident hosts go out of their way to be helpful. Rooms are basic but clean, one with a large balcony overlooking the street. As the surrounding streets are poorly lit, coming home from the bar can seem like a long walk – better take a taxi.

Casa Colonial 'Maruchi'
CASA PARTICULAR $

(Map p412; ☑ 2262-0767, 5-261-3791; maruchib@ yahoo.es; Hartmann No 357, btwn General Portuondo & Máximo Gómez; r USD$30; ✳🛜) This 19th-century colonial with brick walls and museum-worthy furniture is a temple to all things Santería. The three guest rooms feature brass beds with quilts, the upstairs option the most private. All types stay here: *santeros* (priests of Santería), backpackers and foreign students studying for PhDs on the Regla de Ocha. With encyclopedic knowledge of Afro-Cuban religions, Maruchi can organize presentations.

The food is legendary, and the fecund courtyard equally sublime.

Casa Yoyi
CASA PARTICULAR $

(Map p412; ☑ 2262-3166; eulogiadelosmilagros@ nauta.cu; Mariano Corona No 54; r USD$25-30; ✳) A 10-minute walk from the center in the Los Hoyos neighborhood, cheerful Casa Yoyi is modern and tranquil. There are large 1st-floor rooms and an apartment decked out with flat-screen TVs and bright flower prints. Beds vary in quality – some sag – so it pays to see a few rooms. Has a great roof terrace. English and Russian are spoken.

Casa Mili
CASA PARTICULAR $

(Map p412; ☑ 2266-7456; mileidis.rodriguez@nau ta.cu; Calle 8 No 156, btwn Av 5 & 7; r incl breakfast USD$25; ✳) If you can't bear the motorcycle madness of the city center, escape to the residential quarter of Vista Alegre and this spacious, high-ceiling casa with its fine frontal columns and shiny floors. Run by the determined Clara, there are five rooms, with more private ones behind the patio, including an ample family room.

Hotel Las Américas
HOTEL $

(Map p412; ☑ 2264-2011; jcarpeta@hamerica.seu. tur.cu; cnr Avs de las Américas & General Cebreco; r incl breakfast from USD$43; P✳@🌊) The 70 rooms here offer the usual lackluster Islazul interiors, probably not worth it unless you are after the standard hotel amenities. It does offer comprehensive facilities, with a restaurant, 24-hour cafe, small pool and nightly entertainment.

Hotel Rex
HOTEL $$

(Map p406; Av Victoriano Garzón; s/d incl breakfast USD$45/56; ✳🛜) The hotel that once served as a pre-raid base for the Moncadistas in 1953 has been reborn as a comfortable mid-range accommodations option. Suspended above the motorcycle madness and musical backbeat of central Santiago, it maintains a very Cuban flair – rare for hotels here. There's a pleasant roof terrace and an interior bar with soccer on the TV.

Tranquil it isn't; unmistakably Cuba, it most definitely is.

Hotel Versalles
HOTEL $$

(☑ 2269-1016; Alturas de Versalles; s/d incl breakfast USD$79/100; P✳@🌊) Not to be confused with the namesake rumba district of Matanzas, or the resplendent home of Louis XIV, this modest hotel is on the outskirts of town off the road to El Morro. There's a dose of style in its inviting pool and the comfortable rooms with small terraces.

Hotel Casa Granda
HOTEL $$

(Map p406; ☑ 2265-3024; Heredia No 201, cnr General Lacret; s/d incl breakfast USD$66/97; ✳@🛜) This elegant 1914 hotel, artfully described by Graham Greene in his book *Our Man in Havana*, has 58 rooms and classic atmosphere. Greene stayed here in the late 1950s when he enjoyed relaxing on the street-side terrace while his famous pen captured the nocturnal essence of the city. Six decades later, updated rooms are quite luxurious, and the atmosphere remains potent.

Now part of the Iberostar chain, rooms were being renovated at the time of our visit.

Hotel Libertad
HOTEL $$

(Map p406; ☑ 2262-7710; reserva@libertad.tur.cu; Aguilera No 658; s/d USD$61/66; ✳@🛜) Cheap Cuban hotel chain Islazul breaks out of its Soviet-themed concrete-block obsession and goes semi-colonial in this venerable beauty on Plaza de Marte. It has positive staff and 17 clean, uninspiring but high-ceilinged rooms featuring narrow singles. It's quirky in novel ways – don't be surprised if a salesperson is selling clothes out of suitcases in the hall.

Hostal San Basilio BOUTIQUE HOTEL **$$**
(Map p406; ☑2265-1702; reservas@hotelver salles.co.cu; Bartolomé Masó No 403, btwn Pío Rosado & Porfirio Valiente; s/d incl breakfast USD$30/50; ✹@) Acquired by the Encanto chain, the lovely eight-room San Basilio (named for the original name of the street on which it lies) is cozy and refreshingly contemporary – with a romantic colonial setting including a petite patio dripping with ferns. Rooms come with DVD players, umbrellas, bathroom scales and mini bottles of rum. A small restaurant serves breakfast and lunch.

Villa Gaviota HOTEL **$$**
(Map p412; ☑2264-1370; jefe.recepcion@gavi ota.co.cu; Calle 21, Vista Alegre; s/d incl breakfast USD$36/54; P✹❄) Santiago's quiet suburban Vista Alegre district is either an oasis of calm – or a ghost town. Odd duck Villa Gaviota has a number of attractive clustered properties and apartments here with barebones furnishings. With ample greenery, it's private and fairly priced but service can be achingly slow. Features include a swimming pool, bar-restaurant, a billiards room and laundry.

Hotel Balcón del Caribe HOTEL **$$**
(☑2269-1506, 2269-1011; Km 7.5, Carretera del Morro; s/d incl breakfast USD$34/56; P✹❄❄) The tremendous setting next to El Morro fort (p410) is counterbalanced by the usual humdrum Islazul hotel-chain foibles: flowery curtains, ancient mattresses and furnishings salvaged from a 1970s garage sale. But there's a pool and the view is stunning. Get a room inside the complex, not a grottier external cabin. It's located 10km from the city center, making transport a headache.

★**Hotel Imperial** HISTORIC HOTEL **$$$**
(Map p406; ☑2262-8230; José A Saco, btwn Félix Peña & General Lacret; s/d incl breakfast USD$89/144; ✹❄) The return of a Santiago landmark, the eclectic-style 1915 Hotel Imperial has been refurbished to sparkling condition with some welcome concessions to modernity. The 39 rooms are smartly furnished with flat-screen TVs, tall windows and glass showers. Features an elevator to an elegant roof-terrace bar with great city views and live music on weekends.

★**Meliá Santiago de Cuba** HOTEL **$$$**
(Map p412; ☑2268-7070; www.meliacuba.com; cnr Av de las Américas & Calle M; s/d incl breakfast USD$107/126; P✹@❄❄) Sleek on the inside, a blue-mirrored monster on the outside, the 1990s-designed Meliá is Santiago's only 'international' hotel with a laundry list of amenities hard to find elsewhere. Count on real bathtubs in every room, three pools, four restaurants, various shopping facilities and an elegant 15th-floor bar. The downsides are its location on the outskirts and lack of genuine Cuban charm.

Gran Hotel San Felix HOTEL **$$$**
(Map p406; ☑2228-7171; José A Saco, btwn General Lacret & Hartmann; s/d incl breakfast USD$95/134; ✹@) This remake of a classic downtown hotel falls slightly short. The 42 rooms are generally large, and there's a pleasant roof terrace and cyber cafe. Guests can choose from rooms with a balcony overlooking the pedestrian street or interior rooms without windows.

✖ Eating

Despite having more than one million inhabitants and a medley of cultures, the restaurant scene is comparatively lean. However, quality cuisine isn't hard to find.

Ranchon Los Naranjo CUBAN **$**
(Map p412; ☑2271-4068; Pedro Alvarado No 16; CUP$6-10; ☺noon-11pm) On a hilly residential street by Meliá, this open-air restaurant offers great-value meals. Grilled fish and lamb stewed in tomato sauce come recommended. Maybe it's the out-of-the-way location, but it's conducive to chilling. Beware the neon cocktails that run a little too sweet. Prices are in *moneda nacional*.

Bendita Farándula CARIBBEAN **$**
(Map p406; ☑2265-3739; Monseñor Barnada No 513; meals USD$5-9; ☺noon-11pm) You would probably never wander in here unbidden, but with an ambience reminiscent of a provincial French bistro, this cozy two-floored place does Santiago's only *pescado con leche de coco* (fish with coconut sauce; a Baracoan specialty), curried lamb and a really nice *bistek de cerdo con jamon y queso* (pork steak with ham and cheese).

Jardín de las Enramadas ICE CREAM **$**
(Map p412; ☑2265-2205; cnr José A Saco & 10 de Octubre; ice cream USD$1-2; ☺9:45am-11:45pm) Occupying a block just down from the *casco histórico* en route to the port, this garden is

devoted to ornamental plants and great ice cream (which comes with marshmallows and biscuits). Service is exemplary.

La Fortaleza
CUBAN $

(Map p412; ☑ 2264-6296; cnr Av Manduley & Calle 3, Vista Alegre; meals USD$3-7; ☉ noon-11:30pm) In a conducive setting amid Vista Alegre's

mansions, this spacious, inviting shady patio serves above-average food (pay in pesos) alongside live music at lunchtime. But? A big fat zero for the quality of service.

La Arboleda
ICE CREAM $

(Map p412; cnr Avs de los Libertadores & Victoriano Garzón; ice cream USD$1; ☉ 10am-11:40pm

---

MONCADA: THE 26TH OF JULY MOVEMENT

Glorious call to arms or poorly enacted putsch: the 1953 attack on Santiago's Moncada Barracks, while big on bravado, came to within a hair's breadth of destroying Castro's nascent revolutionary movement before the ink was even dry on the manifesto.

With his political ambitions ravaged by Batista's 1952 coup, Castro – who had been due to represent the Orthodox Party in the canceled elections – quickly decided to pursue a more direct path to power by swapping the ballot box for a rifle.

Handpicking and training 116 men and two women from Havana and its environs, the combative Fidel, along with his trusty lieutenant, Abel Santamaría, began to put together a plan so secret that even his younger brother Raúl was initially kept in the dark.

The aim was to storm the Cuartel Moncada, a sprawling military barracks in Santiago (in Cuba's seditious Oriente region) with a shabby history as a Spanish prison. Rather than make an immediate grab for power, Castro's more savvy plan was to capture enough ammunition to escape up into the Sierra Maestra from where he and Santamaría planned to spearhead a wider popular uprising against Batista's malignant Mafia-backed government.

Castro chose Moncada because it was the second-biggest army barracks in the country, yet distant enough from Havana to ensure it was poorly defended. With equal sagacity, the date was set for July 26, the day after Santiago's annual Carnaval, when both police and soldiers would be tired and hungover from the boisterous revelries.

But as the day of attack dawned, things quickly started to go wrong. The plan's underlying secrecy didn't help. Meeting in a quiet rural farmhouse near the village of Siboney, many recruits arrived with no idea that they were expected to fire guns at armed soldiers, and they nervously balked. Secondly, with all but one of the Moncadistas drawn from the Havana region (the only native *santiagüero* was an 18-year-old local fixer named Renato Guitart), few were familiar with Santiago's complex street layout and after setting out at 5am in convoy from the Siboney farm, at least two cars became temporarily lost.

The attack, when it finally began, lasted approximately 10 minutes from start to finish and was little short of a debacle. Splitting into three groups, a small contingent led by Raúl Castro took the adjacent Palacio de Justicia, another headed by Abel Santamaría stormed a nearby military hospital, while the largest group led by Fidel attempted to enter the barracks itself.

Though the first two groups were initially successful, Fidel's convoy, poorly disguised in stolen military uniforms, was spotted by an outlying guard patrol and only one of the cars made it into the compound before the alarm was raised.

In the ensuing chaos, five rebels were killed in an exchange of gunfire before Castro, seeing the attack was futile, beat a disorganized retreat. Raúl's group also managed to escape, but the group in the hospital (including Abel Santamaría) was captured and later tortured and executed.

Fidel escaped into the surrounding mountains and was captured a few days later; but, due to public revulsion surrounding the other brutal executions, his life was spared and the path of history radically altered.

Had it not been for the revolution's ultimate success, this shambolic attempt at an insurrection would have gone down in history as a military nonevent. But viewed through the prism of the 1959 revolution, it has been depicted as the first glorious shot on the road to power.

It also provided Fidel with the political pulpit he so badly needed. 'History will absolve me,' he trumpeted confidently at his subsequent trial. Within six years it effectively had.

Tue-Sun) Santiago's ice cream cathedral is a little out of the center, not that this lessens the queue length. Yell out *¿Quién es último?* (who is last?) and take your place on the Av de los Libertadores side of the parlor. Milkshakes are sometimes sold from the outside window.

Cafe Hotel Casa Granda CAFE $
(Map p406; ☑ 2265-3021; Heredia No 201, Casa Granda; snacks USD$2-8; ⊙ 9am-midnight; 🛜) Positioned like a whitewashed theater box overlooking the unscripted cabaret of Parque Céspedes, the Casa Granda's Parisian-style terrace cafe has to be one of the best people-watching locations in Cuba. Food-wise, you're talking snacks (burgers, hot dogs, sandwiches etc) and service-wise you're talking impassive, verging on grumpy; but the setting beats the grump factor.

Restaurante España SEAFOOD $
(Map p412; Av Victoriano Garzón; meals USD$3-7; ⊙ noon-4pm Mon, noon-4pm & 6-10pm Tue-Sun) Get ready for the Arctic blast of air-conditioning and readjust your Cuban-food preconceptions before you walk into España. It specializes in seafood cooked with panache and – on occasion – fresh herbs. Try the lobster or tangy prawns, but bypass the Cuban wine, which is almost undrinkable.

El Barracón CARIBBEAN $
(Map p412; ☑ 2266-1877; Av Victoriano Garzón; meals USD$3-9; ⊙ noon-11pm) El Barracón tries to reignite the roots of Afro-Cuban culture and cuisine with mixed results. The state-run restaurant's interior, a mix of atmospheric Santería shrine and *cimarrón* is intriguing, but the food can't match its private competition. Stick to the delicious *tostones* (fried plantain patties) filled with chorizo and cheese, or opt for the lamb special.

Panadería Doña Neli BAKERY $
(Map p406; ☑ 2264-1528; cnr Aguilera & General Serafin Sánchez; breads & snacks USD$0.50-1; ⊙ 7am-7pm) Bakery on Plaza de Marte, vending divine-smelling bread and cakes with a scowl.

★ Roy's Terrace Inn
Roof Garden Restaurant CUBAN $$
(Map p406; ☑ 2262-0522; roysterraceinn@gmail.com; Diego Palacios No 177, btwn Padre Pico & Mariano Corona; meals USD$10-15; ⊙ 7-9:30pm; 🛜🍽) If you wish the rest of Cuba could harness this formula: quality homemade food, caring service and excellent atmosphere. Reserve one day ahead for one of only six rooftop tables

surrounded by tumbling flowers in candlelight. Cocktails deliver and family-style servings come overflowing. Fish, chicken or pork are served with sides such as crispy *tamal*es or sautéed eggplant. Vegans and vegetarians welcome.

★ St Pauli INTERNATIONAL $$
(Map p406; ☑ 2265-2292; José A Saco No 605; meals USD$4-15; ⊙ noon-11pm Mon-Thu, to midnight Fri-Sun) In a city of no great culinary tradition, St Pauli arrived like a hurricane. Walk the long, mural-decorated corridor to a bright room featuring blackboard menus and a glass-wall kitchen. Everything is consistently good, particularly the cocktail-glass gazpacho, *pulpo al ajillo* (octopus with garlic) and pineapple chicken fajitas. If you've come behind a group: patience!

★ Madrileño CUBAN $$
(Map p412; ☑ 2264-4138; Calle 8 No 105, Vista Alegre; meals USD$4-15; ⊙ noon-11pm) A well-respected, good-quality option, Madrileño occupies a classy colonial abode in Vista Alegre with interior patio dining with chirping birds. Contrary to the name, this is Cuban *comida criolla* (Creole food). Succulent odors waft from the kitchen. There's an extensive menu with an emphasis on grilled meats.

There's dependable Italian fare such as pasta, or Caribbean flavors that have been marinated on the barbecue and glazed and trussed to spicy perfection. The succulent smoked steaks or seafood *brochetas* are both good. No harm in booking early: it's popular.

Thoms Yadira Restaurante CUBAN $$
(Map p406; ☑ 5-555-1207, 5-267-0196; General Lacret No 705 altos, btwn Heredia & Bartolomé Masó; mains USD$4-16; ⊙ 10am-1:30am) This convivial upstairs restaurant just off Parque Céspedes turns out consistently high-quality seafood favorites including grilled lobster, pasta dishes and salads. A central, reliable spot for dinner before hitting Casa de la Trova; it's popular so expect a wait at peak times.

El Palenquito PARRILLA $$
(☑ 2264-5220; Av del Río No 28, btwn Calle 6 & Carretera de Caney; mains USD$6-12; ⊙ noon-midnight) Barbecue is the specialty of this casual backyard restaurant on the outskirts of Santiago. Grilled pork and chicken are served with the typical sides, but the real star is dessert. Try rich sapote or coconut ice cream in the shells of the original fruit – portions are huge, but you suddenly might not want to share. With good service.

El Holandes CUBAN $$

(Map p406; ☑ 2262-4878; Heredia No 251; mains USD$4-15; ⊙ noon-midnight) A small, pleasing *paladar* (privately owned restaurant) with seating indoors or on a pleasant elevated terrace. The food is classic Cuban, the setting clean and the location prime seating for people-watching and unexpected street concerts.

Restaurante El Morro CARIBBEAN $$

(☑ 2269-1576; Castillo del Morro; mains USD$6-12; ⊙ noon-5pm) Bravo to the spectacular cliffside location sporting huge sea views. Classics, such as roast chicken and pork, are nicely presented. A busload of European and North American 50-somethings can really slow down service, so time your visit. Not that this put off Paul McCartney, who ate here during a whistle-stop 2000 visit (his plate is proudly mounted on the wall).

According to the waiters, the world's most famous vegetarian made do with an omelet. For meat-eaters, the set *comida criolla* (Creole food) lunch is a better bet, a filling spread with soup, main, a small dessert and a drink. Take bus 212 to Ciudamar and walk the last 20 minutes, or take a taxi and combine it with a fort visit.

Compay Gallo CUBAN $$

(Map p412; ☑ 2265-8395; Máximo Gómez No 503 altos; meals USD$4-10; ⊙ noon-11pm) Upstairs in a typical narrow Santiago street on the cusp of the city center, Compay Gallo does classic Cuban food with mixed results. Try the prawn-cocktail starter and the *ragout de codero* (lamb ragu) with ample vegetables.

Ristorante Italiano La Fontana ITALIAN $$$

(Map p412; Meliá Santiago de Cuba, cnr Av de las Américas & Calle M; mains USD$6-18; ⊙ noon-11pm) Pizza *deliciosa* and lasagna *formidable*, ravioli and garlic bread; *mamma mía*, this has to be the number-one option for breaking away from all that chicken and pork! Prices are jacked up on Chilean wines, but it might be worth it anyway.

Restaurante Zunzún CARIBBEAN $$$

(Map p412; ☑ 2264-1528; Av Manduley No 159, Vista Alegre; meals USD$12-18; ⊙ noon-10pm) Dine in bygone bourgeois style in this mansion turned restaurant, Zunzún, in the once upscale Vista Alegre neighborhood. It has always been lauded, though overpriced. Exotic dishes include chicken curry, paella or a formidable cheese plate and cognac. Expect professional, attentive service and entertaining troubadours.

🍷 **Drinking & Nightlife**

★ **Casa Granda Roof Garden Bar** BAR

(Map p406; top fl, Heredia No 201; cover USD$3-10; ⊙ 11am-1am) Slip up to the 5th-floor roof of Casa Granda for the most breathtaking sunset in Cuba. Views of the scene in Parque Céspedes and the dramatically lit cathedral are well worth the charge for nonguests (it increases after 7pm), which credits toward your first drink. Drinks may be double the cost of those elsewhere, but they come garnished with spectacular Santiago views..

Cervecería Puerto del Rey MICROBREWERY

(Map p412; ☑ 2268-6048; cnr Paseo Alameda & Aduana; ⊙ noon-midnight) You know Cuba is changing when you find an actual warehouse-style brewpub filled with locals quaffing pints brewed on-site. The four beers at this noisy, fun spot range from *extra-clara* (light lager) to *negra* (black), which is as diverse an array as you'll see in Cuba. There's decent pub food.

La Gran Sofía CAFE

(Map p406; Plácido; ⊙ 24hr) A local hangout where the coffee is good and *bocaditos* (snacks) won't set you back.

Bar Sindo Garay BAR

(Map p406; ☑ 2265-1531; cnr Tamayo Fleites & General Lacret; ⊙ 11am-11pm) As much a museum to one of Cuba's most famous *trova* musicians (Sindo Garay, most renowned for his composition *Perla marina*) as a bar, this is a smart, usually packed place, serving great cocktails on pedestrianized Tamayo Fleites.

Café La Isabelica CAFE

(Map p406; ☑ 2266-9546; cnr Aguilera & Porfirio Valiente; ⊙ 7am-11pm) Forget the coffee – you've had better at truck stops. It's all about atmosphere: 100% authentic. This smoky, dark cantina-type cafe sells cups of java with prices in pesos.

Club Nautico BAR

(Map p412; off Paseo Alameda; ⊙ noon-midnight) Enlivening Paseo Alameda with its lively *ranchón*-style bar suspended over the water with a great view over the bay, this is a breezy locale to escape the sizzling Santiago heat. Food isn't a highlight – come here for the drinks and the views.

Barrita de Ron BAR

(Map p412; ☑ 2262-5576; Av Jesús Menéndez, btwn Quesada & Narciso López; ⊙ 9am-6pm) A tourist bar attached to the Bacardí Rum Factory (p408); offers rum sales and tastings.

PALO MONTE

Understanding Cuban religions of African origin can be complicated. The most widely practiced and well-known Afro-Cuban religion is Santería. Less studied and infinitely more mysterious is Palo Monte, also known as Regla de Congo or Palo Mayombe.

Like Santería, Palo Monte is a syncretized religion with antecedents in the era of enslaved people. Indentured workers brought over from Africa via the Middle Passage hid their animist beliefs behind a Catholic smokescreen, pretending to venerate Christian saints while worshipping their own pantheon of religious deities in secret.

However, while Santería originated in the Yoruba-speaking regions of present-day Nigeria, Palo Monte is Bantu in origin. Its rites and belief system were introduced by enslaved people brought to Cuba from the Congo Basin in Central Africa.

Another key difference between Palo Monte and Santería is in its essence. Santería emphasizes its deities; Palo Monte revolves around ancestor worship and a belief in natural earthly powers, such as water, mountains and particularly sticks, which are said to yield spiritual powers. Special sticks (*palos*) are used to decorate altars adorned with sacred religious vessels called *nkisi* (human-like dolls or figurines) believed to be inhabited by spirits. You'll know you're in a Palo Monte temple when you see an 'altar' consisting of a cauldron (called a *nganga*) filled with sticks, stones and bones of the dead, often with a crucifix hanging above it.

The Palo Monte has its own deities called Kimpungulu and a creator god known as Nzambi. Though less important and less widely known than Santería orishas, Palo Monte deities are similarly associated with Catholic saints. Kimbabula, god of the wind, relates to St Francis, while Nsasi, god of thunder, is represented by Santa Barbara (Changó in Santería).

Because of its secretive nature, Palo Monte is often misunderstood, and tales of black magic and grave-robbing abound, most of them false. The strongholds of the religion are Santiago de Cuba; Regla and Guanabacoa in Havana; Matanzas; Bahia Honda in Artemisa Province; and Palmira in Cienfuegos Province.

☆ Entertainment

'Spoiled for choice' would be an understatement in Santiago. For what's happening, look for the biweekly *Cartelera Cultural*. The reception desk at Hotel Casa Granda (p415) usually has copies.

★ Casa de las Tradiciones   LIVE MUSIC

(Map p412; ☑ 2265-3892; General Jesús Rabí No 154; USD$1; ⊙ 5pm-midnight) The most discovered 'undiscovered' spot in Santiago still retains its smoke-filled, foot-stomping, front-room feel. Hidden in the genteel Tivolí district, some of Santiago de Cuba's most exciting ensembles, singers and soloists take turns improvising. Friday nights are reserved for straight-up classic *trova*, à la Ñico Saquito and the like. There's a gritty bar and some colorful artwork.

★ Iris Jazz Club   JAZZ

(Map p406; General Serafín Sánchez, btwn José A Saco & Bayamo; USD$5; ⊙ shows 9:30pm-2am) When Santiago gets too hot, noisy and agitated, you need a dose of Iris, one of Cuba's suavest and best jazz clubs, where you can sit in a comfy booth surrounded by pictures of puffing jazz greats and watch some incredibly intuitive exponents of Santiago's small but significant jazz scene.

Noche Santiagüera   LIVE PERFORMANCE

(Map p412; Av Victoriano Garzón, btwn La Alameda & Parque Los Estudiantes; ⊙ 6pm-midnight Sat) **FREE** Every Saturday night, the side streets branching off this main thoroughfare teem with street food, music and crowds for a city-wide outdoor party.

Casa de la Trova   LIVE MUSIC

(Map p406; ☑ 2265-3892; Heredia No 208) Santiago's shrine to the power of traditional music is still going strong five decades on, continuing to attract big names such as Buena Vista Social Club singer Eliades Ochoa. Warming up on the ground floor in the late afternoon, the action slowly gravitates upstairs where, come 10pm, everything starts to simmer. Check current listings on the signboard out front.

The Casa is dedicated to pioneering Cuban *trovador* José 'Pepe' Sánchez (1856–1928) and first opened as Cuba's orginal *trova* (traditional poetic singing/songwriting) house in March 1968.

Santiago Café
CABARET
(Map p412; ☑2268-7070; cnr Av de las Américas & Calle M; USD$5; ☺10pm-2am Sat) This is the hotel Meliá Santiago de Cuba's (p416) slightly less spectacular version of the Tropicana. Cabarets take place on Saturday with a disco afterward. It's on the hotel's 1st floor.

Uneac
ARTS CENTER
(Map p406; ☑2265-3465; Heredia No 266) First stop for art fiends seeking intellectual solace in talks, workshops, encounters and performances – all in a gorgeous colonial courtyard.

Casa de Cultura Josué País García
LIVE MUSIC
(Map p406; ☑2262-7804; Heredia No 204; USD$1; ☺from 9pm Wed, Fri & Sat, 1pm Sun) Grab a seat (or stand in the street) and settle down for whatever this spontaneous place can throw at you: orchestral *danzón* (ballroom dance), folkloric rumba, lovelorn *trovadores* (traditional singers) or rhythmic reggaeton.

Tropicana Santiago
CABARET
(☑2268-7020; from USD$35; ☺from 10pm Wed-Sun) Anything Havana can do, Santiago can do better – or at least cheaper. Styled on the Tropicana original, this 'feathers and baubles' Las Vegas–style floor show is heavily hyped by all the city's tour agencies who offer it for USD$35 plus transport (Havana's show is twice the price, but no way twice as good).

It's located out of town, 3km north of the Hotel Las Américas, so a taxi or rental car is the only independent transport option, making the tour agency deals a good bet. The Saturday night show is superior.

Patio ARTex
LIVE MUSIC
(Map p406; ☑2265-4814; Heredia No 304; ☺11am-1am) Art lines the walls of this shop-and-club combo that hosts live music both day and night in the front room or quaint inner courtyard; a good bet if the Casa de la Trova is full, or too frenetic.

Subway Club
LIVE MUSIC
(Map p406; ☑2266-9119; cnr Aguilera & Mayía Rodriguez; USD$5; ☺8pm-2am) Stylish venue with interesting solo acts singing their hearts out to great piano music come nightfall. Good fun.

Teatro José María Heredia
THEATER
(Map p412; ☑2264-3190; cnr Avs de las Américas & de los Desfiles; ☺box office 9am-noon & 1-4:30pm) Santiago's huge, modern theater and convention center went up during the city

refurbishment in the early 1990s. Rock and folk concerts often take place in the 2459-seat Sala Principal, while the 120-seat Café Cantante Niagara hosts more esoteric events. The Conjunto Folklórico de Oriente (p422) is based here.

Estadio de Béisbol Guillermón Moncada
BASEBALL
(Map p412; ☑2264-2655; Av de las Américas) During the baseball season, from October to April, this stadium hosts games at 7:30pm Tuesday, Wednesday, Thursday and Saturday, and 1:30pm Sunday (CUP$1). The Avispas (Wasps) are the main rivals of Havana's Industriales, with National Series victories in 2005, 2007, 2008 and 2010. On the northeastern side of town.

Patio Los Dos Abuelos
LIVE MUSIC
(Map p406; ☑2262-3267; Francisco Pérez Carbo No 5; USD$2; ☺10pm-2am Mon-Sat) The old-timers label (*abuelos* means grandparents) carries a certain amount of truth. This relaxed live-music house is a bastion for traditional *son* sung the old-fashioned way. The musicians are seasoned pros, and most of the patrons are perfect ladies and gentlemen.

Sala de Conciertos Dolores
LIVE MUSIC
(Map p406; Iglesia de Nuestra Señora de los Dolores, cnr Aguilera & Mayía Rodríguez; ☺from 8:30pm) You can catch the Sinfónica del Oriente at this former church on Plaza de Dolores, plus the impressive children's choir (at 5pm). The event calendar is posted outside.

Teatro Martí
THEATER
(Map p412; ☑2262-0507; Félix Peña No 313; ☒) Children's shows are staged at 5pm on Saturday and Sunday at this theater near General Portuondo, opposite the Iglesia de Santo Tomás.

🔒 Shopping

Fondo Cubano de Bienes Culturales
ARTS & CRAFTS
(Map p406; ☑2265-2358; Félix Peña No 755; ☺8am-5:30pm Mon-Fri) This government-run gallery features a good rotation of local artisans and art exhibitions, a few blocks from Parque Céspedes.

Librería La Escalera Eddy Tamayo
BOOKS
(Map p406; Heredia No 265; ☺10am-10pm) A veritable museum of old and rare books stacked ceiling high, plus vinyl records. Eddy is usually down to make a deal. You'll often find Sombrero-clad *trovadores* sitting on the stairway for a strum.

DON'T MISS

FOLKLÓRICO DANCE GROUPS

Seeing a *folklórico* dance group is a definitive Santiago de Cuba cultural experience. The city is home to a dozen such groups (more than anywhere else in Cuba), which exist to teach and perform traditional Afro-Cuban *bailes* (dances) and pass their traditions on to future generations. Most of the groups date from the early 1960s and all enjoy strong patronage from the Cuban government.

A good place to find out about upcoming *folklórico* events is at the Casa del Caribe (p410) in Vista Alegre where many of the groups hang out and perform.

Santiago's oldest *folklórico* group is the Conjunto Folklórico de Oriente (Map p412; ☑ 2264-3178; Teatro José María Heredia, cnr Avs de las Américas & de los Desfiles) formed in 1959. They perform a huge range of Afro-Cuban dance genres from *gagá* and *bembé* to *tumba francesa* at the Teatro José María Heredia. The Ballet Folklórico Cutumba (Map p412; ☑ 2262-3201; Teatro Galaxia, cnr Avs 24 de Febrero & Valeriano Hierrezuelo; USD$2; ☺ from 8pm Fri & Sun) is an offshoot of the Oriente group formed in 1976. You can usually see them rehearsing at their HQ, the Teatro Galaxia, from 9am to 1pm, Tuesday to Friday.

For pure *tumba francesa* dancing check out the Tumba Francesa La Caridad de Oriente (p403), one of only three of these French-Haitian groups left in Cuba. They can be seen in their rehearsal rooms on Tuesday and Thursday at 9pm.

The Carabalí Olugo (Map p412; Av Eduardo Chibas, cnr Av 24 de Febrero) and the Carabalí Izuama (Map p412; Pío Rosado No 107) are *comparsas* (Carnaval music and dance groups) who represent the Tivolí and Los Hoyos neighborhoods in Santiago's July Carnaval. They are both descendants of 19th-century *cabildos* or mutual aid societies formed along ethnic lines, a factor still reflected in their music.

Compañia Danzaría Folklórica Kokoyé (Map p412) is a more modern group, formed in 1989 to promote Afro-Cuban dance to tourists. They can be seen performing on Saturday evening and Sunday afternoon in the Casa del Caribe (p410).

Album Kafé Egrem   MUSIC
(Map p406; ☑ 2262-6191; José A Saco No 309; ☺ 9am-6pm Mon-Sat, to 2pm Sun) The definitive Cuban specialist music store; this retail outlet of Egrem Studios has a good selection from local musicians.

ARTex   GIFTS & SOUVENIRS
(Map p406; ☑ 2265-4814; Heredia No 208; ☺ 11am-7pm Tue-Sun) Focuses on musical souvenirs, with a respectable selection of CDs and cassettes.

ℹ️ Information

SAFE TRAVEL

Santiago is well known, even among Cubans, for its overzealous *jineteros* (touts), all working their particular angle – be it cigars, private restaurants, *chicas/chicos* (paid sex) or unofficial 'tours.' Sometimes it can seem impossible to shake off the money-with-legs feeling, but a firm 'no' coupled with a little light humor ought to keep the worst of the touts at bay. If needed, seek out the **police** (☑ 116; cnr Mariano Corona & Sánchez Hechavarría).

Santiago's traffic is second only to Havana's in its environmental fallout. Making things worse for pedestrians is the plethora of noisy motorcyclists weaving for position along the city's sinuous 1950s streets. Narrow or nonexistent sidewalks throw further obstacles into an already hazardous brew. Always look before you cross.

INTERNET ACCESS

There's wi-fi in public plazas, major hotels and a few casas particulares. Buy wi-fi scratch cards at Etecsa Telepunto centers or hotel lobbies, though the latter frequently run out.

Etecsa Multiservicios (☑ 2262-4784; cnr Heredia & Félix Peña; internet per hour USD$1.50; ☺ 8:30am-7:30pm) Internet terminals and wi-fi scratch cards in a small office on Plaza Céspedes.

Etecsa Telepunto (☑ 2265-7521; cnr Hartmann & Tamayo Fleites; internet per hour USD$1.50; ☺ 8:30am-7:30pm) Internet terminals, plus sells wi-fi scratch cards.

MEDICAL SERVICES

Santiago has the best access to medicine and related services in the region.

Clínica Internacional de Santiago de Cuba (☑ 2271-4021, 2264-2589; cnr Av Raúl Pujol & Calle 10, Vista Alegre; ☺ 24hr) Capable staff speak some English. A dentist is also present.

Farmacia Clínica Internacional (☑ 2264-2589; cnr Av Raúl Pujol & Calle 10; ☺ 24hr) Best pharmacy in town.

Farmacia Internacional (☑ 2268-7070; Meliá Santiago de Cuba, cnr Av de las Américas

& Calle M; ☺8am-6pm) In the lobby of the Meliá Santiago de Cuba, it sells products in convertibles.

MONEY

The city has plenty of banks and currency-exchange centers.

Banco de Crédito y Comercio (Bandec; ☎2262-8006; Félix Peña No 614; ☺9am-3pm Mon-Fri) In the jarring modern building in Plaza Céspedes.

Banco Financiero Internacional (☎2268-6252; cnr Av de las Américas & Calle 1; ☺9am-3pm Mon-Fri) Has an ATM.

Bandec (cnr José A Saco & Mariano Corona; ☺9am-3pm Mon-Fri) Has an ATM.

Cadeca (☎2265-1383; Aguilera No 508; ☺8:30am-4pm Mon-Fri, to 11:30am Sat) Long lines for currency exchange.

TOURIST INFORMATION

As all tour agencies are government-run, they offer overlapping services and consistent prices.

Asistur (Map p412; ☎2266-7259; www.asistur. cu; cnr Calles 4 & 7, Vista Alegre; ☺9am-5pm Mon-Fri) This office specializes in helping foreigners, mainly in the insurance and financial fields.

Campismo Popular (Map p406; ☎2265-3639; comercial@scu.campismopopular.cu; Cornelio Robert No 163 bajo; ☺8:30am-2pm Mon, Wed & Fri, 10am-3pm Tue & Thu, 8:30am-1pm Sat) For reservations at campismos in the province such as Caletón Blanco, Las Golondrinas, El Saltón and La Mula. Study the varied opening hours before stopping by.

Cubanacán (Map p406; ☎2268-6412; Hotel Casa Granda, Heredia No 201; ☺8am-6pm) Very helpful; sells tours in the Hotel Casa Granda.

Cubatur (Map p406; Heredia No 701; ☺8am-8pm) Sells all number of excursions, for everything from La Gran Piedra to El Cobre. There's another **branch** (Map p412; ☎2265-2560; Av Victoriano Garzón No 364, cnr Calle 4; ☺8am-8pm) on Av Victoriano Garzón.

Infotur (Map p406; ☎2268-6068; Félix Peña No 562; ☺8am-8pm) Helpful location and staff. There's also a branch in Antonio Maceo International Airport.

❶ Getting There & Away

AIR

Antonio Maceo International Airport (☎2269-1053) is 7km south of Santiago de Cuba, off the Carretera del Morro. International flights arrive from Santo Domingo (Dominican Republic), Toronto and Montreal on Cubana (www.cubana.cu). Toronto and Montreal are also served by Sunwing (www.sunwing.ca). With mostly charter service, Sunrise (www.

sunriseairways.net) flies nine times weekly from Port Au Prince, Haiti. American Airlines (www.aa.com) has eight flights a week to and from Miami serving the Cuban-American community.

Internally, Cubana flies nonstop from Havana two or three times a day.

BUS

Víazul buses (www.viazul.cu) leave from the **National Bus Station** (Map p412; Paseo de Martí), opposite the Heredia Monument, 3km northeast of Parque Céspedes.

The Havana bus stops at Bayamo (USD$7, 2¼ hours), Holguín (USD$11, 3½ to four hours), Las Tunas (USD$11, 5½ hours), Camagüey (USD$18, 7½ hours), Ciego de Ávila (USD$24, 9½ hours), Sancti Spíritus (USD$28, 11 hours) and Santa Clara (USD$33, 11 to 12 hours). The Trinidad bus can drop you at Bayamo, Las Tunas, Camagüey, Ciego de Ávila and Sancti Spíritus. The Baracoa bus stops in Guantánamo.

VÍAZUL DEPARTURES FROM SANTIAGO DE CUBA

Destination	Price (USD$)	Duration (hr)	Frequency (daily)
Baracoa	15	4¾	1
Havana	51	15	3
Trinidad	33	11½	1
Varadero	49	15	1

TRAIN

The modern French-style **train station** (☎2262-2836; cnr Av Jesús Menéndez & Martí) is situated near the rum factory northwest of the center. Chinese-made carriages replaced the deteriorating Tren Francés in July 2019 and depart every other day for Havana (15 hours) with stops en route.

Cuban train schedules are fickle, so always verify beforehand what train leaves when and get your ticket as soon as possible thereafter. Arrive at least an hour beforehand to confirm your seat.

TRAIN DEPARTURES FROM SANTIAGO DE CUBA

Havana-bound trains depart from Santiago every other day.

Destination	Price (USD$; 2nd/1st class)	Duration (hr)
Camagüey	26/33	5½
Ciego de Ávila	35/50	7½
Havana	70/95	15
Las Tunas	15/25	3½
Santa Clara	47/61	10

TRUCK

Intermittent passenger trucks leave **Serrano Intermunicipal Bus Station** (Map p412; cnr Av Jesús Menéndez & Sánchez Hechavarría; CUP$5) near the train station to Guantánamo and Bayamo throughout the day. Prices are a few pesos, and early morning is the best time to board. For these destinations, don't fuss with the ticket window; just find the truck parked out front going your way. Trucks for Caletón Blanco and Chivirico also leave from here.

The **Intermunicipal Bus Station** (Map p412; Terminal Cuatro, cnr Av de los Libertadores & Calle 4; CUP$1), 2km northeast of Parque Céspedes, has two buses a day to El Cobre. Two daily buses also leave for Baconao.

❶ Getting Around

TO/FROM THE AIRPORT

A taxi to or from the airport should cost USD$10, but drivers will often try to charge you more. Haggle hard before you get in.

You can also get to the airport on **bus 212** (Map p406; CUP$1), which leaves from Av de los Libertadores opposite the Hospital de Maternidad. **Bus 213** (Map p412; CUP$1) also goes to the airport from the same stop, but visits Punta Gorda first. Both buses stop just beyond the west end of the airport car park to the left of the entrances.

Another option to Havana is **Conectando Cuba** (Map p412; to Havana incl lunch USD$51), a long-distance tourist shuttle.

BOAT

Several ferries depart daily for El Morro from the **ferry terminal** (Malecón; USD$3) along the Malecón. Schedules change often, and the journeys are weather dependent, so confirm plans locally.

BUS & TRUCK

Useful city buses include bus 212 to the airport and Ciudamar, which has a **stop** (CUP$1) in the *casco histórico*, and bus 213 to Punta Gorda: both of these buses start from Av de los Libertadores, opposite Hospital de Maternidad, and head south on Felix Peña in the *casco histórico*.

Other good routes are Bus 214, 401 & 407 to Siboney, from near Av de los Libertadores No 425. **Bus 5 to El Caney** (Map p406; CUP$1) stops on the northwestern corner of Plaza de Marte and at General Cebreco and Calle 3 in Vista Alegre. These buses run every hour or so; more frequent trucks serve the same routes.

Trucks to points north leave from Av de las Américas near Calle M. On trucks and buses you should be aware of pickpockets and wear your backpack in front.

CAR & MOTORCYCLE

Santiago de Cuba suffers from a chronic shortage of rental cars (especially in peak season). You might find there are none available, though the locals have an indefatigable Cuban ability to *conseguir* (to manage or get) and *resolver* (to resolve or work out). The airport offices usually have better availability than those in town.

Cubacar (☑ 2268-7160; Hotel Casa Granda; ◷ 9am-5pm) Rents mopeds for USD$25 per day.

The **Cupet-Cimex gas station** (cnr Avs de los Libertadores & de Céspedes; ◷ 24hr) is open 24 hours. There's an **Oro Negro gas station** (cnr Av 24 de Febrero & Av Eduardo Chibas) on the Carretera del Morro.

TAXI

There's a **Transtur** (Map p412; ☑ 2268-7160; Meliá Santiago de Cuba) taxi stand in front of Meliá Santiago de Cuba. Taxis also wait on Parque Céspedes near the cathedral and hiss at you expectantly as you pass. Hammer out a price beforehand. To the airport, costs range between USD$8 and USD$10 depending on the state of the car. Bici-taxis charge about USD$1 to USD$2 per ride.

Siboney

Playa Siboney is Santiago's answer to Havana's Playas del Este, a low-key seaside town that's more rustic village than deluxe resort. Guarded by precipitous cliffs and dotted with a mixture of craning palms and weather-beaten clapboard houses, the setting here is laid-back. The beach scene mixes fun-seeking Cuban families and young *santi-agüeras* with their older, balder foreign partners. Unfortunately, as of late the town is full of *jejenes* (sand flies) and *jineteros* (touts). Both will bother you.

While the small crescent of grayish sand is none too inspiring, there's consolation in cheap prices and a good location (on the doorstep of Parque Baconao). For those craving a break from Santiago, it's an okay hideaway.

◉ Sights

Granjita Siboney   MUSEUM

(Map p426; USD$1; ◷ 9am-5pm Tue-Sun, to 1pm Mon) Had the revolution been unsuccessful, this unassuming red-and-white farmhouse 2km inland from Playa Siboney on the road to Santiago de Cuba would be the forgotten site of a rather futile putsch. As it is, it's another shrine to the glorious national episode that is Moncada. From this spot, at 5:15am on July 26, 1953, 26 cars under the command of Fidel Castro left to attack the military barracks in Santiago de Cuba.

The house retains many of its original details, including the dainty room used by the two *compañeras* (female revolutionaries)

who saw action, Haydee Santamaría and Melba Hernández. There are also displays of weapons, interesting documents, photos and personal effects related to the attack. Notice the well beside the building, where weapons were hidden.

Overlooking the stony shoreline nearby is an American war memorial dated 1907, recalling the US landing here on June 24, 1898.

🛏️ Sleeping & Eating

There are a good dozen casas particulares in this small seaside settlement.

Ovidio González Salgado   CASA PARTICULAR $
(Map p426; 📱 2239-9340; Av Serrano; r USD$25-35; ⊙Nov-Apr; ❄️) A spacious place with three rooms and multiple terraces. Your best bet is the private top-floor apartment with views of town and sea. With a pleasant owner and great meals.

María Elena González   CASA PARTICULAR $
(Map p426; 📱 2239-9200; rafaelrg47@nauta.cu; Obelisco No 10; USD$25; P ❄️ ❄️) Three slightly disheveled rooms are outshone by the terrace with rockers and giant sea views. The swimming pool may or may not be operating. With busy family life, it can be a bit

chaotic, but the owner has a 1968 Peugeot available as a taxi – handy in these parts.

Sitio del Compay   CARIBBEAN $$
(Bar Rueda; Map p426; Av Serrano; meals USD$5-10; ⊙11am-7pm) Siboney's only real dining option serves no-frills *comida criolla* with friendly service and good beach views. It's in the former house of musical-sage-turned-international-icon Francisco Repilado, aka Compay Segundo, the man responsible for writing the immortal song 'Chan Chan,' which visitors hear on repeat across Cuba.

Born in a small shack by this site in 1907, Compay Segundo shot to superstardom at the age of 90 as the guitarist/winking joker in Ry Cooder's Buena Vista Social Club.

🛈 Getting There & Away

Bus 214 (Map p412; CUP$1) runs from Santiago de Cuba to Siboney from near Av de los Libertadores No 425, opposite Empresa Universal, with a second stop at Av de Céspedes No 110. It leaves about once hourly between 4am and 8:45am (hit-and-miss thereafter). Bus 407 carries on to Juraguá three times a day. Passenger trucks also shuttle between Santiago de Cuba and Siboney.

A taxi to Playa Siboney will cost USD$25 to USD$30.

HISTORY OF COFFEE IN CUBA

The Cubans have always been enthusiastic coffee drinkers. But, while the shade-loving national coffee crop thrives in the cool tree-covered glades of the Sierra del Escambray and Sierra Maestra, it's not indigenous to the island.

Coffee was first introduced to Cuba in 1748 from the neighboring colony of Santo Domingo, yet it wasn't until the arrival of French planters from Haiti in the early 1800s that the crop was grown commercially.

On the run from Toussaint Louverture's revolution of enslaved people, the displaced French found solace in the mountains of Pinar del Río and the Sierra Maestra, where they switched from sugarcane production to the more profitable and durable coffee plant.

Constructed in 1801 in what is now the Sierra del Rosario Reserve in Artemisa Province, the Cafetal Buenavista was the first major coffee plantation in the New World. Not long afterward, planters living in the heavily forested hills around La Gran Piedra began constructing a network of more than 60 *cafetales* (coffee plantations) using pioneering agricultural techniques to overcome the difficult terrain. Their stoic efforts paid off, and by the second decade of the 19th century, Cuba's emergent coffee industry was thriving.

Buoyed by high world coffee prices and aided by sophisticated new growing techniques, the coffee boom lasted from 1800 to about 1820, when the crop consumed more land than sugarcane. At its peak, there were more than 2000 *cafetales* in Cuba, concentrated primarily in the Sierra de Rosario region and the Sierra Maestra to the east of Santiago de Cuba.

Production began to slump in the 1840s with competition from vigorous new economies (most notably Brazil) and a string of devastating hurricanes. The industry took another hit during the War of Independence, though the crop survived and is still harvested today on a smaller scale using mainly traditional methods.

The legacy of Cuba's pioneering coffee industry is best evidenced in the Archeological Landscape of the First Coffee Plantations in the Southeast of Cuba, a Unesco World Heritage Site dedicated in 2000 that sits in the foothills of the Sierra Maestra close to Gran Piedra.

La Gran Piedra & Parque Baconao

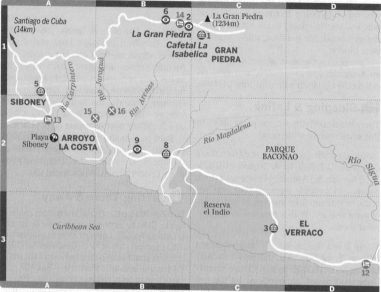

La Gran Piedra & Parque Baconao

La Gran Piedra

Crowned by a 63,000-ton boulder that perches like a grounded asteroid high above the Caribbean, the Cordillera de la Gran Piedra forms part of Cuba's greenest and most biodiverse mountain range. Not only do the mountains have a refreshingly cool microclimate, they also exhibit a unique historical heritage based on the legacy of some 60 or more coffee plantations set up by French farmers in the latter part of the 18th century.

On the run from a bloody rebellion of enslaved people in Haiti in 1791, enterprising Gallic immigrants overcame arduous living conditions and terrain to turn Cuba into the world's number-one coffee producer in the early 19th century. Their craft and ingenuity have been preserved for posterity in a Unesco World Heritage site centered on the Cafetal La Isabelica. The area is also part of Baconao Unesco Biosphere Reserve, instituted in 1987.

⊙ Sights

You can visit the ruins of many of the 100-plus *cafetales* (coffee plantations) on foot. Trails lead out from Cafetal La Isabelica , but

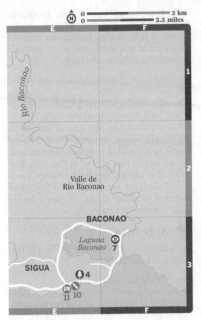

0 ——— 5 km
0 ——— 2.5 miles

Río Baconao

Valle de
Río Baconao

BACONAO

Laguna
Baconao 7

SIGUA

4

11 10

On a clear day, there are excellent views out across the Caribbean, and on a dark night you can see the glow of lights from Jamaica.

Jardín Botánico Gran Piedra   GARDENS
(Map p426; USD$2; ⊙ daylight hours) This garden's cool, misty microclimate fosters species of bromeliads, orchids, anthuriums, tree ferns and other subtropical flora you won't encounter in the Cuban lowlands. While parts of the garden are used as a living lab, the setting is refreshingly organic and unstructured. Bring a picnic and stop here for a relaxed breather before or after climbing the well-trodden path up to La Gran Piedra. The lovely caretakers who live on the grounds welcome visitors during daylight hours.

🛏 Sleeping

Villa La Gran Piedra   HOTEL $
(Map p426; ☑ 2268-6147; Km 14.5, Carretera Gran Piedra; s/d incl breakfast USD$25/30; P ❋) At 1225m, Cuba's highest hotel has plain but comfortable wooden cabins with tile floors and sparse furniture. The cabins' best feature is the abundant vegetation that surrounds them, as well as the panoramic mountain views. Reception is at the on-site restaurant, right by the entrance to the La Gran Piedra viewpoint.

❶ Getting There & Away

A steep, winding paved road climbs 1.5 vertical kilometers from the junction with the coast road near Siboney (on the 214 bus route) through *muchos* potholes.

A taxi from Santiago de Cuba will cost approximately USD$80 to USD$90 (bargain hard) for the round trip. Sturdy Cubans and the odd ambitious foreigner hike up 12km from the bus stop at the road junction in Las Guásimas.

there are no signs. Inquire at La Isabelica about the possibility of hiring a local farmer to show you around for a prearranged fee.

⭐**Cafetal La Isabelica**   MUSEUM
(Map p426; Carretera Gran Piedra; USD$2; ⊙ 8am-4pm) The hub of the Unesco World Heritage site bestowed in 2000 upon the First Coffee Plantations in the Southeast of Cuba is this impressive two-story stone mansion, with its three large coffee-drying platforms, built in the early 19th century by French émigrés from Haiti. It's a 2km hike beyond La Gran Piedra on a rough road.

The complex includes a workshop filled with period tools, the sobering quarters of enslaved people and antique coffee-processing machinery. If available, it's well worth using a guide (be sure to tip) to show you around as there are no explanatory signs. There were once more than 60 such *cafetales* in the area.

⭐**La Gran Piedra**   MOUNTAIN
(Map p426; Carretera Gran Piedra; USD$2) It's worth huffing and puffing the 459 stone steps to the summit of La Gran Piedra at 1234m. The huge rock on top measures 51m long and 25m high and weighs... a lot. Its popularity and commercialization goes a little unchecked (cue the eager trinket salespeople on top).

Parque Baconao

Wondrous and weird, Parque Baconao covers 800 sq km between Santiago de Cuba and the Río Baconao. This Unesco Biosphere Reserve acts as an important haven for a whole ecosystem, and sports an outdoor car museum and a park of life-sized dinosaur sculptures.

Encased in a shallow chasm fenced in by the Sierra Maestra and the placid Caribbean, Baconao's biodiversity is remarkable. More than 1800 endemic species of flora from craning royal palms to prickly cliffside cacti thrive here, and fauna includes many types of endangered bats and spiders.

Beaches are smaller than those on the northern coast, but there's fishing and some 70 scuba-diving sites nearby, including the *Guarico*, a small steel wreck just south of Playa Sigua. Baconao is also famous for its crabs. From mid-March to early May, tens of thousands of large land crabs fill the coast beyond Playa Verraco (also spelled Berraco on local signage).

◉ Sights

There are several beaches along the coast, of which the best is probably Playa Cazonal, by Club Amigo Carisol – Los Corales.

Valle de la Prehistoria   AMUSEMENT PARK

(Map p426; ☑ 2239-9239; USD$1; ⊙ 8am-5pm) The oddest in a plethora of bizarre attractions in Parque Baconao, this Cuban Jurassic Park mixes giant Apatosauruses with concrete cavemen and women, no matter that 57 million years separated their existence. Take in the full 11 hectares of this surreal kitsch park with its 200 life-sized concrete dinosaurs built by inmates from a nearby prison.

There is a rather lame natural history museum on-site, as well as a basic Fred Flintstone–style cafe.

Comunidad Artística El Verraco   GALLERY

(Map p426; ⊙ 9am-6pm) This village of painters, ceramicists and sculptors maintains open studios. Here you can visit the artists and buy original works of art. All it lacks is a good organic cafe.

Laguna Baconao   LAKE

(Map p426; guided hike USD$2) At Laguna Baconao, 2km northeast of Los Corales, you'll find a restaurant, rowboats for hire and several short lakeside hikes, plus a forlorn-looking zoo with crocodiles and the like. The lake supposedly contains 'wild' dolphins. Various trails ply the lakeshore including one that circumnavigates it completely (8km). As it's a flora and fauna reserve, you must first hire a guide. Horse riding may also be available.

From Playa Baconao at the eastern corner of the lake, the paved road continues 3.5km up beautiful Valle de Río Baconao before turning into a dirt track. Soldiers at a checkpoint at the village turn back vehicles from the direct coastal road to Guantánamo because it abuts the US Naval Base. To continue east, backtrack 50km to Santiago de Cuba and take the inland road.

Exposición Mesoamericana   PARK

(Map p426; USD$1) Every Cuban resort area seems to have an attraction replicating indigenous scenes. Here it's the Exposición Mesoamericana, just east of Club Amigo Carisol – Los Corales. Indigenous cave art from Central and South America is arranged in caves along the coastal cliffs.

Museo Nacional de
Transporte Terrestre   MUSEUM

(Map p426; ☑ 2239-9197; Km 8.5, La Punta; USD$1; ⊙ 8am-5pm) Anywhere besides Cuba, this alfresco car museum 2km east of Valle de la Prehistoria would impress. There's Benny Moré's 1958 Cadillac, the Chevrolet Raúl Castro got lost in on the way to Moncada Barracks and Cuban singer Rosita Fornes' lovely Ford T-Bird. But where '50s car relics are as common as cheap cigars, it's like a Toyota Yaris museum in Kyoto.

🏇 Activities

Horseback riding is available at Finca El Porvenir and Laguna Baconao .

Centro Internacional
de Buceo Carisol Los Corales   DIVING

(Map p426; ☑ 2235-6121; www.nauticamarlin.com; Club Amigo Carisol – Los Corales) Situated in the Club Amigo Carisol, this center nevertheless picks up divers at the other hotels daily. Two boats can take up to 20 people to any of the 24 local dive sites. The open-water certification course is USD$375. There are shipwrecks close to shore, and you can feed black groupers by hand.

The water off this bit of coast is some of Cuba's warmest (25°C to 28°C); best visibility is between February and June.

🛏 Sleeping & Eating

All-inclusives usually close in low season (May to October). Check ahead.

You'll find resort dining plus scattered roadside restaurants, most active on weekends.

Club Amigo Carisol
– Los Corales   RESORT $$

(Map p426; ☑ 2235-6121; s/d all-inclusive USD$66/93; P ❄ @ ☄) There's the swim-up bar, umbrellas in the piña coladas, and the government-sponsored band knocking out 'Guantanamera' as you tuck into your lukewarm buffet dinner: you must be back in all-inclusive land. This two-piece Cubanacán resort is situated 44km east of Santiago on the coast's best section of beach (although it's been damaged by successive hurricanes).

Bonuses are a tennis court, a disco, multiple day trips on offer and bright spacious clean rooms. Nonguests can purchase a day pass for USD$25 including lunch.

Hotel Costa Morena   HOTEL $$
(Map p426; ☑ 2235-6126; s/d all-inclusive USD$60/ 80; P ❋ @ ☲) Partly renovated, this long-time hotel has attractive architecture and a large terrace with pool right on the cliffs but no direct beach access. There is good sea swimming, with protection afforded by a reef. A shuttle takes guests to the beach at Club Amigo Carisol – Los Corales, at Sigua, 44km southeast of Santiago de Cuba.

Finca El Porvenir   CARIBBEAN $$
(Map p426; ☑ 2268-6494; Km 18, Carretera de Baconao; meals USD$8-12; ☉ 9am-5pm) Situated on the left of the main road about 4km east of El Oasis, this Palmares-run *finca* (farm) knocks out no-frills *comida criolla* (Creole food). There's also a great swimming pool and horseback-riding excursions. Dining selection is sparse, but the smoked pork chops are surprisingly tasty washed down with a cold Buccanero. The only obstacle to chillaxing is the blaring reggaeton: sound familiar?

Fed by river water constantly circulating out, the swimming pool is clean and refreshingly cool.

Fiesta Guajira   CARIBBEAN $$
(Map p426; ☑ 2239-9586; Carretera Baconao, El Oasis; meals USD$7-10; ☉ 9am-5pm) Once a rodeo; now mainly just a restaurant serving *comida criolla* (typical Cuban food).

❶ Getting There & Away

Most people access Baconao's spread-out sights by private car, taxi or as part of an organized tour from Santiago de Cuba. You can rent a car from the **Cubacar desk** (☑ 2235-6169; Club Amigo Carisol – Los Corales; ☉ 9am-5pm) at Club Amigo Carisol.

Bus 415 from the municipal bus terminal in Santiago's Av de los Libertadores plies this route three times a day, but the bus timetables are not set in stone. Check ahead.

When planning your visit, remember the coastal road from Baconao to Guantánamo is closed to nonresidents. The **Cupet-Cimex gas station** (Complejo La Punta; ☉ 24hr) is 28km southeast of Santiago de Cuba.

El Cobre

☑ 22 / POP 11,438

The Basílica de Nuestra Señora del Cobre, high on a hill 20km northwest of Santiago de Cuba on the old road to Bayamo, is Cuba's most sacred pilgrimage site. It's the shrine of the nation's patron saint: La Virgen de la Caridad (Our Lady of Charity), aka Cachita. In Santería, the Virgin is syncretized with the beautiful *orisha* Ochún, the Yoruba goddess of love and dancing, and a religious icon to almost all Cuban women. Ochún is represented by the color yellow, mirrors, honey, peacock feathers and the number five. In the minds of many worshipers, devotion to the two religious figures is intertwined.

Even for nonbelievers, a visit to the Virgin is a fascinating look in to local culture. The road to the basilica is lined with sellers of elaborate sunflower wreaths, intended as offerings to La Virgen, and hawkers of miniature 'Cachitas.'

History

Legend dictates that the Virgin figurine was first discovered floating on a board in the Bay of Nipe in 1612 by three fishermen called the 'three Juans' caught up in a violent

---

FAMOUS GIFTS TO CACHITA

Many have offered gifts and keepsakes to the Virgin of El Cobre – some of them famous. The most celebrated donor was Ernest Hemingway, who elected to leave the 23-karat gold medal he won for the Nobel Prize for Literature in 1954 to the 'Cuban people.' Rather than hand it over to the Batista regime, Hemingway donated the medal to the Catholic Church who subsequently placed it in the *sanctuario*. The medal was stolen temporarily in the 1980s and, despite being retrieved a few days later, it has since been kept locked away from public view.

In 1957 Lina Ruz left a small guerrilla figurine at the feet of the Virgin to pray for the safety of her two sons, Fidel and Raúl Castro, who were then fighting in the Sierra Maestra. Fate – or was it the spirit of Cachita? – shone brightly. Fidel blazed on until age 90 and Raúl continues carrying the torch into his 90s.

More recently, dissident Cuban blogger Yoani Sánchez visited the Virgin and left her Ortega and Gasset journalistic award in the sanctuary where the arm of censorship can't reach.

storm. With their lives in danger they pulled the figurine from the water and found the words 'I am the Virgin of Charity' inscribed on the board. As the storm subsided and their lives were spared, they assumed a miracle had been granted and a legend was born.

The copper mine at El Cobre has been active since pre-Columbian times and was once the oldest European-operated mine in the western hemisphere (by 1530 the Spanish had a mine here). However, it closed in 2000.

◉ Sights

Basílica de Nuestra Señora del Cobre
CHURCH

(◷6am-6pm) Stunning as it materializes above the village of El Cobre, Cuba's most revered religious site shimmers against the verdant hills behind. Recently renovated – along with many other of Cuba's churches – the church's interior is impressive: light, but not ostentatious with some vivid stained glass. The existing basilica dates to 1927, though a sanctuary has existed on this site since 1648. There's an unending line of pilgrims, many of whom will have traveled from as far as the US.

Visitors maintain a respectful silence and light prayer candles (purchased outside). La Virgen resides in a glass case high above the altar. For such a powerful entity, she's absolutely diminutive, some 40cm from crown to the hem of her golden robe. Check out the fine Cuban coat of arms in the center, a wondrous work of embroidery.

Most of the donations left here (crutches no longer needed, awards gained through prayer) have been removed. In a small chapel at the side of the basilica, there's a small collection drawn from thousands of offerings giving thanks for favors bestowed by the Virgin. Signed baseballs, a TV, a thesis, a tangle of stethoscopes, a raft inner-tube sculpture (suggesting they made it across the Florida Straits safely) and floor-to-ceiling clusters of teeny metal body parts crowd the room.

Monumento Al Cimarrón
MONUMENT

A 10-minute hike up a stone staircase brings you to this anthropomorphic sculpture commemorating the 17th-century copper mine revolt of enslaved people. It's now the location of one of Cuba's most important Santería gatherings in July, Ceremonia a los Cimarrónes (part of the Fiesta del Caribe). Views are superb from up here; walk to the far side of the sculpture for a vista of copper-colored cliffs hanging over the aqua-green reservoir.

The way here is signposted in El Cobre.

✸ Festivals & Events

Ceremonia a los Cimarrónes
RELIGIOUS

(◷Jul) As part of Santiago's Fiesta del Caribe, there's a Santería religious service at the Monumento Al Cimarrón.

⌂ Sleeping

Hospedería El Cobre
HOSTEL $

(☏2234-6246; r CUP$40) This large building behind the basilica has a pleasant sitting room and 15 monk-standard rooms with one to three beds with bath. It's charged in *moneda nacional* (not USD). Meal times are 7am, 11am and 6pm. The nuns are very hospitable. House rules include no drinking or unmarried couples. Donations to the sanctuary are appreciated. Reserve up to 15 days ahead.

The downstairs lobby displays information about the history of the Virgin and the church from the 1600s through to the visit of Pope Benedict XVI in 2012.

ⓘ Getting There & Away

Bus 2 goes to El Cobre (CUP$1) twice a day from Santiago's Intermunicipal Bus Station (p424). Trucks (CUP$5) are more frequent on this route.

You can also take Cubataxi from Santiago de Cuba (around USD$25 round trip).

If you're driving toward Santiago de Cuba from the west, you can join the Autopista Nacional near Palma Soriano but, unless you're in a hurry, it's better to continue on the Carretera Central via El Cobre, which winds through picturesque hilly countryside.

El Saltón

Basking in well-earned eco-credentials, El Saltón is a tranquil mountain escape in the Tercer Frente municipality. Hills that once echoed with the sound of crackling rifle fire now reverberate to the twitter of tropical birds. Secluded and hard to reach, it consists of a lodge, a hilltop *mirador* (viewpoint) and a 30m cascading waterfall with an adjacent natural pool ideal for swimming.

Eco-guides offer horseback riding, hiking to thermal baths or tours into the nearby coffee and cacao plantations. Alternatively, you can just wander off on your own through myriad mountain villages with alluring names such as Filé and Cruce de los Baños. While access is difficult, the reward is ample for nature lovers. Check the state of the waterfall with Campismo Popular (p423) in Santiago; it can seasonally run dry.

CUBA'S BEST & WORST ROAD

The 180km-long coastal road that connects Santiago de Cuba with the small isolated village of Pilón in Granma Province is the best in Cuba for raw natural beauty, but the absolute *worst* for drivers weaned on smooth asphalt instead of endless gaping potholes.

Not surprisingly, traffic on the road is extremely light, and no regular buses operate west of Chivirico. Sturdy taxis and rental cars can ply the route if road conditions are agreeable, but make sure the car is well maintained and check ahead to see if the road is blocked, closed or washed away. Taxi drivers were asking approximately USD$160 for the one-way trip between Santiago and the Marea del Portillo hotels at last visit.

Another option is to use a bicycle. Caught between escarpment and sea, the road makes for a truly epic ride, but beware: there are very few facilities, scant places to eat and drink along the way and, should you have bike problems in the remoter areas, only occasional vehicles pass by. Although the route generally hugs the coast, it periodically ascends and descends steep headlands requiring proper gears and a good level of fitness.

Fortunately, the magnificence of the scenery makes slow travel highly desirable. This remote segment of southeast Cuba has remained completely and utterly unspoiled, a glorious ribbon of hidden bays and crashing surf backed by precipitous cloud-enshrouded mountains. On the land side the road skirts the foothills of Cuba's two highest mountain massifs topped by Pico Turquino and Pico Bayamesa. The mountains create a rain shadow effect rendering their southern slopes dry and speckled with dwarf foliage.

Settlements are bucolic and etched in revolutionary folklore. El Uvero and La Plata were the sites of guerrilla attacks in the 1950s by Castro's nascent army, while just off the coast lie the wrecks of two Spanish destroyers sunk in the Spanish–Cuban–American War.

Those attempting a cycling journey should stock up on food and water in Santiago, and spread the ride over three days with planned stops in Brisas Sierra Mar (p432), Campismo La Mula (p433; check availability in Santiago) and Hotel Marea del Portillo (p397) in Granma Province.

If you're looking to spend the night, Villa El Saltón (2256-6326; Carretera Puerto Rico a Filé; s/d incl breakfast USD$45/65; P✳✈) is a 22-room lodge spread over three blocks, nestled like hidden tree houses amid thick foliage. Invigorating extras include a sauna, hot tub, massage facilities and the hotel's defining feature, a refreshing natural waterfall and pool. The so-so restaurant/bar is popular for billiards, adjacent to a gushing river. Rooms themselves are nothing special.

❶ Getting There & Away

To get to El Saltón, continue west from El Cobre to Cruce de los Baños, 4km east of Filé village. El Saltón is 3km south of Filé. With some tough negotiating in Santiago de Cuba, a sturdy taxi will take you here for USD$90. Ask at Infotur (p423) in Santiago about guided trips.

Chivirico

POP 6661

Chivirico is the only town of any significance on the enticing south coast highway, a roller-coaster of plummeting mountains, crinkled bays and crashing surf that makes up one of Cuba's loveliest road trips. Transport links are relatively good up until Chivirico, but heading west they quickly deteriorate.

Chivirico itself has little to offer besides its remote village bliss, although there's some rugged hiking across the Sierra Maestra if you can get permission.

A difficult trek begins at Calentura, 4km west. It crosses the Sierra Maestra to Los Horneros (20km), from where truck transport to Guisa is usually available. Whether skittish local authorities will let you loose in the area is another matter. Don't just turn up – ask around at somewhere like Cubatur (p423) in Santiago or the Brisas Sierra Mar hotel (p432).

🛏 Sleeping & Eating

Campismo Caletón Blanco CABIN $
(2262-5515; Km 29, Caletón Blanco, Guamá; d incl breakfast USD$30; P✳) One of two handy campismos situated along this route (the other is La Mula). This is one of Cubamar's top campismos, the closest to Santiago (30km) and the newest. Twenty-two bungalows sleep two to four people. There's also

EL UVERO

A major turning point in the revolutionary war took place in this nondescript settlement 23km west of Chivirico, on May 28, 1957, when Castro's rebel army – still numbering less than 50 after six months on the run – audaciously took out a government position guarded by 53 of Batista's soldiers. By the main road are two red trucks taken by the rebels and nearby a double row of royal palms leads to a large monument commemorating the brief but incisive battle. It's a poignant, little-visited spot.

To visit, take a taxi from Chivirico or consult Ecotur (p411) in Santiago.

a restaurant, snack bar, bike rental and facilities for campervans. Make your reservations with Cubamar's Santiago de Cuba office (p423) before arrival.

Brisas Sierra Mar RESORT $$
(☏2232-9110; s/d all-inclusive USD$79/105; P❄@🛜🏊) Isolated but inviting, this big pyramid-shaped resort sits on Playa Sevilla, 15km from Chivirico and 63km west of Santiago (a two-hour drive from the airport). Built into a terraced hillside, a novel elevator leads to a brown-sand beach famous for sand flies. The highlight: a remarkable coral wall superb for snorkeling is just 50m offshore. Dolphins can frequent these waters, too.

As for activities, there are plenty. Horseback riding is available, there's a Marlin Dive Center on the premises, and plenty of special kids' programs (kids under 13 stay free). The hotel gets a lot of repeat visits. Nonguests can buy a day pass (USD$27) that includes lunch, drinks and sports until 5pm. For those cycling the south coast, it's a nice indulgence.

❶ Getting There & Away

Trucks run to Chivirico throughout the day from the Serrano Intermunicipal Bus Station (p424) in Santiago de Cuba. There are also three local buses a day.

Theoretically, one daily truck trundles along to Campismo La Mula and the Pico Turquino trailhead. Transport on to Marea del Portillo is almost unheard of, and road conditions vary from bad to downright impassable unless on two wheels.

Pico Turquino Area

Near the border of Granma and Santiago de Cuba provinces, the pinprick settlement of Las Cuevas is the starting point for arduous ascents of Cuba's highest mountain, Pico Turquino. It's possible in a very long day trip. With guides, visitors can through-hike to Alto del Naranjo and Santo Domingo in Granma Province with an overnight.

◉ Sights

Museo Combate de la Plata MUSEUM
(Map p389; USD$1; ⊙8am-noon & 2-6pm Tue-Sun) Five kilometers west of Las Cuevas (which is 40km west of El Uvero) is this small museum at La Plata, just below the highway. The first successful skirmish of the Cuban Revolution happened here on January 17, 1957. Museum exhibits include the piece of paper signed by the 15 *Granma* survivors who met up at Cinco Palmas in late 1956.

Marea del Portillo is 46km to the west. Don't confuse this La Plata with Comandancia de la Plata, Fidel Castro's Sierra Maestra Revolutionary headquarters.

⚐ Activities

Diving

Cristóbal Colón DIVING
Cuba's greatest wreck dive, the well-preserved Spanish cruiser *Cristóbal Colón* sank in 1898, about 15m down and only 30m offshore at La Mula. This is a genuine remnant of the Spanish–Cuban–American War. Visit with dive centers from Brisas Sierra Mar or Club Amigo Carisol – Los Corales (p428). Without scuba gear, you can see the wreck with a mask and snorkel.

Hiking Turquino

There are two routes to access Pico Turquino. Access via Las Cuevas requires a long ascent to traverse to the trailhead in Santo Domingo in Granma Province.

If summiting the mountain is your main aim, this is probably the quickest, easiest route. If you want to immerse yourself in the area's history and hike to Comandancia de la Plata, set out from Santo Domingo. Both options can be linked in a spectacularly thorough trek with Ecotur (onward transport is better from the Santo Domingo side).

Ecotur (p411) in Santiago offers an intensive day trip (per person USD$130), an overnight (USD$171) and a three-day expedition that includes Comandancia de la Plata (USD$201). Costs include entrance fee, transportation from Santiago, food (BYO snacks and water anyway), basic lodging and guides. It's possible to arrange it as a through-hike, ending in Santo Domingo, or out-and-back. The hike from Las Cuevas may also be organized at relatively short notice at the trailhead.

Camps & Shelters

Located 12km east of the trailhead, Campismo La Mula is handy for those entering the area late or on their way out. Self-sufficient hikers can also pitch tents or use the basic accommodations at Las Cuevas Visitors Center (Map p389; Las Cuevas; entry USD$15, camera fee USD$5). Paid here, the entry fee includes a compulsory Cuban guide.

You can stay overnight at the rudimentary shelter on Pico Cuba (an additional USD$30) if you don't want to descend the same day. There's a basic kitchen, wood-fired stove and plank beds (no mattresses) or floor space if those are taken.

The Route

The trail from Las Cuevas begins on the south coast highway, 7km west of Ocujal and 51km east of Marea del Portillo. This trek also passes Cuba's second-highest peak, Pico Cuba (1872m). Allow at least six hours to go up and four hours to come down, more if it has been raining, as the trail floods and turns slick with mud.

The hike is grueling: you're gaining almost 2km in elevation across only 9.6km of trail. But shade and peek-a-boo views provide plenty of respite. Bring plenty of water before setting out.

Be sure you're on the trail by 6:30am at the latest for the out-and-back day hike.

The well-marked route leads from Las Cuevas to La Esmajagua (600m; 3km; there's water here), Pico Cardero (1265m; quickly followed by a series of nearly vertical steps called Saca La Lengua, literally 'flops your tongue out'), Pico Cuba (1872m; 2km; water and shelter here) and Pico Turquino (1972m; 1.7km). When the fog parts and you catch your breath, you'll behold a bronze bust of José Martí standing on the summit of Cuba's highest mountain.

Record-breakers should note that the (unofficial) summit record by a guide is two hours, 45 minutes.

What to Bring

Hikers should bring sufficient food, warm clothing, a sleeping bag and a poncho – precipitation is common up here (some 2200mm annually), from a soft drizzle to pelting hail. Carry everything you need plus extra food to share if you can carry it and a little something for the *compañeros* (comrades) who take 15-day shifts up on Pico Cuba.

Ask ahead if you would like an English-speaking guide (there are several, but most are based on the Santo Domingo side). Also ask about food provision at Pico Cuba. Drinks are available for purchase at the Las Cuevas trailhead. Tipping the guides is mandatory – CUP$80 to CUP$120 is sufficient.

🛏 Sleeping & Eating

Campismo La Mula   CABIN $
(📞 2232-6262; Km 113, Carretera Granma; r USD$14) On a remote pebble beach 12km east of the Pico Turquino trailhead, La Mula has 50 small cabins popular with holidaying Cubans, hikers destined for Turquino and the odd hitchhiking south coast adventurer. It's pretty much the only option on this isolated stretch of coast. Check with Campismo Popular (p423) in Santiago before turning up.

There's a rustic cafe and restaurant on-site.

❶ Getting There & Away

The Las Cuevas trailhead is located 130km west of Santiago de Cuba on the remote coastal road. If you are headed here with Ecotur (p411), ensure that transportation is included.

Private trucks and the odd rickety bus connect La Mula to Chivirico, but they are sporadic; don't bank on more than one per day. A taxi from Santiago costs USD$100 to USD$120 – at this point you see why booking the trip as a tour offers little price difference.

1. Flamboyant festivalgoer **2.** Joyful carnival musician
3. Women preparing to join in the carnival procession **4.** Member of *conga* (musical group) Los Hoyos, named for the Santiago neighborhood it represents

EVELYN PALEY/ALAMY STOCK PHOTO ©

Carnaval in Santiago de Cuba

Santiago's cultural complexity ensures its raucous July Carnaval (p411) is one of the largest and most authentic in the Caribbean with a kaleidoscope of costumes, copious food stalls, and enough music and noise to summon the dead. If you can brave the heavy heat of summer and hang with a little intrusion of your personal space, this is the real deal.

Unlike most Latin American carnivals, Santiago's annual fiesta did not develop around a Lent-based celebration of deep religious significance. Instead, it was an amalgam of several separate days of fun and diversion called *mamarrachos*, which fell around the time of saints' days but lacked any further religious significance. The festivities, which blossomed in the late 19th century, gave laborers downtime after the January to May period of sugarcane harvesting.

Spanish authorities tolerated the festivities as a means of distracting the poor from more serious forms of rebellion and quickly Carnaval became synonymous with debauchery and scandal. In a delicious touch of modern-day irony, Carnaval now culminates in the Día de la Rebeldía Nacional (July 26), honoring Cuba's most famous (albeit failed) rebellion: the assault on the Moncada Barracks.

These days Carnaval has toned down. A bit.

Don't miss the *comparasas*, parades that are satirical or even antiestablishment in origin. They subdivide into the *congas*, simpler but feistier performances by large groups with manic percussion. Also on show are more-elaborate *paseos*, usually horse-drawn parades, lavish in scale and similar to European-style carnival floats. The Malecón is the hub of parade action.

AT A GLANCE

POPULATION
508,552

OLDEST CITY
Baracoa: 1511

**BEST FOLKLORIC
MUSIC & DANCE**
Tumba Francesa
Pompadour (p442)

BEST NIGHT OUT
Casa de la Trova
Victorino Rodríguez
(p451)

BEST BEACH
Playa Maguana
(p453)

WHEN TO GO

Apr–Aug
Baracoa's Bara-
coesa festival takes
place in early April
with an eruption of
music, dance and
cultural activities.

Sep–Oct
Hurricanes and bad
storms make this
period the best time
to avoid Baracoa.

Nov–Mar
Cooler and
drier. Non-touristy
Guantánamo
lights a fire in mid-
December for the
sultry Changüi
festival.

Parque Nacional Alejandro de Humboldt (p454)
CHRISTIAN_SCHMIDT/SHUTTERSTOCK ©

Guantánamo Province

A fantasy land of crinkled mountains and exuberant foliage, the Cuban Guantánamo remains a galaxy away from modern America in ambience. That doesn't stop most people associating it with the United States' Guantanamo Bay Naval Base, which continues in operation, though downsized. Off the base, the region's valleys and coastal microclimates are Cuba at its most mysterious and esoteric. Herein lie primitive musical subgenres, little-known Afro-Cuban religious rites and echoes of an indigenous Taíno culture supposedly wiped out by the Spanish centuries ago – or so you thought.

Though battered by Hurricane Matthew in 2016, Baracoa and its rural surroundings remain the regional highlight, closely followed by the vibrant endemism of the semivirgin Parque Nacional Alejandro de Humboldt. Further west, the city of Guantánamo, perennially bypassed by most travelers, represents the Cuba rarely tasted by tourists.

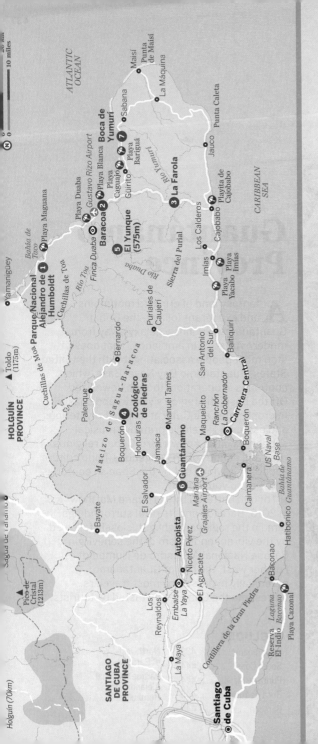

Guantánamo Province Highlights

1 Parque Nacional Alejandro de Humboldt (p454) Searching for the world's smallest frog in the most diverse national park in the Caribbean.

2 Baracoa (p445) Sampling the exotic culinary delights of the city.

3 La Farola (p444) Cycling the ultra-scenic lighthouse road from Cajobabo to Baracoa.

4 Zoológico de Piedras (p442) Getting an eyeful of the homespun artistry of these stony statues.

5 El Yunque (p453) Ascending through tropical jungle to summit Baracoa's mysterious flat-topped mountain.

6 Guantánamo (p439) Uncovering multiple music genres belonging to this forgotten city.

7 Boca de Yumurí (p445) Jumping on board a local boat upstream from the river mouth to navigate through the jaws of a narrow river gorge.

History

Long before the arrival of the Spanish, the Taínos populated the mountains and forests around Guantánamo, living off fishing, hunting and small-scale farming. Columbus first arrived in the region in November 1492, a month or so after his initial landfall near Gibara. He planted a small wooden cross in a beautiful bay ceremoniously christened Porto Santo – after an idyllic island off Portugal where Columbus had enjoyed his honeymoon.

The Spanish returned again in 1511 under the auspices of Columbus' son Diego in a flotilla of four ships and 400 men, including the island's first governor, Diego Velázquez de Cuéllar. Building a makeshift fort constructed from wood, the conquistadors consecrated the island's first colonial settlement, Villa de Nuestra Señora de la Asunción de Baracoa. The astute local *cacique* (chief) known as Hatuey recognized the threat the colonists represented, and he led repeated Taíno incursions on Baracoa to defend their homeland.

Declining in importance after the capital moved to Santiago in 1515, the Guantánamo region became Cuba's Siberia – a mountainous and barely penetrable rural backwater where prisoners were exiled and old traditions survived. In the late 18th century, the area was recolonized by French immigrants from Haiti who used African enslaved people on the difficult terrain to cultivate coffee, cotton and sugarcane.

Following the Spanish–Cuban–American War, a new power took up residence in Guantánamo Bay – the all-powerful Americans, intent on protecting their economic interests in the strategically important Panama Canal region. Despite repeated bouts of mudslinging in the years since, the not-so-welcome *yanquis,* as they are popularly known, have repeatedly refused to budge.

Guantánamo

POP 226,689

Famous for the wrong reasons, Guantánamo is most often bypassed by travelers on the Santiago–Baracoa bus. The malnourished grid of crusty buildings might not look appealing, but a little strolling and attempt at Spanish will uncover Cuban soul aplenty, without the hard sell.

Guantánamo created its own indigenous music genre (*changüí*), claims one of Cuba's three legendary Tumba Francesa (French-Haitian song and dance) troupes, supports an active West Indian social club and exhibits a distinct subgenre of eclectic architecture spearheaded by the intricate work of Leticio Salcines.

'Discovered' by Columbus during his second voyage in 1494, the settlement wasn't built until 1819, when French plantation owners evicted from Haiti founded the town of Santa Catalina del Saltadero del Guaso. In 1843, the burgeoning city became Guantánamo. In 1903, the US Navy took up residence in the bay next door. Sparks have been flying ever since.

◉ Sights

Guantánamo's geometric city grid is easy to navigate. Tree-lined Av Camilo Cienfuegos, a few blocks south of Bartolomé Masó, with its bizarre sculptures and central Rambla-style walkway, is the best place for a stroll.

Parque Martí   SQUARE
(Map p441) Anchored by the tiny **Parroquia de Santa Catalina de Riccis** (Map p441; Parque Martí) from 1863, the renovated Parque Martí features information boards and a clutch of interesting shops, restaurants and entertainment nooks strung along vibrant boulevards. Sitting timelessly amid the action is a seated statue of 'El Maestro,' from whom the square takes its name.

Palacio Salcines   MUSEUM
(Map p441; cnr Pedro A Pérez & Prado; ⊙hours vary) Local architect Leticio Salcines (1888–1973) left a number of impressive works around Guantánamo, including his personal residence built in 1916, a lavish monument said to be the building most representative of the city. The *palacio* is now a museum of colorful frescoes, Japanese porcelain and the like. Opening times can be sporadic.

On the palace's turret is La Fama, a sculpture designed by Italian artist Americo Chine that serves as the symbol of Guantánamo, her trumpet announcing good and evil.

Plaza Mariana Grajales   SQUARE
The huge, bombastic **Monument to the Heroes**, glorifying the Brigada Fronteriza 'that defends the forward trench of socialism on this continent,' dominates Plaza Mariana Grajales, 1km northwest of the train station and opposite Hotel Guantánamo. It's one of the more impressive 'revolution squares' on the island.

GUANTÁNAMO PROVINCE GUANTÁNAMO

Biblioteca Policarpo Pineda Rustán
LIBRARY

(Map p441; ☑ 2132-3352; cnr Los Maceo & Emilio Giro; ☺ 8am-5pm Mon-Sat) An architectural gift from Leticio Salcines is this beautiful provincial library that was once the city hall (1934–51). Trials for Fulgencio Batista's thugs were held here in 1959, and a number were killed when they snatched a rifle and tried to escape.

Museo Provincial
MUSEUM

(Map p441; ☑ 2132-5872; cnr José Martí & Prado; USD$1; ☺ 8am-noon & 1-4:30pm Mon-Fri, 8am-noon Sat) Housed in an old jail guarded by two cannons, the city museum has rooms dedicated to aboriginal culture, local nature, weapons and decorative arts.

✺ Festivals & Events

Festival Nacional de Changüí
MUSIC

(☺ mid-Dec) A celebration of *changüí* music, a regional style considered a predecessor of *son montuno* and modern salsa that employs African rhythms and Spanish guitar.

Noches Guantanameras
FIESTA

(Pedro A Pérez; ☺ 8pm Sat) Saturday night is reserved for this local coming together, when Calle Pedro A Pérez closes to traffic and stalls are set up in the street: come and enjoy whole roast pig, belting music and copious amounts of rum.

🛏 Sleeping

The upside of Guantánamo having little tourism means that hotels come cheap, though casas particulares are the best option.

Casa Norka
CASA PARTICULAR $

(Map p441; ☑ 2135-4512; Calixto García No 766, btwn Prado & Jesús del Sol; r USD$25; ✺ ✺) With just enough zhuzh to keep you interested (hello, Beyoncé and JLo posters). Rooms are large and well kept, and there's a very nice inner patio with plants and tiny pool.

Lissett Foster Lara
CASA PARTICULAR $

(Map p441; ☑ 2132-5970; Pedro A Pérez No 761, btwn Prado & Jesús del Sol; r USD$25; ✺) Like many *guantanameras*, Lissett speaks perfect English, and her house is polished, comfortable and decked out with the kind of plush fittings that wouldn't look amiss in a North American suburb. There are four rooms, including a delightful one on the substantial roof terrace. Lissett also has a private apartment to rent next door.

Hotel Guantánamo
HOTEL $

(☑ 2138-1015; Calle 13 Norte, btwn Ahogados & Calle 3 Oeste; s/d/ste incl breakfast USD$34/41/52; ▣ ✺ ✺ ✺) Hotel Guantánamo is something approaching comfortable. The generic rooms are clean, the pool has water in it, and there's a good lobby bar-cafe mixing up tempting mojitos and serving coffee. It's 1km northwest of the train station.

Hotel Brasil
HOTEL $

(Map p441; ☑ 2132-4332; Calixto García, btwn Giro & Crombet; s/d USD$15/24; ✺) With rates cheaper than many casas particulares, these 35 economical, clean rooms smell only slightly musty, a pleasant surprise given the dark reception area blaring reggaeton. There's an attached restaurant.

Hotel Martí
HOTEL $$

(Map p441; ☑ 2132-9500; magdalaine.borges@hotelmarti.tur.cu; cnr Aguilera & Calixto García; s/d incl breakfast USD$44/59; ✺ ✺) Overlooking Parque Martí, this somewhat refurbished colonial retains some elegance, with not terribly quiet rooms featuring quaint Juliet balconies. Check your room carefully for potential leaks (note water stains on the walls). Entertainment-wise, there's the rooftop-terrace restaurant with deafening music and the street-level bar circled by *jineteras* (female touts).

🍴 Eating & Drinking

At weekends, Parque Martí is an outdoor 'buffet' of mobile food stalls selling cheap, fried *comida ligera* (light food). Because Guantánamo is not a tourism-driven town, it sometimes suffers food shortages and restaurants that can only offer drinks.

★ Sabor Melián
CARIBBEAN $

(☑ 2132-4422; Av Camilo Cienfuegos No 407; meals USD$3-7; ☺ noon-midnight) With a discreet entrance on a busy avenue, this locals' favorite features good service and quality Caribbean chow. Go face-to-face with the whole fried snapper – under crisp skin the meat is incredibly moist. Even if dining solo, you'll feel like a guest at a quinceañera with beribboned chairs and reggaeton videos.

Restaurante Girasoles
CARIBBEAN $

(☑ 2138-4178; Calle 15 Norte, cnr Ahogados; meals USD$1-5; ☺ 10am-10pm) A nude statue rather than a *girasol* (sunflower) marks the entrance to what is, by process of elimination, one of Guantánamo's best restaurants. Behind the Hotel Guantánamo, Girasoles

Guantánamo

Guantánamo

⊙ Sights
1 Biblioteca Policarpo Pineda Rustán.....C4
2 Museo Provincial....................................A3
3 Palacio Salcines.....................................B3
4 Parque Martí..B3
5 Parroquia de Santa Catalina de
Riccis...B3

🛏 Sleeping
6 Casa Norka...B2
7 Hotel Brasil..B3
8 Hotel Martí...B3
9 Lissett Foster Lara................................B2

✗ Eating
10 Bar-Restaurante Olimpia......................B3
11 Restaurante 1870..................................B3

🍸 Drinking & Nightlife
12 La Ruina..B4

🎭 Entertainment
13 Casa de la Trova...................................B3
14 Casa de las Promociones Musicales
'La Guantanamera'..........................B4
15 Casa del Changüí..................................D2
16 Casa del Son...D2
17 Tumba Francesa Pompadour................D2

serves up (albeit at a snail's pace) chicken and fish, occasionally in interesting sauces. The terrace is popular for a drink.

Restaurante 1870　　　　　　CUBAN **$**
(Map p441; ☎2132-0540; Flor Crombet; meals USD$2-7; ◷7-9am, noon-3pm & 6-11pm) The plush setting is grand and befitting of Guantánamo's colonial heyday, and the prices are more than reasonable for good food. But the service leaves much to be desired and tends toward needless pretentiousness. Dress code is no shorts or tank tops.

OFF THE BEATEN TRACK

ZOOLÓGICO DE PIEDRAS

Surreal even by Cuban standards, the Zoológico de Piedras (☎ 2186-5143; Alto de Boquerón; USD$1; ☺9am-6pm Mon-Sat) is an animal sculpture park set amid thick foliage in the grounds of a mountain coffee farm, 20km northeast of Guantánamo. Carved quite literally out of the existing rock by sculptor Angel Iñigo Blanco, starting in the late 1970s, the sculptures now number more than 300 and range from hippos to giant serpents. Señor Blanco passed away in 2014, but the stone zoo continues in his memory.

To get here you'll need wheels or a taxi. Head east out of town and fork left toward Jamaica and Honduras. The 'zoo' is in the settlement of Boquerón.

Bar-Restaurante Olimpia   BURGERS $
(Map p441; cnr Calixto García & Aguilera; mains USD$2; ☺9am-midnight) A celebration of Guantánamo's remarkable Olympic Games performances, this bar-restaurant displays baseball shirts, athletics memorabilia and the boxing vest of three-time Olympic gold medalist Félix Savón (a local boy). Inside there's a small open patio and a mezzanine bar where you can enjoy beers and Cuban-style burgers, all with a vista of adjacent Parque Martí.

La Ruina   BAR
(Map p441; ☎ 2132-9565; cnr Calixto García & Emilio Giro; ☺9:30am-midnight) This shell of a ruined colonial building has 9m ceilings, and there are plenty of benches to prop you up after you've downed your nth beer. There's a popular karaoke scene for those with reality-TV ambitions. The bar menu's good for a snack lunch.

☆ Entertainment

Guantánamo bleeds music. The city's own distinctive musical culture is enshrined in a subgenre of *son* known as *changüí.*

★Tumba Francesa Pompadour   LIVE MUSIC
(Map p441; Serafín Sánchez No 715; ☺9:30am-1pm, from 7pm 2nd & 4th Tue) One of only three Tumba Francesa societies left in Cuba, this house specializes in a unique form of Haitian-style dancing. Programs include *mi tumba baile* (dance) on Tuesdays, *encuentro tradicional*

(traditional get-together) and *peña campesina* (country music). If closed, consult showtimes at the Casa del Changüí opposite.

Casa del Changüí   LIVE MUSIC
(Map p441; ☎ 2132-4178; www.changui.cubava. cu; Serafín Sánchez No 710, btwn Narciso López & Jesús del Sol; ☺9am-noon, 2-6pm & 7pm-midnight Tue-Sun) As primary pulpit for Guantánamo's indigenous music, this is *the* place to experience *changüí* and is a shrine to its main exponent, local *timbalero* (percussionist) Elio Revé. There's a small Sala de Historia museum on-site.

Casa Sandunga (ARTex)   LIVE MUSIC
(☎ 2135-5499; Máximo Gómez No 1062; USD$1; ☺8pm-1am Tue-Sun) Housed in a royal blue building on a quiet street, this spot for variety shows and humor is openly referred to as 'the place.'

Casa del Son   LIVE MUSIC
(Map p441; ☎ 2132-4178; Serafín Sánchez No 710, btwn Narciso López & Jesús del Sol; ☺5pm-midnight) A new venue for old music, this casa shares lovingly restored digs with the Casa del Changüí in Calle Serafín Sánchez, the city's boisterous 'music street.'

Casa de la Trova   LIVE MUSIC
(Map p441; cnr Pedro A Pérez & Flor Crombet; USD$1; ☺9am-noon, 2-6pm & 7pm-midnight) It's hard not to love this scene: a traditional music house with old men in Panama hats dancing athletically.

Casa de las Promociones
Musicales 'La Guantanamera'   LIVE MUSIC
(Map p441; ☎ 2132-7266; Calixto García, btwn Crombet & Giro; ☺hours vary) A well-maintained concert-oriented venue, with Thursday rap *peñas* (performances) and Sunday *trova* (traditional poetic singing) matinees.

❶ Information

INTERNET ACCESS
There's wi-fi in Parque Martí and on the surrounding pedestrian-only blocks. **Etecsa Telepunto** (☎ 2132-7878; cnr Aguilera & Los Maceo; internet per hour USD$1.50; ☺8:30am-7:30pm) sells wi-fi scratch cards.

MEDICAL SERVICES
Hospital Agostinho Neto (☎ 2135-5450; Km 1, Carretera de El Salvador; ☺24hr) This hospital at the west end of Plaza Mariana Grajales near Hotel Guantánamo will help foreigners in emergencies.

Farmacia Internacional (☎ 2135-1129; Flor Crombet No 305, btwn Calixto García & Los Maceo; ⊘ 9am-5pm) On the southeast corner of Parque Martí.

Banco de Crédito y Comercio (☎ 2132-6917; Calixto García No 958, cnr Bartolomé Masó; ⊘ 9am-3pm Mon-Fri) One of two branches on this block, with ATM.

Cadeca (☎ 2135-5909; cnr Calixto García & Prado; ⊘ 8am-4pm)

TOURIST INFORMATION

Cubamar (Campismo Popular; Map p441; ☎ 2132-7356; Crombet, btwn Martí & Pérez; ⊘ 9am-noon & 2-5pm Mon-Fri, 9am-noon Sat) Book any of the region's campismo sites outside the city here.

Havanatur (☎ 2132-6365; Aguilera, btwn Calixto García & Los Maceo; ⊘ 8am-noon & 1:30-4:30pm Mon-Fri, to 11:30am Sat)

Infotur (Map p441; ☎ 2135-1993; infotur@ guantanamo.infotur.tur.cu; Calixto García, btwn Crombet & Giro; ⊘ 8:30am-noon & 1-4:45pm Mon-Sat) Helpful tourist information office.

❶ Getting There & Away

BUS

The rather inconveniently placed **Terminal de Ómnibus** (☎ 2132-9640; www.viazul.com; Carretera a Santiago de Cuba) is 5km west of the center on the old road to Santiago (a continuation of Av Camilo Cienfuegos). A taxi from the Hotel Guantánamo should cost USD$3 to USD$4.

There's one daily Víazul bus to Baracoa departing at 9:30am (USD$10, 3½ hours) and two to Santiago de Cuba (USD$6, 1¾ hours), departing at 5:40pm and 6pm.

GITMO: THE STORY SO FAR

Procured in the aftermath of the Spanish–Cuban–American War via the infamous Platt Amendment in 1903, the US naval base in Guantánamo Bay (dubbed Gitmo by US Marines) was first established primarily to protect the eastern approach to the strategically important Panama Canal.

In 1934, an upgrade of the original treaty reaffirmed the lease terms and agreed to honor them indefinitely unless both governments accorded otherwise. It also set an annual rent of US$4085, a sum that the US continues to cough up, but which the Cubans won't bank on the grounds that the occupation is illegal (Fidel Castro allegedly stored the checks in the top drawer of his office desk).

The US naval base sits at the jaws of Guantánamo Bay with military installations on both sides and the interior of the bay actually inside Cuban territory. Facilities include a dozen beaches, a water desalination plant, two airstrips and Cuba's only McDonald's, KFC and Starbucks. Approximately 8500 military personnel are based here.

The facility's recent history is notorious. In the early '90s, it held thousands of Haitian migrants and Cuban *balseros* (rafters) picked up by the US Coast Guard while trying to reach Florida.

Since 2002, the US has held more than 770 prisoners with suspected Al Qaeda or Taliban links at Camp Delta in Guantánamo Bay without pressing criminal charges. Denied legal counsel and family contact while facing rigorous interrogations, the detainees mounted hunger strikes. Several committed suicide. In 2004, Amnesty International and the UN called to close the base down amid Red Cross reports that aspects of the camp regime were tantamount to torture. The US released 420 prisoners, charging just three of them.

In January 2009, President Barack Obama promised to shut down Guantánamo's detention camps, ending what he termed 'a sad chapter in US history.' Bipartisan opposition in Congress prevented the shutdown. International condemnation of the force-feeding of some 100 inmates on hunger strike in May 2013 renewed pressure, yet Congress successfully blocked all further attempts to move prisoners to the US for trial. The Trump administration had plans to keep the detainment center open indefinitely.

In February 2021, US President Joe Biden announced his administration's intention to close the camp by the end of his term.

As of mid-2021, 40 prisoners remain in Guantánamo. Nine of them are cleared for transfer but, so far, the authorities have struggled to find a country to take them; nineteen are held in indefinite law-of-war detention and are not facing tribunal charges; twelve are being handled by the military commissions war court.

CAR

The Autopista Nacional to Santiago de Cuba ends near Embalse La Yaya, 25km west of Guantánamo, where the road joins the Carretera Central. To drive to Guantánamo from Santiago de Cuba, follow the Autopista Nacional north about 12km to the top of the grade and then take the first turn to the right. Signposts are sporadic and vague, so take a good map and keep alert.

TRAIN

The **train station** (☑ 2132-5518; Pedro A Pérez), five blocks north of Parque Martí, has one departure for Havana (1st/2nd class USD$100/75, 17 hours) every third day via Camagüey, Ciego de Ávila, Santa Clara and Matanzas. Confirm your ticket an hour before departure at the station.

❶ Getting Around

Taxis hang out around Parque Martí. Bus 48 (20 centavos) runs between the center and the Hotel Guantánamo every 40 minutes or so. There are also plenty of **bici-taxis** (Map p441).

Fill up at **Oro Negro Gas Station** (cnr Los Maceo & Jesús del Sol).

South Coast

The long, dry coastal road from Guantánamo to the island's eastern extremity, Punta de Maisí, is Cuba's spectacular semidesert region, where cacti nestle on rocky ocean terraces and prickly aloe vera pokes out from the scrub. Several little stone beaches between Playa Yacabo and Cajobabo make refreshing pit stops for those with time to linger, while the diverse roadside scenery – punctuated at intervals by rugged purple mountains and impossibly verdant riverside oases – impresses throughout.

◉ Sights & Activities

Playita de Cajobabo   BEACH

Cajobabo's main beach is stony and flanked by dramatic cliffs, but nonetheless makes a good snorkeling spot. Follow the road's eastern end over a headland and the asphalt deadends at another beach. Walk east along this beach for 400m and you'll come to a boat-shaped monument commemorating the spot where José Martí landed in 1895 to launch the Second War of Independence.

Martí and Gómez arrived in a rowing boat with four others at 10pm on the night of April 11. The disembarkation served as inspiration for Fidel Castro's subsequent landing in *Granma* 61 years later.

★ La Farola   SCENIC DRIVE

One of the seven modern engineering marvels of modern Cuba, the so-called 'lighthouse road' runs 55km from Cajobabo all the way to Baracoa, connecting cacti-sprinkled semidesert with lush rain forest. There are soaring pines and a lookout at its highest point, Alto de Cotilla.

🛌 Sleeping

Campismo Playita de Cajobabo   CABIN $

(☑ 2188-6304;   www.campismopopular.cu;
USD$20) Vacation among the locals in these rustic but comfortable cabins at Cajobabo's gravelly beach. Reserve through Cubamar (p443) in Baracoa.

❶ Getting There & Away

Buses between Guantanamo and Baracoa ply this road once daily; otherwise, you can get here via bicycle, private transportation or a taxi.

Punta de Maisí

Punta de Maisí is Cuba's easternmost point, and after a long time as an off-limits military zone, the region has opened up to travelers. From here, you can see Haiti 70km away on a clear day. There's not much to do besides climb the spiral stairway of the lighthouse (1862) and share the small, fine white-sand beach with some roaming goats and the few human visitors who trek out here.

The road from Baracoa to the village of La Máquina (55km) is good, and then it's a decent but slightly rougher 13km run from La Máquina to Punta de Maisí. It's popular with cyclists.

◉ Sights

Faro de Maisí   LIGHTHOUSE

(USD$2; ⊙10-11am & 2-4pm) Remove your shoes for the meditative, spiraling climb up 144 wooden stairs to the top of the lighthouse for 360-degree views of the point from 30-some meters high. If you're only one or two people and the lighthouse keeper deems you suitably respectful, he might even let you ascend to the tippy-top to see the light and housing.

🛌 Sleeping & Eating

Hotel Faro de Maisí   HOTEL $

(☑ 2168-9620; www.islazul.cu; La Asunción; s/d incl breakfast USD$20/30; ❋ 🛜) This Islazul hotel with an on-site restaurant is a decent choice in an outstanding, if not particularly convenient location, (about 11km from the actual lighthouse). Modern rooms feature generic graphic images, TVs and phones. Superior rooms have mini fridges with refreshments.

Villa Punta de Maisí CABIN **$**
(☑ 2168-2401; d/ste USD$20/30; P ✳ 🗦 🖭) This remote desert outpost is as quiet as the resident goats want to keep it. Right next to the Faro de Maisí lighthouse and steps from the beach, these prefab cabins come with a pool and restaurant. Atmospheric it ain't, but far-flung it is, and you'll likely have this long stretch of arid beach to yourself.

You *must* reserve in advance by contacting the Hotel Guantánamo (p440).

❶ Getting There & Away

Visitors can come on a day tour from Baracoa or by private transportation.

Boca de Yumurí

Five kilometers south of Baracoa, a road branches east off La Farola and travels 28km along the coast to Boca de Yumurí at the mouth of Río Yumurí. Near the bridge over the river is the **Túnel de los Alemanes** (German Tunnel), an amazing natural arch of trees and foliage. Though lovely, the dark-sand beach here has become *the* day trip from Baracoa. Hustlers hard-sell fried-fish meals, while other people peddle colorful land snails called polymitas. They are endangered as a result of their wholesale harvesting for tourists, so refuse all offers.

◎ Sights & Activities

Boca de Yumurí makes a superb bike jaunt from Baracoa (56km round trip): hot but smooth and flat with great views and many potential stopovers (try **Playa Bariguá** at Km 25). You can arrange bikes in Baracoa – ask at your casa particular.

Playa Manglito BEACH
Sweet and low-key Playa Manglito lies west of Boca de Yumurí, offering dead-easy access, a peaceful stretch of beach and a few restaurant options that will bring the Baracoan feast to you.

Boat Taxis BOATING
(USD$3) From beneath the bridge at the mouth of Río Yumurí, boat taxis head 400m upstream where the steep river banks narrow into a haunting natural gorge. You can arrange to be dropped off here for a picnic on an island in the river delta.

Playa Caguajo HIKING
Near Boca de Yumurí, this little-visited sandy expanse is accessible via a 5km trail from the Río Mata through biologically diverse woodland. Ecotur (p452) in Baracoa runs trips here.

✖ Eating

Restaurant Tato SEAFOOD **$$**
(mains USD$7-10; ⊘ 8am-midnight) On delightful little Playa Manglito, this beach-abutting restaurant will prepare you fresh octopus caught in the shallows just metres from your plate.

❶ Getting There & Away

Visitors can access this area via rental car or taxi from Baracoa, though taxis usually cost more than a tour. Organize an excursion either privately or with Cubatur (p452).

Baracoa
POP 79,797

Beguiling, outlandish and surreal, Baracoa's essence is addictive. On the wet and windy side of the Cuchillas del Toa mountains, Cuba's oldest and most isolated town exudes original atmosphere.

Feast your eyes upon deep green foliage that's wonderfully abundant after the stark aridity of Guantánamo's south coast. Delve into fantastical legends, and acquaint yourself with an unorthodox cast of local characters. There's Cayamba, the self-styled 'Guerrilla troubadour,' who once claimed he was the man with the ugliest voice in the world; La Rusa, an aristocratic Russian émigré who inspired a novel by magic-realist author Alejo Carpentier; and Enriqueta Faber, a French woman who passed herself off as a man to practice as a doctor and marry a local heiress in Baracoa's cathedral in 1819 – likely Cuba's first same-sex marriage. Baracoa – what would Cuba be without you?

While 2016's Hurricane Matthew hit Baracoa hard, most of the town has rebounded.

◎ Sights

★ **Museo Arqueológico 'La Cueva del Paraíso'** MUSEUM
(Moncada; USD$3; ⊘ 9am-4pm) Baracoa's most impressive museum, La Cueva del Paraíso is

Baracoa

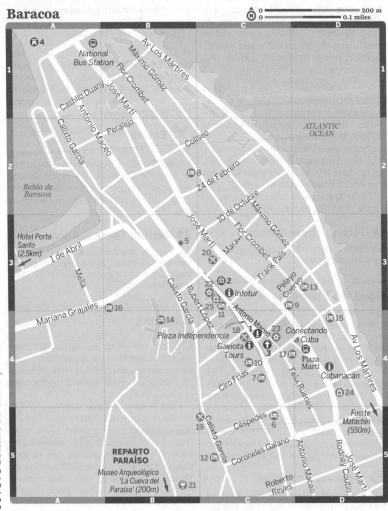

ATLANTIC OCEAN

Bahía de Baracoa

Hotel Porto Santo (2.5km)

Plaza Independencia

REPARTO PARAÍSO

Museo Arqueológico 'La Cueva del Paraíso' (200m)

Fuerte Matachín (550m)

a series of caves that were once Taíno burial chambers. Among nearly 2000 authentic Taíno pieces are unearthed skeletons, ceramics, 3000-year-old petroglyphs and a replica of the Ídolo de Tabaco, a sculpture found in Maisí in 1903 and considered to be one of the most important Taíno finds in the Caribbean.

One of the staff will enthusiastically show you around. The museum is 800m southeast of Hotel El Castillo. Tickets can be purchased at Ecotur (p452).

Casa del Cacao   MUSEUM
(Map p446; ☎2164-2125; Antonio Maceo, btwn Maraví & Frank País; ⊗7am-11pm) FREE Baracoa, you will quickly ascertain (via your nose), is the center of Cuba's chocolate industry; cacao is grown hereabouts and subsequently chocolate-ized in a local factory. Thus this museum with cafe chronicles the history of cacao and its importance in eastern Cuba as well as offering cups full of the pure, thick stuff (hot or cold) in a pleasant indoor cafe. It also sells bars of dark, agreeably bitter Baracoan chocolate.

Baracoa

Parque Natural Majayara PARK

(USD$2, lookout USD$5) 🚶 Southeast of town in the Parque Natural Majayara are a couple of magical hikes and swimming opportunities plus an archaeological trail in the grounds of a lush family farm. It's a very low-key, DIY diversion. Alternatively, Ecotur (p452) leads trips here (USD$20).

Passing the Fuerte Matachín, hike southeast past the baseball stadium and along the dark-sand beach for 20 minutes to the Río Miel, where a long low bridge crosses the river.

On the other side, bear left following a track up through a cluster of rustic houses to another junction. A guard post here is sometimes staffed by a park official collecting entry fees. Turn left again and continue along the vehicle track until the houses clear and you see a signposted, single-track path leading off left to Playa Blanca, an idyllic spot for a picnic.

Staying straight on the track, you'll come to a trio of wooden homesteads. The third of these houses belongs to the Fuentes family. For a donation, Señor Fuentes will lead you on a hike to his family finca (farm), where you can stop for coffee and tropical fruit. Further on he'll show you the Cueva de Aguas, a cave with a sparkling, freshwater swimming hole inside. Tracking back up the hillside you'll come to an archaeological trail with more caves and marvelous ocean views.

Fuerte Matachín FORT

(Museo Municipal; ☎2164-2122; cnr José Martí & Malecón; USD$1; ⊗8am-noon & 2-6pm) Baracoa is protected by a trio of muscular Spanish forts. This one, built in 1802 at the southern entrance to town, houses the Museo Municipal. The small but beautiful building showcases an engaging chronology of Cuba's oldest settlement, including polymita snail shells, the story of Che Guevara and the chocolate factory, and the particular strand of music Baracoa gave birth to: *kiribá*, a forefather of *son*.

There are also exhibits relating to Magdalena Menasse (née Rovieskuya, 'La Rusa'), after whom Alejo Carpentier based his famous book, *La consagración de la primavera* (The Rite of Spring).

Castillo de Seboruco FORT

(Map p446; Loma del Paraíso) Baracoa's highest fort was begun by the Spanish in 1739 and finished by the Americans in 1900. Barely recognizable as a fort these days, it serves as Hotel El Castillo (p450). There's an excellent view of El Yunque's flat top over the shimmering swimming pool. A steep stairway at the southwest end of Calle Frank País climbs directly up.

Bust of Hatuey STATUE

(Map p446; Antonio Maceo) Facing the cathedral is the Bust of Hatuey, a Taíno *cacique* (chief) who was burned at the stake near Baracoa

GUANTÁNAMO PROVINCE BARACOA

in 1512 after resisting Spanish colonization and refusing to convert to Catholicism.

Catedral de Nuestra Señora de la Asunción CHURCH

(Map p446; ☑ 2164-3005; Antonio Maceo No 152; ☺ 7-11am & 4-9pm Tue-Sun) After years of neglect, Baracoa's hurricane-battered historic cathedral has been lovingly restored using primarily Italian funding. There's been a building on this site since the 16th century, though this present, much-altered, incarnation dates from 1833.

The church's most famous artifact is the priceless Cruz de la Parra, the only survivor of 29 wooden crosses erected by Columbus in Cuba on his first voyage in 1492. Carbon dating has authenticated the age of the cross (it dates from the late 1400s), but has indicated it was originally made out of indigenous Cuban wood, thus disproving the legend that Columbus brought the cross from Europe.

Playa Duaba BEACH

Heading north on the Moa road, take the Hotel Porto Santo/airport turnoff and continue for 2km past the airport runway to a black-sand beach at the river mouth where Antonio Maceo, Flor Crombet and others landed in 1895 to start the Second War of Independence. There's a campismo (cheap rustic accommodations), memorial monument and close-up views of El Yunque, though the beach itself isn't sunbathing territory.

Fuerte de la Punta FORT

(Map p446) This Spanish fort has watched over the harbor entrance at the northwestern end of town since 1803. The super thick, hurricane-resistant walls now hide a restaurant (p451).

Tours

Organized tours are a good way to view Baracoa's hard-to-reach outlying sights, and the Cubatur (p452) and Ecotur (p452) offices on Plaza Independencia can book excursions, including to El Yunque (USD$16 to USD$20), Parque Nacional Alejandro de Humboldt (USD$22 to USD$25) and Boca de Yumurí (USD$22).

★ Geovannis Steve Cardosa Matos TOURS

(☑ 5-530-2820; geostevecuba@nauta.cu) The ebullient, English-fluent Steve is a knowledgeable, reliable local guide with a sunny attitude and a menu of professionally led tours to the national park and cacao farm.

He also does walking tours or custom adventures. Contact him directly or via Hostal Nilson (p450).

★ José Ángel Delfino Pérez TOURS

(☑ 2164-1367, 5-425-5819; joseguia@nauta.cu; day tours USD$25-27) Walking plant encyclopedia and enthusiastic geological expert, José has to be Baracoa's best private guide. His professional tours visit El Yunque, Punta de Maisí, Humboldt and – best of all – Boca de Yumurí, a trip that takes in cacao plantations, chocolate tastings and visits to isolated beaches.

Ask to see José's ID, as he has some unwelcome local impersonators. You can contact him by phone, email or at Hostal Nilson (p450).

★★ Festivals & Events

★ Semana de la Cultura Baracoesa CULTURAL

(☺ late Mar) Locals hit the streets to celebrate the 1895 landing of Antonio Maceo. There are feasts and fairs featuring genuine traditions: musical styles and dancing influenced by both indigenous and modern rhythms. It ends with a pilgrimage on April 1.

🛌 Sleeping

★ Casa Colonial Ykira CASA PARTICULAR $

(Map p446; ☑ 2164-3881; ykiram@nauta.cu; Antonio Maceo No 168a, btwn Ciro Frías & Céspedes; r USD$25; ✺) Welcoming and hospitable, Ykira is Baracoa's premier hostess. She also serves a mean dinner made with homegrown herbs. A lovely mural lines the entrance walk, and there are two rooms set in the bosom of family life but with plenty of personal space. Guests enjoy terraces and a *mirador* (viewpoint) with sea views.

★ Casa Yamicel CASA PARTICULAR $

(Map p446; ☑ 2164-1118; neoris70@gmail.com; Martí No 145a, btwn Ciro Frías & Pelayo Cuervo; r USD$25; ✺) Doctor-proprietors that make killer mojitos? You'd better believe it. This colonial house offers six rooms with gorgeous wooden window bars (the best are on the top floor). There's wonderful hospitality, good meals (mains USD$6 to USD$12) and a roof terrace with reviving sea breezes. The superhelpful owners can also hook you up with reliable professional tour guides.

Hostal La Moderna CASA PARTICULAR $

(Map p446; ☑ 2164-3515; elrayo13@nauta.cu; Calixto García No 164a, btwn Galano & Céspedes;

GÜIRITO

Those on a mission to unravel the complex family tree of Cuban music shouldn't skip the tiny village of Güirito, 18km southeast of Baracoa. Herein lie two of the primitive precursors to Cuba's national music, *son*. While *son* and its rhythmic cousin, salsa, got exported around the world, the orphic genres of *kiribá* and *nengón* never got much further than Güirito.

So what exactly are these rugged and rootsy musical forms? Both *kiribá* and *nengón* are rustic antecedents of *son* (rather than variants) passed down orally from generation to generation since the First Independence War in the mid-19th century. Thanks to a local revival in 1982, *kiribá* and *nengón* are still widely practiced in Güirito by a 21-person music and dance group who have meticulously safeguarded the old traditions.

Kiribá's fast beat and relatively free choreography incorporates a couples' dance in which partners move together in broad circular steps. *Nengón* is a slower dance with a distinctive foot-dragging motion said to imitate erstwhile farm-workers who stamped their feet on dried coffee and cacao beans to grind them.

The accompanying music is invariably played by a septet consisting of *tres* (Cuban-style guitar), *güiro* (a ridged, hollowed-out gourd), claves, marimbula, bongos, maracas and voice. *Nengón* has 22 registered songs but in *kiribá* singers make up the words as they go along. The costumes worn at musical gatherings are equally distinctive. Women wear white blouses and long flower-patterned skirts. Men wear *guayabera* (Caribbean dress) shirts and straw *yarey* hats, and carry handkerchiefs.

On most Saturday afternoons the group gets together in Güirito for a traditional fiesta, an informal affair with a wide interchange of Baracoan food. There's *bacán* (crab and plantain tamales), *frangollo* (dried banana mixed with sugar and wrapped in a banana leaf) and rice cooked inside the stomach of a whole roasted pig. Fuelled by rum drawn from oak barrels, the dancing can go on until the small hours. Anyone is welcome.

r USD$20-25; ❁ ☎) Run by the friendly and no-nonsense Dr Ysabel Garrido, this casa has three rooms above the bustling family home. A top-floor seaview terrace has a shaded patio area (which may become a restaurant). The terrace room is the most private (...unless the restaurant does open). The casa is slightly removed from Baracoa's center but only a two-minute walk to the plaza.

Isabel Castro Vilato
CASA PARTICULAR **$**
(Map p446; ☎2164-2267, 5-355-3634; jrosello castro@gmail.com; Mariana Grajales No 35; r USD$25; P ❁) You can't tell from the busy street outside, but this elegant green clapboard-and-stone house has lovely country style and a tranquil atmosphere. There are four massive rooms with minibars and a beautiful backyard garden growing breakfast provisions for your table. The family is helpful and wonderful. Unusually for Baracoa, there's a secure garage/car parking space.

La Casona
CASA PARTICULAR **$**
(Map p446; ☎2164-2133; daliana85@nauta.cu; Félix Ruenes No 1 altos; r USD$20-25; ❁) Rarely is a city's most central casa among its best, but

thus have the young hosts made this place: two spotless 2nd-floor rooms and a knock-out terrace where you can enjoy a cocktail or two.

Casa Dorkis
CASA PARTICULAR **$**
(Map p446; ☎2164-3451, 5-238-5316; dorkis td72@yahoo.es; Flor Crombet No 58 altos, btwn Coliseo & 24 de Febrero; r USD$25; ❁) Though a bit of a walk from the plaza, this is one of your best bets for lodging. This quiet 2nd-story apartment has clean rooms with lovely decor flooded with natural light. There's an *azulejo*-tiled terrace with Atlantic views – ideal for a couple of days of lazy relaxation.

Casa Colonial Lucy
CASA PARTICULAR **$**
(Map p446; ☎5-246-5775, 2164-1061; lucy4708@ nauta.cu; Céspedes No 29, btwn Rubert López & Antonio Maceo; r USD$10-20; ❁) This welcoming home from 1840 exudes character with patios, porches and flowering begonias, though cleanliness could score a little higher. There are two rooms here as well as terraces on different levels, and the atmosphere is quiet and secluded. Lucy's son speaks four languages and offers salsa lessons.

The house was for sale when we visited, so call ahead rather than turning up at the door.

Hostal Las Terrazas Casa Nilson
CASA PARTICULAR $

(Map p446; ☑ 2164-3123, 5-271-8556; www.hostal-nilson.baracoa.co; Flor Crombet No 143, btwn Ciro Frías & Pelayo Cuervo; d USD$20-25, ste USD$35; ❄) With elaborate woodwork, imagery and symbolism of Santería and Baracoan culture, this super-clean house has three quirky rooms over several floors. Ideal for close groups or families, a spacious, suite features a bathroom with two showers and two toilets, face-to-face. No waiting at the door here! Above the restaurant there's a roof terrace with sea views.

Hostal 1511
HOTEL $$

(Map p446; ☑ 2164-5700; reservas@gavbcoa.co.cu; Ciro Frías, btwn Rubert López & Maceo; s/d incl breakfast USD$59/64; ❄🛜) The year 1511 is Baracoa's foundation date, and this diminutive place is a landmark, too, for offering dead-central accommodations with an abundant colonial vibe. The model ship in the lobby sets the tone for an overtly nautical decor that works best in the more charming upstairs rooms. It was under renovation at the time of our visit.

Hostal La Habanera
HOTEL $$

(Map p446; ☑ 2164-5273; Antonio Maceo No 126; s/d incl breakfast USD$59/64; ❄🛜) Atmospheric and inviting in a way only Baracoa can muster, La Habanera sits in a restored and regularly repainted colonial mansion. The four front bedrooms share a street-facing balcony replete with tiled floor and rocking chairs: perfect for imbibing that quintessential Baracoa ambience (street-hawkers, hip-gyrating music, and seafood a-frying in the restaurants).

The downstairs lobby has a bar, a restaurant and a handy Gaviota tour desk. It should be sparkling after renovations happening on our visit.

Hotel El Castillo
HOTEL $$

(Map p446; ☑ 2164-5224; www.gaviotahotels.com; Loma del Paraíso; s/d incl breakfast USD$59/80; 🅿❄🛜🏊) Recline like a colonial-era conquistador in this historic fort-turned-hotel in the hilltop Castillo de Seboruco. Choose your room well: there's some wear and tear, though conquistadors never boasted the privilege of a swimming pool or housekeeping fashioning towels into ships and swans.

The 28 newer rooms in a separate block offer jaw-dropping El Yunque views.

Hotel Río Miel
HOTEL $$

(Map p446; ☑ 2164-1207; www.gaviotahotels.com; Av Malecón, cnr Ciro Frías; s/d incl breakfast USD$59/64; ❄🛜) Stylish and sturdy, this hotel withstood Hurricane Matthew with honors. It's on the Malecón where it faces some of the most inclement weather in Cuba. Run by Gaviota, the service can be slack, but there are remodeled rooms with large safes that fit a laptop.

Hotel Porto Santo
HOTEL $$

(☑ 2164-5106; www.gaviotahotels.com; Carretera del Aeropuerto; s/d incl breakfast USD$59/80; 🅿❄🛜🏊) On the bay where Columbus allegedly planted his first cross is this peaceful, well-integrated low-rise hotel. Situated 4km from the town center and 200m from the airport, there are 36 more-than-adequate rooms all within earshot of the sea. A steep stairway leads down to a tiny, wave-lashed beach. Unfortunately, Hurricane Matthew downed most of the palms shading it.

🍴 Eating & Drinking

Eating in Baracoa is a full-on sensory experience. Cooking here is creative, tasty and – above all – different. To experience the real deal, eat in your casa particular.

Sabor Taíno
CREOLE $

(Map p446; ☑ 5-481-2622; Maraví No 114, btwn Maceo & Martí; meals USD$5-8; ⏱10am-11pm) A lovely family-run *paladar* with the owner's paintings adding to its slightly offbeat vibe, Sabor Taíno serves up delicious, reasonably priced Baracoan classics preceded by soup and followed by dessert. Simply homey, friendly and satisfying.

Cafetería El Parque
FAST FOOD $

(Map p446; ☑ 2164-1206; Antonio Maceo No 142; snacks USD$1-3; ⏱24hr; 🛜) The favored meeting place of just about everyone in town, you're bound to end up at this open terrace at some point, if only to crack open a can of Cristal and tune into the wi-fi.

⭐ Restaurante Las Terrazas Casa Nilson
CUBAN $$

(Map p446; ☑ 2164-3123; Flor Crombet No 143, btwn Ciro Frías & Pelayo Cuervo; meals USD$8-15; ⏱noon-3pm & 6:30-11pm) Up above Hostal Nilson on a spectacular two-level terrace decorated in quirky Afro-Caribbean style, the chef serves some of the best authentic Bar-

BARACOAN CUISINE

Unlike more complex cuisines, Cuban cooking doesn't really have a strong regional identity, at least not until you arrive in Baracoa. Here everything – including the food – is decidedly different. Home to the country's most fickle weather, Baracoa has used its wet microclimate and geographic isolation to jazz up notoriously unambitious Cuban cuisine with spices, sugar, exotic fruits and coconut. Fish anchors most menus yet even the seafood can pull some surprises. Count on tasting tiny tadpole-like *teti* fish drawn from the Río Toa between July to January during a waning moon.

The biggest taste explosion is a locally concocted coconut sauce known as *lechita*, a mixture of coconut milk, tomato sauce, garlic and a medley of spices best served over prawns, *aguja* (swordfish) or dorado. Other main course accompaniments include *bacán*, raw green plantain melded with crabmeat and wrapped in a banana leaf, or *frangollo*, a similar concoction where the ground bananas are mixed with sugar.

Sweets are another Baracoa *tour de force* thanks largely to the ubiquity of the cacao plant and the presence of the famous Che Guevara chocolate factory. Baracoan chocolate is sold all over the island, but the local Casa del Cacao (p446) is an obvious sampling point. You're likely to get it for breakfast in your casa particular, stirred into a local hot chocolate drink made with banana powder known as *chorote*.

Baracoa's most unique culinary invention is undoubtedly *cucurucho*, a delicate mix of dried coconut, sugar, honey, papaya, guava, mandarin and nuts (no concoction is ever quite alike) that is wrapped in an ecologically friendly palm frond. The best stuff is sold by the campesinos on La Farola coming into town from Guantánamo, a stop usually made by buses.

acoan food in town, and hence Cuba. Aside from the typical Baracoan delights, novelties like melt-in-your-mouth octopus with basil ink and homemade *patacon guisado* (a plantain dish), in addition to the secret house sauces, set this place apart. Reserve ahead to ensure a table.

⭐ **El Buen Sabor**   CUBAN **$$**
(Map p446; ☏2164-1400; Calixto García No 134 altos; meals USD$6-15; ☺noon-midnight) Served on a spotless and breezy upstairs terrace, meals come with salad, soup and side included. You can expect the best of Baracoan cuisine at this private restaurant, including swordfish in a coconut sauce, *bacán* (raw green plantain melded with crabmeat and wrapped in a banana leaf) and chocolate-y desserts. Service is attentive.

⭐ **Restaurante La Punta**   CARIBBEAN **$$**
(Map p446; ☏2164-1480; Fuerte de la Punta; meals USD$5-12; ☺10am-11pm) Cooled by Atlantic breezes (and the occasional full-on gale), the Gaviota-run La Punta aims to impress with well-prepared, garnished food in the lovely historical surrounds of the La Punta fort. Go on a Saturday night for live music.

El Ranchón   CLUB
(Map p446; ☏2164-2364; USD$1; ☺9pm-late) Atop a long flight of stairs at the western end of Coroneles Galano, popular El Ranchón mixes an exhilarating hilltop setting with taped disco and salsa music and legions of resident *jineteras* (female touts). Watch your step on the way down – it's a scary 146-step drunken tumble.

☆ Entertainment

⭐ **Casa de la Trova**
Victorino Rodríguez   TRADITIONAL MUSIC
(Map p446; Félix Ruenes No 6; USD$1; ☺matinee 5:30pm, 9pm-midnight) Cuba's smallest, zaniest, wildest and most atmospheric *casa de la trova* (*trova* house) rocks nightly to the Vodou-like rhythms of *changüí-son*. One night the average age of the band is 85, the next it's 22. The common denominator? It's all good. Matinees are usually free. Order a mojito in a jam jar and join in the show.

Casa de la Cultura   LIVE MUSIC
(Map p446; ☏2164-2364; Antonio Maceo No 124, btwn Frank País & Maraví) This venue does a wide variety of shows including some good rumba incorporating the textbook Cuban styles of *guaguancó, yambú* and *columbia* (subgenres of rumba). Go prepared for *mucho* audience participation. There's a good *spectaculo* (show) on the terrace, La Terraza, every Saturday at 11pm: expect rumba, Benny Moré, and the local hairdresser singing Omara Portuondo.

Shopping

Interesting art is easy to find in Baracoa and, like most things in this unique seaside town, it has its own distinctive flavor.

Taller Mirarte   ART
(Map p446; Antonio Maceo; ⏱10am-8pm) An artist's co-op where you'll always find one of the young creative painters sitting at a palette in the window. The local painting style is best described as Gauguin meets Van Gogh in the pages of a Gabriel García Márquez novel.

ARTex   GIFTS & SOUVENIRS
(Map p446; ☎2164-5373; José Martí No 197; ⏱9am-5pm Mon-Sat, to noon Sun) For the usual tourist trinkets, check out this place.

Information

INTERNET ACCESS

There's wi-fi access on Plaza Independencia.
Etecsa Telepunto (☎2164-3182; Antonio Maceo No 182; internet per hour USD$1.50; ⏱8:30am-7pm) sells wi-fi internet scratch cards and offers internet on computer terminals.

MEDICAL SERVICES

There's an international **clinic** (☎2164-1037; José Martí No 237, cnr Roberto Reyes; ⏱24hr) in town and a hospital 2km out of town on the road to Guantánamo.

MONEY

There's no shortage of banks with ATMs.
Banco de Crédito y Comercio (Antonio Maceo No 99; ⏱8am-2:30pm Mon-Fri) Has an ATM.

Banco Popular de Ahorro (☎2164-5209; José Martí No 166; ⏱8-11:30am & 2-4:30pm Mon-Fri) Has an ATM.

Cadeca (☎2164-5345; José Martí No 241; ⏱8:15am-4pm Mon-Fri, to 11:30am Sat & Sun) Short queues for currency exchange.

TOURIST INFORMATION

Cubanacán (Map p446; ☎2164-4383; Martí, btwn Ciro Frías & Céspedes; ⏱8am-noon & 2-6pm Mon-Sat) Sells tours, airline tickets and Conectando a Cuba shuttle tickets. Can also reserve Víazul bus tickets.

Cubatur (☎6132-8342; Antonio Maceo No 181; ⏱8:30am-noon & 1-5pm Mon-Sat) Helpful office that organizes tours to El Yunque and Parque Nacional Alejandro de Humboldt. Can also reserve Víazul bus tickets.

Ecotur (Map p446; ☎2164-2478; Antonio Maceo; ⏱8am-noon & 2-6pm Mon-Sat) Arranges trips to Parque Nacional Alejandro

de Humboldt (USD$22 to USD$25), El Yunque (USD$16 to USD$20), Caño de Yumuri, Rancho Toa, Finca Duaba and area beaches. Find the tiny office on Antonio Maceo at the dead-end T of Mariana Grajales.

Infotur (Map p446; ☎2164-1781; Antonio Maceo No 129a, btwn Frank País & Maraví; ⏱8:30am-noon & 1-4:45pm Mon-Sat) Very helpful office.

Getting There & Away

AIR

Gustavo Rizo Airport is 4km northwest of town, just behind the Hotel Porto Santo. Book flights to Havana with one of the travel agencies. The best way to get to and from the airport is by taxi (USD$8 to USD$10), or bici-taxi (USD$5) if you're traveling light.

The planes (and buses) out of Baracoa can be fully booked, so don't arrive on a tight schedule without outbound reservations.

BUS

The **National Bus Station** (Map p446; ☎2164-3880; cnr Av Los Mártires & Martí) has service with Víazul (www.viazul.com) to Guantánamo and Santiago de Cuba. Reserve your tickets a day in advance (more in high season).
Conectando a Cuba (Map p446; Parque Martí) has a shuttle service that travels to Santiago (USD$17) on Tuesday, Thursday and Sunday at noon, stopping in Guantanamo (USD$12).

TRUCK

Trucks to Moa (departures from 6am) leave from the National Bus Station, traveling along the very bumpy road northwest.

Getting Around

There's a helpful **Via car rental office** (☎2164-1665; Gustavo Rizo Airport) at the airport. The **Cupet-Cimex gas station** (Martí; ⏱24hr) is at the entrance to town 4km from the center, on the road to Guantánamo. If you're driving to Havana, note that the northern route through Moa and Holguín is the most direct, but the road disintegrates rapidly after Playa Maguana – for this reason taxi prices can be astronomical. Most locals prefer the La Farola route.

Bici-taxis around Baracoa charge foreigners USD$2 to USD$5. Negotiate rates for **taxi trips** (☎2164-3737) around the region.

Most casas particulares will be able to procure you a bicycle (USD$5 per day). The ultimate bike ride is the 20km ramble down to Playa Maguana, one of the most scenic roads in Cuba. You can rent mopeds for USD$25 at **Gaviota** (Map p446; ☎2164-5164; Antonio Maceo No 142, Cafetería El Parque; ⏱8am-noon, 2-6pm Mon-Sat) or Hotel El Castillo (p450).

Northwest of Baracoa

The rutted road heading out of town toward Moa is a green paradise flecked with palm groves, rustic farmsteads and serendipitous glimpses of the ocean. There are windswept beaches, coffee farms and rainforest. A new bridge replaced the one knocked out by Hurricane Matthew in 2016.

Much of this region lies within the Cuchillas del Toa Unesco Biosphere Reserve, an area of 2083 sq km that incorporates the Alejandro de Humboldt World Heritage site. Here is Cuba's largest rainforest, with many precious hardwoods and a high number of endemic species.

◉ Sights

★ El Yunque   MOUNTAIN
Baracoa's rite of passage is the 8km (up and down) hike to the top of this moody, mysterious mountain. Views from the summit (575m) and the flora and birdlife along the way are stupendous. Bank on seeing *tocororo* (Cuba's national bird), *zunzúncito* (the world's smallest bird), butterflies and polymitas (colorful endangered snails). The hike is hot (bring 2L of water) and usually muddy. It starts from the campismo 3km past the Finca Duaba (4km from the Baracoa–Moa road).

All visits must be guided. Cubatur (p452) offers this tour almost daily (USD$16 person, minimum four people). The fee covers admission, guide, transport and a sandwich. If you're not up to bagging the peak itself, ask Ecotur (p452) about the 7km Sendero Juncal-Rencontra that bisects fruit plantations and rain forest between the Duaba and Toa rivers.

Río Toa   RIVER
Ten kilometers northwest of Baracoa, the Toa is the third-longest river on the north coast of Cuba and the country's most voluminous. It's also an important bird and plant habitat. Cacao trees and ubiquitous coconut palms grow in the Valle de Toa.

A vast hydroelectric project on the Río Toa was abandoned after a persuasive campaign led by the Fundación de la Naturaleza y El Hombre convinced authorities it would do irreparable ecological damage; engineering and economic reasons also played a part.

Playa Maguana   BEACH
There's magic in this relatively undeveloped Caribbean beach where fun-seeking Cubans roll up in their vintage American cars and haul boomboxes out to the beach. Beyond a food shack (serving cocktails) there's little infrastructure here – which is the attraction of this location. As anywhere, watch your possessions.

Finca Duaba   FARM
(USD$2; ☺8am-7pm) Five kilometers out of Baracoa on the road to Moa and then 1km inland, Finca Duaba offers a fleeting taste of the Baracoan countryside. It's a verdant farm surrounded with profuse tropical plants and embellished with a short cacao (fruit from which chocolate is made) trail that explains the history and characteristics of chocolate. There's also a good *ranchón*-style restaurant and the opportunity to swim in the Río Duaba. A bici-taxi can drop you at the road junction.

🛏 Sleeping & Eating

Campismo Duaba   CABIN $
(☑2132-7356; USD$14; ❄) Ten lovely dollhouse cabins with bathrooms and air-conditioning. From Baracoa, it's on the road to Moa just before the Río Duaba.

Finca La Esperanza   FARMSTAY $
(☑5-218-0735; Km 8, Carretera de Moa-Baracoa; r incl breakfast USD$15) This lovely farmstay also offers meals (USD$8) and excursions. There are boat rides (USD$2) and walks on the Sendero Cayo los Chinos trail (USD$5).

Campismo El Yunque   CABIN $
(☑2164-5262; r USD$14) Simple Cuban-style rustic accommodations offering very basic cabins at the end of the Finca Duaba road, 9km outside of Baracoa. The El Yunque hike starts here.

★ Villa Maguana   HOTEL $$
(☑2164-1204; Km 20, Carretera de Moa-Baracoa; s/d incl breakfast USD$86/103, all-inclusive USD$111/153; 🅿❄) Knocking the socks off any Cuban all-inclusive resort is this delightful place 22km north of Baracoa. Four rustic wooden villas house 16 rooms in total. Guarded by two rocky promontories, it clings precariously to Maguana's famously dreamy setting above a bite-sized scoop of sand. There's a restaurant and amenities such as satellite TV, fridge and air-con.

CUBA'S TALLEST WATERFALL

Little known, even to most Cubans, Salto Fino is the Caribbean's tallest insular waterfall and the 20th tallest in the world. On the Arroyo El Infierno (Stream of Hell), it's surrounded by thick rainforest inside Parque Nacional Alejandro de Humboldt, inaccessible by road and rarely visited on foot.

Split into eight smaller falls, the 93m-high cascade drops off a steep platform in the Cuchillas del Toa Mountains. It was only measured and mapped in 1966 – the first scientific expedition, under prominent Cuban explorer Antonio Núñez Jiménez, bushwhacked a rough path here in 1996. Visitors might glimpse it from a lookout, but there's no public access.

Rancho Toa   CUBAN **$$**
(meals USD$10-12) A Palmares restaurant reached via a right-hand turnoff before the Toa bridge. You can organize boat or kayak trips (USD$5 to USD$10) and watch acrobatic Baracoans scale *cocotero* (coconut palms). A traditional Cuban feast of whole roast pig is available if you can rustle up enough people (eight, usually).

❶ Getting There & Away

A Moa-bound truck can drop you in this area, or you can go via taxi to Playa Maguana (around USD$25 round trip), Campismo El Yunque (USD$18 round trip) and other destinations.

Parque Nacional Alejandro de Humboldt

These steep pine-clad mountains and creeping morning mists guard an astonishing ecosystem that's unmatched in the Caribbean. Cuba's most dramatic and diverse national park was named after German naturalist-explorer Alexander von Humboldt who first visited in 1801. It was designated a Unesco World Heritage site in 2001 as 'one of the most biologically diverse tropical island sites on earth.'

Perched above Bahía de Taco, 40km northwest of Baracoa, lies 600-odd sq km of pristine forest and 2641 hectares of lagoon and mangroves. With 1000 flowering plant species and 145 ferns, it's the Caribbean's most diverse plant habitat. The toxic nature of the underlying rocks in the area has forced plants to survive by adaptation. As a result, 70% of the plants are endemic, as are nearly all 20 species of amphibians, 45% of the reptiles and many birds. Endangered bird species include Cuban Amazon parrots, hook-billed kites and ivory-billed woodpeckers.

🏃 Activities

The park has a network of trails leading to waterfalls, a *mirador* (lookout) and a massive karst cave system around the Farallones de Moa. Four trails are currently open to the public, taking in only a tiny segment of the park's 594 sq km. Typically, you can't just wander around on your own. The longest hike features an eight-hour reconnoiter deeper into the forest, featuring bird and orchid observation.

Each option is accompanied by a highly professional guide. If you're showing up independently, get to the **visitors center** (Carretera de Moa-Baracoa; park entry USD$10) before 10am to secure one. Prices range from USD$5 to USD$10, depending on the hike, but most people organize an excursion through Ecotur (p452), Cubatur (p452) or Gaviota (p452) in Baracoa, which includes transport and a pit stop on Playa Maguana on the way back (USD$24). Ecotur recently added 4WD and ATV excursions.

Balcón de Iberia   HIKING
The park's most challenging loop (7km) bisects both agricultural land and pristine rain forest. It includes a swim in a natural pool near the Salto de Agua Maya waterfall.

Bahía de Taco   HIKING
A circuit hike that incorporates a boat trip through the mangroves and the idyllic horseshoe-shaped bay, plus a 2km hike. Boats use a manatee-friendly motor developed by scientists here.

El Recreo   WALKING
This trail is an easy 2km stroll around the bay.

❶ Getting There & Away

The park visitors center is approximately halfway between Baracoa and Moa. You can arrange a tour through an agency in Baracoa or get there independently. The gorgeously scenic road is a collection of holes but passable in a hire car if driven with care. This road continues into Holguín Province, improving just before Moa.

GUANTÁNAMO PROVINCE PARQUE NACIONAL ALEJANDRO DE HUMBOLDT

Understand
Cuba

History

Embellished by extraordinary feats of revolutionary derring-do, and plagued routinely by the meddling armies of foreign invaders, Cuba has achieved a historical importance far greater than its size would suggest. The underlying and – until the 1960s – ongoing historical themes have been outside interference and internal rebellion, and the results of both have often been bloody.

A Turbulent Historical Trajectory

Since the arrival of Columbus in 1492, Cuba's turbulent historical trajectory has included genocide, slavery, two bitter independence wars, a period of corrupt and violent quasi-independence, and, finally, a populist revolution that, despite early promise, hit a metaphoric pause button. The fallout has led to the emigration of almost one-fifth of the Cuban population, mostly to the US.

For the sake of simplicity, the country's historical eras can be divided into three broad categories: precolonial, colonial and postcolonial. Before 1492 Cuba was inhabited by a trio of migratory civilizations that originated in the Orinoco Basin of South America before island-hopping north. Their cultures have been only partially evaluated to date, primarily because they left very little behind in the way of documentary evidence.

Cuba's colonial period was dominated by the Spanish and the divisive issue of slavery, which spanned the whole era from the 1520s until abolition in 1886. Slavery left deep wounds on Cuba's collective psyche, but its existence and final quashing was integral to the evolution of the country's highly distinctive culture, music, dance and religion. Understand this and you're halfway to understanding the complexities of the contemporary nation.

Postcolonial Cuba has had two distinctive sub-eras, the second of which can be further subdivided in two. The period from the defeat of Spain in 1898 to Castro's revolutionary takeover in 1959 is usually seen as an age of quasi-independence with a strong American influence. It was also a time characterized by violence, corruption and frequent insurrection on the part of opposition groups intent on toppling the government.

TIMELINE	BCE 2000	CE 1100	1492
	The Guanahatabeys, Cuba's earliest known Stone Age civilization, live in the caves along the coast of present-day Pinar del Río Province.	Taíno people start arriving in Cuba after leapfrogging their way across the islands of the Lesser Antilles from the Orinoco Basin in present-day Venezuela.	Christopher Columbus lands in Cuba in modern-day Holguín Province. He sails for a month along the coast, as far as Baracoa, planting religious crosses and meeting with the indigenous Taínos.

The post-1959 Castro epoch breaks conveniently into two stages: the age of Soviet domination from 1961 to 1991, and the modern era that stretches from the Special Period to the present day, when Cuba, despite its devastating economic difficulties, became a truly independent power for the first time.

Pre-Colonial Cuba

The first known civilization in Cuba was that of the Guanahatabeys, a primitive Stone Age people who lived in caves and eked out a meager existence as hunter-gatherers. At some point over a 2000-year period, the Guanahatabeys were gradually pushed west into what is now Pinar del Río Province, displaced by the arrival of another pre-ceramic culture known as the Siboneys. The Siboneys were a slightly more developed group of fishers and small-scale farmers who settled down comparatively peacefully on the archipelago's sheltered southern coast. By the second millennium AD they were similarly displaced by the more sophisticated Taínos, who liked to use Siboneys as domestic servants.

The Taínos first started arriving in Cuba around AD 1050 in a series of waves, concluding a migration process that had begun on mainland South America several centuries earlier. Related to the Greater Antilles Arawaks, the new peace-loving natives were escaping the barbarism of the cannibalistic Caribs who had colonized the Lesser Antibes, pushing the Taínos northwest into Puerto Rico, Hispaniola and Cuba.

The Taínos

Taíno culture was more developed and sophisticated than that of its predecessors; the adults practiced a form of cranial transformation by flattening the soft skulls of their young children, and groups lived together in villages characterized by their thatched *bohíos* (rustic huts) and *bateys* (communal 'plazas').

Their villages, made from mud and thatch, haven't survived, though they have left their imprint in other areas, particularly the language. Words such as hurricane, hammock, guajiro and tobacco are all derived from the Taíno vernacular. The Taínos were also the first of the world's pre-Columbian cultures to nurture the delicate tobacco plant into a form that could easily be processed for smoking.

The Taínos were skillful farmers, weavers, ceramicists and boat-builders, and their complex society exhibited an organized system of participatory government that was overseen by series of local *caciques* (chiefs). Sixty percent of the crops still grown in Cuba today were pioneered by Taíno farmers, who even planted cotton for use in hammocks, fishing nets and bags.

Best Historical Sites

Museo de la Revolución, Havana

Cuartel Moncada, Santiago de Cuba

Comandancia de la Plata, Granma

Fortaleza de San Carlos de la Cabaña, Havana

1494	1508	1511	1519
Columbus returns to Cuba on his second voyage, docking briefly at various points along Cuba's south coast and 'discovering' La Isla de la Juventud.	Spanish navigator Sebastián de Ocampo circumnavigates Cuba, establishing that it's an island and disproving Columbus' long-held idea that it might be a peninsula of the Asian continent.	Diego Velázquez lands at Baracoa with 400 colonizers, including Hernán Cortés (the future colonizer of Mexico). The new arrivals construct a fort and quickly make enemies of the local Taínos.	Havana, the last of Cuba's seven founding 'villas,' is moved to its present site at the mouth of a fine natural harbor. It is inaugurated with a solemn mass under a ceiba tree in what is now Plaza de Armas.

Columbus described the Taínos with terms such as 'gentle,' 'sweet,' 'always laughing' and 'without knowledge of what is evil,' which makes the genocide to come even harder to comprehend. Estimates vary wildly as to how many indigenous people populated Cuba pre-Columbus, though 100,000 is a good consensus figure. Within 30 years, 90% of the Taínos had been wiped out.

Though Cuban culture retains echoes of the Taínos, the independence leaders of later years rarely invoked their erstwhile civilization in the way other Latin Americans celebrated the Aztecs and the Maya, preferring instead to identify with Cuba's African and Spanish roots. Nonetheless, Taíno influences seeped into Cuba's language, eating habits (root vegetables), music (*kiriká* and *changüí*), living space (Taíno-style *bohíos* are still used by Cuban campesinos) and the spirit of resistance.

Colonial Cuba

Columbus & Colonization

Columbus neared Cuba on October 27, 1492, describing it as 'the most beautiful land human eyes had ever seen.' He named it 'Juana' in honor of a Spanish heiress. But deluded in his search for the kingdom of the Great Khan, and finding little gold in Cuba's lush and heavily forested interior, Columbus quickly abandoned the territory in favor of Hispaniola (modern-day Haiti and the Dominican Republic).

The colonization of Cuba didn't begin until nearly 20 years later in 1511, when Diego Velázquez de Cuéllar led a flotilla of four ships and 400 men from Hispaniola to conquer the island for the Spanish Crown. Docking near present-day Baracoa, the conquistadors promptly set about establishing seven *villas* (towns) on the main island – Havana, Trinidad, Baracoa, Bayamo, Camagüey, Santiago de Cuba and Sancti Spíritus – in a bid to bring their new colony under strong central rule. Watching nervously from the safety of their *bohíos* (thatched huts), a scattered population of Taínos looked on with a mixture of fascination and fear.

Despite Velázquez' attempts to protect the local Taínos from the gross excesses of the Spanish swordsmen, things quickly got out of hand and the invaders soon found that they had a full-scale rebellion on their hands. Leader of the embittered and short-lived Taíno insurgency was the feisty Hatuey, an influential *cacique* (chief) and archetype of the Cuban resistance, who was eventually captured and burned at the stake, Inquisition-style, for daring to challenge the iron fist of Spanish rule.

With the resistance decapitated, the Spaniards set about emptying Cuba of its relatively meager gold and mineral reserves, using the beleaguered natives as forced labor. As slavery was nominally banned under a papal edict, the Spanish got around the various legal loopholes by

In the 17th century the Spanish forced the remaining indigenous population into towns known as *pueblos indios*. Old and New World cultures cross-fertilized, allowing indigenous practices and words to seep into everyday Cuban life.

1522	1555	1607	1741
The first enslaved people arrive in Cuba from Africa, ushering in an era that is to last for 350 years and having a profound effect on the development of Cuban culture.	The age of piracy is inaugurated. French buccaneer Jacques de Sores attacks Havana and burns it to the ground. In response, the Spanish start building a huge network of forts.	Havana is declared capital of Cuba and becomes the annual congregation point for Spain's Caribbean treasure fleet, loaded up with silver from Peru and gold from Mexico.	A British Navy contingent under the command of Admiral Edward Vernon briefly captures Guantánamo Bay during the War of Jenkins' Ear, but is sent packing after a yellow fever epidemic.

introducing a ruthless *encomienda* system, whereby thousands of natives were rounded up and forced to work for Spanish landowners on the pretext that they were receiving free 'lessons' in Christianity.

The brutal system lasted 20 years before the 'Apostle of the Indians,' Fray Bartolomé de Las Casas, appealed to the Spanish Crown for more humane treatment, and in 1542 the *encomiendas* were abolished for the indigenous people. For the unfortunate Taínos, the call came too late. Those who had not already been worked to death in the gold mines quickly succumbed to fatal European diseases such as smallpox, and by 1550 only about 5000 scattered survivors remained.

The Independence Wars

With its brutal system of slavery established, the Spanish ruled their largest Caribbean colony with an iron fist for the next 200 years, despite a brief occupation by the British in 1792. Cuba's creole landowners, worried about a repetition of Haiti's brutal 1791 rebellion of enslaved people, held back when the rest of Latin America took up arms against the Spanish in the 1810s and 1820s. As a result, the nation's independence wars came more than half a century after the rest of Latin America had broken away from Spain. But when they arrived, they were no less impassioned – or bloody.

The First War of Independence

Fed up with Spain's reactionary colonial policies and enviously eyeing Lincoln's new American dream to the north, *criollo* (Spaniards born in the Americas) landowners around Bayamo began plotting rebellion in the late 1860s. On October 10, 1868, Carlos Manuel de Céspedes, a budding poet, lawyer and sugar-plantation owner, launched an uprising from his Demajagua sugar mill near Manzanillo in the Oriente.

Calling for the abolition of slavery and freeing his own enslaved people as an example, Céspedes proclaimed the famous *Grito de Yara*, a cry of liberty for an independent Cuba, encouraging other disillusioned separatists to join him. For the colonial administrators in Havana, such an audacious bid to wrest control was an act tantamount to treason. The furious Spanish reacted accordingly.

Fortunately for the loosely organized rebels, the cagey Céspedes had done his military homework. Within weeks of the historic *Grito de Yara*, the diminutive lawyer-turned-general had raised an army of more than 1500 men and marched defiantly on Bayamo, taking the city in a matter of days. But initial successes soon turned to lengthy deadlock. A tactical decision not to invade western Cuba, along with an alliance between *peninsulares* (Spaniards born in Spain but living in Cuba) and the Spanish, soon put Céspedes on the back foot.

Che Guevara – whose father's family name was Guevara Lynch – can trace his Celtic roots back to a Patrick Lynch, born in Galway in Ireland in 1715, who emigrated to Buenos Aires via Bilbao in 1749.

1762	1791	1808	1850
Spain joins France in the Seven Years' War, provoking the British to attack and take Havana. They occupy Cuba for 11 months before exchanging it for Florida in 1763.	A bloody rebellion of enslaved people in Haiti causes thousands of white French planters to flee west to Cuba, where they set up the earliest coffee plantations in the New World.	Pre-empting the Monroe Doctrine, US president Thomas Jefferson proclaims Cuba 'the most interesting addition which could be made to our system of states,' thus beginning a 200-year US fixation.	Venezuelan filibuster Narciso López raises the Cuban flag for the first time in Cárdenas during an abortive attempt to 'liberate' the colony from Spain.

Temporary help arrived in the shape of *mulato* (mixed-race) general Antonio Maceo, a tough and uncompromising Santiagüero, nicknamed the 'Bronze Titan' for his ability to defy death on countless occasions, and the equally formidable Dominican, Máximo Gómez. But despite economic disruption and the periodic destruction of the sugar crop, the rebels lacked a dynamic political leader capable of uniting them behind a singular ideological cause.

With the loss of Céspedes in battle in 1874, the war dragged on for another four years, reducing the Cuban economy to tatters and leaving an astronomical 200,000 Cubans and 80,000 Spanish dead. Finally, in February 1878 a lackluster pact was signed at El Zanjón between the uncompromising Spanish and the exhausted separatists, a rambling and largely worthless agreement that solved nothing and acceded little to the rebel cause. Maceo, disgusted and disillusioned, made his feelings known in the antidotal 'Protest of Baraguá,' but after an abortive attempt to restart the war in 1879, both he and Gómez disappeared into a prolonged exile.

The Spanish–Cuban–American War (Second War of Independence)

Cometh the hour, cometh the man. José Martí – poet, patriot, visionary and intellectual – had grown rapidly into a patriotic figure of Bolívarian proportions in the years following his ignominious exile in 1871, not just in Cuba but in the whole of Latin America. After his arrest at the age of 16 during the First War of Independence for a minor indiscretion, Martí had spent 20 years formulating his revolutionary ideas abroad in places as diverse as Guatemala, Mexico and the US. Although impressed by American business savvy and industriousness, he was equally repelled by the country's all-consuming materialism and was determined to present a workable Cuban alternative.

In the 1880s there were over 100,000 Chinese people living in Cuba, mainly as cheap labor on sugar plantations in and around the Havana region.

Dedicating himself passionately to the cause of the resistance, Martí wrote, spoke, petitioned and organized tirelessly for independence for well over a decade and by 1892 had enough momentum to coax Maceo and Gómez out of exile under the umbrella of the Partido Revolucionario Cubano (PRC; Cuban Revolutionary Party). At last, Cuba had found its spiritual leader.

Predicting that the time was right for another revolution, Martí and his compatriots set sail for Cuba in April 1895, landing near Baracoa two months after PRC-sponsored insurrections had tied down Spanish forces in Havana. Raising an army of 40,000 men, the rebels promptly regrouped and headed west, engaging the Spanish for the first time on May 19 at a place called Dos Ríos.

On this bullet-strafed and strangely anonymous battlefield, Martí, conspicuous on his white horse and dressed in his trademark black tunic, was

1868	1878	1886	1892
Céspedes frees his enslaved people in Manzanillo and proclaims the *Grito de Yara*, Cuba's first independence cry and the beginning of a 10-year war against the Spanish.	The Pact of El Zanjón ends the First War of Independence. Cuban general Antonio Maceo issues the Protest of Baraguá and resumes hostilities the following year before disappearing into exile.	After more than 350 years of exploitation and cross-Atlantic transportation, Cuba becomes the second-last country in the Americas to abolish slavery.	From exile in the US, José Martí galvanizes popular support and forms the Cuban Revolutionary Party, laying the groundwork for the resumption of hostilities against Spain.

shot and killed as he charged suicidally toward the Spanish lines. Had he lived he would certainly have become Cuba's first president; instead, he became a hero and a martyr whose life and legacy would inspire generations of Cubans in years to come.

Conscious of mistakes made during the First War of Independence, Gómez and Maceo stormed west with a scorched-earth policy that left everything from the Oriente to Matanzas in flames. Early victories quickly led to a sustained offensive and, by January 1896, Maceo had broken through to Pinar del Río, while Gómez was tying down Spanish forces near Havana.

The Spaniards responded with an equally ruthless general named Valeriano Weyler, who built countrywide north–south fortifications to restrict the rebels' movements. In order to break the underground resistance, *guajiros* (country people) were forced into camps in a process called *reconcentración*, and anyone supporting the rebellion became liable for execution.

The brutal tactics started to show results. On December 7, 1896, the Mambís (the name for the 19th-century rebels fighting Spain) suffered a major military blow when Antonio Maceo was killed south of Havana trying to break out to the east.

Enter the Americans

By this time Cuba was a mess: thousands were dead, the country was in flames, and William Randolph Hearst and the US tabloid press were leading a hysterical war campaign characterized by sensationalized, often inaccurate reports about Spanish atrocities.

Preparing perhaps for the worst, the US battleship *Maine* was sent to Havana in January 1898, on the pretext of 'protecting US citizens.' Its touted task never saw fruition. On February 15, 1898, the *Maine* exploded out of the blue in Havana Harbor, killing 266 US sailors.

The Spanish claimed it was an accident, the Americans blamed the Spanish, and some Cubans accused the US, saying it provided a convenient pretext for intervention. Despite several investigations conducted over the following years, the real cause of the explosion may remain one of history's great mysteries, as the hulk of the ship was scuttled in deep waters in 1911.

After the *Maine* debacle, the US scrambled to take control. They offered Spain US$300 million for Cuba and, when this deal was rejected, demanded a full withdrawal of the Spanish from the island. The long-awaited US–Spanish showdown that had been simmering imperceptibly beneath the surface for decades had finally resulted in war.

The only important land battle of the conflict was on July 1, when the US Army attacked Spanish positions on San Juan Hill just east of Santiago de Cuba. Despite vastly inferior numbers and limited, antiquated weaponry, the under-siege Spanish held out bravely for over 24 hours before future US President Theodore Roosevelt broke the deadlock by

1895	1896	1898	1902
José Martí and Antonio Maceo arrive in Cuba to ignite the Second Independence War. Martí is killed at Dos Ríos in May and is quickly elevated to martyr status.	After sustaining more than 20 injuries in a four-decade military career, Antonio Maceo meets his end at Cacahual, Havana, where he is killed in an ambush.	Following the loss of the battleship USS *Maine,* the US declares war on Spain and defeats its forces near Santiago. A four-year US occupation begins.	Cuba gains nominal independence from the US and elects Tomás Estrada Palma as its president. US troops are called back three times within the first 15 years of the republic.

leading a celebrated cavalry charge of the Rough Riders up San Juan Hill. It was the beginning of the end for the Spaniards, and an unconditional surrender was offered to the Americans on July 17, 1898.

Post-Colonial Cuba

Independence or Dependence?

On May 20, 1902, Cuba became an independent republic – or did it? Despite three years of blood, sweat and sacrifice during the Spanish–Cuban–American War, no Cuban representatives were invited to the historic peace treaty held in Paris in 1898 that had promised Cuban independence *with conditions*.

The conditions were contained in the infamous Platt Amendment, a sly addition to the US 1901 Army Appropriations Bill that gave the US the right to intervene militarily in Cuba whenever it saw fit. The US also used its significant leverage to secure itself a naval base in Guantánamo Bay in order to protect its strategic interests in the Panama Canal region.

Despite some opposition in the US and a great deal more in Cuba, the Platt Amendment was passed by Congress and was written into Cuba's 1902 constitution. For Cuban patriots, the US had merely replaced Spain as the new colonizer and enemy. The repercussions have been causing bitter feuds for over a century and still continue today.

The Batista Era

Fulgencio Batista, a *holguiñero* (from Holguín province) of mixed race from the town of Banes, was a wily and shrewd negotiator who presided over Cuba's best and worst attempts to establish an embryonic democracy in the 1940s and '50s. After an army officers' coup in 1933, he had taken power almost by default, gradually worming his way into the political vacuum it left amid the corrupt factions of a dying government. From 1934 onwards, Batista served as the army's chief of staff and, in 1940 in a relatively free and fair election, he was duly elected president.

Given an official mandate, Batista began to enact a wide variety of social reforms and set about drafting Cuba's most liberal and democratic constitution to date. But neither the liberal honeymoon nor Batista's good humor were to last. After the 1944 election, the former army sergeant reluctantly handed power over to the politically inept President Ramón Grau San Martín, and left Cuba to live in New York City. Soon, corruption and inefficiency soon reigned like never before.

The Revolutionary Spark is Lit

Aware of his erstwhile popularity and sensing an easy opportunity to line his pockets with one last big paycheck, Batista made a deal with the

---

US Presidents Who Tried to Buy Cuba

1808 – Thomas Jefferson (undisclosed sum)

1848 – James Polk ($100 million)

1854 – Franklin Pierce ($130 million)

1898 – William McKinley ($300 million)

1920	1925	1933	1940
Sharp increases in world sugar prices after WWI spearhead the so-called 'Dance of the Millions' in Cuba. Huge fortunes are made overnight. A heavy economic crash quickly follows.	Gerardo Machado is elected president and institutes a massive program of public works, but his eight-year reign turns increasingly despotic and his declining popularity leads to resentful unrest.	The 1933 revolution is sparked by an Army Officers' Coup that deposes the Machado dictatorship and installs Fulgencio Batista in power.	Cuba adopts the '1940 Constitution,' considered one of the most progressive documents of its era, guaranteeing rights to employment, property, minimum wage, education and social security.

American Mafia, promising to give them carte blanche in Cuba in return for a cut of their gambling profits, and positioned himself for a comeback.

On March 10, 1952, three months before scheduled elections he looked like losing, Batista staged a military coup. Wildly condemned by opposition politicians inside Cuba, but recognized by the US government two weeks later, Batista quickly let it be known, when he suspended various constitutional guarantees including the right to strike, that his second incarnation wouldn't be as enlightened as his first.

After Batista's coup, a revolutionary circle formed in Havana around the charismatic figure of Fidel Castro, a lawyer by profession and a gifted orator who had been due to stand in the canceled 1952 elections. Supported by his younger brother Raúl and aided intellectually by his trusty lieutenant Abel Santamaría (later tortured to death by Batista's thugs), Castro saw no alternative to the use of force in ridding Cuba of its dictator.

Low on numbers but determined to make a political statement, Castro led 119 rebels in an attack on the strategically important Moncada army barracks in Santiago de Cuba on July 26, 1953. The audacious and poorly planned assault failed dramatically when the rebels' driver (who was from Havana) took the wrong turning in Santiago's badly signposted streets and the alarm was raised.

Fooled, flailing and hopelessly outnumbered, 64 of the Moncada conspirators were rounded up by Batista's army and brutally tortured and executed. Castro and a handful of others managed to escape into the nearby mountains, where they were found a few days later by a sympathetic army lieutenant named Sarría, who had been given instructions to kill them. 'Don't shoot, you can't kill ideas!' Sarría is alleged to have shouted on finding Castro and his exhausted colleagues.

By taking Castro to jail instead of murdering him, Sarría ruined his military career, but saved Fidel's life. (One of Fidel's first acts after the revolution triumphed was to release Sarría from prison and give him a commission in the revolutionary army.) Castro's capture soon became national news, and he was put on trial in the full glare of the media spotlight. Fidel defended himself in court, writing an eloquent and masterfully executed speech that he later transcribed into a comprehensive political manifesto entitled *History Will Absolve Me*.

Basking in his newfound legitimacy and backed by a growing sense of dissatisfaction with the old regime in the country at large, Castro was sentenced to 15 years imprisonment on Isla de Pinos (a former name for Isla de la Juventud). Cuba was well on the way to gaining a new national hero.

In February 1955 Batista won the presidency in what were widely considered to be fraudulent elections and, in an attempt to curry favor with growing internal opposition, agreed to an amnesty for all political prisoners, including Castro. Believing that Batista's real intention was to

Cuba's First Three Presidents

Tomás Estrada Palma (1902–06)

José Miguel Gómez (1909–13)

Mario García Menocal (1913–21)

HISTORY POST-COLONIAL CUBA

In December 1946 the Mafia convened the biggest ever get-together of North American mobsters in Havana's Hotel Nacional, under the pretense that they were going to see a Frank Sinatra concert.

1952	1953	1956	1958
Batista stages a bloodless military coup, canceling the upcoming Cuban elections in which an ambitious young lawyer named Fidel Castro was due to stand.	Castro leads a band of rebels in a disastrous attack on the Moncada army barracks in Santiago. He uses his subsequent trial as a platform to expound his political plans.	The *Granma* yacht lands in eastern Cuba with Castro and 81 rebels aboard. Decimated by the Cuban Army, only about a dozen survive to regroup in the Sierra Maestra.	Che Guevara masterminds an attack against an armored train in Santa Clara, a military victory that finally forces Batista to concede power. The rebels march triumphantly on Havana.

HUMAN RIGHTS

'Human rights' in Cuba has long been the revolution's Achilles heel. To speak out against the government in this tightly controlled, politically paranoid society is a serious and heavily punishable crime that – if it doesn't first land you in jail – is likely to lead to job stagnation, petty harassment and social ostracism.

The Castro era got off to a bad start in January 1959 when the revolutionary government – under the auspices of Che Guevara – rounded up Batista's top henchmen and summarily executed them inside Havana's La Cabaña fort with barely a lawyer in sight. Within a matter of months the Cuban press had been silenced and worried onlookers in the US were vociferously calling 'foul.'

In the years since, Cuba has scored badly on most global human rights indices with the world's two most respected human rights bodies, Amnesty International and Human Rights Watch, regularly berating the government for its refusal to respect the rights of assembly, association and expression, and other basic civil liberties.

Cuba's international image took another hit during 2003's 'Black Spring' when the government rounded up 75 dissidents, who they claimed were agents of the US, and handed them all lengthy jail terms. After an international outcry, all of the dissidents were eventually released, the last in 2011. Notwithstanding, harassment and intimidation of dissidents, including peaceful protesters such as the 'Ladies in White,' continues.

Cuba's supporters often justify the alleged human rights violations with tit-for-tat arguments. When the US questioned the 2011 jailing of American development contractor Alan Gross, they pointed to the incarceration of the 'Cuban Five' (five Cubans imprisoned in the US on equally flimsy spying charges). Gross and the Cuban Five were finally released in a prisoner swap in December 2014.

There have been other improvements in recent years. Gay persecution, once rife at all levels of Cuban society, is largely a thing of the past. Religious persecution is similarly rare. Freedom of expression and the press, however, remain frustratingly stifled, although, in the internet age, some high-profile bloggers, most notably Yoani Sánchez, have managed to reach an international audience.

---

assassinate him once out of jail, Castro fled to Mexico, leaving Baptist schoolteacher Frank País in charge of a fledgling underground resistance campaign that the vengeful Moncada veterans had christened the 26th of July Movement (M-26-7).

The Revolution

In Mexico City, Castro and his compatriots plotted and planned afresh, drawing in key new figures such as Camilo Cienfuegos and the Argentine doctor Ernesto 'Che' Guevara, both of whom added strength and panache to the nascent army of disaffected rebel soldiers. On the run from the Mexican police and determined to arrive in Cuba in time for an uprising

1959	1960	1961	1962
Castro is welcomed ecstatically in Havana. The new government passes the historic First Agrarian Reform Act. Camilo Cienfuegos' plane goes missing over the Cuban coast off Camagüey.	Castro nationalizes US assets on the island, provoking the US to cancel its Cuban sugar quota. Castro immediately sells the sugar to the Soviet Union.	US-backed Cuban mercenaries stage an unsuccessful invasion at the Bay of Pigs. The US declares a full trade embargo. Cuba embarks on a highly successful literacy campaign.	The discovery of medium-range nuclear missiles in Cuba, installed by the Soviet Union, brings the world to the brink of nuclear war in the so-called Cuban Missile Crisis.

that Frank País had planned for late November 1956 in Santiago de Cuba, Castro and 81 companions set sail for the island on November 25 in an old and overcrowded leisure yacht named *Granma*.

After seven dire days at sea they arrived at Playa Las Coloradas near Niquero in Oriente on December 2 (two days late). Following a catastrophic landing – 'It wasn't a disembarkation; it was a shipwreck,' a wry Guevara later commented – they were spotted and routed by Batista's soldiers in a sugarcane field at Alegría de Pío three days later.

Of the 82 rebel soldiers who had left Mexico, little more than a dozen managed to escape. Splitting into three tiny groups, the survivors wandered around hopelessly for days half-starved, wounded and assuming that the rest of their compatriots had been killed in the initial skirmish. 'At one point I was Commander in Chief of myself and two other people,' Fidel commented years later. However, with the help of the local peasantry, the dozen or so hapless soldiers finally managed to reassemble two weeks later in Cinco Palmas, a clearing in the shadow of the Sierra Maestra, where a half-delirious Fidel gave a rousing and premature victory speech. 'We will win this war,' he proclaimed confidently. 'We are just beginning the fight!'

The comeback began on January 17, 1957, when the guerrillas scored an important victory by sacking a small army outpost on the south coast in Granma Province called La Plata. This was followed in February by a devastating propaganda coup when Fidel persuaded *New York Times* journalist Herbert Matthews to come up into the Sierra Maestra to interview him. The resulting article made Castro internationally famous and gained him much sympathy among liberal Americans.

By this point he wasn't the only anti-Batista agitator. On March 13, 1957, university students led by José Antonio Echeverría attacked the Presidential Palace in Havana in an unsuccessful attempt to assassinate Batista. Thirty-two of the 35 attackers were shot dead as they fled, and reprisals were meted out on the streets of Havana with a new vengeance. Cuba was rapidly disintegrating into a police state run by military-trained thugs.

Elsewhere passions were running equally high. In September 1957 naval officers in the normally tranquil city of Cienfuegos staged an armed revolt and set about distributing weapons among the disaffected populace. After some bitter door-to-door fighting, the insurrection was brutally crushed and the ringleaders rounded up and killed, but for the revolutionaries the point had been made. Batista's days were numbered.

Back in the Sierra Maestra, Fidel's rebels overwhelmed 53 Batista soldiers at an army post in El Uvero in May and captured more badly needed supplies. The movement seemed to be gaining momentum and despite losing Frank País to a government assassination squad in Santiago de Cuba in July, support and sympathy around the country was starting to mushroom. By the beginning of 1958 Castro had established a fixed

A 1976 book entitled *How the Battleship Maine Was Destroyed* concluded that the explosion of the *Maine* in Havana Harbor in 1898 was caused by the spontaneous combustion of coal in the ship's bunker.

Of the 12 or so men that survived the disastrous *Granma* landing in December 1956, only two were still alive in 2021: Raúl Castro and Ramiro Valdés.

1967	1968	1970	1976
Che Guevara is hunted down and executed in Bolivia in front of CIA observers after a 10-month abortive guerrilla war in the mountains.	The Cuban government nationalizes 58,000 small businesses in a sweeping socialist reform package. Everything falls under strict government control.	Castro attempts to achieve a 10-million-ton sugar harvest. The plan fails and Cuba begins to wean itself off its unhealthy dependence on its mono-crop.	Terrorists bomb a Cuban jet in Barbados, killing all 73 people aboard. A line is traced back to anti-Castro activists with histories as CIA operatives working out of Venezuela.

headquarters in a cloud forest high up in the Sierra Maestra he christened 'La Plata,' and was broadcasting propaganda messages from Radio Rebelde (710AM and 96.7FM) all across Cuba. The tide was starting to turn.

Sensing his popularity waning, Batista sent an army of 10,000 men into the Sierra Maestra in May 1958, on a mission known as Plan FF (*Fin de Fidel* or End of Fidel). The intention was to liquidate Castro and his merry band of loyal guerrillas who had now burgeoned into a solid fighting force of 300 men. The offensive became something of a turning point as the rebels – with the help of the local campesinos (country people) – gradually halted the onslaught of Batista's young and ill-disciplined conscript army.

With the Americans increasingly embarrassed by the no-holds-barred terror tactics of their one-time Cuban ally, Castro sensed an opportunity to turn defense into offense and signed the groundbreaking Caracas Pact with eight leading opposition groups calling on the US to stop all aid to Batista. Che Guevara and Camilo Cienfuegos were promptly dispatched to the Escambray Mountains to open up new fronts in the west, and by December, with Cienfuegos holding down troops in Yaguajay (the garrison finally surrendered after an 11-day siege) and Guevara closing in on Santa Clara, the end was in sight.

It was left to Che Guevara to seal the final victory, employing classic guerrilla tactics to derail an armored train in Santa Clara and split the country's battered communications system in two. By New Year's Eve 1958, the game was up: a sense of jubilation filled the country, and Che and Camilo were on their way to Havana unopposed.

In the small hours of January 1, 1959, Batista fled by private plane to the Dominican Republic. Meanwhile, materializing in Santiago de Cuba the same day, Fidel made a rousing victory speech from the town hall in Parque Céspedes before jumping into a 4WD and traveling across the breadth of the country to Havana in a Caesar-like cavalcade. The 'triumph' of the revolution was seemingly complete.

Post-Revolutionary Realities

Cuba's history since the revolution has been a David and Goliath tale of confrontation, rhetoric, Cold War stand-offs and an omnipresent US trade embargo that has featured 11 US presidents and three Cuban leaders – two of them called Castro. For the first 30 years, Cuba allied itself with the Soviet Union as the US used various retaliatory tactics (all unsuccessful) to bring Fidel Castro to heel, including a botched invasion, 600-plus assassination attempts and one of the longest economic blockades in modern history.

When the Soviet bloc fell in 1989–91, Cuba stood alone behind an increasingly defiant and stubborn leader, surviving, against all odds, through a decade of severe economic austerity known as the Special

Castro's government passed over 1000 laws in its first year (1959), including rent and electricity cost reductions, the abolition of racial discrimination and the First Agrarian Reform Act.

1980	1991	1993	1996
Following an incident at the Peruvian embassy, Castro opens the Cuban port of Mariel. Within six months, 125,000 have fled the island for the US in the so-called Mariel Boatlift.	The Soviet Union collapses and Cuba heads toward its worst economic collapse of modern times, entering what Castro calls a 'Special Period in a Time of Peace.'	Attempting to revive itself from its economic coma, Cuba legalizes the US dollar, opens up the country to tourism and allows limited forms of private enterprise.	Miami 'Brothers to the Rescue' planes are shot down by Cuban jets, provoking Bill Clinton to sign the Helms-Burton Act, further tightening the terms of the US embargo.

Period. GDP fell by more than half, luxuries went out the window, and a wartime spirit of rationing and sacrifice took hold among a populace that, ironically, had prized itself free from foreign (neo)colonial influences for the first time in its history.

The worst years of the Special Period were from 1991–1994, though the recovery was slow with proper progress only possible after Cuba forged closer ties with Venezuela (and its oil) in the early 2000s.

The Era of Raúl

In July 2006, the unimaginable happened. Fidel Castro, rather than dying in office and paving the way for an American-led capitalistic re-opening (as had long been predicted), retired from day-to-day governing due to poor health and passed power quietly onto his younger brother, Raúl. Inheriting the country's highest office on the cusp of a major world-wide recession, Raúl began a slow package of reforms.

It kicked off modestly in 2008 when Cubans were permitted access to tourist hotels, and allowed to purchase mobile phones and myriad electronic goods – rights taken for granted in most democratic countries, but long out of reach to the average Cuban. These moves were followed in January 2011 by the biggest economic and ideological shake-up since the country waved *adiós* to Batista. Radical new laws laid off half a million government workers and tried to stimulate the private sector by granting business licenses to 178 state-recognized professions – everything from hairdressers to disposable-lighter refillers.

By 2013, Cuba had witnessed its most dramatic economic shift in decades with nearly 400,000 people working in the private sector, 250,000 more than in 2010, though it was still far from anything like Western-style capitalism.

The apogee of Raúl's 10-year 'reign' came in 2016 when US President Barack Obama visited Cuba hot on the heels of announcing the loosening of US trade and travel restrictions to Cuba for the first time in decades. The two leaders met at a baseball game in a trip that heralded telecom agreements, mutual cooperation in law enforcement and the environment and the reinstatement of commercial flights to and from the US.

Goodbye Castro, Hello Trump

In November 2016, the US election was surprisingly won by Donald Trump. In what seemed like a nano-second, Cuban–American relations went from sweet to sour. The Trump administration started battening down the hatches as early as June 2017 ending a halcyon if short-lived era when American travelers had visited the country in their thousands. Within two years, US cruises had been suspended, numerous Cuban hotels had been put on a banned list and – due to an unrelated series of

2002	2006	2008	2011
Half of Cuba's sugar refineries are closed, signaling the end of a three-century-long addiction to the boom-bust mono-crop. Laid-off sugar workers continue to draw salaries and are offered free education.	Castro is taken ill just before his 80th birthday with diverticulitis disease and steps down from the day-to-day running of the country. He is replaced by his brother Raúl.	Raúl Castro is officially inaugurated as Cuban president and embarks on his first set of reforms, permitting Cubans access to tourist hotels and allowing them to purchase mobile phones and electronic goods.	Raúl Castro signals an economic thaw by announcing that the government plans to cut half a million jobs from the state sector and open up private enterprise to over 175 licensed businesses.

THE PASSING OF FIDEL

Fidel's omnipresence for the past half-century made the man seem invincible, yet on November 25, 2016, Raúl Castro announced his brother's passing at the age of 90. His cremated remains were laid to rest in Santiago de Cuba after a cross-island procession that recalled the march of his revolutionary triumph, done in reverse. Throughout Cuba, crowds lined the streets to pay homage to their longtime leader as exiles celebrated in Miami.

His remains were laid to rest under a large boulder-shaped stone simply engraved 'Fidel.' Orders were left to not use his likeness for statues or souvenirs, nor his name for streets, institutions or public sites. Perhaps the commodification of Che Guevara rested heavy on his shoulders.

'sonic attacks' – the US embassy (reopened under Obama) was down to a skeleton staff.

Amid all the kerfuffle, Raúl Castro bowed out in February 2018, handing the reins over to the first non-Castro leader in 59 years, Miguel Díaz-Canel, who was officially inaugurated as the President of the Republic of Cuba in October 2019. The Villa Clara native faced a baptism of fire with a stagnating economy, flailing allies abroad (Venezuela) and an increasingly grumpy US on the doorstep. Then came the coronavirus pandemic.

Down, But Not Out

In a country heavily reliant on tourism, Covid-19 hit Cuba hard. Already reeling from a tightened US trade embargo and the collapse of the country's former benefactors in Venezuela, Cuba was plunged into its biggest economic crisis since the Special Period. In January 2021, matters were complicated further when Diaz-Canal announced that Cuba's two currencies would be amalgamated with convertibles being phased out and replaced by the considerably less valuable Cuban peso.

Food shortages, which had been a way of life before the pandemic began, quickly worsened as everyday basics such as cooking oil, chicken and toothpaste became increasingly scarce. Frustrated and hungry, Cubans often queued for hours outside shops only to be told to come back the next day.

In a slightly healthier subplot, the country fared relatively well in mitigating Covid-19 with low death rates and hospitalizations compared to other Latin American countries. Hedging its bets in the race for a cure, the government came up with several of its own vaccine candidates and launched it first mass immunizations in May 2021.

Since his inauguration in January 2021, President Joe Biden's administration lifted some restrictions on business and travel and renewed diplomatic talks.

2014	2016	2017	2020
Following a prisoner swap, Barack Obama announces the reestablishment of diplomatic ties with Cuba and a raft of measures including telecommunications aid and the easing of financial restrictions.	Fidel Castro passes away on November 25, 2016 at the age of 90. After one week of mourning and a cross-island procession, he is laid to rest in Santiago de Cuba.	While not nearly a full rollback of his predecessor's Cuba policies, US President Donald Trump's directives limit travelers from the US to group tours and seek to clamp down on travel-related transactions with the Cuban military.	Cuba legalizes the US dollar and opens 80+ 'dollar stores' around the country where citizens can buy imported consumer goods with bank cards.

Food & Drink

Good food in Cuba has a short history. Until recently, basic ingredients were thin on the ground and the nation's default 'snack' was an anemic cheese and spam sandwich with the consistency of melted rubber. A change in the privatization laws in 2011 quickly turned the culinary world on its head. In the last decade, private restaurants have proliferated, chefs have sharpened their creative knives and Cuba has discovered that its homegrown, home-produced *comida cubana* (traditional Cuban food) is actually rather tasty.

The Culinary Challenge

Señores and señoras, we are pleased to announce that Cuba is no longer the proverbial 'leftover' plate of the culinary world. The turnaround has been astronomical and unprecedented. The economic reforms of 2011, when the Cuban government allowed private restaurants (until then limited to 12 people) to expand and diversify, has been a massive game changer. Taste-deprived travelers who once wisely elected to skip the

Top: La Bodeguita del Medio (p214), Varadero

A typical Cuban breakfast

appetizer and main course and proceed directly to rum and cigars can now tuck into honey-glazed chicken, rabbit in chocolate sauce, and new takes on old Cuban favorites such as *ropa vieja* (spicy shredded beef). Feeding the trend, Havana and other cities are awash with creative new private restaurants experimenting with cooking methods and ingredients previously unheard of on the island. Free from the shackles of austere 1990s rationing, Cuban chefs bandy around words like 'fusion' and 'medium-rare', and inscribe their menus with dishes such as eggplant caviar.

For first-time visitors accustomed to French-style creativity or American abundance, the food might not seem very remarkable. But if you last visited Cuba in the early 2000s, in the days when all chickens were fried to smithereens and 'salad' meant undressed cabbage and green beans from a tin, you're in for a rather pleasant surprise.

Stewing 500 Years

The pain and shortages of the 1990s didn't do Cuban cuisine any favors, starving it of all but the most basic of ingredients and obscuring what, beneath the surface, has always been a rich and diverse food culture.

FRUIT, GLORIOUS FRUIT

Stay in a Cuban casa particular (rooms in a private home) and you'll nearly always be offered a massive breakfast. The first thing to arrive is usually an ambrosial plate of tropical fruit. Its contents vary according to season and location, but the classic selection consists of a juicy quintet of banana, papaya, mango, pineapple and guava. Of these only guava and pineapple predate the arrival of the Spanish on the isles. Bananas and mangoes, both Asian in origin, were brought to Cuba during the colonial period, where they thrive in the tropical climate. The papaya is indigenous to South America.

Moros y cristianos (black beans & rice)

Cuba's cuisine is a creative stew of selective morsels, recipes and cooking techniques left behind by successive travelers since the epoch of Columbus and Velázquez. Imagine a bubbling cauldron filled with ingredients plucked from Spain, Africa, France, precolonial Taínos, and cultures from various other islands in the Caribbean that has been left to intermingle and marinate for 500 years.

From the original Taínos came indigenous root vegetables such as yucca and sweet potato, and native fruits such as guava; from the Spanish came pork, rice, flavor-enhancing spices and different frying techniques; the culture of African slavery brought plantains in their various guises along with *congrí* (rice and beans cooked together with spices in the same pot); while, from its island neighbors, Cuba shares the unmistakable taste of the Caribbean enshrined in *sofrito*, a base sauce of tomatoes seasoned with onions, peppers, garlic, bay leaf and cumin.

Mix it all together and you get *comida cubana*, the simple, hearty but healthy food that's light on spice (cumin and oregano predominate), but has no shortage of flavor. Whole roast pork is the meat of choice, closely followed by chicken, fried or roasted and often flavored with citrus sauces or honey.

Never far from the sea, the Cubans love fish: lobster, crab, prawns, *aguja* (swordfish) and *pargo* (snapper) are common. The key starch is rice usually mixed with beans as either *moros y cristianos* (made with black beans) or *congrí* (made with red beans). Root vegetables are another mainstay and are complemented by plantains, cooked many ways. In season, Cuban avocados are sublime and tropical fruit is abundant.

Don't leave Cuba without trying the national dish, *ropa vieja* (spicy shredded beef), whole roast pork with all the trimmings, *picadillo* (ground beef with olives and capers), *tostones* (twice-fried plantains), and *moros y cristianos*.

Farm-to-Table Restaurants

Ajiaco Café –
Cojímar, Havana

El Olivo – *Viñales*

Finca Coincidencia –
Matanzas Province

El Cimarrión –
Vedado, Havana

REGIONAL SPECIALTIES

Caibarién This small town in Villa Clara province is Cuba's crab capital.

Baracoa A completely different food universe to the rest of Cuba. Specialties include *cucurucho* (sweet blend of honey, coconut, guava and nuts), *bacán* (tamale with mashed banana, crab and coconut), *teti* (tiny fish indigenous to Toa River) and *lechita* (spicy coconut sauce).

Playa Larga & Zapata Peninsula Crocodiles are farmed and consumed in stews in designated hotels and restaurants in southern Matanzas Province.

Bayamo *Ostiones* (oysters usually served in a tomato sauce) are a staple street-food in Granma's main city.

Oriente *Congrí* (rice and red beans seasoned with cumin, peppers and pork chunks) has its roots in the African-influenced culture of eastern Cuba. In the west, you're more likely to get *moros y cristianos* (with black beans but no pork).

Las Tunas Birthplace of *La Caldosa,* a soup-like stew made with root vegetables, chicken and spices.

Rum Tales

Pioneers in the field of rum manufacture in the mid-19th century, the Cubans successfully transformed *aguardiente,* the coarse and unrefined 'fire water' imbibed by sailors and pirates on the Spanish Main, into the smooth, clear 'Ron Superior' used today in sophisticated cocktails such as mojitos and daiquiris.

Guarapo is pure sugarcane juice mixed with ice and lemon that is served from road-side stalls called *guaraperos;* you'll find them all over rural Cuba.

The man behind the metamorphosis was a Spanish immigrant from Catalonia called Don Facundo Bacardí Massó (1814–86). Don Facundo's Santiago de Cuba rum factory was inaugurated in a bat-infested dockside warehouse in 1862 where he experimented with the region's high-quality sugarcane to create a new kind of aged rum that was delicate, crisp and fruity on the palate. Winning instant popularity, Bacardí's name quickly became a byword for rum and the family emerged as powerful and influential voices in Cuban politics.

Yet the Bacardís ultimately fell out with the Castro regime in the early 1960s and fled abroad, moving their headquarters to Bermuda. Although you won't find any Bacardí rum sold in Cuba today, the company's old factory in Santiago still produces the domestically popular Ron Caney (the so-called 'rum of the revolution'), stored in Don Facundo's barrels.

The other famous Cuban rum dynasty, Havana Club was founded by José Arechabala in the town of Cárdenas in 1878. The Arechabala family also fled Cuba after the revolution although they were less successful in maintaining their trademark, which was seized by the Cuban government in 1973. Today, Havana Club accounts for 40% of Cuba's alcohol market.

Aside from the Ron Caney factory in Santiago and the Havana Club operation with two factories in Mayabeque province near Havana, Cuba supports more than 100 rum factories. Tap a local and they'll probably wax poetically about Ron Santiago de Cuba, Ron Mulata (made in Villa Clara) or Ron Varadero.

The 'holy trinity' of cocktails consists of the mojito, the daiquiri and the Cuba Libre.

Rum is made from molasses, a by-product of sugarcane. Its production in Cuba has been overseen by generations of skillful *maestros romeros* ('rum masters'), who must have a minimum of 25 years of rum-tasting experience (there are currently only eight in Cuba). The drink is classified by both color (dark, golden or clear) and age *(añejo).* Good rums can range from anything from three years to 14 years in age. As a rule, rum cocktails (always made with clear rum) are more popular with tourists than Cubans. Cubans prefer to drink their rum dark, neat and without ice in order to enjoy the full flavor.

Cuban Way of Life

Blurring past the outskirts of a provincial city on a tour bus, Cuba can seem bleak and austere. But what you see isn't always what you get in this complex country. Cuba requires patience, sleuthing and a little bit of detached observation. Decipher the elaborate codes that keep local life ticking and you'll quickly uncover Cuba's irrepressible musical energy, a nonstop dance that carries on in spite of everything.

A Recipe for Being Cuban

Take a dose of World War II rationing and a pinch of Soviet-era austerity. Fold in the family values of Latin America, the educational virtues of Canada and the bawdy bar humor of the Irish. Mix with the tropical vibe of Jamaica and the innate musicality of sub-Saharan Africa before dispersing liberally around the streets of Havana, Santiago de Cuba, Trinidad and Viñales.

Life in Cuba is an open and interactive brew. Spend time in a local home and you'll quickly start to piece together an archetype. There's the pot of coffee brewing on the stove and the well-used rocking chair creaking on the porch, a faded print of José Martí hung strategically above the TV and a doll-like statue of the venerated Virgin of El Cobre standing like a shrine in the corner. Aside from the house-owner and their mother, brother, sister and niece, every Cuban home has a seemingly endless queue of visitors traipsing through day and night: a bare-chested neighbor who's popped over to borrow a hammer; a guy with a battered street-cart selling plump avocados; the local busybody from the CDR (Committee for the Defense of the Revolution) gathering gossip; the parish priest dropping by for a glass of rum *sin hielo* (no ice); plus the cousin, the long-lost friend, the third cousin twice removed... You get the picture. Then there are the sounds: a cock crowing, a trombonist practicing his scales, dogs barking, car engines exploding, a salsa beat far off, and those all-too-familiar shouts from the street: *Dime asere?* (What's up, mate?); *Que pasa, mi amor?* (What's wrong, my love?); *Ah mi vida – no es fácil!* (It ain't easy, my love!). Yes, *no es fácil* – it ain't easy. Life in Cuba is anything but easy but, defying all logic, it's rarely dull.

Cuba leads the world with the lowest patient to doctor ratio. It has almost three times as many doctors to patients as in the United States.

Lifestyle

Survivors by nature and necessity, Cubans have long displayed an almost inexhaustible ability to bend the rules and 'work things out' when it matters. The two most overused verbs in the national phrasebook are *conseguir* (to get, manage) and *resolver* (to resolve, work out). Cubans are experts at doing both. Their intuitive ability to bend the rules and make something out of nothing is borne out of economic necessity. In a small nation bucking modern sociopolitical realities, where monthly salaries top out at around the equivalent of US$30, survival can often mean getting innovative as a means of supplementing personal income.

Cruise the crumbling streets of Centro Habana and you'll see people *conseguir*-ing and *resolver*-ing wherever you go. There's the off-duty doctor using their car as a taxi, or the street cartoonist scribbling sketches of unsuspecting tourists in the hope of earning a tip. Other schemes may be ill-gotten or garnered through trickery, such as the *compañero* (comrade) who pockets the odd blemished cigar from their day job to sell to snowbirds from Toronto who don't know any better. Old Cuba hands know one of the most popular ways to make extra cash is working with (or over) tourists.

In Cuba, hard currency (ie convertible pesos) rules, primarily because it is the only way of procuring the modest luxuries that make living in this austere socialist republic more comfortable. Paradoxically, the post-1993 double economy has reinvigorated the class system the revolution worked so hard to neutralize, and it's no longer rare to see Cubans with access to convertibles touting designer clothing while others beg tourists for bars of soap. This stark re-emergence of 'haves' and 'have-nots' is striking.

Other social traits that have emerged since the revolution are more altruistic and less divisive. In Cuba sharing is second nature and helping out your *compañero* with a lift, a square meal or a few convertibles when they're in trouble is considered a national duty. See the way that strangers interact in queues and observe neighbors share everything from tools, to food, to babysitting time without a second thought.

As an outsider, the best way to get to know Cuba is to reserve comment and watch it unfold before you. While long lines and poor service infuriate tourists, Cubans remain unflappable. Rushing doesn't make things happen any faster. But there are richer ways to pass the time: shooting the breeze in rocking chairs, spending Sundays with families or inviting their cousins, friends and neighbors over when a bottle of rum comes your way.

Cubans are informal. The *tú* form of Spanish address is much more common that the formal *usted,* and people greet each other with a variety of friendly addresses. Don't be surprised if a complete stranger calls you *mi amor* (my love) or *mi vida* (my life), and expect casa particular (private homestay) owners to regularly open the front door shirtless (men), or with their hair in curlers (women). To confuse matters further, Cuban Spanish is rich in colloquialisms, irony, sarcasm and swear words.

Main Cuban Crops

....

Bananas

....

Citrus fruit

....

Coffee

....

Mangos

....

Pineapples

....

Rice

....

Sugarcane

....

Tobacco

The Home Front

While Cuban homes sport the basics (fridges, cookers, microwaves), they still lack the expensive trappings of 21st-century consumerism. Car ownership is approximately 38 per 1000, compared to 800 per 1000 in the US; few households sport clothes dryers (spot the flapping clotheslines). That impressive breakfast laid out by your casa particular owner at 8am probably took three hours of searching and queuing to procure (Cuban supermarkets have nothing like the variety and abundance of goods as their counterparts in the US or Europe).

Not that this dents home pride; gathered ornaments and mementos, however old and kitschy, are displayed with love and kept ruthlessly clean. To most outsiders, the local lifestyle seems old-fashioned and austere.

What makes Cuba different from somewhere like Mexico City or Philadelphia, though, is the government's heavy subsidizing of every facet of life, meaning there are few mortgages, no health-care bills, no college fees and fewer taxes. Expensive nights out cost next to nothing in Cuba, where tickets for the theater, the cinema, the ballpark or a music concert are state-subsidized and considered a right of the people.

Habana Vieja is one of the most crowded quarters in Latin America with over 82,000 people living in an area of just 4.5 sq km.

The Winds of Change

Fueled by cautious reform, the Cuban way of life has been changing slowly and subtly since Raúl Castro took the reins from Fidel in 2008. Though the progress may seem sluggish to insiders, a returning exile who has spent the last decade in Miami or Madrid would have some illuminating epiphanies.

Barely anyone had a cell phone in Cuba in the mid-2000s; today, the devices are almost as ubiquitous as they are in the rest of the world. The recent addition of public wi-fi hotspots has turned parks into vibrant collective one-sided conversations held loudly with relatives abroad. A diaspora of families separated for decades are getting to know one another again.

Electronic goods legalized in 2008 have also found their way into Cuban households. These days, it is not unusual to see a DVD player and a modern flat-screen TV beneath a yellowing picture of José Martí. The ability of Cubans to travel abroad since January 2013 has enabled a lucky few who can afford it to shop overseas. Panama is jokingly referred to as Cuba's largest supermarket. Some of the more successful casas particulares come equipped with shiny sandwich makers and top-notch coffee machines.

Cuba's improved culinary scene (p471) is one of the most visible changes for people who remember the hunger of the 1990s. Notwithstanding, the dilemma of any new private restaurant owner is how to pitch their pricing – at foreigners or Cubans, or a mix of both? Some keep two menus with different pricing in both currencies. Top restaurants in Havana are still generally the preserve of tourists and diplomats, while private restaurants in the smaller provincial towns are patronized primarily by locals and are thus more reasonably priced.

Until 2008, Cubans were inexplicably barred from staying in tourist hotels. While high prices still keep out many, some of the more economical resorts like Playa Santa Lucía welcome plenty of Cuban guests during the long hot summer holiday.

Markets and shops, though still far from lavish, have improved and there has been a surge in shops selling large household items such as fridges and washing machines. In urban centers, private business resonates everywhere, from street-side barbers to sophisticated tour guides with their own business cards and websites.

The economic and social changes introduced since the 1990s, while almost universally welcomed, have accentuated income divisions in a country long accustomed to socialism. People with ready access to convertibles – primarily those working in the tourist sector – have prospered; indeed, some casas particulares in Havana (who were limited to renting just two rooms until 2011) have morphed into mini-hotels in all but name. Meanwhile, the lives of people in the more isolated parts of rural Cuba have changed little. In small towns in the Oriente, the foibles that have haunted Cuba since the Special Period – shortages of bottled water, crumbling public buildings and awful roads – continue to bite.

And what of the future? In modern Cuba, better access to the internet has fueled a youth culture of expectation and aspiration. Millennials and their younger cohorts, serenaded by the escapist culture of reggaeton, sport tattoos, wear bling (even if it's fake) and court Miami dreams. It's a sharp contrast to the tightly controlled 'waste not want not' attitude of their parents. Notwithstanding, worsening relations with the US and the economic collapse of close ally Venezuela brought new shortages to Cuba in 2019 with long lines, empty shelves and the reintroduction of rationing in basic foodstuffs.

Sport

Considered a right of the masses, professional sport was abolished by the government after the revolution. Performance-wise it was the best thing the new administration could have done. Since 1959, Cuba's Olympic medal haul has rocketed into the stratosphere, though in recent years its flagging performance is blamed on lack of funding.

Elements of French culture imported via Haiti in the 1790s are still visible in Cuba today, particularly in the French-founded settlements of Guantánamo and Cienfuegos.

Cuba high-jumper Javier Sotomayor has held the world record (2.45m) for the event since 1993, and has recorded 17 of the 24 highest jumps ever.

The crowning moment came in 1992 when Cuba – a country of 11 million people languishing low on the world's rich list – brought home 14 gold medals and ended fifth on the overall medals table. It's a testament to Cuba's high sporting standards that its 11th-place finish in Athens in 2004 was considered something of a national failure.

Characteristically, the sporting obsession starts at the top. Fidel Castro was once renowned for his baseball-hitting prowess, but what is lesser known was his personal commitment to the establishment of a widely accessible national sporting curriculum at all levels. In 1961 the National Institute of Sport, Physical Education and Recreation (INDER) founded a system of sport for the masses that eradicated discrimination and integrated children from a young age. By offering paid leisure-time to workers and dropping entrance fees to major sports events, the organization caused participation in popular sports to multiply tenfold by the 1970s and the knock-on effect to performance was tangible.

Cuban *pelota* (baseball) is legendary and the country is riveted during the October to March regular season, turning rabid for the playoffs in April. You'll see passions running high in the main square of provincial capitals, where fans debate minute details of the game with lots of finger-wagging in what is known as a *peña deportiva* (fan club) or *esquina caliente* (hot corner).

Cuba is also a giant in amateur boxing, as indicated by champions Teófilo Stevenson, who brought home Olympic gold in 1972, 1976 and 1980, and Félix Savón, another triple medal winner, most recently in 2000. Every sizable town has an arena called *sala polivalente,* where big boxing events take place, while training and smaller matches happen at gyms, many of which train Olympic athletes.

Multiculturalism

A convergence of three different races and numerous nationalities, Cuba is a multicultural society that, despite difficult challenges, has been relatively successful in forging racial equality.

The annihilation of the indigenous Taínos by the Spanish and the brutality of the system of slavery left a bloody mark in the early years of colonization, but the situation had improved significantly by the second half of the 20th century. The revolution guaranteed racial freedom by law, though black Cubans are still far more likely to be stopped by the police for questioning, and over 90% of Cuban exiles in the US are of white descent. Blacks are also under-represented in politics; of the victorious rebel army officers that took control of the government in 1959, only a handful (Juan Almeida being the most obvious example) were black or mixed race.

In June 2008 the Cuban government legalized sex-change operations and agreed to provide them free to qualifying parties.

According to the most recent census, Cuba's racial breakdown is 27% *mulato* (mixed race), 64% white, 8% black and 1% Chinese. Aside from the obvious Spanish legacy, many of the so-called 'white' population are the descendants of French immigrants who arrived on the island in various waves during the early part of the 19th century. Indeed, the cities of Guantánamo, Cienfuegos and Santiago de Cuba were all either pioneered or heavily influenced by French *émigrés,* and much of Cuba's coffee and sugar industries owe their development to French entrepreneurship.

The black population is also an eclectic mix. Numerous Haitians and Jamaicans came to Cuba to work in the sugar fields in the 1920s and they brought many of their customs and traditions with them. Their descendants can be found in Guantánamo and Santiago in the Oriente or places such as Venezuela in Ciego de Ávila Province, where Haitian Vodou rituals are still practiced.

Religion

Religion is among the most misunderstood and complex aspects of Cuban culture. Before the revolution, 85% of Cubans were nominal Roman Catholics, though only 10% attended church regularly. Protestants made up most of the remaining church-going public, though a smattering of Jews and Muslims have always practiced in Cuba and still do. Soon after the 1959 revolution, 140 Catholic priests were expelled for reactionary political activities and another 400 left voluntarily, while the majority of Protestants, who represented society's poorer sector, had less to lose and stayed.

When the government declared itself Marxist-Leninist and therefore atheist, life for *creyentes* ('believers') took on new difficulties. Though church services were never banned and freedom of religion never revoked, Christians were sent to Unidades Militares de Ayuda a la Producción (UMAPs; Military Production Aid Units), where it was hoped hard labor might reform their religious ways; homosexuals and vagrants were also sent to the fields to work. This was a short-lived experiment, however. More trying for believers were the hard-line Soviet days of the '70s and '80s, when they were prohibited from joining the Communist Party and few, if any, believers held political posts. Certain university careers, notably in the humanities, were off-limits as well.

Things have changed dramatically since then, particularly in 1992 when the constitution was revised, removing all references to the Cuban state as Marxist-Leninist and recapturing the laical nature of the government. This led to an aperture in civil and political spheres of society for religious adherents, and to other reforms (eg believers are now eligible for party membership).

Cuba is one of the few small nations graced with the visit of the past three popes. Since Cuban Catholicism gained the papal seal of approval with Pope John Paul II's visit in 1998, church attendance surged, rewarded further with the arrival of his successor Pope Benedict XVI in 2012. Pope Francis, the first pontiff from Latin America, was received by a thrilled public in a nine-day visit in 2015 as he urged more freedom to worship. He also is credited with brokering the diplomatic thaw in US–Cuba relations.

It's worth noting that church services have a strong youth presence. There are currently 400,000 Catholics regularly attending Mass and 300,000 Protestants from 54 denominations. Other denominations such as the Seventh Day Adventists and Pentecostals are rapidly growing in popularity.

Santería

Of all Cuba's cultural mysteries (and there are many), Santería is the most complex, cloaking an inherent 'African-ness' and leading you down an unmapped road that is at once foggy and fascinating.

A syncretistic religion that hides African roots beneath a symbolic Catholic veneer, Santería is a product of the era of slavery, but remains deeply embedded in contemporary Cuban culture, where it has had a major impact on the evolution of the country's music, dance and rituals. Today more than three million Cubans identify as believers, including numerous writers, artists and politicians.

Santería's misrepresentations start with its name; the word is a historical misnomer first coined by Spanish colonizers to describe the 'saint worship' practiced by 19th-century African enslaved people. A more accurate moniker is Regla de Ocha (way of the *orishas*), or Lucumí, named for the original adherents who hailed from the Yoruba ethno-linguistic group in southwestern Nigeria, a prime looting ground for brutal traders of enslaved people.

The Committees for the Defense of the Revolution (CDRs) are Cuba's controversial local political committees. On the one hand, CDRs act as prime government tools in quashing dissent and maintaining a compliant population; on the other, they organize important community festivals, blood banks and vaccination campaigns.

THE ORISHAS

The *orishas* (deities) are central to the understanding of Santería. There are over 400 of them in the traditional Yoruba religion, though only about a dozen are significant in contemporary Cuba. The most important are known as the Siete Potencias (seven powers) which, between them, control all aspects of daily life.

They are: Changó, the Zeus-like king of the gods; Yemayá, mother of the gods; Elegguá, god of destiny and travelers; Oggún, god of war; Ochún, god of love and sensuality; Oyá, guardian of cemeteries; and Obalatá, the white-clad god of peace and intellect. Two additional *orishas* important in Cuba are Babalú Ayé, god of healing; and Orula, god of fortune and wisdom, through whom the high priests of Santería *(babalawos)* interpret the oracles (Ifá).

The most popular *orishas* in Cuba are combative Changó, represented by Santa Bárbara; loving Ochún syncretized with Cuba's patron saint, the black Virgen de la Caridad; and motherly Yemayá, the patron saint of sailors and fisherfolk twinned with Our Lady of Regla. The *orisha* Babalú Ayé or San Lázaro is also widely venerated by the sick for his healing powers. Every December 17 thousands of pilgrims make a procession to El Rincón, a church near Havana, in the hope of achieving better health.

Santeros believe that the *orishas* control every aspect of daily life and can bring both good and bad fortune. To garner their favor, people build altars, offer food or animal sacrifices, and summon up their spirits during drumming and initiation ceremonies. It is believed that by successfully harnessing the power of the *orishas,* a person can achieve a healthy balance between the forces of nature and the conflicting tugs on their personality. The ultimate goal is to determine your personal destiny.

Every practicing *santero* has an *orisha* special to them. The choice is usually determined by one's personal attributes; a strong man is a son of Changó, a bright child the offspring of Obalatá, and a sensuous woman a daughter of Ochún.

Fully initiated adherents of Santería (called *santeros*) believe in one God known as Oludomare, the creator of the universe and the source of Ashe (all life forces on earth). Rather than interact with the world directly, Oludomare communicates through a pantheon of *orishas,* various imperfect deities similar to Catholic saints or Greek gods, who are blessed with different natural (water, weather, metals) and human (love, intellect, virility) qualities. *Orishas* have their own feast days, demand their own food offerings, and are given numbers and colors to represent their personalities.

Santería has no equivalent to the Bible or Koran. Instead, religious rites are transmitted orally and, over time, have evolved to fit the realities of modern Cuba. Another departure from popular world religions is the abiding focus on 'life on earth' as opposed to the afterlife, although Santería adherents believe strongly in the powers of dead ancestors, known as *egun,* whose spirits are invoked during initiation ceremonies.

Santería's syncretism with Catholicism occurred surreptitiously during the colonial era when African animist traditions were banned. In order to hide their faith from the Spanish authorities, African enslaved people secretly twinned their *orishas* with Catholic saints. Thus, Changó the male *orisha* of thunder and lightning was hidden somewhat bizarrely behind the feminine form of Santa Bárbara, while Elegguá, the *orisha* of travel and roads, became St Anthony de Padua. In this way an erstwhile enslaved person praying before a statue of Santa Bárbara was clandestinely offering his/her respects to Changó, while Afro-Cubans ostensibly celebrating the feast day of Our Lady of Regla (September 7) were, in reality, honoring Yemayá. This syncretization, though no longer strictly necessary, is still followed today.

Literature & the Arts

Leave your preconceptions about 'art in a totalitarian state' at home. The breadth of Cuban cinema, painting and literature could put many far more politically libertarian nations to shame. The Cubans seem to have a habit of taking almost any artistic genre and making it better. You'll pick up everything here: Spanish-quality flamenco, world-class ballet, uplifting classical music, alternative cinema, Shakespearean theater and genre-reinventing art.

Literary Cuba

Cubans *love* conversation and extend their loquaciousness to the page. Maybe it's something in the rum, but since time immemorial, writers in this highly literate Caribbean archipelago have barely paused for breath, telling and retelling their stories with characteristic zeal. In the process they have spewed forth some of Latin America's most groundbreaking and influential literature.

The Classicists

Any literary journey should begin in Havana in the 1830s. Cuban literature found its earliest voice in *Cecilia Valdés,* a novel by Cirilo Villaverde (1812–94), published in 1882 but set 50 years earlier in a Havana divided by class, slavery and prejudice. It's widely considered to be the greatest 19th-century Cuban novel.

Preceding Villaverde, in publication if not historical setting, was romantic poet and novelist Gertrudis Gómez Avellaneda. Born to a rich Camagüeyan family of privileged Spanish gentry in 1814, Avellaneda was a rare female writer in a rigidly masculine domain. Eleven years before *Uncle Tom's Cabin* woke up America to the same themes, her novel *Sab*, published in 1841, tackled the prickly issues of race and slavery. It was banned in Cuba until 1914 due to its abolitionist rhetoric. What contemporary critics chose not to see was Avellaneda's subtle feminism, which depicted marriage as another form of slavery.

Heberto Padilla (1932–2000) was a Cuban poet whose dissident writings in the 1960s led to his imprisonment, inspiring the 'Padilla Affair.'

MARTÍ – A CATEGORY OF HIS OWN

The writing of José Julián Martí Pérez (1853–95) stands alone. A pioneering philosopher, revolutionary and modernist writer, Martí broadened the political debate in Cuba beyond slavery (which was abolished in 1886) to issues such as independence and – above all – freedom. His instantly quotable prose remains a rare unifying force among Cubans around the world, whatever their political affiliations. He is similarly revered by Spanish speakers globally for his internationalism, which has put him on a par with Simón Bolívar.

Martí's writing covered a huge range of genres: essays, novels, poetry, political commentaries, letters and even a hugely popular children's magazine called *La edad de oro* (Golden Age). An accomplished master of aphorisms, his powerful one-liners still crop up in everyday Cuban speech. His two most famous works, published in 1891, are the political essay *Nuestra América* (Our America) and his collected poems, *Versos sencillos* (Simple Verses), both of which laid bare his hopes and dreams for Cuba and Latin America.

Further east, neoclassical poet and native of Santiago de Cuba, José María de Heredia lived and wrote mainly from exile in Mexico. He was banished for allegedly conspiring against the Spanish authorities. His poetry, including the seminal *Himno del desterrado,* is tinged with a nostalgic romanticism for his homeland.

The Experimentalists

Cuban literature grew up in the early 1900s. Inspired by a mixture of Martí's modernism and new surrealistic influences wafting over from Europe, the first half of the 20th century was an age of experimentation for Cuban writers. The era's literary legacy rests on three giant pillars: Alejo Carpentier (1904–80), a baroque wordsmith who invented the much-copied style of *lo real maravilloso* (magic realism); Guillermo Cabrera Infante (1929–2005), a Joycean master of colloquial language who pushed the parameters of Spanish to barely comprehensible boundaries; and José Lezama Lima (1910–76), a gay poet of Proustian ambition, whose weighty novels are rich in layers, themes and anecdotes.

None are easy to read, but all broke new ground inspiring erudite writers far beyond Cuban shores (Márquez and Rushdie among them). Swiss-born Carpentier's magnum opus was *El siglo de las luces* (Explosion in a Cathedral), which explores the impact of the French revolution in Cuba through a veiled love story. Many consider it to be the finest novel ever written by a Cuban author. Infante, from Gibara, rewrote the rules of language in *Tres tristes tigres* (Three Trapped Tigers), a study of street life in pre-Castro Havana. Lezama, meanwhile, took an anecdotal approach to novel writing in *Paradiso* (Paradise), a multilayered, widely interpreted evocation of Havana in the 1950s with homoerotic undertones.

Grasping at the coattails of this virtuosic trio was Miguel Barnet, an anthropologist from Havana, whose *Biografía de un cimarrón* (Biography of a Runaway Slave), published in 1963, gathered testimonies from 103-year-old former enslaved person Esteban Montejo and crafted them into a fascinating written documentary of the brutal system of slavery nearly 80 years after its demise.

Best Cuban Classics

Cirilo Villaverde: *Cecelia Valdés* (1882)

Alejo Carpentier: *El siglo de las luces* (1962)

Guillermo Cabrera Infante: *Tres tristes tigres* (1967)

Reinaldo Arenas: *Antes que anochezca* (1992)

Enter Guillén

Born in Camagüey in 1902, *mulato* (mixed race) poet Nicolás Guillén was far more than just a writer: he was a passionate and lifelong champion of Afro-Cuban rights. Rocked by the assassination of his father in his youth, and inspired by the drum-influenced music of former black enslaved people, Guillén set about articulating the hopes and fears of dispossessed black laborers with the rhythmic Afro-Cuban verses that would ultimately become his trademark. Famous poems in a prolific career included the evocative *Tengo* (I Have) and the patriotic *Che Comandante, Amigo* (Commander Che, Friend).

Working in self-imposed exile during the Batista era, Guillén returned to Cuba after the revolution whereupon he was given the task of formulating a new cultural policy and setting up the Writers and Artists Union, UNEAC (Unión de Escritores y Artistas de Cuba).

Contemporary writer Leonardo Padura Fuentes is well known for his quartet of Havana-based detective novels, *Los cuatro estaciones* (Four Seasons), now a riveting Netflix miniseries.

The Dirty Realists

In the 1990s and 2000s, baby boomers that had come of age in the era of censorship and Soviet domination began to respond to radically different influences in their writing. Some fled the country, others remained; all tested the boundaries of artistic expression in a system weighed down by censorship and creative asphyxiation.

Stepping out from the shadow of Lezama Lima was Reinaldo Arenas, a gay writer from Holguín Province, who, like Guillermo Cabrera Infante, fell out with the revolution in the late '60s and was imprisoned for his

WIFREDO LAM

In the international context, art in Cuba is dominated by the prolific figure of Wifredo Lam (1902–82), painter, sculptor and ceramicist of mixed Chinese, African and Spanish ancestry. Born in Sagua La Grande, Villa Clara Province, in 1902, Lam studied art and law in Havana before departing for Madrid in 1923 to pursue his artistic ambitions in the fertile fields of post–WWI Europe. Displaced by the Spanish Civil War in 1937, he gravitated toward France, where he became friends with Pablo Picasso and swapped ideas with the pioneering surrealist André Breton. Having absorbed various cubist and surrealist influences, Lam returned to Cuba in 1941, where he produced his own seminal masterpiece *La Jungla* (Jungle), considered by critics to be one of the developing world's most representative paintings.

efforts. Arenas finally escaped to the US in 1980 during the Mariel Boatlift. He went on to write his hyperbolic memoir, *Antes que anochezca* (Before Night Falls), about his imprisonment and homosexuality. Published in the US in 1993, it met with huge critical acclaim.

The so-called 'dirty realist' authors of the late '90s and early 2000s took a more subtle approach to challenging contemporary mores. Pedro Juan Gutiérrez earned his moniker, 'tropical Bukowski,' for the *Dirty Havana Trilogy,* a sexy, sultry study of Centro Habana during the Special Period. The trilogy held a mirror up to the desperate economic situation but steered clear of direct political polemics.

Zoé Valdés, born the year Castro took power, has been more direct in her criticism of the regime, particularly since leaving Cuba for Paris in 1995. Her most readily available novels (translated into English) are *I Gave You All I Had* and *The Weeping Woman*.

The Fascinated Foreigners

Cuba also inspires foreign writers to pen fiction, most notably Ernest Hemingway and Graham Greene. Hemingway first visited Cuba in the late 1930s on his boat *El Pilar*, partly as a break from his soon-to-be ex-wife. His love affair with the country continued until his death. His novels *The Old Man and the Sea* (1952; a portrayal of an old man's quest to bag a giant fish) and *Islands in the Stream* (1970; a harrowing trilogy following the fortunes of writer Thomas Hudson) were based on his experiences fishing – and, during WWII, hunting for German submarines – off Cuba's coast.

Greene visited the island several times in the 1950s and it became the setting for his book *Our Man in Havana* (1958), a tongue-in-cheek look at espionage that casts an interesting light on pre–Cuban Missile Crisis Havana.

Graham Greene originally set his comic take on British espionage in Soviet-occupied Tallinn, Estonia. But a chance visit to Havana changed his mind. The novel ultimately became *Our Man in Havana.*

While none of his novels take place in Cuba, Colombian author Gabriel García Márquez developed a long-standing friendship with Fidel Castro during the 1960s, and wrote several articles on Cuba including *Memories of a Journalist* (1981), which recalls the Bay of Pigs invasion.

Cinema

Cuban cinema has always been closer to European art-house traditions than to the formula movies of Hollywood, especially since the revolution, when cultural life veered away from American influences. Few notable movies were made until 1959, when the new government formed the Instituto Cubano del Arte e Industria Cinematográficos (Icaic), headed up by longtime film sage and former Havana University student, Alfredo Guevara, who held the position on and off until 2000.

The 1960s were Icaic's *Década de oro* (Golden Decade) when, behind an artistic veneer, successive directors were able to test the boundaries of state-imposed censorship and, in some cases, gain greater creative license. Innovative movies of this era poked fun at bureaucracy, made pertinent comments on economic matters, questioned the role of intellectualism in a socialist state and, later on, tackled previously taboo gay issues. The giants behind the camera were Humberto Solás, Tomás Gutiérrez Alea, and Juan Carlos Tabío, who, working under Guevara's guidance, put cutting-edge Cuban cinema on the international map.

Cuba's first notable post-revolutionary movie, the joint Cuban-Soviet *Soy Cuba* (I am Cuba; 1964) was directed by a Russian, Mikhail Kalatozov, who dramatized the events leading up to the 1959 revolution in four interconnecting stories. Largely forgotten by the early '70s, the movie was resurrected in the mid-1990s by American director Martin Scorsese, who was astounded by its cinematography, atmospheric camera work and technically amazing tracking shots. The film gets a rare 100% rating on the Rotten Tomatoes website and has been described by one American film critic as 'a unique, insane, exhilarating spectacle.'

The 2010 movie *Memories of Overdevelopment* about a jaded Cuban living in New York where he's troubled by memories of his socialist past was the first dramatic feature to be filmed on location in both Cuba and the US.

Serving his apprenticeship in the 1960s, Cuba's most celebrated director, Tomás Gutiérrez Alea, cut his teeth directing art-house movies such as *La muerte de un burócrata* (Death of a Bureaucrat; 1966), a satire on excessive socialist bureaucratization; and *Memorias de subdesarrollo* (Memories of Underdevelopment; 1968), the story of a Cuban intellectual too idealistic for Miami, yet too decadent for the austere life of Havana. Teaming up with fellow director Juan Carlos Tabío in 1993, Gutiérrez went on to make another movie classic, the Oscar-nominated *Fresa y chocolate* (Strawberry and Chocolate) – the tale of Diego, a skeptical homosexual who falls in love with a heterosexual communist militant. It remains Cuba's cinematic pinnacle.

Humberto Solás, a master of low budget *(cine pobre)* movies, first made his mark in 1968 with the seminal *Lucía*. It explored the lives of three Cuban women at key moments in the country's history: 1895, 1932 and the early 1960s. Solás made his late-career masterpiece, *Barrio Cuba,* the tale of a family torn apart by the revolution, in 2005.

Since the death of Gutiérrez Alea in 1996 and Solás in 2008, Cuban cinema has passed the baton. Fernando Pérez leaped onto the scene in 1994 with the Special Period classic *Madagascar,* focusing on an intergenerational struggle between a mother and daughter, and followed it up with 2003's *Suite Habana,* a moody documentary about a day in the life of 13 real people in the capital that uses zero dialogue. Pérez's closest 'rival' is Juan Carlos Cremata, whose 2005 road movie *Viva Cuba,* a study of class and ideology as seen through the eyes of two children, garnered much international praise.

The last few years have seen few classics of the same clout, but 2011's *Juan of the Dead,* Cuba's version of UK horror-comedy *Shaun of the Dead,* broke ground as Cuba's first zombie movie. In a thinly veiled critique on the regime, an idler-turned-slayer-of-the-undead fights for survival in a Havana overrun by zombies.

RAÚL MARTÍNEZ & THE GRUPO DE LOS ONCE

Ciego de Ávila, born Raúl Martinez (1927–1995), spearheaded the Cuban pop art movement during the 1950s and '60s with iconic depictions of José Martí, Camilo Cienfuegos and Che Guevara, although his work was inspired by Soviet socialism as much as by the American pop art movement. Martinez was a member of the Grupo de los Once, a group of groundbreaking abstract painters and sculptors who exhibited together between 1953 and 1955 and left a lasting impression on Cuban art. You can see much of the work of Martínez in Ciego de Ávila's Centro de Promoción Cultural Guiarte (p308) as well as Havana's Museo Nacional de Bellas Artes (p85).

Reflecting the expanded options of distribution in the digital age, director Arturo Sotto's entertaining 2014 comedy *Boccaccerías Habaneras* is available in its entirety on YouTube.

Havana's significant influence on the film culture of the American hemisphere is highlighted each year in the Festival Internacional del Nuevo Cine Latinoamericano held every December in Havana. Described as the ultimate word in Latin American cinema, this annual get-together of critics, sages and filmmakers has been fundamental in showcasing recent Cuban classics to the world.

Painting & Sculpture

Thought-provoking and visceral, modern Cuban art combines lurid Afro-Latin American colors with the harsh reality of the revolution. For foreign art lovers visiting Cuba, it's a unique and intoxicating brew. Forced into a corner by the constrictions of the culture-redefining Cuban revolution, modern artists have invariably found that, by co-opting (as opposed to confronting) the socialist regime, opportunities for academic training and artistic encouragement are almost unlimited. Encased in such a volatile, creative climate, abstract art in Cuba – well established in its own right before the revolution – has flourished.

The first flowering of Cuban art took place in the 1920s when painters belonging to the so-called Vanguardia movement relocated temporarily to Paris to learn the ropes from the avant-garde European school then dominated by the likes of Pablo Picasso. One of the Vanguardia's earliest exponents was Victor Manuel García (1897–1969), the genius behind one of Cuba's most famous paintings, *La gitana tropical* (Tropical Gypsy; 1929), a portrait of an archetypal Cuban woman with her luminous gaze staring into the middle distance. The canvas, displayed in Havana's Museo Nacional de Bellas Artes, is often referred to as the Latin Mona Lisa.

Victor Manuel's contemporary, Amelia Peláez (1896–1968), also studied in Paris, where she melded avant-gardism with more primitive Cuban themes. Though Peláez worked with many different materials, her most celebrated work was in murals, including the 670-sq-meter tile mural on the side of the Hotel Habana Libre.

After the high-water mark of Wifredo Lam, Cuban pop art was a major influence during the 1950s and 1960s. Art has enjoyed strong government patronage since the revolution (albeit within the confines of strict censorship), exemplified with the opening of the Instituto Superior de Arte in 1976 and the Fábrica de Arte Cubano in 2014.

Top Contemporary Artists

José Villa

Joel Jover

Flora Fong

José Rodríguez Fúster

2+2=5

Julia Valdéz

Leo D'Lázaro

Architecture

There is nothing pure about Cuban architecture. Rather like its music, the nation's eclectic assemblage of buildings exhibits an unashamed hybrid of styles, ideas and background influences. Over time, and through a process of architectural osmosis, the country has created its own individualistic building form, an inherent 'Cubaness' perceptible alongside more recognizable baroque, neoclassical and art deco features.

Styles & Trends

Emerging relatively unscathed from the turmoil of three revolutionary wars and buffered from modern globalization by its peculiar economic situation, the nation's well-preserved cities have survived into the 21st century with the bulk of their colonial architectural features intact. The preservation has been helped by the nomination of Havana Vieja, Trinidad, Cienfuegos and Camagüey as Unesco World Heritage sites, and aided further by foresighted

Top: Castillo de San Pedro de la Roca del Morro (p410), Santiago de Cuba

local historians who have created a model for self-sustaining historical preservation that might well go down as one of the revolutionary government's greatest achievements.

Cuba's classic and most prevalent architectural styles are baroque and neoclassicism. Baroque designers began sharpening their quills in the 1750s; neoclassicism gained the ascendency in the 1820s and continued, amid numerous revivals, until the 1920s. Trademark buildings of the American era (1902–59) exhibited art deco and, later on, modernist styles. Art nouveau played a cameo role during this period influenced by Catalan *modernisme;* recognizable art nouveau curves and embellishments can be seen on pivotal east–west axis streets in Centro Habana. Ostentatious eclecticism, courtesy of the Americans, characterized Havana's rich and growing suburbs from the 1910s onwards.

Building styles weren't all pretty, though. Cuba's brief flirtation with Soviet architectonics in the 1960s and '70s threw up plenty of breeze-block apartments and ugly utilitarian hotels that sit rather jarringly alongside the beautiful relics of the colonial era. Havana's Vedado neighborhood maintains a small but significant cluster of modernist 'skyscrapers' constructed during a 10-year prerevolutionary building boom in the 1950s.

Rare examples of Cuban Gothic architecture can be seen at Iglesia del Sagrado Corazón de Jesús in Havana and its namesake church in the nation's most devoutly religious city, Camagüey.

Coastal Fortifications

While European kings were hiding from the hoi polloi in muscular medieval castles, their Latin American cousins were building up their colonial defenses in a series of equally colossal Renaissance forts.

The protective ring of fortifications that punctuates Cuba's coastline stretching from Havana in the west to Baracoa in the east forms one of the finest ensembles of military architecture in the Americas. The construction of these sturdy stone behemoths by the Spanish in the 16th, 17th and 18th centuries reflected the colony's strategic importance on the Atlantic trade routes and its vulnerability to attacks by daring pirates and competing colonial powers.

As Cuban capital and the primary Spanish port in the Caribbean, Havana was the grand prize to ambitious would-be raiders. The sacking of the city by French pirate Jacques de Sores in 1555 exposed the weaknesses of the city's meager defenses and provoked the first wave of fort building.

Havana's authorities called in Italian military architect Bautista Antonelli to do the job and he responded with aplomb, reinforcing the harbor mouth with two magnificent forts, El Morro and San Salvador de la Punta. The work, which started in the 1580s, was slow but meticulous; the forts weren't actually finished until after Antonelli's death in the 1620s. Antonelli also designed the Castillo de San Pedro de la Roca del

---

HAVANA'S PARISIAN INFLUENCE

French landscape architect Jean-Claude Forestier added a Parisian flavor to Havana's modern urban layout in the 1920s. Fresh from high-profile commissions in the French capital, Forestier arrived in Havana in 1925 where he was invited to draw up a master plan to link the city's disparate urban grid. He spent the next five years sketching broad tree-lined boulevards, Parisian-style squares and a harmonious city landscape designed to accentuate Havana's iconic monuments and lush tropical setting.

Forestier's plans were unhinged by the Great Depression, but his Parisian vision was ultimately realized 30 years later with the vast construction projects enacted in the 1950s. The focal point was Plaza de la Revolución with its grand Martí Memorial, which sits atop a small hill, with broad avenues radiating on all sides. The best boulevards for strolling are Paseo and Avenida de los Presidentes (Calle G), both adorned with tree-lined central walkways and punctuated with heroic statues.

Teatro Tomás Terry (p243), Cienfuegos

Morro in Santiago, started around the same time but, thanks to ongoing attacks, most notoriously by British buccaneer Henry Morgan in 1662, not finished until 1700.

More forts were added in the 18th century, most notably at Jagua (near present-day Cienfuegos) on the south coast and Matanzas in the north. Baracoa in the far east was encircled with a bulwark of three small fortifications, all of which survive.

With their thick walls, and polygon layout designed to fit in with the coastal topography, Cuba's forts were built to last (all still survive) and largely served their purpose at deterring successive invaders until 1762. In that year the British arrived during the Seven Years War, blasting a hole in San Severino in Matanzas and capturing Havana after a 44-day siege of El Morro. Spain's response when it got back Havana from the British in 1763 was to build the humungous La Cabaña, the largest fort in the Americas. Not surprisingly, its heavy battlements were never breached.

In the 1980s and '90s, Havana's and Santiago's forts were named Unesco World Heritage sites.

Theatrical Architecture

Attend a dance or play in a provincial Cuban theater and you might find your eyes flicking intermittently between the artists on the stage and the equally captivating artistry of the building.

As strong patrons of music and dance, the Cubans have a tradition of building iconic provincial theaters and most cities have an historic venue where you can view the latest performances. By popular consensus, the most architecturally accomplished Cuban theaters are the Teatro Sauto (p221) in Matanzas, the Teatro la Caridad (p263) in Santa Clara, and the Teatro Tomás Terry (p243) in Cienfuegos.

Teatro la Caridad (p263), Santa Clara

All three gilded buildings were constructed in the 19th century (in 1863, 1885 and 1890 respectively) with sober French neoclassical facades overlaying more lavish Italianate interiors. A generic defining feature is the U-shaped three-tiered auditoriums that display a profusion of carved wood-paneling and wrought iron, and are crowned by striking ceiling frescoes. The frescoes of angelic cherubs in the Caridad and Tomás Terry were painted by the same Philippine artist, Camilo Salaya, while the Sauto's was the work of the theater's Italian architect, Daniele Dell'Aglio. Other features include ornate chandeliers, gold-leafed mosaics and striking marble statues: the Sauto's statues are of Greek goddesses, while the Tomás Terry sports a marble re-creation of its eponymous financier, a Venezuelan-born sugar baron.

Philanthropy played a major part in many Cuban theaters in the 19th century, none more so than Santa Clara's Caridad (the name means 'charity'), which was paid for by local benefactor, Marta Abreu. In an early show of altruism, Abreu, who donated to many social and artistic causes, ensured that a percentage of the theater's ongoing profits went to charity.

Lack of funds in recent times has left many Cuban theaters in dire need of repair. Some buildings haven't survived. The Colesio, Cuba's earliest modern theater built in 1823 in Santiago de Cuba, was destroyed by fire in 1846. The Teatro Brunet in Trinidad built in 1840 is now a ruin used as an atmospheric social center. Havana's oldest theater, the Tacón, survives, but was overlaid by a Spanish social center (the Centro Gallego) in the 1910s. Pinar del Río's recently refurbished Teatro Milanés (1838) has a lovely Sevillan patio, while the neoclassical Teatro Principal (1850) in Camagüey is the home of Cuba's most prestigious ballet company.

Most Architecturally Attractive Hotels

Hotel Ordoño
(Gibara)

Hotel Sagua
(Sagua La Grande)

Hotel Raquel
(Havana)

Hostal del Rijo
(Sancti Spíritus)

Hotel Camino de
Hierro (Camagüey)

Cuban Baroque

Baroque architecture arrived in Cuba in the mid-1700s, via Spain, a good 50 years after its European high-water mark. Fueled by the rapid growth of the island's nascent sugar industry, nouveau riche owners of enslaved people and sugar merchants plowed their juicy profits into grandiose urban buildings. The finest examples of baroque in Cuba adorn the homes and public buildings of Habana Vieja, although the style didn't reach its zenith until the late-1700s with the construction of the Catedral de la Habana (p67) and the surrounding Plaza de la Catedral (p67).

Due to climatic and cultural peculiarities, traditional baroque (the word is taken from the Portuguese noun *barroco,* which means an 'elaborately shaped pearl') was quickly 'tropicalized' in Cuba, with local architects adding their own personal flourishes to the new municipal structures that were springing up in various provincial cities. Indigenous features included: *rejas,* metal bars secured over windows to protect against burglaries and allow for a freer circulation of air; *vitrales,* multicolored glass panes fitted above doorways to pleasantly diffuse the tropical sun's rays; *entresuelos,* mezzanine floors built to accommodate the live-in enslaved families; and *portales,* galleried exterior walkways that provided pedestrians with shelter from the sun and the rain.

Signature baroque buildings, such as the Palacio de los Capitanes Generales in Plaza de Armas in Havana, were made from hard local limestone dug from the nearby San Lázaro quarries and constructed using the labor of enslaved people. As a result, the intricate exterior decoration that characterized baroque architecture in Italy and Spain was noticeably toned down in Cuba, where local workers lacked the advanced stonemasonry skills of their more accomplished European cousins.

Some of the most exquisite baroque buildings in Cuba are found in Trinidad and date from the early decades of the 19th century when designs and furnishings were heavily influenced by the haute couture fashions of Italy, France and Georgian England.

Neoclassicism

Neoclassicism first evolved in the mid-18th century in Europe as a reaction to the lavish ornamentation and gaudy ostentation of baroque. Conceived in the progressive academies of London and Paris, the movement's early adherents advocated sharp primary colors and bold symmetrical lines, coupled with a desire to return to the perceived architectural 'purity' of ancient Greece and Rome.

The style eventually reached Cuba at the beginning of the 19th century, spearheaded by groups of French émigrés who had fled west from Haiti following a violent rebellion of enslaved people in 1791. Within a couple of decades, neoclassicism had established itself as the nation's dominant architectural style.

By the mid-19th century sturdy neoclassical buildings were the norm among Cuba's bourgeoisie in cities such as Cienfuegos and Matanzas, with striking symmetry, grandiose frontages and rows of imposing columns replacing the decorative baroque flourishes of the early colonial period.

Havana's first true neoclassical building was El Templete (p74), a diminutive Doric temple constructed in Habana Vieja in 1828 next to the spot where Father Bartolomé de las Casas is said to have conducted the city's first Mass. As the city gradually spread westward in the mid-1800s, outgrowing its 17th-century walls, the style was adopted in the construction of more ambitious buildings, such as the famous Hotel Inglaterra (p86) overlooking Parque Central. Havana grew in both size and beauty during this period, bringing into vogue new residential design features

Top: Palacio de los Capitanes Generales (p69), Havana

Bottom: Capitolio Nacional (p85), Havana

Edificio Bacardí (p81), Havana

such as spacious classical courtyards and rows of imposing street-facing colonnades, leading seminal Cuban novelist Alejo Carpentier to christen it the 'city of columns.'

A second neoclassical revival swept Cuba at the beginning of the 20th century, spearheaded by the growing influence of the US on the island. Prompted by the ideas and design ethics of the American Renaissance (1876–1914), Havana underwent a full-on building explosion, sponsoring such gigantic municipal buildings as the Capitolio Nacional (p85) and the Universidad de la Habana. In the provinces, the style reached its high-water mark in a series of glittering theaters.

Art Deco

Notable Art Deco Buildings

....
Edificio Bacardí (Havana)
....
Teatro América (Havana)
....
Iglesia de Nuestra Señora de la Caridad (Banes)
....
Cuartel Moncada (Santiago de Cuba)

Art deco was an elegant, functional and modern architectural movement that originated in France at the beginning of the 20th century and reached its apex in America in the 1920s and '30s. Drawing from a vibrant mix of Cubism, futurism and African art, the genre promoted lavish yet streamlined buildings with sweeping curves and exuberant sun-burst motifs such as the Chrysler building in New York and the architecture of the South Beach neighborhood in Miami.

As the United States' then ally, Cuba quickly acquired its own clutch of 'tropical' art deco buildings with the lion's share residing in Havana. One of Latin America's finest examples of early art deco is the Edifico Bacardí in Habana Vieja, built in 1930 to provide a Havana headquarters for Santiago de Cuba's world-famous rum-making family.

Another striking creation was the 14-story Edificio López Serrano in Vedado, constructed as the city's first real *rascacielo* (skyscraper) in 1932, using New York's Rockefeller Center as its inspiration. Other more functional art deco skyscrapers followed, including the Teatro América on

Palacio de Valle (p244), Cienfuegos

Av de la Italia, the Teatro Fausto on Paseo de Martí and the Casa de las Américas on Calle G. A more diluted and eclectic interpretation of the genre can be seen in the famous Hotel Nacional, whose sharp symmetrical lines and decorative twin Moorish turrets dominate the view over the Malecón.

Eclecticism

Eclecticism is the term often applied to the nonconformist and highly experimental architectural zeitgeist that grew up in the United States during the 1880s. Rejecting 19th-century ideas of 'style' and categorization, the architects behind this revolutionary new genre promoted flexibility and an open-minded 'anything goes' ethos, drawing their inspiration from a wide range of historical precedents.

Thanks to the strong US presence in the decades before 1959, Cuba quickly became a riot of modern eclecticism, with rich American and Cuban landowners constructing huge Xanadu-like mansions in burgeoning upper-class residential districts. Expansive, ostentatious and, at times, outlandishly kitsch, these fancy new homes were garnished with crenelated walls, oddly shaped lookout towers, rooftop cupolas and leering gargoyles. For a wild tour of Cuban eclecticism, head to the neighborhoods of Miramar in Havana, Vista Alegre in Santiago de Cuba and the Punta Gorda in Cienfuegos.

Music & Dance

Rich, vibrant, layered and soulful, Cuban music has long acted as a standard-bearer for the sounds and rhythms emanating out of Latin America. This is the birthplace of salsa, where European dances adopted black rhythms, and where the African drum first courted the Spanish guitar. From the down-at-heel docks of Matanzas to the bucolic villages of the Sierra Maestra, the amorous musical fusion went on to fuel everything from *son*, rumba, mambo, *chachachá, charanga, changüí, danzón* and more.

Into the Mix

Aside from the obvious Spanish and African roots, Cuban music has drawn upon a number of other influences. Mixed into an already exotic melting pot are genres from France, the US, Haiti and Jamaica. Conversely, Cuban music has also played a key role in developing various melodic styles and movements in other parts of the world. In Spain they called this process *ida y vuelta* (return trip) and it is most clearly evident in a style of flamenco called *guajira*. Elsewhere the 'Cuban effect' can be traced back to forms as diverse as New Orleans jazz, New York salsa and West African Afrobeat.

Described by aficionados as 'a vertical representation of a horizontal act,' Cuban dancing is famous for its libidinous rhythms and sensuous close-ups. Inheriting a love for dancing from birth and able to replicate perfect salsa steps by the age of two or three, most Cubans are natural performers who approach dance with a complete lack of self-consciousness – a notion that can leave visitors from Europe or North America feeling as if they've got two left feet.

Danzón Days

Best Places for Música Cubana

Son Casa de la Trova (Santiago de Cuba)

Nueva Trova Casa de la Trova (Trinidad)

Rumba Callejón de Hamel (Havana)

Jazz Jazz Café (Havana)

The invention of the *danzón* is usually credited to innovative Matanzas band leader, Miguel Faílde, who first showcased it with his catchy dance composition *Las Alturas de Simpson* in Matanzas in 1879. Elegant and purely instrumental in its formative days, the *danzón* was slower in pace than some of Cuba's earlier homegrown fusion dances, and its intricate steps required dancers to circulate in couples rather than groups, a move that scandalized polite society at the time. From the 1880s onward, the genre exploded, expanding its peculiar syncopated rhythm, and adding such improbable extras as conga drums and vocalists.

By the early 20th century, the *danzón* had evolved from a stately ballroom dance into a more jazzed-up free-for-all known alternatively as *charanga, danzonete* or *danzón-chá*. Not surprisingly, it became Cuba's national dance, though since it was primarily a bastion of moneyed white society, it was never considered a true hybrid.

Africa Calling

While drumming in the North American colonies was ostensibly prohibited, Cuban enslaved people were able to preserve and pass on many of their musical traditions via influential Santería *cabildos,* religious brotherhoods that re-enacted ancient African percussive music on simple *batá* drums or *chequeré* rattles. Performed at annual festivals or on special Catholic saints' days, this rhythmic yet highly textured dance music was offered up as a form of religious worship to the *orishas* (deities).

Over time the ritualistic drumming of Santería evolved into a more complex genre known as rumba. Rumba was first concocted on the docks of Havana and Matanzas during the 1890s when ex-enslaved people, exposed to a revolving series of outside influences, began to knock out soulful rhythms on old packing cases in imitation of various African religious rites. As the drumming patterns grew more complex, vocals were added, dances emerged and, before long, the music had grown into a collective form of social expression for all black Cubans.

Spreading in popularity throughout the 1920s and '30s, rumba gradually spawned three different but interrelated dance formats: *guaguancó,* an overtly sexual dance; *yambú,* a slow dance; and *columbia,* a fast, aggressive dance often involving fire torches and machetes. The latter originated as a devil dance of the Náñigo rite, and today it's performed only by solo males.

Pitched into Cuba's cultural melting pot, these rootsy yet highly addictive musical variants slowly gained acceptance among a new audience of middle-class whites, and by the 1940s the music had fused with *son* in a new subgenre called *son montuno,* which, in turn, provided the building blocks for salsa.

Indeed, so influential was Cuban rumba by the end of WWII that it was transposed back to Africa with experimental Congolese artists, such as Sam Mangwana and Franco Luambo (of OK Jazz fame), using ebullient Cuban influences to pioneer *soukous,* their own variation on the rumba theme.

Raw, expressive and exciting to watch, Cuban rumba is a spontaneous and often informal affair performed by groups of up to a dozen musicians. Conga drums, *claves, palitos* (sticks), *marugas* (iron shakers) and *cajones* (packing cases) lay out the interlocking rhythms, while the vocals alternate between a wildly improvising lead singer and an answering *coro* (chorus).

> The *danzón* was originally an instrumental piece. Words were added in the late 1920s and the new form became known as the *danzonete.*

DANCE FUSION

Cuban dance is as hybridized as the country's music; indeed many dance genres evolved from popular strands of Cuban music.

Early dance forms mimicked the European-style ballroom dances practiced by the colonizers, but added African elements. This unorthodox amalgamation of styles can be seen in esoteric genres such as the French-Haitian *tumba francesa,* a marriage between 18th-century French court dances and imported African rhythms: dancers wearing elegant dresses wave fans and handkerchiefs while shimmying to the drum patterns of Nigeria and Benin.

Other dances reflected the working lives of Cuba's enslaved people. The *pilón* in Granma province copies the motion of pounding sugarcane. *Nengón* and *kiribá* in Baracoa mimic the crushing of cocoa and coffee beans beneath the feet.

The first truly popular dance hybrid was the *danzón,* a sequence dance involving couples whose origins lay in the French and English *contradanza,* but whose rhythm contained a distinctive African syncopation.

The mambo and *chachachá* evolved the *danzón* further, creating dances that were more improvised and complicated. Mambo's creator, Pérez Prado, specifically pioneered mambo dancing to fit his new music in the 1940s, while the *chachachá* was codified as a ballroom dance in the early 1950s by a Frenchman named Monsieur Pierre.

Rising Son

Cuba's two most celebrated 19th-century sounds, rumba and *danzón,* came from the west – specifically the cities of Havana and Matanzas. But as the genres remained largely compartmentalized between separate black and white societies, neither can be considered true hybrids. The country's first real musical fusion came from the next great sound revolution, *son.*

Son emerged from the mountains of the Oriente region in the second half of the 19th century, though the earliest known testimonies go back as far as 1570. It was one of two genres to arise at around the same time (the other was *changüí*), both of which blended the melodies and lyricism of Spanish folk music with the drum patterns of recently freed African enslaved people. *Son's* precursor was *nengón,* an invention of black sugarplantation workers who had evolved their percussive religious chants into a form of music and song.

The leap from *nengón* to *son* is unclear and poorly documented, but at some point in the 1880s or '90s the *guajiros* (country folk) in the mountains of present-day Santiago de Cuba and Guantánamo provinces began blending *nengón* drums with the Cuban *tres* guitar while over the top a singer improvised words from a traditional 10-line Spanish poem known as a *décima.*

In its pure form, *son* was played by a sextet consisting of guitar, *tres* (guitar with three sets of double strings), double bass, bongo and two singers who played maracas and claves (sticks that tap out the beat). Coming down from the mountains and into the cities, the genre's earliest exponents were the legendary Trio Oriental, who stabilized the sextet format in 1912 when they were reborn as the Sexteto Habanero. Another early *sonero* was singer Miguel Matamoros, whose self-penned *son* classics such as 'Son de la Loma' and 'Lágrimas Negras' are de rigueur among Cuba's ubiquitous musical entertainers, even today.

In the early 1910s *son* arrived in Havana, where it adopted its distinctive rumba *clave* (rhythmic pattern), which later went on to form the basis of salsa. Within a decade it had become Cuba's signature music, gaining wide acceptance among white society and destroying the myth that black music was vulgar, unsophisticated and subversive.

By the 1930s the sextet had become a septet with the addition of a trumpet, and exciting new musicians such as blind *tres* player Arsenio Rodríguez – a songwriter who Harry Belafonte once called the 'father of salsa' – were paving the way for mambo and *chachachá.*

Filin' is a term derived from the English word 'feeling.' It was a style of music showcased by jazz crooners in the 1940s and '50s. In Cuba *filin'* grew out of bolero and *trova* (traditional poetic singing).

Barbarians of Rhythm

Cuba's first hybrid musical genre was the *habanera,* a traditional European-style dance with a syncopated drumbeat, that rose to the fore in the mid-19th century and lasted until the 1870s.

In the 1940s and '50s the *son* bands grew from seven pieces to eight and beyond, until they became big bands incorporating full horn and percussion sections that played rumba, *chachachá* and mambo. The reigning mambo king was Benny Moré, who with his sumptuous voice and rocking 40-piece all-black band was known as El Bárbaro del Ritmo (Barbarian of Rhythm).

Mambo grew out of *charanga* music, which itself was a derivative of *danzón.* Bolder, brassier and more exciting than its two earlier incarnations, the music was characterized by exuberant trumpet riffs, belting saxophones and regular enthusiastic interjections by the singer (usually in the form of the word *dilo!* or 'say it!').

The style's origins are mired in controversy. Some argue that it was invented by native *habanero* Orestes López after he penned the new rhythmically dextrous 'Mambo' in 1938. Others give the credit to Matanzas band leader Pérez Prado, the first musician to market his songs under the increasingly lucrative mambo umbrella in the early '40s. Whatever the case, mambo soon spawned the world's first universal dance craze, and from New York to Buenos Aires, people couldn't get enough of its infectious rhythms.

A variation on the mambo theme, the *chachachá,* was first show-cased by Havana-based composer and violinist Enrique Jorrín in 1951 while playing with the Orquesta América. Originally known as 'mambo-rumba,' the music was intended to promote a more basic kind of Cuban dance that less-coordinated North Americans would be able to master, but it was quickly mambo-ized by overenthusiastic dance competitors, who kept adding complicated new steps.

Charangas were Cuban musical ensembles that showcased popular *danzón-*influenced pieces.

Salsa & Its Offshoots

Salsa is an umbrella term used to describe a variety of musical genres that emerged out of the fertile Latin New York scene in the 1960s and '70s, when jazz, *son* and rumba blended to create a new, brassier sound. While not strictly a product of Cubans living in Cuba, salsa's roots and key influences are descended directly from *son montuno* and indebted to innovators such as Pérez Prado, Benny Moré and Miguel Matamoros.

The self-styled Queen of Salsa was Grammy-winning singer and per-former Celia Cruz. Born in Havana in 1925, Cruz served the bulk of her musical apprenticeship in Cuba before leaving for self-imposed exile in the US in 1960. But due to her longstanding opposition to the Castro regime, Cruz' records and music have remained largely unknown on the island, despite her enduring legacy elsewhere.

Far more influential on their home turf is the legendary salsa outfit Los Van Van, a band formed by Juan Formell in 1969 and one that still performs regularly at venues across Cuba. With Formell at the helm as the group's great improviser, poet, lyricist and social commentator, Los Van Van were one of the few modern Cuban groups to create their own unique musical genre – that of songo-salsa. The band also won top honors in 2000 when it memorably took home a Grammy for its classic album, *Llegó Van Van.* Despite the death of Formell in 2014, the band continues to play, record and tour.

Modern salsa mixed and merged further in the '80s and '90s, allying itself with new cutting-edge musical genres such as hip-hop, reggaeton and rap, before coming up with some hot new alternatives, most notably *timba* and songo-salsa.

Timba is, in many ways, Cuba's own experimental and fiery take on traditional salsa. Mixing New York sounds with Latin jazz, *nueva trova,* American funk, disco, hip-hop and even some classical influences, the music is more flexible and aggressive than standard salsa, incorporating greater elements of the island's potent Afro-Cuban culture. Many *timba* bands such as Bamboleo and La Charanga Habanera use funk riffs and rely on less-conventional Cuban instruments such as synthesizers and kick drums. Others – such as NG La Banda, formed in 1988 – have in-fused their music with a more jazzy dynamic.

Traditional jazz, considered the music of the enemy in the revolu-tion's most dogmatic days, has always seeped into Cuban sounds. Jesús 'Chucho' Valdés' band Irakere, formed in 1973, broke the Cuban music scene wide open with its heavy Afro-Cuban drumming laced with jazz and *son,* and the Cuban capital has a number of decent jazz clubs. Other musicians associated with Cuban jazz include pianist Gonzalo Rubalca-ba, Isaac Delgado and Adalberto Álvarez y Su Son.

Nueva Trova – the Soundtrack of a Revolution

The 1960s were heady days for radical new forms of musical expression. In the US Dylan released *Highway 61 Revisited,* in Britain the Beatles concocted *Sgt Pepper* while, in the Spanish-speaking world, musical activists such as Chilean Víctor Jara and Catalan Joan Manuel Serrat were turning their politically charged poems into passionate protest songs.

Determined to develop their own revolutionary music apart from the capitalist West, the innovative Cubans – under the stewardship of Haydee Santamaría, director at the influential Casa de las Américas – came up with *nueva trova.*

A caustic mix of probing philosophical lyrics and folksy melodic tunes, *nueva trova* was a direct descendant of pure *trova*, a bohemian form of guitar music that had originated in the Oriente in the late 19th century. Post-1959, *trova* became increasingly politicized and was taken up by more sophisticated artists such as Manzanillo-born Carlos Puebla, who provided an important bridge between old and new styles with his politically tinged ode to Che Guevara, 'Hasta Siempre Comandante' (1965).

Nueva trova came of age in February 1968 at the Primer Encuentro de la Canción Protesta, a concert organized at the Casa de las Américas in Havana and headlined by such rising stars as Silvio Rodríguez and Pablo Milanés. In a cultural context, it was Cuba's mini-Woodstock, an event that resounded forcefully among leftists worldwide as a revolutionary alternative to American rock 'n' roll.

In December 1972, the nascent *nueva trova* movement gained official sanction from the Cuban government during a music festival held in Manzanillo city commemorating the 16th anniversary of the *Granma*

CONTEMPORARY SOUNDS

Orishas Veteran rappers based mainly in France these days, Orishas returned after a hiatus in 2018 with the album *Gourmet,* featuring reggaeton artist Jacob Forever.

Jacob Forever A hot young reggaeton artist originally from Camagüey; his hit 'Hasta Que Se Seque El Malecón' (Until the boardwalk dries up) made waves in 2016.

Gente de Zona Collaborating with Marc Anthony and Enrique Iglesias, this reggaeton-salsaton group hit the roof winning Latin Grammys and other awards with recent energy-infused hits.

Interactivo An artist's collective that has showcased countless individual talent since its formation in 2001, including hip-hop artist Kumar, jazzy poet and instrumentalist Yusa, and founder jazz pianist Roberto Carcassés. Cuban fusion personified.

Buena Fe Creative rock duo from Guantánamo whose penetrating lyrics appeal to Cuba's awakening youth movement.

Haydée Milanés Jazzy singer and daughter of *trova* great, Pablo Milanés.

X-Alfonso The man behind Havana's exciting Fábrica de Arte Cubano is a king of many genres from Hendrix-style rock to Latin hip-hop. Listen out also for his sister M-Alfonso, another great fusion singer.

Diana Fuentes Singer with an R&B and funk bent who has worked with everyone who's anyone in the Cuban music scene, including X-Alfonso.

Yissy Probably Cuba's most talented drummer, Yissy García lays down her beat with a strong nod to Yoruba tradition.

landing. Highly influential throughout the Spanish-speaking world during the '60s and '70s, *nueva trova* has often acted as an inspirational source of protest music for the impoverished and downtrodden populations of Latin America, many of whom looked to Cuba for spiritual leadership in an era of corrupt dictatorships and US cultural hegemony. This solidarity was reciprocated by the likes of Rodríguez, who penned numerous internationally lauded classics such as 'Canción Urgente para Nicaragua' (in support of the Sandinistas), 'La Maza' and 'Canción para mi Soldado' (about the Angolan War).

Rap, Reggaeton & Beyond

The contemporary Cuban music scene is an interesting mix of enduring traditions, modern sounds, old hands and new blood. With low production costs, solid urban themes and lots of US-inspired crossover styles, rap and reggaeton have taken the younger generation by storm.

Born in the ugly concrete housing projects of Alamar, Havana, Cuban hip-hop, rather like its US counterpart, has gritty and impoverished roots. First beamed across the nation in the early 1980s when American rap was picked up on homemade rooftop antennae from Miami-based radio stations, the new music quickly gained ground among a young urban black population who were culturally redefining themselves during the inquietude of the Special Period. By the '90s groups such as Public Enemy and NWA were de rigueur on the streets of Alamar and by 1995 there was enough hip-hop to throw a festival.

Tempered by Latin influences and censored by the parameters of strict revolutionary thought, Cuban hip-hop has shied away from US stereotypes, instead taking on a progressive flavor all its own. Instrumentally the music uses *batá* drums, congas and electric bass, while lyrically the songs tackle important national issues such as sex tourism and the difficulties of the stagnant Cuban economy.

Despite being viewed early on as subversive and anti-revolutionary, Cuban hip-hop has gained unlikely support from inside the Cuban government, whose art-conscious legislators consider the music to have played a constructive social role in shaping the future of Cuban youth. Fidel Castro went one step further, describing hip-hop as 'the vanguard of the revolution' and – allegedly – trying his hand at rapping at a Havana baseball game.

The same cannot be said for reggaeton, a melding of hip-hop, Spanish reggae and Jamaican dance hall that emerged out of Panama in the 1990s and gained mainstream popularity in Puerto Rico in the mid-2000s. The Cuban government banned explicit reggaeton songs from TV and radio in 2012, and many hip-hop artists have expressed their discomfort with the genre's overtly sexist and narcissistic lyrics that glorify sex, violence and drug culture.

Nonetheless, reggaeton is the soundtrack of Cuban youth who share its cravings for Miami-style escapism and bling-like material goods. Pushing it underground has only increased reggaeton's popularity, spearheaded by homegrown artists such as Osmani Garcia, Jacob Forever and Gente de la Zona. These days, you'll hear it everywhere: around swimming pools, on street corners and booming out of car windows.

'Guajira Guantanamera' means 'country girl from Guantánamo.' Written by *trovador* (traditional singer/guitarist) Joseito Fernández, most of the original lyrics have been replaced with words from José Martí's *Versos sencillos*.

Landscape & Wildlife

Some 1250km long and between 31km and 193km wide, Cuba is the Caribbean's largest island with a total land area of 110,860 sq km. Shaped like one of its signature crocodiles and situated just south of the Tropic of Cancer, the country is actually an archipelago made up of 4195 smaller islets and coral reefs. Its unique ecosystems have been fascinating and perplexing scientists and naturalists ever since Alexander von Humboldt first mapped them in the early 1800s.

The Cuban Landscape

Formed by a volatile mixture of volcanic activity, plate tectonics and erosion, Cuba's landscape is a lush, varied concoction of mountains, caves, plains and *mogotes* (flat-topped hills). The highest point, Pico Turquino (1972m), is situated in the east among the Sierra Maestra's lofty triangular peaks. Further west, in the Sierra del Escambray, ruffled hilltops and gushing waterfalls straddle the borders of Cienfuegos, Villa Clara and Sancti Spíritus provinces. Rising like purple shadows in the far west, the 175km-long Cordillera de Guanguanico is a more diminutive range that includes the protected Sierra del Rosario Biosphere Reserve and the distinctive pincushion hills of the Valle de Viñales.

Lapped by the warm turquoise waters of the Caribbean Sea in the south, and the chop of the Atlantic Ocean in the north, Cuba's 5746km of coastline shelters more than 300 natural beaches and features one of the world's largest tracts of coral reef. Home to approximately 900 reported species of fish and more than 410 varieties of sponge and coral, the country's unspoiled coastline is a marine wonderland and a major reason why Cuba has become renowned as a diving destination.

Cuba's Isla Grande (main island) is the 17th-largest island in the world by area; slightly smaller than Newfoundland, but marginally bigger than Iceland.

The 7200m-deep Cayman Trench between Cuba and Jamaica forms the boundary of the North American and Caribbean plates. Tectonic movements have tilted the island over time, creating uplifted limestone cliffs along parts of the north coast and low mangrove swamps on the south. Over millions of years Cuba's limestone bedrock has been eroded by underground rivers, creating interesting geological features including the 'haystack' hills of Viñales and more than 20,000 caves countrywide.

As a sprawling archipelago, Cuba contains thousands of islands and keys (most uninhabited) in four major offshore groups: the Archipiélago de los Colorados, off northern Pinar del Río; the Archipiélago de Sabana-Camagüey (or Jardines del Rey), off northern Villa Clara and Ciego de Ávila; the Archipiélago de los Jardines de la Reina, off southern Ciego de Ávila; and the Archipiélago de los Canarreos, around Isla de la Juventud. Most visitors will experience one or more of these island idylls, as the majority of resorts, scuba diving and beaches are found in these regions.

As a narrow island, Cuba is never wider than 200km north to south. The longest river, the 343km-long Río Cauto, flows from the Sierra Maestra in a rough loop north of Bayamo, only navigable by small boats for 110km. To compensate, 632 *embalses* (reservoirs) or *presas* (dams), covering an area of more than 500 sq km altogether, have been created for irrigation and water supply; these supplement the almost unlimited groundwater held in Cuba's limestone bedrock.

Lying in the Caribbean's main hurricane region, Cuba has been hit by some blinders in recent years, notably 2012's Sandy, which wrought more than US$2 billion in damage and Hurricane Irma in 2017, a devastating category five, which gained the ominous title of Cuba's costliest ever storm.

Unesco & Ramsar Sites

The highest level of environmental protection in Cuba is provided by Unesco, which has created six biosphere reserves over the last 30 years. Biosphere reserves are areas of high biodiversity that rigorously promote conservation and sustainable practices. After a decade and a half of successful reforestation, the Sierra del Rosario became Cuba's first Unesco Biosphere Reserve in 1985. It was followed by Cuchillas del Toa (1987), Península de Guanahacabibes (1987), Baconao (1987), Ciénaga de Zapata (2000) and the Bahía de Buenavista (2000). Additionally, two of Cuba's nine Unesco World Heritage sites are considered 'natural' sites, ie nominated primarily for their ecological attributes. They are Parque Nacional Desembarco del Granma (1999), hailed for its uplifted marine terraces, and Parque Nacional Alejandro de Humboldt (2001), well known for its extraordinary endemism. Complementing the Unesco sites are half a dozen Ramsar Convention sites earmarked in 2001–02 to conserve Cuba's vulnerable wetlands. These lend added protection to the Ciénaga de Zapata and Bahía de Buenavista, and throw a lifeline to previously unprotected regions such as Isla de la Juventud's Lanier Swamp (prime crocodile territory), the expansive Río Cauto delta in Granma/Las Tunas, and the vital flamingo nesting sites on the north coasts of Camagüey and Ciego de Ávila provinces.

On top of its national parks and Unesco sites, Cuba protects land in flora and fauna reserves, eco-reserves and areas of managed resources, including the Sierra del Chorrillo in Camagüey and the Reserva Ecológica Varahicacos in Varadero.

National Parks

The definition of a national park is fluid in Cuba (some are referred to as natural parks or flora reserves) and there's no umbrella organization as in Canada or the USA. A handful of the 14 listed parks – most notably Ciénaga de Zapata – now lie within Unesco biosphere reserves or Ramsar Convention sites, meaning their conservation policies are better monitored. The country's first national park was Sierra del Cristal, established in 1930 (home to Cuba's largest pine forest), though it was 50 years before the authorities created another, Gran Parque Nacional Sierra Maestra (also known as Turquino), which safeguards Cuba's highest mountain. Other important parks include Viñales, with its *mogotes* (limestone monoliths), caves and tobacco plantations and Gran Piedra, near Santiago de Cuba, which is overlaid by the Baconao Unesco Biosphere Reserve. Two important offshore national parks off the south coast are the Jardines de la Reina, an archipelago diving haven off Ciego de Ávila Province's coast, and the rarely visited Cayos de San Felipe off the coast of Pinar del Río Province.

Parque Nacional Alejandro de Humboldt is named for the German naturalist Alexander von Humboldt (1769–1859) who visited the island between 1801 and 1804.

Agriculture

Agricultural land accounts for some 30% of the Cuban landmass and one in every five Cubans is engaged in some form of agricultural work.

Tobacco, grown primarily in prosperous Pinar del Río Province, is the third-most important industry for the Cuban economy. Like most farming in Cuba, it's still carried out in a way that's changed little in centuries, with fields plowed by yoked oxen, and is as photogenic to watch as it is gut-busting to do.

Sugar was an economic powerhouse before the US embargo. Production recovered during the Soviet era, peaking in 1970 but collapsing again in the 1990s. Many mills were closed during restructuring of the industry in 2002. Production has recently recovered slightly due to increased demand from China but still struggles to top two million tonnes per year.

The other big crop grown is rice, a staple in the Cuban diet, while coffee is cultivated on the Cordillera de la Gran Piedra near Santiago de Cuba.

Wildlife

Cuba has an unusual share of indigenous fauna to lure serious animal-watchers. Birds are the biggest draw and Cuba has over 350 different varieties, two dozen endemic. Head to the mangroves of Ciénaga de Zapata in Matanzas Province or to the Península de Guanahacabibes in Pinar del Río for the best sightings of *zunzuncito* (bee hummingbird), the world's smallest bird. At 6.5cm, it's not much longer than a toothpick. These areas are also home to the *tocororo* (Cuban trogon), Cuba's national bird. Other popular bird species include *cartacubas* (indigenous to Cuba), herons, spoonbills, parakeets and rarely seen Cuban pygmy owls.

Flamingos are abundant in Cuba's northern keys, though the largest nesting ground in the western hemisphere, located in Camagüey Province's Río Máximo delta, has been compromised by contamination.

Land mammals have been hunted almost to extinction with the largest indigenous survivor the friendly *jutía* (tree rat), a 4kg edible rodent that scavenges on isolated keys living in relative harmony with armies of inquisitive iguanas. The vast majority of Cuba's other 38 species of mammal are from the bat family.

Cuba harbors a species of frog so small and elusive that it wasn't discovered until 1996 in what is now Parque Nacional Alejandro de Humboldt near Baracoa. Still lacking a common name, the endemic amphibian is known as *Eleutherodactylus iberia;* it is less than 1cm in length, and has a range of only 100 sq km.

Other odd species include the *mariposa de cristal* (Cuban clear-winged butterfly), one of only two clear-winged butterflies in the world; the rare *manjuarí* (Cuban alligator gar), an ancient fish considered a living fossil; the *polimita*, a unique land snail distinguished by its festive yellow, red and brown bands and, discovered only in 2011, the endemic *Lucifuga,* a blind troglodyte fish.

Reptiles are well represented in Cuba. Aside from iguanas and lizards, there are 15 species of snake, none poisonous. Cuba's largest snake is the *majá,* a constrictor related to the anaconda that grows up to 4m in length; it's nocturnal and doesn't usually mess with humans. The endemic Cuban crocodile *(Crocodylus rhombifer)* is relatively small but agile on land and in water. Its 68 sharp teeth are specially adapted for crushing turtle shells. Crocs have suffered from major habitat loss in the last century though greater protection since the 1990s has seen numbers increase. Cuba has established a number of successful crocodile breeding farms *(criaderos),* the largest of which is at Guamá near the Bay of Pigs. Living in tandem with the Cuban croc is the larger American crocodile *(Crocodylus acutus)* found in the Zapata Swamps and in various marshy territories on Cuba's southern coast.

Cuba's marine life compensates for what the island lacks in land fauna. The manatee, the world's only herbivorous aquatic mammal, is found in the Bahía de Taco and the Península de Zapata, and whale sharks frequent the María la Gorda area at Cuba's western tip from November to February. Four turtle species (leatherback, loggerhead, green and hawksbill) are found in Cuban waters and they nest annually in isolated keys or on protected beaches in Península de Guanahacabibes.

Endangered Species

Due to habitat loss and persistent human hunting, many of Cuba's animals and birds are listed as endangered species. These include the critically endangered Cuban crocodile, which has the smallest habitat range

---

Cuba's Longest River

Name *Río Cauto*

Length *343km*

Navigable length *110km*

Basin area *8928 sq km*

Source *Sierra Maestra Mountains*

Mouth *Caribbean Sea*

of any crocodile, existing only in 300 sq km of the Ciénaga de Zapata (Zapata Swamp) and in the Lanier Swamp on Isla de la Juventud. Protected since 1996, wild numbers now hover at around 3000.

Other vulnerable species include the *jutía* (tree rat), which was hunted mercilessly during the Special Period, when hungry Cubans tracked them for their meat (they still do – in fact, it is considered a delicacy); the tree boa, a native snake that lives in rapidly diminishing woodland areas; and the elusive *carpintero real* (ivory-billed woodpecker) spotted after a 40-year gap in the Parque Nacional Alejandro de Humboldt near Baracoa in the late 1980s, but not seen since.

The seriously endangered West Indian manatee, while protected from illegal hunting, continues to suffer from a variety of human threats, most notably from contact with boat propellers, suffocation caused by fishing nets and poisoning from residues pumped into rivers from sugar factories.

Cuba has an ambiguous attitude toward turtle hunting. Hawksbill turtles are protected under the law, though a clause allows for up to 500 of them to be captured per year in certain areas (Camagüey and Isla de la Juventud). Travelers will occasionally encounter *tortuga* (turtle), caught illegally, on the menu in places such as Baracoa.

The Caribbean manatee can grow 4.5m long and weigh up to 600kg. It can consume up to 50kg of plant life a day.

Plants

Cuba is synonymous with the palm tree; through songs, symbols, landscapes and legends the two are inextricably linked. The national tree is the *palma real* (royal palm), and it's central to the country's coat of arms and the Cristal beer logo. It's believed there are 20 million royal palms in

CUBA'S PROTECTED AREAS

AREA NAME	YEAR DESIGNATED	OUTSTANDING FEATURES
UNESCO BIOSPHERE RESERVES		
Sierra del Rosario	1985	eco practices
Cuchillos del Toa	1987	primary rainforest
Península de Guanahacabibes	1987	turtle nesting site
Baconao	1987	coffee culture
Ciénaga de Zapata	2000	largest wetlands in Caribbean
Buenavista	2000	karst formations
RAMSAR CONVENTION SITES		
Ciénaga de Zapata	2001	largest wetlands in Caribbean
Buenavista	2002	karst formations
Ciénaga de Lanier	2002	unusual mosaic of ecosystems
Humedal del Norte de Ciego de Ávila	2002	unique coastal lakes
Humedal Delta del Cauto	2002	large population of aquatic birds
Humedal Río Máximo-Cagüey	2002	significant flamingo nesting site
'NATURAL' UNESCO WORLD HERITAGE SITES		
Parque Nacional Desembarco del Granma	1999	pristine marine terraces
Parque Nacional Alejandro de Humboldt	2001	high endemism

Cuba and locals will tell you that wherever you stand on the island, you'll always be within sight of one of them. These majestic trees reach up to 40m in height and are easily identified by their lithe trunk and green stalk at the top. There are also *cocotero* (coconut palm); *palma barrigona* (big-belly palm) with its characteristic bulge; and the extremely rare *palma corcho* (cork palm). The latter is a link with the Cretaceous period (between 65 and 135 million years ago) and is cherished as a living fossil. You can see examples of it on the grounds of the Museo de Ciencias Naturales Sandalio de Noda in Pinar del Río. Cienfuegos' Jardín Botánico also exhibits some 280 different palm varieties. Cuba itself has 90 types of palm tree.

It is estimated that Cuba harbors between 6500 and 7000 different species of plant, almost half of which are endemic.

Other important trees include mangroves, which protect the Cuban shoreline from erosion and provide an important habitat for small fish and birds. Mangroves account for 26% of forests and cover almost 5% of the coast; Cuba ranks ninth in the world in terms of mangrove density, with the most extensive swamps situated in the Ciénaga de Zapata.

The largest native pine forests grow on Isla de la Juventud (the former Isle of Pines), in western Pinar del Río, in eastern Holguín's Sierra Cristal and in central Guantánamo. These forests are especially susceptible to fire damage, and pine reforestation has been a particular headache for Cuba's environmentalists.

Rainforests exist at higher altitudes – between approximately 500m and 1500m – in the Sierra del Escambray, Sierra Maestra and Macizo de Sagua-Baracoa mountains. Original rainforest species include ebony and mahogany, but today most reforestation is in eucalyptus, which is graceful and fragrant, but invasive.

Dotted liberally across the island, ferns, cacti and orchids contribute hundreds of species, many endemic, to Cuba's cornucopia of plant life. For the best concentrations check out the botanical gardens in Santiago de Cuba for ferns and cacti and Soroa in Artemisa Province for orchids. Most orchids bloom from November to January, and one of the best places to see them is in the Reserva Sierra del Rosario. The national flower is the graceful *mariposa* (butterfly jasmine); you'll know it by its white floppy petals and strong perfume.

Endemic Fauna

Cuban crocodile

Bee hummingbird

Tocororo (bird)

Jutía (tree rat)

Cuban gar (fish)

Eleutherodactylus Iberia (frog)

Cuban boa (snake)

Cuban red bat

Medicinal plants are widespread in Cuba due largely to shortages of prescription medicines. Pharmacies are well stocked with effective tinctures such as aloe (for cough and congestion) and a bee by-product *propólio*, used for everything from stomach amoebas to respiratory infections. On the home front, every Cuban patio has a pot of *orégano de la tierra* (Cuban oregano), a cold remedy whipped up into a wonder elixir with lime juice, honey and hot water.

Environmental Issues

Most of Cuba's environmental threats are of human origin and relate either to pollution or habitat loss, often through deforestation. Efforts to conserve the archipelago's diverse ecology really began in 1978, when Cuba established the National Committee for the Protection and Conservation of Natural Resources and the Environment (Comarna).

To reverse 400 years of deforestation and habitat destruction, the body created green belts and initiated ambitious reforestation campaigns. Comarna oversees national and international environmental legislation, including adherence to international treaties that govern Cuba's Unesco Biosphere Reserves and Unesco World Heritage sites.

Cuba's greatest environmental problems are aggravated by an economy struggling to survive. As the country pins its hopes on tourism, a contradictory environmental policy has evolved. All-inclusive resorts may be good for jobs and the economy, but their continued rollout (a good half-dozen opened between 2017 and 2019 alone) has placed added strain on the ecosystems of Cuba's northern keys. With ally Venezuela ailing, Cuba's oil supply has destabilized. The government has plans to start drilling for oil off the northwest coast, though a spill would be devastating. Therein lies the dilemma: how can a developing nation provide for its people *and* maintain ecological standards?

Deforestation

At the time of Columbus' arrival in 1492, 95% of Cuba was covered in virgin forest. By 1959, thanks to wholesale land-clearing for sugarcane and citrus plantations, this area had been reduced to 16%. Large-scale tree-planting and the organization of protected parks has seen this figure creep back up to 36%, although only 9% of this is undisturbed primary forest.

Las Terrazas in Pinar del Río Province provided a blueprint for reforestation in the late 1960s, restoring hectares of denuded woodland to prevent ecological disaster. More recent efforts have focused on safeguarding the Caribbean's last virgin rainforest in Parque Nacional Alejandro de Humboldt and adding protective forest fringes to wetlands in the Río Cauto delta.

Wildlife & Habitat Loss

Maintaining healthy animal habitats is crucial in Cuba, a country with high levels of endemism and hence a higher threat of species extinction. The problem is exacerbated by the narrow range of endemic animals, such as the Cuban crocodile that lives almost exclusively in the Ciénaga de Zapata, or the equally rare *Eleutherodactylus iberia* (the world's smallest frog). The latter has a range of just 100 sq km and exists only in the Parque Nacional Alejandro de Humboldt, whose formation in 2001 undoubtedly saved it from extinction. Other areas under threat include the giant flamingo nesting sites on the Archipiélago de Sabana-Camagüey, and Moa, where contaminated water runoff has played havoc with the coastal mangrove ecosystems favored by manatees.

Building new roads and airports, and the frenzied construction of giant resorts on virgin beaches, exacerbate the clash between human activity and environmental protection. The grossly shrunken extent of the Reserva Ecológica Varahicacos in Varadero due to encroaching resorts is one example. Cayo Coco – part of an important Ramsar-listed wetland that sits adjacent to a fast-developing hotel strip – is another.

Cuba's Highest Mountains

Pico Turquino
1972m, Santiago de Cuba Province

Pico Cuba
1872m, Santiago de Cuba Province

Pico Bayamesa
1730m, Granma Province

LANDSCAPE & WILDLIFE ENVIRONMENTAL ISSUES

BIRDWATCHING

Cuba offers a birdwatching bonanza year-round and no serious ornithologist should enter the country without their binoculars. Your experience will be enhanced by the level of expertise shown by many of Cuba's naturalists and guides in the key birdwatching zones.

Areas with specialist birdwatching trails or trips include the Cueva las Perlas (p201) trail in Parque Nacional Península de Guanahacabibes, the Maravillas de Viñales (p190) trail in Parque Nacional Viñales, the Sendero la Serafina (p156) in the Reserva Sierra del Rosario, the Observación de Bermejas (p233) tour in Gran Parque Natural Montemar and the Sendero de las Aves in Hacienda la Belén (p338) in Camagüey Province.

Must-sees include the *tocororo* (Cuban trogon), the *zunzuncito* (bee hummingbird), the Cuban parakeet, the Antillean palm swift, the *cartacuba* (Cuban tody; an indigenous Cuban bird) and, of course, the flamingo – preferably in a flock. Good spots for some DIY birdwatching are on Cayo Romano and adjacent Cayo Sabinal, although you'll need a car to get there. Specialists and ivory-billed-woodpecker seekers will enjoy Parque Nacional Alejandro de Humboldt.

Overfishing (including turtles and lobster for tourist consumption), agricultural runoff, industrial pollution and inadequate sewage treatment have contributed to the decay of coral reefs. Diseases such as yellow band, black band and nuisance algae have begun to appear. The rounding up of wild dolphins as entertainers in tourist-oriented *delfinarios* (dolphinariums) has also rankled many activists.

Aging Infrastructure & Pollution

As soon as you arrive in Havana or Santiago de Cuba, the air pollution hits you like a sharp slap on the face. Airborne particles, old trucks belching black smoke and by-products from burning garbage are just some of the culprits. Havana's century-old sewer system – built for a population that has since quadrupled – is on the point of complete breakdown. Sewage blockages affect over half of city residents and drinking-water leaks sabotage conservation efforts. Cement factories, sugar refineries and other heavy industries have also made their (dirty) mark.

The nickel mines engulfing Moa serve as stark examples of industrial concerns taking precedence: some of Cuba's wildest landscape has turned into a barren wasteland of lunar proportions. Unfortunately there are no easy solutions; nickel is one of Cuba's largest exports, a raw material the economy couldn't do without.

While old American cars paint a romantic picture to tourists, they're hardly fuel efficient. Add to that the use of substandard fuels due to economic constraints. Then there's the public transport – even Fidel Castro went on the record to lament the adverse health effects of Cuba's filthy buses.

> Approximately 2% of Cuba's arable land is given over to coffee production and the industry supports a workforce of 265,000.

Environmental Successes

On the bright side of the environmental equation is the Cuban government's enthusiasm for reforestation and protecting natural areas – especially since the mid-1980s – along with its willingness to confront mistakes from the past. Its most stunning achievement is reef conservation in Marine Protected Areas. Cuba has also taken on climate change and rising sea levels with preparatory measures.

Havana Harbor, once Latin America's most polluted, has been undergoing a massive cleanup, as has the Río Almendares, which cuts through the heart of the city. Sulfur emissions from oil wells near Varadero have been reduced, and environmental regulations for developments are now enforced by the Ministry of Science, Technology and the Environment. Fishing regulations have become increasingly strict. Striking the balance between Cuba's immediate needs and the future of its environment is a pressing challenge.

Las Terrazas is the nation's most obvious eco-success, though there have been others, including the implementation of wind farm sites and the first solar farm, opened in Cienfuegos Province in 2014. In terms of fauna, the nation can point to major crocodile reintroduction programs and successful sea turtle conservation. A more recent development has been a surge in eco-fincas and farm-to-table restaurants, mostly inspired by the growing private sector.

Survival Guide

Hurricane Planning

Caribbean hurricanes are born 3000km away off the west coast of Africa, where pockets of low pressure draw high winds toward them and the Earth's rotation molds them into their familiar counterclockwise swirl. The official hurricane season in Cuba runs from June to November. The strongest and rarest of hurricanes, Category 5, typically build up in July and August and pack winds that exceed 250km/h. Cuba is hit by a major hurricane, on average, once every four years. Recent ones include Irma (2017), Sandy (2012) and Gustav (2008).

Before You Go

➡ Always check that your travel insurance covers hurricanes. This is inexpensive and must be purchased at least 24 hours before a hurricane is named; it will cover you for changes in your travel plans. If you have booked a vacation package with an overseas operator, there are usually procedures in place vis-à-vis hurricanes. This might involve options to change your dates, relocate to another destination, or cancel your trip altogether. If you are traveling in hurricane season, always check ahead when booking.

➡ If a storm is developing when you are due to travel, begin monitoring local television and radio or the website of the US National Hurricane Center (www.nhc.noaa.gov) run by the US National Oceanic and Atmospheric Administration. Embassies also usually post warnings on their homepages.

➡ If your trip is after a hurricane, it may or may not be appropriate to travel. Where widespread infrastructural damage has been done, your trip may not be possible or desirable. If your destination got off relatively lightly, sticking to your plans may be a good idea, as many islands affected by hurricanes have suffered a 'second disaster' through loss of tourism.

On the Ground

➡ Cuba has an excellent record in dealing with hurricanes and, as a result, casualties are usually mercifully light. Indeed, it has been estimated that you are 15 times more likely to be killed by a hurricane in the US than in Cuba. A high level of preparedness coupled with good meteorological predictions and well-rehearsed drills from a disciplined population ensure things generally run smoothly. Stay tuned and obey all instructions. Locals are invariably well-versed in what to do.

➡ If you are staying in a tourist resort when a hurricane approaches, you will be evacuated in advance to a safe area with help from the Cuban authorities.

➡ When a storm is a day or more out, be sure to stock up on bottled water, non-perishable food and prescription medications, plus a flashlight, batteries and first-aid kit. If driving a rental car, be sure the tank is full of gas. In assessing the danger, keep an eye on rain and wind speed forecasts.

➡ When the storm approaches, be sure your mobile phone is fully charged, as well as any other devices you might need. Place your cash, passport and any important identification in a safe place. Stay away from trees and power lines.

➡ Check updates online or on the radio frequently.

➡ After the storm hits, have plenty of patience. Prepare to stand in line for hours for basic supplies or wait for aid to arrive. If you have been evacuated from a resort, procedures will be in place to relocate you, or get you home safely. If you are traveling independently, wait for government announcements and follow the locals.

Directory A–Z

Accessible Travel

Cuba's inclusive culture extends to disabled travelers, and while facilities may be lacking, the generous nature of Cubans generally compensates when it can.

However, with battered buses, potholed sidewalks and poorly maintained buildings, some of which haven't been renovated since the 1950s, independent travel can be difficult for people with physical challenges. Many older buildings in Cuba don't have elevators or, if they do, they are regularly out of order. Similarly, public buses lack facilities for the physically impaired. For comfort and reliability, modern Cubataxis are the best way of getting around.

Steps and curbs are a perennial problem. Ramps are often not available and, when they are, they can be ridiculously steep. Only the more expensive hotels offer specially designed accessible rooms with wide doors and customized bathrooms. If it's your first time in Cuba, it might be better to book into an all-inclusive resort that caters for physically challenged travelers. Start your inquiries at the part foreign-owned Meliá and Iberostar chains in places like Varadero, Cayo Coco and Guardalavaca.

Sight-impaired travelers will be helped across streets and given priority in lines. Etecsa phone centers have telephone equipment for the hearing-impaired, and TV programs are broadcast with closed captioning.

Hotels with special facilities for the physically impaired include:

Hotel Iberostar Parque Central (Map p78; ☑7-860-6627; www. iberostar.com; Neptuno, btwn Agramonte & Paseo de Martí; r incl breakfast USD$490-570; P@☎☀), Havana

Hotel Saratoga (Map p78; ☑7-868-1000; www.hotel-saratoga. com; Paseo de Martí No 603; d/ ste USD$506/605; P@☎☀), Havana

Meliá Internacional (Map p206; ☑45-62-31-00; www.melia. com; Av Las Américas Km 1; s/d USD$323/465; @☎☀), Varadero

Meliá Varadero (Map p206; ☑45-66-70-13; Carretera las Morlas; s/d all-inclusive USD$283/405; P@☎☀), Varadero

Download Lonely Planet's free Accessible Travel guide from https://shop.lonely-planet.com/categories/accessible-travel

Customs Regulations

Cuban customs regulations are complicated. For the full up-to-date scoop see www. aduana.gob.cu.

Entering Cuba

Travelers are allowed to bring in personal belongings including photography equipment, binoculars, a musical instrument, radio, personal computer, tent, fishing rod, bicycle, canoe and other sporting gear, and up to 10kg of medicines. Canned, processed and dried food are no problem, nor are pets (as long as they have veterinary certification and proof of rabies vaccination).

Items that do not fit into the categories mentioned above are subject to a 100% customs duty to a maximum of USD$1000.

Items prohibited from entry into Cuba include narcotics, explosives, pornography, electrical appliances broadly defined, light motor vehicles, car engines and products of animal origin.

Leaving Cuba

You are allowed to export 50 boxed cigars duty-free (or 23 singles) and up to US$5000 (or the equivalent) in cash.

Exporting undocumented art and items of cultural patrimony is restricted and involves fees. Normally, when you buy art you will be given an official 'seal' at the point of sale. Check this before you buy. If you don't get one, you'll need to obtain one from the **Registro Nacional de Bienes Culturales** (Calle 17 No 1009, btwn Calles 10 & 12; ☉9am-noon Mon-Fri) in

Havana. Bring the objects here for inspection, fill in a form, pay a fee of between USD$10 and USD$30, which covers from one to five pieces of artwork, and return 24 hours later to pick up the certificate.

Travelers should check local import laws in their home country regarding Cuban cigars. Some countries, including Australia, charge duty on imported Cuban cigars.

Discount Cards

There are no tourist discount cards in Cuba.

Students who can provide proof of enrollment at a Cuban university or college for a minimum stay of six months should be issued with a *carnet* – the identification document that allows foreigners to pay for museums, transport (including *colectivos*; shared taxis) and theater performances in Cuban pesos (CUP).

Electricity

The electrical current in Cuba is 110V, with 220V in many tourist hotels and resorts.

110V/220V/60Hz

Embassies & Consulates

All embassies are in Havana, and most are open from 8am to noon on weekdays. Australia is represented in the Canadian Embassy. New Zealand is represented in the UK Embassy. Canada has additional consulates in Varadero and Guardalavaca.

Austrian Embassy (☎7-204-2825; Av 5A No 6617, cnr Calle 70, Miramar)

Canadian Embassy (☎7-204-2516; Calle 30 No 518, Miramar)

Danish Consulate (☎7-866-8128; Paseo de Martí No 20, 4th fl)

Dutch Embassy (☎7-204-2511; Calle 8 No 307, btwn Avs 3 & 5, Miramar)

French Embassy (☎7-201-3131; Calle 14 No 312, btwn Avs 3 & 5, Miramar)

German Embassy (☎7-833-2539; Calle 13, cnr Calle B)

Italian Embassy (☎7-204-5615; Av 5 No 402, cnr Calle 4, Miramar)

Japanese Embassy (☎7-204-3355; Miramar Trade Center, cnr Av 3 & Calle 80, Miramar)

Mexican Embassy (☎7-204-7722; Calle 12 No 518, cnr Av 7, Miramar)

Spanish Embassy (☎7-866-8025; Cárcel No 51)

Swedish Embassy (☎7-204-2831; Calle 34 No 510, Miramar)

Swiss Embassy (☎7-204-2611; Av 5 No 2005, btwn Avs 20 & 22, Miramar)

UK Embassy (☎7-214-2200; Calle 34 No 702, Miramar)

US Embassy (☎7-839-4100; Calzada, btwn Calles L & M)

Food

Cuban cuisine – popularly known as *comida criolla* – has improved immensely since privatization laws, passed in 2011, inspired a plethora of pioneering restaurants to take root, particularly in Havana. Travel in rural areas, however, and Cuban food can still be limited and insipid.

Cuban meals are characterized by *congrí* (rice flecked with black beans), meat (primarily pork, closely followed by chicken and beef), fried plantains (green bananas), salad (limited to seasonal ingredients) and root vegetables, usually yuca (cassava) and *calabaza* (pumpkin-like squash).

Pescado (fish) is also readily available. Though you'll come across dorado, *aguja* (swordfish), and occasionally octopus and crab in some of the specialist seafood places, you're more likely to see *pargo* (red snapper), lobster or prawns.

Cubans are also aficionados of ice cream and the nuances of different flavors are heatedly debated. Coppelia ice cream is legendary, but ridiculously cheap tubs of other brands (440g for USD$1) can be procured almost everywhere, and even the machine-dispensed peso stuff ain't half bad.

Vegetarians

In a land with a recent history of rationing and food shortages, strict vegetarians and vegans will have a hard time. Cubans don't traditionally understand vegetarianism, and when they do (or when they *say* they do), it can be summarized rather adroitly with one key word: omelet – or, at a stretch, scrambled eggs. However, things are changing. Cooks at casas particulares (rooms in private homes), who may already have had experience cooking meatless dishes for other travelers, are usually pretty good at accommodating vegetarians. The same goes for private restaurants, many of which have started to develop menus with vegetarian sections. Havana and Viñales have recently sprouted Cuba's first decent full-blown vegetarian restaurants.

Climate

Havana

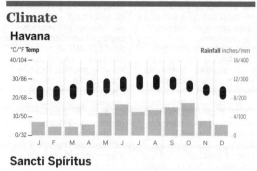

Sancti Spíritus

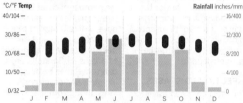

Santiago De Cuba

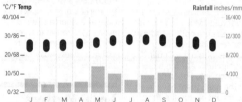

Where to Dine

GOVERNMENT-RUN RESTAURANTS

Government-run restaurants vary wildly. The cheaper ones are often pretty grim and are notorious for handing you a nine-page menu (in Spanish) when the only thing available is fried chicken. Food is often limp and unappetizing and discourse with bored waiters can be worthy of a *Monty Python* sketch (whatever you do, don't complain about a dirty fork). That said, things have got progressively better in the last decade. The state-run Palmares group manages a wide variety of restaurants countrywide from bog-standard beach shacks to the *New York Times*–lauded **El Aljibe** (📞7-204-1583/4; Av 7, btwn Calles 24 & 26, Miramar; mains USD$12-15; ⏰noon-mid-night) in Miramar, Havana. There are a few highlights among the government-run restaurants in Habana Vieja, and the state-run Gaviota company has recently tarted up some of its old staples around the country.

State-run restaurants generally charge in Cuban pesos. However, as employees also earn their salaries in Cuban pesos, tips (preferably in US$) are highly appreciated.

PRIVATE RESTAURANTS

First established in 1995 during the economic chaos of the Special Period, private restaurants (sometimes called *paladares*) owe much of their success to the sharp increase in tourist traffic in Cuba, coupled with the bold experimentation of local chefs who, despite a paucity of decent ingredients, have heroically managed to keep the age-old traditions of Cuban cooking alive. They have proliferated since new business laws were passed in 2011, especially in Havana. Private restaurant meals are generally more expensive than their state-run equivalents, costing anything between USD$8 and USD$30.

In the last decade, private restaurants have become more adventurous, plying an increasing array of international and fusion dishes. Italian-themed and, to a lesser extent, Spanish-themed restaurants are popular all over the island. Havana has recently sprouted places specializing in Lebanese, Russian and Iranian food.

Health

From a medical point of view, Cuba is generally safe as long as you're reasonably careful about what you eat and drink.

Prevention is the key to staying healthy while traveling around Cuba. Travelers who receive the recommended vaccines and follow commonsense precautions usually come away with nothing more than a little diarrhea.

Before You Go

HEALTH INSURANCE

Since May 2010, Cuba has made it obligatory for all foreign visitors to have medical insurance. Random checks are made at the airport, so ensure you bring a printed copy of your policy.

Should you end up in hospital, call **Asistur** (📞7-866-4499, emergency 7-866-8527; www.asistur.cu; Paseo de Martí No 208; ⏰9am-3pm Mon-Fri) for help with insurance and medical assistance. In addition to its office in Havana, it has offices in Varadero, Cayo Coco, Guardalavaca and Santiago de Cuba.

Outpatient treatment at international clinics is reasonably priced, but emergency and prolonged hospitalization gets expensive (the free medical system for Cubans should only be used when there is no other option).

Should you have to purchase medical insurance on arrival, you will pay from USD$3 per day for coverage of up to USD$25,000 in medical expenses (for illness) and USD$5000 for repatriation of a sick person.

RECOMMENDED VACCINATIONS

There are no mandatory vaccinations. Check with your GP before you go regarding personal requirements.

In Cuba

AVAILABILITY & COST OF HEALTHCARE

The Cuban government has established a for-profit health system for foreigners called Servimed (www.smcsalud.cu), which is entirely separate from the free, not-for-profit system that takes care of Cuban citizens. There are more than 40 Servimed health centers across the island, offering primary care as well as a variety of specialty and high-tech services. If you're staying in a hotel, the usual way to access the system is to ask the manager for a physician referral. Servimed centers accept walk-ins. While Cuban hospitals provide some free emergency treatment for foreigners, this should only be used when there is no other option. Remember that in Cuba medi-

cal resources are scarce and the local populace should be given priority in free health-care facilities.

Almost all doctors and hospitals expect payment in cash, regardless of whether you have travel health insurance or not. The cost for a consultation is between USD$35 and USD$50. Hotel clinics tend to be the more expensive options. If you develop a life-threatening medical problem, you'll probably want to be evacuated to a country with state-of-the-art medical care. Since this may cost tens of thousands of dollars, be sure you have insurance to cover this before you depart.

INFECTIOUS DISEASES

The most common travel-related diseases, such as dysentery and hepatitis, are acquired by the consumption of contaminated food and water. Mosquito-borne illnesses are not a significant concern on most of the islands within the Cuban archipelago. Although the Zika virus has been present in the past, there have been no recent outbreaks. Pregnant women or women who plan to get pregnant and their partners should check travel advisories before going to Cuba.

TAP WATER

Tap water in Cuba is not reliably safe to drink and outbreaks of cholera have been recorded in recent years. Bottled water called Ciego Montero rarely costs more than USD$1, but is sometimes not available in small towns. Stock up in the cities when going on long bus or car journeys.

Internet Access

State-run telecommunications company Etecsa has a monopoly as Cuba's internet service provider. For public internet access, almost every provincial town has an

Etecsa *telepuntos* (internet cafe–cum call center) where you can wait in line to enter and buy a one-hour user card (USD$1) with scratch-off *usuario* (code) and *contraseña* (password) to use at computers on-site or in a public wi-fi area (usually the central plaza of a town). Cards can be used for multiple internet sessions.

There are no independent internet cafes outside the *telepuntos*. However, these days most hotels and a growing number of casas particulares (private homestays) have wi-fi (although the signal is often weak and you'll need an Etecsa scratch-card to access it). Scratch-cards can sometimes be bought in hotels and casas particulares, though often at inflated rates.

Although connections are often slow and temperamental, particularly at peak times (late afternoon and early evening), internet in Cuba has improved greatly in the last five years and is likely to continue to do so.

Legal Matters

Cuban police are everywhere and they're usually very friendly – more likely to ask you for a date than a bribe. Corruption is a serious offense in Cuba, and typically no one wants to get mixed up in it. Getting caught out without identification is never good; carry some around just in case (a driver's license, a copy of your passport or a student ID card should be sufficient).

Drugs are prohibited in Cuba, though you may still get offered marijuana and cocaine on the streets of Havana. Penalties for buying, selling, holding or taking drugs are serious, and Cuba is making a concerted effort to treat demand and curtail supply; it is only the foolish traveler who partakes while on a Cuban vacation.

LGBTIQ+ Travelers

While Cuba isn't a full-blown queer destination (yet), it's more tolerant than many other Latin American countries. The hit movie *Fresa y Chocolate* (Strawberry and Chocolate; 1994) sparked a national dialogue about homosexuality. Activist Mariela Castro, the daughter of Raúl, has led the way in much-needed LGBT reforms and changing social perceptions. Today Cuba is pretty tolerant, all things considered, and LGBT travelers shouldn't have many problems.

Same-sex marriage isn't yet legal in Cuba, although it's probably only a matter of time before it becomes so (President Díaz-Canel has expressed his support). Discrimination on the basis of sexual orientation and gender is illegal.

Lesbianism is less tolerated and seldom discussed and you'll see very little open displays of affection between female partners. There are occasional *fiestas para chicas* (not necessarily all-girl parties but close); ask around at the **Cine Yara** (Map p90; cnr Calles 23 & L) in Havana.

The best gay nightlife scenes are in Havana and Santa Clara, where drag shows are weekly occurrences in **Cafe Cantante Mi Habana** (Map p90; ☑7-879-0710; cnr Paseo & Calle 39, Havana; cover USD$10; ☺8pm-3am), **Cabaret Las Vegas** (Map p90; Calzada de la Infanta No 104, btwn Calles 25 & 27, Havana; entry USD$5; ☺10pm-4am) and **Club Mejunje** (Map p262; Marta Abreu No 107, Santa Clara; ☺4pm-1am Tue-Sun),. Countrywide, many of Cuba's best casas particulares (private homestays) have gay owners.

Maps

Signage is awful in Cuba, so a good map is essential for drivers and cyclists alike.

The comprehensive *Guía de Carreteras,* published in Italy, includes the best maps available in Cuba. If it doesn't come free when you rent a car, you can download it at www.cubamappa.com. It has a complete index, a detailed Havana map and useful information in English, Spanish, Italian and French. Handier still is the all-purpose *Automapa Nacional,* available at hotel shops and car-rental offices.

The best map published outside Cuba is the Freytag & Berndt 1:1.25 million *Cuba* map. The island map is good, and it has indexed town plans of Havana, Playas del Este, Varadero, Cienfuegos, Camagüey and Santiago de Cuba.

For good basic maps, pick up one of the provincial *Guías* available in Infotur offices.

Money

Cuba's official currency is the Cuban peso (CUP$). The country's erstwhile 'second' currency, Cuban convertibles (CUC$) was abolished and taken out of circulation between January and June 2021. Since 2020, it has also been legal to use US dollars in Cuba.

At the time of writing, Cuban pesos were pegged 24:1 with the US dollar, although there was a rampant black market.

The best currency to bring to Cuba is US dollars which circulate widely especially among private businesspeople. Canadian dollars, euros and pounds sterling can also be readily exchanged. Australian dollars are not accepted anywhere in Cuba.

State-run businesses in Cuba deal in Cuban pesos (CUP$). Private sector businesses generally prefer payment in US dollars. As a result, it is best to travel around the country with a mix of the two currencies.

You cannot buy Cuban pesos outside the country.

Cadeca branches in every city and town sell Cuban pesos. There is almost always a branch at the local *agropecuario* (vegetable market). Since the abolition of convertibles, there has been rampant black market in money changing in Cuba with CUP$/US$ rates running as high as 50:1. We do not recommend changing money on the black market.

ATMs & Credit Cards

Cuba has traditionally been a cash economy, but credit cards have become more readily accepted in the last few years, especially in resorts and other state-run hotels. There are a growing number of ATMs.

US debit and credit cards, or cards connected to US banks, cannot be used.

While services can still be booked with credit cards from the USA on the internet, inside Cuba it's another story.

When weighing up whether to use a credit card or cash, bear in mind that the charges levied by Cuban banks are similar for both (around 3%). However, your home bank may charge additional fees for ATM/credit-card transactions. An increasing number of debit cards work in Cuba, but it's best to check with both your home bank and the local Cuban bank before using them. 'Visa debit' is usually the best bet.

Ideally, it pays to arrive in Cuba with a stash of cash and a credit and debit card as backup.

Almost all private business in Cuba, such as at *casas particulares* (private homestays), is still conducted in cash, preferably US dollars.

Cash advances can be drawn from credit cards, but the commission is the same. Check with your home bank before you leave, as many banks won't authorize large withdrawals in foreign countries unless you notify them of your travel plans first.

ATMs are becoming more common. This being Cuba, it is wise to only use ATMs when the bank is open, in case any problems occur.

Cash

Credit cards have become more common in Cuba in the last few years, although it's still necessary to bring some cash. Use a concealed money belt and keep the cash on you or in your hotel's safety deposit box at all times.

It's better to ask for small bills when you're changing money, as many Cuban businesses (taxis, restaurants etc) can't change anything bigger and the words *no hay cambio* (no change) echo everywhere. If desperate, you can always break big bills at hotels.

DENOMINATIONS

Cuban pesos (CUP$) are sometimes called *moneda nacional* (abbreviated MN) or *pesos Cubanos* or simply pesos.

The peso comes in notes of one, five, 10, 20, 50 and 100 pesos; and coins of one (rare), five and 20 centavos, and one and three pesos. The five-centavo coin is called a *medio*, the 20-centavo coin a *peseta*. Centavos are also called *kilos*.

Tipping

Tipping in Cuba is important. Since most Cubans earn their money in Cuban pesos (CUP$), leaving a tip of US$1 (CUP$24) or more makes a huge difference.

Resorts/hotels Tip for good service with bellhops, service staff.

Musicians Carry small notes to tip musicians in bars/restaurants.

Restaurants Standard 10%, or up to 15% if service is excellent.

Taxis Tip 10% if you are on the meter, otherwise agree full fare beforehand.

Post

Letters and postcards sent to Europe and the US take about a month to arrive. While *sellos* (stamps) are sold in Cuban pesos and convertibles, correspondence bearing the latter has a better chance of arriving. Postcards cost USD$0.75 to all countries. Letters cost around USD$0.75 to the Americas, USD$0.85 to Europe and USD$0.95 to all other countries. Prepaid postcards, including international postage, are available at most hotel shops and post offices and are the surest bet for successful delivery. For important mail, you're better off using DHL, which is located in all the major cities.

Public Holidays

Officially Cuba has nine public holidays. Other important national days to look out for include January 28 (anniversary of the birth of José Martí); April 19 (Bay of Pigs victory); October 8 (anniversary of the death of Che Guevara); October 28 (anniversary of the death of Camilo Cienfuegos); and December 7 (anniversary of the death of Antonio Maceo).

January 1 Triunfo de la Revolución (Liberation Day)

January 2 Día de la Victoria (Victory of the Armed Forces)

May 1 Día de los Trabajadores (International Worker's Day)

July 25–27 Día de la Rebeldía Nacional (Commemoration of Moncada Attack)

October 10 Día de la Independencia (Independence Day)

December 25 Navidad (Christmas Day)

December 31 New Year's Eve

Safe Travel

Cuba is safer than most Latin American countries. Indeed, it has been voted among the safest country in the world for tourists. Violent attacks are extremely rare and city streets are generally chill, even after dark. Be aware of the following.

➡ Petty theft and pickpockets

➡ Short-changing in bars and restaurants

➡ Street hustlers selling cigars

➡ Dual currency scams

➡ For women, sexist banter and unwanted attention from men

Things to Look Out For

➡ Petty theft (eg rifled luggage in hotel rooms or unattended shoes disappearing from the beach) is common.

➡ To prevent pickpocketing wear your bag in front of you on crowded buses and at busy markets, and only take the money you will need when you head out at night. Always check your change in bars and restaurants.

➡ Short-changing is not uncommon, especially in state-run businesses. Cuba has two currencies and the notes are easy to confuse. Check change in banks, restaurants and shops and never change money on the street.

➡ Begging is subtle but it exists and is exacerbated by tourists who hand out money, soap, pens, chewing gum and other things to people on the street. If you truly want to do something to help, pharmacies and hospitals will accept medicine donations, schools happily take pens, paper, crayons etc, and libraries will gratefully accept books. Alternatively, pass stuff onto your casa particular owner or leave it at a local church.

➡ Hustlers are called *jineteros/jineteras* (male/female touts), and can be a nuisance in some cities. Their main line is selling fake cigars. For the real thing, only ever buy cigars from official government outlets.

Telephone

Cell phone usage has become relatively widespread in Cuba in the last few years. Normally a recorded message will inform you of phone number changes. Etecsa *telepuntos* (internet-cafes-cum-call-centers) have air-conditioned phone and internet terminals in almost every provincial town.

Cell Phones

Cubacel has a wide range of roaming agreements. See the full list online at: www.etecsa.cu/telefonia_movil/roaming.

You can use your own GSM or TDMA phones in Cuba with a local SIM card, though you'll need to ensure your phone is unlocked first. Buy a SIM card (USD$40 including USD$10 worth of data) at an Etecsa *telepunto*. Bring your passport. There are numerous offices around the country (including at the Havana airport) where you can do this.

Costs run between USD$0.35 per minute for calls within Cuba, USD$0.09 for texts. You pay the same amount if a fixed line calls you. International calls start at USD$1.10 per minute; texts USD$0.60. To rent a phone in Cuba costs from USD$10 per day. You'll also need to pay a USD$100 deposit. Charges after this amount to around USD$0.35 per minute. For up-to-date costs and information on cell phones see www.etecsa.cu.

All said and done, to communicate with people abroad, it may be cheaper to buy a USD$1 per hour internet card, find a wi-fi signal and use Skype or WhatsApp.

Phone Codes

➡ To call Cuba from abroad, dial your international access code, Cuba's country code (53), the city or area code, and the local number.

➡ To call internationally from Cuba, dial the international access code '00,' followed by the country code, the area code and the number; to call the US, just dial ⏻119, then 1, the area code and the number.

➡ To call cell phone to cell phone or cell phone to landline just dial the eight-digit number (which always starts with a '5').

➡ To call cell phone to landline (or landline to landline) dial the provincial code plus the local number.

Phone Rates

Local calls cost from CUP$0.10 to CUP$1 depending on the time of day and distance. Since most coin phones don't return change, common courtesy means that you should push the 'R' button so that the next person in line can make their call with your remaining money.

International calls made with a card cost CUP$25 per minute regardless of destination.

Hotels with three stars and up usually offer slightly pricier international phone rates.

Phonecards

Etecsa is where you buy phonecards, use the internet

and make international calls. Blue public Etecsa phones accepting magnetized or computer-chip cards are everywhere. The cards are rechargeable in values of CUP$5, CUP$10, CUP$30 and CUP$100.

You will also see coin-operated phone booths that accept coins of CUP$0.05, CUP$0.20 and CUP$1 for local and national long-distance calls only.

Tourist Information

Cuba's official tourist information bureau is called Infotur (www.infotur.cu). It has offices in all the main provincial towns and desks in most of the bigger hotels and airports. Travel agencies, such as Cubanacán, Cubatur, Gaviota and Ecotur can usually supply some general information.

Visas & Tourist Cards

Package tourists receive their tourist card with their other travel documents. Those going 'air only' usually buy the tourist card from the travel agency or airline office that sells them the plane ticket, but policies vary (eg Canadian airlines give out tourist cards on their airplanes), so you'll need to check ahead with the airline office via phone or email.

In some cases you may be required to buy and/or pick up the card at your departure airport, sometimes at the flight gate itself some minutes before departure. Some independent travelers have been denied access to Cuba flights because they inadvertently haven't obtained a tourist card.

Tourist cards are light green, and cost US$25 if they're not included in your flight deal. Travelers flying from the US get a pink tourist card that costs significantly more (between US$50 and US$85 depending on which airline you fly with).

Once in Havana, tourist-card extensions or replacements cost another USD$25. You cannot leave Cuba without presenting your tourist card. If you lose it, you can expect to face at least a day of frustrating Cuba-style bureaucracy to get it replaced.

You are not permitted entry to Cuba without an onward ticket.

Fill the tourist card out clearly and carefully, as Cuban customs are particularly fussy about crossings out and illegibility.

Business travelers and journalists need visas. Applications should be made through a consulate at least three weeks in advance (longer if you apply through a consulate in a country other than your own).

Extensions

For most travelers, obtaining a tourist card extension once in Cuba is potentially easy: you just go to the *inmigración* (immigration office) and present your documents (passport, tourist card, details of where you're staying) and USD$25 in stamps. Obtain these stamps from a branch of Bandec or Banco Financiero Internacional beforehand. You'll only receive an additional 30 days after your original 30 days (apart from Canadians who get an additional 90 days after their original 90), but you can exit and re-enter the country for 24 hours and start over again (some travel agencies in Havana have special deals for this type of trip). Attend to extensions at least a few business days before your visa is due to expire and never attempt travel around Cuba with an expired visa. Be aware that immigration offices – like all offices in Cuba – can be slow and infested with queues.

Cuban Immigration Offices

Nearly all provincial towns have an immigration office (where you can extend your visa), though the staff rarely speak English and aren't always overly helpful. Try to avoid Havana's office if you can, as it gets ridiculously crowded.

Bayamo (☏2357-2584; Km 2, Carretera Central; ☺8am-7pm Mon, Wed & Fri, to 5pm Tue, to noon Thu & Sat) In a big complex 200m south of the Hotel Sierra Maestra.

Camagüey (Calle 3 No 156, btwn Calles 8 & 10, Reparto Vista Hermosa; ☺8am-7pm Mon, Wed & Fri, to 5pm Tue, to noon Thu & Sat)

Ciego de Ávila (Independencia, btwn Marcial Gómez & Delgado; ☺8am-7pm Mon, Wed & Fri, to 5pm Tue, to noon Thu & Sat)

Cienfuegos (☏43-55-36-41; Av 46, btwn Calles 29 & 31, Cienfuegos; ☺8am-7pm, to 5pm Tue, to noon Thu & Sat, closed Sun)

Guantánamo (Calle 1 Oeste, btwn Calles 14 & 15 Norte; ☺8am-7pm Mon, Wed & Fri, to 5pm Tue, to noon Thu & Sat) Directly behind Hotel Guantánamo.

Havana (Calle 17 No 203, btwn Calles J & K; ☺8am-5pm Mon-Wed & Fri, to noon Thu & Sat)

Holguín (Fomento No 256, cnr Peralejo; 8am-7pm Mon, Wed & Fri, to 5pm Tue, to noon Thu & Sat)

Las Tunas (Av Camilo Cienfuegos, Reparto Buenavista; ☺8am-7pm Mon, Wed & Fri, to 5pm Tue, to noon Thu & Sat)

Sancti Spíritus (☏4132-4729; Independencia Norte No 107; ☺8am-7pm Mon, Wed & Fri, to 5pm Tue, to noon Thu & Sat)

Santa Clara (cnr Av Sandino & Sexta, Santa Clara; ☺8am-7pm, to 5pm Tue, to noon Thu & Sat, closed Sun) Three blocks east of Estadio Sandino.

Santiago de Cuba (☏2264-1983; Av Pujol No 10, btwn Calles 8 & 10; ☺8am-7pm Mon, Wed & Fri, to 5pm Tue, to noon Thu & Sat) Stamps for visa extensions are sold at the Banco de Crédito y Comercio at Felix Peña No 614 on Parque Céspedes.

Trinidad (☏4134-2708; Julio Cueva Díaz; ☺8am-7pm Mon, Wed & Fri, to 5pm Tue, to noon Thu & Sat) Off Paseo Agramonte.

Varadero (cnr Av 1 & Calle 39, Varadero; ☺8am-7pm Mon, Wed & Fri, to 5pm Tue, to noon Thu & Sat)

Volunteering

There are a number of bodies offering volunteer work in Cuba, though it is always best to organize things in your home country first. Just turning up in Havana and volunteering can be difficult, if not impossible.

Cuban Solidarity Campaign (www.cuba-solidarity.org) Head office in London, UK.

Global Volunteers (https://globalvolunteers.org/cuba) With programs in Havana, Ciego de Avila and Sancti Spríritus.

Go Overseas (www.gooverseas.com) A catalog of around 20 programs in Cuba organized by length of stay, area and program rating, many officially licensed by the US.

Imagine Cuba Travel (www.imaginecubatravel.ca)

Canada-based sustainable agriculture organization offers trips that focus on visiting Cuba farms.

Pastors for Peace (www. ifconews.org) Collects donations across the US to take to Cuba.

Witness for Peace (www. witnessforpeace.org) Brings delegations to Cuba, some studying the impact of US policy.

Women Travelers

In terms of physical safety, Cuba is a dream destination for women travelers. Most streets can be walked alone at night, violent crime is rare and the chivalrous part of machismo means you'll never step into oncoming traffic.

But machismo cuts both ways, protecting on one side and pursuing – relentlessly – on the other. It can be tiresome to go out alone at night and steel yourself against the onslaught of *pretendientes* (men courting), unless you're really keen on them or improving your Spanish. There's also relatively few solo travelers in Cuba and no youth hostels, which means fewer travelers to keep company with.

Cuban women are used to *piropos* (the whistles, kissing sounds and compliments constantly ringing in their ears), and might even reply with their own if they're feeling frisky. For foreign women, however, it can feel like an invasion.

Ignoring *piropos* is the first step. But sometimes ignoring isn't enough. Learn some rejoinders in Spanish so you can shut men up. *No me moleste* (don't bother me), *está bueno ya* (all right already) or *que falta respeto* (how disrespectful) are good ones. As is the withering 'don't you dare' stare that is also part of the Cuban woman's arsenal. Wearing plain, modest clothes might help lessen unwanted attention; topless sunbathing is out. An absent partner, invented or not, seldom has any effect. If you go to a disco, be very clear with Cuban dance partners whether or not you are interested.

Women must bring their own tampons (non-existent in Cuba) or pads (called *íntimos*, literally 'intimates').

Transportation

GETTING THERE & AWAY

Entering the Country

Whether it's your first or 50th time, descending low into José Martí International Airport, over rust-red tobacco fields, is an exciting and unforgettable experience. Entry procedures are relatively straightforward, and with over four million visitors a year, immigration officials are used to dealing with foreign arrivals.

Outside Cuba, the capital city is called Havana, and this is how travel agents, airlines and other professionals will refer to it. Within Cuba, it's almost always called La Habana. For the sake of consistency, we use the former spelling.

Flights, tours and rail tickets can be booked online at lonelyplanet.com/bookings.

Air

Cuba has 10 international airports. The largest by far is **Aeropuerto Internacional José Martí** (www.havana-airport.org; Av Rancho Boyeros, Rancho Boyeros) in Havana. The only other sizable airport is **Juan Gualberto Gómez International Airport** (VRA; ☑45-61-30-16, 45-24-70-15) in Varadero.

In Havana most airline offices are situated in one of two clusters: the **Airline Building** (Calle 23 No 64) in Vedado, or in the **Miramar Trade Center** (Map p96; Av 3, btwn Calles 76 & 80, Miramar; ☺hours vary) in Playa.

Cubana de Aviación (☑7-649-0410; www.cubana.cu; Airline Bldg, Calle 23 No 64, Vedado, Havana; ☺8:30am-4pm Mon-Fri, to noon Sat), the national carrier, grounded half its fleet after a crash in May 2018. After this and considering the ongoing impacts of the COVID-19 pandemic, the airline was operating at reduced capacity the time of writing. Its airfares are usually among the cheapest, though overbooking and delays are nagging problems. Overweight baggage is strictly charged for every kilogram above the 20kg allowance. If you have the option, book with another airline.

For safety recommendations, check the latest at www.airsafe.com.

Flights to/from Cuba

AFRICA

Direct flights from Africa originate in Luanda, Angola, with TAAG (www.taag.com). From all other African countries you'll need to connect in London, Paris, Madrid, Amsterdam or Rome.

ASIA & AUSTRALIA

There are no direct flights to Cuba from Australia. Travelers can connect through Europe, Canada, the US or Mexico. Air China (www.airchina.com) flies from Beijing.

CLIMATE CHANGE & TRAVEL

Every form of transport that relies on carbon-based fuel generates CO_2, the main cause of human-induced climate change. Modern travel is dependent on airplanes, which might use less fuel per miles per person than most cars but travel much greater distances. The altitude at which aircraft emit gases (including CO_2) and particles also contributes to their climate change impact. Many websites offer 'carbon calculators' that allow people to estimate the carbon emissions generated by their journey and, for those who wish to do so, to offset the impact of the greenhouse gases emitted with contributions to portfolios of climate-friendly initiatives throughout the world. Lonely Planet offsets the carbon footprint of all staff and author travel.

CANADA

Flights from Canada serve 10 Cuban airports from 22 Canadian cities. Toronto and Montreal are the main hubs. Other cities are served by direct charter flights. Airlines include Air Canada (www.aircanada.com), Air Transat (www.airtransat.com), Sunwing (www.sunwing.ca) and Westjet (www.westjet.com). Travel agency A Nash Travel (www.nashtravel.com/travel-cuba) can be helpful with bookings.

CARIBBEAN

Cubana is the main airline serving the Caribbean, flying to the Dominican Republic and Haiti (the latter from Santiago de Cuba). As of 2019, schedules are limited, so check ahead. Bahamasair (www.bahamasair.com) and Cayman Airways (www.caymanairways.com) have regular flights to Nassau and Grand Cayman, respectively.

EUROPE & UK

Regular flights to Cuba depart from Belgium, France, Germany, the Netherlands, Italy, Russia, Spain, Switzerland and the UK. The following airlines serve Europe:

Aeroflot (☎7-204-3200; www.aeroflot.ru; Miramar Trade Center, Av 5 & Calle 76, Havana; ◷9am-3pm Mon-Fri)

Air Europa (☎7-204-6904; www.aireuropa.com; Miramar Trade Center, Av 5 & Calle 76, Havana; ◷9am-5pm Mon-Fri)

Air France (☎7-206-4444; www.airfrance.com; Miramar Trade Center, Av 5 & Calle 76, Havana; ◷8:30am-4:30pm Mon-Fri)

Blue Panorama (www.blue-panorama.com)

Condor (www.condor.com)

Edelweiss (www.flyedelweiss.com)

Iberia (www.iberia.com)

KLM (www.klm.com)

Neos (www.neosair.it)

TUI Fly Netherlands (www.tuifly.com)

Virgin Atlantic (☎7-204-0747; www.virgin-atlantic.com; Miramar Trade Center, Av 5 & Calle 76, Havana; ◷9am-4:30pm Mon-Fri)

MEXICO

Mexico City and Cancún are good places to connect with a wide number of US cities. Interjet (www.interjet.com.mx) serves Mexico.

SOUTH & CENTRAL AMERICA

There are good connections to airports throughout South America. Central American airports provide the best link to other parts of the Caribbean. The following airlines serve Latin America:

Avianca (www.avianca.com), Colombia.

Conviasa (www.conviasa.aero), Venezuela.

Copa Airlines (www.copaair.com), Panama.

LATAM Peru (www.latam.com), Peru.

UNITED STATES

The first commercial flights between the US and Cuba started in November 2016, following moves by the Obama administration to ease travel restrictions. Those traveling on a US passport still must be traveling under the authorized travel categories. The following airlines now serve Cuba:

American Airlines (☎in the USA 800-433-7300; www.aa.com; Miramar Trade Center, Av 5 & Calle 76, Havana; ◷9am-5pm Mon-Fri, to 1pm Sat), from Miami.

Delta Airlines (www.delta.com) From Miami and Atlanta.

Jet Blue (www.jetblue.com) From Fort Luaderdale and New York.

Southwest Airlines (www.southwest.com) From Fort Lauderdale and Tampa.

United Airlines (www.united.com) From New York and Houston.

Sea

Cruises

With US–Cuban cruises off the menu since June 2019, you're once again limited to mainly European-based cruise lines if you want to visit Cuba by ship. German-run Hapag-Lloyd Cruises (www.hl-cruises.com) runs an interesting 12-day 'Best of Cuba' cruise out of Mexico that calls at Havana, La Isla de la Juventud and Santiago de Cuba. UK-run Marella Cruises (www.tui.co.uk/cruise) has a seven-night 'Flavours of the Caribbean' trip that starts and finishes in Jamaica but does a loop around Havana, the Cayman Islands and Mexico. British-Norwegian Fred Olsen Cruise Lines (www.fredolsencruises.com) runs a comprehensive two-week trip from Barbados to the Dominican Republic that calls at both Santiago de Cuba and Havana.

Private Yacht

Cuba has eight international entry ports equipped with customs facilities:

➡ Marina Hemingway (Havana)

➡ Marina Dásena (Varadero)

➡ Marina Cienfuegos

Commercial Air Routes

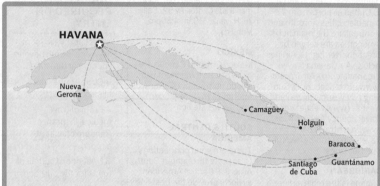

- ➡ Marina Cayo Guillermo
- ➡ Marina Santiago de Cuba
- ➡ Puerto de Vita (near Guardalavaca in Holguín Province)
- ➡ Cayo Largo del Sur
- ➡ Cabo San Antonio (far western tip of Pinar del Río Province)

Boat owners should communicate with the Cuban coast guard on VHF 16 and 68 or the tourist network 19A.

Tours

Cuba is popular on the organized-tour circuit, especially in the realm of soft adventure. There are also specialist tours focusing on culture, the environment, adventure, photography, cycling, birdwatching, architecture and hiking. Some popular agencies include:

Cuban Adventures (www. cubagrouptour.com) Australian-based company specializing in Cuba travel, running small tours with mainly local guides. It also runs licensed trips for American travelers.

Exodus (www.exodus.co.uk) British-based adventure-travel company offering a nine-day cultural trip or a nine-day cycle ride staying in a mixture of hotels and casas particulares (private homestays).

Explore (www.explore.co.uk) Offers over half-a-dozen packages up to 15 days long, including specialist hiking, biking and family-oriented trips.

GETTING AROUND

Air

There are no internal connections between Cuban airports, except via Havana. At the time of writing, these flights were plagued by delays and cancellations.

Cubana de Aviación (☑7-649-0410; www.cubana. cu; Airline Bldg, Calle 23 No 64, Vedado, Havana; ☺8:30am-4pm Mon-Fri, to noon Sat) theoretically has flights between Havana and 11 regional airports. However, domestic flight schedules have been pared back drastically since a plane crash in May 2018. More reliable Cubana routes include La Isla de la Juventud, Holguín and Santiago de Cuba.

One-way flights are half the price of round-trip flights and weight restrictions are strict (especially on smaller planes). You can purchase tickets at most hotel tour desks and travel agencies for the same price as at the

airline offices, which are often chaotic.

Aerogaviota (☑7-203-0668; www.aerogaviota.com) runs more expensive charter flights between Havana and Cayo Coco, Holguín, Baracoa and Santiago de Cuba. However, the company also experienced a plane crash in 2017 and has posted pared back schedules since.

Bicycle

Cuba is a cyclist's paradise, with bike lanes, bike workshops and drivers accustomed to sharing the road countrywide. Spare parts are difficult to find – you should bring important spares with you. Still, Cubans are grand masters at improvised repair and, though specific parts may not be available, something can surely be jury-rigged. *Poncheros* (puncture repair stalls) fix flat tires and provide air; every small town has one.

Helmets are unheard of in rural Cuba, although upscale resorts and Havana renters now offer them. If in doubt, bring your own. A lock is imperative, as bicycle theft is rampant. *Parqueos* are bicycle parking lots located wherever crowds congregate (eg markets, bus terminals, downtown etc). Pay one

Cuban peso and someone 'official' will guard your bike.

Throughout the country, the 1m-wide strip of road to the extreme right is reserved for bicycles, even on highways. It's illegal to ride on sidewalks and against traffic on one-way streets and you'll be ticketed if caught. Road lighting is deplorable, so avoid riding after dark (over one-third of vehicle accidents in Cuba involve bicycles); carry lights with you just in case.

Trains with *coches de equipaje* or *bagones* (baggage carriages) should take bikes for around CUC$10 per trip. These compartments are guarded, but take your panniers with you and check over the bike when you arrive at your destination. Víazul buses also take bikes.

Purchase

Limited selection and high prices make buying a bike in Cuba through official channels unattractive. Better to ask around and strike a deal with an individual to buy their *chivo* (Cuban slang for bike) and trade it or resell it when you leave. With some earnest bargaining, you might be able to get one for around CUC$50 – although the more you pay, the less your bones are likely to shake. Despite the obvious cost savings, bringing your own bike is still the best bet by far.

Rental

Official bike rental places are scant in Cuba, but with the private economy taking off so rapidly, things are changing. You can usually procure something roadworthy for between CUC$5 per hour or CUC$20 per day. Bikes are usually included as a perk in all-inclusive resort packages, but beware of bad brakes and zero gears.

For long-distance cycling, it's always best to bring your own bike.

Boat

The most important ferry service for travelers is the slow, tatty (though relatively safe) catamaran from Surgidero de Batabanó to Nueva Gerona on the Isla de la Juventud. Suffice to say, the boat is little used by non-Cubans who – if they visit the Isla at all – usually elect to fly.

Several other ferries make short hops across various harbors and bays. The most relevant for travelers is the passenger ferry from Havana to Regla and Casablanca. Post a 2003 hijack attempt, security on this ferry is still fairly tight. Expect bag checks.

Bus

Bus travel is a dependable way of getting around Cuba, at least in the more popular areas. Víazul (www.viazul. com) is the main long-distance bus company available to non-Cubans, with fairly punctual and reliable air-conditioned coaches going to destinations of interest to travelers.

Víazul charges for tickets in convertibles. Buses schedule regular stops for lunch/dinner and always carry two drivers. Bring warm layers – the air-conditioning blasts an Arctic chill. Reserve ahead on the more popular routes, particularly in high season.

Note that the demand in high season often outstrips availability. If you can't get a seat on the bus you want, look for other stranded travelers to join for a shared taxi to your destination.

Conectando, run by Cubanacán, is a newer option set up to relieve some of Víazul's overcrowding. The pros are that it runs between city center hotels and can be booked head of time at Infotur and Cubanacán offices. The cons are that the schedules aren't as reliable or extensive as Víazul. Check ahead that your bus is running.

Many of the popular tourist areas now have 'bus tours,' hop-on/hop-off buses that link all the main sights in a given area and charge between CUC$2 and CUC$10 for an all-day ticket. The services are run by government transport agency Transtur. Havana and Varadero both have open-topped double-decker buses. Smaller minibuses are used in Viñales, Trinidad, Cayo Coco, Guardalavaca, Cayo Santa María and Baracoa (seasonal).

Cubans travel over shorter distances in provincial

DOMESTIC FLIGHTS FROM HAVANA

DESTINATION	FREQUENCY	DURATION (HR)
Baracoa	2 weekly	2½
Camagüey	1 weekly	1½
Guantánamo	2 weekly	2
Holguín	1 daily	1½
Nueva Gerona	2 daily	35 min
Santiago de Cuba	1–2 daily	1½

buses. These buses sell tickets in *moneda nacional* (Cuban pesos) and are a lot less comfortable and reliable than Víazul. They leave from the provincial bus stations in each province. Schedules and prices are usually chalked up on a board inside the terminal. Sometimes travelers are not allowed on these buses or preference is given to locals getting a seat.

Reservations

Reservations with Víazul are necessary during peak travel periods (June to August, Christmas and Easter) and on popular routes (Havana–Trinidad, Trinidad–Varadero, and Santiago de Cuba–Baracoa). You can usually book a day or two beforehand.

The Víazul bus out of Baracoa is almost always booked, so reserve a seat on this service when you arrive. It is now possible to make reservations online at www.viazul.com if you register with the site. However, like all Cuban websites, it is prone to 'crashing.'

Car & Motorcycle

Renting a car in Cuba is technically easy, but once you've factored in gas, insurance, hire fees etc, it isn't cheap. Furthermore, a countrywide shortage of cars means rentals are often unavailable. Prices vary with car size, season and length of rental. Bank on paying an average of CUC$75 per day for a medium-sized car. It's actually cheaper to hire a taxi for distances of under 150km (at the time of writing taxis were charging CUC$0.55 per kilometer for intercity routes).

There is no full-blown motorcycle rental in Cuba. In resort areas it is often possible to rent mopeds to zip between beaches and/or make short road journeys. Scooter rental costs around CUC$25 a day and you'll need to present your driver's license.

Driver's License

Your home license is sufficient to rent and drive a car in Cuba.

Fuel

Gas sold in convertibles (as opposed to pesos) is widely available in stations all over the country (the north coast west of Havana being the notable exception). Gas stations are often open 24 hours and may have a small parts store on site. Gas is sold by the liter and comes in *regular* (CUC$1 per liter) and *especial* (CUC$1.20 per liter) varieties. Rental cars are advised to use *especial*. All gas stations have efficient pump attendants, usually in the form of *trabajadores sociales* (students in the process of studying for a degree).

VÍAZUL BUS ROUTES

ROUTE	DURATION (HR)	PRICE (CUC$)	STOPPING AT...
Cayo Santa María–Trinidad	6½	20	Caibarién, Remedios, Santa Clara, Cienfuegos
Havana–Guantánamo	15½	57	Camagüey, Santiago de Cuba
Havana–Holguín	10½	44	Santa Clara, Sancti Spíritus, Ciego de Ávila, Camagüey, Las Tunas
Havana–Santiago de Cuba	15½	51	Santa Clara, Sancti Spíritus, Ciego de Ávila, Camagüey, Las Tunas, Holguín, Bayamo
Havana–Trinidad	6	25	Playa Larga, Playa Girón, Cienfuegos
Havana–Varadero	3	10	Matanzas, Varadero Airport
Havana–Viñales	3¼	12	Las Terrazas, Pinar del Río
Santiago de Cuba–Baracoa	4¾	15	Guantánamo
Trinidad–Santiago de Cuba	12	33	Sancti Spíritus, Ciego de Ávila, Camagüey, Las Tunas, Holguín, Bayamo
Trinidad–Varadero	6	20	Santa Clara, Cienfuegos
Varadero–Santiago de Cuba	16	49	Santa Clara, Sancti Spíritus, Ciego de Ávila, Camagüey, Las Tunas, Holguín, Bayamo
Viñales–Trinidad	10	37	Pinar del Río, Cienfuegos

Insurance

Rental cars come with a required CUC$15 to CUC$30 per day insurance, which covers everything but theft of the radio (store in the trunk at night) and tires.

If you do have an accident, you must get a copy of the *denuncia* (police report) to be eligible for the insurance coverage, a process that can take all day. If the police determine that you are the party responsible for the accident, say *adiós* to your deposit.

Rental

Renting a car in Cuba is relatively straightforward, as long as there are cars available. Endemic shortages mean that it's best to book at least a month in advance. You can browse the options on the Transtur website (www. transturcarrental.com) or book through an off-shore third party such as A Nash Travel (www.nashtravel. com) or Cuba Travel Services (www.cubatravelservices. com).

There are essentially four rental companies in Cuba – Cubacar, Havanautos, Via and Rex. All have countrywide offices and representation in most top-end hotels and resorts. The first three companies charge similar prices. Rex offers luxury cars at higher rates.

Aspiring renters will need to show up with a passport, driver's license and a refundable deposit of between CUC$150 and CUC$250 (cash or credit card). You can rent a car in one city and drop it off in another for a reasonable fee. Note that there are very few rental cars with automatic transmission.

In Cuba, you pay for the first tank of gas when you rent the car and return it empty (a suicidal policy that sees many tight-fisted tourists running out of gas a kilometer or so from the drop-off point). You will not

RENT A CAR & DRIVER

Sure, there's not a lot of traffic on the roads, but driving in Cuba isn't as easy as many people think, especially when you factor in teetering cyclists, baseball-chasing children, galloping horses, pedestrians with limited or no peripheral vision, and – worst of all – a serious lack of signposts.

To avoid hassle, you can hire both a comfortable, modern car and a driver with a growing number of companies, most notably **Car Rental Cuba** (☑5-447-2822; www.carrental-cuba.com; Maceo No 360-1, btwn Serafin García & EP Morales, Santa Clara; per day from CUC$75).

be refunded for any gas left in the tank.

Petty theft of mirrors, antennas, taillights etc is common, so it's worth it to pay someone a convertible or two to watch your car for the night. If you lose your rental contract or keys you'll pay a penalty (usually CUC$50). Drivers under 25 pay a CUC$5 fee, while additional drivers on the same contract pay a CUC$3 per day surcharge.

Check over the car carefully with the rental agent before driving into the sunset, as you'll be responsible for any damage or missing parts. Make sure there is a spare tire of the correct size, a jack and a lug wrench. Check that there are seatbelts and that all the doors lock properly.

While agents are usually accommodating, you might end up paying more than you planned or have to wait for hours until someone returns a car. The more Spanish you speak and the friendlier you are, the more likely problems will be resolved to everyone's satisfaction (tips to the agent might help). As with most Cuban travel, always have a plan B, C and Z.

Road Conditions

Driving here isn't just a different ballpark, it's a different sport. The first problem is that there is limited signage – although things have got better in recent years. Major junctions and turnoffs to

important resorts or cities are often not indicated at all. Not only is this distracting, it's also incredibly time-consuming. The lack of signage also extends to highway instructions. Often a one-way street is not clearly indicated or a speed limit not highlighted, which can cause problems with the police (who won't understand your inability to telepathically absorb the road rules), and road markings are nonexistent everywhere.

The Autopista, Vía Blanca and Carretera Central are generally in a good state, but be prepared for roads suddenly deteriorating into chunks of asphalt and unexpected railroad crossings everywhere else (especially in the Oriente). Rail crossings are particularly problematic, as there are hundreds of them and there are never any safety gates. Beware: however overgrown the rails may look, you can pretty much assume that the line is still in use. Cuba's trains, rather like its cars, defy all normal logic when it comes to mechanics.

While motorized traffic is refreshingly light, bicycles, pedestrians, oxcarts, horse carriages and livestock are a different matter. Many old cars and trucks lack rearview mirrors and traffic-unaware children run out of all kinds of nooks and crannies. Stay alert, drive with caution and use your horn when passing or on blind curves.

Driving at night is not recommended due to variable roads, drunk drivers, crossing cows and poor lighting. Drunk-driving remains a troublesome problem despite a government educational campaign. Late night in Havana is particularly dangerous, as it seems there's a passing lane, cruising lane and drunk lane.

Traffic lights are often busted or hard to pick out and right-of-way rules are thrown to the wind. Take extra care.

Road Rules

Cubans drive how they want, where they want. It seems chaotic at first, but it has its rhythm. Seatbelts are supposedly required and maximum speed limits are technically 50km/h in the city, 90km/h on highways and 100km/h on the Autopista, but some cars can't even go that fast and those that can, go faster still.

With so few cars on the road, it's hard not to put the pedal to the floor and just fly. Unexpected potholes are a hazard, however, and watch out for police. There are some clever speed traps, particularly along the Autopista. Speeding tickets start at CUC$30 and are noted on your car contract; the fine is deducted from your deposit when you return the car. When pulled over by the police, you're expected to get out of the car and walk over to them with your paperwork. An oncoming car flashing its lights means a hazard up ahead (and usually the police).

Spare Parts

While you cannot count on spare parts per se to be available, Cubans have decades of experience keeping old wrecks on the road without factory parts and you'll see them do amazing things with cardboard, string, rubber and clothes hangers to keep a car mobile.

If you need air in your tires or you have a puncture, use a gas station or visit the local *ponchero* (puncture repair stall). They often don't have measures, so make sure they don't overinflate your tires.

Hitching & Ride-Sharing

The transportation crisis, culture of solidarity and low crime levels make Cuba a popular hitchhiking destination. Here, hitchhiking is more like ride-sharing, and it's legally enforced. Traffic lights, railroad crossings and country crossroads are regular stops for people seeking rides.

In the provinces and on the outskirts of Havana, the *amarillos* (official state-paid traffic supervisors, so-named for their mustard yellow uniforms) organize and prioritize ride seekers, and there's nothing to stop you standing in line. Rides cost MN$5 to MN$20 depending on distance. Travelers hitching rides will want a good map and some Spanish skills. Expect to wait two or three hours for rides in some cases.

Hitchhiking is never entirely safe in any country in the world, and we don't recommend it. Travelers who decide to hitchhike should understand that they are taking a small but potentially serious risk. People who do choose to hitchhike will be safer if they travel in pairs and let someone know where they are planning to go.

Local Transportation

Bici-Taxi

Bici-taxis are big pedal-powered tricycles with a double seat behind the driver. They are common in Havana, Camagüey, Holguín and a few other cities. In Havana drivers want a CUC$2 minimum fare (Cubans pay MN$5 to

MN$10). Some *bici-taxistas* ask ridiculous amounts. The fare should be clearly understood before you hop aboard.

Boat

Some towns, such as Havana, Cienfuegos, Gibara and Santiago de Cuba, have local ferry services that charge in *moneda nacional* (Cuban pesos).

Bus

Very crowded, very steamy, very challenging, very Cuban – *guaguas* (local buses) can be useful in bigger cities. Buses work fixed routes, stopping at *paradas* (bus stops) that always have a line, even if it doesn't look like it. You have to shout out *¿el último?* to find out who was the last in line when you showed up as Cuban queues form in loose crowds.

Buses cost a flat MN$0.40 or five centavos if you're using convertibles. Havana and Santiago de Cuba are kitted out with newer fleets of Chinese-made metro buses. You must always walk as far back in the bus as you can and exit through the rear. Make room to pass by saying *permiso,* always wear your pack in front and watch your wallet.

Colectivo

Colectivos are shared taxis running on fixed, long-distance routes, leaving when full. They are often pre-1959 American cars that belch diesel fumes and can squash in at least three people across the front seat. It's often faster and safer to pay a little more for a modern state-owned *colectivo* (maximum four passengers). *Colectivos* hang about bus stations or you can organize one through your casa particular (private homestay) or the local Infotur office.

Horse Carriage

Many provincial cities have *coches de caballo* (horse carriages) that trot on fixed routes, often between train/bus stations and city centers. They cost around MN$1. Many horses are overworked and in lamentable condition. It's best to give your business to healthy ones if there's an option (or better yet, a bici-taxi).

Taxi

Official yellow taxis (Cubataxi) are metered and cost CUC$1 to start and CUC$1 per kilometer in cities. However, taxi drivers are in the habit of offering foreigners a flat, off-meter rate that generally works out very close to what you'll pay with the meter. Older taxis (usually Russian Ladas) don't have meters and usually charge less, although you'll probably have to do without air-conditioning and seatbelts.

Train

Public railways operated by Ferrocarriles de Cuba serve all of the provincial capitals and are a unique way to experience Cuba, as long as you have time, patience and a flexible itinerary.

Old trains and fuel shortages have traditionally led to delays and Cubans who have the budget to travel by other means often do so. However, the situation improved immeasurably in July 2019 when the rail network received its first proper upgrade for over 20 years with the importation of 80 modern train carriages from China.

Getting a ticket is usually no problem, as there's a quota for tourists paying in convertibles on trains numbered 1 to 8 (there are no reservations on other trains). Foreigners must pay for their tickets in cash, but prices are reasonable. The carriages are a mix of worn-out facilities on older trains and reasonably comfortable air-conditioned coaches on the latest 2019 models. Toilets can be iffy – bring toilet paper. Watch your luggage on overnight trips and bring extra food in case of emergencies The newer trains serve refreshments, but individual stations usually don't

For Cuban train times and types, consult The Man in Seat Sixty-One (www.seat61.com).

At time of research, the Estación Central of Havana was closed for renovation. In the meantime, most services depart through the La Coubre station.

Classes

The newer coaches have two classes: 1st (which is air-conditioned) and 2nd. First-class tickets cost CUC$20 to CUC$25 more than 2nd.

Costs

Regular trains cost under CUC$3 per 100km. The newer trains are more expensive, but still a bargain compared to other countries. First-/second-class tickets between Havana and Santiago de Cuba cost CUC$70/95. Sample 2nd-class fares are:

Havana–Matanzas CUC$10

Havana–Santa Clara CUC$25

Havana–Camagüey CUC$45

Havana–Las Tunas CUC$55

The Hershey Train (between Havana and Matanzas; see p160) is priced like the *regular* trains.

Rail Network

Cuba's train network is comprehensive, running almost the full length of the main island from Guane in Pinar del Río Province to Caimanera, just south of the city of

TRAIN SERVICES FROM HAVANA

All trains stop at Matanzas, Santa Clara, Ciego de Ávila, Camagüey and Las Tunas en route.

ROUTE	TRAIN NUMBER	PRICE (2ND/1ST CLASS)	DURATION (HR)	FREQUENCY
Havana–Santiago de Cuba	1	70/95	15	every other day
Santiago de Cuba–Havana	2	70/95	15	every other day
Havana–Guantánamo	3	75/100	17	every third day
Guantánamo–Havana	4	75/100	17	every third day
Havana–Holguín	5	60/80	14	every third day
Holguín–Havana	6	60/80	14	every third day
Havana–Bayamo–Manzanillo	7	60–65/85–90	15–17¼	every third day
Manzanillo–Bayamo–Havana	8	60–65/85–90	15–17¼	every third day

Guantánamo. There are also several poorly served branch lines heading out north and south and linking up places such as Nuevitas, Morón and Cienfuegos. Baracoa is one of the few cities without a train connection. Other trainless enclaves are the Isla de la Juventud, the far west of Pinar del Río Province and the northern keys. Trinidad has been detached from the main rail network since a storm brought down a bridge in 1992.

Reservations

Reservations for Cuba's newer trains (numbered 1 to 8) can be made up to 30 days in advance. A quota of tickets for foreigners is set aside for each carriage.

In most train stations, you just go to the ticket window and buy a ticket. In La Coubre station in Havana, there's a separate waiting room and ticket window for passengers paying in convertibles. Be prepared to show your passport when purchasing tickets.

Services

Many additional local trains operate at least daily and some more frequently. There are also smaller trains linking Las Tunas and Holguín, Holguín and Santiago de Cuba, Santa Clara and Nuevitas,

Cienfuegos and Sancti Spíritus, and Santa Clara and Caibarién. However, there are no printed timetables for any of these services, just cheap blackboards at individual stations.

The Hershey Train is the only electric railway in Cuba and was built by the Hershey Chocolate Company in the early 20th century; it's a fun way to get between Havana and Matanzas.

Train Stations

Cuban train stations, despite their occasionally grandiose facades, are invariably dingy, chaotic places with little visible train information, although things have been looking up a little since the network's 2019 upgrade. Departure times are displayed on black chalkboards or handwritten notices; there are no electronic or printed timetables. Always check train info two to three days before your intended travel.

Truck

Camiones (trucks) are a cheap, fast way to travel within or between provinces. Every city has a provincial and municipal bus stop with *camiones* departures. They run on a (loose) schedule and you'll need to take your

place in line by asking *¿el último?* (to find out who was the last in line when you showed up); you pay as you board. For many destinations, the majority of departures leave in the early morning.

Camion traveling is hot, crowded and uncomfortable, but is a great way to meet local people, fast; a little Spanish will go a long way. A truck from Santiago de Cuba to Guantánamo costs around five pesos (CUC$0.20), while the same trip on a Víazul bus costs CUC$6.

Sometimes terminal staff tell foreigners they're prohibited from traveling on trucks. As with anything in Cuba, smile and never take 'no' as your final answer. Striking up a conversation with the driver or appealing to other passengers for aid usually helps.

Language

Spanish pronunciation is pretty straight-forward – Spanish spelling is phonetically consistent, meaning that there's a clear and consistent relationship between what you see in writing and how it's pronounced. Also, most Latin American Spanish sounds are pronounced the same as their English counterparts. Note though that the kh in our pronunciation guides is a throaty sound (like the 'ch' in the Scottish *loch*), v and b are similar to the English 'b' (but softer, between a 'v' and a 'b'), and r is strongly rolled. If you read our colored pronunciation guides as if they were English, you'll be understood just fine. The stressed syllables are in italics.

Spanish nouns are marked for gender (masculine or feminine). Endings for adjectives also change to agree with the gender of the noun they modify. Where necessary, both forms are given for the phrases in this chapter, separated by a slash and with the masculine form first, eg *perdido/a* (m/f).

Spanish has two words for the English 'you': an informal (*tú*) and polite form (*Usted*) which are accompanied by a different form of the verb. When talking to people familiar to you or younger than you, use the informal form of 'you', *tú*, rather than the polite form *Usted*. In all other cases use the polite form. The polite form is used in the phrases provided in this chapter; where both options are given, they are indicated by the abbreviations 'pol' and 'inf'.

WANT MORE?

For in-depth language information and handy phrases, check out Lonely Planet's *Latin American Spanish Phrasebook*. You'll find it at **shop.lonelyplanet.com**, or you can buy Lonely Planet's iPhone phrasebooks at the Apple App Store.

BASICS

English	Spanish	Pronunciation
Hello.	Hola.	o·la
Goodbye.	Adiós.	a·dyos
How are you?	¿Qué tal?	ke tal
Fine, thanks.	Bien, gracias.	byen gra·syas
Excuse me.	Perdón.	per·don
Sorry.	Lo siento.	lo syen·to
Yes./No.	Sí./No.	see/no
Please.	Por favor.	por fa·vor
Thank you.	Gracias.	gra·syas
You're welcome.	De nada.	de na·da

My name is ...
Me llamo ...   me *ya*·mo ...

What's your name?
¿Cómo se llama Usted?   ko·mo se ya·ma oo·ste (pol)
¿Cómo te llamas?   ko·mo te ya·mas (inf)

Do you speak English?
¿Habla inglés?   a·bla een·gles (pol)
¿Hablas inglés?   a·blas een·gles (inf)

I don't understand.
Yo no entiendo.   yo no en·tyen·do

ACCOMMODATIONS

I'd like to book a room.
Quisiera reservar una   kee·sye·ra re·ser·var oo·na
habitación.   a·bee·ta·syon

How much is it per night/person?
¿Cuánto cuesta por   kwan·to kwes·ta por
noche/persona?   no·che/per·so·na

Does it include breakfast?
¿Incluye el desayuno?   een·kloo·ye el de·sa·yoo·no

campsite	terreno de camping	te·re·no de kam·peeng
hotel	hotel	o·tel
guesthouse	pensión	pen·syon
youth hostel	albergue juvenil	al·ber·ge khoo·ve·neel

I'd like a ... room.	Quisiera una habitación ...	kee-sye-ra oo-na a-bee-ta-syon ...
single	individual	een-dee-vee-dwal
double	doble	do-ble
air-con	aire acondicionado	ai-re a-kon-dee-syo-na-do
bathroom	baño	ba-nyo
bed	cama	ka-ma
window	ventana	ven-ta-na

DIRECTIONS

Where's ...?
¿Dónde está ...? — don-de es-ta ...

What's the address?
¿Cuál es la dirección? — kwal es la dee-rek-syon

Could you please write it down?
¿Puede escribirlo, por favor? — pwe-de es-kree-beer-lo por fa-vor

Can you show me (on the map)?
¿Me lo puede indicar (en el mapa)? — me lo pwe-de een-dee-kar (en el ma-pa)

at the corner	en la esquina	en la es-kee-na
at the traffic lights	en el semáforo	en el se-ma-fo-ro
behind ...	detrás de ...	de-tras de ...
far	lejos	le-khos
in front of ...	enfrente de ...	en-fren-te de ...
left	izquierda	ees-kyer-da
near	cerca	ser-ka
next to ...	al lado de ...	al la-do de ...
opposite ...	frente a ...	fren-te a ...
right	derecha	de-re-cha
straight ahead	todo recto	to-do rek-to

EATING & DRINKING

What would you recommend?
¿Qué recomienda? — ke re-ko-myen-da

What's in that dish?
¿Que lleva ese plato? — ke ye-va e-se pla-to

I don't eat ...
No como ... — no ko-mo ...

That was delicious!
¡Estaba buenísimo! — es-ta-ba bwe-nee-see-mo

Please bring the bill.
Por favor nos trae la cuenta. — por fa-vor nos tra-e la kwen-ta

Cheers!
¡Salud! — sa-loo

I'd like to book a table for ...	Quisiera reservar una mesa para ...	kee-sye-ra re-ser-var oo-na me-sa pa-ra ...
(eight) o'clock	las (ocho)	las (o-cho)
(two) people	(dos) personas	(dos) per-so-nas

Key Words

appetisers	aperitivos	a-pe-ree-tee-vos
bottle	botella	bo-te-ya
bowl	bol	bol
breakfast	desayuno	de-sa-yoo-no
children's menu	menú infantil	me-noo een-fan-teel
(too) cold	(muy) frío	(mooy) free-o
dinner	cena	se-na
food	comida	ko-mee-da
fork	tenedor	te-ne-dor
glass	vaso	va-so

highchair	trona	tro·na
hot (warm)	caliente	kal·yen·te
knife	cuchillo	koo·chee·yo
lunch	comida	ko·mee·da
main course	segundo plato	se·goon·do pla·to
market	mercado	mer·ka·do
menu (in English)	menú (en inglés)	me·noo (en een·gles)
plate	plato	pla·to
restaurant	restaurante	res·tow·ran·te
spoon	cuchara	koo·cha·ra
vegetarian food	comida vegetariana	ko·mee·da ve·khe·ta·rya·na
with/without	con/sin	kon/seen

Meat & Fish

beef	carne de vaca	kar·ne de va·ka
chicken	pollo	po·yo
duck	pato	pa·to
fish	pescado	pes·ka·do
lamb	cordero	kor·de·ro
pork	cerdo	ser·do
turkey	pavo	pa·vo
veal	ternera	ter·ne·ra

Fruit & Vegetables

apple	manzana	man·sa·na
apricot	albaricoque	al·ba·ree·ko·ke
artichoke	alcachofa	al·ka·cho·fa
asparagus	espárragos	es·pa·ra·gos
banana	plátano	pla·ta·no
beans	judías	khoo·dee·as
beetroot	remolacha	re·mo·la·cha
cabbage	col	kol
carrot	zanahoria	sa·na·o·rya
celery	apio	a·pyo
cherry	cereza	se·re·sa
corn	maíz	ma·ees
cucumber	pepino	pe·pee·no
fruit	fruta	froo·ta
grape	uvas	oo·vas
lemon	limón	lee·mon
lentils	lentejas	len·te·khas
lettuce	lechuga	le·choo·ga
mushroom	champiñón	cham·pee·nyon
nuts	nueces	nwe·ses
onion	cebolla	se·bo·ya

orange	naranja	na·ran·kha
peach	melocotón	me·lo·ko·ton
peas	guisantes	gee·san·tes
(red/green) pepper	pimiento (rojo/verde)	pee·myen·to (ro·kho/ver·de)
pineapple	piña	pee·nya
plum	ciruela	seer·we·la
potato	patata	pa·ta·ta
pumpkin	calabaza	ka·la·ba·sa
spinach	espinacas	es·pee·na·kas
strawberry	fresa	fre·sa
tomato	tomate	to·ma·te
vegetable	verdura	ver·doo·ra
watermelon	sandía	san·dee·a

Other

bread	pan	pan
butter	mantequilla	man·te·kee·ya
cheese	queso	ke·so
egg	huevo	we·vo
honey	miel	myel
jam	mermelada	mer·me·la·da
oil	aceite	a·sey·te
pasta	pasta	pas·ta
pepper	pimienta	pee·myen·ta
rice	arroz	a·ros
salt	sal	sal
sugar	azúcar	a·soo·kar
vinegar	vinagre	vee·na·gre

Drinks

beer	cerveza	ser·ve·sa
coffee	café	ka·fe
(orange) juice	zumo (de naranja)	soo·mo (de na·ran·kha)
milk	leche	le·che
tea	té	te
(mineral) water	agua (mineral)	a·gwa (mee·ne·ral)
(red/white) wine	vino (tinto/ blanco)	vee·no (teen·to/ blan·ko)

EMERGENCIES

Help!	¡Socorro!	so·ko·ro
Go away!	¡Vete!	ve·te
Call ...!	¡Llame a ...!	ya·me a ...
a doctor	un médico	oon me·dee·ko

| the police | *la policía* | la po·lee·*see*·a |

I'm lost.
Estoy perdido/a. es·toy per·*dee*·do/a (m/f)

I'm ill.
Estoy enfermo/a. es·toy en·*fer*·mo/a (m/f)

I'm allergic to (antibiotics).
Soy alérgico/a a soy a·*ler*·khee·ko/a a
(los antibióticos). (los an·tee·*byo*·tee·kos) (m/f)

Where are the toilets?
¿Dónde están *don*·de es·*tan*
los servicios? los ser·*vee*·syos

SHOPPING & SERVICES

I'd like to buy ...
Quisiera comprar ... kee·*sye*·ra kom·*prar* ...

I'm just looking.
Sólo estoy mirando. so·lo es·toy mee·*ran*·do

May I look at it?
¿Puedo verlo? *pwe*·do *ver*·lo

I don't like it.
No me gusta. no me *goos*·ta

How much is it?
¿Cuánto cuesta? *kwan*·to *kwes*·ta

That's too expensive.
Es muy caro. es mooy *ka*·ro

Can you lower the price?
¿Podría bajar un po·*dree*·a ba·*khar* oon
poco el precio? *po*·ko el *pre*·syo

There's a mistake in the bill.
Hay un error ai oon e·*ror*
en la cuenta. en la *kwen*·ta

ATM	*cajero automático*	ka·*khe*·ro ow·to·ma·*tee*·ko
credit card	*tarjeta de crédito*	tar·*khe*·ta de *kre*·dee·to
internet cafe	*cibercafé*	see·ber·ka·*fe*
post office	*correos*	ko·*re*·os
tourist office	*oficina de turismo*	o·fee·*see*·na de too·*rees*·mo

TIME & DATES

What time is it?	*¿Qué hora es?*	ke *o*·ra es
It's (10) o'clock.	*Son (las diez).*	son (las dyes)
It's half past	*Es (la una)*	es (la *oo*·na)

How?	*¿Cómo?*	*ko*·mo
What?	*¿Qué?*	ke
When?	*¿Cuándo?*	*kwan*·do
Where?	*¿Dónde?*	*don*·de
Who?	*¿Quién?*	kyen
Why?	*¿Por qué?*	por ke

SIGNS

Abierto	Open
Cerrado	Closed
Entrada	Entrance
Hombres/Varones	Men
Mujeres/Damas	Women
Prohibido	Prohibited
Salida	Exit
Servicios/Baños	Toilets

(one).	*y media.*	ee *me*·dya
morning	*mañana*	ma·*nya*·na
afternoon	*tarde*	*tar*·de
evening	*noche*	*no*·che
yesterday	*ayer*	a·*yer*
today	*hoy*	oy
tomorrow	*mañana*	ma·*nya*·na
Monday	*lunes*	*loo*·nes
Tuesday	*martes*	*mar*·tes
Wednesday	*miércoles*	*myer*·ko·les
Thursday	*jueves*	*khwe*·ves
Friday	*viernes*	*vyer*·nes
Saturday	*sábado*	*sa*·ba·do
Sunday	*domingo*	do·*meen*·go
January	*enero*	e·*ne*·ro
February	*febrero*	fe·*bre*·ro
March	*marzo*	*mar*·so
April	*abril*	a·*breel*
May	*mayo*	*ma*·yo
June	*junio*	*khoon*·yo
July	*julio*	*khool*·yo
August	*agosto*	a·*gos*·to
September	*septiembre*	sep·*tyem*·bre
October	*octubre*	ok·*too*·bre
November	*noviembre*	no·*vyem*·bre
December	*diciembre*	dee·*syem*·bre

TRANSPORTATION

Public Transportation

boat	*barco*	*bar*·ko
bus	*autobús*	ow·to·*boos*
plane	*avión*	a·*vyon*
train	*tren*	tren
first	*primero*	pree·*me*·ro

last · último · *ool·tee·mo*

next · próximo · *prok·see·mo*

I want to go to ...
Quisiera ir a ... · kee·*sye*·ra eer a ...

Does it stop at ...?
¿Para en ...? · pa·ra en ...

What stop is this?
¿Cuál es esta parada? · kwal es *es*·ta pa·*ra*·da

What time does it arrive/leave?
¿A qué hora llega/ · a ke o·ra ye·ga/
sale? · *sa*·le

Please tell me when we get to ...
¿Puede avisarme · pwe·de a·vee·*sar*·me
cuando lleguemos · kwan·do ye·ge·mos
a ...? · a ...

I want to get off here.
Quiero bajarme aquí. · kye·ro ba·*khar*·me a·*kee*

a ... ticket	un billete de ...	oon bee·ye·te de ...
1st-class	primera clase	pree·*me*·ra *kla*·se
2nd-class	segunda clase	se·*goon*·da *kla*·se
one-way	ida	ee·da
return	ida y vuelta	ee·da ee *vwel*·ta
airport	aeropuerto	a·e·ro·*pwer*·to
aisle seat	asiento de pasillo	a·*syen*·to de pa·*see*·yo
bus stop	parada de autobuses	pa·*ra*·da de ow·to·*boo*·ses
canceled	cancelado	kan·se·*la*·do
delayed	retrasado	re·tra·*sa*·do
platform	plataforma	pla·ta·*for*·ma
ticket office	taquilla	ta·*kee*·ya
timetable	horario	o·*ra*·ryo
train station	estación de trenes	es·ta·*syon* de *tre*·nes
window seat	asiento junto a la ventana	a·*syen*·to *khoon*·to a la ven·*ta*·na

Driving & Cycling

I'd like to hire a ...	Quisiera alquilar ...	kee·*sye*·ra al·kee·*lar* ...
4WD	un todo-terreno	oon to·do-te·*re*·no
bicycle	una bicicleta	oo·na bee·see·*kle*·ta
car	un coche	oon *ko*·che

motorcycle	una moto	oo·na mo·to
child seat	asiento de seguridad para niños	a·*syen*·to de se·goo·ree·da pa·ra nee·nyos
diesel	petróleo	pet·ro·le·o
helmet	casco	kas·ko
hitchhike	hacer botella	a·ser bo·te·ya
mechanic	mecánico	me·ka·nee·ko
petrol/gas	gasolina	ga·so·lee·na
service station	gasolinera	ga·so·lee·ne·ra
truck	camion	ka·myon

Is this the road to ...?
¿Se va a ... por · se va a ... por
esta carretera? · es·ta ka·re·te·ra

(How long) Can I park here?
¿(Por cuánto tiempo) · (por kwan·to tyem·po)
Puedo aparcar aquí? · pwe·do a·par·kar a·kee

The car has broken down (at ...).
El coche se ha averiado · el ko·che se a a·ve·rya·do
(en ...). · (en ...)

I have a flat tyre.
Tengo un pinchazo. · ten·go oon peen·cha·so

GLOSSARY

altos – upstairs apartment; caps when in an address

agropecuario – vegetable market; also sells rice, fruit

amarillo – a roadside traffic organizer in a yellow uniform

americano/a – in Cuba this means a citizen of any Western hemisphere country (from Canada to Argentina); a citizen of the US is called a *norteamericano/a* or *estado- unidense*; also gringo/a and yuma

Arawak – linguistically related Indian tribes that inhabited most of the Caribbean islands and northern South America

Autopista – the national highway that has four, six or eight lanes depending on the region

babalawo – a *Santería* priest; also *babalao*; see also *santero*

bahía – bay

bailes – dances

barbuda – name given to Castro's rebel army; literally 'bearded one'

barrio – neighborhood

bici-taxi – bicycle taxi

bodega – stores distributing ration-card products

bohío – thatched hut

bolero – a romantic love song

botella – hitchhiking; literally 'bottle'

cabaña – cabin, hut

cabildo – a town council during the colonial era; also an association of tribes in Cuban religions of African origin

cacique – chief; originally used to describe an Indian chief and today used to designate a petty tyrant

Cadeca – exchange booth

cafetal – coffee plantation

caliente – hot

calle – street

camión – truck

campesinos – people who live in the *campo*

campismo – national network of 82 camping installations, not all of which are open to foreigners

casa particular – private house that lets out rooms to foreigners (and sometimes Cubans); all legal casas must display a green triangle on the door

casco histórico – historic center of a city (eg Trinidad, Santiago de Cuba)

CDR – Comités de Defensa de la Revolución; neighborhood-watch bodies originally formed in 1960 to consolidate grassroots support for the Revolution; they now play a decisive role in health, education, social, recycling and voluntary labor campaigns

chachachá – cha-cha; dance music in 4/4 meter derived from the rumba and mambo

Changó – the *Santería* deity signifying war and fire, twinned with Santa Barbara in Catholicism

chivo – Cuban slang for 'bike'

cimarrón – a runaway slave

claves – rhythm sticks used by musicians

coches de caballo – horse carriages

Cohiba – native Indian name for a smoking implement; one of Cuba's top brands of cigar

colectivo – collective taxi that takes on as many passengers as possible; usually a classic American car

comida criolla – Creole food

compañero/a – companion or partner, with revolutionary connotations (ie 'comrade')

congrí (rice flecked with black beans)

conseguir – to get, obtain

convertibles – convertible pesos

coppelia – Cuban ice creamery

criollo – Creole; Spaniard born in the Americas

Cubanacán – soon after landing in Cuba, Christopher Columbus visited a Taíno village the Indians called Cubanacán (meaning 'in the center of the island'); a large Cuban tourism company uses the name

danzón – a traditional Cuban ballroom dance colored with African influences, pioneered in Matanzas during the late 19th century

décima – the rhyming, eight-syllable verse that provides the lyrics for Cuban son

duende – spirit/charm; used in flamenco to describe the ultimate climax to the music

El Líder Máximo – Maximum Leader; title often used to describe Fidel Castro

el último – literally 'the last'; this term is key to mastering Cuban queues (you must 'take' *el último* when joining a line and 'give it up' when someone new arrives)

entronque – crossroads in rural areas

finca – farm

Gitmo – American slang for Guantánamo US Naval Base

Granma – the yacht that carried Fidel and his companions from Mexico to Cuba in 1956 to launch the Revolution; in 1975 the name was adopted for the province where the Granma arrived; also name of Cuba's leading daily newspaper

guajiros – country folk

guarapo – fresh sugarcane juice

habanero/a – someone from Havana

herbero – seller of herbs, natural medicines and concocter of remedies; typically a wealth of knowledge on natural cures

ingenio – an antiquated term for a sugar mill; see central

inmigración – immigration office

jardín – garden

jinetera – a female tout; a woman who attaches herself to male foreigners

jinetero – a male tout who hustles tourists; literally 'jockey'

M-26-7 – the '26th of July Movement,' Fidel Castro's revolutionary organization, was named for the abortive assault on the Moncada army barracks in Santiago de Cuba on July 26, 1953

maqueta – scale model

máquina – private peso taxi

mercado – market

mirador – lookout or viewpoint

mogote – a limestone monolith found at Viñales

Moncada – a former army barracks in Santiago de Cuba named for General Guillermo Moncada (1848–95), a hero of the Wars of Independence

moneda nacional – abbreviated to MN; Cuban pesos

mudéjar – Iberian Peninsula's Moorish-influenced style in architecture and decoration that lasted from the 12th to 16th centuries and combined elements of Islamic and Christian art

nueva trova – philosophical folk/guitar music popularized in the late '60s and early '70s by Silvio Rodríguez and Pablo Milanés

Operación Milagros – the un-official name given to a pioneering medical program hatched between Cuba and Venezuela in 2004 that offers free eye treatment for impoverished Venezuelans in Cuban hospitals

Oriente – the region comprised of Las Tunas, Holguín, Granma, Santiago de Cuba and Guantánamo provinces; literally 'the east'

orisha – a *Santería* deity

paladar – a privately owned restaurant

parada – bus stop

parque – park

PCC – Partido Comunista de Cuba; Cuba's only political party, formed in October 1965 by merging cadres from the Partido Socialista Popular (the pre-1959 Communist Party) and veterans of the guerrilla campaign

peña – musical performance or get-together in any genre: son, rap, rock, poetry etc.

período especial – the 'Special Period in Time of Peace' (Cuba's economic reality post-1991)

pregón – a singsong manner of selling fruits, vegetables, brooms, whatever; often comic, they are belted out by *pregoneros/as*

puente – bridge

quinceañera – Cuban rite of passage for girls turning 15 (*quince*), whereby they dress up like brides, have their photos taken in gorgeous natural or architectural settings and then have a big party with lots of food and dancing

ranchón – rural farm/restaurant

reggaetón – Cuban hip-hop

Regla de Ocha – set of related religious beliefs popularly known as *Santería*

resolver – to resolve or fix a problematic situation; along with *el último*, this is among the most indispensable words in Cuban vocabulary

río – river

salsa – Cuban music based on son

salsero – salsa singer

Santería – Afro-Cuban religion resulting from the syncretization of the Yoruba religion of West Africa and Spanish Catholicism

santero – a priest of *Santería*; see also babalawo

santiagüero – someone from Santiago de Cuba

s/n – *sin número;* indicates an address that has no street number

son – Cuba's basic form of popular music that jelled from African and Spanish elements in the late 19th century

Taíno – a settled, Arawak-speaking tribe that inhabited much of Cuba prior to the Spanish conquest; the word itself means 'we the good people'

tambores – *Santería* drumming ritual

telepunto – Etecsa (Cuban state-run telecommunications company) telephone and internet shop/call center

temporada alta/baja – high/low season

Behind the Scenes

SEND US YOUR FEEDBACK

We love to hear from travelers – your comments keep us on our toes and help make our books better. Our well-traveled team reads every word on what you loved or loathed about this book. Although we cannot reply individually to your submissions, we always guarantee that your feedback goes straight to the appropriate authors, in time for the next edition. Each person who sends us information is thanked in the next edition – the most useful submissions are rewarded with a selection of digital PDF chapters.

Visit **lonelyplanet.com/contact** to submit your updates and suggestions or to ask for help. Our award-winning website also features inspirational travel stories, news and discussions.

Note: We may edit, reproduce and incorporate your comments in Lonely Planet products such as guidebooks, websites and digital products, so let us know if you don't want your comments reproduced or your name acknowledged. For a copy of our privacy policy visit lonelyplanet.com/privacy.

OUR READERS

Many thanks to the travelers who used the last edition and wrote to us with helpful hints, useful advice and interesting anecdotes:

A Angie Cohn, Amj Kriens, Alley Lloyd, Ann Steinmetz, Antoine D Levy-Lambert, Arent Van Gent **B** Bob Goodall **C** Carolina Teixeira & Adriano Meneghetti, Caroline Halembert & Jérôme Mausen, Catherine Smith **D** Daniela De Armas, Dave Reid, David Gutteridge, David Lisbona, Debra Loevy **E** Eleanor Pole **F** Felix Guzman, Francesca Mangione **G** Garry Bargh, Guus Dekking **H** Helena Granziera, Howard Smukler **J** Jasmijn Nicolaes, Jennifer Wright, Jonathan Harris, Joseph T Stanik, Julia Heinz **K** Katerina Alegria **L** Lyndell Newman **M** Manchan Magan, Marco Ferrari, Maria Corbett, Maria Luisa Colledani, Maria Uleskog, Mark Fisher, Mark Nunan, Martin Hellwagner, Martin Winter, Martine De Vos, Michal Rudziecki, Mark Shuttleworth **N** Nina Mardell, Noemi La Torre **P** Paolo Votino, Peter Coggins, Philip Schilling **R** Reigo Tamm, Richard Brunt, Richard Harris, Rosa Playford, Rossella Squillace, Rousee Magali, Rowena Gillow, Ruth Thomas, Ruthie Garelik **S** Sara Turner, Sarah Tankard, Simone Theunissen, Sonia Langford, Steffen Enggaard Kristensen, Stephen Hockley, Sussie Carlson **T** Tamara Smith, Terry Allsop, Thijs Wesselink **V** Vicky Jassey **Z** Zoe Dobell

WRITER THANKS

Brendan Sainsbury

Special thanks to all my many Cuban *amigos*, especially Julio & Elsa Roque and Luis Miguel in Havana, Julio & Rosa Muñoz in Trinidad, Julio & Lidia in Playa Girón, Roberto in Viñales, Moreno & Mercy in Santa Clara, Yoel in Matanzas, and Carlos for his careful driving and excellent company everywhere. An extra gracias to my wife, Liz, for accompanying me on the road and enjoying La Isla de la Juventud.

Wendy Yanagihara

My deepest gratitude goes to Diego and Rudens for uber-Cuban language lessons, unforgettable adventures (including the immigration office), and hiking beers. *Muchas gracias* also to Maité, Idolka, Nilson and Ramses for local insight and friendship; to Anna for sparkly companionship; to the many guides and patient *taxistas* who made this assignment feasible in two months on the ground; to Brendan and Carolyn for invaluable intel; and to the ones who always make my travels possible: Laura, Victoria, Jason and Jasper.

ACKNOWLEDGEMENTS

Climate map data adapted from Peel MC, Finlayson BL & McMahon TA (2007) 'Updated World Map of the Köppen-Geiger Climate Classification', *Hydrology and Earth System Sciences*, 11, 1633–44.

Cover photograph: View of Spanish colonial rooftops, Trinidad. Joshua Davenport/Shutterstock ©

Illustrations p72-3 by Michael Weldon.

THIS BOOK

This 10th edition of Lonely Planet's *Cuba* guidebook was researched and written by Brendan Sainsbury and Wendy Yanagihara. The previous edition was also written by Brendan and Carolyn McCarthy. This guidebook was produced by the following:

Destination Editors Bailey Freeman, Alicia Johnson

Senior Product Editors Daniel Bolger, Martine Power, Saralinda Turner

Senior Cartographer Corey Hutchison

Product Editors Hannah Cartmel, Jenna Myers

Book Designers Fergal Condon, Clara Monitto

Cartographer: Rachel Imeson

Assisting Editors Janet Austin, Judith Bamber, Sarah Bailey, Michelle Coxall, Melanie Dankel, Lauren Keith

Assisting Cartographer James Leversha

Cover Researcher Brendan Dempsey-Spencer

Thanks to Ronan Abayawickrema, Karen Henderson, Catherine Naghten, Monique Perrin, Vicky Smith, Amanda Williamson

Index

Map Legend

Sights

- Beach
- Bird Sanctuary
- Buddhist
- Castle/Palace
- Christian
- Confucian
- Hindu
- Islamic
- Jain
- Jewish
- Monument
- Museum/Gallery/Historic Building
- Ruin
- Shinto
- Sikh
- Taoist
- Winery/Vineyard
- Zoo/Wildlife Sanctuary
- Other Sight

Activities, Courses & Tours

- Bodysurfing
- Diving
- Canoeing/Kayaking
- Course/Tour
- Sento Hot Baths/Onsen
- Skiing
- Snorkeling
- Surfing
- Swimming/Pool
- Walking
- Windsurfing
- Other Activity

Sleeping

- Sleeping
- Camping
- Hut/Shelter

Eating

- Eating

Drinking & Nightlife

- Drinking & Nightlife
- Cafe

Entertainment

- Entertainment

Shopping

- Shopping

Information

- Bank
- Embassy/Consulate
- Hospital/Medical
- @ Internet
- Police
- Post Office
- Telephone
- Toilet
- Tourist Information
- Other Information

Geographic

- Beach
- Gate
- Hut/Shelter
- Lighthouse
- Lookout
- Mountain/Volcano
- Oasis
- Park
- Pass
- Picnic Area
- Waterfall

Population

- Capital (National)
- Capital (State/Province)
- City/Large Town
- Town/Village

Transport

- Airport
- Border crossing
- Bus
- Cable car/Funicular
- Cycling
- Ferry
- Metro station
- Monorail
- Parking
- Petrol station
- Subway/Subte station
- Taxi
- Train station/Railway
- Tram
- Underground station
- Other Transport

Routes

- Tollway
- Freeway
- Primary
- Secondary
- Tertiary
- Lane
- Unsealed road
- Road under construction
- Plaza/Mall
- Steps
- Tunnel
- Pedestrian overpass
- Walking Tour
- Walking Tour detour
- Path/Walking Trail

Boundaries

- International
- State/Province
- Disputed
- Regional/Suburb
- Marine Park
- Cliff
- Wall

Hydrography

- River, Creek
- Intermittent River
- Canal
- Water
- Dry/Salt/Intermittent Lake
- Reef

Areas

- Airport/Runway
- Beach/Desert
- Cemetery (Christian)
- Cemetery (Other)
- Glacier
- Mudflat
- Park/Forest
- Sight (Building)
- Sportsground
- Swamp/Mangrove

Note: Not all symbols displayed above appear on the maps in this book

OUR STORY

A beat-up old car, a few dollars in the pocket and a sense of adventure. In 1972 that's all Tony and Maureen Wheeler needed for the trip of a lifetime – across Europe and Asia overland to Australia. It took several months, and at the end – broke but inspired – they sat at their kitchen table writing and stapling together their first travel guide, *Across Asia on the Cheap*. Within a week they'd sold 1500 copies. Lonely Planet was born.

Today, Lonely Planet has offices in Franklin, Dublin and Beijing, with a network of over 2000 contributors in every corner of the globe. We share Tony's belief that 'a great guidebook should do three things: inform, educate and amuse'.

OUR WRITERS

Brendan Sainsbury

Havana, Artemisa & Mayabeque Provinces, Cienfuegos Province, Isla de la Juventud & Cayo Largo del Sur, Matanzas Province, Pinar del Río Province, Villa Clara Province Born and raised in the UK in a town that never merits a mention in any guidebook (Andover, Hampshire), Brendan spent the holidays of his youth caravanning in the English Lake District and didn't leave Blighty until he was 19. Making up for lost time, he's since squeezed 70 countries into a sometimes precarious existence as a writer and professional vagabond. His rocking chair memories will probably include staging a performance of 'A Comedy of Errors' at a school in war-torn Angola, running 150 miles across the Sahara Desert in the Marathon des Sables, and hitchhiking from Cape Town to Kilimanjaro with an early, dog-eared copy of Lonely Planet's *Africa on a Shoestring*. In the last 11 years, he has written over 40 books for Lonely Planet, covering everything from Castro's *Cuba* to the canyons of *Peru*. When not scribbling research notes, Brendan likes partaking in ridiculous 'endurance' races, strumming old Clash songs on the guitar, and experiencing the pain and occasional pleasures of following Southampton Football Club.

Wendy Yanagihara

Camagüey Province, Ciego de Ávila Province, Granma Province, Guantánamo Province, Holguín Province, Las Tunas Province, Sancti Spíritus Province, Santiago de Cuba Province Wendy serendipitously landed her dream job of writing for Lonely Planet in 2003 and has spent the intervening years contributing to titles including *Vietnam*, *Japan*, *Mexico*, *Costa Rica*, *Ecuador*, *Indonesia* and *Grand Canyon National Park*. In the name of research, she has explored remote valleys of West Papua, explored tiny Tokyo alleys and hiked the Grand Canyon from rim to rim. For work and pleasure, she has traveled six continents and lived in three, Antarctica being the exception to date. Top experiences include gorilla tracking in Uganda, rafting the Nile, spotting pink river dolphins in the Amazon, trekking on a Patagonian glacier and, closer to home in southern California, stand-up paddling with common dolphins. She hopes that writing for Lonely Planet encourages travelers to connect with indigenous people, cultures, wildlife and the environment as a whole, to motivate conservation of the world's rich diversity. Wendy has also written for *BBC Travel*, The *Guardian*, *Lonely Planet Magazine* and lonelyplanet.com, and intermittently freelances as a graphic designer, illustrator and visual artist.

Published by Lonely Planet Global Limited
CRN 554153
10th edition – Nov 2021
ISBN 978 1 78701 374 2
© Lonely Planet 2021 Photographs © as indicated 2021
10 9 8 7 6 5 4 3 2 1
Printed in Malaysia